Integrated Computer Graphics

Bruce Mielke
University of Wisconsin - Green Bay

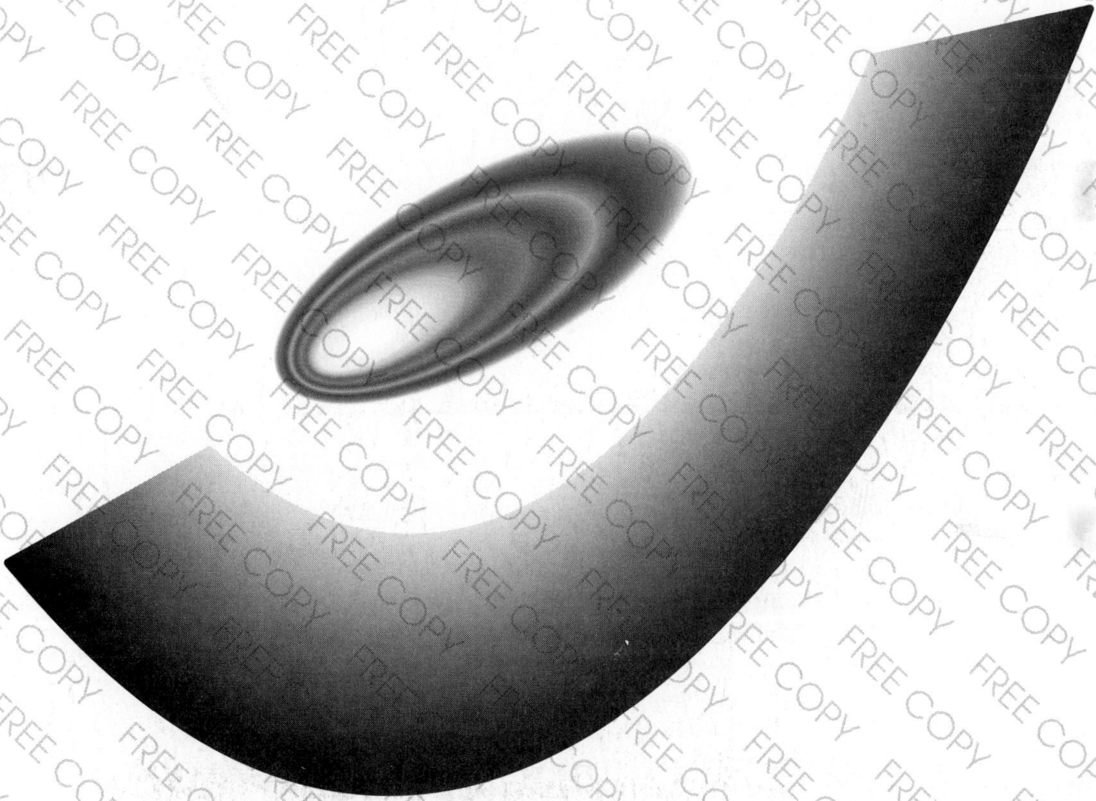

WEST PUBLISHING COMPANY
St. Paul New York San Francisco Los Angeles

Copyeditor: Fran Haselstiener
Compositor: The Clarinda Company
Dummie Artist: Hespenheide Design
Cover Image: by H. Jürgens, H.-O. Peitgen, D. Saupe, from: "The Beauty of Fractals", H.-O. Peitgen, D. Richter, Springer-Verlag, Heidelberg, 1986

…

Printed in the United States of America

98 97 96 95 94 93 92 91 8 7 6 5 4 3 2 1 0
Library of Congress Cataloging-in-Publication Data

Mielke, Bruce W.
Integrated computer graphics/Bruce W. Mielke.
p. cm.
Includes Index
ISBN 0-314-78431-4 (hard)
1. Computer graphics. I. Title
T385.M53 1991
006.6—dc20

∞
90-21879
CIP

Photo Credits

1.2.8 (left) Created using MIRAGE Professional Graphics Software by Zenographics; **1.2.8** (right) Created using MIRAGE Professional Graphics Software by Zenographics; **1.2.10** Courtesy of Autodesk, Inc.; **1.2.11** Reprinted with permission COMPUTER GRAPHICS WORLD, June 1989, copyrighted by PennWell Publishing Company; **1.2.12** Reprinted with permission COMPUTER GRAPHICS WORLD, May 1989, copyrighted by PennWell Publishing Company; **1.2.13** Courtesy of Takenaka Corporation and Intergraph Corporation; **1.2.17** Reprinted with permission COMPUTER GRAPHICS WORLD, January 1989, copyrighted by PennWell Publishing Company; **1.2.18** Reprinted with permission COMPUTER GRAPHICS WORLD, January 1989, copyrighted by PennWell Publishing Company; **1.2.23** Reprinted with permission COMPUTER GRAPHICS WORLD, March 1989, copyrighted by PennWell Publishing Company; **1.2.24** Reprinted with permission COMPUTER GRAPHICS WORLD, March 1989, copyrighted by PennWell Publishing Company; **D.2.2** Reprinted with permission COMPUTER GRAPHICS WORLD, December 1989, copyrighted by PennWell Publishing Company; **D.2.3** Reprinted with permission COMPUTER GRAPHICS WORLD, July 1989, copyrighted by PennWell Publishing Company; **1.2.14** (left) Courtesy of Selles-Yoko and Intergraph Corporation; (right) Courtesy of Fluar Daniel and

Table of Contents

Preface

Background and Objectives

In an era of specialization and compartmentalization of knowledge, computer graphics is an area in which many diverse specialties come together. Mathematicians create images of their works to display in art galleries, while artists, who once shunned technology, now embrace one of the most sophisticated, high technology tools, the computer, in their work. Contributors of images for this book include artists, physical and biological scientists, mathematicians, cinematographers, graphic designers and business people. To each of these people, and many others, computer graphics has become a tool for expressing their innermost thoughts and feelings as well as a means of serving diverse applications.

Less costly hardware and easy to use software have contributed to the growth of computer graphics by encouraging a broad spectrum of people to become interested. The growth in computer graphics would not have occurred without the decreasing cost of hardware; easy to use software encourages a broad spectrum of people to try computer graphics. There are two central pillars on which software development rests. The first is the classification and standardization of operations used in computer graphics. The second is the evolution of user interfaces that give easy access to standard operations. This book concentrates on the principles of software development in both PC and workstation environments.

Organization

Chapters 2 and 3 take the reader from graphics hardware through the creation of a simple, two-dimensional graphics package. This package has many of the main output primitives found in various graphics standards. The chapter also covers representation and transformation of two-dimensional graphics objects. The simple package is applied to create fractals and graftals.

Many of the most popular graphics programs have user interfaces based on bitmap graphics. Chapter 4 introduces the basic bit operations and the most important bitmap procedure, Bitblt. Pull-down menus are created and implemented using Bitblt.

Chapters 5 and 6 give a step-by-step development of a graphics paint/draw-type program. Chapter 5 begins by classifying interactive input devices and giving a simple example of how such a device can be implemented and used to create animations. In chapter 6, the interactive techniques of chapters 4 and 5 are combined with the graphics primitives of chapter 3 to create graphic tools. These tools are accessed from an event-driven paint/draw program.

Chapter 7 introduces two-dimensional spline curves. Three of the most common classes of spline-type curves (B-splines, Bézier curves and Catmull-Rom curves) are compared and contrasted. This chapter shows how to create graphic tools for interactive spline curve drawing and reshaping.

The last four chapters of the book concentrate on three-dimensional graphics. Chapter 8 presents the representation and transformation of graphic objects in various three-dimensional coordinate systems. To create line drawing procedures that show three-dimensional objects on a two-dimensional screen, the objects must be projected to the screen. Chapter 9 introduces various types of projections and discusses their uses. The chapter begins with a historical development of various types of projections and their uses. This allows students to see that non-perspective projections were used in part because people in other eras viewed the world differently. The chapter ends with the implementation of a simple, three-dimensional, wire-frame graphics package.

The last two chapters concentrate on creating realistic three-dimensional drawings. Chapter 10 surveys techniques used to remove surfaces and lines hidden behind surfaces nearer to the viewer. The chapter starts with back-face removal, the simplest technique, and includes discussions of other methods, such as the z-buffer method, which are more complicated but can be used when back-face removal fails. Images created using the techniques in Chapter 10 give enough visual cues to be understood, but do not appear very realistic. To create more realistic images, one must incorporate texture, light and shadow, reflective characteristics and color. Chapter 11 introduces many of the techniques used to add these qualities. In addition to the standard methods for creating flat and interpolated shading, this chapter covers a simple example of ray-tracing and introduces radiosity. The chapter also presents the major color models, their applications in graphics and the new bitmap technique, compositing. The chapter ends with an introduction to volume-rendering data structures and applications.

Possible Orderings and Coverage of Topics

An undergraduate, one-semester course in two-dimensional graphics can be taught using Chapters 2 through 7. In sections where more than one algorithm for the same operation is given, the instructor can cover one algorithm in-depth to give the students an understanding of the problem, then sketch the reasons for the other algorithms in less detail. It is possible to do all of the material in the first seven chapters without linear algebra, but section 3.6 gives an introduction to matrix operations and their application in two-dimensional problems. The detailed implementation of Bitblt (section 4.2) is given for completeness. In most undergraduate classes, this section can be used to show the underlying problems of representing rectangular bit images in memory that has a linear organization. These problems limit the types of operations that Bitblt can do easily. Chapter 5 introduces the problems encountered when building a user interface, while allowing the user to develop a simple program to create animations. Chapter 6 introduces some of the solutions to the user interface problem. If object-oriented Pascal is available, the techniques presented in section 6.6 may be applied when creating the tools in section 6.1. If you want to develop a color graphics application, section 11.6 on color models can be included at any point after Chapter 2. Chapter 7 introduces spline curves and shows how to construct B-splines, Bézier and Catmull-Rom curves using interactive techniques.

For more advanced undergraduate students with a solid background in linear algebra (especially linear and affine transformations) and data structures, the instructor may choose to cover the material in Chapters 2 through 7 in more depth. An alternate syllabus including three-dimensional graphics can be achieved by spending less time on the details of maintaining a segmented graphics system and/or covering only one of the spline types found in Chapter 7. This would allow time to include Chapters 8, 9, one or more of the hidden-surface algorithms in Chapter 10 and selected topics from Chapter 11.

Chapter 11 may be sampled in a variety of ways. The first four sections of this chapter cover the traditional shading techniques (flat, Gouraud and Phong) as well as ray-tracing and radiosity. If the goal of the instructor is to give an overview of techniques used to create realistic images, sections 11.7 and 11.8 survey some of the newer techniques. This information may be presented quickly or assigned for reading.

Features of the Text

Complete coverage of the fundamental techniques used in creating and manipulating computer images is essential in any computer graphics textbook, but a discussion of the methods used to present the material is also necessary if the students are to be motivated to learn about graphics. The following are some of the important features that present, organize, integrate, summarize and reinforce the material in the book:

- Color images in Chapters 1, 2, 3 and 11 are included in the text, where the techniques used to create them are discussed, not detached from the text in a separate section of the book. While it is not always possible for students to create these images, they will see the techniques used. Additionally many images are state of the art, created in 1990 and obtained from wide-ranging international sources.
- Chapters 2 through 11 begin with sections called "Directions." These sections survey applications of computer graphics related to topics covered in the chapter. The Directions for Chapter 3, for example, includes a discussion of the impact of computer graphics on mathematical modeling. Fractals, the most famous mathematical entities visualized using computer graphics, are also introduced. The graphics primitives needed to draw fractals are then developed in Chapter 3, with the last section of the chapter devoted to the programs used to create fractals and graftals. The Directions for Chapter 5 surveys the use of computer graphics in producing motion pictures. The last section of Chapter 5 shows students how create a simple animation program they can use to draw poses for two-dimensional cartoons.
- Summary boxes at the end of many sections give the correspondence between procedures discussed in the section and similar procedures in such standard graphics packages as GKS, PHIGS, Turbo Pascal, and the Macintosh Toolbox.
- The exercises at the end of each section range from short answer questions that review material to programming exercises that challenge students to apply the techniques presented.
- Programming projects that have students integrate techniques found in more than one section of the book are given in Chapters 5 through 7, 9 and 10.

Ancillary Materials for Instructors

1. The *Instructor's Manual* contains hints on solutions to some of the exercises and suggestions for teaching some of the material such as bitmap graphics.
2. In addition to the color used in the book, a set of transparencies from SIGGRAPH 89 and 90 is provided to instructors.
3. Instructors will receive a disk (either PC or Macintosh compatible) with all of the code figures from the book in text files.
4. *Transparency Masters* provided to instructors include over 100 figures from the book.

Acknowledgments

Many people were involved in creating this book. I want to thank the people and organizations who furnished the images used. I also want to thank the reviewers whose suggestions have greatly improved the presentation of material.

Bruno Andriamanualimana
Department of Computer Science
SUNY College of Technology at Utica

Cyrus Azarbod
Department of Computer Science
Mankato State University

Brian Barsky
Dept. of Electrical Engr. & C.Science
University of California–Berkeley

Hedley Bond
Department of Computer Science
University of Tennessee–Knoxville

Wayne Carlson
Department of Computer Science
Ohio State University

John Cross
Department of Computer Science
Indiana University of Pennsylvania

Steve Cunningham
Department of Computer Science
California State University–Stanislaus

Wanda Dann
Department of Computer science
SUNY-Morrisville College

Eudice Feder
Department of Computer Science
California State University–Northridge

Dieter Felner
Department of Computer Science
Memorial University

Eugene Fiume
Department of Computer Science
University of Toronto

Jack Goldfeather
Department of Computer Science
Carlton College

Lein Harn
Department of Computer Science
University of Missouri–Kansas City

Marek Holynski
Department of Computer Science
Boston University

Thomas Kiesler
Department of Computer Science
University of Missouri–Kansas City

Ann Kirch
Quantitive Methods & C. Science
College of St. Thomas

Daniel Lamet
Department of Computer Science
Boise State University

Suzanne Lea
Department of Mathematics
University of North Carolina–Greensboro

Jia-Guu Leu
Department of Computer Science
Wayne State University

John Lowther
Department of Computer Science
Michigan Technological University

Michael Main
Department of Computer Science
University of Colorado–Boulder

Christopher Morgan
Dept. Of Math & Computer Science
California State University–Hayward

Rosalee Nerheim
Department of Computer Science
De Paul University

Jeff Perotti
Department of Math & Computer Science
DePauw University

Darleen Pigford
Department of Computer Science
Western Kentucky University

Cornel Pokorny
Department of Computer Science
California Polytechnic State University

David Salomon
Department of Computer Science
California State University–Northridge

Bruno Schmidt
Department of Computer Science
Southwest Missouri State University

Stephanie Smullen
Department of Computer Science
University of Tennessee–Chattanooga

William I. Thacker
School of Business Administration
Winthrop College

A special thanks to all of the students who have commented on the book, from the time it existed as a set of supplemental notes through the first three classroom versions. Without their enthusiastic support I would not have tried to write it. I give special thanks to Greg Swain and Kevin Koehne, who spent many hours implementing Bitblt before it was widely available, and to Ernie Colantonio, who helped implement many of the algorithms on PCs. I want to thank all of the people at West for their assistance. Very special thanks to my acquisitions editor Jerry Westby for his vision of what this book could be; to my developmental editors Liz Lee and Denis Ralling for their encouragement and organizational skills; and to my production editor Janine Wilson for putting together a fantastic final product. Finally, I want to thank my wife Jan without whose patient cooperation, editorial and graphic design skills this book would not have been possible.

CHAPTER

1

Introduction to Computer Graphics

1.1 The Changing Role of Graphics in Computing

Computer graphics has been a part of computing from its earliest days, but it was only in the late 1970s and early 1980s that computer graphics became cost effective. In the sixties the cathode ray tubes (CRTs) used to display pictures contained phosphors that had to be refreshed quickly or the images would fade. One way to achieve this quick refresh was to store the picture in the main computer memory, but memory was expensive. The only alternative to extensive memory use was expensive hardware that redrew lines many times per second from a list of end points [Berg 86].

The cost of computer graphics was dramatically reduced by the introduction of the storage-tube CRT by Tektronix in 1968. This CRT retained an image until the user erased it and required no extra memory or redraw hardware. The storage-tube CRT made it possible for large firms to create engineering or technical drawings on in-house computers.

The seventies saw a significant drop in the cost of computer memory and other graphics hardware, making memory-intensive raster scan graphics viable. Raster scan systems made realistically shaded color images a reality; however, graphics systems were still too expensive to permit their extensive use outside of some specialized applications.

Computer graphics finally entered the mainstream of computing in the eighties with the widespread use of low-priced personal computers. Manufacturers of PCs used graphics as one way to sell computers. Promotion programs of the early eighties were filled with pie charts, bar graphs, animated horse races, and fractal mountains. By the mid eighties graphics moved from its status as a limited-purpose tool to become an integral part of computer systems. The Macintosh computer, with its extensive use of graphics and the mouse, has helped integrate every aspect of computer use, from the developing data relationships in data bases to debugging programs. PCs with more memory than many mainframe computers of the seventies are now found in most offices and many homes.

Graphics workstations have made Computer Aided Design (CAD) cost effective for a wide variety of companies. These workstations combine interactive graphics' ease of use with the computing power of a mainframe. The workstation itself may be a simple personal computer or a high-end workstation with its own local processor, mass storage, and high-resolution display device. A wide range of interactive input devices cater to the diversity of user requirements and resources.

1.2 A Sampling of Computer Graphics Applications

The first decades of computer graphics were dominated by engineering applications. While access to computer graphics systems was restricted, computer art dates from the early sixties. Ivan Sutherland developed interactive sketch software in 1963 [Sutherland 1963], and the first computer art exhibitions ran simultaneously in the United States and Germany in 1965 [Dietrich 1985]. The number and variety of computer graphics applications has grown as the cost of graphics systems has decreased.

The following examples of computer art submitted for competitions and exhibits reflect the diversity of styles and techniques developed by computer artists (figures 1.2.1–.5).

FIGURE 1.2.1

"Circus" by Barbara Joffe, © 1989.

FIGURE 1.2.2

"Son" by Luz Bueno, © 1989.

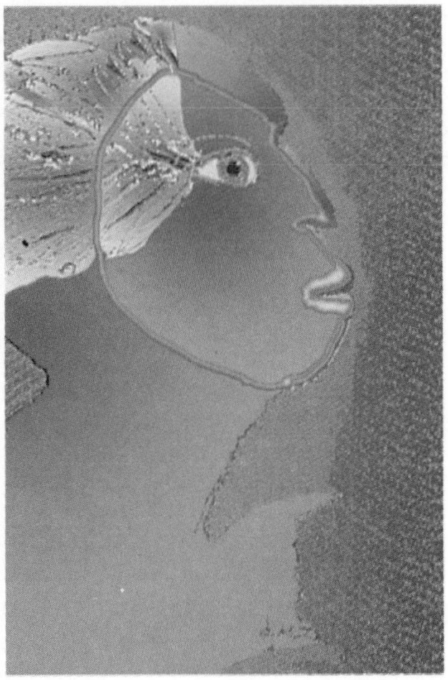

FIGURE 1.2.3

"Warhol Portait," 36" × 48", Computer generated, plotter output, © Kamran Moojedi, 1985.

FIGURE 1.2.4

"Settignano Series: Religion" by *Copper Giloth.*

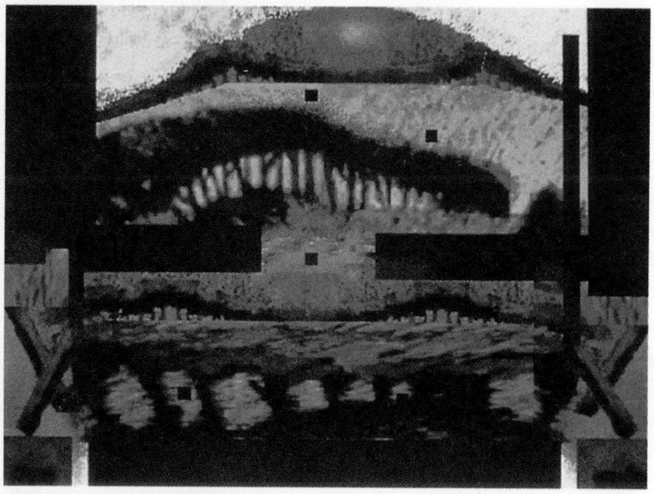

FIGURE 1.2.5

"Mask of Fear" by *Charles Csuri.*

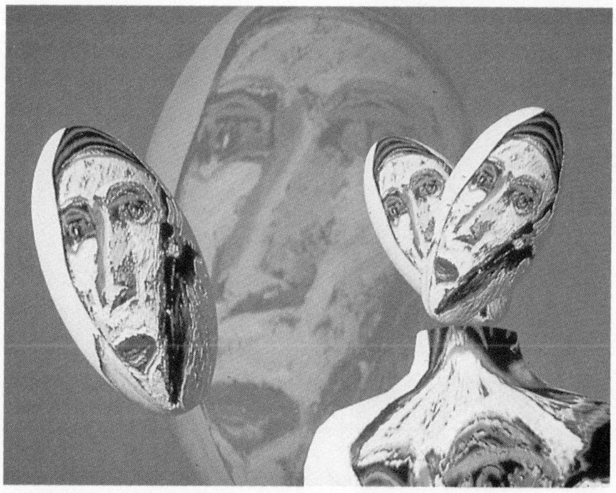

Computer animation is another art form that has developed in recent years. It can be seen in commercial films such as *The Abyss* (figure 1.2.6), as well as in experimental films such as Aliza Corsan's *Under the Puddle* (figure 1.2.7).

FIGURE 1.2.6

The special-effect water tentacle, seen in the film The Abyss, *took six months to create using computer graphics.*

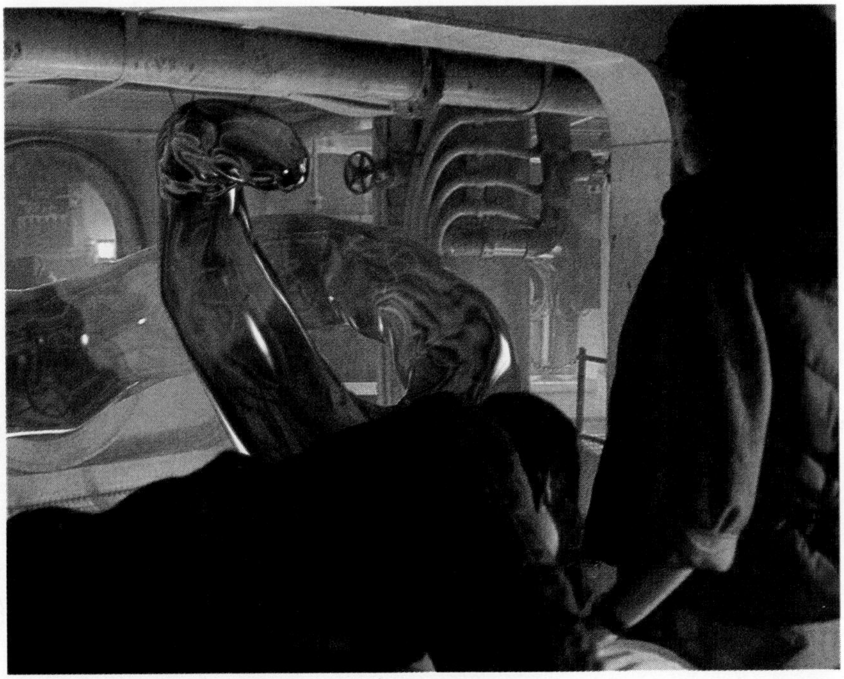

FIGURE 1.2.7

"Under the Puddle" by Aliza Corson (1990). This experimental animation presents an underwater observation of a rainstorm. The final scene depicted here shows the puddle as the storm dissipates revealing a clear sky and surrounding trees. Particle system software (S. Amkraut) was used to generate the raindrop motion. Blurring and wave effects were achieved with image processing (J. M. Fujii). The final scene is composited with a photographic image (D. Remler). Produced at the Ohio State University, Advanced Center for the Arts and Design.

Computer graphics has also revolutionized commercial art. Computer-generated presentation graphics give statistics visual impact (figure 1.2.8). Computer graphics images are commonly used in advertising to give products a modern look (figure 1.2.9).

FIGURE 1.2.8

Creative business graphics help present facts in an eye-catching manner. The bar graphs, pie chart, and linegraphs are examples of presentation graphics which do more than present the facts.

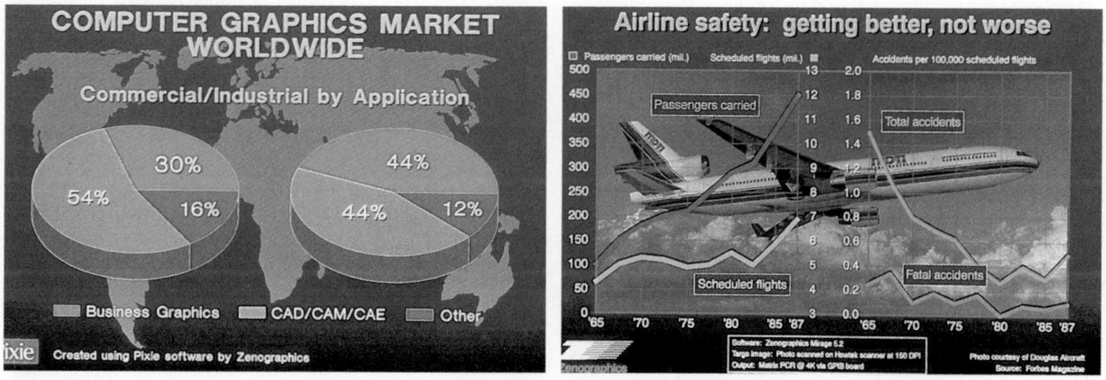

FIGURE 1.2.9

This image of Radio City Music Hall created by WAVEFRONT Technologies a construction company's ad shown during the halftime of Super Bowl XXII.

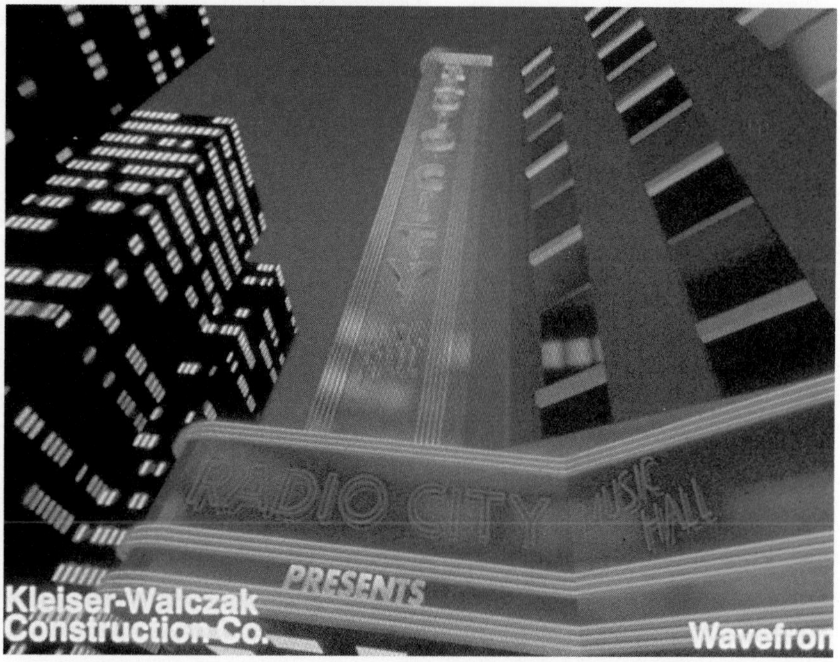

The development of software that encourages use by nontechnical individuals along with affordable PC-based computer graphics systems have spurred the widespread use of computers in the graphic arts. The rapid growth of desktop publishing has fueled the demand for higher-quality graphic printing as well as for better interfaces between PCs and traditional typesetting equipment.

Another applied art form, architecture, has also benefited from computer graphics. Using computer technology, architects can produce construction plans (figures 1.2.10 and 1.2.11) and realistic renderings of buildings under varying lighting conditions (figures 1.2.12–14).

FIGURE 1.2.10

Architectural drawings can be taken from floor plans to wire frame drawings to shaded drawings using CAD software. (AutoCAD by Autodesk).

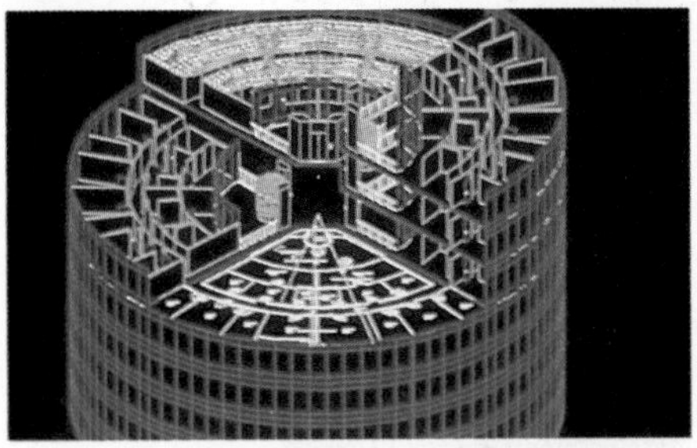

FIGURE 1.2.11

A wire frame drawing created on an MS-DOS based "Autocad workstation" by Trillian Computer Corp.

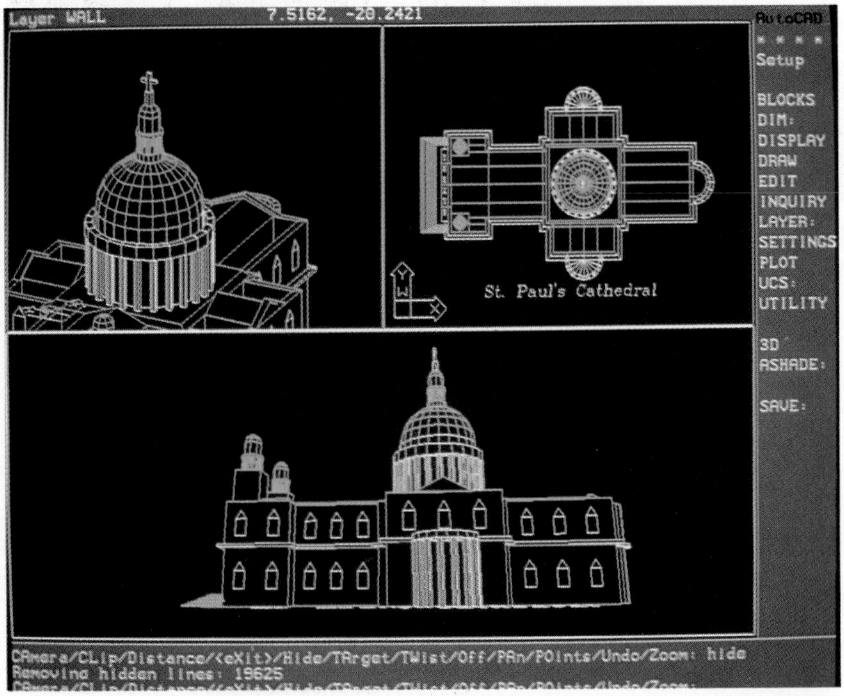

FIGURE 1.2.12

An example of a rendered architectural drawing created by Design Vision using an Alias/2 system.

FIGURE 1.2.13

This simulation of lighting was created using ray tracing with multiple light sources and surface mapping of foliage on Intergraph's Modelview package.

FIGURE 1.2.14

Interior lighting modeled using the Modelview package.

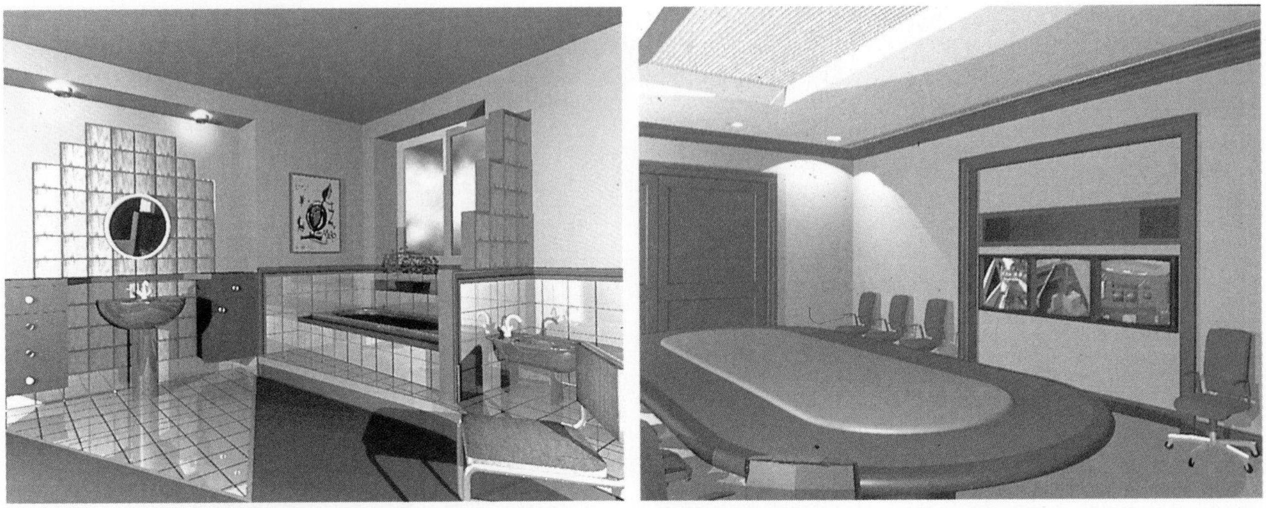

As in architecture, engineering applications of computer graphics have progressed far beyond line drawings. CAD programs allow engineers to go directly from three-dimensional wire-frame models of parts (figure 1.2.15) to shaded images (figure 1.2.16).

FIGURE 1.2.15

Detailed plans with specifications created using VersaCAD.

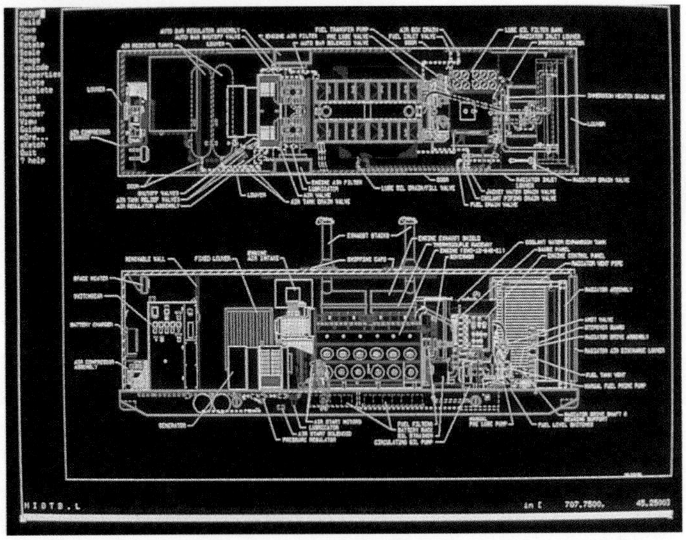

FIGURE 1.2.16

Wire frame drawings and shaded surface drawings created in Computer Vision's Personal Designer.

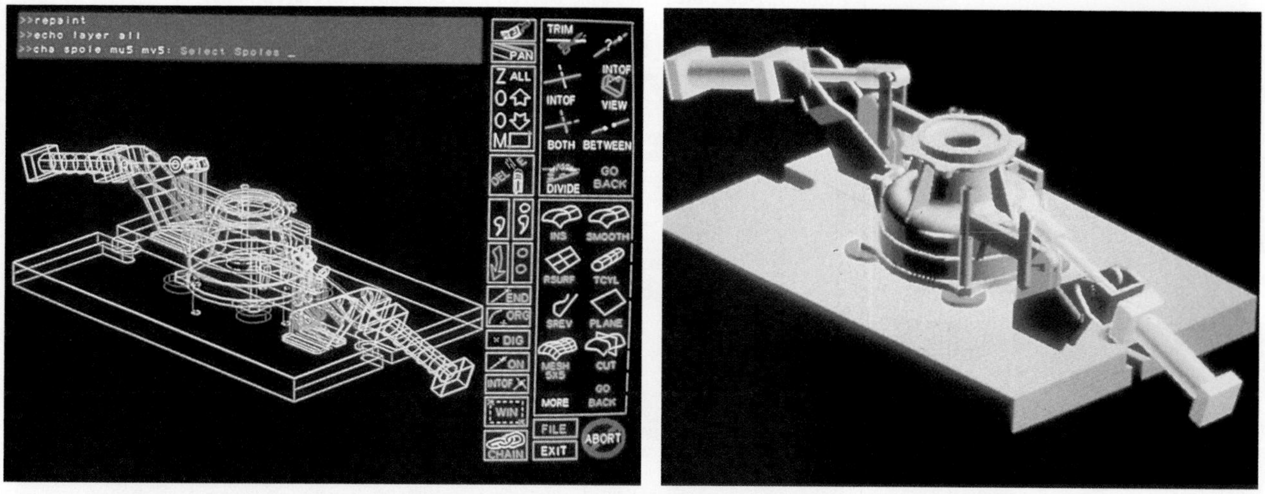

Computer graphics has allowed scientists to reprocess images, such as X rays of the human body (figures 1.2.17 and 1.2.18) and digital images of celestial bodies (figure 1.2.19), to reveal previously undetectable details. Mathematical models of things that cannot be seen, such as black holes (figure 1.2.20) and the pressure on the hull of a sailing yacht, are simulated by computer graphics systems.

FIGURE 1.2.17

Peripheral venogram shows increased vascularization in the leg at the right. (Dr. Aton Pogany, Winthrop Pharmaceuticals)

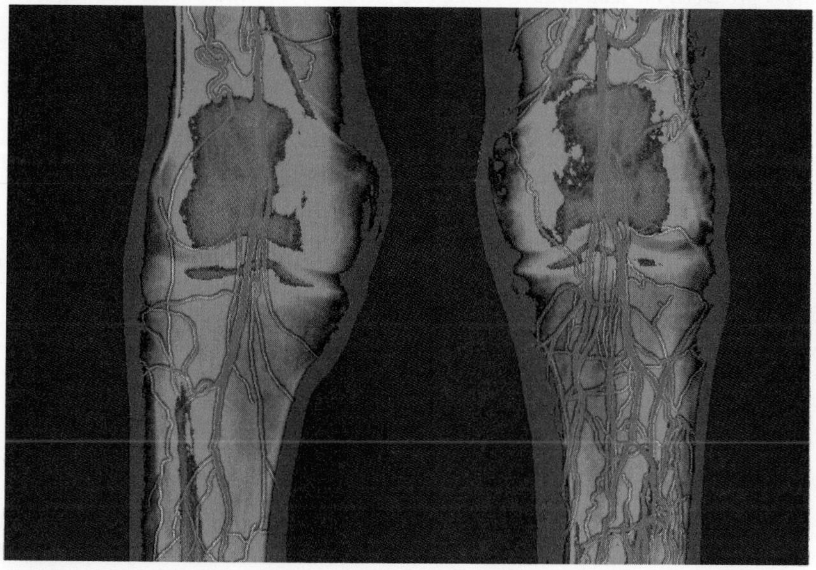

FIGURE 1.2.18

Aortogram shows blockage of abdominal blood vessels. (Dr. Aton Pogany, Alta Bates Hospital, Berkeley; Winthrop Pharmaceuticals)

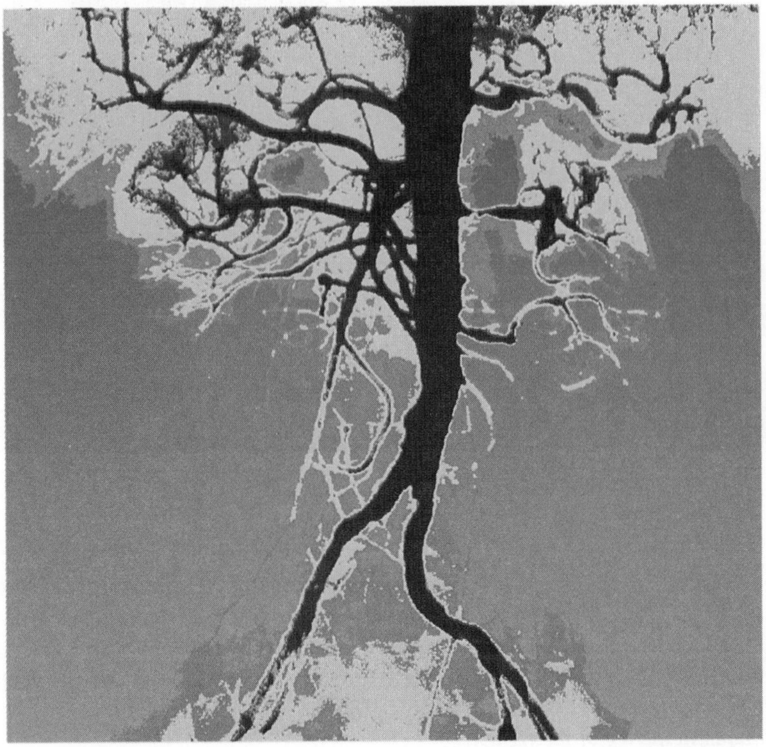

FIGURE 1.2.19

Enhanced pictures of Neptune's moon Triton. (NASA's Jet Propulsion Laboratory)

FIGURE 1.2.20

A solution of Einstein's numerical relativity equations produced the data used to create this picture of a Schwarzschild black hole. (David Hobill, Larry Smarr, David Bernstein, Donna Cox, and Ray Idaszak, NCSA, Univ. of Illinois, at Urbana-Champaign)

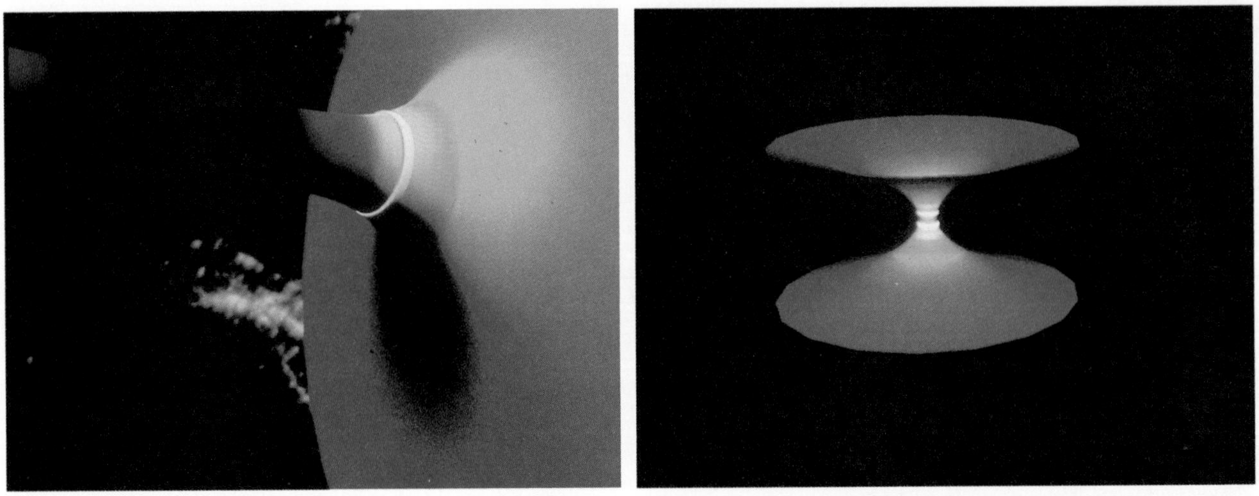

Graphic representations of mathematical models allow engineers to test designs without going to the expense of constructing models. Flight simulators (figure 1.2.21) using computer graphics give pilots the experience of emergency situations without risking life or property.

Computer graphics has spread throughout the business world and is now invading athletics. Golfers, gymnasts, and discus throwers are among those who have had their athletic performance improved by motion capture technology.

Reflective markers are placed at important reference locations on an athlete's body, and a videotape is made of the athlete in action. [figure 1.2.22] From the positions of the markers on each frame of the video the athlete's performance can be analyzed. Bar charts are graphs used to display data such as motion, position, and orientation. Wire-frame figures (figure 1.2.23 or stick figures (figure 1.2.24) give athletes an animated view of their performance. This type of analysis has also been used to improve the appearance of a new, animated Muppet character [Cramblitt 1989].

FIGURE 1.2.21

A flight simulator created by Evans and Sutherland.

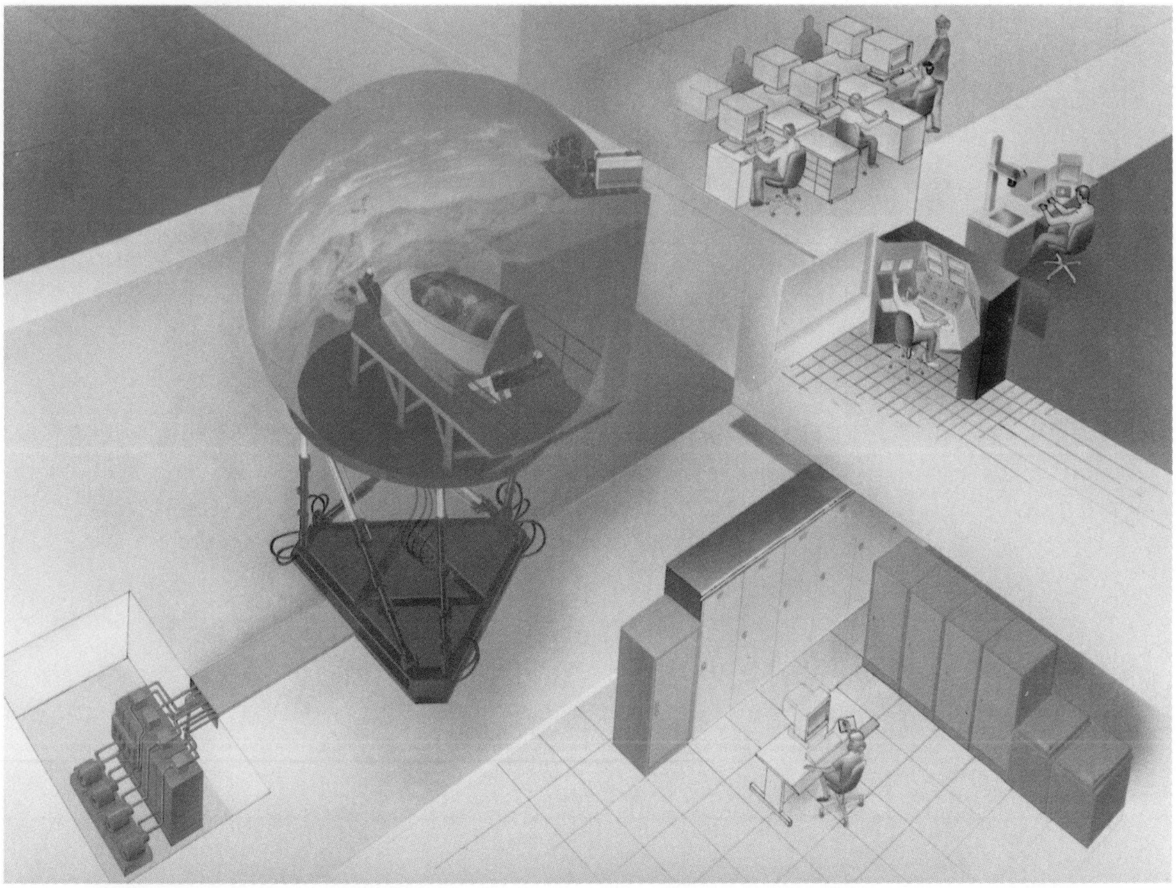

FIGURE 1.2.22

Reflective patches were placed at reference points on the body of discus thrower Jordi Guich as part of a motion capture study. An animation created from this study was used to promote the Barcelona Olympic Games (Cabezas 1989).

FIGURE 1.2.23

Golfers can take many strokes off their scores by having their swings analyzed by the Biomechanics System (Cramblitt 1989).

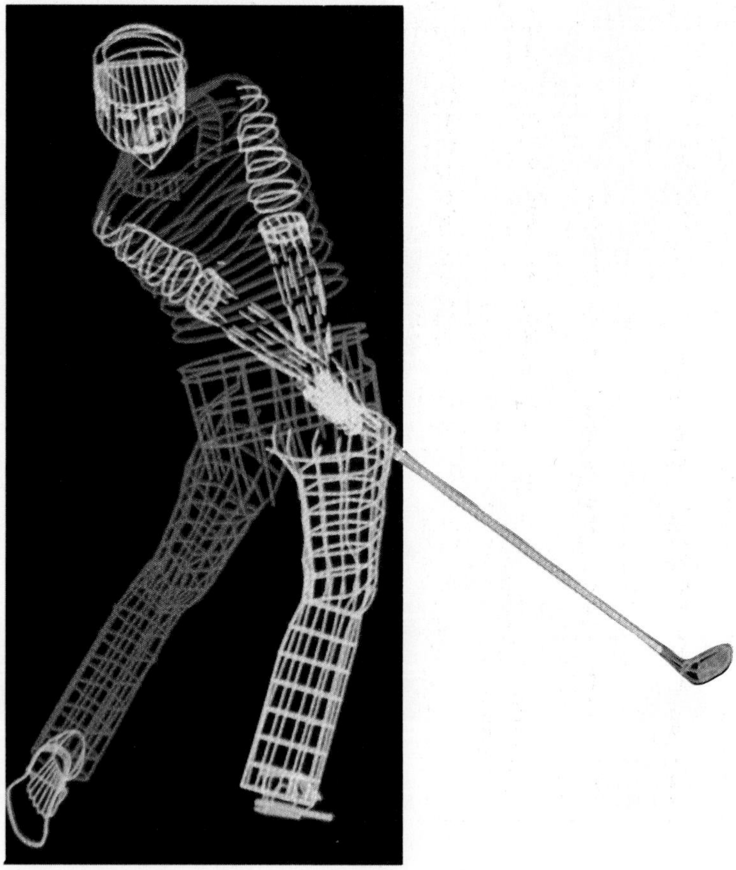

FIGURE 1.2.24

Stick figure drawings of athletes created from motion capture videos show where problems occur in their performance. These figures show a gymnast making a front somersault and a layout back somersault (inset) (Peak Performance Technologies (Cramblitt 1989).

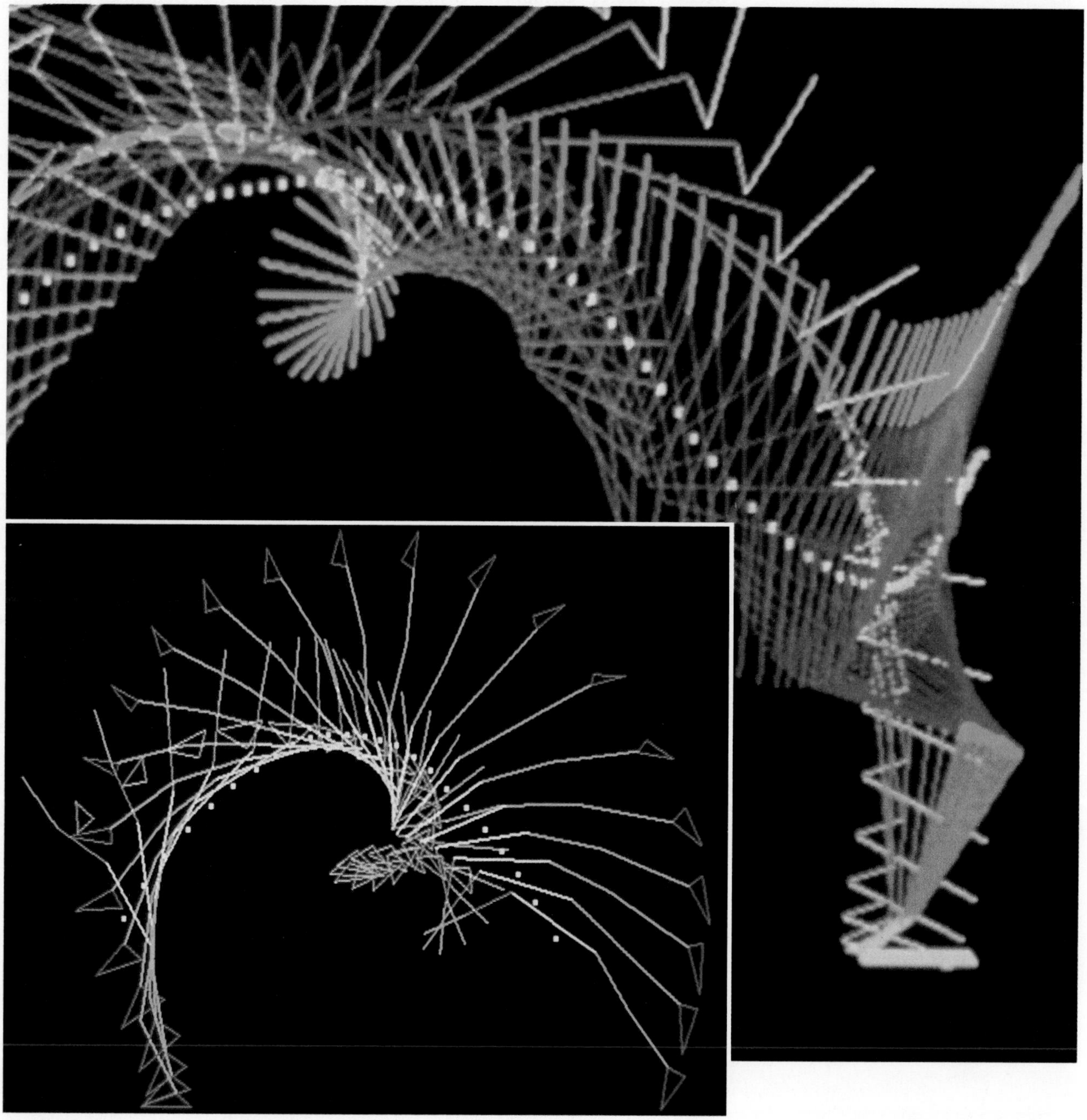

BIBLIOGRAPHY

Berger, Marc, *Computer Graphics with Pascal* The Benjamin/Cummings Publishing Company, Menlo Park, CA 1986.

Bézier, P. *Numerical Control: Mathematics and Applications*. Translated by A.R. Forrest, London: Wiley, 1979.

Cabezas, Roger, ''From Seoul to Barcelona,'' *IEEE CG&A* 9 (4): 6–9[July 1989].

Cox, Donna J. ''The Tao of Postmodernism: Computer Art, Scientific Visualization and Other Paradoxes,'' *Leonardo* [Supplemental Issue 1989]: 7–12.

Cramblitt, Bob, ''Computers Capture Moments of Motion,'' *Computer Graphics World* 12 (3): 50–58[March 1989].

Dietrich, Frank, ''Visual Intelligence: The First Decade of Computer Art (1965–1975),'' *IEEE CG&A* 5 (7): 33–45[July 1985].

LeWinter, Renee, and Cynthia Barron, ''Artistic Challenge Establishing Aesthetic Standards in Computer Art,'' *Computer Graphics World* 13 (2): 49–54[February 1990].

Sutherland, I.E. ''Sketchpad: A Man-Machine Graphics Communication System,'' *AFIPS Spring Joint Computer Conference* 23 329–46[1963]. Available from Spartan Books, Baltimore, Maryland.

Wright, Richard, ''The Image in Art and Computer Art,'' *Leonardo* [Supplemental Issue, 1989]: 49–53.

CHAPTER

2

Graphics Hardware and Software

DIRECTIONS

—*Virtual Reality*

The ancient Greek philosopher Plato believed that all we perceive is merely shadows on the inside of a cave. For him the quest for the nature of reality was academic. Today, researchers in computer graphics are creating artificial reality with head-mounted stereo display devices. (see figure D.2.1). These display devices measure changes in head position or orientation and adjust the displayed images in real time to reflect head movements. Users can wear a data glove which allows them to reach into this simulated space to move objects about.

While **virtual reality** is in its infancy, it has been used for many years to create realistic flight simulators. Yet there is still a big difference between today's flight simulators and the ultimate version of virtual reality, the ''HoloDeck'' in ''Star Trek: The Next Generation,'' where people can interact with simulated objects and beings as if they were real. Although improvements in computer graphics hardware have not made the HoloDeck a reality, virtual reality has reached a level where, in one experiment, people could play a simulated game of racquetball. In another virtual reality experiment, a treadmill helped create the sense of walking about in a simulated building (Wright 1989) (see figure D.2.2).

The level of reality simulated by current systems can be amazing. In a series of experiments carried out at Silicon Graphics (Conn et al. 1989), two or more people shared the virtual world they created. A game of tag in this world can be similar to a real game of tag with some exceptions: as one of the participants discovered, hiding inside another person's head was a tough strategy to beat. In a more serious experiment, two architects enter a children's center they are designing, trying the light switches to see if they are at the correct level and generally viewing the environment from the child's perspective. This same experiment could be repeated with two teachers. One would assume the role of a child, while the other would have the role of teacher. In such an environment, role playing would be much more effective as a tool for understanding a student's point of view.

An extension of the two-person virtual reality suggested by Wright (1989) is a person-machine virtual reality. A robot in an inaccessible place, such as the ocean floor, could be controlled by a person through an interface of virtual reality. The person would see body movements in the virtual reality, which would then be translated into robot actions. The robot need not move like a human because its actions would be translated back into human movements in virtual reality. (see figure D.2.3).

Virtual reality could also provide a new way to view art: viewers would be able to interact with the work, experience it, and change it to suit their personal backgrounds. Likewise, movies of the future would not need to have a fixed plot. Viewers could assume any part and change the movie to fit personal tastes.

This leads us back to the HoloDeck. Today's technology is far from that level of sophistication. The headset in the experiments discussed earlier normally uses liquid crystal displays that are far from lifelike. Recently, however, some examples of this technology have been coupled with optical disks to create more realistic images. When graphics techniques for creating realistic three-dimensional images are improved, a realistic, interactive virtual reality may no longer be purely science fiction.

FIGURE D.2.1

The View Interface Environmental Workstation shows a 3-dimensional scene that changes in response to user head movements. (NASA Ames Research Center).

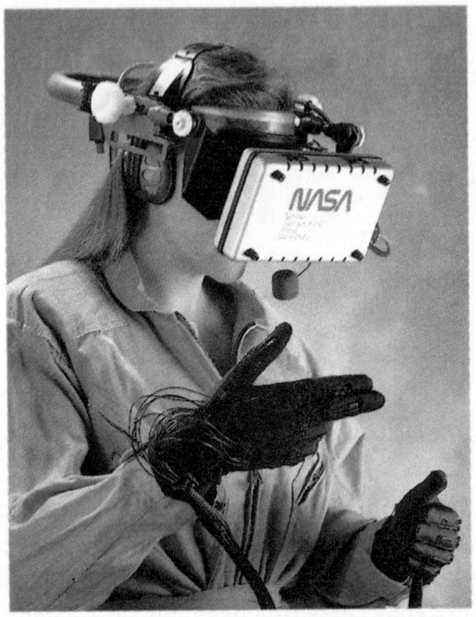

FIGURE D.2.2

Virtual reality technology made it possible to simulate tours of Sitterson Hall at the University of North Carolina before the hall was built. (Wright 1989, 77.)

Introduction

Computer science is hardware dependent by its very nature, but few branches of computer science are more hardware dependent than computer graphics. The saying "A picture is worth a thousand words" is an understatement when it comes to computer-generated images. Pictures generated on high-resolution graphics systems often use more than a million words of computer memory. When large amounts of memory were not as readily available as they are today, highly specialized display and printing devices were required to create graphic images. Even with low-cost memory, the sheer volume of data needed to create or modify a picture places a strain on systems not designed for graphics. Add

FIGURE D.2.3

The data glove from VPL Research translates user hand movements into hand movements of a simulated hand. (Orr 1989, 89).

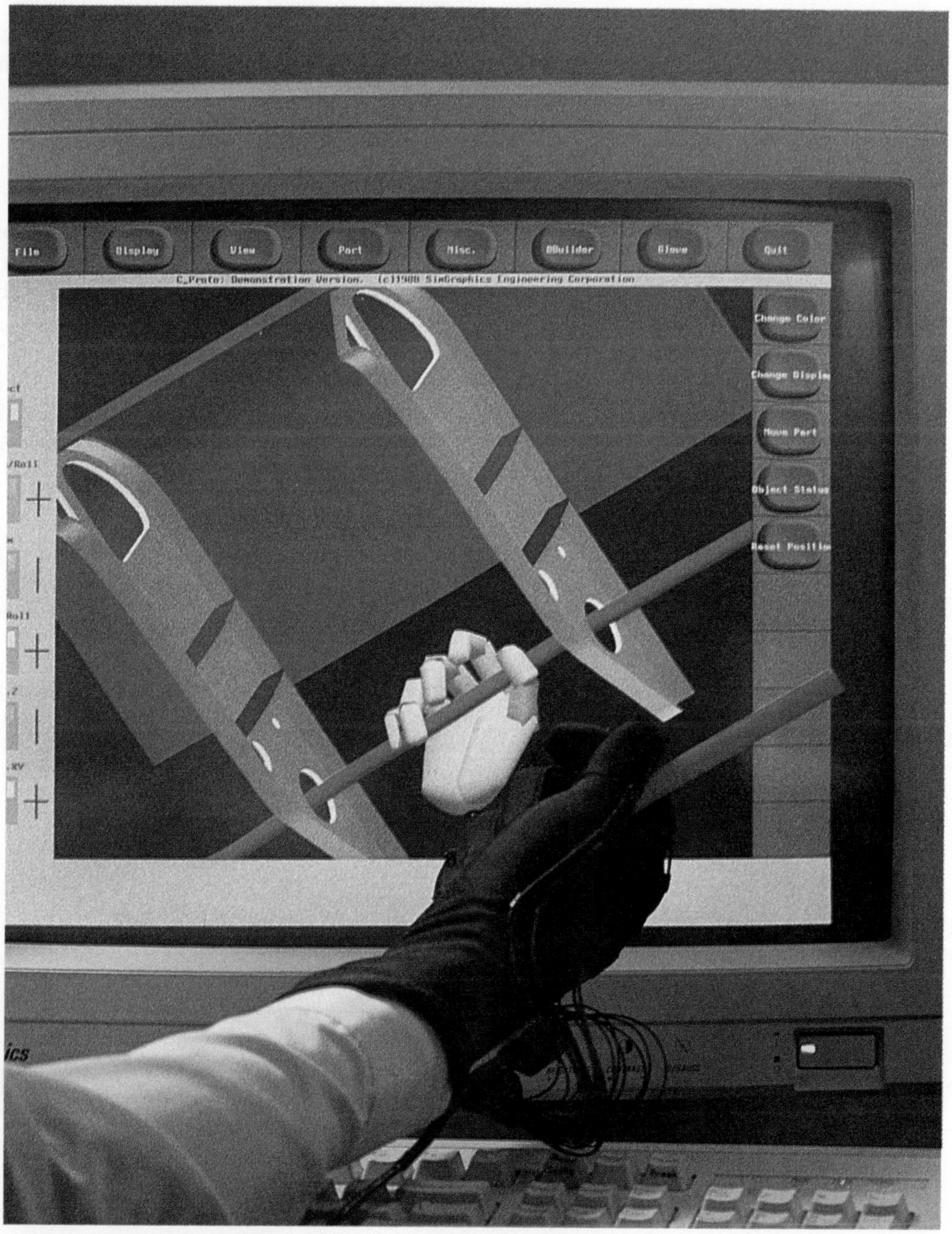

to this problem the challenge to make the process of image creation interactive, and the result is very specialized hardware.

The heavy dependence on hardware often masked the types of activities graphics programs were used for. Standard graphics interface systems were devised in the seventies and eighties to list standard graphics processes. Implementations of these standards allow programmers to create device-independent graphics programs. This chapter gives a broad overview of graphics hardware and software standards.

2.1 Display Devices

Computer graphic images usually originate on some type of display device. The wide variety of display devices available is a direct result of both rapidly changing technology and the diverse needs of users. The most commonly used display device is the **refresh cathode ray tube(CRT).**

The picture tubes on television sets are CRTs. The CRT creates an image by bombarding a phosphor on the inside of its screen with a beam of electrons created in the neck of the tube (figure 2.1.1). The electron beam causes the phosphor's atoms to be put into a higher energy state, and as they return to their stable state they give off energy as light.

The main tasks carried out by a CRT are

- Creating a beam of electrons of an appropriate energy level
- Directing the beam in a regular path focused on the screen
- Creating an image that is clear and that neither flickers nor remains on the screen when it is replaced by the next image

The electrons forming the beam are generated by heating a negatively charged surface, called a **cathode,** in a vacuum. An electric coil heater is surrounded by

FIGURE 2.1.1

Simplified cross-section of a CRT

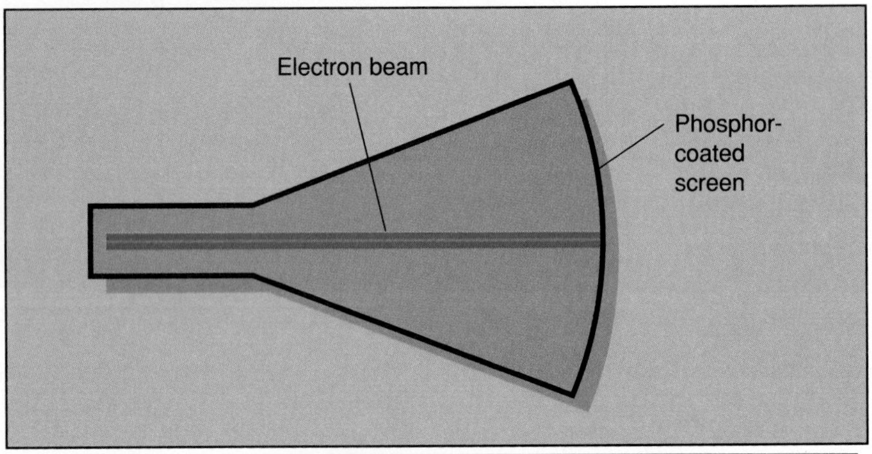

a cylindrical cathode. When a current is passed through the coil it heats up, causing electrons to "boil off" of the cathode (figure 2.1.2). Because electrons are negatively charged, they are repelled from the cathode and move toward the screen.

The intensity of the beam is determined by the number of electrons reaching the screen. A negatively charged grid placed between the cathode and the focusing mechanism controls the intensity of the beam. This **control grid** has a variable charge controlled by the brightness knob on the CRT. The higher the negative charge on the grid, the fewer electrons that are energetic enough to pass through the grid. Those electrons that do get through the grid are repelled by it and sent toward the focusing device. The complete system of cathode and control grid is often called an **electron gun.**

Electrons that get through the grid are focused into a beam by either a **positively charged (anode) focusing device** or a **magnetic focusing device** (figure 2.1.3). In either case, the beam is focused so that its smallest cross-section occurs at the screen surface (figure 2.1.4). The distance from the focusing device to the place where the beam has its smallest cross-section is called the **focal distance.** The electrons cannot be focused into parallel paths because they repel one another and the beam would spread out before it got to the screen.

One difficulty with focusing the electron beam is that the radius of curvature of most CRTs is greater than the focal distance. If the focal distance were set as the distance from the focusing device to the center of the screen, the beam would not focus at the edge of the screen (figure 2.1.5). Most CRTs vary focusing to fit the curvature of the screen.

Even a well-focused beam has a cross-sectional area larger than a single phosphor atom. The size of this cross-section determines the number and size of distinct dots on the screen. The individual dots that the beam controls are grouped into **pixels** (short for "picture elements"), positions addressable by the

FIGURE 2.1.2

The electron gun in a CRT

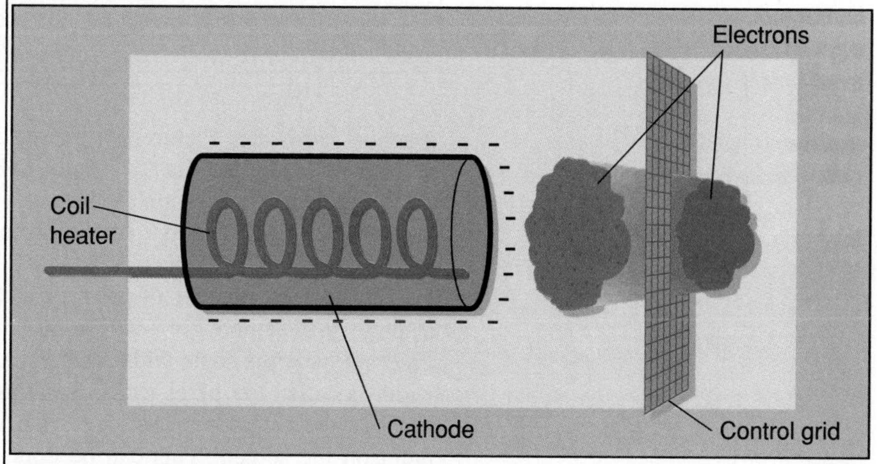

FIGURE 2.1.3

After passing through the grid, the electron cloud is focused into a narrow beam and directed to a desired location on the screen.

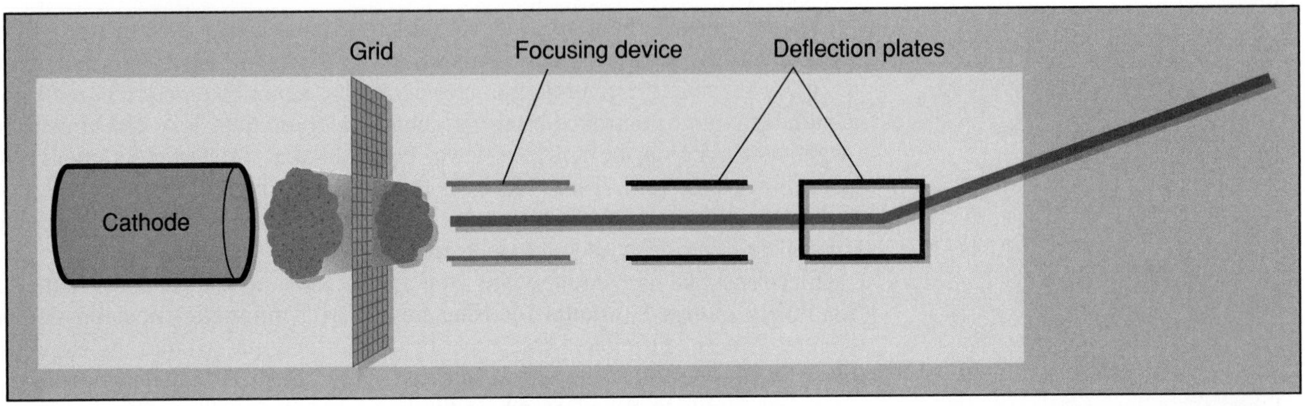

FIGURE 2.1.4

The electron beam is focused so that it strikes the inside surface of the screen at the point of its smallest cross-section.

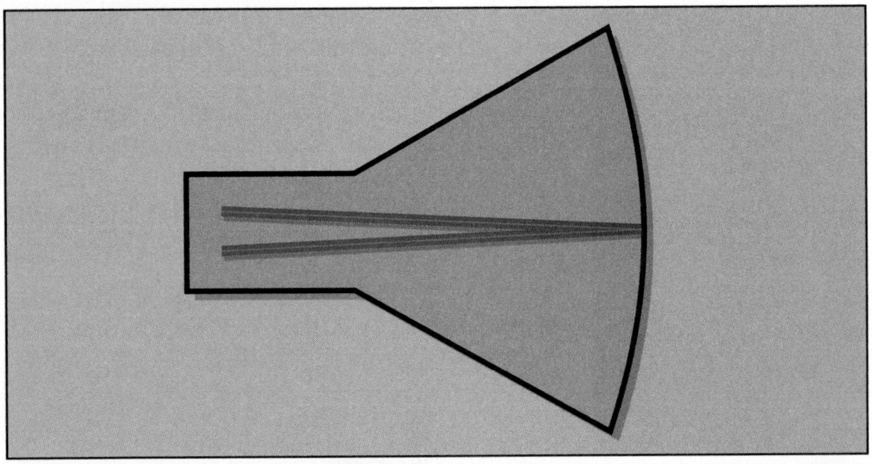

graphics hardware. Picture sharpness, called **resolution,** is determined by the number of pixels per linear distance. More dots generally mean higher resolution. Resolution of a graphics system is normally specified by of the number of pixels in a horizontal row of the screen followed by the number of rows of pixels. A typical specification is 640 × 400-pixel display. The **aspect ratio** is the ratio of the number of rows of a display to the number of columns of a display. While there are often more pixels horizontally than vertically, pixels need not have the same width as height. The ratio of the height of a pixel to its width is called the **pixel ratio.** Systems with square pixels have pixel ratio 1.

Once the electron beam leaves the focusing device, it must be aimed at a point on the screen. This can be done in two different ways; by a system of

FIGURE 2.1.5

CRTs must vary focusing to accommodate the screen's curvature or the beam will be out of focus in some parts of the screen.

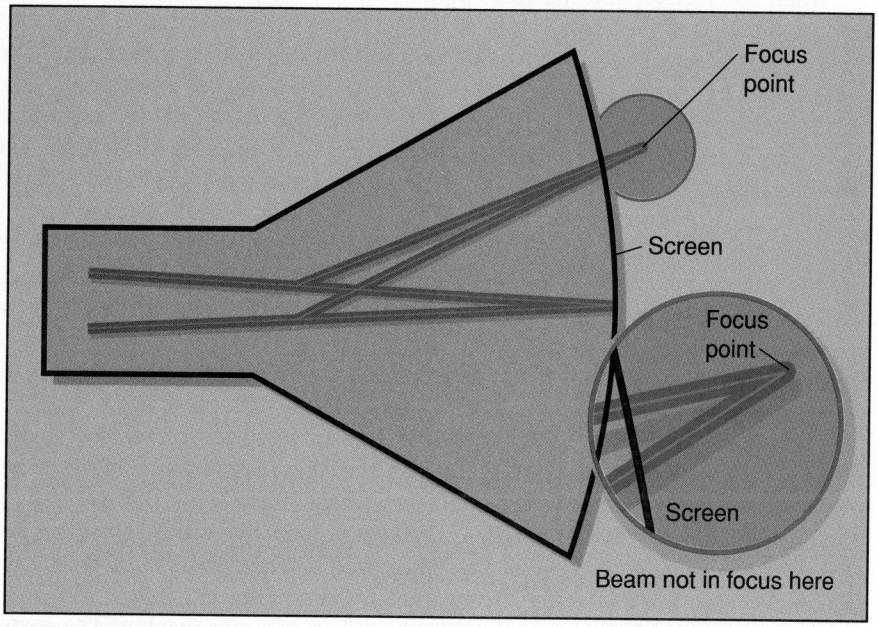

adjustable voltage plates or by a system of two magnetic coils. Either system is used to control the horizontal and vertical coordinates of the beam's destination (figure 2.1.3).

The inside surface of the CRT often contains positively charged metal surfaces that help accelerate the beam onto the screen (figure 2.1.6). Picture

FIGURE 2.1.6

The inside surface of the CRT often contains charged metal places that help accelerate the beam.

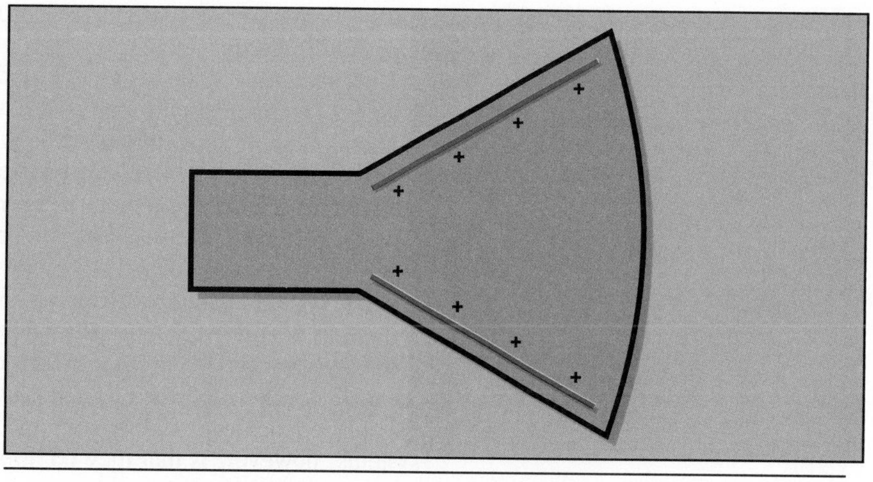

intensity may be controlled by varying the charge on these plates. Intensity is increased if the charge is increased.

When an electron finally strikes a phosphor atom on the screen, the kinetic energy (energy derived from motion) of the electron is converted to heat. This heat causes electron in the phosphor atom to be raised to a higher, unstable quantum state. Some of these higher quantum states are so unstable that the electron instantly returns to a stable level. Other states are more stable, so that the electron returns to a stable state after only a short time. In either case, the energy released by the return of the electron to a stable state is given off as light.

Different phosphors have different sets of quantum states. Specific energy and stability levels are associated with each quantum state. The amount of energy released by the jump from one quantum state to another determines which color of light will be given off. The stability of the state determines the number of atoms that will be giving off light at a given time after the electron beam strikes them. The length of time needed to reduce the light output to 10 percent of its initial output is called the **persistence** of a phosphor.

Phosphors with higher persistence give a steadier image that has less **flicker** than those with lower persistence. This is a desirable feature when an image has many fine details, such as an engineering drawing. Applications such as animated pictures, in which the image changes quickly, require phosphors that are not as persistent. Persistent phosphors would leave an after-image on the screen, resulting in a poor-quality picture for animation.

There are two different ways to use the CRT in graphics display. The **raster scan** system is very similar to a television set. The beam in this type of system traces a regular pattern on the screen. It usually starts at the upper-left corner of the screen and is directed across the screen in the horizontal direction. After completing one pass across the screen, it moves down one line and traces the next line. Each line in this type of system is called a **scan line.** Raster scan systems refresh the entire screen with this pattern 30–60 times per second. Raster scan systems normally re-create a pattern stored in memory, so every pixel corresponds to one or more bits of memory (figure 2.1.7) As you may recall, the block of memory used to store the screen pattern is called the **frame buffer.** The size of the frame buffer is determined by multiplying the number of pixels per scan line by the number of scan lines. Thus, a system with 640×400 resolution would have 256,000, or 256K, pixels. This represents at least 32K bytes of memory.

Until recently, 32K was a large portion of the memory in many mainframe systems. To create graphics on a CRT without using large amounts of memory, a second method the **random scan** system was developed. In this system, the picture is described in terms of line segments rather than pixels. The electron beam traces the lines in a picture (figure 2.1.8). Random scan systems are also called **vector** systems because they store the lines being drawn as a series of end points interpreted as vectors to be drawn by the scan system. The electron gun in these systems is not restricted to horizontal and vertical motion. The list of end points is converted into instructions that cause the electron gun to trace the given line directly on the screen. Random scan is more efficient than raster scan because pictures described as a series of end points of lines require much less memory to achieve high resolution. One drawback of most random scan systems, however, is that they do no allow for patterned shading except when it is described as a series of lines.

F I G U R E 2.1.7

Consecutive passes of the raster scan duplicate patterns in memory.

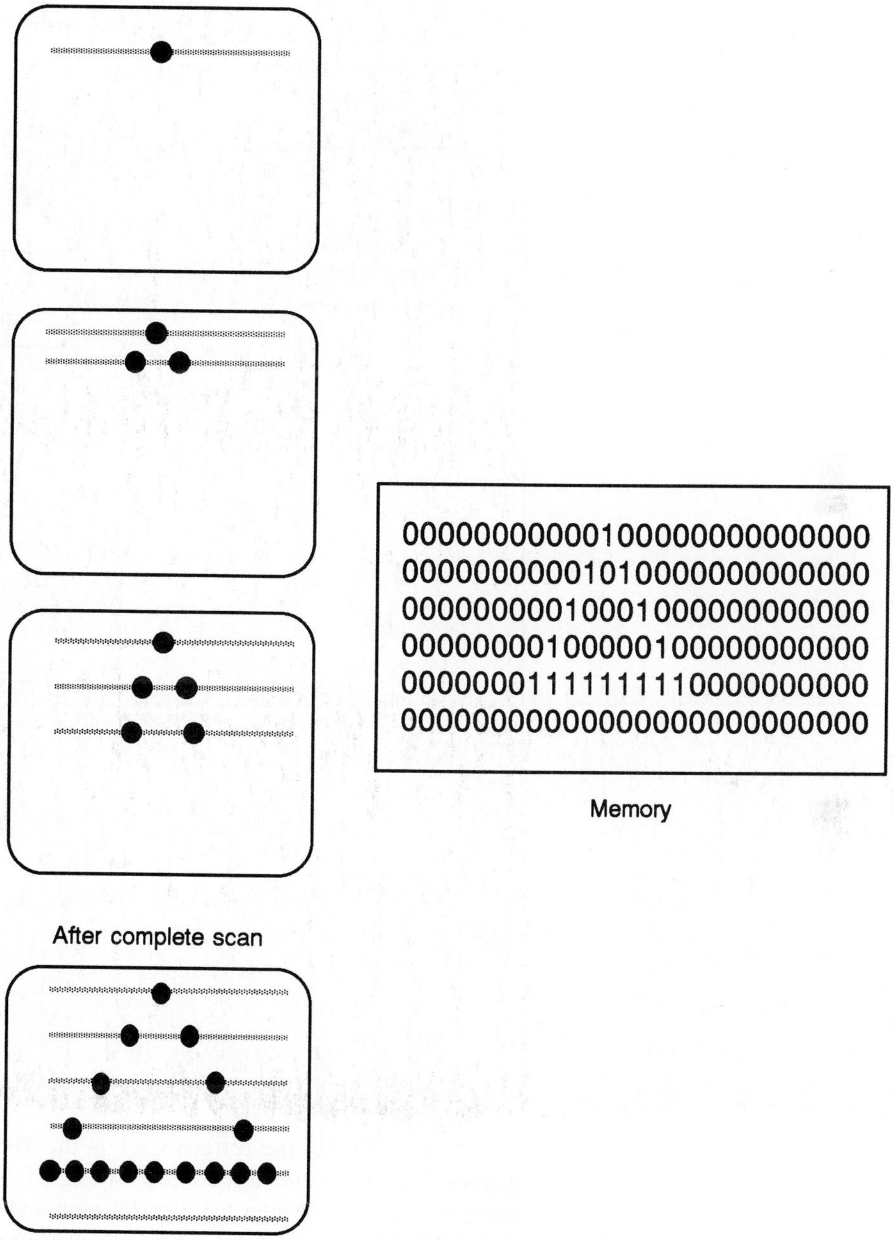

FIGURE 2.1.8

A sequence of instructions direct a random scan system to create an image on the screen.

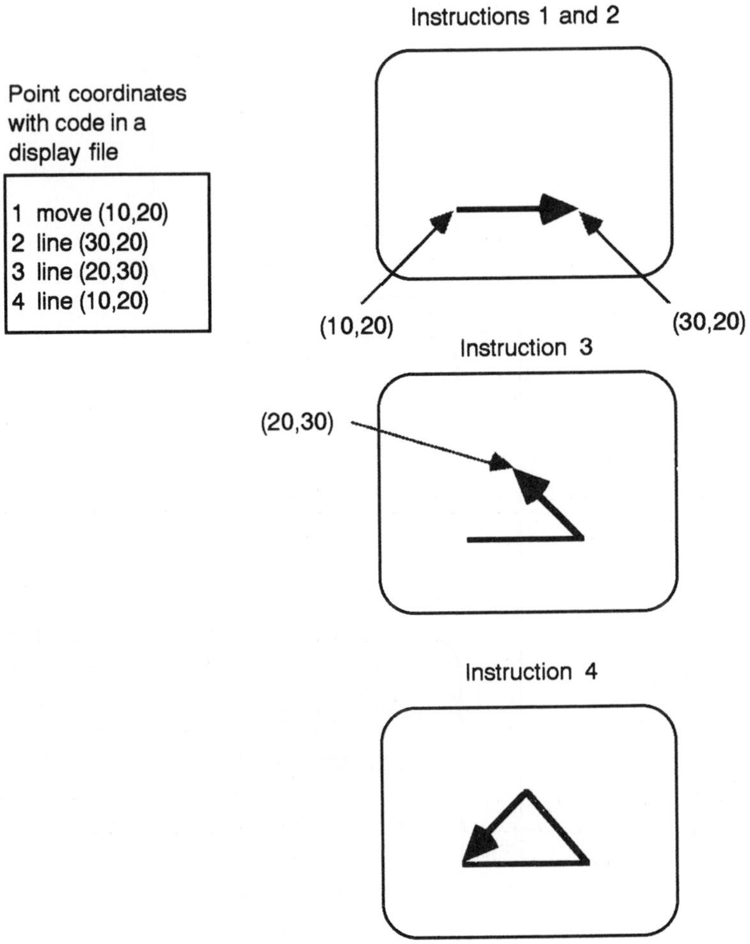

An alternative to the refresh CRT is the **direct-view storage tube (DVST)** (figure 2.1.9). In the direct-view storage tube, the picture is created on a **storage surface** between the electron gun and the phosphors on the screen.

DVSTs have two electron guns, the **primary gun** and the **flood gun.** The primary gun draws a sequence of lines with a beam of high-energy electrons. These electrons pass through a positively charged collector grid to strike the uniformly negatively charged storage surface. Electrons dislodged from the

FIGURE 2.1.9

Cross-section of a direct-view storage tube

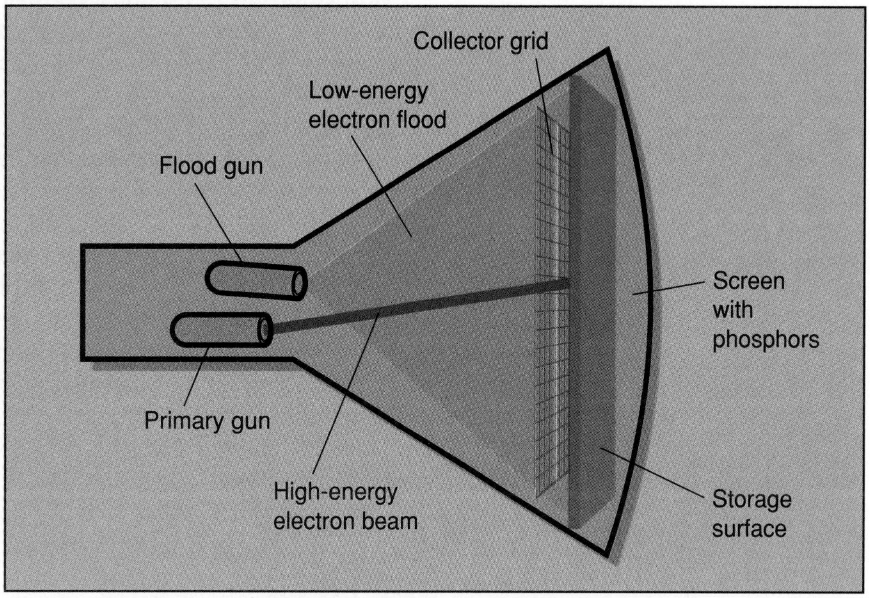

surface by the electron beam are attracted to the collector grid, while electrons on the storage surface cannot migrate to even out the charge because this surface is a nonconductor. This leaves a positively charged pattern of lines on the storage surface wherever the electron beam strikes it.

The flood gun emits a constant cloud of low-energy electrons that are not focused or deflected. These low-energy electrons flood (are uniformly spread) over the whole storage surface. The low-energy electrons passing near the positively charged areas of the storage surface are attracted to them and pass through them to strike the phosphor screen. The charge on the storage surface is not appreciably altered by these low-energy electrons. Electrons approaching the negatively charged areas of the storage surface are repelled and collected by the collector grid.

Because the screen is constantly flooded with electrons from the flood gun, the DVST requires no refresh cycle and has no flicker. It is not possible, however, to erase lines on the DVST selectively; the whole screen must be erased to change the picture. To erase the screen, a positive charge is stored on the entire storage surface, causing the flood gun to erase the entire picture with a flash. Next, the storage surface is given its normal, even, negative charge, and the picture is redrawn without the erased lines. This problem and the reduction in the cost of memory have led to a decline in the use of DVST systems.

Adding color to a graphics system requires both a change in hardware and a change in software. It takes more than the addition of a color CRT to create a color system. When color is added, the pixel may be on or off but it also has a color associated with it. Each color on the system must have a numerical representation. A combination of software and hardware converts these numerical values into color on the CRT screen.

Most **color CRTs** use three phosphors, one for each of the primary additive colors—red, green, and blue **(RGB monitors).** One these color CRTs, each pixel has one or more groups of dots each of which contains a red, a green, and a blue dot. Three electron beams, one for each color phosphor, are aimed at the screen. The intensity of each beam determines just how much of each primary color will appear in an area, and this in turn determines the overall color effect. See chapter 11 for more details on color mixing.

The alignment and focusing of the three beams is critical to achieving a sharp image on a color CRT, so screen sharpness does not wholly depend on the number of dots on the screen. Many color CRTs employ a **shadow mask** behind the screen, which helps align the electron beams so that each strikes the appropriate phosphor dot (figure 2.1.10).

Sony has recently replaced the shadow mask with an **aperture grille** in some of its monitors. This structure uses long vertical slits (figure 2.1.11) instead of the holes of the shadow mask to help align the beams. While the aperture grille is expensive, it leads to a brighter screen with less rolling flicker because of slight vertical shifts of the picture.

FIGURE 2.1.10

The shadow mask behind the screen of a color CRT helps align the electron beams so that each strikes the phosphor dot of the appropriate color.

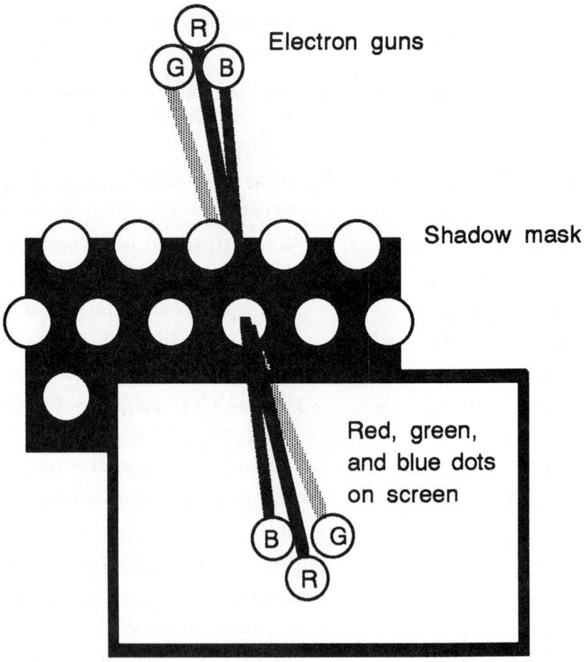

FIGURE 2.1.11

Sony replaces the shadow mask with an aperture grill of vertical slits. This structure produces a brighter screen with less rolling flicker.

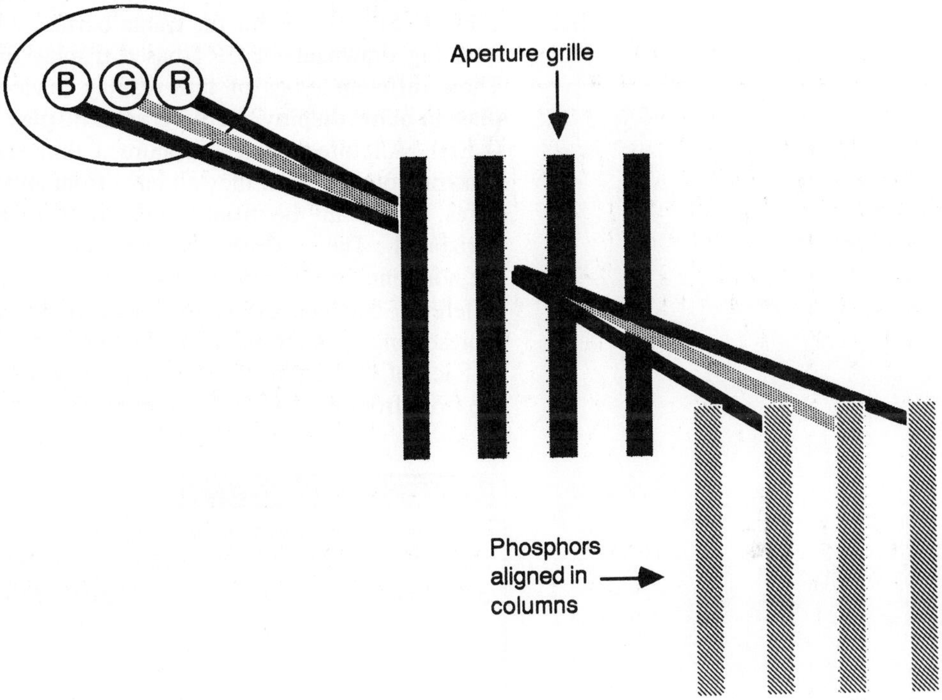

Another color technology is **beam penetration.** With this method a single beam is directed at a screen that has two phosphor layers. Each layer contains phosphors of a different color, usually red or green. The intensity of the beam determines whether the electrons will excite the phosphors in the layer closest to the electron gun or will pass through it to excite the phosphors in the layer farther from the gun. If the beam is adjusted to an intermediate energy level, some electrons will excite both of the phosphors, with the result that the color displayed will be a mixture of the two basic phosphor colors. This usually adds two more colors to this type of display.

The typical PC color system may allow 16 colors (including black and white). Each of these colors is a predetermined combination of red, green, and blue, and is assigned a number between 0 and 15. Four bits ar needed to represent the numbers between 0 and 15, so each pixel is represented by 4 bits. While it is possible to store these bits in consecutive memory locations, that is not the usual way. A commonly used method for storing color codes is to use multiple banks of memory. Each bank of memory has 1 bit per pixel in the frame buffer. The displacement of a bit from the beginning of a bank is its **bank address.** Each pixel is assigned a bank address, and each bit of the color code for a pixel is stored in a separate bank, at the bank address of the pixel (figure 2.1.12). There are as many banks of memory as there are bits in the color code. The reason this storage strategy is adopted is that graphics cards may be designed to access all bits with the same bank address simultaneously. A graphics system with 640 × 400 resolution and 16 colors require at least 2 × 256K = 512K bytes for the frame buffer.

A big drawback of CRT-based display units is the depth of the monitor. Three different types of thin display devices are currently in common use: **plasma panel display, liquid crystal display (LCD),** and **light-emitting diode (LED).** All three devices feature a thin screen system and have a similar construction—that is, they all have front and back glass panels embedded with wires. Wires in the front panel are vertical, wires in the back panel are horizontal . The vertical wires represent the x-coordinates on the screen while the horizontal wires represent y-values. To light the pixel (x_0,y_0), the voltage difference between the vertical wire representing x_0 and the horizontal wire representing y_0 is raised enough to cause a current flow between the two wires.

Each of the display devices mentioned contains a third panel that separates the front from the back panel. In the plasma panel display (figure 2.1.13), this

FIGURE 2.1.12

One commonly used method for storing a color code is to assign each pixel a bank address (the distance from the beginning of a bank). The code for the pixel is stored 1 bit per bank at the bank address of the pixel. If the code for a pixel is 1100, it can be stored as shown.

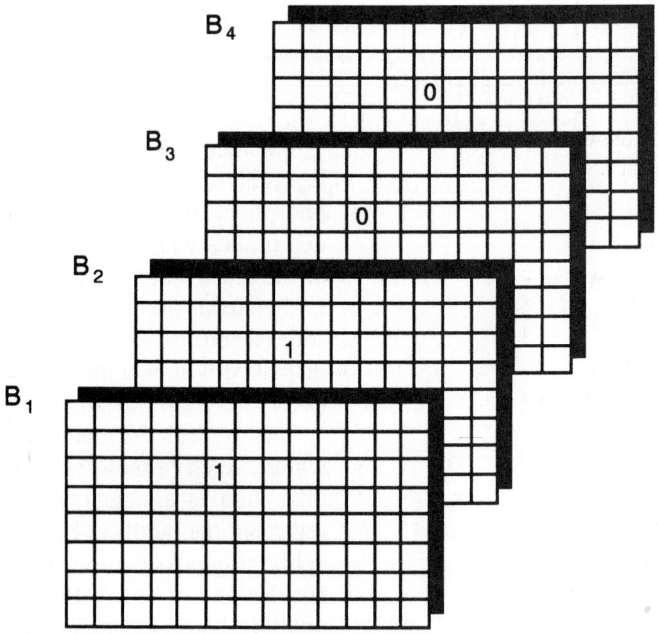

FIGURE 2.1.13

The three layers of a gas plasma display fit together closely so that when there is a large voltage drop between the y-coordinate wire in the back panel and the x-coordinate wire in the front panel, a current runs through the neon tubes.

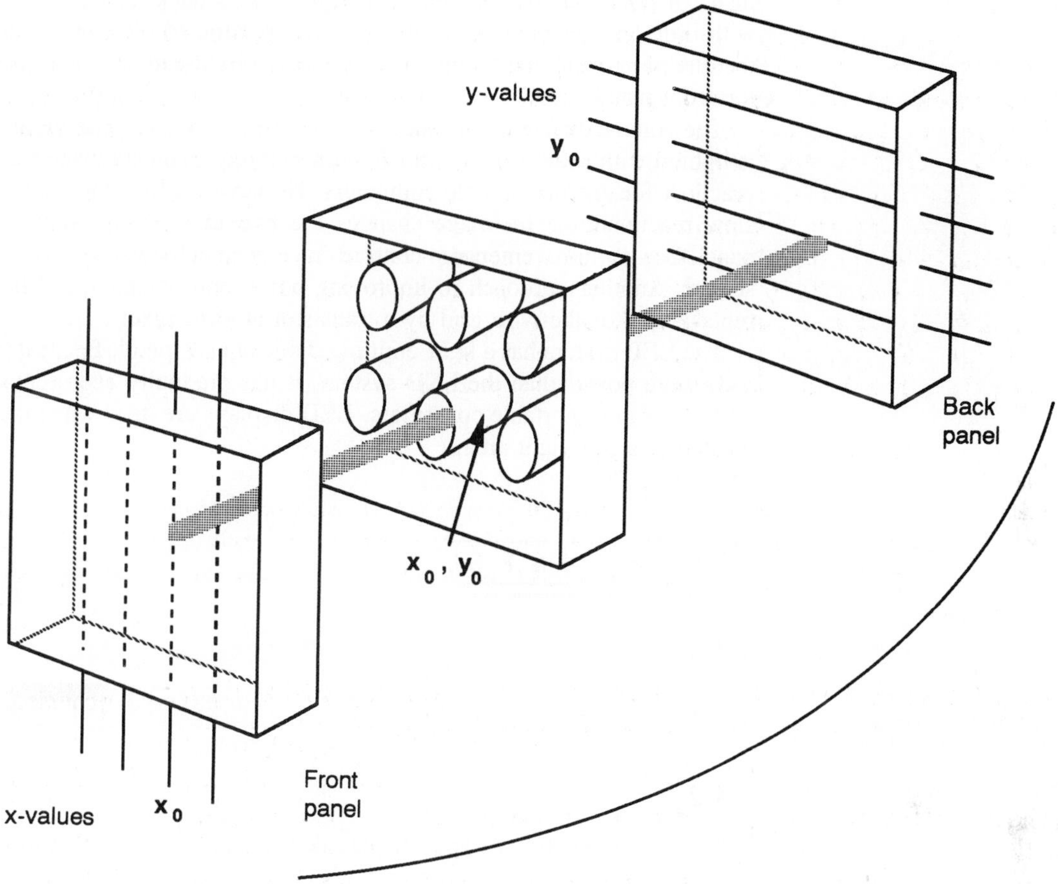

panel contains neon tubes (bulbs) that begin to glow when the voltage difference between the front and back is large enough to initiate a current. Once the current is started, it will continue as long as a sustaining current lower than the initiating current is present. If the voltage difference is allowed to drop below that which is needed for the sustaining current, then the neon will stop glowing. Plasma panels require relatively high voltages to work and are very expensive, so they are not normally used on portable machines. The flicker-free performance of these displays is desirable for use in engineering applications. Because the plasma panel is transparent, it can be combined with a rear-projection system, which allows slides to be projected on the panel so diagrams can be merged with photographic images.

In the LCD system, the middle panel contains pockets of clear liquid crystals that can be aligned by the current passing between the front and back panels. The front panel of the LCD is polarized glass, so light entering the system is polarized. In one method of creating images, if the crystals are aligned in one direction the polarized light is reflected off the back panel without having its plane of polarization modified. This light passes back through the front panel with little loss of intensity. If the crystals are aligned differently, they modify the direction of polarization, and the reflected light can no longer pass through the front panel.

The voltage differences needed in LCD displays are very small, and the panel is lighted with room light. These low-energy requirements make LCD displays practical for use on portable computers. However, a low contrast image and a slow reaction time to image changes are two major drawbacks of the LCD panel. Some improvements in contrast have been achieved by back-lighting the screen. Another approach to improving both contrast and speed has been the replacement of the wire grid by a transistor at each pixel.

The LED system has a light-emitting diode at each pixel. Because this system uses more power than the LCD system, it has gradually been replaced by the LCD display in portable computers. LED displays are used when the display is located in a low-light area.

EXERCISES

2.1.1

Find out what type of graphics system will be used in your course. What types of display devices will you use?

2.1.2

What is the resolution of your display device, and how many Pixels does your display device use?

2.1.3

If you are using a raster scan system, how many colors are available on your system? Calculate the amount of memory needed for your frame buffer.

2.2 Hard-Copy Devices

Many applications of computer graphics require that an image on a graphics screen be reproduced in a noncomputer medium. Such reproductions are called **hard copies.** Images projected as slides or overhead transparencies for classroom or conference use, called **presentation graphics,** are an example of hard-copy images. Many other applications, such as engineering, graphic design, and architecture, also require hard copies. To accommodate this diversity of need, several different types of hard-copy devices are available.

These devices differ in cost, in the techniques used to create an image, in the quality of the image, and in the colors they can reproduce.

The simplest way to capture a graphics screen image on photographic film is to use a **film recorder.** This device aligns a camera with the video display and shields the screen so no reflected light degrades the image. Film recorders are ideal for creating color presentation graphics because some degree of color control can be achieved by the use of an appropriate color film. Photographic copiers are available to make transparencies for most commonly used projectors.

Many computer **printers** can be used to print graphic images. Some printers require additional hardware or software to produce acceptable graphic images, but even with these additional costs, they often are the cheapest hard-copy devices available.

Printers can be divided into two classes: **impact** and **non-impact printers.** The **dot-matrix printer** is the impact printer most often used to create graphic images. In this type of printer, the print head contains a column of pins. Selected pins are activated during printing, creating a pattern. These pins strike an inked ribbon, which in turn reproduces the pin pattern on paper behind the ribbon (figure 2.2.1). The pin patterns are not restricted to type faces or type spacing, so dot-matrix printers are more versatile than printers such as **daisy-wheel printers** or **line printers,** which are restricted to typefaces.

The most common non-impact printers are the **ink-jet printers** and **laser printers** (figure 2.2.2). Ink-jet printers shoot an electrically charged stream of ink onto paper wrapped on a drum. An electric field directs the stream, forming patterns of dots. Laser printers use a laser beam to create an electronically charged image on a light-sensitive drum. Toner attracted to the image on the drum is deposited on paper. Non-impact printers are popular with businesses because they are quiet and have excellent reproduction quality.

FIGURE 2.2.1

A column of pins in the head of a dot-matrix printer strikes an inked ribbon, creating an image on paper.

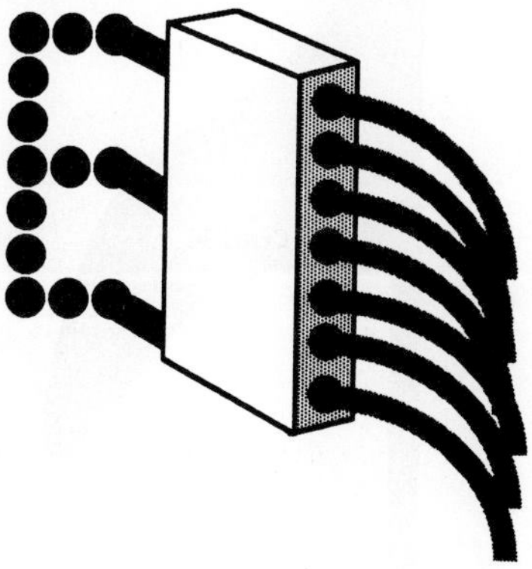

FIGURE 2.2.2

A laser printer

On both dot-matrix and ink-jet printers the image created has, until recently, been a reproduction of the dot patterns on the screen. A form created from 20 dots on the screen was re-created with 20 dots on the printer. Screen resolutions of 75 dots per inch (dpi) resulted in printed images with a resolution of 75 dpi. This is very low quality when compared with laser printers, which normally have a resolution of 300 dots per inch, or typesetting equipment, which normally has a resolution of 1200 or more dots per inch (figure 2.2.3). Page description languages such as Adobe's **PostScript** allow the resolution of the output to be matched to the resolution of the output devices. These languages store an image as a list describing components such as lines, fonts, and curves. Most laser printers and many ink-jet printers can receive instructions in such a language and print a reconstructed image with resolution of 300 dpi or better. Many typesetting machines also accept input in PostScript and create true typeset hard copy.

FIGURE 2.2.3

The figure on the left was printed with a dot-matrix printer. On the right, the same figure was printed with a laser printer.

Other types of non-impact printers include **thermal printers** (figure 2.2.4) and **thermal transfer printers.** Both printers use heat to create an image. Thermal printers heat a chemically treated paper. These printers are slow and require a special paper that is costly and has a short shelf life. They are also restricted to one-color printing. Thermal transfer printers apply heat to a waxed ink ribbon, melting the wax and making it stick to regular paper. Thermal transfer printers are relatively expensive but produce high-quality color prints.

In recent years, color printing on ink-jet and laser printers has improved greatly, but it is still far from magazine quality.

Plotters are used to create line drawings. Frequently plotters use pens to draw lines, but they can also use laser, ink-jet, or electrostatic techniques. A plotter creates images by moving the carriage or cross bar on which a pen or other drawing tool is mounted across a sheet of paper. The pen is then moved back and forth on the bar to create the image.

All movements of the drawing mechanism are controlled by a special set of plotter directives. Applications programs often require special interface software to convert their draw commands into plotter commands. Typical plotter commands raise and lower the pen as well as move the pen to a specific position. The number of directions that pens can move is normally between 4 and 16. When microprocessors are added to plotters, standard geometric figures such as circles and ellipses can be generated automatically. The plotters use paper that is either stretched flat or rolled on a drum or belt.

Flatbed plotters have a large, flat surface over which the paper is held flat by clamps, a vacuum, or an electrostatic charge. The carriage is mounted above the paper and moves back and forth over it while the pen moves along the carriage. Flatbed plotters vary in size from 12 by 18 inches to 6 by 10 feet.

FIGURE 2.2.4

Color electrostatic printers can produce high-quality, wide format, dry color plots directly from random vector data. (CalComp).

Drum plotters (figure 2.2.5) have a stationary carriage. The paper moves back and forth on a drum under the carriage while the pens on the carriage move to appropriate positions to draw on the paper. Drum plotters tend to be smaller than flatbed plotters, ranging in size from 1 to 3 feet across. The drum plotter has the advantage of not taking up as much floor space as a flatbed plotter with similar-size output.

The **beltbed plotter** is an attempt to combine the large, flat surface of the flatbed plotter with the space-saving feature of the drum plotter. With this type of plotter, both the pen carriage and the paper move as a drawing is generated.

Color can be added to a plotter simply by changing the pen for different parts of the drawing procedure. Some plotters allow more that one pen to be mounted at the same time; for these machines the command language includes pen-color changes. Several tools can replace pens on plotters; these include a ''pen light'' which exposes photographic film, and a ''pen stylus,'' which can be used for cutting lines in soft material.

FIGURE 2.2.5

A drum plotter

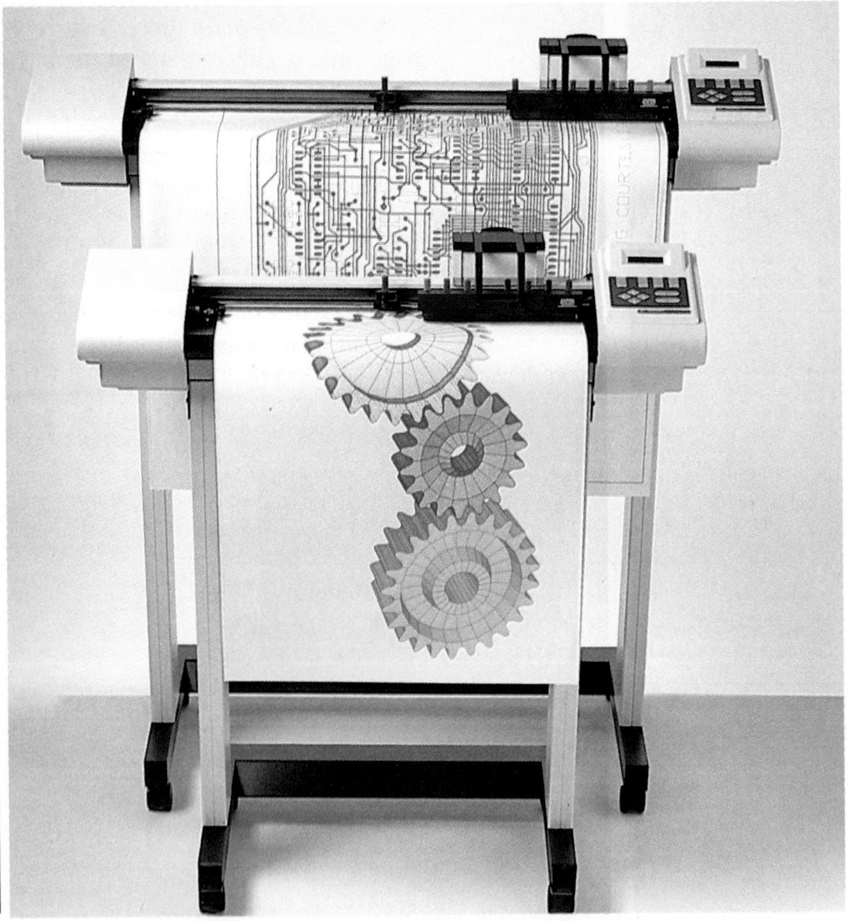

EXERCISES

2.2.1

What types of graphics printers will you use?

2.2.2

Are there special functions which allow you to print directly from a graphics program? If not, write a procedure to transfer the image on your graphics screen to your printer.

2.2.3

If you are using a plotter, find out what commands you use to create images on the plotter.

2.2.4

Is the resolution of your printer different from the resolution on your screen? If so, is there any way to print an image from your screen in higher resolution?

2.3 Interactive Graphics Input Devices

The current popularity of computer graphics can be largely attributed to the many interactive graphics applications available. These programs use at least one interactive input device to read the user's draw commands. Large graphics systems may use many input devices, each performing a specific set of tasks. This section presents the operation of various physical devices. The actual integration of these devices into applications programs is discussed in chapter 5.

The most commonly used input device is the **alphanumeric keyboard.** Keyboards are primarily used to enter text, but they can also be used to create, manipulate, and destroy graphic images. Even the simplest keyboard can be used for this purpose if keys representing letters and numbers are assigned special tasks. Extended keyboards, found on many computers, have arrow keys for directing the movements of a cursor. Many of these keyboards also have function keys that may be given special assignments.

Special-purpose keyboards that have keys labeled with graphics operations are often packaged with large graphics systems. Some of these systems also have a keyboard of dials for entering analog values.

Thumb wheels have been a common extension found on graphics terminal keyboards for many years. These dials, used to position crosshairs on the screen, usually occurs in pairs. One wheel controls the horizontal movement of the crosshairs, while the other controls the vertical movement.

The **mouse** (figure 2.3.1), a hand-sized device used to move a cursor on the screen, has gained popularity as one of the prime input devices for many graphics systems. As the mouse is moved across a flat surface, its movements are converted to digital values that determine relative movements of the screen

FIGURE 2.3.1

A mouse is commonly used with microcomputers for interactive graphics manipulation.

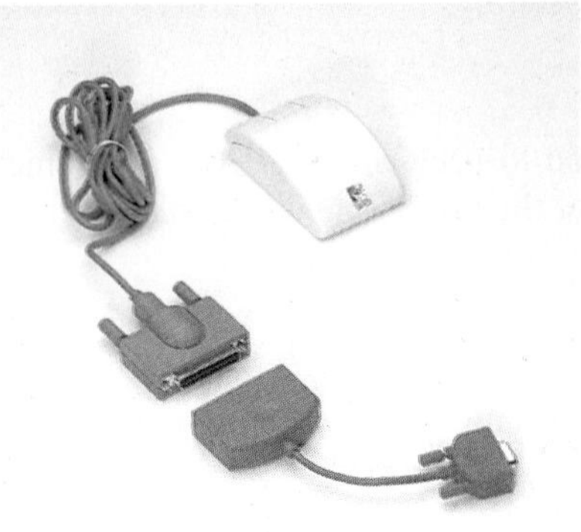

cursor. Two methods are used to capture the movements of the mouse. In the mechanical mouse, a rolling ball or wheels in the base transmit the mouse's movements to potentiometers. Optical mice are moved across a surface with a light and dark pattern. A light from within the mouse is reflected from the patterned surface, and photo cells in the mouse detect motion as changes in the pattern under the mouse. The mouse may be lifted from the flat surface and moved with no effect on the screen cursor because it only relates movements with respect to a starting position. One or more buttons on the mouse are used to report the coordinates of the current cursor position to the computer. Buttons can also be programmed to represent keyboard input.

Efficient use of the mouse depends on having a clear area on a nonskid flat surface such as desktop. When such a surface is not available, the mouse may be replaced by the **trackball** (figure 2.3.2). The trackball is similar to the mouse except the ball and buttons are on the top of the device. The ball is moved by the user's finger, causing the cursor to move on the screen while the trackball base remains stationary. Trackball movements can be more accurately controlled than the movements of the mouse, so it is often preferred for applications requiring fine adjustments.

The **joystick** is another device used to move the cursor on a screen. Joysticks have a shaft that is moved from a centered, vertical position to a position indicating the direction the cursor is to move. The more the user moves the joystick, the faster the cursor moves. Small movements of the joystick often make the cursor move farther than desired, so joysticks are often used to control the cursor's velocity rather than its absolute position. A third degree of movement may be indicated by rotating the shaft in a clockwise or counterclockwise direction.

FIGURE 2.3.2

A trackball is used with laptop computers, some microcomputers, and some workstations. It can also replace a mouse when improved user control is needed.

FIGURE 2.3.3

Touch panels allow the user to point at objects on the screen with a finger.

Two devices, **touch panels** and **light pens,** allow the user to point directly at points on the screen. A touch panel (figure 2.3.3) is a transparent plate on the CRT screen that responds to the user's touch. The location the user touches is reported optically, electronically, or acoustically.

Optical touch panels have a grid of horizontal and vertical light beams created by sources along one vertical edge and one horizontal edge of the panel. Detectors along opposite sides of the panel record interruptions of the beams, which occur when the panel is touched. One or two vertical and horizontal beams are broken when the panel is touched. If two parallel beams are broken, the finger is assumed to be centered between them. Optical touch panels are low-resolution devices with positions to within about one-quarter of an inch.

Acoustical and electronic touch panels have much better resolution than optical touch panels. Acoustical panels transmit bursts of high-energy shock waves through a flat plate of glass. Vertical and horizontal bursts alternate at high frequency, so when the plate is touched, waves are reflected from the finger to senders on both the vertical and horizontal sides of the plate. The time required for the waves to make the round trip is recorded, and the distance to the finger is calculated from the duration of the round trip.

Electronic touch panels use two slightly separated, transparent sheets, one of which is coated with a conducting material, and the other with a resistive substance. When the panel is touched, the two sheets come into contact with each other, causing a voltage drop across the resistive side. The location of this voltage drop is then calculated to determine the position of the touch.

The light pen is shaped like a pen, but it does not emit light the way a normal pen emits ink. Rather, it detects the light of an excited phosphor on a CRT screen. The light pen is pointed at the screen, the phosphor under the pen is excited, and the position of the refresh beam is recorded. Because the screen is refreshed 30–60 times per second, the position if recorded instantly. A light pen is activated by a switch that is engaged by pressing the pen on the screen, by manually moving a button, or by simply touching a specific area of the pen itself.

One of the main difficulties with light pens is that some pixels in the area at which the pen is pointed must be lit. If a low-level background screen color is used, this does not cause a problem; but in systems that use black as a background, the light pen cannot be used to select points in the background area.

To overcome this problem, some systems repeatedly draw a small target (a single point or character, for example) on different parts of the screen when the light pen does not record any light. When the pattern moves into the light pen's field of view, the position is recorded. The field of view for a light pen is larger than a pixel, so the position recorded will not necessarily be at the center of the pen. Larger patterns produce more accurate results in such systems.

An alternative to creating a pattern that seeks the pen is to create a cursor that follows pen movements. The pattern, normally a cross, is displayed on the screen. The user moves the light pen from the position of the cross toward the desired selection point. As the pen moves, its position relative to the current location of the cross is noted, and the cross is redrawn either at the current pen position or at a position where the pen is projected to be if its current motion is continued. The position of the pen is determined by taking an average of the pixels from the previous tracking cross that are in the pen's field of view.

The pen must be moved slowly enough to permit repositioning of the cross. If the pen is moved so that the cross is no longer in its field of view, tracking must be restarted. One way to do this is to have the system try to find the pen by moving a pattern in a spiral around the last known pen position until the pen is found, and then repositioning the cross at the current pen position.

Other types of search patterns, such as the raster scan pattern or a character burst, in which the screen is filled with a pattern, are used to reestablish contact with the light pen. Another alternative is to leave the cross stationary or return it to its beginning position, and require the user to move the pen to the area of the cross. The one drawback of this procedure is that the user may have intended to discontinue tracking by withdrawing the pen from the screen. In this case, the continued appearance of the cross on the screen can be annoying.

For some applications, such as mapdigitizing, it is necessary to translate points on an existing document to a digital representation suitable for computer use. **Graphics tablets** or **digitizers,** which use a pointing device such as a stylus or a hand cursor, have long been used for this purpose. The stylus or hand cursor (figures 2.3.4 and 2.3.5) is moved over a tablet until the user indicates, by pressing a button, that the desired point has been located. Several buttons are normally available on the pointing device so that the user can choose one point or a sequence of points.

FIGURE 2.3.4

Graphics tablets allow artists to draw using a pencil-like stylus.

FIGURE 2.3.5

Digitizers can be used to coordinate sample points from an existing image.

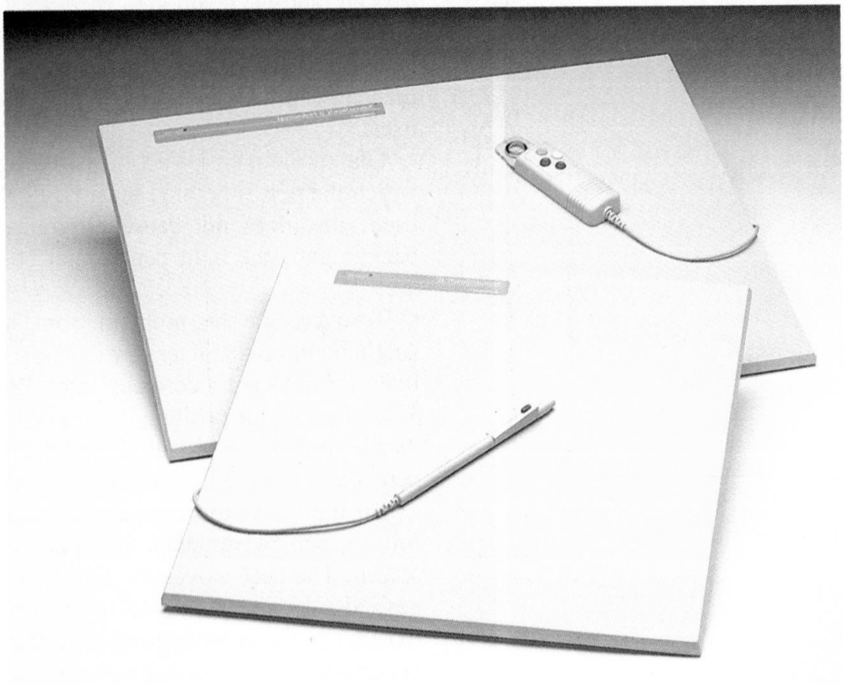

An electronic sensing system determines the position of the pointing device. An electrified grid of wires in the tablet creates a magnetic field. The pointing device contains a coil of wire that cuts the field and creates a current. When strength of the current indicates that the stylus or cursor is close to the tablet, a screen cursor is displayed to show the screen position corresponding to the current tablet position. The position of the pointing device on the tablet is determined by coded pulses in the current. Another method for specifying the position of the pointing device is for each wire to have a slightly different voltage. The pointing device can record the voltage differences between the vertical and horizontal wires. These differences correspond to coordinate differences on the screen.

Acoustic graphics tablets are composed of an L-frame assembly, two strip microphones positioned in an L-shape. A stylus creates sound by generating an electric spark at its tip and its position is tracked by comparing the times the sound from the spark reaches each microphone. Three-dimensional objects may be digitized by a similar device called a sonic digitizer. Three-dimensional sonic digitizers use three or more microphones to record the position of the stylus. To record the position of the stylus correctly, at least three microphones must have a clear line to the stylus. Because solid objects may block the path from the stylus to some of the microphones, more than three microphones are normally used in these systems.

Scanners have become an increasingly important means of digitizing two-dimensional graphic images. These systems can either read images directly off paper or videotape at low to relatively high resolution. Most scanners come with software that allows the user to alter the digitized image.

EXERCISES

2.3.1

What types of interactive graphics input devices will you use?

2.3.2

If you want to read command keys such as the arrow keys, are there any special functions other than read which you use to read these keys? What ASCII codes do you get when you read these special keys?

2.3.3

If you have other interactive devices, find out how to read the results from these devices.

2.3.4

Which of the devices that you have access to do you find easiest to use? Why?

2.4 The Hardware/Software Interface

Output from programs must be converted into an appropriate format before it can be displayed on the devices discussed in this chapter. The diversity of display devices means there are several organizations for the conversion process. Most systems, however, have a collection of special software and hardware, called the **display processor** (figure 2.4.1), that is responsible for controlling output to display devices.

Applications programs generally attempt to represent images in a real-world coordinate system. Graphic objects such as points and lines described in world coordinates must be reproduced on the display device in coordinates belonging to the display device screen. The screen is essentially a plane surface that can be described by the usual coordinate system. The y-coordinate represents vertical positions and the x-coordinate represents horizontal positions. One point on the screen, usually the upper- or lower-left corner, represents the point with coordinates (0,0). This point is called the **origin,** and other points are described by their distances from the origin. The **x-distance** and **y-distance** are both measured in pixels so that these coordinates always have integer values.

The display processor receives descriptions of graphic images from applications programs as screen coordinates and causes the image to be displayed with the appropriate gray levels or colors. In addition, the display processor displays text in a style specified by the user and draws lines of an appropriate type (dotted, dashed, or solid). Interactive input devices may also be connected directly to the display processor.

The image on a refresh CRT must be restored at a regular interval. The display processor may be responsible for picture restoration, or a separate **display controller** may take on this task.

While the set of tasks specified for the display processor is fairly standard, the processes required to perform those tasks vary considerably from display device to display device. In raster scan systems, a binary image exists in the computer's memory, and the **CRT controller** uses this information to decide whether a pixel is turned on or not. The random scan display system requires that the display processor position the electron beam to draw lines. The distinct nature of these two systems leads to considerably different implementations of such graphics primitives as line drawing.

FIGURE 2.4.1

The display processor is a collection of software and hardware devices designed to assist the applications programmer in making the best use of the graphics display device.

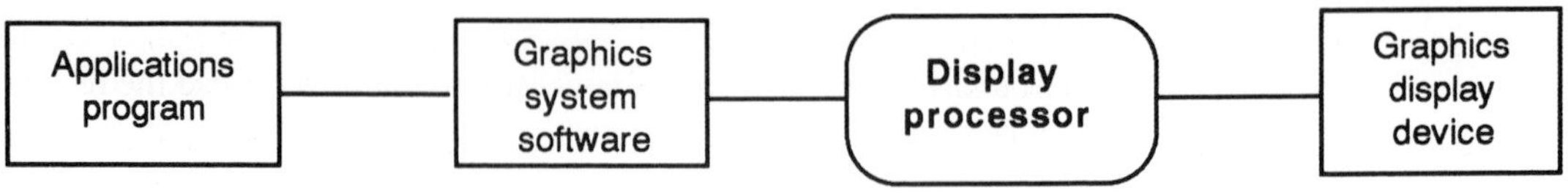

The processor unit of random scan devices normally receives **a display-file program,** a set of line and move instructions stored in device-dependent OpCodes. The output of applications programs (figure 2.4.2) is translated into a display-file program by a program called the **display-file translator.** It is stored in the **refresh display file** and executed once during every refresh cycle by the display processor. The processor adds interactive updates of the image to the display-file program between refresh cycles.

Lines are the basic graphic objects created on random-access systems. The **vector generator** directs the electron beam to move between the end points of the desired line. Vector generators can be implemented as hardware or simulated by software. An **analog vector generator** is a hardware device that creates lines by generating a linear change in voltage in the deflection devices. This causes the beam to be deflected in a continuous motion from one end point to the other. This line-generating method produces the smoothest lines.

The software alternative, called the **digital vector generator,** calculates the coordinates of a sequence of pixels that closely approximates points on the line segment, and then is directed to turn on each of these pixels. All pixels have integer coordinates, so these points only approximate points on the line. The result of this approximation is a line that is not as smooth as that generated by the analog generator. Digital vector generators are much cheaper than analog vector generators, and in recent years the density of points used by them has increased substantially. This increase has resulted in a considerable improvement in line quality.

Line styles such as dotted or dashed lines are created by turning the electron beam off and on during the draw cycle. Curved lines, including those used to draw text characters, are approximated by short line segments. Various types of shading are created by using solid, dotted, or dashed line segments.

Raster scan systems generate a display image directly from the contents of a special block of memory called the frame buffer (figure 2.4.3). In monochrome systems each bit in the frame buffer represents 1 pixel on the CRT, while in color systems 4 or more bits are typically used to represent each pixel. The display processor on raster scan systems is responsible for converting graphics commands into an appropriate binary representation of a given image. The binary image is, in turn, displayed on the screen by the **CRT controller.**

FIGURE 2.4.2

The display processor for a vector system

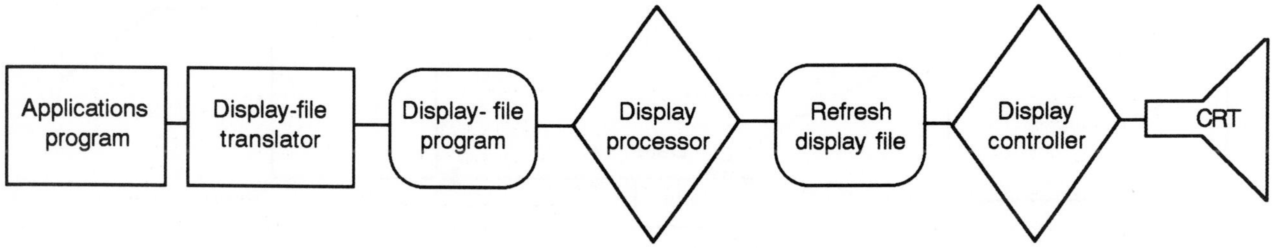

FIGURE 2.4.3

The frame buffer is the portion of memory that stores a numerical version of the graphic image in a raster graphics system.

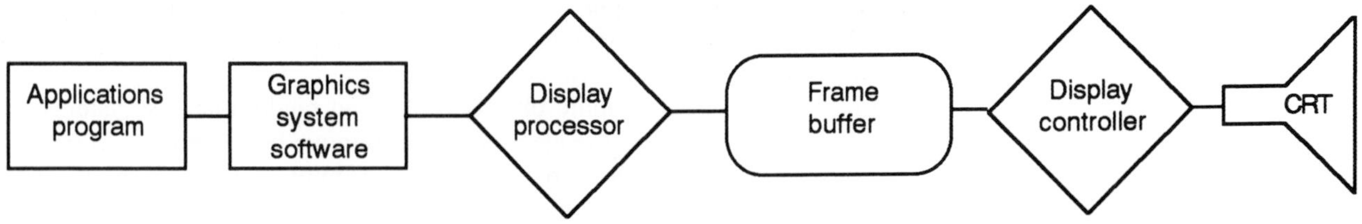

The CRT controller must scan data in the frame buffer at the same rate that the electron beam is scanning the CRT screen (figure 2.4.4). Data is transferred from the frame buffer to a **shift register** 1 byte at a time. Bits are shifted one at a time from the shift register to the CRT circuitry. The CRT controller counts the number of bytes sent to the CRT circuitry, and each time the count equals the number of bytes in a scan line the controller sends a horizontal synchronization signal to the CRT circuitry. The controller also counts the number of horizontal synchronization signals, and after a specified number of these signals, the controller sends a vertical synchronization signal to the CRT circuitry. The synchronization signals allow the controller to maintain a constant CRT scanning rate.

FIGURE 2.4.4

The CRT controller transfers data from the frame buffer to the shift register. The data is transferred 1 bit at a time from the register to the CRT circuitry. The CRT controller also maintains synchronization of data flow and electron beam scanning with horizontal and vertical synchronization signals.

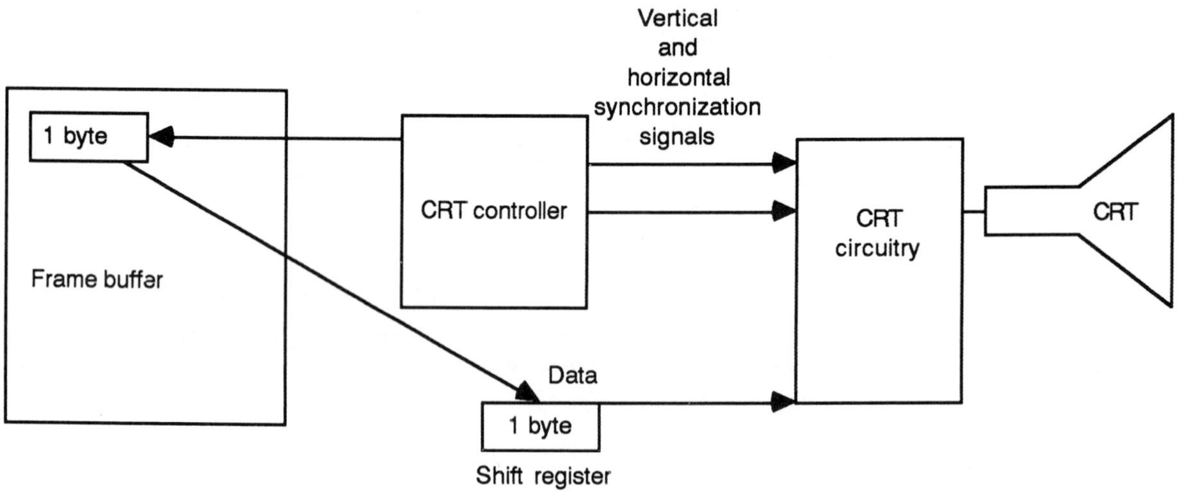

Primitive instructions to the display processor on a raster scan system set the color of individual pixels or perform logical operations on two blocks of pixels. Because these operations are more flexible that the line-oriented operations of random scan systems, the display processors on raster scan systems normally have more flexible operation sets. Text, for example, may be generated by transferring blocks of pixels or by re-creating letter shapes with curve generators.

EXERCISES

2.4.1

What graphics software will you use?

2.4.2

How do you access the graphics library from the programs you will write?

2.4.3

Get a list of the basic graphics functions with parameters.

2.5 Computer Graphics Interface Standards

Applications programs could create graphic images by direct calls on the display processor of a system, but such programs would not be portable to other systems even if they were written in a high-level language such as Pascal, C, or FORTRAN. In addition, the complicated nature of display-file programs in random scan systems makes it difficult for the applications programmer to utilize such a system to its fullest.

To improve the productivity of applications programmers, professional and government standards organizations and other groups have tried to create standard graphics interfaces (see figure 2.5.1). At present there are five major graphics interface standards (figure 2.5.2) on which future graphics standards will be based. Each standard fills the role of a device-independent support package at some level in a computer graphics system.

In the mid 1970s, ACM SIGGRAPH (Special Interest Group on Computer Graphics of the Association for Computing Machinery) set out to establish a graphics **Core System** to address the problems of transportability. The purpose of the Core System and its successors has been twofold: first, to provide applications programmers with a standard set of graphics primitives; and second, to give manufacturers of graphics equipment a set of guidelines for offering a useful set of graphics primitives.

FIGURE 2.5.1

The device-independent support package or graphics standard makes applications programs independent of the machine used.

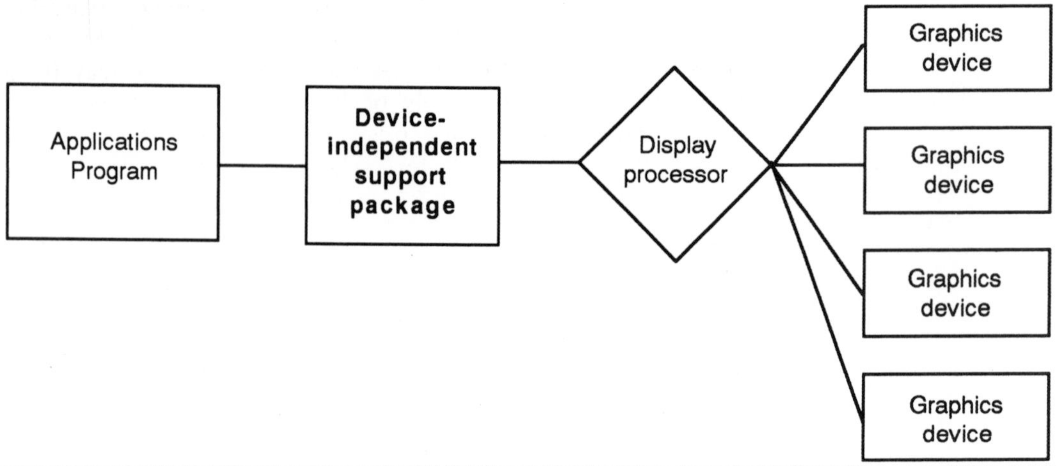

FIGURE 2.5.2

Some current computer graphics standards

Graphics standards

GKS
GKS-3D
CGI
PHIGS
CGM

The Core System was created when the vector scan CRT and line-drawing devices were the standard graphics output devices and when most graphics were created on large mainframe computers. The Core System has been used for high-performance, mainframe-driven CAD/CAM systems, and it was the first standard to include three-dimensional functions.

At the time the Core System was developed, the widespread use of raster graphics systems on microcomputers was not foreseen, so the Core does not define the tools necessary to utilize all the capabilities of those systems. With many of the functions once reserved for mainframe computers now being transferred to micro systems, the use of the Core System is declining.

The **Graphics Kernel System (GKS)** and its three-dimensional extension **GKS-3D** are task-oriented systems designed to define the operations of a **workstation.** The GKS was originally developed in Germany in 1978. It has been extensively redesigned by a working group of the International Standards Organization (ISO). While the ACM Core System and GKS were developed about the same time, the GKS was influenced by the Core System. The GKS, like the Core System, does not make full use of raster systems. Unlike the Core, the GKS is strictly a two-dimensional standard. Many implementations of the GKS are available, and the GKS functions may be accessed through most of the major programming languages. A workstation as defined by the GKS is not a stand-alone graphics terminal but a precisely defined collection of graphics input and output devices.

The **Programmers Hierarchical Interactive Graphics System (PHIGS)** is yet another task-oriented graphics standard created by an ISO working group. This standard is useful for applications that manipulate complex displays in a dynamic, highly interactive environment. PHIGS uses the same set of graphics primitives as GKS and GKS-3D. But while the GKS primitives are organized into linear list structures, PHIGS groups its primitives into tree structures. These tree structures are used to represent the relationships between various parts of a picture.

The **Computer Graphics Virtual Device Interface (CGI)** was created by a task group sanctioned by the ISO in the mid 1980s. This standard describes a device-independent interface at the level of primitive drawing operations. The **VDI** (virtual device interface) created by this standard attempts to unify the GKS and PHIGS systems by incorporating functions common to both standards (figure 2.5.3). It also recognizes some of the shortcomings of these standards by adding some primitive functions not found in these systems. The virtual device created by the CGI may be implemented by either software or hardware and specifies functions in the following areas:

- Control, negotiation, and errors
- Output and attributes
- Segmentation
- Input and echoing
- Raster

The CGI virtual device accepts only two-dimensional data, leaving the conversion of three-dimensional data to two-dimensional data to modeling software and graphics support systems. This implies that a device that makes the conversion directly cannot be covered by the CGI. To circumvent this problem, CGI devices are theoretical devices contained in a graphics system. This system is a collection of interfaces, one of which is CGI. Physical devices supporting the three-dimensional/two-dimensional projection are considered part of the system containing the CGI interface.

The controls specified by CGI functions include those that initialize and terminate a graphics session, and reset attribute and control functions. Geometric or constructive primitives in the CGI system use a **virtual device coordinate space (VDC),** a device-independent coordinate system. The CGI also provides a function for transforming VDC coordinates to device-dependent coordinates.

Output primitives are the functions used to draw objects—such as polygons (POLYLINE), arcs of circles (CIRCULAR ARC), and ellipses (ELLIPTICAL ARC)—and filled versions of closed polygons and curves (POLYGON,

FIGURE 2.5.3

The CGI specifies the standard primitive functions of a graphics system used by the higher-level standards.

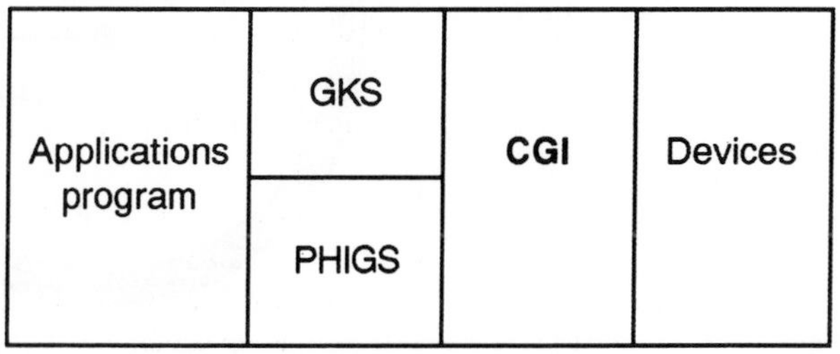

RECTANGLE, CIRCLE, AND ELLIPTICAL ARC CLOSED). A function called POLYMARKER draws the vertices of a polygon but not the lines joining the vertices. A sample of the instructions used to create a torus (doughnut) is given in figure 2.5.4. Character strings can also be drawn to the screen (TEXT), and images stored in arrays may be mapped to the screen by CELL ARRAY.

Lines may be drawn in different colors and styles (dotted or solid). Different fill colors and textures may be used to fill a closed figure. Text comes in different families (called **fonts**), styles (bold, italic, and plain), sizes (points), and colors. These variations and others are covered by attribute functions in the CGI standard.

Segments and **rasters** are structures used to store graphic images. A segment is a data structure used to store the instructions for creating a set of related graphic objects. Objects stored in a segment are manipulated in a group, such as the pair of circles forming the torus in figure 2.5.4. Segments can be transformed (moved on the screen) or made visible or invisible. A list containing all the segments in a picture is stored with the first segments in the list at the front of the picture; those at the end of the list are at the back of the picture.

The major difference between the PHIGS and GKS is in the structure used to define relationships between graphic objects. The GKS uses segments that are linear list structures, while the PHIGS organizes graphic objects into hierarchical **structures.** This hierarchical organization allows graphic objects in PHIGS to inherit properties from one or more other graphics objects (figure 2.5.5). Figure 2.5.6 shows a PHIGS structure for the human body. Whereas parts of a structure can be manipulated, the parts of a segment cannot be altered.

FIGURE 2.5.4

Example of a graphic image constructed with the CGI closed polygon primitive CIRCULAR ARC CENTER CLOSE

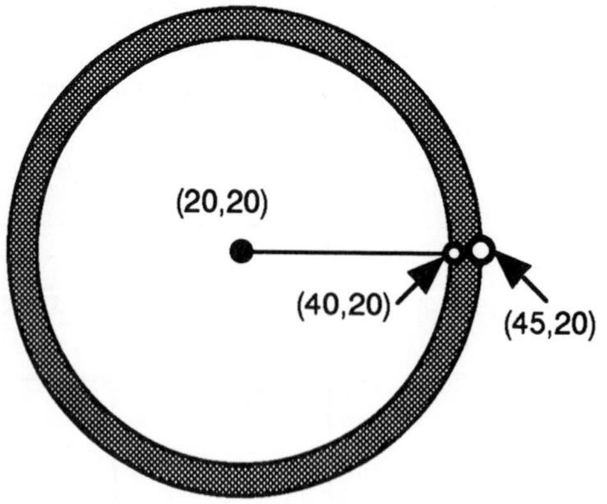


```
BeginFig;
  ArcCtr 20,20  1,0  1,0  25
  Close;
  ArcCtr 20,20  1,0  1,0  20
EndFig;
```

F I G U R E 2.5.5

CGI and GKS use lists of segments to store pictures; PHIGS uses a multilevel, hierarchical organization to store its structures.

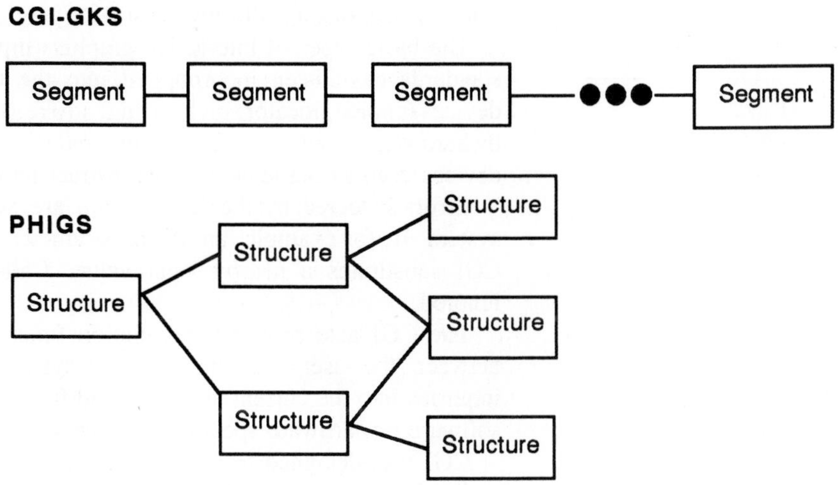

F I G U R E 2.5.6

An example of the hierarchical relationship between structures in the PHIGS system

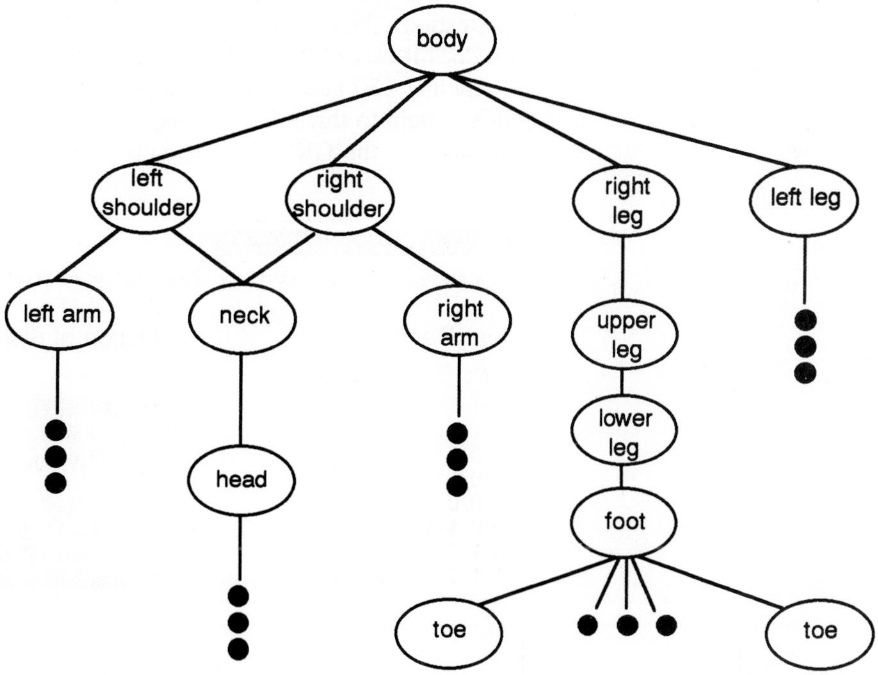

The CGI can also store pictures as snapshots of a raster image (figure 2.5.7). The pixels of a raster image are grouped into a rectangular arrangement called a **bitmap.** Each pixel is mapped to a memory unit large enough to describe its appearance. For a simple black-and-white image, one bit is sufficient to indicate whether the pixel is black or white. Color images usually require one or more bytes of memory to hold the color of a pixel.

The basic types of interactive graphics input given in the GKS and PHIGS standards have been incorporated into the CGI system. The six classes of devices (choice, locator, pick, string, stroke, and valuator) may be implemented by hardware or software. The mouse and the keyboard are examples of physical devices used to implement some abstract input devices.

Errors detected by the CGI system are either ignored or corrected by the system. If, for example, an illegal parameter value is passed to the system, the CGI substitutes a nearby legal value. Calls to nonsupported functions are ignored.

The CGI also provides negotiation functions for two-way communication between the user and the graphics system. This communication includes inquiries into the current attributes and functions available. Functions allowing software or hardware specifications are also included.

CGI was designed to be a broad standard, and most implementations will include a subset of the functions available. Neither the GKS not the PHIGS standards use a complete implementation of the CGI.

In addition to those tasks covered in the CGI, GKS systems formalize the purposes of input devices and extend the structure of segments. The transformation between real-world coordinate systems, called **world coordinates (WC)** and **Normalized Device Coordinates (NDC)** (GKS's version of VDC), allows GKS programmers to work in coordinates appropriate for a given application. The GKS does not support a full range of raster graphics functions, nor does it extend the CGI to three-dimensions.

Another 150 task force developed GKS-3D in the mid 1980s to extend the GKS system to three-dimensions. While the GKS-3D system appears to be an extension of the GKS, it is actually a stand-alone system. In GKS-3D, GKS

FIGURE 2.5.7

Raster storage with a corresponding section of display

Raster

1 1 1 1 1 1 1 1
0 1 1 1 1 1 1 0
0 0 1 1 1 1 0 0
0 0 0 1 1 0 0 0
0 0 0 1 1 0 0 0
0 0 1 1 1 1 0 0
0 1 1 1 1 1 1 0
1 1 1 1 1 1 1 1

Section of display

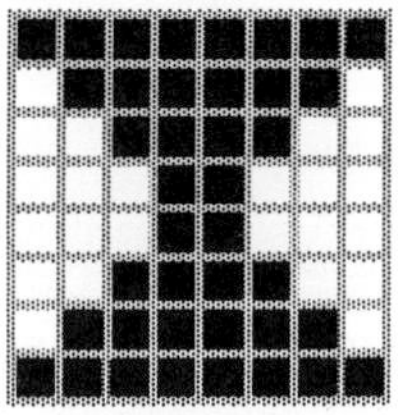

functions are simulated. The two-dimensional objects created by these functions are actually three-dimensional objects restricted to the plane $z = 0$. Lines created by calls to POLYLINE, for example, are created by calls to POLYLINE3 with z component 0. In addition to the two-dimensional primitives, GKS-3D has a full complement of line- and curve-drawing functions in three-dimensions. GKS-3D also provides the transformations that allow the user to select a point of view as well as the method of projection used to transform three-dimensional images to images in two-dimensions. Programmers may set the world coordinate system they wish to use and the area of the screen that the picture will occupy. Segments and input devices are essentially unchanged from the GKS.

The Computer Graphics Metafile (CGM) is an attempt to give a standard definition of a file structure for the capture, transfer, and archiving of pictorial information. Properties the graphics metafile provides include the following:

- A graphic protocol for off-line and off-site plotting
- A single format for spooling to multiple dissimilar plotting devices
- The possibility and impetus for a single standard interface to picture-generating devices
- A method for reusing the same picture without recomputing it
- A structure for unifying and integrating distinct graphics systems

Each of these graphics standards is given in a language-independent setting. In the past this has led to a plethora of implementations in various high-level languages. To circumvent this, the GKS has established language bindings for FORTRAN, Pascal, Ada, and C. Language bindings are standard names and formats for GKS functions usually given as procedures in a given language (figure 2.5.8). Some formats included in these bindings are the number and types of parameters and the order in which they are listed when a procedure or function is called. At this time, the ISO has two different Pascal standards, each allowing different data structures. This means there are two different bindings for Pascal. The C standard has a restriction of six-character externals, but current compilers allow longer names. Some examples of the bindings in Pascal are given in figure 2.5.9. Figure 2.5.10 gives the same calls in full FORTRAN 77.

FIGURE 2.5.8

The language binding of a graphics standard is the specification of the standard's functions in a high-level programming language. These procedures and functions are used by the applications programmer.

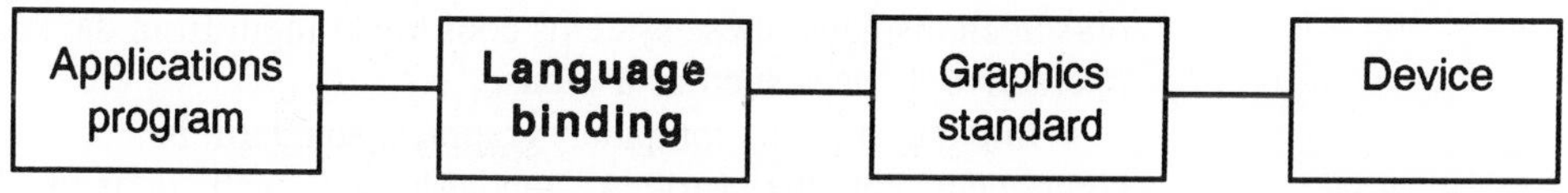

FIGURE 2.5.9

Examples of GKS Pascal bindings

```
ISO Pascal:Level 1
var
   p1 : array [1..40] of GRPoint;
   p2 : array [1..2000] of GRPoint;
   tp : GRPoint;

   GPolyline(40,p1);
   GPolyline(2000,p2);
   GText(tp,'Temperature in degrees');
```

```
ISO Pascal:Level 0
var
   p1,p2 : GAPointArray;
   tp    : GRPoint;

   GPolyline(40,p1);
   GPolyline(2000,p2);
   GText(tp,'Temperature in degrees');
```

FIGURE 2.5.10

Example of GKS language bindings for full FORTRAN 77

```
REAL XA(40), YA(40, XA2(2000),YA2(2000)
REAL TX, TY

CALL GPL(40, XA, YA)
CALL GPL(2000, XA2, YA2)
CALL GTX(TX, TY, 'TEMPERATURE IN DEGREES')
```

Standards are also being developed for subdividing a bitmap graphics screen into regions called **virtual display devices** or **windows.** These standards, called **windowing systems,** provide the user with a graphic interface to multiple applications displayed in various windows. They also allow a program to run on one system, while its user interface appears on a different system. Most windowing systems are based on work done at Xerox in the seventies. The Macintosh finder was the first such system to gain widespread use, but today Microsoft windows is used on PCs, and X11 (figure 2.5.11) has become the standard window system for workstations. In addition to supporting multiple on-screen displays, these systems coordinate input from the keyboard and other interactive devices such as a mouse.

While no overall computer graphics standard is currently in place, the components of the various standards are well defined. Throughout the remainder of this book the components of a graphics system will be developed and illustrated with applications. These applications will often suggest other components that we will then add.

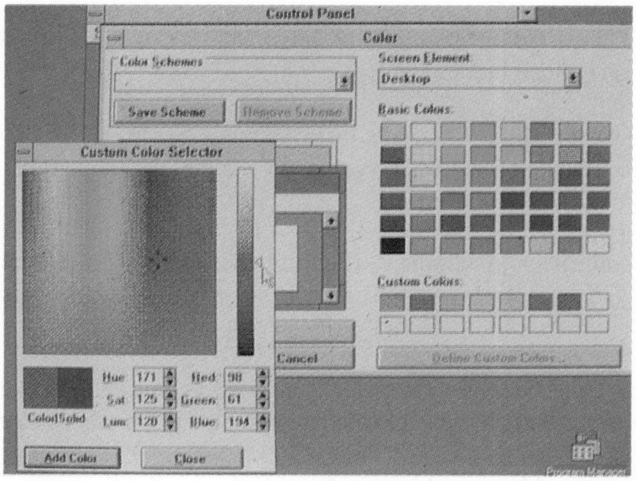

FIGURE 2.5.11

Microsoft Windows (left), XWindows OSF/Motif (center), and PEX (right) are three examples of user interfaces that rely on graphic windows.

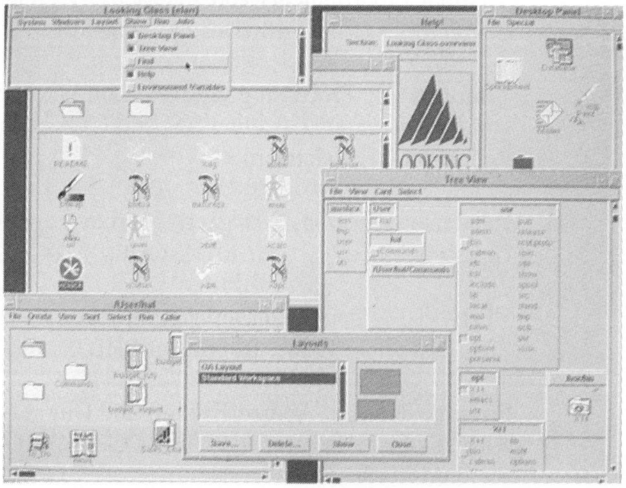

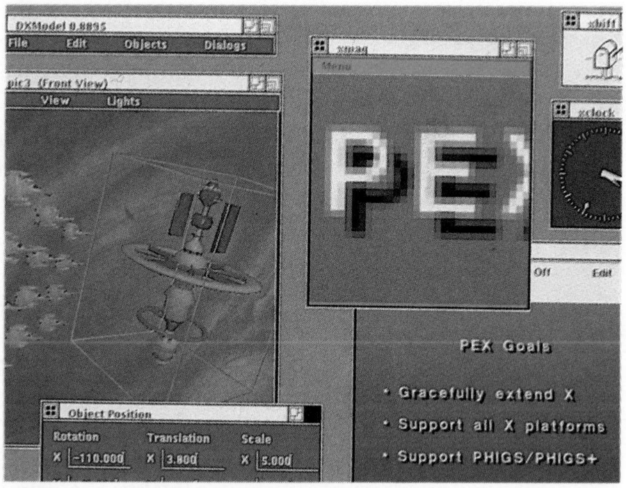

BIBLIOGRAPHY

Abernathy, Aileen. "True Colors," *MacUser* 4(10):236–71 (October 1988). Excellent overview of various color monitors.

Bono, Peter R. "Guest Editor's Introduction: Graphic Standards," *IEEE CG&A* 6(8): 12–16 (August 1986). Development of the various graphics standards.

Carson, George S., and Eileen McGinnis. "The Reference Model for Computer Graphics," *IEEE CG&A* 6(8): 17–24 (August 1986). Relationships among standards.

Chin, Janet S. "New Procedures for Graphics Standardization," *IEEE CG&A* 8(6): 74–76 (November 1988). Review of standards process at the end of 1988.

Conn, Coco, Jaron Lanier, Margaret Minsky, Scott Fisher, and Allison Druin. "Virtual Environments and Interactivity: Windows to the Future." *Computer Graphics* 23 (5): 7–18 (December 1989).

"Information Processing System Computer Graphics Graphical Kernel System," *Computer Graphics* (Special GKS Issue): 1–130 (February 1984). Report on GKS standard.

Henderson, Lofton, Margaret Journey, and Chris Osland. "The Computer Graphics Metafile," *IEEE CG&A* 6(8): 24–32 (August 1986).

"PHIGS + Functional Description Revision 3.0," *Computer Graphics* 22(3): 125–218 (July 1988). Report on PHIGS standard.

Powers, Thomas, Andrea Fankel, and David Arnold. "The Computer Graphics Virtual Device Interface," *IEEE CG&A* 6(8): 33–41 (August 1986). The CGI standards.

Puk, Richard F., and John I. McConnel. "GKS-3D: A Three-Dimensional Extension of the Graphics Kernel Standard," *IEEE CG&A* 6(8): 42–49 (August 1986).

Shuey, David, David Bailey, and Thomas P. Morrissey. "PHIGS: A Standard, Dynamic, Interactive Graphics Interface," *IEEE CG&A* 6(8): 50–57 (August 1986).

Skall, Mark W. "NBS's Role in Computer Graphics Standards," *IEEE CG&A* 6(8): 66–70 (August 1986).

Sparks, Madeleine R., and Julian R. Gallop. "Language Bindings for Computer Graphics Standards," *IEEE CG&A* 6(8): 58–65 (August 1986).

Wright, Jeff. "Altered States: A Software Developer's Vision of Virtual Reality," *Computer Graphics World* 12 (12): 77–83 (December 1989).

CHAPTER

3

Developing a Simple Graphics Package

DIRECTIONS

—*Fractals: A New Window on Mathematics*

In the Classical period, the Greeks used the geometry of regular shapes, such as straight lines, circles, and polygons, to bring order to their world. With the advent of high-powered computing in the 1970s and 1980s the need for simplification diminished. Freed from these constraints, contemporary mathematician Benoit Mandelbrot wondered:

> *Why is geometry often described as cold and dry? One reason lies in its inability to describe the shape of a cloud, a mountain, a coastline, or a tree. Clouds are not spheres, mountains are not cones, coastlines are not circles, and bark is not smooth, nor does lightning travel in a straight line.*
>
> *More generally, I claim that many patterns of Nature are so irregular and fragmented, that, compared with Euclid . . . Nature exhibits not simply a higher degree, but an altogether different level of complexity. [Mandelbrot 83]*

The geometry of Euclid has thoroughly influenced both art and science. While artists have used the straight line, they have never felt constrained to draw spherical clouds or conical mountains. Nevertheless, physicists and other mathematical scientists have had no choice other than to use linear approximations in many problems.

Over the years, techniques used in the arts and sciences have fostered the division between these disciplines. The reward for mathematicians such as Gaston Julia and Pierre Fatou, who worked with complex geometric sets, was relative obscurity. How could mathematicians use words to describe objects such as those pictured in figure D.3.1? How could physicists use mathematics to describe radio interference?

Work similar to that shown in figure D.3.1 has appeared in art galleries and has sparked debates as to whether such work should be considered art or science. Mathematicians and physicists have always thought in terms of pictures; the computer has given broader audiences access to these images. Images such as this make it possible for a non-mathematician to understand what the twentieth-century German mathematician Hermann Weyl conceded on his one-hundredth birthday:

> *My work has always tried to unite the true with the beautiful, and when I had to choose one or the other, I usually chose the beautiful.*

The advent of modern computer graphics not only provided a new way to display data, but also furnished scientists with a tool that enabled them to look at clouds as something other than spheres. The picture of a tornado-spawning cloud in figure D.3.2 was created by applying an atmospheric model to data taken during a storm in 1977.

Today mathematicians and scientists from diverse fields of study are creating algorithms to help themselves and others visualize theoretical models. This chapter develops many of the algorithms necessary to display two-dimensional data in such models.

FIGURE D.3.1

Computers have made it possible for mathematicians to show the beauty of mathematical objects to everyone. This fractal image has been displayed in art museums.

FIGURE D.3.2

An image of a tornadic storm developing. Temperature and moisture structures and the atmosphere during an actual storm formation on May 20, 1977 in Del City, Oklahoma are real data. To trigger the storm, data of a small artificial cumulus cloud were added.

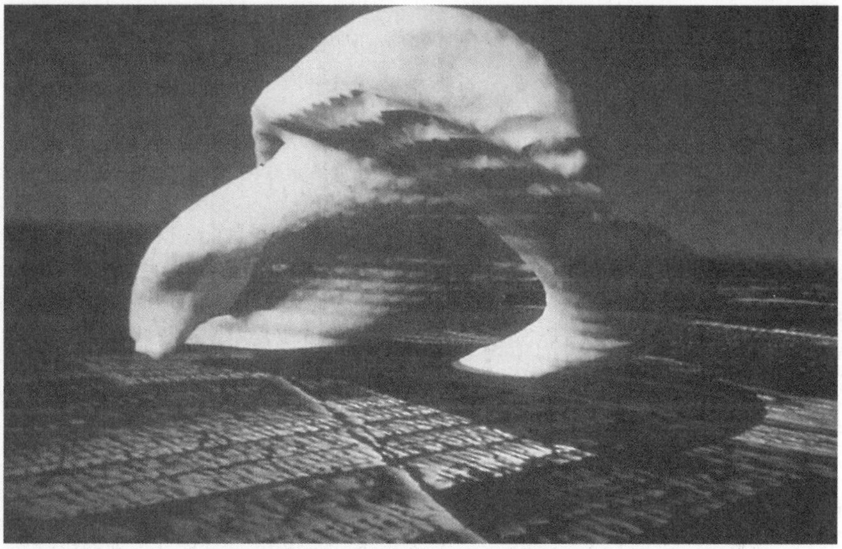

Introduction

The intricate relationship between graphics hardware, software interfaces, and applications programs were outlined in chapter 2. As an illustration of this relationship, in this chapter you will build a basic graphics interface package for line drawing and apply it to simple graphics problems.

The discussion begins by presenting methods for the creation of several line-drawing primitives that can be used by raster scan graphics systems. These line-drawing primitives are found at the machine level and use a system-dependent coordinate system. The first step in creating a device-independent interface is to implement system-independent coordinates. Translation and scaling are needed to convert from application-dependent coordinates to system-dependent coordinates.

Line- and point-drawing procedures for the device-independent coordinate system correspond to the line- and point-drawing functions of the graphics software interfaces introduced in section 2.5. These functions are applied to some simple problems where there is need to rotate graphic objects.

Translation, scaling, and rotation can be described as matrix operations if homogeneous coordinate systems are used. While matrices provide a unified theoretical approach to transformations in two dimensions, they are more powerful when applied to three-dimensional transformations in chapter 8.

Your simple graphics package is given an additional test: the creation of fractal images. These complex images can be generated by relatively simply programs that test parts of the graphics package not used in the other applications.

3.1 Line-drawing Algorithms

This chapter presents graphics methods for the representation of lines in a plane. Spaces have an infinite number of points in plane geometry. Lines, polygons, and curves are infinite subsets of the set of points. In all computer representations of infinite geometries, the major problem is translating those infinite sets of points into finite sets that give suitable representations.

Some applications require that lines be drawn as accurately as possible. In other applications, images must appear on a screen quickly and often disappear just as quickly. The rough representation of a line is sufficient for such applications. Generally, realism is gained at the expense of speed, so developers must choose algorithms that maintain the balance of speed and realism appropriate for a particular application.

Efficient algorithms are essential because graphics programs tend to repeat small sections many times. A programmer can improve the efficiency of a program in a number of ways. For example, values invariant in a loop should be assigned outside of the loop. Geometric properties like symmetry often allow the programmer to compute one point on a figure and get others by simple operations, such as multiplying one or both coordinates of the point by -1. Operations used within a loop also affect the speed of an algorithm because they are performed more than once. Floating-point operations are generally slower than integer operations, so integer operations are substituted whenever possible. Finally, an optimizing compiler can improve the performance of the program by substituting more efficient operations—for example, right and left shifts for integer multiplication.

The line-drawing algorithms given in this section illustrate the problems that occur when you are transferring mathematical techniques directly into programs that generate computer graphics. The first algorithm is an example of a direct transfer from mathematical theory to a graphics program. It uses the floating-point arithmetic necessary to generate the infinite number of points in the mathematical model. The second algorithm makes use of the fact that only a finite number of points are on the graphics screen, so that the best point may be selected from the set of possible candidates by using integer arithmetic. The last part of the section discusses a method that makes lines appear more realistic. These algorithms will be presented in the context of a frame-buffer graphics system because that is the context in which a programmer is most likely to apply them. A line-drawing procedure is a graphics primitive and as such is part of graphics systems. POLYLINE is the line-drawing function specified in the CGI system.

Most graphics systems address pixels as pairs of positive integers (x,y) and provide a procedure called **SetPixel** to set the screen color of a given pixel to a previously set color, usually called the **PenColor**. SetPixel is usually implemented as a call to the CRT controller. Assume, for simplicity, that the PenColor is either black or white, and that it has been set so that the line will stand out from a solid background. An alternate algorithm making the line visible on a varying background is the subject of an exercise (3.1.2).

The coordinate systems may have the origin, (0,0), either at the upper- or lower-left corner of the screen. The x-coordinate values for points on the right of the screen are larger than the values for those on the left. The normal

FIGURE 3.1.1

Coordinate system for a graphics screen with the origin at the lower-left corner

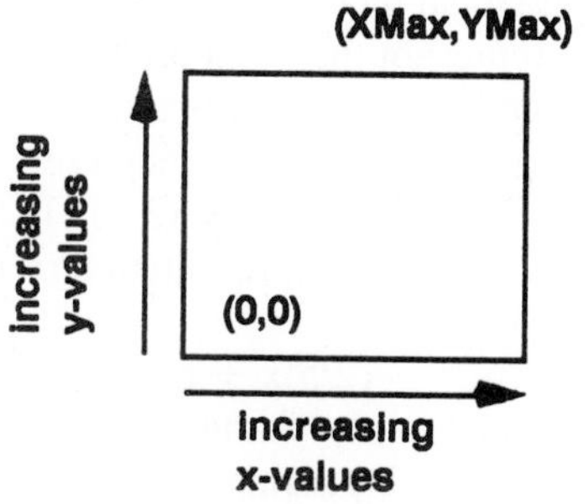

mathematical coordinate system can be simulated by placing the origin in the lower-left corner with y-values increasing from the origin upward. If the origin is at the upper left, y-values increase as one moves to the bottom of the screen. Although the origin is at the upper-left corner in many of the newer graphics systems, assume that the origin is at the lower left because that coincides with the standard mathematical arrangement. Also assume that the largest x-value for a system is the constant XMax and that the largest y-value is the constant YMax (figure 3.1.1). Converting from one system to the other is left as an exercise (3.1.3).

In algebra, lines are usually described by the slope-intercept equation $y = mx + b$, where (0,b) is the point where the line crosses the y-axis (the y-intercept) and m is the slope of the line. Recall that the slope of a line may be considered the amount of change in y associated with an increase of x. Given a point on a line, you can use the slope to find a second point on the line. For example, if you have the point (1,3) on the line $y = (2/5)x + b$, you know that if x increases by 5, y will increase by 2, so that the point (6,5) will also be on the line (figure 3.1.2). Similarly, if the point (1,3) is on the line $y = -(2/5)x + b$, and if you increase x by 5, y will decrease by 2. In this case the point (6,1) will be on the line (figure 3.1.3). While this technique for plotting a line is a serviceable paper-and-pencil technique, it will not work in computer graphics because points in between the two computed points are not plotted.

FIGURE 3.1.2

If the line $y = (2/5)x + b$ passes through point (1,3), then it also passes through point (6,5).

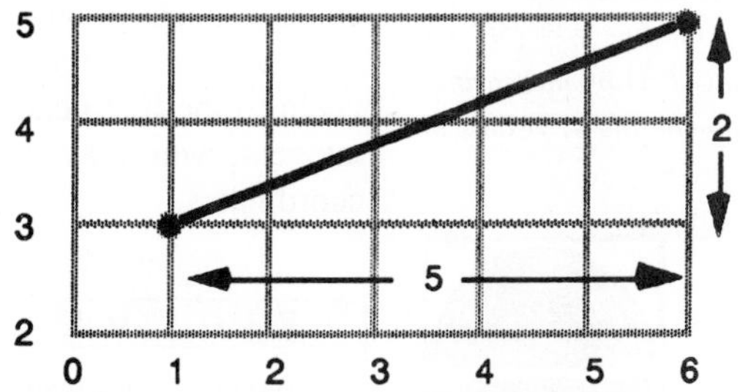

FIGURE 3.1.3

If the line $y = -(2/5)x + b$ passes through point (1,5), then it also passes through point (6,1).

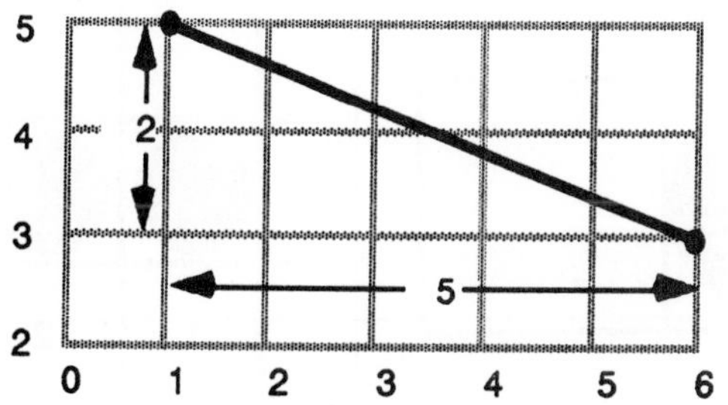

FIGURE 3.1.4

The points (2,3) and (2,4) are the two candidates to represent the point (2,3 2/5) on the line y = (2/5)x + b.

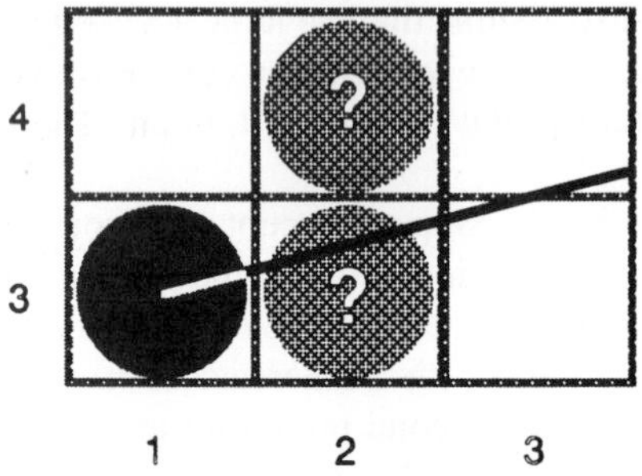

3.1.a Digital Differential Analyzer (DDA)

If you restrict the increase in x to 1, then the point $(x + 1, y + m)$ is on the line. In the first example, where $y = (2/5)x + b$, this means the point $(2,3 + 2/5)$ is on the line. While this point exists in the mathematical model, it does not on the graphics screen. The most likely candidates to represent the point are (2,3) and (2,4) (figure 3.1.4). One way to make the choice between them is to apply the round function on 3 plus 2/5, and choose the point (2,3). You can increase x by 1 again and get the point $(3,3 + 4/5)$, which is represented by (3,4). If the process is continued through three more steps, you have a representation of the line between the points (1,3) and (6,5) (figure 3.1.5).

If you try this process on the second example, $y = -(2/5)x + b$, it will also work well. In both cases an x-increase of 1 resulted in a y-change of less than 1. If you repeat the process with the line $y = (5/3)x + b$ passing through (1,3), an x-increase of 1 is accompanied by a y-increase of 5/3. The resulting point, $(2,3 + 5/3)$, is closest to the pixel with coordinates (2,5), and the line once again has a hole in it (figure 3.1.6). The reason is that an increase in 1 of x results in an increase of more than 1 in y because the slope is greater than 1. It seems reasonable at this point to increase y by 1 and compute x. Fortunately, this can be done with just a slight revision of the earlier computation; that is, if (x,y) is on the line $y = mx + b$, then $(x + 1/m, y + 1)$ is also on that line. This time y is incremented from 3 to 5, and the values of x are computed and rounded. This example suggests that if the absolute value of the slope is greater than 1, you should increment y and compute x. Otherwise, you will increment x and compute y.

Until now you have assumed partial knowledge of the equation of the line under consideration—that is, the slope and a point on the line. Your line-generating algorithm will assume that only the end points of a segment are given to the line generator. Because all coordinates on the graphics screen are integers, you may assume that the algorithms will only deal with integer coordinates.

FIGURE 3.1.6

An attempt to plot the line y = (5/3)x + b, starting at point (1,3) by increasing x by 1 and then computing y, results in a hole in the line.

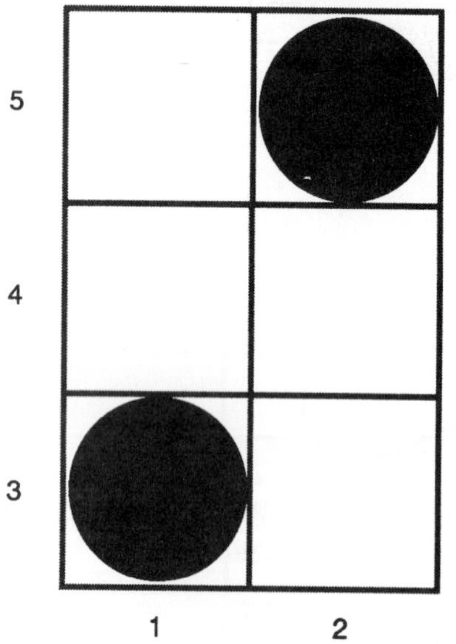

FIGURE 3.1.5

A graphical representation of the line joining (1,3) and (6,5)

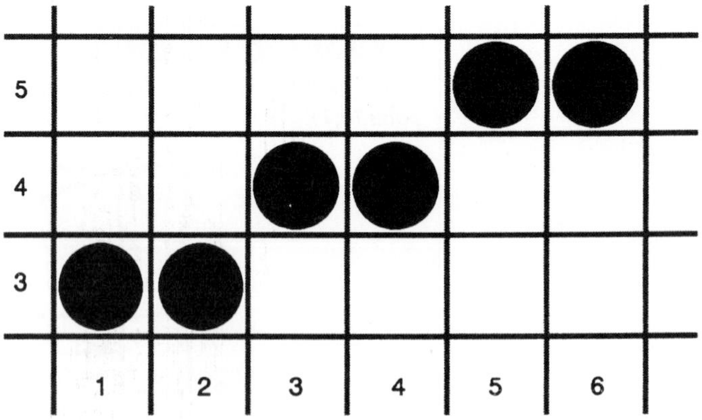

The **Digital Differential Analyzer (DDA)** applies the technique discussed previously to generate a line segment given its end points (figure 3.1.7). First, recall that a line joining points (x_1,y_1) and (x_2,y_2) has slope $m = (y_2 - y_1)/(x_2 - x_1)$.

You now have all the information that the previous examples used except the relationship of the points to each other. If, for example, (x_1,y_1) is above and to the right of (x_2,y_2), whether you increment x or increment y you will be beyond the end of the segment. Another problem occurs if the line is vertical. Then x_1 equals x_2, and a computation of the slope leads to a runtime error.

The DDA avoids these problems by computing the numerator, $dx = x_2 - x_1$, and the denominator, $dy = y_2 - y_1$, of m separately. It then computes the absolute value of each and chooses the larger value, which is the number of

FIGURE 3.1.7

DDA line-drawing algorithm

```
(* Pascal implementation of the DDA line-drawing algorithm *)

procedure DDA (x1,y1,x2,y2 : integer);
var
   dx, dy : integer;                  (* change in x and y between the end points of the line         *)
   Steps, StepCounter : integer;      (* largest change and the number of points to be plotted        *)
   XIncrement,YIncrement : real;      (* amount added to a point to get the next point                *)
   x,y : real;                        (* coordinates of intermediate points                           *)
begin (*DDA*)
   dx := x2 - x1;                     (*compute the change in each variable over the line segment     *)
   dy := y2 - x1;
   if abs(dx) > abs(dy) then          (* the variable with the largest change will be incremented by  *)
      Steps := abs(dx)                (* one and the other variable by its change divided by Steps    *)
   else
      Steps := abs(dy);
   XIncrement := dx / Steps;          (* the increments are real so there is no loss in accuracy      *)
   YIncrement := dy / Steps;
   x := x1;
   y := y1;
   SetPixel(round(x),round(y));
   for StepCounter := 1 to Steps do
      begin
         x := x + XIncrement;
         y := y + YIncrement;
         SetPixel(round(x),round(y))
      end
end; (*DDA*)
```

steps the algorithm will need. The increment for x is computed by dividing dx by the number of steps, and the increment for y by dividing dy by the number of steps.

For example, if the larger value was dx, then the number of steps would be the absolute value of dx. If the point (x_1,y_1), which is assumed to be the beginning point, is to the left of (x_2,y_2), the x should be incremented by 1. If the relationship is reversed, then x should be incremented by -1. These are exactly the relationships that occur if you compute dx/abs(dx). Notice in this case that dy/abs(dx) is either m or $-m$, depending on the relationship of the two points, so it will be the correct increment for y.

Are there ways in which the efficiency of DDA may be improved? The operations contained in the loop are those most likely to affect the operating speed of an algorithm. In this case, all the arithmetic in the loop is floating-point arithmetic, and the round procedure was used to decide which point should be in the representation of the line. When fixed-point arithmetic is available, it can be used in place of floating-point arithmetic to gain speed. If an alternate method using only integer arithmetic were available, then both the floating-point operations and the round function could be eliminated from the loop.

3.1.b Bresenham's Line Generator

When an algorithm must determine which point will be used in the construction of an object, it is often possible to make the decision without computing the actual value of the point. The algorithm developed by **Bresenham** uses one of the important point-selection techniques, that of computing the difference of the distances between integer coordinates of a pixel and the real coordinates of the actual point. It would seem that this is even more work because the actual point is needed to calculate the distance. The technique works because all you need to know is whether the difference is positive or negative, and this can be determined without floating-point arithmetic.

To simplify the process assume that the line you want to graph has a positive slope of less than 1. This restriction allows you to increment x by 1 and not miss any points. If (x_1,y_1) is on the line $y = mx + b$, your problem is to decide which of the points, $(x_1 + 1,y_1)$ or $(x_1 + 1,y_1 + 1)$, is closer to $(x_1 + 1, m(x_1 + 1) + b)$, the actual point on the line (figure 3.1.8). If d_1 is the distance between (x_1,y_1) and $(x_1 + 1, m(x_1 + 1) + b)$,

FIGURE 3.1.8

A comparison of the distances d_1 and d_2 can be computed by integer arithmetic. Integer arithmetic is one factor that increases the speed of the Bresenham line generator.

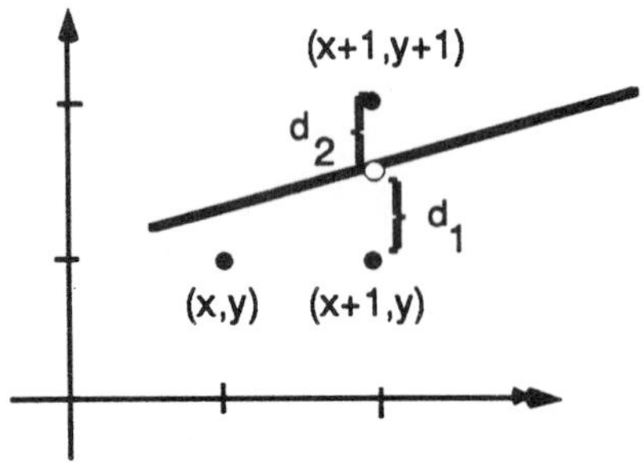

$$d_1 = m(x_1 + 1) + b - y_1$$

Similarly, d_2, the distance between $(x_1 + 1,y_1 + 1)$ and $(x_1 + 1, m(x_1 + 1) + b)$, is

$$d_2 = (y_1 + 1) - m(x_1 + 1) - b$$

The difference is

$$d_1 - d_2 = 2m(x_1 + 1) - 2y_1 + 2b - 1$$

If this difference is positive, then d_1 is larger than d_2 and you would choose the point $(x_1 + 1,y_1 + 1)$; otherwise, you would choose the point $(x_1 + 1,y_1)$. Both m and b are real variables, however, so even though you no longer need the round function, you still are using floating-point arithmetic. Recall that $m = dy/dx$. Even if m is negative, you may calculate m in such a way to ensure that dx is positive by relabeling the points so that $x_2 > x_1$. If you multiply the difference $d_1 - d_2$ by dx, the resultant expression (let's call it an indicator), will be positive exactly when the difference is positive.

$$\begin{aligned} r &= dx\,(d_1 - d_2) \\ &= 2\,dy\,(x_1 + 1) - 2\,dx\,y_1 + 2\,dx\,b - dx\ (*) \\ &= 2\,dy\,x_1 - 2\,dx\,y_1 + c \end{aligned}$$

where c is the real constant,

$$2\,dy + dx\,(2b - 1)$$

At this point you are still required to use floating-point arithmetic.

Because this algorithm will compute the indicator r_i for every point (x_i,y_i), the indicator r_{i+1} may be calculated with r_i as long as $i>=1$. If you again use the trick of taking the difference of the indicators in this case, you can eliminate the constant c.

$$r_{i+1} - r_i = 2\,dy\,(x_{i+1} - x_i) - 2\,dx(y_{i+1} - y_i)$$

In this derivation, $x_{i+1} = x_i + 1$, so that the indicator r_{i+1} may be calculated by

$$r_{i+1} = r_i + 2\,dy - 2\,dx(y_{i+1} - y_i)$$

Recall that y_{i+1} was calculated from y_i using r_i. If r_i is positive, then $y_{i+1} = y_i + 1$; otherwise $y_{i+1} = y_i$. Substituting for y_{i+1}, you get

$$r_{i+1} = r_i + 2\,dy - 2\,dx$$

if r_i is positive; otherwise

$$r_{i+1} = r_i + 2\,dy$$

Notice that for a given line the values $2\,dy - 2\,dx$ and $2\,dy$ are integer constants that may be calculated prior to entering the main loop.

To compute r_1, use the fact the (x_1,y_1) is on the line so that $y_1 = mx_1 + b$, where $m = dx/dy$. The equation (*) with this value for y_1 and m substituted simplifies to

$$r_1 = 2\,dy - dx$$

You have derived the Bresenham's algorithm for the case of a line with slope between 0 and 1.

To modify Bresenham's algorithm to handle lines with slope larger than 1, recall that in the DDA algorithm, all that was necessary was to increment y by 1 and then determine which x-value would be plotted. This is equivalent to interchanging the roles of x and y in the algorithm. For lines with negative slopes, one of the coordinates is decreased while the other is incremented by 1.

In algorithms that calculate an indicator to choose the next representation point, the decision as to which point will be included is not always clear. Points

FIGURE 3.1.9

Bresenham's line-generating algorithm

```
(* Bresenham's line-drawing algorithm for 0 <= m <= 1 *)

procedure BresenhamLine(x1,y1,x2,y2 : integer);
var
   dx,dy,x,y,EndX,r,PositiveAddon, NegativeAddon : integer;
begin (* DrawLine *)
   dx := abs(x2 - x1);
   dy := abs(y2 - y1);
   r := 2 * dy - dx;                (* the initial value of the indicator          *)
   PositiveAddon := 2 * (dy - dx);  (* constant added if previous indicator >=0    *)
   NegativeAddon := 2 * dy;         (* constant added if previous indicator < 0    *)
                                    (* determine the starting and ending points    *)
   if x1 > x2 then                  (* start at (x2,y2)                            *)
      begin
         x := x2;
         y := y2;
         EndX := x1
      end
   else
      begin
         x := x1;
         y := y1;
         EndX := x2
      end;
   SetPixel(x,y);
   while x < EndX do
      begin
         x := x + 1;
         if r < 0 then              (* choose current y-value and compute r        *)
            r := r + NegativeAddon
         else                       (* increment y-value and compute r             *)
            begin
               y := y + 1;
               r := r + PositiveAddon
            end;
         SetPixel(x,y)
      end (* while x < EndX *)
end; (* DrawLine *)
```

equidistant from the actual point on the line are equally good representatives of the point. Bresenham's algorithm arbitrarily chooses not to increment y in such cases. This process often leads to different representations of a line when it is drawn in the reverse direction (Bresenham 1987); that is, a line drawn from (x_1,y_1) to (x_2,y_2) may have a different representation than if it were drawn from

(x_2,y_2) to (x_1,y_1). This is particularly important if a line is being erased with the same algorithm (exercise 3.1.2). Care must be taken to erase in the same direction in which the line was originally drawn.

3.1.c Antialiasing

While Bresenham's algorithm is a good example of how an efficient algorithm may be constructed from a less efficient one, the problem of realistic representation of a line or any other geometric object on the screen has not yet been addressed. The most obvious problem in transferring images to the screen is the steplike appearance of lines (the "jaggies"), but there are other problems, such as the actual disappearance of objects that are too small to be represented by a dot. These representation problems are called **aliasing.** The term *aliasing* is used in sampling theory applied to signal processing. If too few samples of a waveform are taken, the precise nature of the waveform is lost. When you plot a line, you are sampling points on the line that correspond to pixels, and as in the signal sampling, the precise nature of the line is lost.

The obvious solution to some of these difficulties is to pack the points in the graphic representation closer together. As computer memory has become less expensive, frame buffers have become larger and more points can be put in the same area, resulting in improved resolution. Another solution has been to make the graphic screen smaller, which increases the density of the dots without increasing their number.

While screen resolution may be increased, it is usually more important that the hard copy have better resolution than the screen. This problem has been addressed by hard-copy devices that rebuild the image before drawing it. These printing devices receive a coded signal, not the image of the line from the screen, to draw a line between two points. In machines such as plotters, this is translated into movements of a pen. Other printers, such as laser printers, reconstruct lines by using many more points than are available on the screen.

FIGURE 3.1.10

If the intensity of a pixel is set to represent the percentage of that pixel covered by a line, the jaggies are softened.

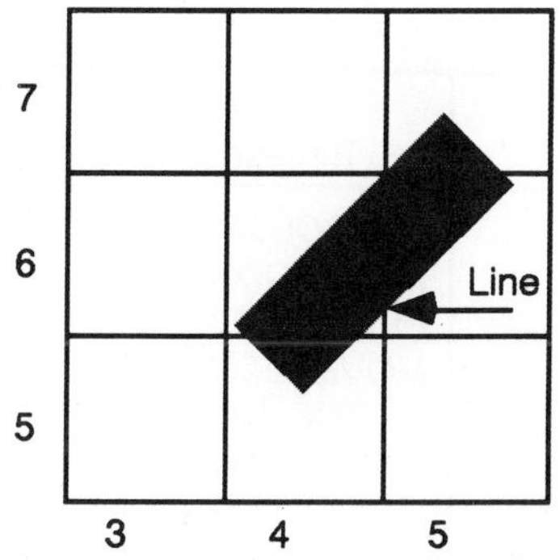

If the image is to be reproduced directly off of the screen or if realism is very important, you may want to incorporate **antialiasing** techniques. Developed to improve the image on the screen, antialiasing techniques reduce the effects of sampling errors by adjusting each pixel's gray level to better match the pixel's position relative to the actual line. While line segments in geometry consist of an infinite number of infinitesimal points, the representation of a line is a sequence of a finite number of pixels, each of them small in size. As a result, lines on the screen have width and may be considered rectangles. The percentage of a pixel actually covered by the rectangle may be computed by using sampling theory. Altering the gray level of a pixel to approximate this percentage will soften the jaggies.

In figure 3.1.10 the rectangle representing (4,6) is roughly 50 percent covered by the line, so its gray level would be set at 50 percent. The pixel (4,5) is covered to a lesser extent, so its gray level will be set at a lower percent. This type of computation will improve the appearance of the line, but the computations required to achieve this improvement are still time consuming (figure 3.1.11).

Altering the gray value of a pixel can make yet another improvement in the quality of line drawings. Lines with slopes near 1 and -1 have fewer pixels per

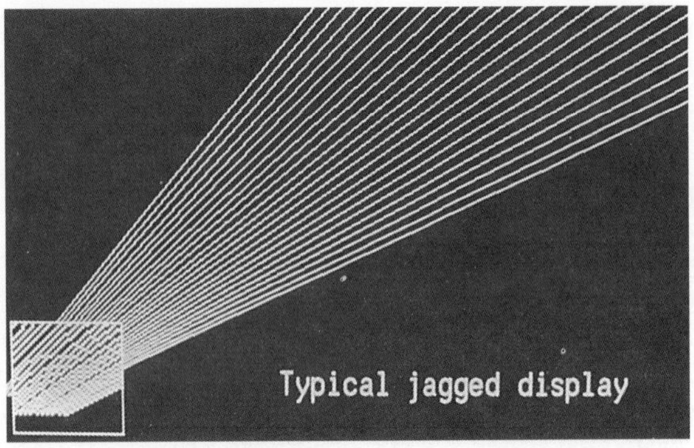

FIGURE 3.1.11

The affects of antialiasing.

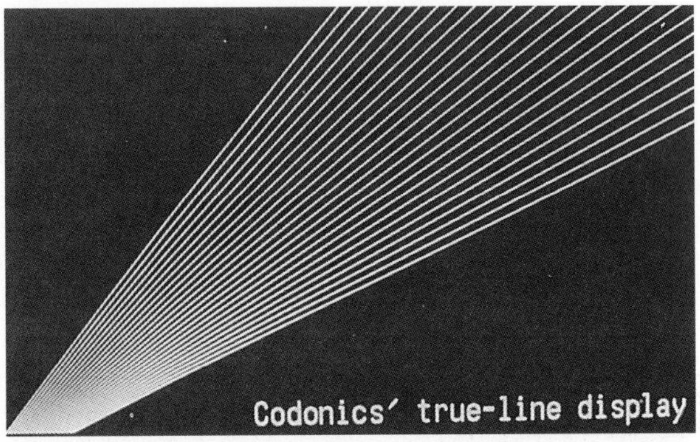

FIGURE 3.1.12

Lines with slopes near 1 and −1 have fewer pixels per unit length than do horizontal or vertical lines.

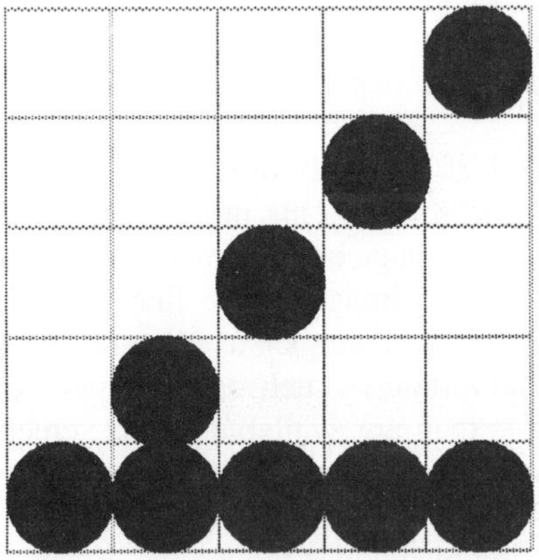

unit length than do horizontal or vertical lines (figure 3.1.12). The algorithms that you used to create lines use the same number of pixels to draw the line between (1,1) and (3,1) as they do to draw the line from (1,1) to (3,3). Clearly, the line from (1,1) to (3,3) is the diagonal of a square that has the line from (1,1) to (3,1) as its side, and the diagonal of a square is longer than one of its sides. If the gray value used to draw lines is increased when the slope is closer to 1 or −1, the comparative appearance of the lines will improve.

Figure 3.1.13 lists line-drawing and color-setting functions for some popular systems.

FIGURE 3.1.13

Line-drawing procedures available on various systems

Graphic system

	GKS and PHIGS	Turbo Pascal 4.0–5.5 IBM	Macintosh Toolbox	Apple II Turtlegraphics
Function	set polyline, colour index, x and y polyline(n,x,y) (n = 1)	SetColor SetWriteMode Line(x1,y1,x2,y2); or MoveTo(x,y); LineTo(x,y);	PenPat MoveTo(x1,y1); LineTo(x2,y2);	PENCOLOR(NONE); MOVETO(X1,Y1); PENCOLOR(WHITE); MOVETO(X2,Y2);

EXERCISES

3.1.1

Extend the Bresenham line-drawing algorithm to include lines with arbitrary slope.

FIGURE 3.1.14

The line algorithm may be written so that pixels along the line are not set to a predetermined color but instead have their color reversed.

3.1.2

In a system that allows pixels to be only black or white, the line algorithm may reverse the pixel color for points on the line rather than set them to the PenColor. Such algorithms may be used to display a line on a varying background (figure 3.1.14) or to draw a line that will later be erased. Lines drawn by this algorithm are erasable because a second application of the algorithm with the same beginning and end points will return all pixels to their original state. Assume that a graphics system has a boolean function TestPixel(x,y) that returns true if the pixel is not black and false if it is. Revise Bresenham's line-drawing algorithm to change the pixel color for points on the line. In graphic systems with a PenColor or PenMode **reverse** or **xor,** no special algorithm is needed.

3.1.3

Write a procedure to convert coordinates of a system with origin at the lower left of the display to coordinates of a system with origin at the upper left.

3.1.4

Draw the line from the point (10,10) to the point (70,30) with the primitive line-drawing procedure of your system. Set the PenColor to the background color, and draw the line from (70,30) to (10,10). Is the line completely erased? If not, why?

3.1.5

Implement the DDA given in figure 3.1.7 on your system.

3.1.6

Modify the DDA to draw solid, dashed, or dotted lines upon request.

3.1.7

The DDA can be modified so that one of the coordinates is updated by integer arithmetic. Implement the DDA with this modification. Does it run faster than the DDA implemented in exercise 3.1.5?

3.1.8

Is there a way to do fixed-point arithmetic on your machine? If so, can your compiler access this arithmetic directly? If so, implement the DDA with fixed-point arithmetic. If you cannot access fixed-point arithmetic directly, implement assembly-level routines to do fixed-point arithmetic, and implement the DDA with these routines. Is there a speed improvement over the DDA implemented in exercise 3.1.5 or 3.1.7?

3.1.9

Find out where the origin is in your graphics system.

3.1.10

What are your YMax and XMax?

3.1.11

How does your system enter the graphics mode?

3.1.12

What procedures for drawing lines are available on your system?

3.1.13

Give approximate coordinates for the vertices of each of the polygons in figure 3.1.14 if the rectangle represents your entire graphics screen.

FIGURE 3.1.15

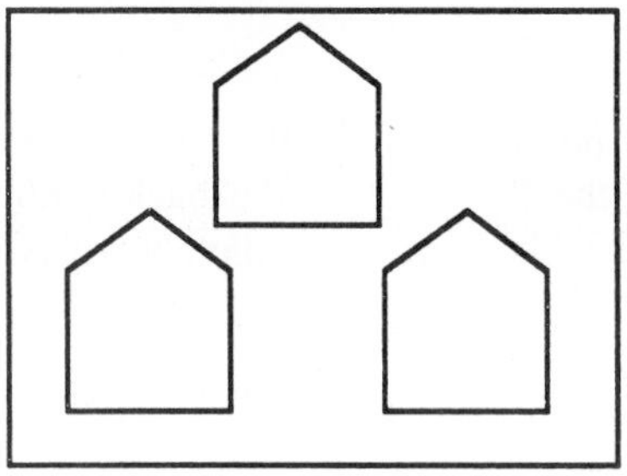

3.1.14

Write the code to create the picture in figure 3.1.15 on your graphics system.

3.1.15

Find out how to print from your system.

3.1.16

Print your picture.

3.1.17

a. Trace the Bresenham algorithm for the line between (1,1) and (7,3) (figure 3.1.16). b.Repeat this process using the DDT.

FIGURE 3.1.16

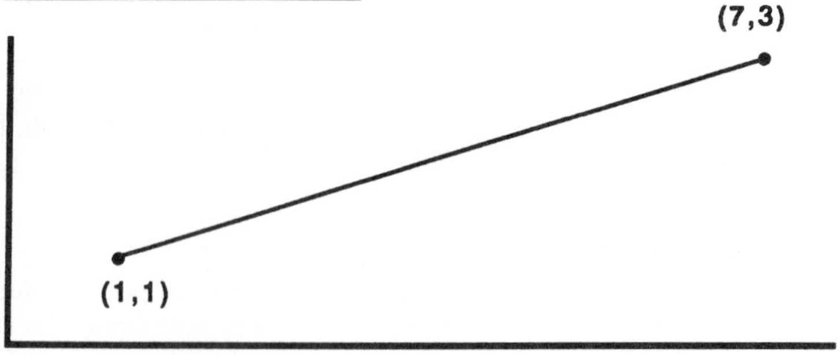

3.2 Windows and Viewports

The user who wants to draw a line from the point (−5,−5) to the point (5,5), will not be able to display this line because of the coordinate systems of most display devices. Pixels are normally labeled with positive integer coordinates. Even if this line is translated to a line between pixels (0,0) and (10,10), it will only appear as a tiny speck in a corner of the screen. Clearly, translation is not the only transformation needed. You must provide a way to scale drawings and position them on the screen so that in this case, the line from (−5,−5) to (5,5) may be represented by a line on the screen from pixel (50,50) to pixel (150,150). All these transformations should be transparent to the user; that is, even though the line joins pixels with coordinates (50,50) and (150,150), the user still works with the line from (−5,−5) to (5,5).

FIGURE 3.2.1

Users specify the window and viewport used to display their drawings.

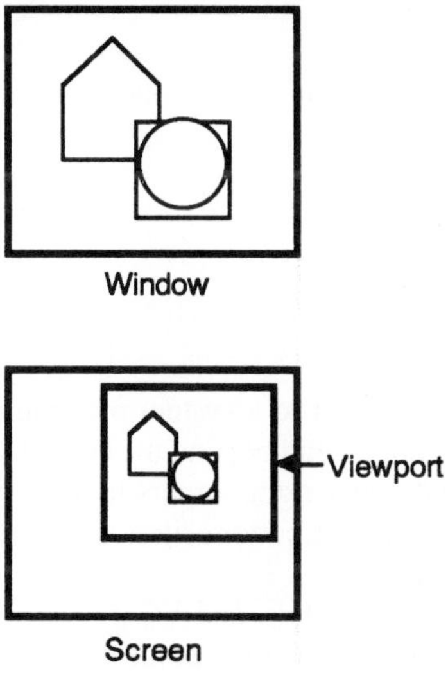

In order to specify the coordinate system that best suits a situation, you will create procedures using application-specific coordinate systems. These coordinates are world coordinates, as opposed to the system coordinates that are called **screen coordinates.** To establish the relationship between world and screen coordinates, the user first specifies, in world coordinates, a rectangle that surrounds the drawing. This rectangle is called a **window,** and coordinates of objects in the window are given in **window coordinates.** The section of the screen where the window will be drawn is called a **viewport** (figure 3.2.1).

Your system will do the transformations between the window and viewport, so the boundaries of both must be stored in the system. You store the conversion factors needed to convert from world coordinates to screen coordinates in order to save computation time during actual drawing. All of this current data is stored in a structure called a **window** (figure 3.2.2).

The line-drawing procedure DrawLine uses the screen coordinates of the end points to draw a line. Sometimes it is easier to describe a line in terms of its starting point and the x- and y-distance to the end point. To facilitate this type of operation, called a **relative** operation, you will keep track of a point called the **cursor.** The coordinates of the cursor are stored in CurrentX and CurrentY.

FIGURE 3.2.2

The structure used to hold the information necessary to make conversions from world to screen coordinates, the boundaries of the window in world and screen coordinates, and other information needed to maintain a window.

```
type
   Window = record
      CurrentX, CurrentY          : real;          (* world coordinates of the cursor           *)
      ViewLeft,ViewRight          : real;          (* left and right boundaries of viewport     *)
      ViewTop,ViewBottom          : real;          (* top and bottom viewport boundaries        *)
      WindowLeft,WindowRight      : real;          (* world coordinates, viewport sides         *)
      WindowTop,WindowBottom      : real;          (* world coordinates of viewport top         *)
                                                   (* and bottom                                *)
      XConvertMult,XConvertAdd    : real;          (* conversion factors for x                  *)
      YConvertMult,YConvertAdd    : real;          (* conversion factors for y                  *)
      PenColor, FillColor         : ScreenColor    (* pen and fill colors                       *)
   end;
```

FIGURE 3.2.3

Normalized device coordinates range between 0 and 1, while screen coordinates range between 0 and XMax or YMax.

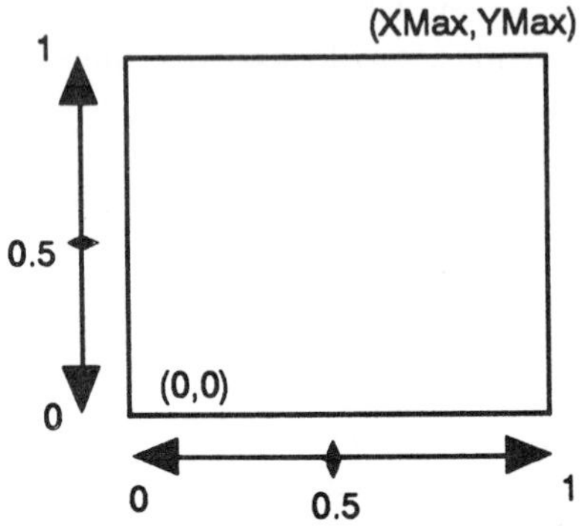

The first step in building a machine-independent coordinate system is to free the viewport procedure from the screen coordinates. To make it easier to locate the viewport, you replace the screen coordinates with normalized device coordinates, for which the lower-left corner is (0,0) and the upper-right corner is (1,1). The corners of the viewport will be specified as pairs of real numbers between 0 and 1 (figure 3.2.3). This will allow you to write your conversion code without reference to specific graphic systems.

The procedure for setting the viewport is called **SetViewport.** It has five parameters: the four real numbers between 0 and 1 that represent the left, bottom, right, and top of the viewport; and the record holding your Window information. A sample call to SetViewport follows:

(SetViewport(0.5,0.7,1.0,0.9,TheWindow)

If the parameter representing the frame is called TheWindow, this call to SetViewport will compute corners of the viewport as real numbers closest to the actual screen coordinates for the corners. For this example the computations are

TheWindow.ViewLeft:= 0.5 * XMax

TheWindow.ViewBottom := 0.7 * YMax

The Window.ViewRight := 1.0 * XMax

TheWindow.ViewTop := 0.9 * YMax

These numbers are then rounded to integers and passed to a system procedure called **Viewport.** Viewport ensures that lines do not extend beyond the specified screen rectangle. You will use the lower-left and upper-right corners to specify viewports, so a call to viewport will be Viewport(left,bottom,right,top). All parameters for viewport are in screen coordinates.

The fields XConvertMult, XConvertAdd, YConvertMult, and YConvertAdd of the window are used to convert the world coordinates of a point to screen coordinates. The conversion factors ending in Mult are **scaling factors,** and those ending in Add are **translation factors.** These conversion factors are calculated when the window coordinates are set in order to speed up conversions done during line drawing.

The **x-translation factor** is the x-distance from the world coordinate origin to the screen coordinate of the origin. The **y-translation factor** is defined similarly. For example, if the world origin (0,0) is at (2,1) (in screen coordinates), then the translation factor XConvertAdd is 2 and the translation factor YConvertAdd is 1.

The **x-scaling factor** is the ratio of the x-distance between two points in screen coordinates to the x-distance in world coordinates between the two points that the screen points represent. The **y-scaling factor** is defined similarly. For example, if the points (0,0) and (2,3) in world coordinates are represented by the screen points (0,0) and (1,1), the scaling factor XConvertMult is ½ because the x-distance between the two points, 1, in screen coordinates is ½ of this x-distance in world coordinates. The scaling factor YConvertMult is ⅓.

When both a translation and a scaling take place, the formulas for the factors become more complicated. Consider converting the world coordinates (xw,yw)

FIGURE 3.2.4

When window coordinates are converted to viewport coordinates, the distance between a point and the lower-left corner of a window is computed in window coordinates. This distance is multiplied by the conversion factor for window to viewport. The resulting number is the distance from the lower-left corner to the point in viewport coordinates. This is added to the viewport coordinates of the lower-left corner to get the viewport coordinates of P.

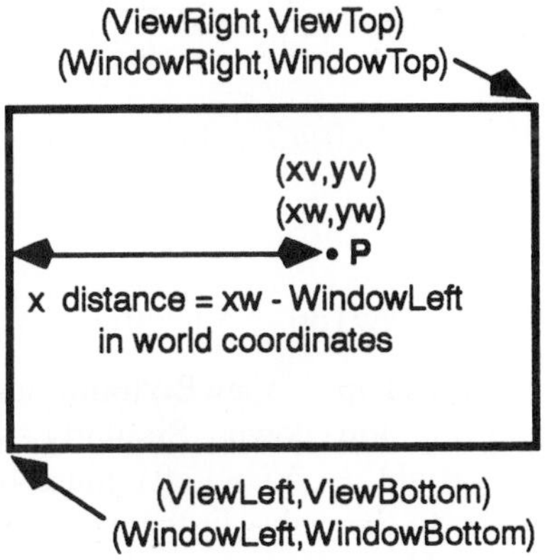

FIGURE 3.2.5

The viewport in this picture is adjusted to reflect the square window.

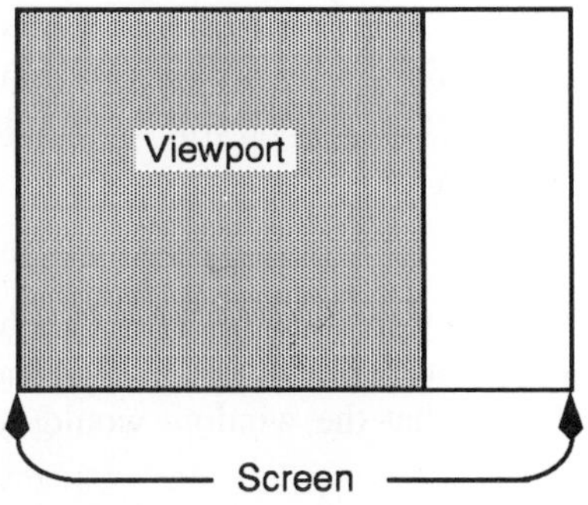

Viewport set for the whole screen, with the Window set at (0,0) and (20,20)

of a point, P, to the pair of real numbers (xv,yv) nearest the viewport coordinates of P. In figure 3.2.4, the pairs (ViewLeft,ViewBottom) and (ViewRight,ViewTop) represent the real-number coordinates computed by SetViewport. The pairs (WindowLeft,WindowBottom) and (Window-Right,WindowTop) represent the world coordinates (in real numbers) of the viewport's corners. When computing xv, first notice that the x-scaling factor for this picture can be computed by dividing the length of the viewport given in viewport coordinates by the length given in world coordinates.

XConvertMult = (ViewRight − ViewLeft)/(WindowRight − WindowLeft)

Once your have this scaling factor, you use it to convert the world distance of the point P from the corner of the viewport into the viewport distance.

ViewportDistance = (xw − WindowLeft)*XConvertMult

To get xv, the screen coordinates of P, you only need to add the number ViewLeft.

xv = (xw − WindowLeft)*XConvertMult + ViewLeft

This simplifies to

xv = xw*XConvertMult + XConvertAdd

with

XConvertAdd = ViewLeft − WindowLeft*XConvertMult

Similar computations yield the following equations for YConvertMult and YConvertAdd:

YConvertMult = (ViewTop − ViewBottom)/(WindowTop − WindowBottom)

and

YConvertAdd = ViewBottom − WindowBottom*YConvertMult

These computations work well as long as you do not compare line lengths in the x- and y-directions. If you want to maintain a one-to-one relationship between distances in the x- and y-directions, then the multipliers must be the same for each direction. If they are not, then a square in world coordinates will have one side longer than the other in screen coordinates. Suppose, for example, that a user specifies that the viewport is to be the whole screen, that the world coordinates of the lower-left corner are (0,0), and that the coordinates of the upper-right corner are (20,20). If the user draws the ''square'' that surrounds the viewport, it will have lower-left-corner screen coordinates of (0,0) and upper-right-corner screen coordinates of (XMax, YMax). Since for most systems XMax > YMax, this rectangle will not be the square desired (figure 3.2.5).

Many systems allow the user to specify the relationship between the vertical and horizontal coordinates. Let's keep your system relatively simple by requiring equivalent vertical and horizontal distances. To make the necessary corrections, assume that the user has in mind a general area of the screen where the image is to appear and wants to impose an exact set of coordinates on that area. This means that SetViewport will be advisory, and that SetWindow, the procedure used to establish world coordinates, will take precedence over it. Also assume that the height and width of pixels are equal. If they are not equal, additional corrections must be made. (These corrections will be made in a later exercise 3.2.6.)

Adjustments to the viewport will be made by decreasing the x- or y-coordinate of the upper-right corner. By restricting the adjustment to one of these values you construct the largest viewport consistent with the given world coordinate system. In the example given in figure 3.2.5, the x-coordinate of the upper-right corner of the viewport will be reduced to YMax. The viewport in this case will be the largest square viewport allowed on the screen.

The procedure SetWindow computes the width-to-height ratios of both the window and the viewport and saves these in WindowRatio and ViewRatio, respectively.

$$\text{WindowRatio} = (\text{WindowRight} - \text{WindowLeft})/(\text{WindowTop} - \text{WindowBottom})$$

and

$$\text{ViewRatio} = (\text{ViewRight} - \text{ViewLeft})/(\text{ViewTop} - \text{ViewBottom})$$

If WindowRatio is larger than ViewRatio, (ViewTop − ViewBottom) must be reduced by moving the viewport from the top down. Similarly, if WindowRatio is less than ViewRatio, (ViewRight − ViewLeft) must be reduced by moving the left side of the viewport to the right. In the example, WindowRatio = 20/20 = 1 and ViewRatio = Xmax/YMax > 1. Because WindowRatio < ViewRatio, ViewRight is reduced to YMax and then ViewRatio = YMax/YMax = 1.

You would like WindowRatio = ViewRatio; if WindowRatio < ViewRatio, you want to alter ViewRight so that

$$\text{WindowRatio} = \text{ViewRatio} = (\text{ViewRight} - \text{ViewLeft})/(\text{ViewTop} - \text{ViewBottom})$$

—that is, ViewRight = ViewLeft + (ViewTop − ViewLeft) * WindowRatio. A similar computation when WindowRatio > ViewRatio gives the new formula for ViewTop as

$$\text{ViewTop} = \text{ViewBottom} + (\text{ViewRight} - \text{ViewLeft})/\text{WindowRatio}$$

The actual procedures SetViewport and SetWindow are given in figure 3.2.6. After these corrections, the window will be located in the lower-left part of the original viewport. How would you change this so that the window would be centered in the specified viewport?

Notice that when the viewport is set, you assume that the window is maintained so that the conversion factors must be adjusted to reflect the new window. Therefore, SetWindow is called from SetViewport, and it, in turn, calls the system primitive Viewport.

FIGURE 3.2.6

SetViewport and SetWindow

```
procedure SetViewport(left,bottom,right,top: real;     (* corners of viewport                   *)
                      var ThisWindow: Window);          (* the frame of this viewport            *)

begin (* SetViewPort *)
   with ThisWindow do
      begin
         ViewLeft := XMax * left;          (* compute left screen coordinate of the viewport    *)
         ViewBottom := YMax * bottom;      (* compute bottom screen coordinate of the viewport  *)
         ViewRight := XMax * right;        (* compute right screen coordinate of the viewport   *)
         ViewTop := YMax * top;            (* compute top screen coordinate of the viewport     *)
                                           (* compute the conversion factors and adjust scale   *)
         SetWindow(WindowLeft,WindowBottom,WindowRight,WindowTop,ThisWindow)
      end;
end; (*SetViewPort*)

procedure SetWindow(left, bottom, right, top : real;   (* corners of the window                 *)
                    var ThisWindow : Window);           (* the frame of this window              *)
var
   WindowRatio, ViewRatio : real;                       (* ratio of the x and y scaling factors  *)
                                                        (* in the window and the viewport        *)
   vleft, vbottom, vright, vtop : integer;              (* local values used to set the viewport *)
begin (* SetWindow *)
   with ThisWindow do
      begin
         (* record the sides of the window *)
         WindowLeft := left;
         WindowBottom := bottom;
         WindowRight := right;
         WindowTop := top;

         (* compute conversion factors *)
         WindowRatio := (WindowRight - WindowLeft) / (WindowTop - WindowBottom);
         ViewRatio := (ViewRight - ViewLeft) / (ViewTop - ViewBottom);

         (* adjust scale to avoid distortion *)
         if WindowRatio > ViewRatio then
            ViewTop := ViewBottom + (ViewRight - ViewLeft) / WindowRatio
         else if WindowRatio < ViewRatio then
            ViewRight := ViewLeft + (ViewTop - ViewBottom) * WindowRatio;

         (* compute x -scale and translation factors *)
         XConvertMult := (ViewRight - ViewLeft) / (WindowRight - WindowLeft);
         XConvertAdd := ViewLeft - WindowLeft * XConvertMult;

         (* compute y -scale and translation factors *)
         (* note that y-scale has been adjusted to be the same as x-scale*)
         YConvertMult  := XConvertMult;
         YConvertAdd := ViewBottom - WindowBottom * YConvertMult;

         (* set the system viewport *)
         vleft := round(ViewLeft);
         vbottom := round(ViewBottom);
         vright := round(ViewRight);
         vtop := round(ViewTop);
         Viewport(vleft,vbottom,vright,vtop)     (* the system primitive to maintain a viewport   *)
      end
end; (* SetWindow *)
```

Now that the coordinate system has been standardized, you must write your own graphics procedures to use them. Figure 3.2.7 depicts the relationships among the system's various parts.

While all graphics systems provide at least a procedure comparable to the Viewport procedure, some also provide the procedures SetWindow and SetViewport. A summary of some popular systems is given in figure 3.2.8.

FIGURE 3.2.7

An overview of the transformation from world to screen coordinates

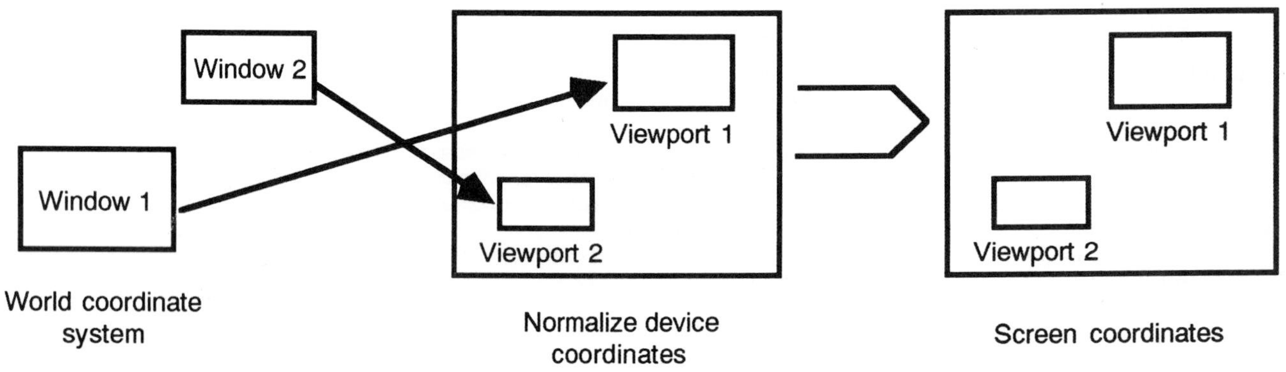

FIGURE 3.2.8

Window/viewport procedures available in various systems

Graphic system

Function	Book	GKS and PHIGS	TurboPascal 4.0–5.5 IBM	Macintosh Toobox	Apple II Turtlegraphics	Coordinate system
	SetWindow	SET WINDOW				World
	SetViewPort	SET VIEWPORT				Normalized device
	ViewPort		SetViewPort	ClipRect	VIEWPORT	Device

EXERCISES

3.2.1.

Develop equations to convert screen coordinates to world coordinates.

3.2.2.

Write a procedure SetWindow that allows the user to determine the x-scale and y-scale.

3.2.3.

How would you change the conversion factors computed in this section if your system had its origin (0,0) at the upper-left corner?

3.2.4.

How would you change the conversion factors computed in this section if your system's viewports used local coordinates with the upper-left corner (0,0) and lower-right corner (ViewRight − ViewLeft, ViewTop − ViewBottom)?

3.2.5.

Change the SetWindow procedure so that the resulting viewport will be centered on the selected viewport.

3.2.6.

The pixel ratio is the ratio of the height of a pixel to its width. In some systems, such as the CGA high-resolution, black-and-white graphics system, this ratio is not 1. If the pixel ratio is not 1, vertical and horizontal lines covering the same number of pixels have different lengths on the screen. In the CGA high-resolution, black-and-white system, for example, the line from (0,0) to (0,10) is about 2.3 times the length of the line from (0,0) to (10,0). To correct for this, you could lengthen lines in the x-direction or shorten lines in the y-direction.

a. What are the advantages and disadvantages of each approach?
b. How would the conversion factors be changed when the y-direction length of a line is shortened? How would the conversion factors be changed if the x-direction length of a line is lengthened?
c. If you are changing the length of a line in the x-direction, what problems can occur when the viewport is set?
d. Could this correction be made at the time you convert from NDCs to screen coordinates?
e. Incorporate corrections for the pixel ratio of your system in your conversion from world to screen conversion factors.

3.2.7

Give values for the parameters a, b, c, d in SetViewPort(a,b,c,d,TheWindow) that will locate your viewport in each of the locations in figure 3.2.9.

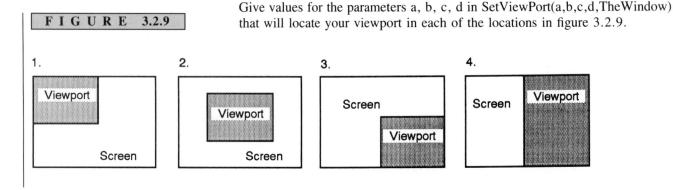

FIGURE 3.2.9

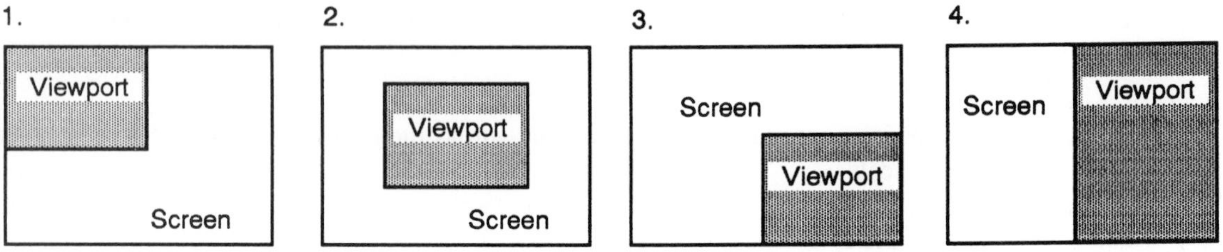

3.2.8

If your system has a function for setting viewports, what coordinate system is used in the viewport?

3.2.9

Try to draw a square with the line-drawing functions provided by your system. Did you actually get a square?

FIGURE 3.2.10

3.2.10

If your square looks like the diagram in figure 3.2.10, you can get a square by multiplying distances in the x-direction by a number larger than 1. To compute this number, increase the length of the horizontal side until you get a square; then divide the length of this horizontal side by the vertical side length. Find the number.

FIGURE 3.2.11

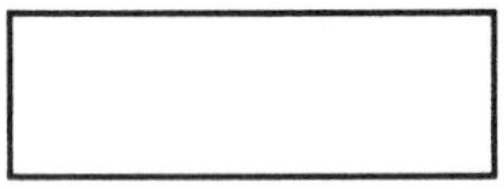

3.2.11

If your square looks like the one in figure 3.2.11, you can get a square by multiplying distances in the y-direction by a number larger than 1. To compute this number, increase the length of the vertical side until you get a square; then divide the length of this vertical side by the horizontal side length.

3.2.12

If your viewport is the whole screen and the lower left corner of your window is at $(-5,-5)$ while the upper right corner is at (10,10), calculate the conversion factors XMult, XAdd, YMult, and YAdd for your system. If you want to draw a line between the points $(-1,2)$ and $(5,-1)$, what will the screen coordinates of the endpoints be?

3.2.13

Repeat problem 6 if the viewport is changed so its lower left corner has NDCs (0.25,0.75) and its upper right corner has NDCs (0.5,1).

3.3 Clipping Lines

The line-drawing procedures you considered in section 3.1 had two points as parameters. No checking was done to see if those parameters were actually points on the screen. The portion of the screen used for drawing is further restricted when a viewport is specified. If coordinates of either end point did not represent a point in the viewport, a lot of time could be wasted in computing values that SetPixel would not be able to plot correctly. It would make sense to see which part of the line can be plotted and apply the line-drawing procedure on that line segment only. The process of finding those parts of a picture that will be visible in a given window is called **clipping.** The clipping functions described in this section may be applied either at the window or viewport level. For consistency with your use of procedure Viewport in section 3.2, you will clip at the viewport level.

FIGURE 3.3.1

Clipping is used to restrict line drawing to that portion of a line segment that lies within the viewport.

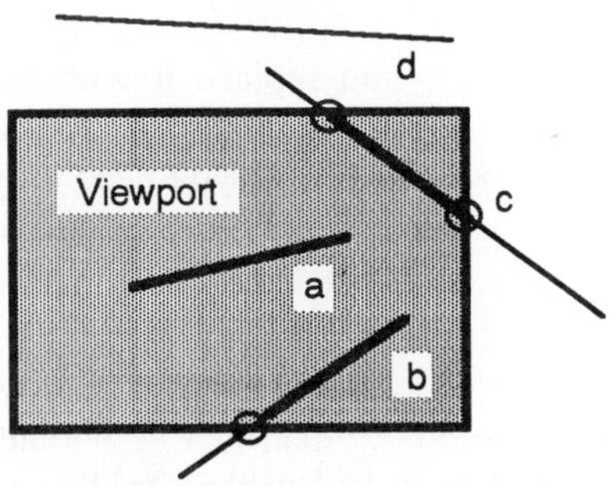

To determine which part of a line will be plotted, it is necessary to find out if either end point is not on the viewport. When both are on the viewport, the line may be plotted with no difficulty (line *a* in the figure 3.3.1). If an end point is not on the viewport (lines *b, c,* and *d* in the figure 3.3.1), you should try to replace it with the intersection of the line segment and the viewport boundary close to that end point. This technique for replacing end points works well as long as there is a segment of the line on the viewport. If the line does not intersect the viewport, a method of determining when to stop the replacement process is needed. Assume the screen coordinates of the lower-left corner of a viewport (XVMin,YVMin) and the upper-right corner of a viewport (XVMax-,YVMax) (figure 3.3.2).

The Cohen-Sutherland clipping algorithm classifies the relationship between points in the plane and points in the viewport by dividing the plane into nine regions determined by the viewport boundaries (figure 3.3.3). Every point may then be given a set of codes based on its position. The point P_2 in figure 3.3.3

FIGURE 3.3.2

The corners of a viewport specified in screen coordinates

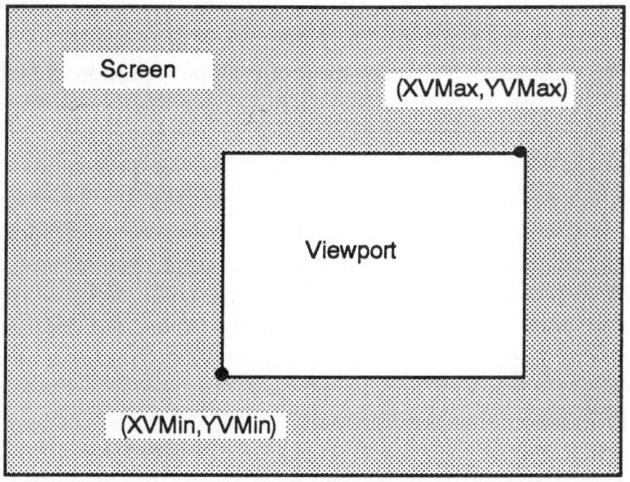

FIGURE 3.3.3

The regions used in clipping

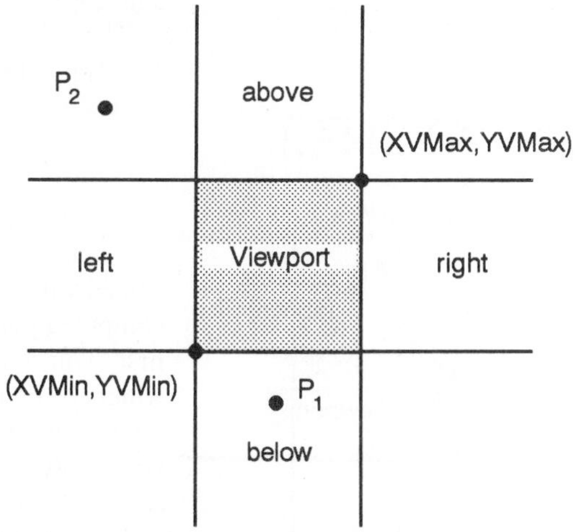

FIGURE 3.3.4

If both end points of a line are above the viewport, then the whole line will be above the viewport.

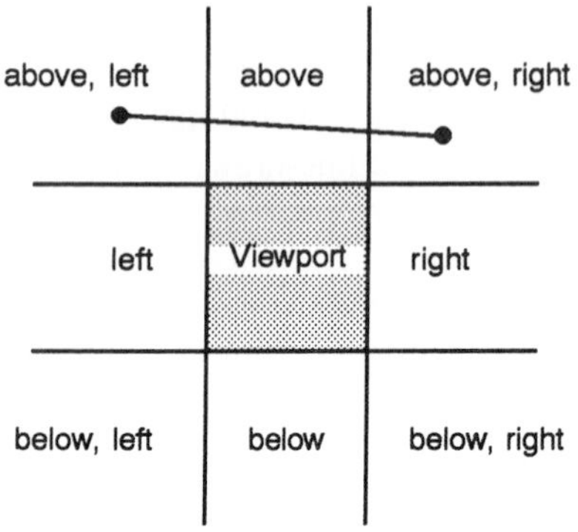

FIGURE 3.3.5

Sequence of points generated by the Cohen-Sutherland clipping algorithm

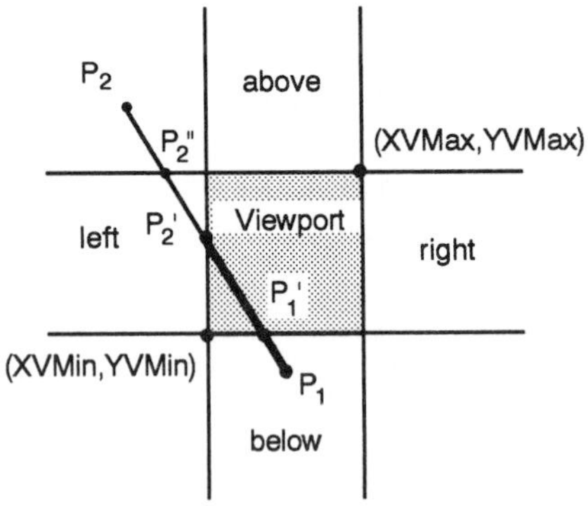

FIGURE 3.3.6

The sequence of computations in the Cohen-Sutherland algorithm

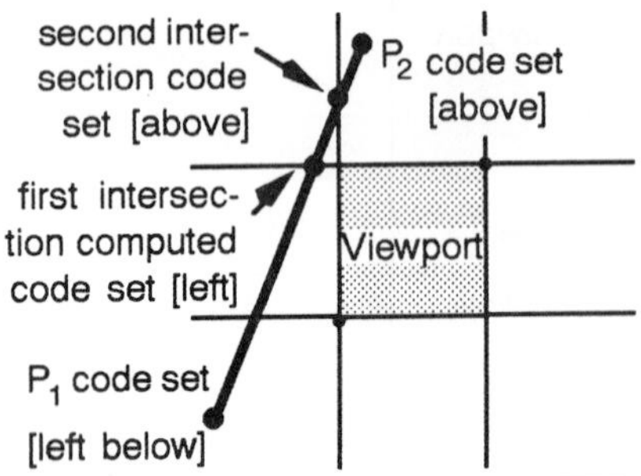

would have the code set [above,left], while the point P_1 would have the code set [below]. Points on the viewport have an empty code set. To determine if a point has above in its code set, you simply find out if its y-coordinate is larger than YVMax. Not only does the point P_1 have this property, but also its x-coordinate is less than XVMin, so it has left in its code set.

Once the end points of a line segment have been coded, it is possible to determine if the line may be drawn. If both end points have empty code sets, then both points are in the viewport and the line may be drawn between these points. If the intersection of the code sets is not empty, then the line will not appear in the viewport and no line will be drawn. Suppose, for example, that two points have above (figure 3.3.4) in their code sets, so all points on the line between the two will have above in their code sets. In this case, the line will be entirely above the viewport.

In the case that neither situation occurs, at least one of the points is not in the viewport; that is, its code set is not empty. The end point P_1 with coordinates (x_1,y_1) in figure 3.3.5 has code set [below], and the end point P_2 with coordinates (x_2,y_2) has the code set [above,left]. You would like to replace P_1 with the point P_1' and the point P_2 with the point P_2', so draw the line l joining P_1' and P_2'.

Because the point P_1 has below in its code set, you replace it with the intersection of l and the lower boundary of the viewport, the line y = YVMin. Clearly the y-coordinate of the intersection will be YVMin, so you need only find its x-coordinate. To get the x-coordinate, you solve the point-slope form of the equation of a line for x

$$x = x_1 + (y - y_1)/m$$

where $m = (y_2 - y_1)/(x_2 - x_1)$. Notice that the result will be real, so that the round function must be applied to get $x = \text{round}(x_1 + (\text{YVMin} - y_1)/m)$.

Plotting line l now means plotting the line segment from P_1' to P_2. You calculate the code set for P_1' and find that P_1' has an empty code set. To eliminate above from P_2's code set, you must find the intersection of l with the line y = YVMax. The x-coordinate must be calculated again, this time using y = YVMax and $x = \text{round}(x_1 + (\text{YVMax} - y_1)/m)$. The point P_2'', which is still not in the viewport, has the code set [left].

The next replacement point is clearly the intersection of l with the line x = XVMin, which may be computed by using the point-slope equation solved for y.

$$y = y_1 + m(x - x_1)$$

This time the point computed is P_2', the desired second point in the viewport.

As this example illustrates, finding the intersection of the line under consideration and a viewport boundary does not always mean that the newly computed point is in the viewport. In this case, had you chosen to eliminate left first, you would have reached the point P_2' immediately. Thus, the order in which you consider the code-set elements helps to determine how often a new intersection must be sought. Finally, it may be necessary to calculate new end points several times to discover that the line will not appear in the viewport (figure 3.3.6).

Figure 3.3.7 contains a Pascal implementation of the Cohen-Sutherland algorithm.

FIGURE 3.3.7

The Cohen-Sutherland clipping algorithm

```
(* The Cohen-Sutherland clipping algorithm's  special types*)
type
   Location= (Above, Below, Left, Right);
   PointCode= set of Location;

(* This procedure draws clipped lines.              *)
(* The procedure Line calls on one of the line-     *)
(* drawing algorithms discussed in section 3.1.     *)
(* Assume a rectangular viewport with               *)
(* corners (XVMin,YVMin) and (XVMax,YVMax).         *)

procedure ClipLine1 (x1,y1,x2,y2 : integer);

var
   code1,code2 , code: PointCode;      (* code sets associated with given points                          *)
   x,y                 : integer;      (* used to hold the coordinates of the point changed               *)
   m                   : real;         (* slope of line between the points                                *)
   Accept, Reject      : boolean;      (* used to indicate whether or not clipping is complete            *)

(* this procedure establishes the code set for a given point. *)

procedure SetCode(x,y : integer;  var c : PointCode);

begin  (* SetCode *)
   c := [ ];
   if x < XVMin  then
      c :=  [Left]
   else  if x > XVMax  then
      c :=  [Right];
   if  y < YVMin then
      c := c +  [Below]
   else  if  y > YVMax   then
      c := c + [Above ]
end;  (* SetCode *)

(* This procedure computes the intercept for the boundary indicated by a code entry .*)
procedure GetBoundaryPoint(var x,y : integer; code : PointCode);
begin (* GetBoundaryPoint *)
   if Left in code then
      begin
         x := XVMin;
         y :=  round (y1 + m *(XVMin - x1))
      end
   else  if  Right in code then
      begin
         x := XVMax;
         y :=  round (y1 + m * (XVMax - x1))
      end
   else  if  Above in code then
      begin
         x := round(x1 + (YVMax - y1)/m);
         y := YVMax
      end
```

(continued)

FIGURE 3.3.7 continued

```
   else
      begin
         x := round(x1 + (YVMin- y1)/m);
         y := YVMin
      end
end; (* GetBoundaryPoint *)

begin (* ClipLine1 *)
   m := (y2 - y1)/(x2 - x1);
   repeat
      SetCode(x1,y1,Code1);
      SetCode(x2,y2,Code2);
      Accept := (Code1 = [ ])  and (Code2 = [ ]);  (* are both points in the viewport?      *)
      Reject := (Code1 * Code2 <> [ ]);            (* is the line invisible?               *)
      if not (Accept or Reject) then
         begin
            if code1 = [ ] then                    (* first point in bounds, check the second *)
               code := code2
            else                                   (* work with the first point            *)
               code := code1;
            GetBoundaryPoint(x,y,code);
            if code = code1 then
               begin
                  x1 := x;
                  y1 := y
               end
            else
               begin
                  x2 := x;
                  y2 := y
               end
         end                                       (* if not (Accept or Reject), then      *)
   until Accept or Reject;

   if Accept then
      Line(x1,y1,x2,y2)

end; (* ClipLine1 *)
```

Many graphics algorithms have hardware implementations. These algorithms either take advantage of built-in operations that are fast, or they have specially constructed hardware to perform difficult operations. An example of an algorithm that was constructed to take advantage of a fast built-in operation is the **Sproull-Sutherland clipping algorithm.** This variation of the Cohen-Sutherland algorithm applies the code test on midpoints of line segments in what amounts to a binary search for line segments that will be in the viewport.

The Sproull-Sutherland clipping algorithm repeatedly computes the intersection of the given line segment with the boundaries of the viewport. These computations use floating-point arithmetic and the round function. It would appear that computing midpoints that have coordinates

$$((x_2 - x_1)/2, (y_2 - y_1)/2)$$

also uses floating-point arithmetic and would eventually need the round function. The numerators in the fractions are integers, so that the problem is division by 2. This may be accomplished on integers by using a right shift operation that is fast and gives integer results so that no floating-point arithmetic is needed.

The Sproull-Sutherland algorithm first considers the end points of the given line segment. If both end points are visible, the line is drawn. Lines for which neither end point is visible and for which the code sets have non-empty intersections are not drawn. In the case that one end point is visible or the code sets have empty intersections, the midpoint of the segment is computed. If the midpoint coincides with one of the end points, the algorithm terminates. Otherwise, the code set for the midpoint is calculated, and the two segments created by the bisection are checked for visibility. If a segment is visible, the segment is accepted; if the midpoint is the intersection of the segment and the viewport boundary, then the procedure terminates successfully. Segments that are not visible have the codes of their end points tested to see if the line can be discarded. If it cannot be discarded, the midpoint of this segment is computed and the algorithm continues; otherwise the algorithm terminates.

FIGURE 3.3.8

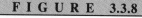

When applying the mid-point algorithm, you must take into account that lines can intersect a viewport in different ways.

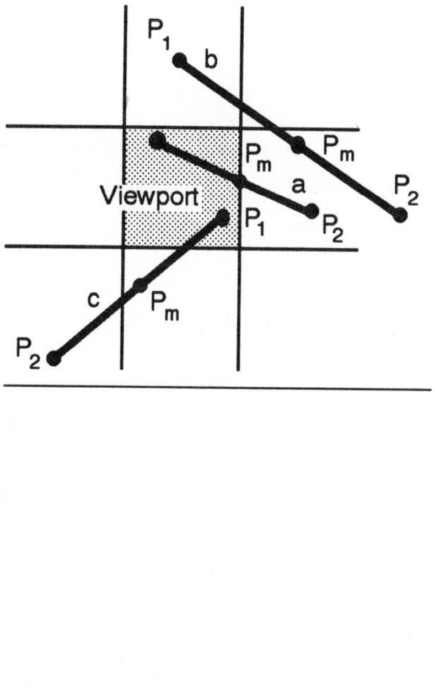

Figure 3.3.8 shows examples of the application of this algorithm. The half line P_2P_m on line *b* and line *c* would be rejected while the other half line has an inconclusive test, so the algorithm would continue by calculating the midpoint of P_1P_m and checking the segments created by this midpoint. The half line P_1P_m on line *a* would be accepted, and P_m would be, in fact, the intersection of the segment and the viewport boundary.

Liang and Barsky have created an alternative algorithm that uses floating-point arithmetic but finds the appropriate end points with at most four computations. This algorithm uses the parametric equations for a line and solves four inequalities to find the range of the parameter for which the line is in the viewport.

The parametric representation of the line between (x_1,y_1) and (x_2,y_2) gives x- and y-values for every point in terms of a parameter t that ranges from 0 to 1. The equations are

$$x = x_1 + (x_2 - x_1)*t = x_1 + dx*t$$

and

$$y = y_1 + (y_2 - y_1)*t = y_1 + dy*t$$

Notice that when $t = 0$, the point computed is (x_1,y_1); and when $t = 1$, the point computed is (x_2,y_2).

A point is visible if its coordinates are within the bounds of the viewport. This requirement leads to the following inequalities:

$$XVMin \leq x_1 + dx*t \leq XVMax$$

$$YVMin \leq y_1 + dy*t \leq YVMax$$

These inequalities may be rewritten as four separate inequalities

$$-dx*t \le x_1 - XVMin$$

$$dx*t \le XVMax - x_1$$

$$-dy*t \le y_1 - YVMin$$

$$dy*t \le YVMax - y_1$$

with the general form $m*t \le c$. The range of values of t that satisfy these inequalities and the inequality $0 \le t \le 1$ determine the final range of t to be $TMin \le t \le TMax$, for which the line segment is visible. Start with TMin = 0 and TMax = 1.

In solving the general form $m*t \le c$, first note that the multiplier m is zero when dx = 0 or dy = 0. This occurs exactly when the line is parallel to one of the boundaries. You need only restrict t so that the remaining variable coordinate stays within the boundaries.

If the value of $m > 0$, you just divide the inequality by m to get $t \le c/m$. In this case, the ratio $r = c/m$ may be used in three different ways. When the ratio is less than TMin, the line will be invisible. If $TMin \le r \le TMax$, set TMax = r. Finally, if $r \ge TMax$, the inequality does not affect the range of t.

For values of $m < 0$, the direction of the inequality is changed when you divide by the negative number m. Thus, the solution to the inequality is

$$t \ge c/m.$$

This time values of the ratio $r = c/m$ larger than TMax indicate that the line is not visible. Values of r within the range $TMin \le r \le TMax$ result in a reassigning of TMin to r. Other values of r have no effect on the range of t. The following examples will illustrate the actions of this algorithm. In figure 3.3.9, the line segment between (10,1) and (2,8) is to be drawn in a viewport with

FIGURE 3.3.9

The sequence of t-values chosen in an application of the Liang-Barsky algorithm

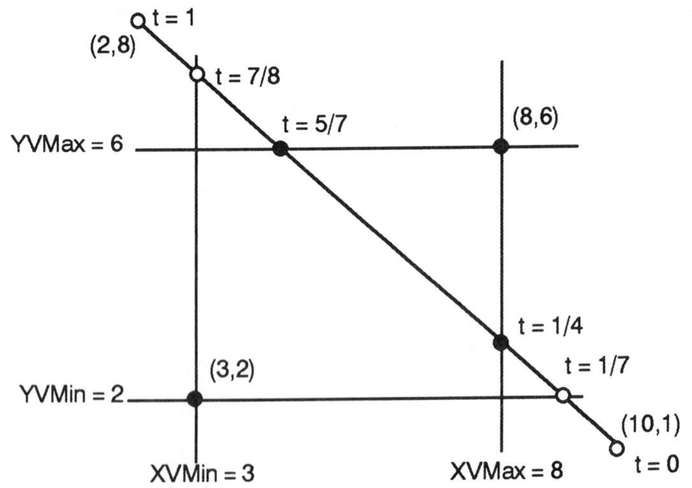

FIGURE 3.3.10

The Liang-Barsky algorithm applied to an invisible line segment

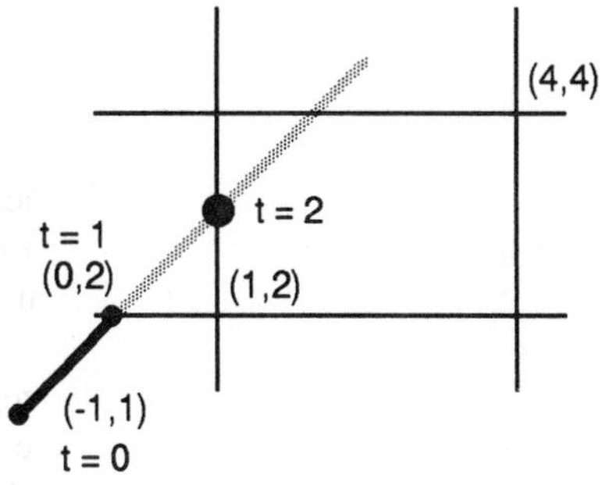

opposite corners (3,2) and (8,6). The point (10,1) is (x_1,y_1) in the computation, dx = −8, and dy = 7. The initial value for TMin is 0 and TMax = 1. Substituting into the inequality $dx*t \leq XVMax - x_1$ and solving for t results in $t \geq 1/4$. The smallest value t may take, TMin, must be at least 1/4, so at this point TMin is set to 1/4. Evaluation of $-dx*t \leq x_1 - XVMin$ yields $t \leq 7/8$. This indicates that TMax is at most 7/8, so it is set to that value.

The inequality $dy*t \leq YVMax - y_1$ restricts t to be less than or equal to 5/7, and TMax is once again adjusted, this time so TMax = 5/7. The solution to $-dy*t \leq y_1 - YVMax$ yields $t \geq 1/7$. All t between TMin and Tmax satisfy this inequality, so that this restriction is ignored.

To find the segment of the line that will be visible, you need only compute the values for x and y when t = TMin and t = TMax. In this case, the point (8,2 3/4) corresponds to t = 1/4; when t = 5/7, the corresponding point is (4 2/7, 6). The line is then plotted between (8,3) and (4,6).

An example of how the algorithm handles an invisible line segment is illustrated in figure 3.3.10. The line segment from (−1,1) to (0,2) is not visible in the viewport with corners (1,2) and (4,4). In this example dx = 1, and the solution of $-dx*t \leq x_1 - XVMin$ is $t \leq 2$. This is impossible because $t \leq$ TMax and TMax is always less than or equal to 1. The contradiction indicates that the line is not visible in this viewport. A Pascal implementation is given in figure 3.3.11.

FIGURE 3.3.11

The Liang-Barsky clipping algorithm

```
(* Procedure ClipLine2 uses the Liang-Barsky clipping algorithm      *)
(* to create a clipped line.                                          *)

procedure ClipLine2 (x1,y1,x2,y2 : integer);

var
   TMax,TMin   :   real;
   dx,dy       :   integer;
   Accept      :   boolean;
(* The function TRangeTest computes the restrictions on t            *)
(* induced by the boundary inequalities. It returns false if the     *)
(* line is determined to be invisible, and true otherwise.           *)

function TRangeTest(m,c : real; var TMax, TMin : real):boolean;
var
   r            :   real;
   TestResult   :   boolean;
begin (*TRangeTest *)
   TestResult := true;
   if m < 0 then
      begin
         r := c / m;
         if r > TMax then          (* t forced out of range           *)
            TestResult := false
         else if TMin < r then     (* t has a larger minimum          *)
            TMin := r
      end (* if m < 0 *)
```

(continued)

FIGURE 3.3.11 continued

```
  else if m>0then
     begin
        r := c / m;
        if r<TMin then              (* t forced out of range          *)
           TestResult := false
        else if r<TMax  then        (* t has a smaller maximum        *)
           TMax := r
     end (* if m > 0 *)
  else if  c<0then                  (* point outside of the boundary and line parallel to boundary*)
     TestResult := false
  TRangeTest := TestResult
end; (*TRangeTest *)

begin (* ClipLine2 *)
   Accept := false;
   (* set the initial range of t *)
   TMin := 0;
   TMax := 1;
   dx := x2 - x1;
   if TRangeTest(-dx, y1 - YVMin,TMin,TMax)  then
      if TRangeTest(dx,  YVMax  - y1, TMin, TMax)  then
         begin
            dy := y2 - y1;
            if TRangeTest(-dy,  x1 - XVMin,  TMin, TMax) then
               if TRangeTest(dy,  XVMax - x1, TMin, TMax ) then
                     (* all boundary tests passed, TMin and TMax ready                    *)
                     (* for computation of end points of the line                         *)
                  begin
                     Accept := true;
                     (* x2 and y2 must be computed first, since the values of x1 and y1 must be    *)
                     (* the original values x1 and y1 for both computations                         *)
                     if TMax < 1 then (* new values for x2 and y2 must be computed            *)
                        begin
                           x2 := round (x1 + TMax * dx);
                           y2 := round (y1 + TMax * dy)
                        end
                     if TMin > 0 then     (* new values for x1 and y1 must be computed       *)
                        begin
                           x1 := round ( x1 + TMin * dx);
                           y1 := round (y1 + TMin * dy)
                        end;
               end (* TRangeTest on dy *)
         end; (* TRangeTest on dx *)
      if Accept  then
         Line(x1,y1,x2,y2)
end; (* ClipLine2 *)
```

Now assume that you have a line-drawing procedure DrawLine(x1,y1,x2,y2) that draws properly clipped lines. This procedure will be used in section 3.4 when you create a line-drawing procedure that uses world coordinates. Many graphics packages provide line-drawing procedures at this level (figure 3.3.12).

Variations of the clipping algorithms dealing with viewports that are convex polygons were developed by Cyrus and Beck [CyBe 78].

FIGURE 3.3.12

Low-level line-drawing procedures and viewport procedures.

Implementations of DrawLine and Viewport

	GKS and PHIGS	Turbo Pascal Graphics 4.0 -5.5	Macintosh Graphics	Turtlegraphics

DrawLine (x1,y1,x2,y2)	set polyline, colour index, x and y
	n := 2;
	polyline(n,x,y);
		Line(x1,y1,x2,y2)
		or
		MoveTo(x1,y1);
		LineTo(x1,y1);
			MoveTo(x1,y1);
			LineTo(x2,y2);
				PENCOLOR(NONE);
				MOVETO(X1,Y1);
				PENCOLOR(COLOR);
				MOVETO(X2,Y2);

Viewport (XVMin,YVMin, XYMax,YVMax)	set_viewport (XVMin,YVMin, XYMax,YVMax)	SetViewPort(XVMin,YVMin, XYMax,YVMax))	Viewport := NewRgn; SetRect(ViewRect, XVMin,YVMin, XYMax,YVMax); RectRgn(Viewport,ViewRect); SetClip(Viewport);	VIEWPORT (XVMIN,XVMAX, YVMIN,YVMAX)

EXERCISES

3.3.1

Trace the Cohen-Sutherland algorithm for the example given in figure 3.3.9.

3.3.2

Implement DrawLine and Viewport on your system. Is there a simple way to implement FillPort on your system?

3.3.3

Write a procedure on your system to implement the Liang-Barsky algorithm.

3.3.4

Trace the Sproull-Sutherland algorithm on the example given in figure 3.3.9.

3.3.5

Write a procedure to implement the Sproull-Sutherland algorithm on your system. Check to see if the language you are using has shift commands that you may use instead of division.

3.3.6

Does your system allow you to turn clipping on and off? If so, how is it done? If not, is there a way to modify our procedure SetWindow so that clipping may be turned on and off?

3.3.7

a. Trace the Cohen-Sutherland clipping algorithm for each line and the window given below.
b. Trace the Liang-Barsky clipping algorithm for each line and the window given below (see figure 3.3.13).

3.3.8

Does your system do clipping on world or screen coordinates?

3.4 The Simple Graphics Package

In section 3.2 you created a new coordinate system that freed the user from the coordinate system of the screen. In order to use this system, you must create your own basic graphics procedures. Your objective will be to create procedures that facilitate the writing of graphics programs.

Most graphics systems have a procedure to turn on the graphics mode. The one you create here will be called **GraphOn.** A procedure **TextOn** for returning to the normal text mode is also needed.

Next you will need to have a procedure, **OpenWindow** (see figure 3.4.1), that initializes a window. OpenWindow will use the screen coordinates as default world coordinates, so the translation factors will be 0 and the scaling factors will be 1. Many graphics systems set the window defaults to range from 0 to 1. You will fix your initial current position at (0,0) and start with the pen color white and the fill color black.

Once the window has been opened, you will need procedures for moving from place to place, drawing lines, and drawing points. All these operations assume that both the cursor and a second end point are given in window coordinates that must be converted to screen coordinates. You will use the procedure **WorldToScreen** to convert from world to screen coordinates, and the procedure **DrawWorldLine** to do the actual work (see figure 3.4.2). Each procedure sets the cursor position to the final end point.

There are also two line-drawing procedures: **LineAbs(x,y,TheWindow)** and **LineRel(dx,dy,TheWindow)**. LineAbs draws a line from the cursor position to the point (x,y). LineRel draws a line from the cursor position to the point

FIGURE 3.4.1

The procedure OpenWindow initializes the data structure window.

```
procedure OpenWindow(var TheWindow : Window);
begin (* OpenWindow*)
   with TheWindow do
      begin
         (*initialize the cursor*)
         CurrentX := 0;
         CurrentY := 0;
         (*set the viewport and window constants to whole screen*)
         Viewport(0,0,XMax,YMax);
         ViewLeft := 0; ViewRight := XMax; ViewBottom := 0; ViewTop := YMax;
         WindowLeft := 0; WindowRight := XMax; WindowBottom := 0; WindowTop := YMax;
         (*set the conversion factors*)
         XConvertMult := 1; XConvertAdd := 0; YConvertMult := 1; YConvertAdd := 0;
         (*set the pen and fill colors *)
         PenColor := white; FillColor := black;
      end
end; (* OpenWindow*)
```

FIGURE 3.4.2

The procedure WorldToScreen converts world coordinates to screen coordinates. This procedure is used by DrawWorldLine to draw a line when the end points of the line are given in world coordinates.

```
(*This procedure converts the world coordinates of a point into screen coordinates which are returned    *)

procedure WorldToScreen(WorldX, WorldY : real;
                        var ScreenX, ScreenY : integer;
                        var TheWindow : Window);
begin
   with TheWindow do
      begin
         ScreenX := round(XConvertMult * WorldX + XConvertAdd);
         ScreenY := round(YConvertMult * WorldY + YConvertAdd)
      end
end; (* WorldToScreen *)

(*This procedure draws the line from the cursor point to the specified point given in world coordinates.    *)

procedure DrawWorldLine(WorldX,WorldY : real; var TheWindow : Window);
var
   StartX,StartY,EndX,EndY: integer; (* screen coordinates of end points of line *)
begin (* DrawWorldLine*)
   with TheWindow do
      WorldToScreen(CurrentX,CurrentY,StartX,StartY,TheWindow)
   WorldToScreen(WorldX,WorldY,EndX,EndY,TheWindow);
   DrawLine(StartX,StartY,EndX,EndY);
   with TheWindow do
      begin
         CurrentX := WorldX;
         CurrentY := WorldY
      end
end; (*DrawWorldLine*)
```

FIGURE 3.4.3

The procedures LineAbs and MoveRel are representative of the types of procedures in your simple graphics package.

```
(* This procedure draws a line from the current cursor position to the position on the screen     *)
(* which has world coordinates (WorldX, WorldY) in the window TheWindow.                            *)

procedure LineAbs (WorldX, WorldY : real; var TheWindow : Window);
begin
   DrawWorldLine(WorldX,WorldY,TheWindow)
end;  (* LineAbs*)

(* This procedure moves the cursor position from the current position to the position where       *)
(* the world x and y coordinates are incremented by WorldX and WorldY respectively.                *)

procedure MoveRel (dWorldX, dWorldY : real; var TheWindow : Window);
begin
   with TheWindow do
      begin
         CurrentX := CurrentX + dWorldX;
         CurrentY := CurrentY + dWorldY
      end
end;  (*MoveRel*)
```

computed by adding dx to the cursor's x-coordinate and dy to the cursor's y-coordinate. Both basic line-drawing procedures call on DrawWorldLine with TheWindow.PenColor. The procedure LineAbs is given in figure 3.4.3.

The procedures **PointAbs(x,y,TheWindow)** and **PointRel(dx,dy,TheWindow)** are used to put a point at world coordinates (x,y) and at the cursor point plus the distances dx and dy. The procedure PointAbs(x,y,TheWindow) displays a point at the screen location corresponding to the point with world coordinates (x,y). PointRel(dx,dy,TheWindow) displays the point whose world coordinates are computed by adding dx to the cursor's x-coordinate and dy to the cursor's y-coordinate. The cursor is adjusted to be at the point plotted. This may be accomplished by using WorldToScreen and applying SetPixel if it is available on the system. An alternative is first to set the cursor to the point where the point is to be plotted and then to call on DrawWorldLine at the same point.

While the line-drawing procedures are a natural extension of the work done in earlier sections of this chapter, the move procedures **MoveAbs(x,y,TheWindow)** and **MoveRel(dx,dy,TheWindow)** are needed to establish the position of the cursor without drawing a line to that position. These procedures alter the value of TheWindow.CurrentX and TheWindow.CurrentY. As in the line procedures, MoveAbs sets the current position to x and y while MoveRel (figure 3.4.3) computes the current positions by adding dx and dy to the appropriate coordinates.

In addition to the drawing procedures, you need a procedure **SetPenColor** to set the pen color in a given window and a procedure **SetFillColor** to set the fill

FIGURE 3.4.4

The procedures and functions of the simple graphics package

Simple graphics package

GraphOn
TextOn
OpenWindow
SetViewPort
SetWindow
ActivateWindow
LineAbs
LineRel
MoveAbs
MoveRel
PointAbs
PointRel
SetPenColor
SetFillColor
FillPort

color in a given window. As it will be possible to have more than one viewport active on the screen at the same time, you will also need a procedure **FillWindow,** which fills the current window with FillColor.

For more than one window to be on the screen at a given time, you will also need a procedure **ActivateWindow** to activate a given window. This procedure ensures that the system viewport is set to the given window's viewport. If ActivateWindow is not used when you are changing windows, any drawing done is converted to screen coordinates either outside the current viewport or in the wrong viewport.

Functions available in the simple graphics packages are given in figure 3.4.5.

EXERCISES

3.4.1.

Implement the simple graphics package on your system.

3.4.2.

Test your package by creating the drawing in figure 3.4.5. Set your window coordinates slightly larger or your boundary rectangle may not be completely drawn because of round-off error.

FIGURE 3.4.5

Drawing for problem 3.4.2

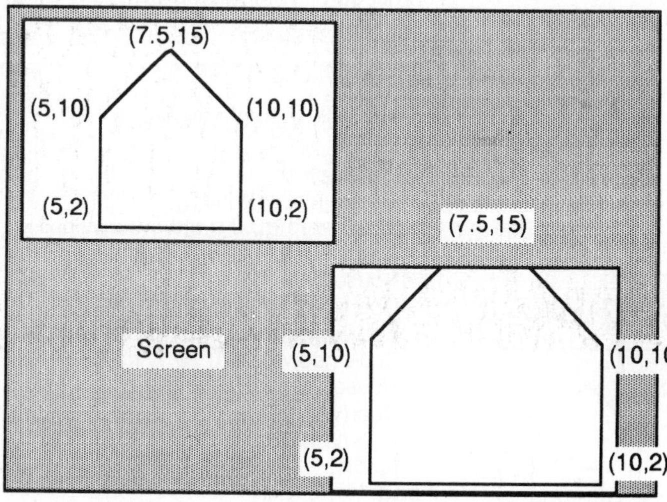

3.4.3.

Draw the picture in figure 3.4.5 by using the LineRel and MoveRel procedures rather than LineAbs and MoveAbs.

3.4.4

Suppose the procedure ''house'' draws the polygon with vertices at the points (3,3), (3,7), (5,9), (7,7), and (7,3). What window corner settings would you use to ensure that the whole house would be drawn as large as possible? With your window settings, are the walls of the house the same length as the base of the house?

3.4.5

How would you create the drawing with the procedure House which draws only the polygon given above (see figure 3.4.6)?

FIGURE 3.4.6

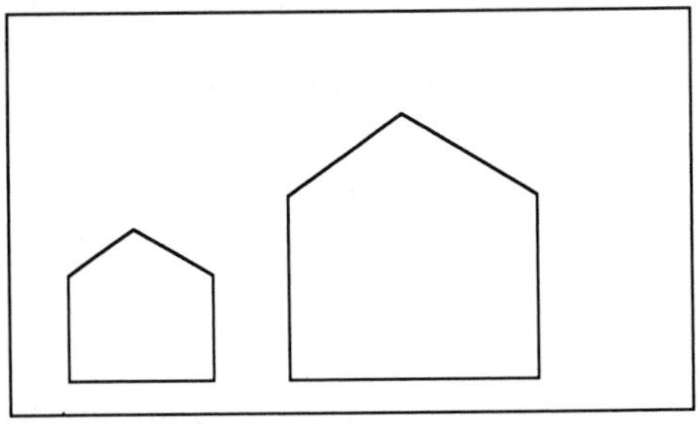

3.4.6

Suppose you write the following program, in which the procedure House draws a house in the designated window, and Door draws a door on the house in the designated window (see figure 3.4.7). If you decide to put a door on each of the houses in the diagram after drawing the house in Wind2 and inserting the procedure Door in the program as shown, what will happen? Why does this happen?

```
program DrawHouse;
  var
    Wind1, Wind2 : Window;
begin
  InitGraphics;
  OpenWindow(Wind1);
  SetViewport(0.0,0.0,0.5,0.5,Wind1);
  SetWindow(0,0,20,20,Wind1);
  House(Wind1);
  OpenWindow(Wind2);
  SetViewport(0.5,0.5,1.0,1.0,Wind2);
  SetWindow(0,0,20,20,Wind2);
  House(Wind2);
  Door(Wind2);
  Door(Wind1);
  readln
end.
```

FIGURE 3.4.7

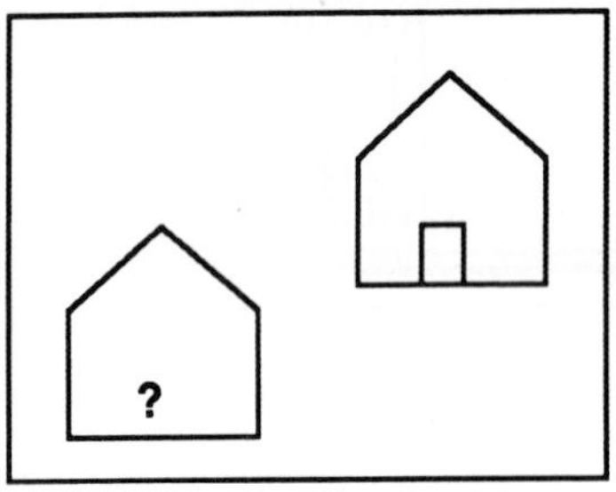

3.4.7

Why is it important to open a window before you use it even if you have used InitGraphics?

FIGURE 3.5.1

Example of a picture created with the simple graphics package

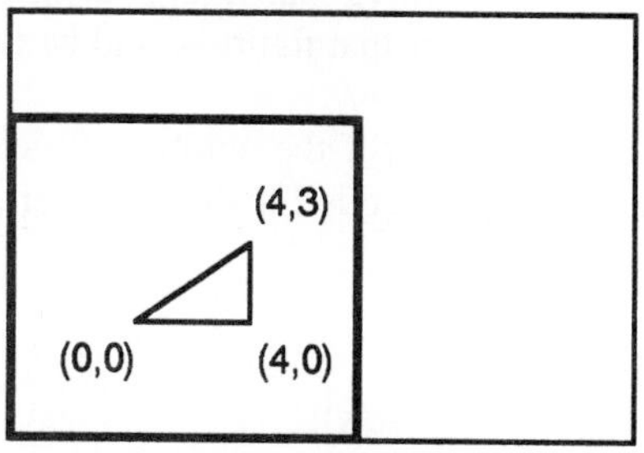

FIGURE 3.5.2

Figure 3.5.1 with the window corners specified

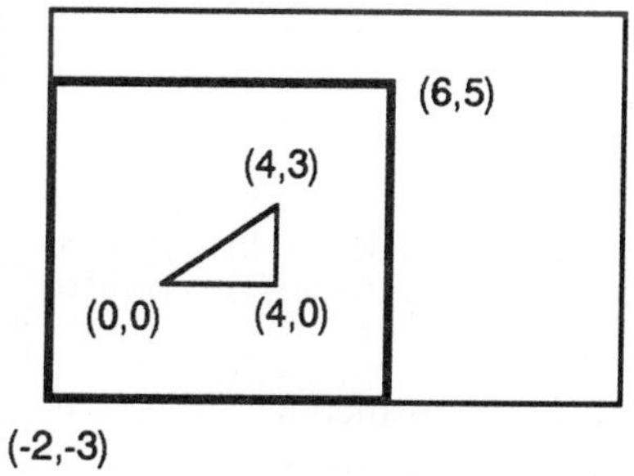

3.5 Representation of Graphic Objects and Their Rotations

Now that you have a simple graphics package, you can put it into use to see how the various parts work together. Remember, your goal was to create a set of procedures that would make your programs independent of the particular hardware system in use. In this section you will decompose your images into meaningful components. These components will be created both as procedures and as data structures. This not only makes altering a picture easier, it also helps document the program. Reading this type of program, even without reading the documentation, should be easier.

The first picture (figure 3.5.1) that you will create with your package is not very complicated.

Note that if this picture were drawn in terms of the screen's coordinate system, the triangle would be a spot in the corner of the screen. It is up to the programmer to pick both the viewport and the world coordinates for that viewport. To pick the viewport, simply assume that the drawing will be in the lower-left corner of the screen. Also assume that the drawing will extend a little more than half the distance to the top of the screen and half the distance to the right side of the screen. A suitable choice of viewport would be obtained by SetViewPort(0,0,0.75,0.75,TheWindow) if TheWindow is the window of the drawing (figure 3.5.2).

Next, an appropriate set of world coordinates must be selected for this viewport. A square with the lower-left corner at $(-2,-3)$ and upper-right corner at (6,5) might seem reasonable. It would be, but with the small number of integer values available and the tendency of the programmer to draw all objects with integer coordinates, an attempt to draw the rectangle around the picture might result in one or more of the lines not being drawn because of round-off error. In this case, it probably would be better to choose the corners of the window at $(-2.2,-3.2)$ and $(6.2,5.2)$. With these choices the picture can be drawn by the sequence of steps listed in figure 3.5.3.

FIGURE 3.5.3

The Pascal code used to create the drawing in figure 3.5.2

```
GraphOn;
OpenWindow(TheWindow);
SetViewport(0,0,0.75,0.75,TheWindow);
SetWindow(-2.2,-3.2,6.2,5.2,TheWindow);
(* draw a rectangle around the picture *)
MoveAbs(-2,-3,TheWindow);
LineAbs(6,-3,TheWindow);
LineAbs(6,5,TheWindow);
LineAbs(-2,5,TheWindow);
LineAbs(-2,-3,TheWindow);
(* draw the triangle *)
MoveAbs(0,0,TheWindow);
LineAbs(4,0,TheWindow);
LineAbs(4,3,TheWindow);
LineAbs(0,0,TheWindow);
```

This fragment of code illustrates two of the problems encountered in using this package without any additional procedures. First, it is clear that the code for both the triangle and the rectangle is just a call to MoveAbs followed by a sequence of calls to LineAbs. If you consider any polygonal figure (a figure composed of a sequence of line segments), the code for that figure would be the same except for the number of calls to LineAbs.

The regularity of the code for polygons suggests that if the number of sides and the vertices of the polygon were known, then the code for that polygon P might be

```
with P do
  begin
    MoveAbs(Vertex[1].x, Vertex[1].y, TheWindow);
    for i := NumberOfSides downto 1 do
      LineAbs(Vertex[i].x, Vertex[i].y, TheWindow);
  end;
```

where the loop is reversed to allow for a simple return to the first vertex. The storage types suggested by this example are

```
point = record
  x : real; (* x-coordinate of a point *)
  y : real (* y-coordinate of a point *)
end;

polygon = record
  NumberOfSides : integer; (* number of side of the polygon *)
  Vertex : array[1..maxside] of point (* coordinates of vertices *)
end;
```

There is a flaw in this technique for polygon construction. In most cases when you draw polygons, you want a polygon of a specified size in a given place—for example, a rectangle with length 5 and width 3 that has its upper-right corner at the point (10,15). If you were to use the polygon code and require another rectangle of the same size, this time with an upper-right corner at (30,10), you would need two separate data structures. Quite often the same figure is repeated many times at different places in one diagram. If, for example, a landscape architect uses a 1-foot square to represent a planter, there might be 20 such planters in a given plan. With the technique you are using to draw polygons, you would have to store 20 squares. All the squares would be the same, but they would be located at different spots.

To rectify this problem, replace the LineAbs in your code with LineRel. In the drawing algorithm with LineAbs, each point was plotted to ensure correct placement of the polygon. When you replace these absolute coordinates with relative coordinates, it is important that you properly locate the initial position in order to place the figure correctly. The initial position on such a polygon is called the **hotspot.** Once a hotspot is established, drawings are based on this position. The code for drawing one of these polygons is

```
with P do
  begin
    MoveAbs(Vertex[1].x, Vertex[1].y, TheWindow); (* move
    to the hotspot*)
    for i : NumberOfSides downto 1 do
      LineRel(Vertex[i].x, Vertex[i].y, TheWindow); (* draw the sides *)
  end;
```

There is still one problem with this drawing that has not yet been addressed: What if the polygon is rotated so that the sides are not parallel to those stored for the polygon? The simplest solution is to have one representation of the polygon for each of the different rotations. For most applications this the most efficient solution because only a few rotations are usually needed. If, however, the number and angles of rotation are not known beforehand, or if there are many different angles of rotation, one may use trigonometry to solve the problem. *Because all distances now used are moves relative to the hotspot, all rotations are around the hotspot*. The hotspot is the origin for these coordinates, so these rotations can be pictured as rotations about the origin (figure 3.5.4). The original x-coordinate, X, can be represented as $X = r\cos\theta$ and the y-coordinate as $Y = r\sin\theta$. If the coordinates of the rotated point are (X',Y'), each coordinate can be computed as $X' = r\cos(\theta + \Phi)$ and $Y' = r\sin(\theta + \Phi)$. A simple application of the formulas for sin and cos of the sum of two angles gives the following equations for the coordinates (X',Y') of a point (X,Y) after it is rotated through an angle Φ:

$$X' = X\cos\phi - Y\sin\phi$$

and

$$Y' = X\sin\phi + Y\cos\phi$$

FIGURE 3.5.4

The points (x,y) and (x′,y′) can be represented in terms of r and the angles θ and (θ + ϕ).

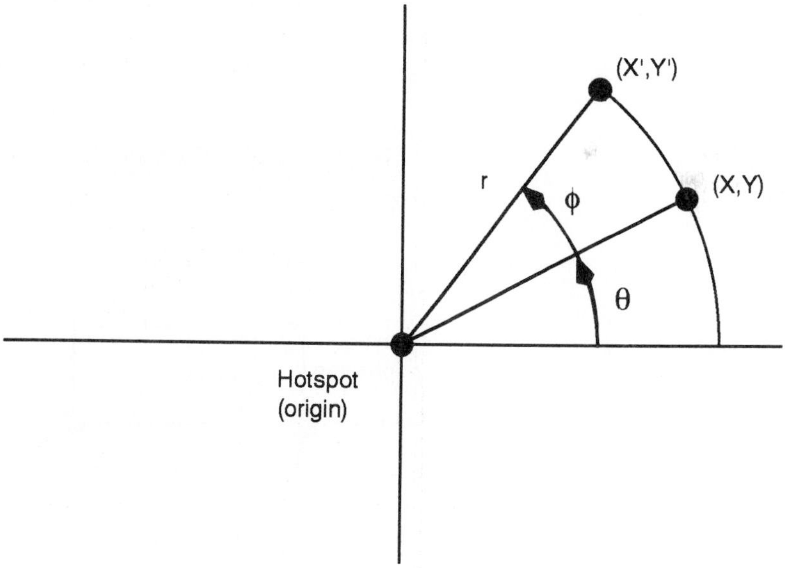

Notice how the location of the hotspot affects the final position of the figure. If the hotspot is at the center (as in figure 3.5.5.a), then the position of the center stays fixed. If, however, the position of the hotspot is at a corner, that corner stays in the same spot and the entire rectangle is moved (see figure 3.5.5b).

In the case of the general rotation, the fact that the hotspot need not be one of the actual vertices of the polygon requires that you add vertex index 0 to represent the distance from the hotspot to the first actual vertex. You also add a MoveRel from the hotspot to the first vertex. The complete procedure to draw a polygon in any alignment is given in figure 3.5.6.

FIGURE 3.5.5.a

Rotation of a rectangle through 90° when the hotspot is at the center of the rectangle

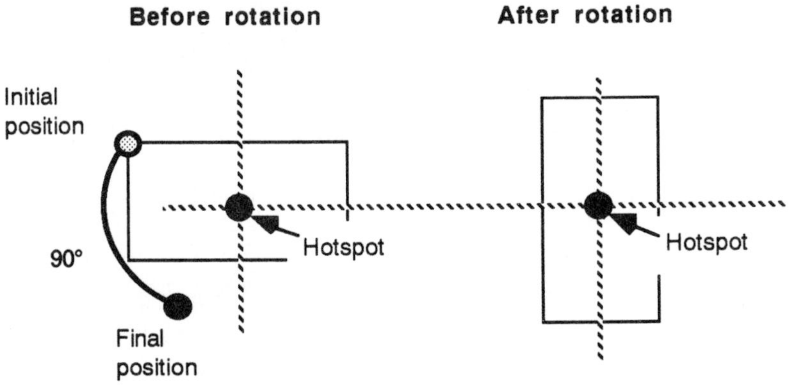

FIGURE 3.5.5.b

Rotation of 90° when the hotspot is at a corner

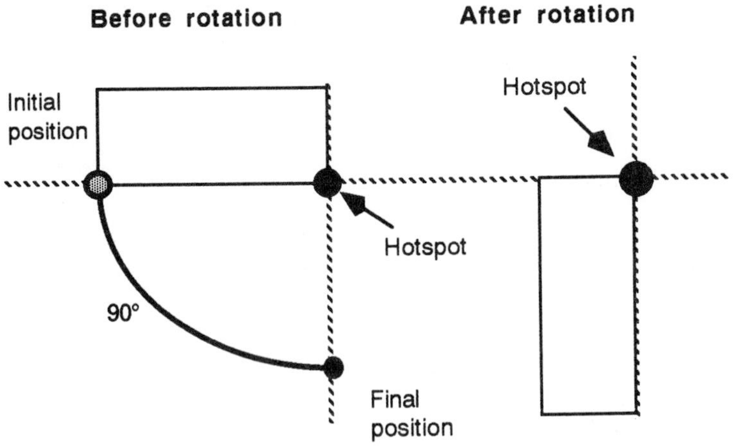

FIGURE 3.5.6

Procedure used to draw a polynomial that may be rotated through an angle

```
type
   point = record
      x : real; (* x coordinate of a point *)
      y : real  (* y coordinate of a point *)
   end;

   polygon = record
      NumberOfSides : integer;                  (* number of side of the polygon      *)
      Vertex : array[0..maxside] of point       (* coordinates of vertices            *)
   end;

procedure DrawPoly( LocX, LocY : real;          (* location of the hotspot            *)
                    Poly : Polygon:             (* the polygon                        *)
                    Theta : real;               (* angle of rotation                  *)
                    TheWindow : window;         (* window of the polygon              *)
var
   I : integer;       (* counter for drawing                                          *)
   P : Polygon;       (* local polygon used to hold rotation of Poly                  *)

procedure Rotate(P1 : Polygon;                  (* polygon that will be rotated       *)
                 var P2 : Polygon;              (* rotated polygon                    *)
                 Theta : real ;                 (* angle of rotation                  *)
const
   RadiansPerDegree = 0.017453;                 (* number of radians per degree       *)
var
   I : integer;              (* counter for number of sides                           *)
   SinTheta : real;          (* holds value of the sin of Theta                       *)
   CosTheta : real;          (* holds value of the cos of Theta                       *)
   RadianTheta : real;       (* angle Theta given in radians for the Trig functions   *)
begin (* rotate *)
   RadianTheta := RadiansPerDegree * Theta; (* convert the degree measure of Theta to radians       *)
   SinTheta := sin(RadianTheta);            (* because Trig functions work only on radian measure angles *)
   CosTheta := cos(RadianTheta);            (* store these values to speed up rotation              *)
   P2.NumberOfSides := P1.NumberOfSides;
   for I := 0 to  P2.NumberOfSides do
      begin
         P2.Vertex[I].X := P1.Vertex[I].X * CosTheta - P1.Vertex[I].Y * SinTheta;
         P2.Vertex[I].Y := P1.Vertex[I].X * SinTheta + P1.Vertex[I].Y * CosTheta
      end
end; (* rotate *)

begin (* DrawPoly *)
   if Theta <> 0 then                       (* if there is a non-zero angle of rotation, rotate   *)
      Rotate(Poly,P,Theta)
   else
      P := Poly;
   MoveAbs(LocX,LocY,TheWindow);            (* move to the hotspot                                *)
   with P do
      begin
         (* move from hotspot to first vertex  *)
         MoveRel(Vertex[0].X,Vertex[0].Y,TheWindow);
         (* draw the sides of the polygon      *)
         for I := NumberOfSides downto 1 do
            LineRel(Vertex[I].X,Vertex[I].Y,TheWindow)
      end
end; (*DrawPoly *)
```

FIGURE 3.5.7.a

Rotations of a planter by multiples of 90°

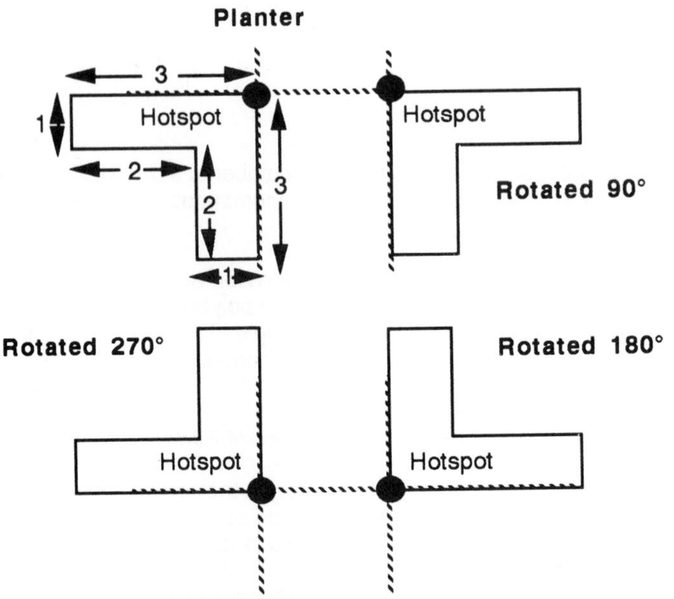

If it were possible to rotate the planter only in multiples of 90° (figure 3.5.7a,b), then you could have used the version of DrawPoly without the call to procedure Rotate. In this case the polygon does not have vertex 0, and each of the positions must be specifically stored (figure 3.5.7.c).

In the actual garden (figure 3.5.7.d), you would use the general form of DrawPoly with the Rotate procedure included. To get the given diagram, you would simply call on DrawPoly(Planter, 1.25,6.25,270,TheWindow).

FIGURE 3.5.7.b

The planter defined in relative coordinates

```
with Planter do
  begin
    SetVertex(Vertex[0],  0,  0 );
    SetVertex(Vertex[1], -3,  0 );
    SetVertex(Vertex[2],  0, -1 );
    SetVertex(Vertex[3],  2,  0 );
    SetVertex(Vertex[4],  0, -2 );
    SetVertex(Vertex[5],  1,  0 );
    SetVertex(Vertex[6],  0,  3 )
  end;
```

FIGURE 3.5.7.c

The relative coordinates of the corners of the planter's four rotations

```
with Planter_0 do
   begin
      SetVertex ( Vertex[1], -3,  0 );
      SetVertex ( Vertex[2],  0, -1 );
      SetVertex ( Vertex[3],  2,  0 );
      SetVertex ( Vertex[4],  0, -2 );
      SetVertex ( Vertex[5],  1,  0 );
      SetVertex ( Vertex[6],  0,  3 )
   end;

with Planter_90 do
   begin
      SetVertex ( Vertex[1],  3,  0 );
      SetVertex ( Vertex[2],  0, -1 );
      SetVertex ( Vertex[3], -2,  0 );
      SetVertex ( Vertex[4],  0, -2 );
      SetVertex ( Vertex[5], -1,  0 );
      SetVertex ( Vertex[6],  0,  3 )
   end;

with Planter_180 do
   begin
      SetVertex ( Vertex[1],  0,  3 );
      SetVertex ( Vertex[2],  1,  0 );
      SetVertex ( Vertex[3],  0, -2 );
      SetVertex ( Vertex[4],  2,  0 );
      SetVertex ( Vertex[5],  0, -1 );
      SetVertex ( Vertex[6], -3,  0 )
   end;

with Planter_270 do
   begin
      SetVertex ( Vertex[1],  0,  3 );
      SetVertex ( Vertex[2], -1,  0 );
      SetVertex ( Vertex[3],  0, -2 );
      SetVertex ( Vertex[4], -2,  0 );
      SetVertex ( Vertex[5],  0, -1 );
      SetVertex ( Vertex[6],  3,  0 )
   end;
```

FIGURE 3.5.7.d

The hotspot is located at a position on an object that allows for the object's easy placement.

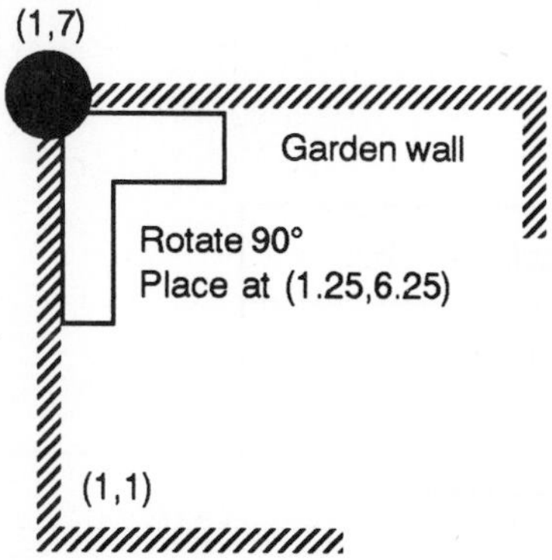

FIGURE 3.5.8

The procedure SetVertex simplifies the assignment of values to polygon vertices.

```
(* this procedure is used to set the values of a polygon vertex *)

procedure SetVertex(var P : point; XValue, YValue : real);

begin (* SetVertex *)
  with P do
    begin
      x := XValue;
      y := YValue
    end
end; (* SetVertex *)
```

The procedure SetVertex sets the values for a given vertex (figure 3.5.8).

Polygon-drawing procedures are available in many graphics packages. Figure 3.5.9 gives a sample of these functions.

Polygons drawn using your graphics package primitive LineAbs will automatically be clipped to fit into the current window. The resulting polygon may not be a closed polygon (figure 3.5.10) because some of its vertices may be outside the current window. If the polygon must be maintained as a closed polygon, you must employ an alternative method of clipping.

The **Sutherland-Hodgman** polygon-clipping algorithm seeks to clip a polygon against a convex polygon by connecting the intersections of polygon sides with clipping-region edges (figure 3.5.11). Your rectangular windows are convex polygons, so the clipping algorithm given here is a special case of the Sutherland-Hodgman algorithm.

This algorithm clips each side of the polygon against each of the four window boundaries. The sequence in which the clipping is performed is called the **clipping pipe.** You first clip against the left side, then the right side, followed by the bottom and finally the top (figure 3.5.12). Figure 3.5.13 shows the succession of clips. At each stage the clipped polygon is passed to the next stage of clipping.

FIGURE 3.5.9

A sample of the polygon drawing procedures available in some standard graphics packages.

Polygon Drawing Procedures

	GKS and PHIGS	Turbo Pascal Graphics 4.0–5.5	Macintosh Toolbox
DrawPoly(P);	polyline(n,x,y);	DrawPoly(n,p);	FramePoly(p);

FIGURE 3.5.10

If a polygon is clipped by simply applying the line-clipping algorithms to each edge of the polygon, the resulting figure will not be closed. Most filling algorithms only work on closed polygons, so if the polygon is to be filled, you must close a clipped polygon.

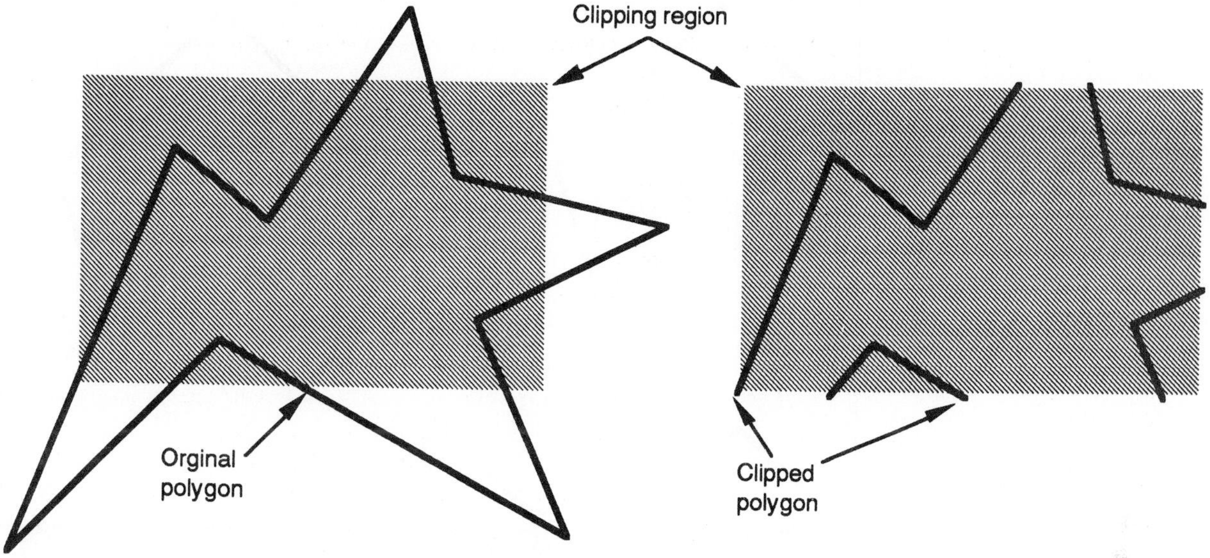

FIGURE 3.5.11

To close the clipped polygon created in figure 3.5.10, you must add the bold line segments when clipping.

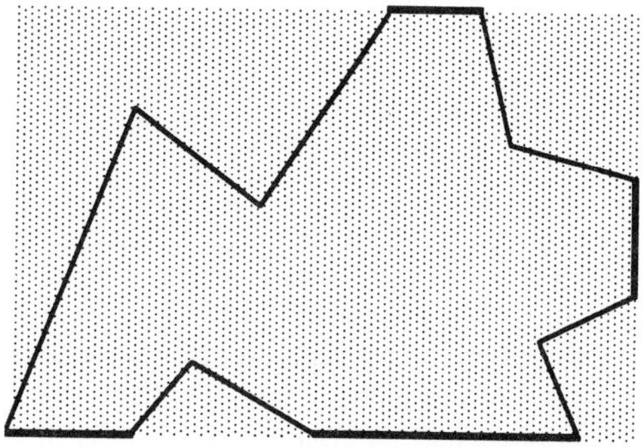

FIGURE 3.5.12

The clipping pipe for the Sutherland-Hodgman polygon-clipping algorithm

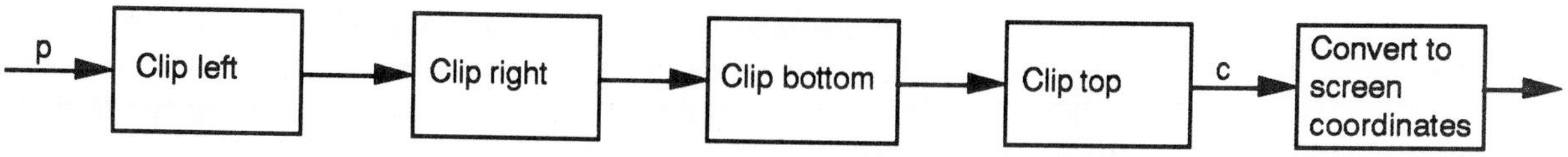

FIGURE 3.5.13

Each segment of the Sutherland-Hodgman clipping pipe applied to a polygon

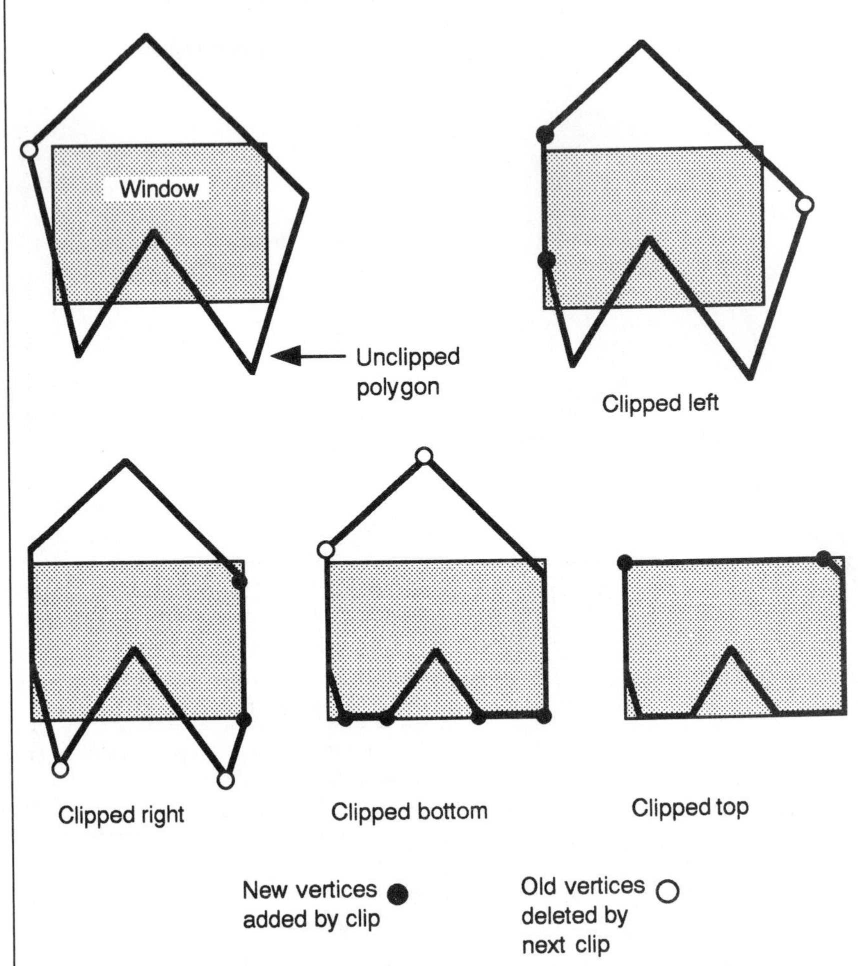

Actual clipping of a polygon side is a fairly simple task. Each pair of vertices is considered in turn. One vertex is designated as last while the other is designated as first. If the last vertex and the first vertex are both inside the boundary, last is put into the clipped polygon. If the vertex last is inside the boundary but the vertex first is not, the intersection of the polygon side and the window boundary is inserted into the clipped polygon and then the vertex last is inserted. If the vertex last is outside the current window edge and the vertex first is inside, then the intersection of the polygon side and the window edge is added to the clipped polygon. If both vertices are outside the region, then nothing is added to the clipped polygon. This process is summarized in figure 3.5.14. Before the next side is clipped, vertex last is renamed as first and the next vertex in the original polygon is designated as first.

FIGURE 3.5.14

The location of the end points of an edge determines what will be added to the clipped polygon at a given time.

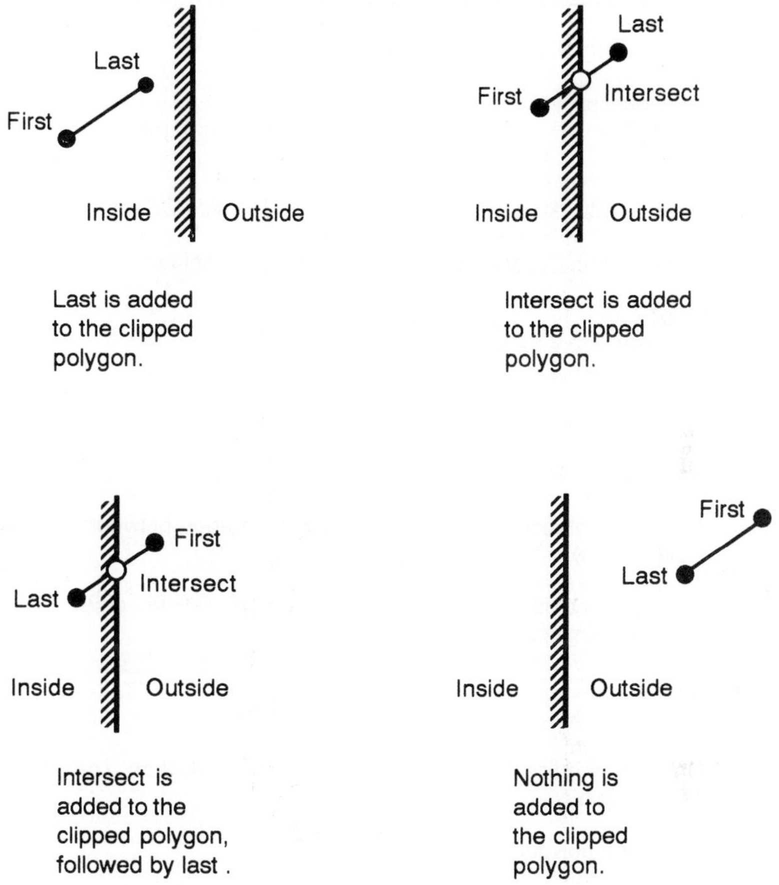

FIGURE 3.5.15

When the side of a polygon crosses the current clipping boundary, vertices of the polygon outside of that boundary are dropped from the clipped polygon. The next entry in the clipped polygon is the next intersection of a polygon side with the clipping boundary.

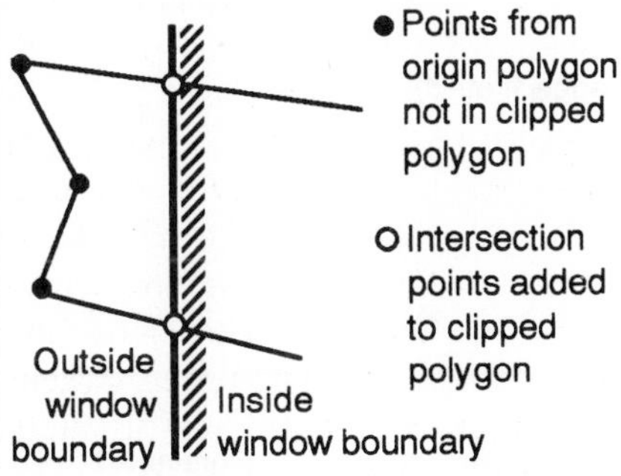

If a polygon crosses a clipping boundary, the clipped polygon coincides with this boundary between the point where the polygon crosses the boundary and the next point where it crosses the boundary (figure 3.5.15). After the polygon is clipped at a given step in the pipe, this clipped polygon is passed to the next step in the pipe for clipping. Thus, if the segments added to the clipped polygon cross other window boundaries, they will be clipped to conform to these boundaries (shown in figure 3.5.13). The Pascal implementation of the Sutherland-Hodgman algorithm is given in figure 3.5.16.

FIGURE 3.5.16

The Sutherland-Hodgman polygon-clipping algorithm

```
type
   Sides = (left,right,bottom,top);
   Extent : array[Sides] of integer;

(* The procedure AddVertex adds the point p as a vertex of polygon c.                    *)

procedure AddVertex(p:point; var c : Polygon);
begin
   c.numvert := c.numvert+1;
   c.verts[c.numvert] := p;
end;

(* The function Inside returns true if the point p is inside the side CSide of the Clipper.  *)

function Inside(p : point; Clipper : extent; CSide : sides) : boolean;
begin
   case CSide of
     top     : Inside := p.y >= Clipper[top];
     bottom  : Inside := p.y <= Clipper[bottom];
     left    : Inside := p.x >= Clipper[left];
     right   : Inside := p.x <= Clipper[right]
   end
end;

(* The procedure FindIntersect finds the intersection of the edge between first and        *)
(* last with the given edge of the clipping rectangle.                                     *)

procedure FindIntersect(first, last : point; Clipper : Extent; CSide : sides;
                        var Intersect : point);
begin
{ left to reader}
end;

(* The procedure ClipOne clips the polygon p in the direction of CSide. The result is      *)
(* returned in the polygon c.                                                              *)

procedure ClipOne(p:polygon; var c : polygon;
                  Clipper:Extent;  CSide:Sides);
var
   first,last       : point;         (* the first and last vertices of a given side   *)
   intersect        : point;         (* point of intersection with window edge         *)
   VertexNumber     : integer;       (* counter used to proceed through vertices      *)
begin
   c.numvert := 0;
   first := p.verts[p.numvert];      (* prime the pump by doing the last edge first   *)
   for VertexNumber := 1 to p.numvert do
     begin
       last := p.verts[VertexNumber];
       if Inside(last,Clipper,CSide) then
         begin
           if Inside(first,Clipper,CSide) then  (* both points in the clipping region *)
             AddVertex(last,c)
           else
```

(continued)

FIGURE 3.5.16 continued

```
            begin                           (* first outside, last inside region            *)
              FindIntersect(last,first,Clipper,CSide,Intersect);
              AddVertex(Intersect,c);
              AddVertex(last,c)
            end
        end
      else
        if Inside(first,Clipper,CSide) then    (* first inside, last outside region            *)
          begin
            FindIntersect(first,last,Clipper,CSide,Intersect);
            AddVertex(Intersect,c)
          end;
      first := last
    end
  end;

procedure ClipPoly (p:polygon; var c : polygon;
                    Clipper:extent);
var
  CSide : Sides;
begin
  for CSide := left to top do
    begin
      ClipOne(p,c,Clipper,CSide);
      p:= c                                 (* clip the clipped version of the polygon      *)
    end;
end;
```

EXERCISES

3.5.1

Create more polygonal objects that represent garden objects, such as planters, benches, and gazebos. Using the Rotate form of DrawPoly, write a program that will display these objects in a garden setting.

3.5.2

Repeat exercise 3.5.1. with different hotspots for your objects.

3.5.3

Create the rotations of the objects needed in exercise 3.5.1 as prestored polygons and using the form of DrawPoly without the Rotate procedure, repeat exercise 3.5.1.

3.5.4

Using the prestored rotations of your polygons as in exercise 3.5.3, repeat exercise 3.5.2.

3.5.5

Repeat exercises 3.5.1–3.5.4, this time creating office furniture and drawing an office floor plan.

3.5.6

Write a procedure that computes the values of the sine function at a selected number of points between $x = 0$ and $x = \pi$ and that stores these values in a polygon. Use DrawPoly to display the graph of the sine function.

FIGURE 3.5.17

Trace the polygonal clipping algorithm for this polygon.

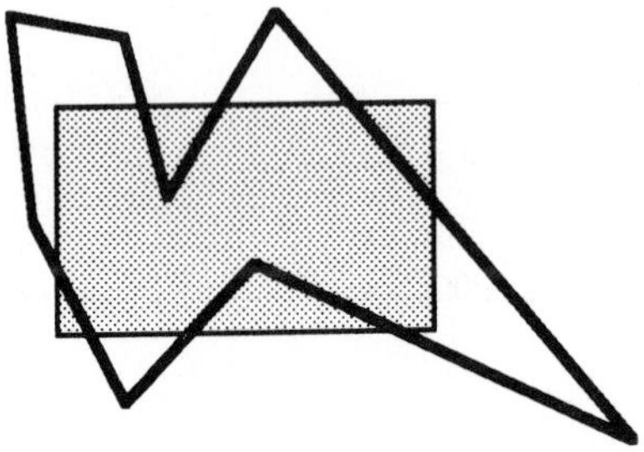

3.5.7

Trace the Sutherland-Hodgman algorithm for the polygon and window shown in figure 3.5.17.

3.5.8

Implement the Sutherland-Hodgman algorithm.

3.5.9

Give the relative coordinates of the vertices of the rectangle (30,30), (30,36), (40,36), and (40,30) if the vertex (30,30) is used as the hotspot.

3.5.10

Use rotation techniques covered in this section to compute the following rotations of the rectangle in exercise 1 about the given hot spot:

a. Rotate it 90° about (33,36)
b. Rotate it −90° about (33,36)
c. Rotate it 180° about (35,33)

Sketch your results to see if you have used the formula correctly.

3.5.11

Write the code necessary to store the rectangle in problem 1 with hot spot (35,33) in each of the relative coordinate polygon formats given in the chapter.

3.5.12

Does your graphics library have a predefined polygon procedure? If so in what format are polygons stored for this procedure? Does this procedure use world coordinates or some other type of coordinates? If the polygon procedure uses a coordinate system other than world coordinates, write a procedure to draw a polygon in world coordinates which calls on the library's polygon procedure.

3.6 Matrix Algebra and Its Application in Two-Dimensional Transformations

The transformations of two-dimensional objects were introduced in section 3.5. When an object is described in terms of coordinates relative to a hotspot, rotations about that hotspot are actually rotations about the origin. It is more difficult to compute the coordinates of a point rotated about an arbitrary point. This section explains how complex transformations can be decomposed into a product of matrices, each representing a simpler transformation. While matrices provide a way to investigate transformations, programs written to describe these transformations usually condense the results in code similar to that given in the last section. You will briefly review matrix multiplication before applying it.

The **size of a matrix** with m rows and n columns is given as m × n. The matrix A, given by

$$A = \begin{bmatrix} 1 & 2 & 3 \\ 4 & 5 & 6 \end{bmatrix}$$

has 2 rows and 3 columns and is therefore a 2 × 3 matrix, while the matrix B, given by

$$B = \begin{bmatrix} 1 & 2 \\ 3 & 4 \\ 5 & 6 \end{bmatrix}$$

is a 3 × 2 matrix. *A point with coordinates (x,y) may be represented as the 1 × 2 matrix [xy].* Two matrices are equal if and only if they are the same size and all the corresponding entries are equal.

The matrix C, given by

$$C = \begin{bmatrix} 1 & 4 \\ 2 & 5 \\ 3 & 6 \end{bmatrix}$$

is obtained from the matrix A described above by converting the ith row of A into the ith column of C. The matrix C is called the **transpose** of A, written A^t.

The product XY of two matrices X and Y can only be computed if the number of columns of the first matrix, X, is the same as the number of rows of the second matrix, Y. The resulting matrix XY has the same number of rows as X and the same number of columns as Y. The product of the two matrices given above, AB, is a 2 × 2 matrix, while the product BA of the same matrices is a 3 × 3 matrix. Clearly AB ≠ BA in this case. Even if the product XY of two matrices is defined, the product YX need not be defined because the number of columns of the first matrix must equal the number of rows of the second matrix.

To calculate the entry in the ith row and j^{th} column of the product matrix, multiply corresponding entries in the ith row of the first matrix and the jth column of the second matrix and add the products. The product AB of matrices $A = [a_{ij}]$ and $B = [b_{ij}]$ can be described formally as $AB = [c_{ij}]$ where

$$c_{ij} = \sum_{k=1}^{n} (a_{i,k}\, b_{kj})$$

FIGURE 3.6.1

Computing the entry in the first row, second column of the product of two matrices

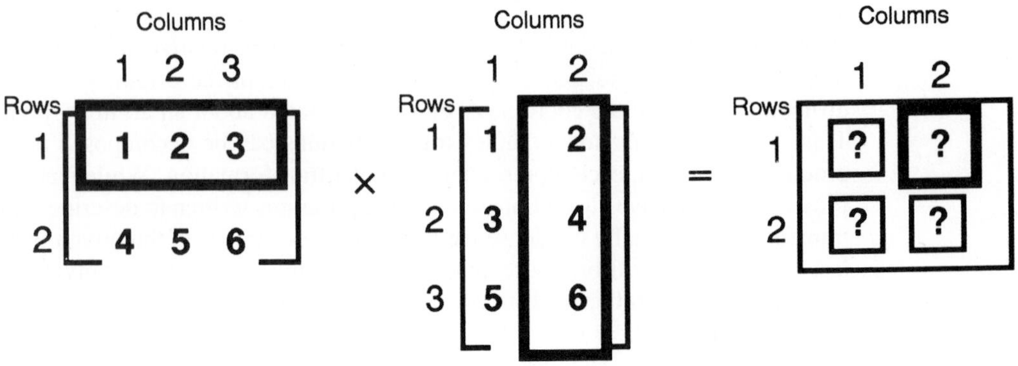

The entry in the first row and second column of the product, AB, given in figure 3.6.1, is

$$(1 \times 2) + (2 \times 4) + (3 \times 6) = 2 + 8 + 18 = 28$$

The entry in the second row and second column of the product BA is computed by multiplying corresponding members of the highlighted row from B and the highlighted column from A (figure 3.6.2). The value of the entry is

$$(3 \times 2) + (4 \times 5) = 26$$

One of the simplest applications of matrix multiplication is **scaling** a graphic object. Figure 3.6.3 shows a rectangle with one of its corners at the origin. Each corner has its coordinates changed to $x' = x\ S_x$ and $y' = y\ S_y$, where S_x and S_y are the scaling factors. This set of equations can be given as the single matrix equation

FIGURE 3.6.2

Compute the entry in the second row, second column of a matrix.

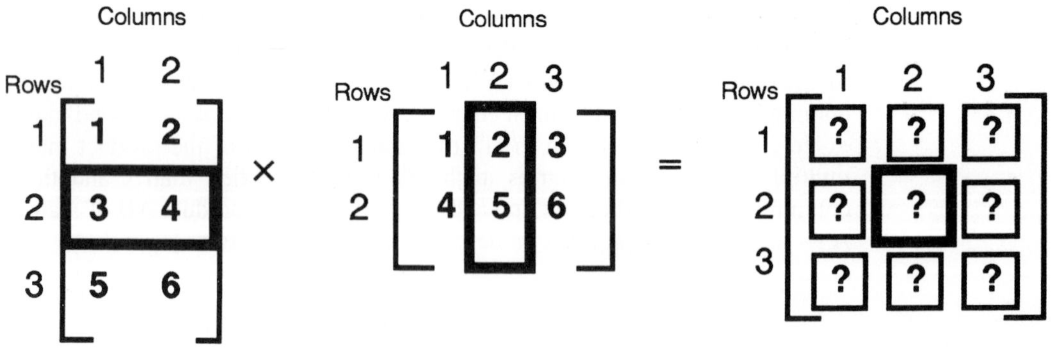

FIGURE 3.6.3

Scaling a rectangle with one corner at the origin

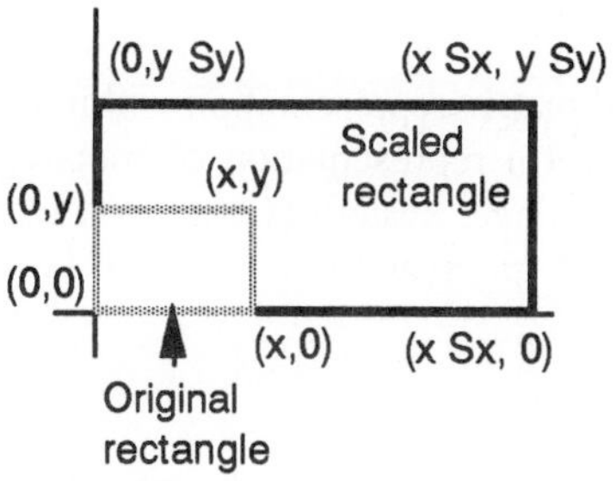

$$[x'y'] = [xy] \begin{bmatrix} S_x & 0 \\ 0 & S_y \end{bmatrix}$$

Similar matrix equations can be used to represent **reflections;** for example, the reflection through the origin, $x' = -x$ and $y' = -y$ (figure 3.6.4), and the reflection through the line $y = x$, $x' = y$ and $y' = x$.

Recall that if a point (x,y) is rotated through an angle ϕ about the origin (figure 3.6.5), then the coordinates of its new position, (x′,y′), can be calculated by the following equations:

$$x' = x \cos \phi - y \sin \phi$$

$$y' = y \cos \phi + x \sin \phi$$

Application of matrix multiplication shows that this transformation can also be represented by the following matrix equation:

$$[x'y'] = [xy] \begin{bmatrix} \cos \phi & \sin \phi \\ -\sin \phi & \cos \phi \end{bmatrix}$$

Here the matrices [x′y′] and [xy] represent the points (x′,y′) and (x,y) respectively, and the matrix

$$\begin{bmatrix} \cos\phi & \sin \phi \\ -\sin \phi & \cos \phi \end{bmatrix}$$

is the **representation of the rotation.**

FIGURE 3.6.4

Reflection through a line and reflection through a point

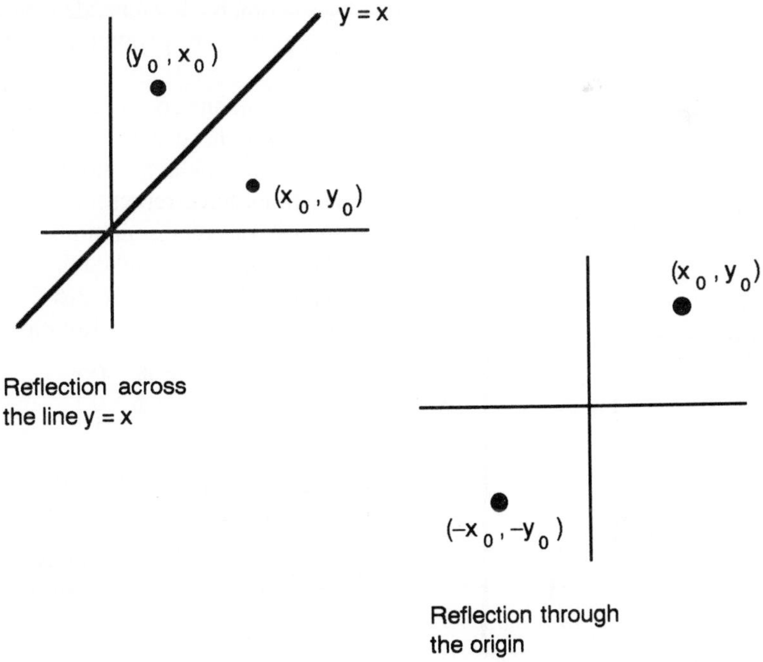

FIGURE 3.6.5

Rotation about the origin

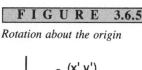

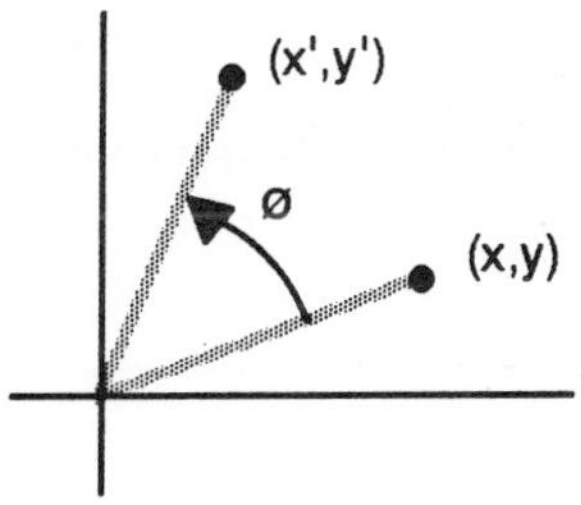

FIGURE 3.6.6

The translation of the point (x,y) to the point ($x+T_x$,$y+T_y$)

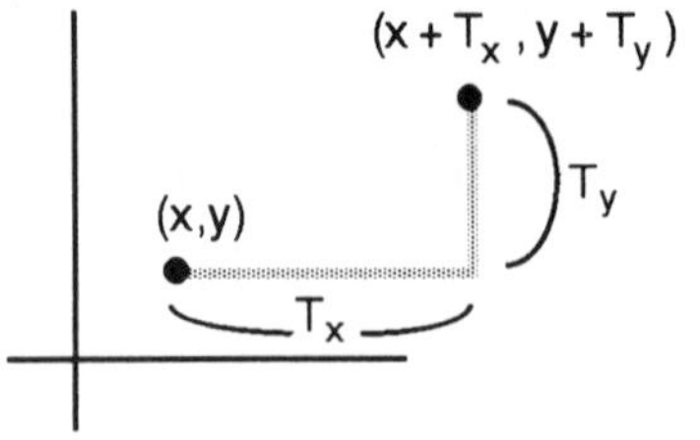

Another basic transformation is **translation** (figure 3.6.6). The equations for this transformation are

$$x' = x + T_x$$

$$y' = y + T_y$$

These equations cannot be converted to a useful matrix representation within the usual coordinate system. To facilitate the uniform representation of transformations as matrix equations, the standard coordinate system is extended to a system known as **homogeneous coordinates.** A point with coordinates (x,y) has homogeneous coordinates $[x_h y_h]$ where

$$x_h = x\,w,\ y_h = y\,w$$

All of your applications in two-dimensions will use w = 1, so the point (x,y) has homogeneous coordinates [x y 1]. As long as w is not zero, the point with coordinates [x y w] can be normalized to [x/w y/w 1]. Translation can now be represented with homogeneous coordinates as

$$[x'y'1] = [x\ y\ 1]\begin{bmatrix}1 & 0 & 0\\ 0 & 1 & 0\\ T_x & T_y & 1\end{bmatrix}$$

The result of this multiplication is the point with homogeneous coordinates

$$[x + T_x\ y + T_y\ 1]$$

No point with finite coordinates can have homogeneous coordinates [x y 0], because if any translation is applied to such a point, it will remain fixed. Points with coordinates [x y 0] are said to be **points at infinity.** The term *point at infinity* comes from projective geometry, where all lines must intersect. Normal Euclidean geometry is embedded into a projective plane by adding a point at infinity for each set of parallel lines. This point is where the set of parallel lines meet.

It appears that one coordinate system is necessary to do most transformations while another is needed to do translations. But if this were indeed the case, matrix notation would be more of a detriment than an aid. Fortunately, all transformations have representations in the homogeneous coordinate system. The homogeneous representations can be derived from matrix representations in standard coordinates by embedding these matrices in the upper-left corner of the 3 × 3 matrix given in figure 3.6.7.

FIGURE 3.6.7

The matrix representation of a transformation embedded into the matrix representing the transformation in homogeneous coordinates

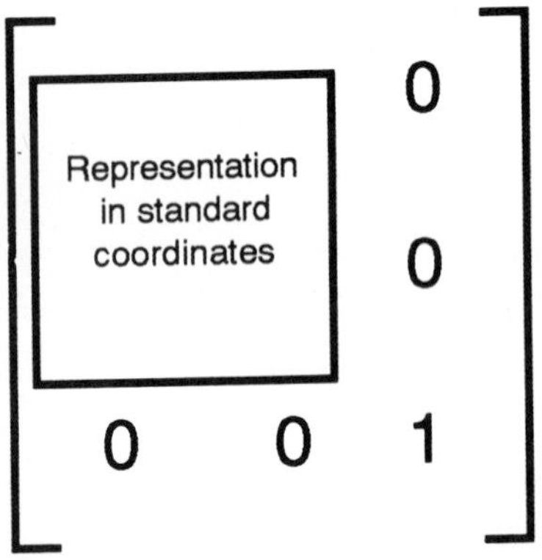

The representation of the Rotation matrix in homogeneous coordinates is

$$\begin{bmatrix}\cos\phi & \sin\phi & 0\\ -\sin\phi & \cos\phi & 0\\ 0 & 0 & 1\end{bmatrix}$$

It is easy to verify that the following matrix equation gives the equations for rotation about the origin.

$$[x'y'1] = [x\ y\ 1]\begin{bmatrix}\cos\phi & \sin\phi & 0\\ -\sin\phi & \cos\phi & 0\\ 0 & 0 & 1\end{bmatrix}$$

FIGURE 3.6.8

Rotation of an object around a hotspot realized as a composition of transformations

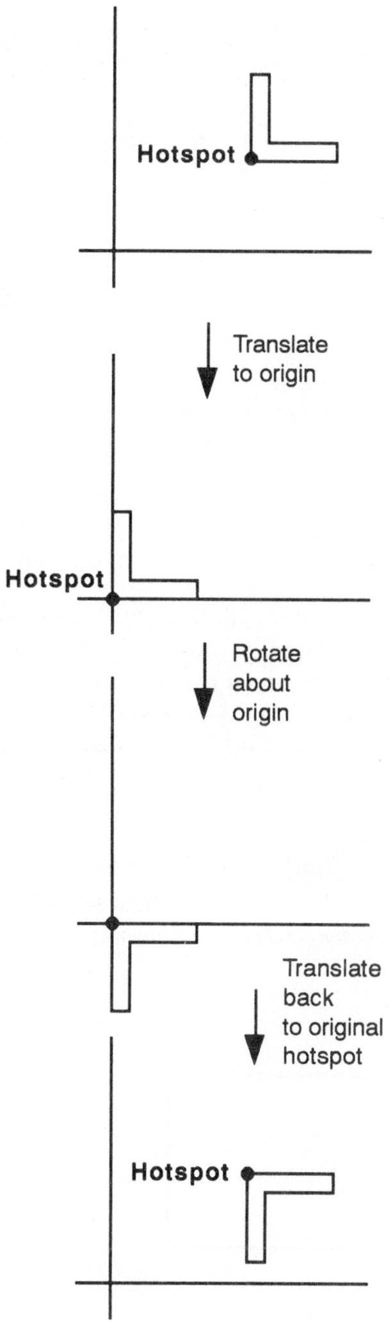

Matrices provide more than just a notational device for sets of equations: they also give a simple way to compute the effect of a sequence of operations. If, for example, you want to rotate a triangle around a hotspot different from the origin, you can translate the hotspot to the origin, rotate, and then translate the hotspot back to its original location (figure 3.6.8). If the hotspot is located at the point (5,7), then the translation to the origin is represented by

$$\begin{bmatrix} 1 & 0 & 0 \\ 0 & 1 & 0 \\ -5 & -7 & 1 \end{bmatrix}$$

The matrix representing the translation back to the hotspot is the matrix.

$$\begin{bmatrix} 1 & 0 & 0 \\ 0 & 1 & 0 \\ 5 & 7 & 1 \end{bmatrix}$$

If these transformations are applied consecutively on a point, the resulting point will be at the same location. These transformations are inverses of each other. Notice that the product of the matrices representing the two transformations is the **multiplicative identity matrix**

$$\begin{bmatrix} 1 & 0 & 0 \\ 0 & 1 & 0 \\ 0 & 0 & 1 \end{bmatrix}$$

Thus, the matrix representations of these inverse transformations are **multiplicative inverses** of each other.

Calculating the multiplicative inverse of a matrix when it exists is, in general, a lengthy procedure. For the transformations used in computer graphics, however, the geometric interpretations provide shortcuts for calculating these inverses. A rotation about the origin through an angle has the inverse transformation of a rotation through an angle of $-\phi$. The equations

$$\cos(-\phi) = \cos\phi$$

$$\sin(-\phi) = -\sin\phi$$

can be substituted into the matrix representation of the rotation through $-\phi$ to get the matrix representing that transformation:

$$\begin{bmatrix} \cos\phi & -\sin\phi & 0 \\ \sin\phi & \cos\phi & 0 \\ 0 & 0 & 1 \end{bmatrix}$$

Notice that the rows of the matrix representing a rotation are equal to the corresponding columns of the matrix representing the inverse of the rotation. The multiplicative **inverse of a rotation** representation is its transpose. Computation of other inverse matrices is left for the reader.

In light of this discussion, the problem of rotating a graphic object around a hotspot other than the origin can be reduced to multiplication by a matrix, T, to translate to the origin. The resulting point is multiplied by a matrix, R, to rotate through angle ϕ. Finally, this result is multiplied by T^{-1}. The entire transformation for a point **p** to point **p′** is given by

$$\mathbf{p}' = \mathbf{p}\, T\, R\, T^{-1}$$

Matrix multiplication is associative; thus, the product matrix TRT^{-1} represents the transformation, and the product needs to be calculated only once before the transformation is applied to the points of a graphic object. The product TRT^{-1} follows.

$$\begin{bmatrix} 1 & 0 & 0 \\ 0 & 1 & 0 \\ -T_x & -T_y & 1 \end{bmatrix} \begin{bmatrix} \cos\phi & \sin\phi & 0 \\ -\sin\phi & \cos\phi & 0 \\ 0 & 0 & 1 \end{bmatrix} \begin{bmatrix} 1 & 0 & 0 \\ 0 & 1 & 0 \\ T_x & T_y & 1 \end{bmatrix}$$

$$\begin{bmatrix} \cos\phi & \sin\phi & 0 \\ -\sin\phi & \cos\phi & 0 \\ (1-\cos\phi)T_x + T_y\sin\phi & (1-\cos\phi)T_y + T_x\sin\phi & 1 \end{bmatrix}$$

In general, if a transformation can be decomposed into a sequence of transformations, then the original transformation is represented by the product of the matrices representing the transformations in the sequence. Another application of this technique is the scaling of a geometric figure while maintaining one of its corners in a fixed position.

If the square with opposite corners (1,1) and (2,2) is to be scaled so that its horizontal side is tripled while its vertical side is doubled, simple scaling creates a new rectangle with opposite corners (3,2) and (6,4) (figure 3.6.9). Suppose the lower-left corner (1,1) of the original rectangle is to remain fixed under the scaling (figure 3.6.10). A simple way to achieve this is to translate the lower-left corner of the rectangle to the origin with the matrix.

FIGURE 3.6.9

A rectangle scaled without fixing one of its corners

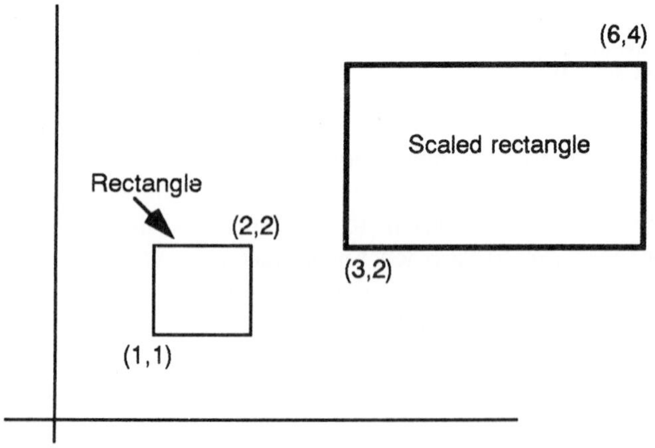

FIGURE 3.6.10

Scaling the rectangle (1,1) (2,2) by 4 in the x-direction and 3 in they y-direction; (1,1) is a fixed point.

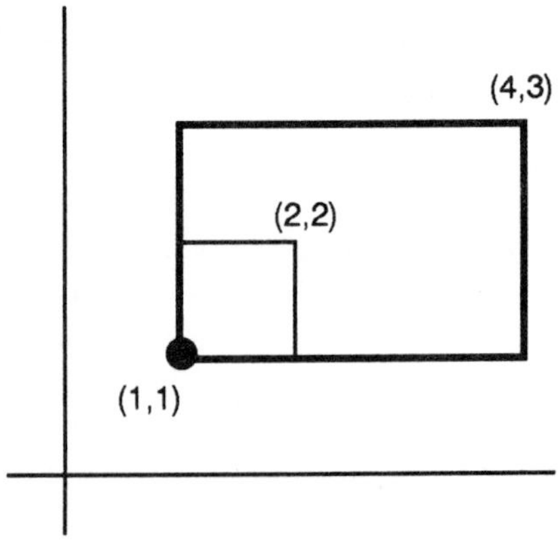

$$\begin{bmatrix} 1 & 0 & 0 \\ 0 & 1 & 0 \\ -1 & -1 & 1 \end{bmatrix}$$

Next, apply the scaling matrix

$$\begin{bmatrix} 3 & 0 & 0 \\ 0 & 2 & 0 \\ 0 & 0 & 1 \end{bmatrix}$$

Finally, multiply that result by the inverse of the original translation matrix

$$\begin{bmatrix} 1 & 0 & 0 \\ 0 & 1 & 0 \\ 1 & 1 & 1 \end{bmatrix}$$

This sequence of transformations is illustrated in figure 3.6.11.

The scaling depicted in the last example can be generalized to scaling relative to an arbitrary fixed point (x_0,y_0). This general transformation is characterized by the matrix product

$$\begin{bmatrix} 1 & 0 & 0 \\ 0 & 1 & 0 \\ -x_0 & -y_0 & 1 \end{bmatrix} \begin{bmatrix} S_x & 0 & 0 \\ 0 & S_y & 0 \\ 0 & 0 & 1 \end{bmatrix} \begin{bmatrix} 1 & 0 & 0 \\ 0 & 1 & 0 \\ x_0 & y_0 & 1 \end{bmatrix}$$

which equals

$$\begin{bmatrix} S_x & 0 & 0 \\ 0 & S_y & 0 \\ (1-S_x)x_0 & (1-S_y)y_0 & 1 \end{bmatrix}$$

FIGURE 3.6.11

The sequence of transformations needed to scale a rectangle and keep the point (1,1) fixed

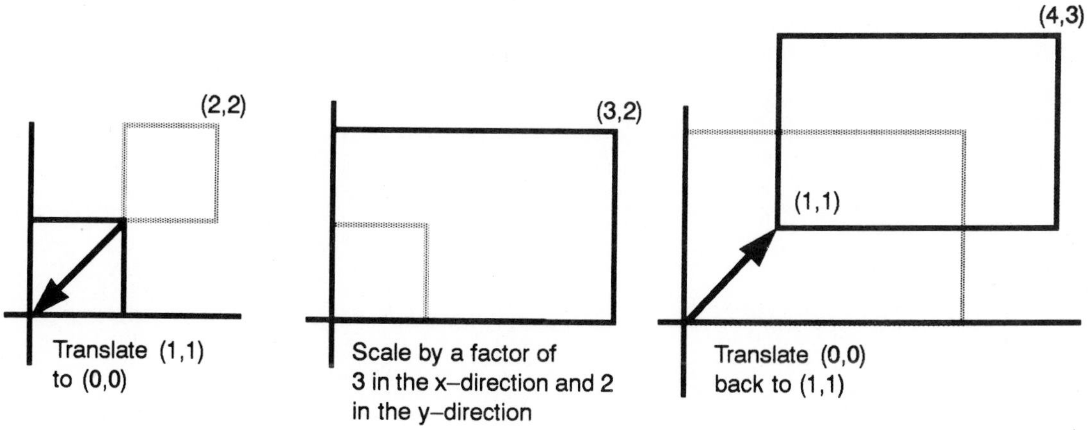

FIGURE 3.6.12

Shearing a rectangle in the x-direction by a factor of 3

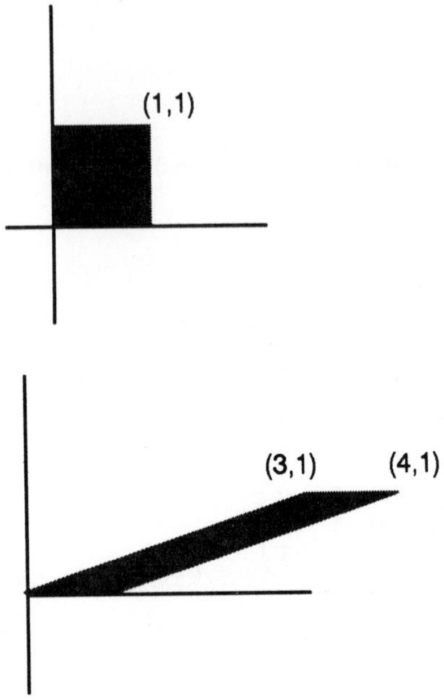

Another transformation, **shearing,** alters the shape of an object by adding a multiple of one coordinate to the other coordinate of a point. The matrix representation for a shear with shear factor SH_x in the x-direction is

$$\begin{bmatrix} 1 & 0 & 0 \\ SH_x & 1 & 0 \\ 0 & 0 & 1 \end{bmatrix}$$

Figure 3.6.12 shows an x-direction shear with shear factor 3.

Shear in the y-direction has the matrix representation

$$\begin{bmatrix} 1 & SH_y & 0 \\ 0 & 1 & 0 \\ 0 & 0 & 1 \end{bmatrix}$$

Once a transformation is expressed as a matrix equation of the form **P′ = PM,** it is possible to implement this transformation directly with the procedure in listed in figure 3.6.13. In this transformation the coordinates of a point **P** are stored in a matrix [**P**[1],**P**[2],**P**[3]], and the coordinates of the transformed point are normalized.

If one were to apply this function with the matrix representing the shear in the y-direction, five of the multiplications in the loop are by 0 and three are by 1. Even when simple translation is performed, homogeneous coordinates are not needed. Matrix representations allow the programmer to discover transformation equations. The programmer then transfers these equations to efficient procedures. Figure 3.6.14 gives a procedure for the y-shear in which the usual definition of a point is used and no matrix references are needed.

Scaling and rotation about an arbitrary point can also be implemented without matrix multiplication or homogeneous coordinates. A scaling procedure is given in figure 3.6.15. The rotation procedure is left as an exercise (3.6.9).

FIGURE 3.6.13

Procedure to implement an arbitrary two-dimensional transformation on a point represented by a matrix in homogeneous coordinates

```
(* Procedure to compute the transformation of the point OldPoint to the point NewPoint              *)
(* using the transformation represented by the matrix TransformationMatrix                          *)
const
   dimension = 3;                (* number of homogeneous coordinates                              *)
type
   CoordinateRange   = 1..3;     (* number of homogeneous coordinates                              *)
   point       = array[CoordinateRange] of real;                (* coordinates of a point          *)
   matrix      = array [CoordinateRange,CoordinateRange] of real; (* transformation matrix         *)

procedure Transform (OldPoint : point; TransformationMatrix : matrix; var NewPoint : point);
var
   row       : CoordinateRange;                           (* index used for rows of the matrix    *)
   column    : CoordinateRange;                           (* index used for columns of the matrix*)
begin (*Transform *)
   for column := 1 to dimension do                        (* calculate each coordinate            *)
      begin
         (* Each coordinate is a sum. Initialize the sum with the first product.                   *)
         NewPoint[column] := OldPoint[column] * TransformationMatrix[1,column];
         for row := 2 to dimension do                     (*compute the rest of the sum           *)
            NewPoint[column] := OldPoint[column] * TransformationMatrix[row,column];
      end;
   (* normalize the resulting coordinates*)
   for column := 1 to dimension do
      NewPoint[column] := NewPoint[column] / NewPoint[dimension]
end; (* Transform*)
```

FIGURE 3.6.14

The y-shear operation implemented by a procedure on the normal two-dimensional representation of a point

```
(* Procedure to transform an OldPoint to a NewPoint by a y-shear of ShearFactor *)
type
   point = record
      x : real;
      y : real
   end;
procedure YShear(OldPoint : point; ShearFactor : real; var NewPoint : point);
begin (*YShear*)
   NewPoint.x := OldPoint.x;                          (* x-coordinate not changed     *)
   NewPoint.y := OldPoint.y + ShearFactor*OldPoint.x; (* change y  by shear factor    *)
end; (* YShear*)
```

FIGURE 3.6.15

Procedure to implement the scale transformation represented by the matrix given

```
(* Procedure to transform a point OldPoint to a point NewPoint by scaling factors ScaleX and      *)
(* ScaleY.  The point FixedPoint remains fixed under this transformation.                          *)

procedure Scale(OldPoint, FixedPoint : point; ScaleX,ScaleY : real; var NewPoint : point);
begin (*Scale*)
   NewPoint.x := ScaleX*OldPoint.x + (1 - ScaleX) * FixedPoint.x;
   NewPoint.y := ScaleY*OldPoint.y + (1 - ScaleY) * FixedPoint.y
end; (* Scale*)
```

EXERCISES

3.6.1

Try to compute each of the following matrix products. If the product cannot be computed, explain why.

a. $\begin{bmatrix} 1 & 0 & 2 \\ -3 & 2 & 1 \end{bmatrix} \begin{bmatrix} 3 & 0 & 7 \\ 0 & 2 & 1 \end{bmatrix}$

b. $\begin{bmatrix} 1 & 0 \\ -3 & 2 \end{bmatrix} \begin{bmatrix} 0 & 3 & -7 \\ 2 & 1 & 1 \end{bmatrix}$

c. $\begin{bmatrix} 1 & 2 & 3 \end{bmatrix} \begin{bmatrix} 0 & 2 & 3 \\ 1 & 0 & 0 \\ 4 & 0 & 1 \end{bmatrix} \begin{bmatrix} 2 \\ 1 \\ 2 \end{bmatrix}$

3.6.2

Give the matrix representations of the following transformations:

a. Reflection across the y-axis ($x' = -x$, $y' = y$).
b. Reflection across the x-axis ($x' = x$, $y' = -y$).
c. Reflection through the origin ($x' = -x$, $y' = -y$).
d. Reflection across the line $y = x$ ($x' = y$, $y' = x$).
e. Reflection across the line $y = -x$ ($x' = -y$, $y' = -x$).

3.6.3

For each of the transformations given in exercise 3.6.2, give a geometric interpretation of the inverse operation. Use this to find the multiplicative inverse of each of the matrices found in 3.6.2.

3.6.4

Give a geometric interpretation of the inverse of x-direction shear. Use this to give the multiplicative inverse of the matrix representing that operation.

3.6.5

Show that a point with homogeneous coordinates [x y 0] is invariant under translation.

3.6.6

Show that the reflection across the line $y = x$ is equivalent to a reflection across the x-axis followed by a rotation of $-90°$. (*Hint:* Show that the two matrix representations are equal.)

3.6.7

Show that the reflection across the line $y = -x$ is equivalent to reflection across the y-axis followed by a rotation of $-90°$.

3.6.8

What is the matrix representation for a reflection across an arbitrary line $y = mx + b$?

3.6.9

Write a Pascal procedure to rotate a point around an arbitrary point. Write this procedure without using matrix operations or homogeneous equations.

3.6.10

Use matrix multiplication on the rectangle (30,30), (30,36), (40,36) and (40,30) to:

a. rotate it 90° about (33,36)
b. rotate it −90° about (33,36)
c. rotate is 180° about (35,33)

3.6.11

If a transformation T is accomplished by multiplying by two matrices $\mathbf{M_1}$ and $\mathbf{M_2}$, that is for any point **p**, T((**p**) = $(\mathbf{pM_1})\mathbf{M_2}$, what law of matrix multiplication makes it possible to accomplish the same transformation by multiplying by the matrix $\mathbf{M} = \mathbf{M_1M_2}$?

3.7 Fractals and Related curves

Fractals are a class of graphic objects that presents a good test for the simple graphics package. Fractals range from the space-filling curves, named after the mathematicians **Hilbert** and **Sierpinski** (figure 3.7.1), to the abstract shapes of the **Mandelbrot set** and **Julia sets.** In addition to fractals, this section introduces a closely related class of curves called **graftals** which are generated by grammars called **L-systems.** Some of the pictures generated will appear to be three-dimensional, but no three-dimensional graphics functions are used.

Fractal curves may be used to model natural shapes. Mandelbrot, in his book *The Fractal Geometry of Nature* (1983), discusses the nature of measurement. He sets out to prove by example that measurement is not absolute but depends on the size of the measuring unit.

For example, a geographer looking at a map of United States might measure the length of Maine's coast as several hundred miles. When the measurement is repeated with a map of Maine, peninsulas and inlets that are not visible on the United States map are revealed, adding substantially to the length of the coastline. The coastline measurement would continue to increase if the magnification were increased to measure at the level of grains of sand, molecules, or atoms.

FIGURE 3.7.1

The Sierpinski curve

The following discussion looks at representations of fractal curves that are similar to geographers' maps in that the curves drawn will be finite representations of fractal curves. An advantage you have over the geographer is that you can always change your window coordinates to reveal more detail, whereas a geographer has a limited number of maps available.

The problem of measuring coastlines or borders of countries may be viewed as measuring the same object using progressively finer measuring devices. Mandelbrot points out that the length of the frontier between Portugal and Spain is listed differently in the encyclopedias of the two countries. Portugal, the smaller country, gives a larger value for this length, so perhaps it used a larger scale map, in other words, a smaller measuring unit.

In this instance, the fact that the length of coastlines and borders depended on the length of the measuring device is a curiosity, but Mandelbrot noticed that the length varied in nearly the same way for other coastlines and borders. These computations led to a new view of the dimension of a geometric object: that the curve being measured is divided into a number of units of length r. The Euclidean dimension of a straight line is one, since it can be characterized by its length.

There is an alternative method for characterizing dimension. If you start with a line of length 1 and divide it into copies of itself scaled by a factor r, the line will be composed to (1/r) scaled copies. If $r = 1/3$, the line will contain 3 copies of itself. This leads to the trivial equality $1 = r(r^{-1})$. Similarly, a square of side length 1 can be divided into $(1/r)^2$ copies of itself in which each of its measurements has been scaled by r. Again, if $r = 1/3$, it takes 9 copies of a square 1/3 on a side to cover a square of side length 1. This results in the trivial equation $1 = (1/r)^2r^2$. The scaling relationship can be described by $1 = Nr^D$, where N is the number of copies of the object scaled by r that is needed to decompose the object.

If you decompose a piece of a shoreline into copies of itself scaled by r and try to solve the equation $1 = Nr^D$, what value will you get for D? At first this would seem to be a simple question to answer. The shoreline is composed of lines; therefore D should be 1. This is true for a straight line. But no matter how small the scale of the copy of the line, the length of the line is the same. The length of the shoreline increases as the scale of the measuring device is decreased. Mandelbrot discovered that even though the measured length of shorelines changes, D stays nearly constant. For curves such as coastlines the value of D is not an integer but a fraction between 1 and 2. The value D is called the **fractal dimension** of the curve.

In the case of a line, the fractal dimension is one just like its Euclidean dimension. A comparison of published lengths of borders and coastlines showed that as the scale varied, the lengths varied in such a way that the fractal dimension D turned out to be very close to $3/2$(Mandelbrot 1983). Coastlines and borders may be thought of as curves in the plane of a map; hence they have a Euclidean (normal) dimension of 1. Mandelbrot defined a **fractal curve** as a curve that has fractal dimension greater than its Euclidean dimension.

When geographers depict coastlines on maps of increasing scale, coastlines continue to show more of similar features—such as bays, inlets, and promontories—when they are depicted on maps of increasing scale. This property is formalized in a collection of mathematically defined curves in which sections of each curve reproduce the whole curve on a smaller scale. Such curves are called **self-similar.** It is possible to create self similar artificial coastlines mathematically. Theoretically, measurements of these curves may be carried down to any level.

An example of a self-similar curve is the **Koch arc.** The measuring unit r for this curve starts at 1 and is reduced to one-third of the current value at each level of higher resolution. The first-level curve is a straight line of length 1 with $r = 1$ (figure 3.7.2). The next level of Koch curve has $r = 1/3$ and is drawn by replacing the middle third of the line in level 1 with two segments, each of length 1/3. The length of this curve is clearly 4/3. At the third level, each of the line segments is replaced by a level-1 curve of length 4/9. The length of this curve is 16/9, which is 4/3 the length of the level-2 curve. This process may be carried to any level, but in all cases the next level has a measuring unit equal to one-third of the previous level's unit and a length four-thirds of the previous level's length. If the length at a level is L(r), where r is the measuring unit of that level, then the length of the next level is given by

$$L(r/3) = 4/3L(r)$$

In many self-similar curves such as the Koch curve, the dimension D is fairly easy to calculate. Note that a single copy of the Koch curve is replaced by 4

FIGURE 3.7.2

Three levels of the Koch arc

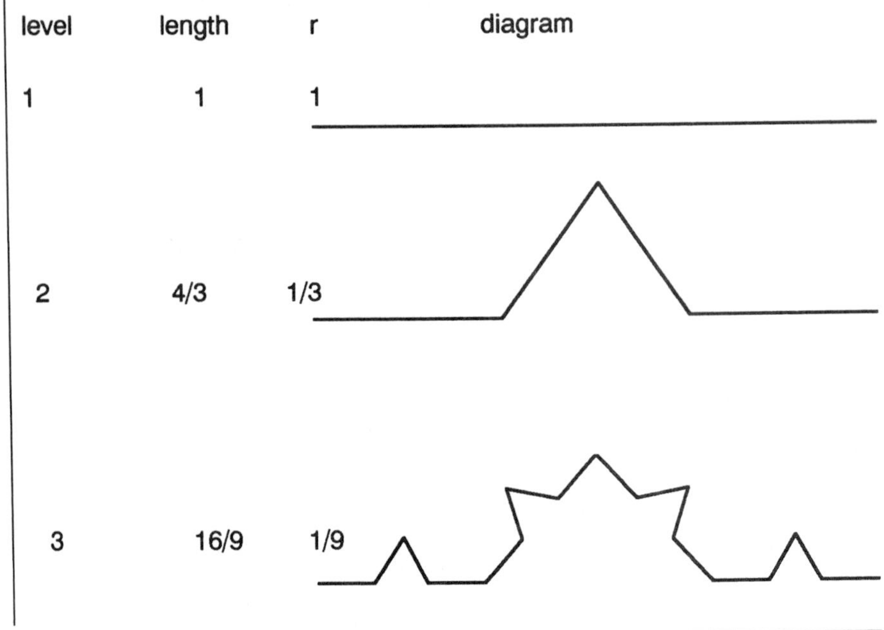

copies of itself scaled by r = 1/3, so you solve the dimension equation $1 = 4 (1/3)^D$ to get $D = \log(4)/\log(3) \approx 1.2857$.

The D-value is surprisingly close to the values of D computed in the geographic curves presented above. This fact may be cited as the reason that variations of the Koch curve can be used to simulate islands. The formula for computing the dimension of the Koch curves may be used to compute the dimension of any self-similar curve that consists of N line segments, each of length r. For such curves, $D = \log N/\log(1/r)$.

The Sierpinski curve shown in figure 3.7.1 is generated from pieces similar to the curve in figure 3.7.3. This curve is constructed by dividing each of the line segments for a given level into three segments, each with a length one-half of the original segment. The dimension of this simple version of the curve is $D = \log 3/\log 2 \approx 1.5849$.

This construction of Sierpinski curve is described in terms of the three 90° rotations of the base curve A (figure 3.7.4), called the level-1 curves. These rotations are labeled B, C, and D. The 270° rotation is B, the 180° rotation is C, and the 90° rotation is D. The curves can be described recursively. At level 0, no curve is generated. For each level n, the end points of the line segments in the level-1 diagram for A may be labeled with the n-1 level of the rotation that would appear at that point (figure 3.7.5). This labeling may be considered the general description of the curve A. The level-1 drawing of A consists of level-0 calls to the procedures listed with lines drawn between the calls. The level-2 drawing of A would consist of the same line drawings, but they would include calls to the labeled procedures at level 1.

FIGURE 3.7.3

The level-1 Sierpinski A curve

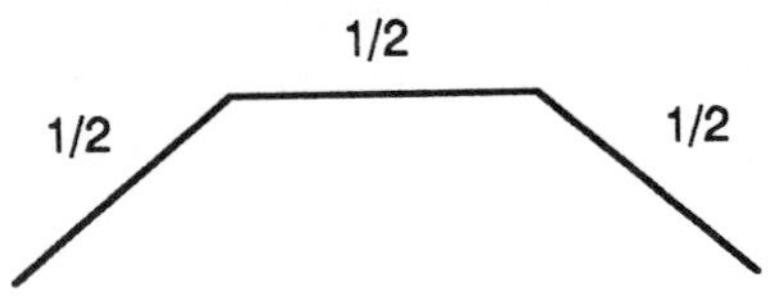

FIGURE 3.7.4

All four level-1 Sierpinski curves

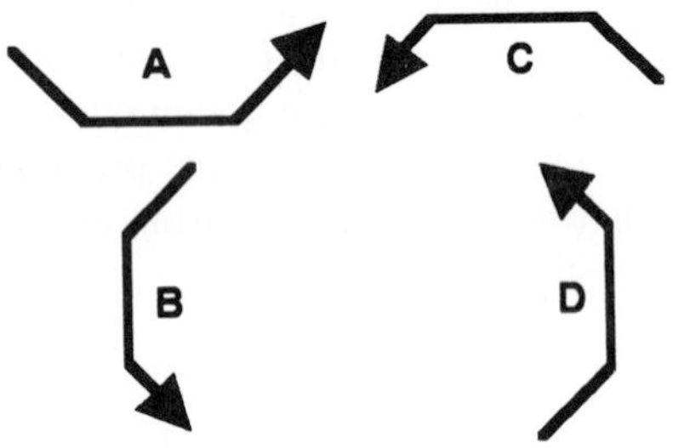

FIGURE 3.7.5

The level-1 Sierpinski A curve with labels used to create the procedure A

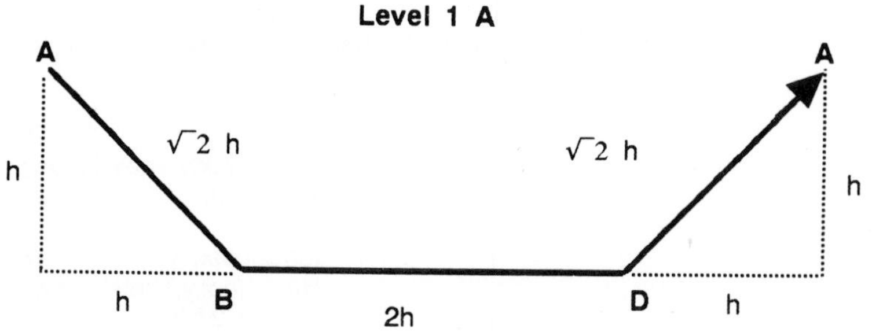

Consider the level-1 approximation of A. All calls to procedures at this level are 0-level calls that result in nothing being drawn; so at level 1, A consists of three line segments. If the leftmost point labeled A in figure 3.7.5 has coordinates (x,y), then the first line is drawn to the point (x + h, y − h). In procedure A, this is accomplished by a MoveAbs(x,y) followed by a call to LineAbs(x,y) after assigning x = x + h and y = y − h. Next, x is assigned to x + 2h and LineAbs is called again for (x,y). Finally, x is set to x + h and y to y + h, and a last call to LineAbs(x,y) is made.

If you want to create the level-2 curve for A, repeat the process above, only this time calling on the curves A, B, D, and A again at level 1. Figure 3.7.6 shows the level-2 curve A with the connecting lines emphasized. The procedure that draws A is given in figure 3.7.7, and descriptions of all the curves are given in figures 3.7.8 and 3.7.9.

FIGURE 3.7.6

The level-2 Sierpinski A curve

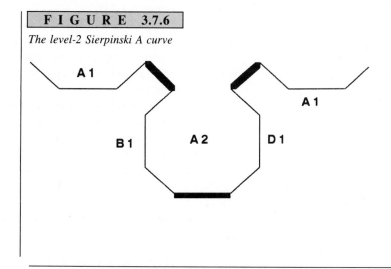

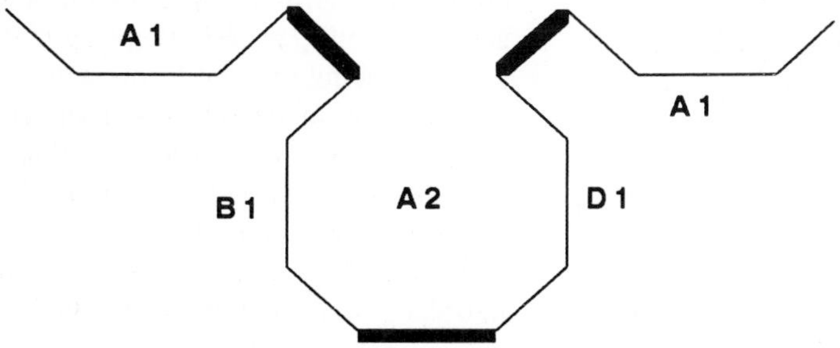

FIGURE 3.7.7

The procedure that generates the Sierpinski A curve for any level i

```
procedure A(i,h : integer;var x,y : real; var TheWindow : Window);
   begin
      if i>0 then
         begin
            A(i - 1,h,x,y,TheWindow);
            x := x + h;
            y := y - h;
            LineAbs(x,  y,TheWindow);
            B(i - 1,h,x,y,TheWindow );
            x := x + 2 * h;
            LineAbs(x,  y,TheWindow);
            D(i - 1,h,x,y,TheWindow );
            x := x + h;
            y := y + h;
            LineAbs(x,  y,TheWindow);
            A(i - 1,h,x,y,TheWindow )
         end
   end;
```

FIGURE 3.7.8

Shorthand notation for the lines used to draw the Sierpinski curves

Line from (x,y) to:

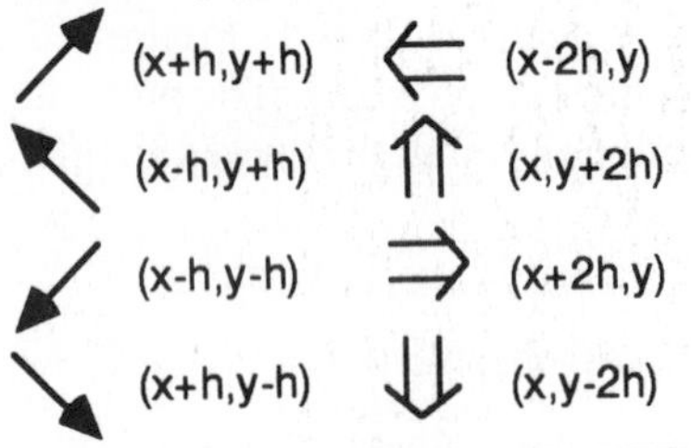

FIGURE 3.7.9

Shorthand notation for the four Sierpinski curves

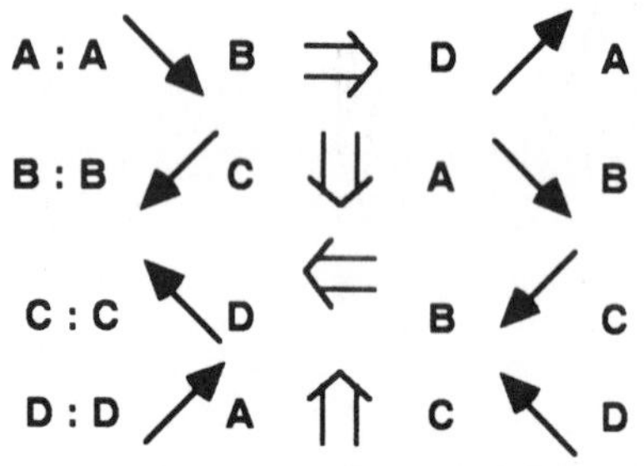

If the distance h remains constant you get longer curves; magnification will not reveal any finer detail. If, however, the value h is reduced as the level is reduced, then the overall size of the diagram may be roughly maintained while both the length of the curve and low-level detail will be increased. The Sierpinski curves for A at levels 2, 3, and 5 are shown in figure 3.7.10. The size of h is divided by 2 on each recursive call.

In order to make the slightly more interesting curve in figure 3.7.1, the program in Appendix A draws the curves, each with a line connecting it to the next curve figure 3.7.11).

A second class of curves, those related to self-similar fractals and generated by recursive procedures, are the graftals. Figure 3.7.12 is a tree generated by a graftal. The term *graftal* was introduced by Smith (1984) to describe curves generated by **parallel graph grammars.** Graftals can be used to create natural-looking organic forms without the use of a random number generator.

The ideas of parallel rewriting grammars and **bracketed L-systems** were introduced by Lindenmayer in 1968 to model developing biological systems. Languages in the original bracketed L-system consisted of a set of symbols such as 0 and 1 with left and right brackets ([,]). The left bracket indicated a branch to the left after a given symbol; the right bracket indicated an end to that branch. In order to make interesting pictures, the left and right parentheses are added to indicate branches to the right.

The language that generated figure 3.7.12 may be given as the set of symbols {0, 1, [,], (,)} with the grammar rules {0 → 1 [0] 1 (0) 0, 1 →11,[→[,]→],(→(,) →)}. Figure 3.7.13 shows the first two generations of the tree produced if you represent 0 as a dotted line and 1 as a solid line.

FIGURE 3.7.10

The Sierpinski A curves for levels 2, 3, and 5

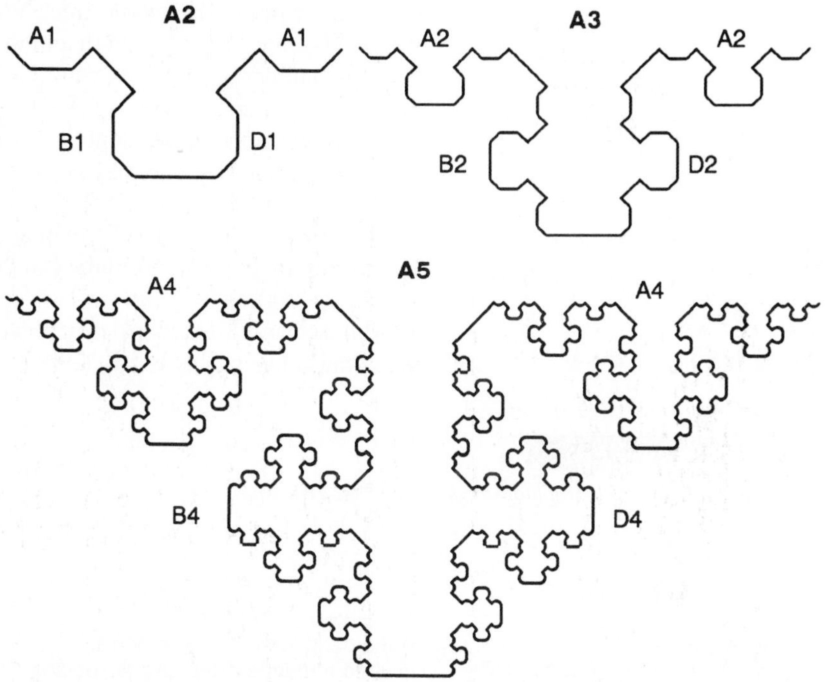

FIGURE 3.7.11

An interesting method for joining the four Sierpinski curves into one diagram is given in appendix 1. This demonstrates the construction at level 1.

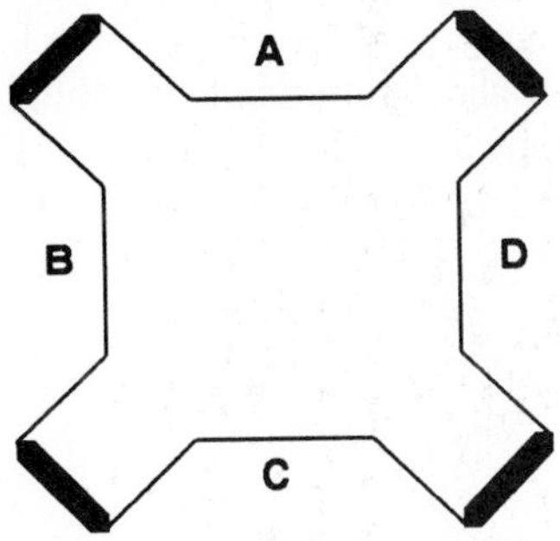

FIGURE 3.7.12

A graphtal tree generated by a bracketed L-system

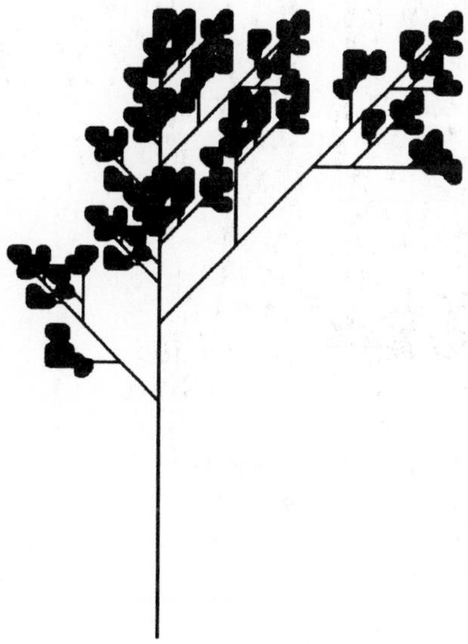

FIGURE 3.7.13

The first two generations of the tree in figure 3.7.12

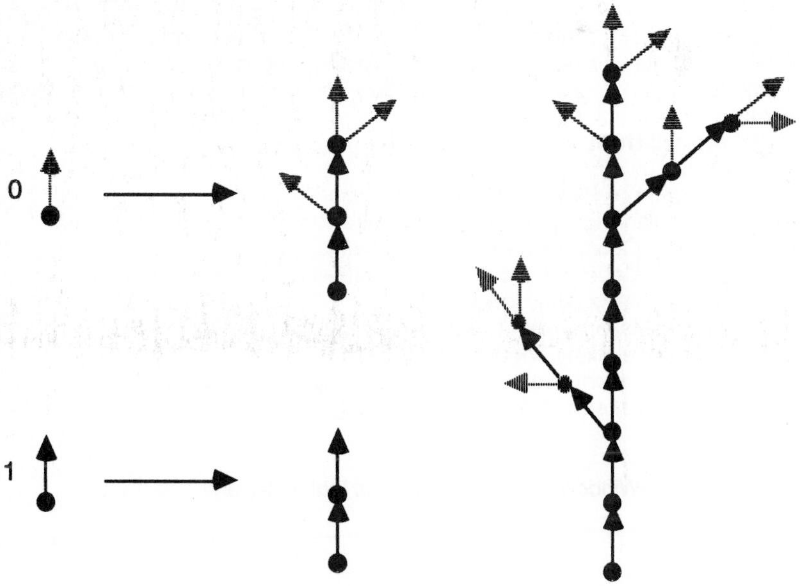

A less mathematical way of viewing this grammar is to think of 0 as a bud and 1 as an actual branch of length 1. Branches can double in size, hence the production 1 → 11, while buds can produce a new branch with essentially the same structure as the whole tree. With this view of 0, the production 0 → 1[0]1(0)0 represents a tree with an initial trunk growth, a bud for a left-growing branch, another growth of trunk, a bud for a right-growing branch, and a terminal bud for next year's growth.

Each year the branches double in length and the buds sprout into trees of level 1. From the diagram one may deduce that a given generation of tree, say T(n), can be given recursively by the formula T(n) = 2**(n − 1) [T(n − 1)] 2**(n − 1) (T (n − 1)) T(n − 1), where 2**n represents 2 raised to the nth power repetitions of 1. This formula can be converted into a recursive procedure (figure 3.7.14).

Rather than writing separate procedures for left and right branching, simply pass the branch angle to T as a value parameter. The formulas x =

FIGURE 3.7.14

This procedure draws the graphtal tree for the bracketed L-system given in the text

```
const
   DeltaAngle = 30;                 (* the branch angle is 30°                  *)
   BranchLength = 1;                (* the base length of a branch is 1         *)
   DegreesToRadians = 0.017453;     (* used to convert degrees to radians       *)
var
   PowerOf2 : array[0..8] of integer; (* PowerOf2[n] is the nth power of 2      *)

procedure TreeMaker (Level : integer;
                     Angle : integer;
                     TheWindow : Window);
   var
      Count         : integer;      (* number of segments for a branch          *)
      RadianAngle   : real;         (* The angle in radians                     *)
      dx,dy         : real;         (* Size of the change in x and y for branch *)
   begin
      if Level > 0 then
         begin
            Count := PowerOf2[Level];
            RadianAngle := Angle * DegreesToRadians;
            dx := Count * BranchLength * cos(RadianAngle);
            dy := Count * BranchLength * sin(RadianAngle);
            LineRel(dx, dy,TheWindow);
            TreeMaker(Level - 1, Angle + DeltaAngle,TheWindow);
            LineRel(dx,dy,TheWindow);
            TreeMaker(Level - 1, angle - DeltaAngle,TheWindow);
            TreeMaker(n - 1, angle,TheWindow)
         end
      else
         Leaf(TheWindow);        (* draws a leaf at the end of a branch         *)
   end;
```

1*cos(BranchAngle) and y = 1*sin(BranchAngle), where 1 is the current branch length, can be used to compute the relative coordinates of the end of the branch. If the change in angle at which the branches grow, DetaAngle, is changed and the branching sequence is changed, different types of plants can be created (Prusinkiewicz, Lindenmayer, and Hanan 1988; de Reffye et al. 1988) (figure 3.7.15).

The triangle has also been used to generate realistic fractal images. In this construction a right triangle is rotated and resized (figure 3.7.16), both randomly and deterministically, to build mountains (figured 3.7.17) (Smith 1984).

Fractals that are not self-similar may be generated by considering the effect of iterated applications of a function on a regular complex number. Many mathematical models consist of a beginning value for a variable and a function for calculating the next value of that variable. Population models used in biology typically assume a starting population and then compute the population

FIGURE 3.7.15

"Water Lilies"—copyright © 1990, D. R. Fowler, J. Hanan, P. Prusinkiewicz, N. Fuller, University of Regina—was created using L-systems.

FIGURE 3.7.16

Triangles are rotated and resized to create the mountains in figure 3.7.17

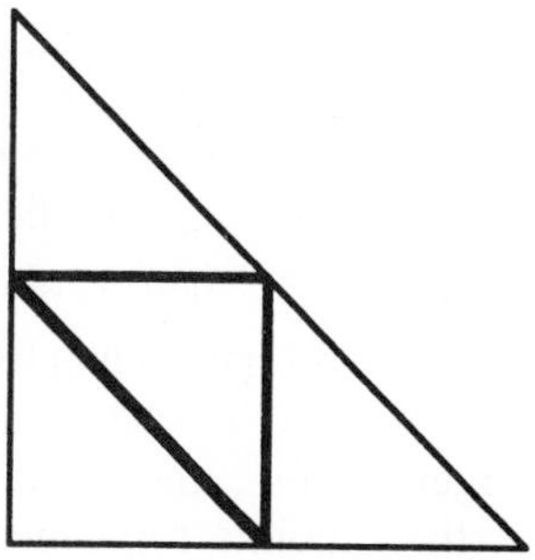

FIGURE 3.7.17

Kenton Musgrave used fractals to create the mountains in his image "Nimbus."

at the end of a given time period by using a formula that takes into account factors in the growth and decline of that population. The population at the end of the first time period is used as the initial population for the next time period, so it is substituted into the formula to calculate the population at the end of the next interval. This iterated calculation led, in most cases, to populations that eventually settled into a stable cycle of growth and decline. In some cases, however, the cycle of growth and decline did not have predictable maxima and minima. These unpredictable cycles were labeled **chaotic.**

Population models use real numbers. The extension of the study of iterated functions into complex numbers has not only helped explain problems encountered with iterated real-valued functions, but also produced a new way of visualizing problems in the branch of mathematics known as dynamic systems.

For a complex number given as $z = a + ib$, where a and b are real and $i^2 = -1$, the value for function $f(z) = z^2$ is $(a^2 - b^2) + i(2ab)$. Iteration of this function results in three different behaviors depending on the magnitude, $\sqrt{a^2+b^2}$, of the initial value of z. If the magnitude is less than 1, the magnitude of each z^2 will be smaller than the magnitude of z, so that eventually the iterated values will tend toward 0. The complex point 0 is called an **attractor.** If, however, the magnitude of z_0 is larger than 1, the values computed will continue to grow without bound for those points for which infinity is an attractor. The set of points that converge to a given attractor is called its **domain of attraction.** A number on the boundary between these two domains of attraction—that is, a number with magnitude 1—will always square to another number of magnitude 1. This boundary is the unit circle that is not a fractal. For other complex functions, the boundary between domains of attraction is often a fractal.

If the complex function $f(z) = z^2 + c$—where c is a complex constant—is applied iteratively to 0, the resulting sequence of complex numbers, $S = \{c, c^2 + c, (c^2 + c)^2 + c \ldots\}$, may converge to a point 0, grow larger, or cycle around a given value. The set of complex numbers c for which the sequence S converges to a finite attractor is called the Mandelbrot set (figure 3.7.18). The

FIGURE 3.7.18

A sequence of enlargements of an area of the Mandelbrot set's boundary

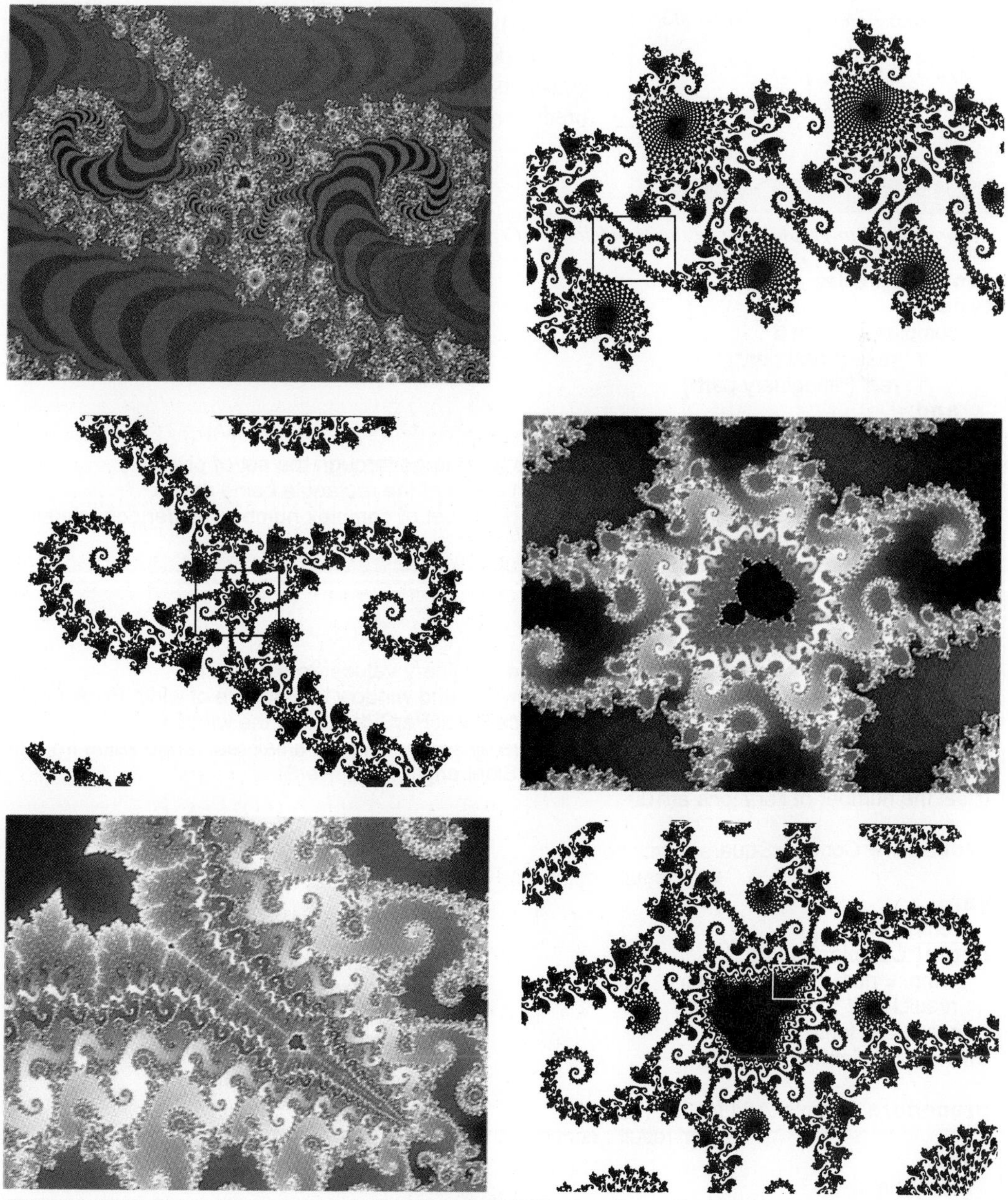

FIGURE 3.7.19

Rectangles bounded by these values contain pictorially exciting areas of the Mandelbrot set's boundary.

Interesting Mandelbrot regions	
real	imaginary
-.76 to -.74	.01 to .03
-1.26 to -1.24	.01 to .03

boundary of the Mandlebrot set is a pictorially interesting fractal curve. Exploration of this boundary under increasing magnification has resulted in some of the most exciting computer graphics ever created (Peitgen and Richter 1986).

Even with a monochrome system, it is possible to produce interesting results by zooming in on parts of the curve. Dewdney (1985) suggests exploring the rectangles with real part between .26 and .27 and imaginary part between 0 and .01. Figure 3.7.19 lists other regions with rich curves. Figure 3.7.20 is a Pascal representation of the program that generates parts of the Mandlebrot set given in Dewdney (1985). Figure 3.7.18 is a sequence of zooms generated by repeated application of that program.

The points plotted in programs such as that given in figure 3.7.20 are initial constants c for which part of the sequence S stays within a given bound for a predetermined number of iterations. The sequence is assumed to converge for

FIGURE 3.7.20

Program used to graph areas of the Mandelbrot set

```
program fractal;
type
   complex = record
      r : real; (* real part*)
      i : real (*imaginary part*)
   end;
var
   ct1, ct2, x, y          : integer;   (* counters used to go through the set of pixels                  *)
   PixelsPerSide           : integer;   (* pixels on a side of the rectangle being drawn                  *)
   BottomLeft, TopLeft : complex;   (* corners of the set of complex numbers under consideration      *)
   SideLength, Scale   : real;
   iterations              : integer;

procedure initialize;

(* set the range of real values from .26 to .27 and imaginary values from 0 to .01                        *)
(* read the number of PixelsPerSide, set the viewport and window to a square of width PixelsPerSide       *)
(* so that points between (1,1) and (PixelsPerSide,PixelsPerSide) are in the window                       *)
(* compute the SideLength of the complex square by subtracting the small real range value from the       *)
(* large real range value, and compute Scale := SideLength/PixelsPerSide                                  *)
(* set the number of iterations at 100                                                                    *)

procedure ComplexSquare (num : complex;
                         var result : complex);
var
   temp : real;
begin(*ComplexSquare *)
   temp := num.r * num.r - num.i * num.i;
   result.i := 2 * num.r * num.i;
   result.r := temp
end; (*ComplexSquare *)

procedure ComplexAdd (c1, c2 : complex;
                      var result : complex);
var
   temp : real;
```

(continued)

FIGURE 3.7.20 continued

```
begin (* ComplexAdd *)
   temp := c1.r + c2.r;
   result.i := c1.i + c2.i;
   result.r := temp
end; (* ComplexAdd *)

function PrintPixel (c1, c2 : real) : boolean;
var
   z, c          : complex;
   count         : integer;
   TestValue     : boolean;
begin (*PrintPixel*)
   c.r := c1;
   c.i := c2;
   z := c;
   count := 0;
   repeat
      count := count + 1;
      ComplexSquare(z, z);
      ComplexAdd(c, z, z);
      TestValue := ((z.r * z.r + z.i * z.i) < 4)
   until (count = iterations) or (NOT TestValue);
   PrintPixel := TestValue
end; (* PrintPixel *)
begin (*fractal*)
   Initialize;
   for ct1 := 1 TO PixelsPerSide do
      for ct2 := 1 TO PixelsPerSide do
         if PrintPixel(ct1 * Scale + BottomLeft.r, ct2 * Scale + BottomLeft.i) then
            PointAbs(ct1, ct2)
end (*fractal*).
```

such points. When you are using this method to plot points in the Mandelbrot set, there is no guarantee that the magnitude of the entries in the sequence S will not remain small for a large number of iterations and then explode. There is also no guarantee that the points you plot actually represent the constants you are looking for. All that can be said is that the fractal curve is contained in the plotted set. For higher iteration numbers, fewer points will have bounded magnitude; thus fewer points will be printed and more detail will be revealed. On large computers 1000 iterations are suggested, but on small computers interesting results have been generated with as few as 30 iterations.

If c is in the Mandlebrot set or on its boundary and $f(z) = z^2 + c$, then for different complex numbers z_0, the values taken by entries in the sequence $S = \{z_0, f(z_0), f(f(z_0)), f(f(f(z_0))), \ldots\}$ can converge to a single point, cycle through a set of points, or grow without bound. The boundaries between domains of attraction are Julia sets. For points c on the interior of the Mandelbrot set, the Julia set, which looks like a wrinkled and squashed circle around one attractor, is a fractal. When the point c is on or near the boundary of the Mandelbrot set, the resulting Julia sets are fractally bound regions surrounding multiple attractors. Figure 3.7.22 gives samples of the sets of z_0 with convergent S for the c value shown.

FIGURE 3.7.21

The top picture shows an enlargement of the area called the valley of the sea horses. This is the area of the Mandelbrot set shown as a rectangle in the bottom picture. Both images were generated using a modified version of the program given in figure 3.7.20.

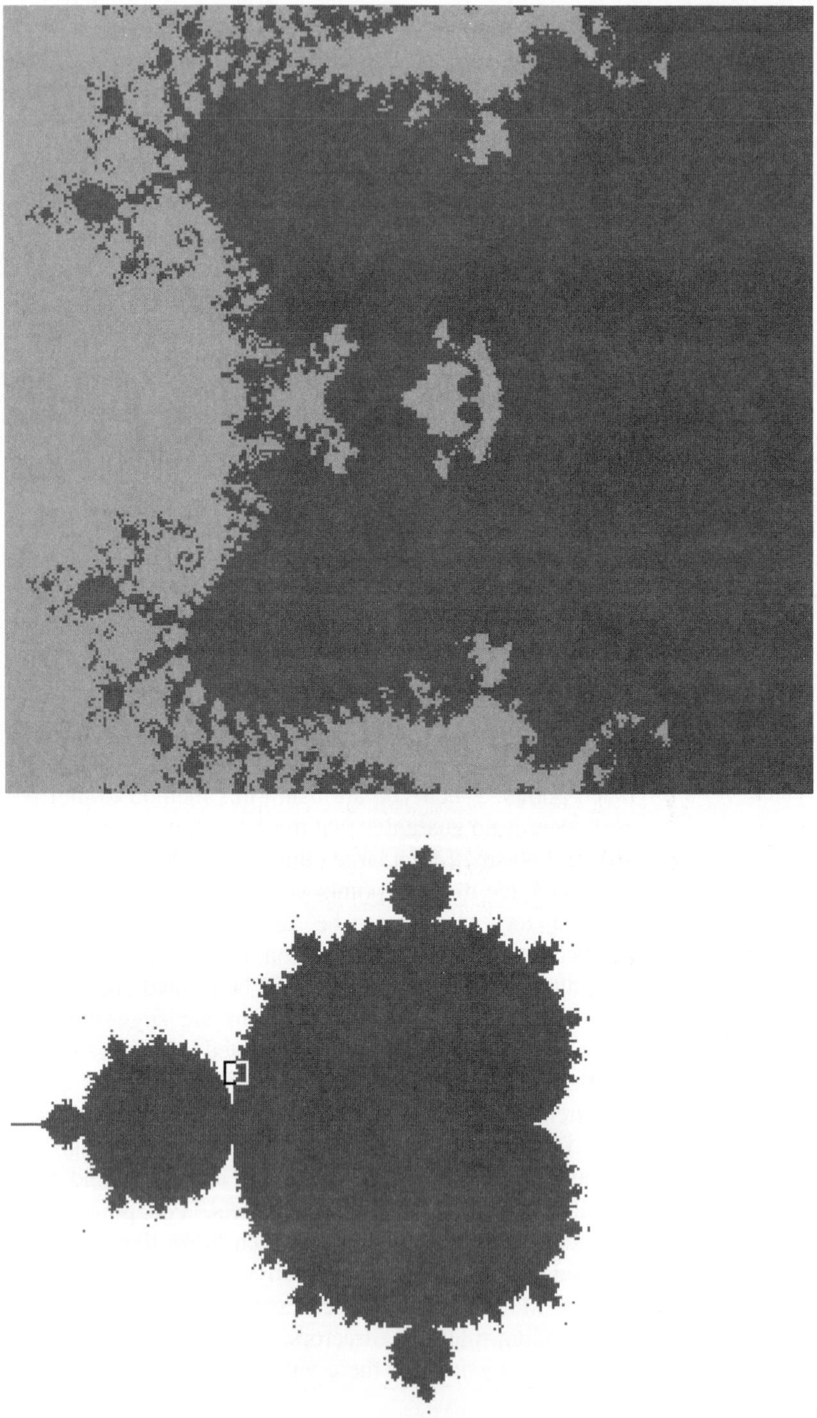

FIGURE 3.7.22

A sampling of the Julia sets and Mandelbrot boundaries and their locations

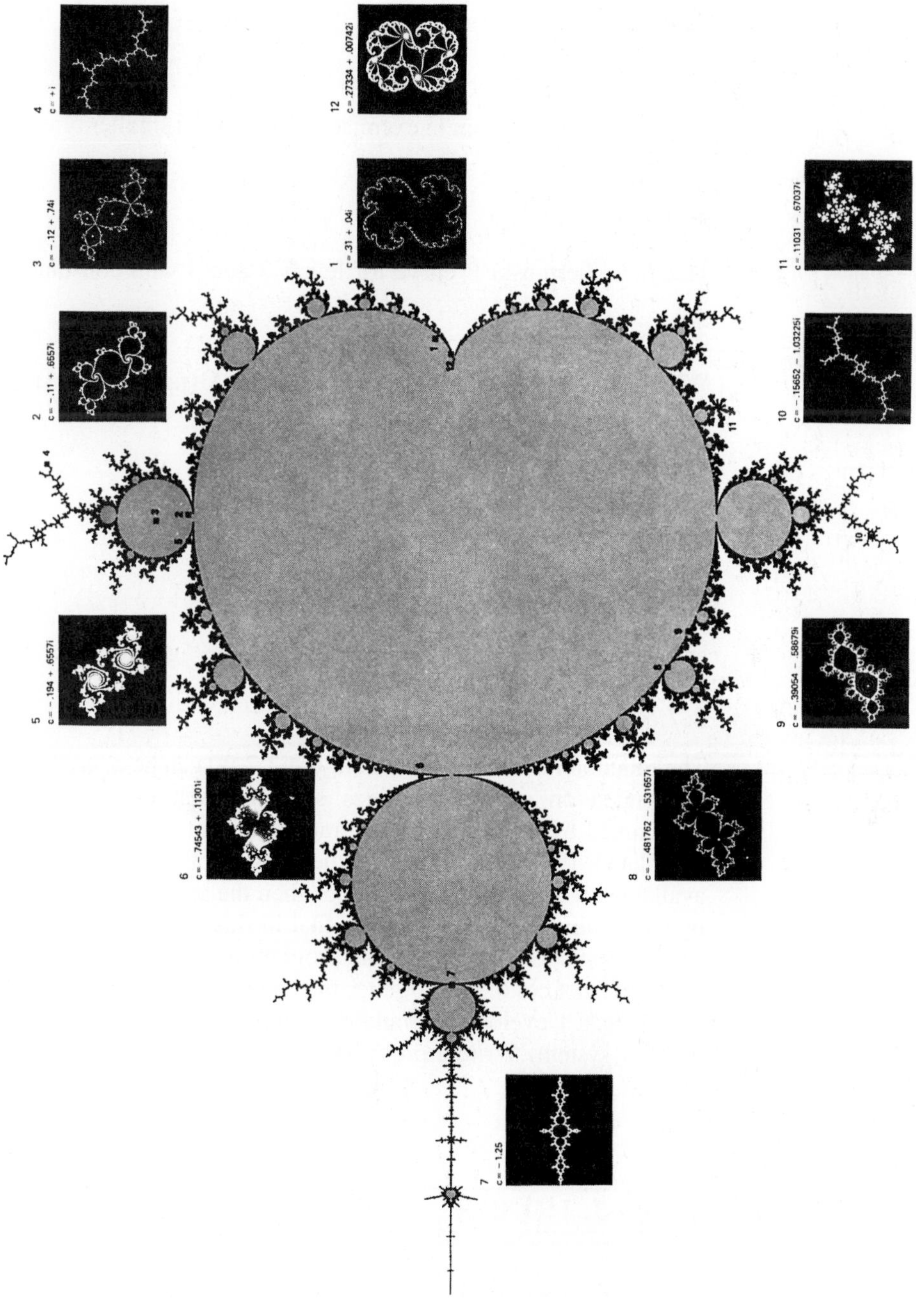

EXERCISES

3.7.1

Write a program on your system to draw the tree shown in figure 3.7.12.

3.7.2

Change the tree program in exercise 3.7.1 to use a smaller branch angle at lower levels.

3.7.3

Trace the Sierpinski B curve for levels 2 and 3 with constant h.

FIGURE 3.7.23

Hilbert's space-filling curve is based on the four curves A, B, C, and D. The level-1 versions of these curves are shown here.

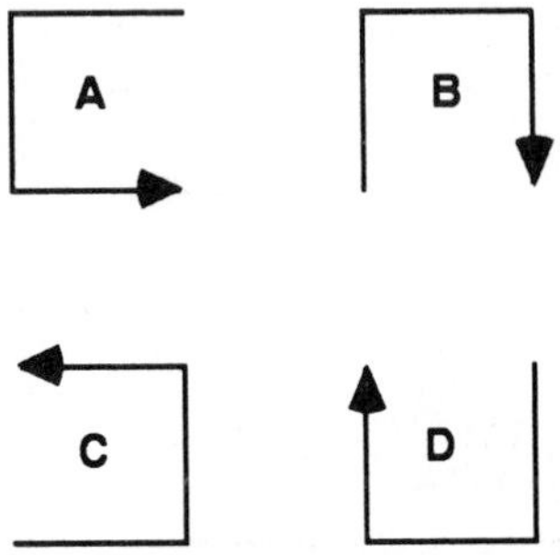

3.7.4

Write a program to draw the Hilbert curve A (figure 3.7.23) if the curves are described by

$$A : D \leftarrow A \downarrow A \rightarrow B ;$$
$$B : C \uparrow B \rightarrow B \downarrow A ;$$
$$C : B \rightarrow C \uparrow C \leftarrow D ;$$
$$D : A \downarrow D \leftarrow D \uparrow C,$$

and the arrows represent lines as given in the figures for the Sierpinski curve.

3.7.5

The function PrintPixel given in figure 3.7.20 can be altered to return a color to be printed on a color graphics system. Each pixel is printed in a color determined by the number of iterations, count, when the repeat-until loop is completed. If the upper limit on the number of iterations is 100 and the colors available are numbered from 0 to 5, then the color returned could be computed by (count **div** 20) **mod** 5. Notice that in this formulation, the points that were originally plotted in black by the program in 3.7.21 are now plotted in color 5. If black is not color 5 but 0, alter the color computation to print the Mandelbrot set in black. Develop a formula for computing colors from count that will work on your system. Write a program to print the Mandlebrot set in color.

BIBLIOGRAPHY

Barnsley, Michael. *Fractals Everywhere,* San Diego: Academic Press, 1988.

Barnsley, Michael, et al. "Harnessing Chaos for Image Synthesis." *Computer Graphics* (SIGGRAPH '88) 22(4): 131–40 (August 1988).

Bresenham, Jack E. ''Ambiguities in Incremental Line Rastering.'' *IEEE CG&A* 7 (5): 31–43 (May 1987).
Discusses reasons erasures cannot be made in reverse direction.

Cyrus, M. and J. Beck ''Generalized Two- and Three Dimensional Clipping,'' *Computers and Graphics* Vol 3 (L) 1978 pp. 23–28.

Demko, Stephen, Laurie Hodges, and Bruce Naylor. ''Construction of Fractal Objects with Iterated Function Systems.'' *Computer Graphics* (SIGGRAPH '85) 19 (3): 271–78 (July 1985).

de Reffye, Philippe, et al. ''Plant Models Faithful to Botanical Structure and Development.'' *Computer Graphics* (SIGGRAPH '88) 22 (4): 151–58.

Dewdney, A. K. ''A Computer Microscope Zooms in for a Look at the Most Complex Object in Mathematics.'' *Scientific American* 253 (2): 16–24 (August 1985).

Dreiling, Leslie. ''Fractal Art: The Power of Computer Graphics Images, an Elegant Abstraction.'' *Computer Graphics World* 9 (7): 91–92 (July 1986).
Mandelbrot images; a simple explanation of Mandelbrot sets.

Kawaguchi, Yoichiro. ''A Morphological Study of the Form of Nature.'' *Computer Graphics* (SIGGRAPH '82) 16 (3): 223–32 (July 1982).
Construction of naturally occurring objects.

Magnenat-Thalmann, N., and D. Thalmann. ''An Indexed Bibliography on Image Synthesis.'' *IEEE CG&A* 7 (8): 27–38 (August 1987).
Bibliography includes work on fractals and antialiasing in animation.

Mandelbrot, B. *The Fractal Geometry of Nature*. New York: W. H. Freeman, 1983.
The classic book on fractals.

Nicholl, Tina, D. T. Lee, and Robin A. Nicholl. ''An Efficient New Algorithm for 2-D Line Clipping: Its Development and Analysis.'' *Computer Graphics* (SIGGRAPH '87): 253–62 (July 1987).
A fast but complicated clipping algorithm that depends on rotations and reflections to reduce the number of zones in which a point may appear; includes uses of viewport boundaries to cut down intersections computed.

Oppenheimer, Peter E. ''Real Time Design and Animation of Fractal Plants and Trees.'' *Computer Graphics* (SIGGRAPH '86) 20 (4): 55–64 (August 1986).
Random factors in generating self-similar objects.

Peitgen, H. O., and P. H. Richter. *The Beauty of Fractals: Images of Complex Dynamical Systems*. Heidelberg, Springer-Verlag: 1986.
Fantastic color photos and excellent explanations of Mandelbrot and related sets.

Pickover, Clifford A. ''Math and Beauty.'' *Computer Graphics World* 10 (7): 143–47 (July 1987).
Pictures generated with bounds on real and imaginary parts of z rather than the magnitude of z.

———. ''Pattern Formation and Chaos in Networks.'' *Comm of the ACM* 31 (2): 136–51 (February 1988).
Gives an application of fractals to network feedback analysis.

Prusinkiewicz, Przemyslaw, and Glen Sandness. ''Koch Curves as Attractors and Repellers.'' *IEEE CG&A* 8 (6): 26–41 (November 1988).

Prusinkiewicz, Przemyslaw, Aristid Lindenmayer, and James Hanan. ''Developmental Models of Herbaceous Plants for Computer Imagery Purposes.'' *Computer Graphics* (SIGGRAPH '88) 22 (4): 144–50 (August 1988).

Smith, Alvy Ray. ''Plants, Fractals, and Formal Languages.'' *Computer Graphics* (SIGGRAPH '84) 18 (3): 1–10 (July 1984).
Defines and uses graftals.

Stevens, Roger T. *Fractal Programming in C*. Redwood City, Calif.: M & T Publishing, 1989.

CHAPTER

4

Bitmap Graphics

DIRECTIONS

Pull-down Menus

Alice, it's your turn to learn word processing!

With these words the high tribunal of management condemned the unwilling office worker to that most fearful fate. In the television ad (figure D.4.1) for a word processor, Alice was dragged from the boardroom directly to a torture chamber to begin her training in a device resembling the electric chair.

Why do the words "it's your turn to learn word processing" strike fear in the hearts of so many? The keyboard on a word processor is, for the most part, the familiar typewriter keyboard, and the CRT screen, when properly used, does not cause great tribulation. Explanations of both devices occupy but a few pages of word processor user manuals.

In the past, however, the manual itself was an obstacle the novice user had to overcome. Finding the menu for a simple operation, such as setting tabs or margins, could be difficult because individual operations were hidden in a hierarchy of menus. Even if the appropriate menu item could be seen on the screen, the keys used to move among the choices often differed from menu to menu. With impediments like these, is it any wonder that the average office worker dreaded that infamous sentence?

In most cases, the source of the problem was not the user, but the creators of the software, who would defend their work saying, "You have to make accommodations for the computer." The developers were actually paraphrasing A. Chapanis, who once stated:

"It is easy to make things hard.
It is hard to make things easy."

Increasing competition in the software market brought about a change of attitude in the software industry as developers began writing **user-friendly** programs. Much time has been spent investigating every aspect of the **user interface** to discover ways to make programs easier to use. The overriding principle behind user-friendly program development seemed to be "Learning to use a computer system is like learning to use a parachute - if a person fails on the first try, odds are he won't try again."
(Computer Graphics Consultants, 1984.)

Faced with a dictionary-size manual, the first-time user might have preferred parachute jumping to learning a new system. When Apple first introduced its Macintosh computer, one of its television ads compared the stack of manuals accompanying "the other computer" to the Macintosh's single, thin manual. One way the Macintosh overcame the extensive manual problem was by eliminating menu hierarchies. Using a mouse, the user simply points to an entry in a **pull-down menu.** All menus are accessed by exactly the same technique, and there are no lengthy lists of control characters for the novice to learn.

Microsoft Windows now provides a similar environment for IBM-compatible PCs. Pull-down menus in these systems have their titles listed in a **menu bar,** and all menus are accessed in the same way. The user points to the title, causing the menu to be displayed in full, and then points to the desired entry in the menu in order to make a selection.

The display and use of pull-down menus are applications of a relatively new form of computer graphics, **bitmap graphics.**

FIGURE D.4.1

Example of a pull-down menu in a workstation word processor

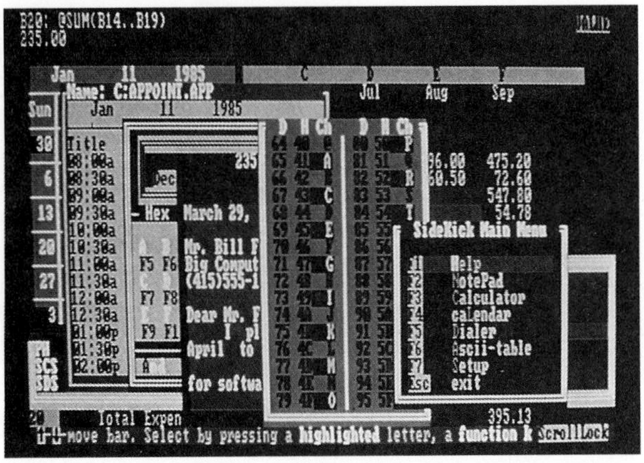

4.1 Introduction to Bitmap Graphics

The algorithms in the last chapter displayed representations of graphic objects such as lines and polygons. These objects have an abstract existence outside of their screen images. For example, the line from the point (1,2) to the point (3,5) may be moved to any window on the screen and appears to have different lengths depending on the world coordinates of that window. If the image on the screen is simply a pattern of pixels, such as a scanned image, it is difficult to manipulate. In some cases it is possible to decompose pixel patterns into geometric pieces, each of which may be described by an algorithm similar to those discussed in chapter 3. These pieces may then be manipulated by using the techniques given in chapter 3. Images that are too complicated to decompose must be manipulated as sets of pixels. This manipulation of sets of pixels is called bitmap graphics.

During the mid 1970s, researchers at Xerox PARC (Palo Alto Research Center) were experimenting with different ways to copy regions of a graphics screen, either to other regions of the screen or into parts of the main memory (other than those used to store the image on the screen). In 1975, Dan Ingalls and Diana Merry developed an operator that could copy one row (string of bits) to various places in memory. An outer loop was added to this operator so that more than one row could be moved at a time. This resulted in the transfer of a matrix-like rectangular region by a function named **Bitblt (Bit-boundary Block transfer).** While Bitblt is not the only function used on bitmaps (Guibas and Stolfi 1982; Kornfield 1987), it is the most important such function.

Figure 4.1.1 shows the coordinate system used for bitmap graphics that reflects the matrix-like structures manipulated by Bitblt. The coordinates of x and y are both zero at the upper-left corner of the diagram, and they reach their maximum at the lower-right corner of the diagram. The standard unit moved by Bitblt is the **rectangle.** The upper-left corner of such a rectangle is called the **origin,** and the lower-right corner is called the **corner.**

The type **Point** is defined by

FIGURE 4.1.1

The coordinate system used for bitmap graphics has its origin in the upper-left corner. Bitmaps describe rectangular regions; the upper-left corner is called the origin, and the lower-right corner is called the corner.

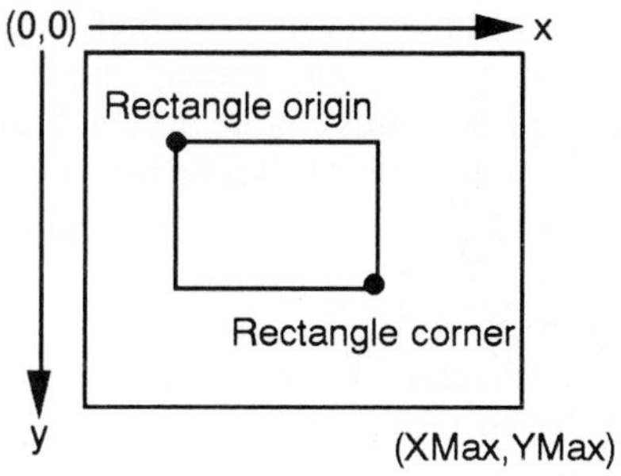

Point = **record**
  X : integer;
  Y : integer
end;

The type **Rectangle** is defined by

Rectangle = **record**
  Origin : Point;
  Corner : Point
end;

Because a bitmap has a matrix-like structure, it would seem reasonable to assume that a bitmap is a matrix. This structure would be too restrictive, however, especially if one is trying to manipulate data in the frame buffer. Most compilers will not allow the frame buffer to be assigned a variable name and structure. In Pascal and other languages that require strict typing, matrix representation would require that each size of bitmap be a different type. These problems may be overcome by representing bitmaps as an extended pointer type. This representation contains fields for the address of the data as well as fields that tell Bitblt the structure of the rectangle for the type **BitMap.**

BitMap = **record**
  Base : WordAdd;
  Width : integer;
  Rect : Rectangle
end;

FIGURE 4.1.2

The parts of a bitmap and the storage of a bitmap in memory

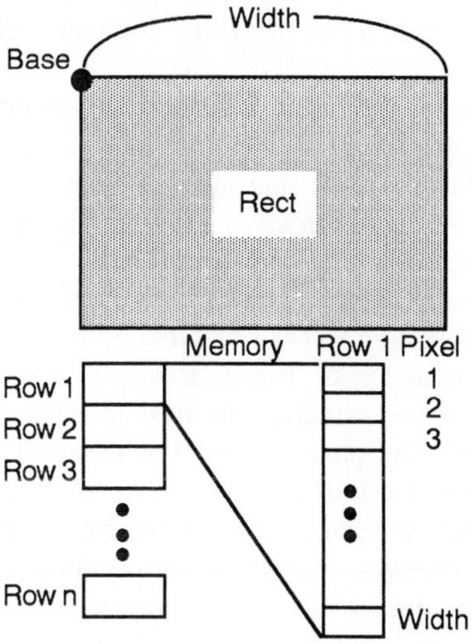

The Base is the address of the memory location that holds the origin. This address is usually stored in two parts; the first is the offset from the beginning of the memory page on which the bitmap is stored, and the second is the page address (figure 4.1.2). The type **WordAdd** is typically an **array**[1..2] **of** integer.

Bitmaps, like arrays, are normally stored in row-normal form—that is, pixels that are adjacent in the same row are stored in successive memory locations. This approach works well in bitmap graphics because the raster refresh is row oriented. The linear nature of memory makes it necessary to know the row length when computing the address of a matrix element. The speed of the Bitblt operator can normally be increased by using the largest memory unit possible. The operators used to implement Bitblt determine which memory unit is chosen. Width is usually measured in bytes or words. The width of a self-contained bitmap may be computed from the coordinates of the bitmap rectangle's corners by the formula

$$Width = (corner.x - origin.x + (PixelsPerUnit - 1)) \textbf{ div } PixelsPerUnit$$

PixelsPerUnit is the number of pixels per memory unit. The term (PixelsPerUnit − 1) in the formula for width is used to round up to the next full unit. The number of pixels per unit of memory is very machine dependent. The Apple II system uses the byte as its memory unit because it has byte-oriented

FIGURE 4.1.3

When a bitmap represents part of a larger bitmap, such as the screen, its width is the width of the larger bitmap. This is because the rows of the smaller bitmap are contained in the rows of the larger bitmap and do not occupy contiguous memory locations.

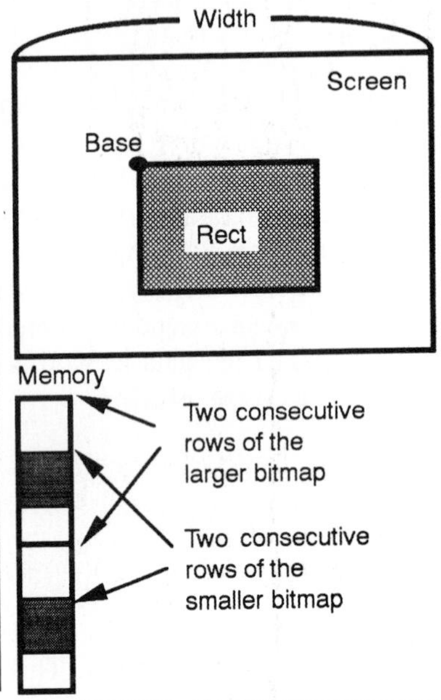

FIGURE 4.1.4

The address of a pixel is computed as an offset from the address at the beginning of the row.

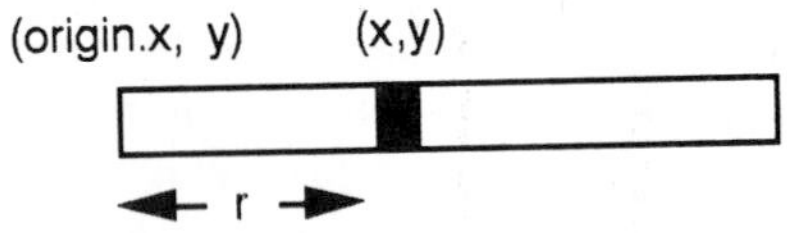

machine operations. Only bits per byte are used to represent pixels because the last bit of each byte is used to indicate color. Turbo Pascal has fast word-oriented operations on the IBM. This makes it possible to implement BitBlt to move 16 bits efficiently. In black-and-white graphics this means there are 16 pixels per unit. Storage methods for color boards on the same machine differ dramatically from manufacturer to manufacturer (Defanti, Frankel, and Leske 1987).

The width is computed separately because a bitmap may represent a part of a larger bitmap. In this case, the width would be the width of the larger map. If, for example, the width of the screen is 40 words, any bitmap used to represent part of the screen would have a width of 40 words (figure 4.1.3). This type of bitmap would have its rectangle determined by the larger bitmap to maintain the correct relationship between the coordinate system and the memory addressing.

Computing the address of an individual pixel, (x,y), is a relatively easy process once the address, a, of the memory unit holding the first pixel in a row is known. First compute the number of bits from the origin to x : $r = x - origin.x + 1$ (figure 4.1.4). The memory unit address for the bit is then

$$UnitAddress = a + (r \textbf{ div } PixelsPerUnit)$$

Because each row of a bitmap begins on a unit boundary, the bit address is independent of the row value and can be computed by

$$BitAddress = r \textbf{ mod } PixelsPerUnit$$

Computing the row address for (x,y) is often a difficult problem. When you are dealing with normal memory, the computation is relatively straightforward. First compute the row number with

$$RowNumber = y - origin.y + 1$$

The row address is just $(RowNumber - 1) * Width + BaseAddress$, where *BaseAddress* is the address of the first unit in the bitmap. The variables in memory used to store black-and-white bitmaps normally fit on one page of memory. If the variable does extend over more than one page, the computation will be very system dependent.

Computing the row address of a point (x,y) in the frame buffer is often more complicated. Microcomputers such as the Apple II and IBM PC use interleaving in the buffer to reduce screen flicker. In systems that use interleaving, consecutive rows on the screen are not stored in consecutive memory blocks. Row addresses for these machines should be calculated and stored in an array subscripted on y. Some samples of the formulas used are given in figure 4.1.5. Problems in obtaining these formulas and other addressing problems with color boards are discussed in (Defanti, Frankel, and Leske 1987). Because of the difficulties involved in getting addresses for the screen, it is best to have a predefined bitmap, Display, for the screen. The page part of the base of a bitmap is used to determine location of the frame buffer.

Obtaining the base address for a variable is system dependent, but most programming languages provide an address function that returns the address of a variable. Screen addresses must be found in the system documentation, or, as

FIGURE 4.1.5

Samples of screen address formulas used by graphics systems

ScreenAddress[y]

IBM — CGA
8192* (y mod 2) + ((y **div** 2)*80)

IBM - Hercules card
8192 + (y **mod** 4)) + (90* (y **div** 4))

Apple II/III Turtlegraphics (screen 1)

8192 + 128* ((y **mod** 64) div 8) + 40* (y **div** 64) +
1024* (y **mod** 8)

in the case of the Macintosh, the system must be told which block of memory will appear on the screen.

Finally, the rectangle *Rect* in the definition of Bitmap defines the coordinate system that you wish to use on the given bitmap. In the predefined bitmap Display, the origin is (0,0) and the corner is (XMax,YMax). Coordinate systems for other bitmaps may have any coordinates for the origin and the corner, as long as both coordinates of the corner are larger than the corresponding coordinates of the origin.

We will implement the procedure Bitblt in the following form:

```
procedure Bitblt(SourceMap,DestinationMap:Bitmap;
   Destination : Point;
   SourceRec   : Rectangle;
   Code        : OpCode);
```

Bitblt alters the DestinationMap by applying the operation given by Code on paired bits from the SourceMap and the DestinationMap. The SourceRec determines the region of the SourceMap that will be used. Destination gives the location in the DestinationMap that is synchronized with the origin of the SourceRec for the operation. Figure 4.1.6 illustrates the other parameters with the exception of Code. Many implementations of Bitblt use a source point and a destination rectangle. These implementations are very similar to the one presented here. Often a texture parameter is also added; this will be done as an exercise in section 4.2.

We will also employ a commonly used subset of the possible codes that we will store as the scalars

OpCode = (**cXor, cOr, cAnd, cLr, cStore**)

FIGURE 4.1.6

An illustration of Bitbit using the **xor** *code*

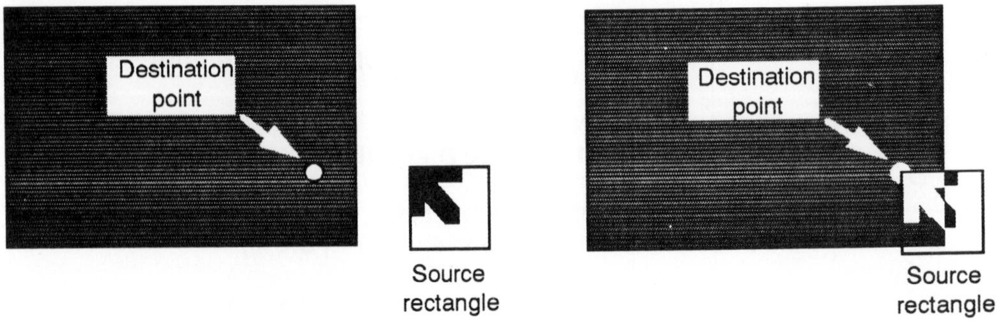

Each of these codes except cLr is the name of an operation. The letter *c* is added to the front to avoid conflict with predefined language operations. Thus cStore stores data. Some of the other operations are more complicated. In figure 4.1.7 the number 1 represents a bit that is on, and the number 0 represents a bit that is off. For those familiar with logical operators, 1 also represents true while 0 represents false. The operation cLr is clear. It is implemented by negating the bitmap and then **and**ing the bitmap. In figure 4.1.7, the numbers along the left side represent the bit values for the source, the numbers at the top represent the original values of the destination bit, and the numbers inside the diagram represent the values in the destination bit after the operation is complete.

FIGURE 4.1.7

A summary of the opcodes used in Bitbit

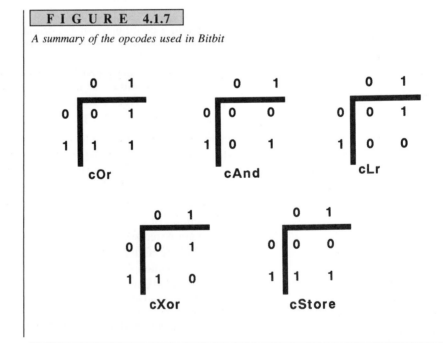

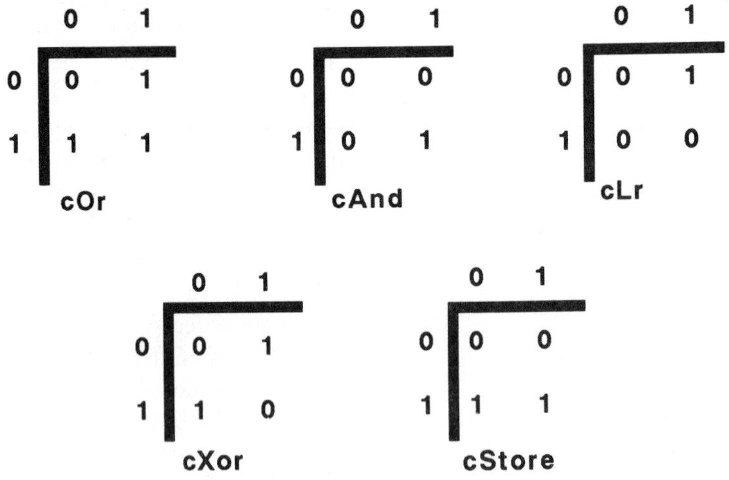

EXERCISES

4.1.1

Does your graphics system have a procedure or procedures for manipulating blocks of pixels?

4.1.2

What operations do these functions implement?

4.1.3

What coordinate system do these funtions use?

4.1.4

How will you specify rectangles on your system?

4.1.5

Is there a special bitmap which represents the screen, or do you have one set of procedures which map to the screen and another which map from the screen to memory?

4.1.6

Can you specify a block of memory as a frame buffer?

4.2 Implementation of the Procedure Bitblt

The procedure Bitblt is designed to apply an operator on pairs of corresponding bits in two bitmaps and to store the results in the destination bitmap. Pairing of the bits is accomplished by superimposing a copy of the source rectangle on the destination bitmap so that the origin of this rectangle corresponds to the destination point. Each bit in the source rectangle is paired with its counterpart in the superimposed rectangle. Rows of the source rectangle begin on the same bit of a word and end on the same bit of a word. The rows of the image of the source rectangle also begin and end on the same bit of a word, but these bits will probably not be the same bits that the source rectangle begins and ends on.

Figure 4.2.1 shows that the rows of the source rectangle and its image may even intersect a different number of words. If the source rectangle is too large to be superimposed on the destination bitmap at the destination point, the source rectangle is clipped to get the largest rectangle that will fit. Once the pairing is established, the operations on successive rows are very similar. The major responsibility of Bitblt is to compute the appropriate starting address of each row. Actual row operations are given to another procedure, **Rowblt.**

Implementation of the procedure Rowblt on commercial graphics systems is very machine dependent. Because this procedure often moves thousands of bits, the importance of highly refined code cannot be overemphasized. Different uses

FIGURE 4.2.1

The rows of the image of the source rectangle begin and end on the same bit of a word, but these bits will probably not be the same bits that the source rectangle begins and ends on.

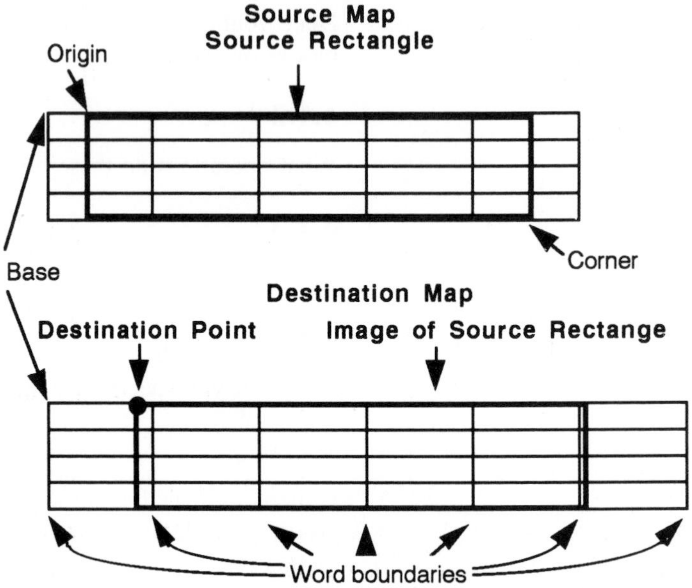

for Bitblt may be made more efficient if Rowblt is altered for a specific purpose. Some systems actually compile Rowblt on the run to ensure top-quality code for a specific application. Our implementation of Bitblt, based on that found in (Pike and Ingalls 1984), will stress general considerations over the efficiency of a specific implementation.

The efficiency of Rowblt can be improved even if machine considerations are ignored. If Rowblt operates on individual bits, the operation must be repeated thousands of times. If it operates on larger memory units, the number of operations is reduced by a factor corresponding to the size of the memory unit. Employing these larger units is often the single most important improvement that can be made. Examples of such operations are Pascal's Boolean operators. While these operators work on a variable that stores its value in one bit of a word, the operators actually are applied to each bit in the affected word.

Improvements gained by operating on more than one bit at a time are tempered by alignment problems. Suppose, for example, that we have two, one-word bitstrings that are to have the operation **and** applied to them. Assume that the source rectangle starts on the sixth bit of a 16-bit word and ends at bit 12 of the same word. Also assume that the destination point is on the fourth bit of a word (figure 4.2.2). Before we can apply **and** to the pair, the bits must be aligned so that the bit at the origin of the source rectangle is **and**ed with the bit at the destination point.

Rowblt should leave the source unchanged, so a copy of the source is made. Once a copy of the word has been made, a shift operation may be applied to move the bits in the copy so that they occupy bits 4 through 10 (figure 4.2.3).

FIGURE 4.2.2

When the bit addresses of the source origin and the destination point are not the same, a copy of the source is made with the origin shifted. The bit address of the origin of the copy is then the same as the bit address of the destination point.

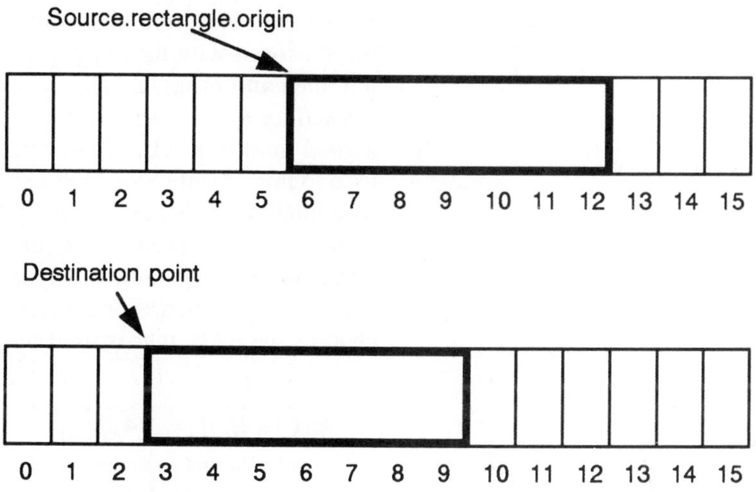

FIGURE 4.2.3

A copy of the source shifted 2 bits to the left is created so the original source is not altered directly by Bitbit.

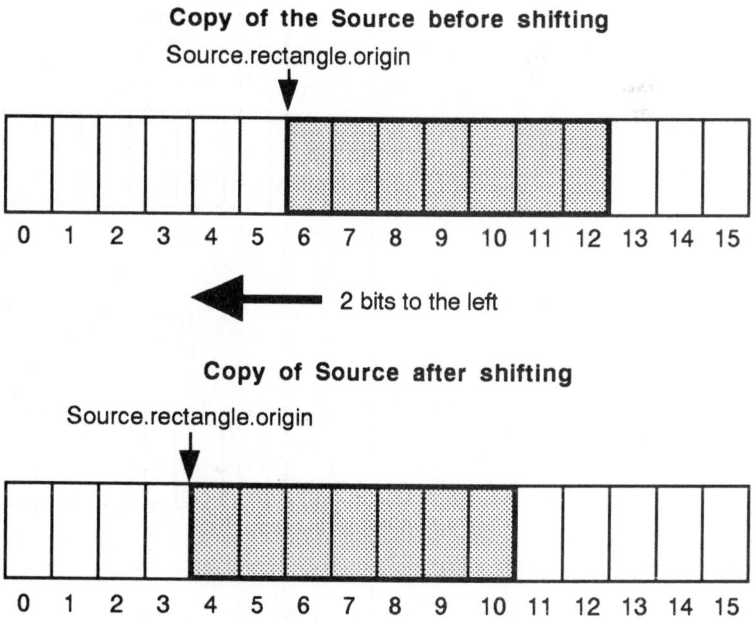

If **and** is now applied, the source rectangle's origin will match its destination point. Notice that if **and** is applied at this point, bits that precede and follow the image of the source rectangle are altered. Bitblt, whence Rowblt, should affect a string that is at most the width in bits of the source rectangle.

To protect those bits of the destination map that should not be affected by this application, you apply Rowblt **masks** to the copy. These masks ensure that Rowblt will leave the bits unaltered. In the example, the mask given in figure 4.2.4 is **or**ed with the copy of the source after it has been shifted 2 bits to the left; then **and** is applied (figure 4.2.5). The mask created here would also have worked for the cLr operation, which is actually an **and.** It would not have been a good mask for cOr, cXor, or cStore. Straightforward assignment cannot be used to implement cStore because the masks would be stored in the destination. You implement cStore by **xor**ing the source and destination, **and**ing this result with the mask if needed, and then **xor**ing this result with the destination. The mask for these operations (figure 4.2.6) is **and**ed with the copy before the operation is applied. For efficiency, the masks are stored in arrays, and Bitblt chooses the mask that is used by Rowblt.

FIGURE 4.2.4

The operation **and** *is performed on the copy of the source and destination. To avoid altering parts of the destination outside the source rectangle, all bits of the source outside the rectangle are set to 1. This is done by creating a mask and applying it to the shifted copy of the source.*

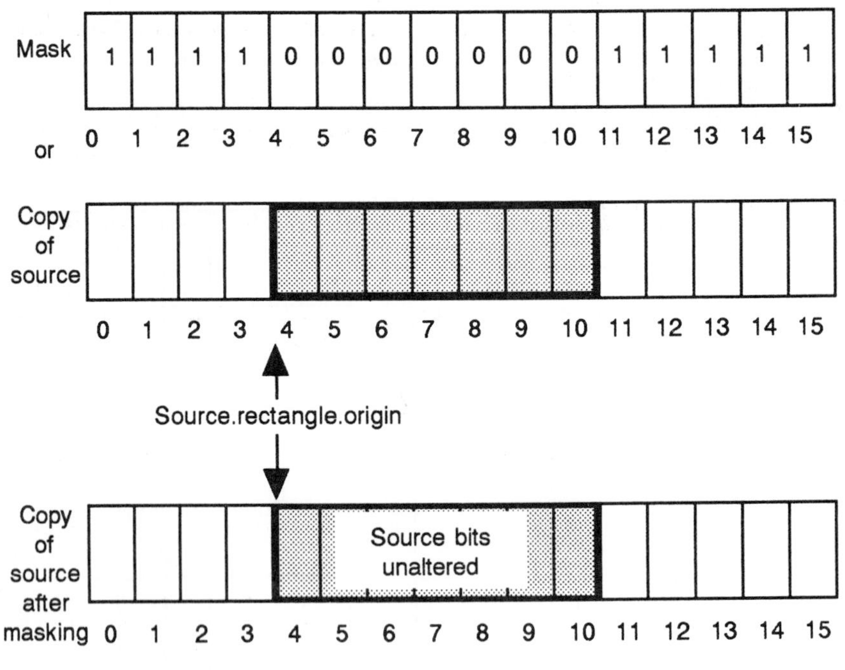

FIGURE 4.2.5

The Bitbit operation **and** *with actual values substituted*

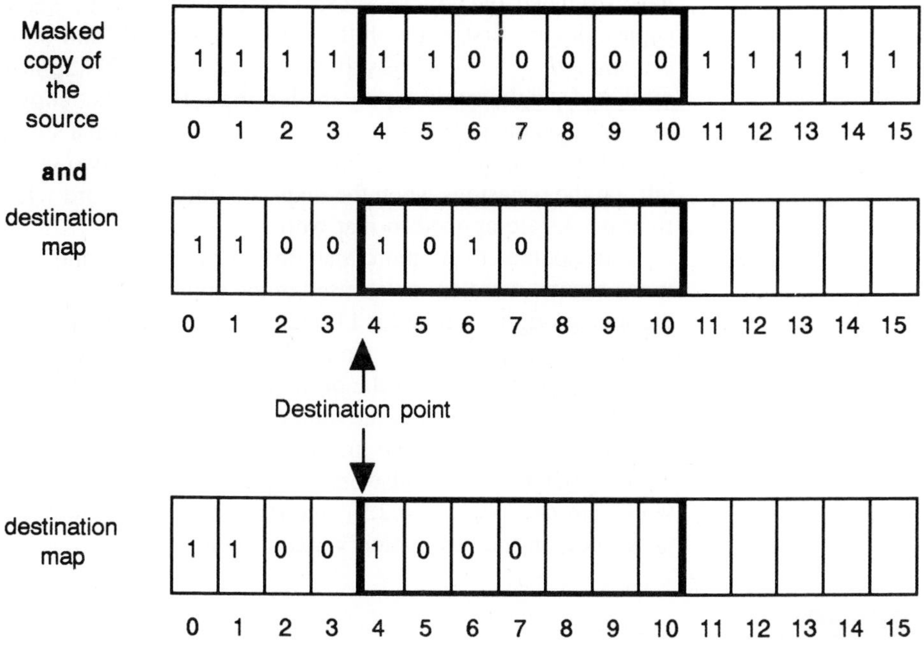

FIGURE 4.2.6

When the Bitbit operation is **or,** *a mask of zeros is used to protect values outside the source rectangle. To get the zeros and maintain source values inside the source rectangle, a mask with zeros outside the rectangle and one's inside the rectangle is anded with the shifted copy of the source.*

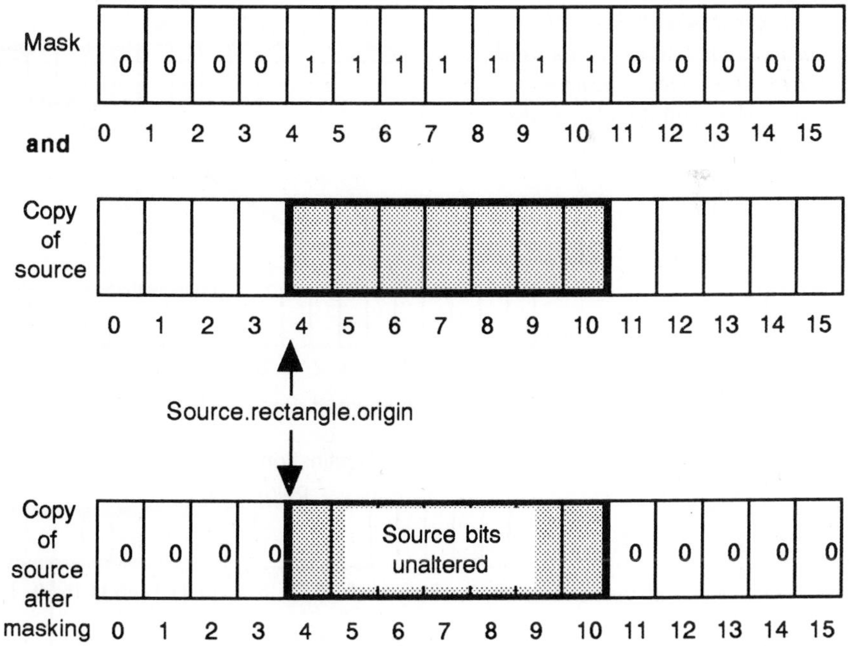

Even if you ignore clipping problems, this version of Rowblt will only suffice if all of your bitmaps are one word or less in width. If, in the example, the destination point had been at bit 12 of the word, and if there had been a second word in the row of the destination, then the set of bits altered by Rowblt would have extended over two words. This problem can be solved by making two copies. In the first copy shift 6 bits to the right, and shift the second copy (*wordlength* − 6) = 10 bits to the left (figure 4.2.7). Split the mask into a left mask and a right mask. Apply the left mask to the first copy; then use this copy to operate on the first word in the destination. Perform a similar operation on the second copy (figure 4.2.8). Notice that if you create two sets of masks, right and left, on the occasions when the maps are only one word wide, both the left and right masks are applied to that word.

If the source covers more than one word, there is another problem. The bits in the second word are never used in the computation. In the example, suppose the source origin were at bit 11 and the destination point at bit 12. You process the first word of the source simply by shifting a copy of it 1 bit to the right and operating on the pair after the mask has been applied. The second word has bits from both the first word of the source and the second word of the source. A copy of each word is made. The first word is shifted (*wordlength* − 1) = 15 bits to the left, while the second word's copy is shifted 1 bit to the right. These two words are **or**ed (figure 4.2.9), the right mask is applied, and the operation is performed on the destination's second word.

FIGURE 4.2.7

In cases where the shifted image of the source extends over word boundaries, the bits moved beyond the word boundary are put into a second word. These bits are shifted a distance (wordlength − shift distance) *in the opposite direction.*

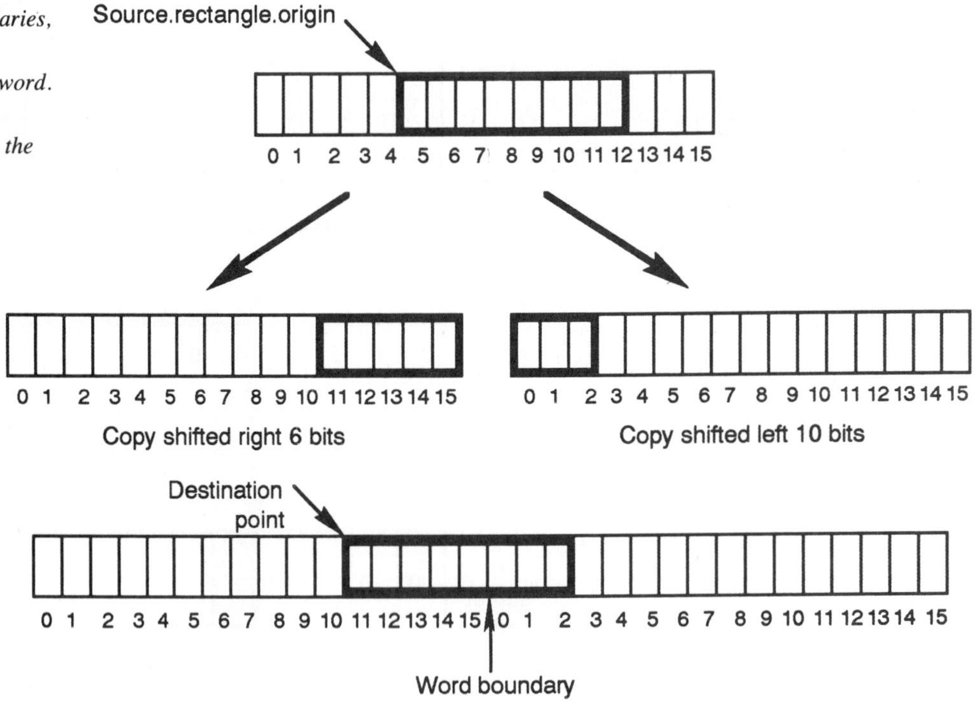

For bit strings that cover more than two words, the previous operation is repeated with the masks applied to only the first and last words. If the shift had been to the left, the second word would have been used in the computation of the first word, and the last word would have been used by itself. It is possible for the number of words per row of the source and destination to be different. Figure 4.2.10 is a chart of the possibilities.

Shifts never move the left edge of the row outside of its word, so some of the combinations cannot occur in our procedures. In the shift right, if the source row is shorter than the destination, you obtain the last word of the destination without using the word following the source. In the case where the number of words in the source row is larger than the number of words in the destination

FIGURE 4.2.8

When the source extends over more than one word, two masks are needed. One mask is used on the leftmost word and the other is used on the rightmost word.

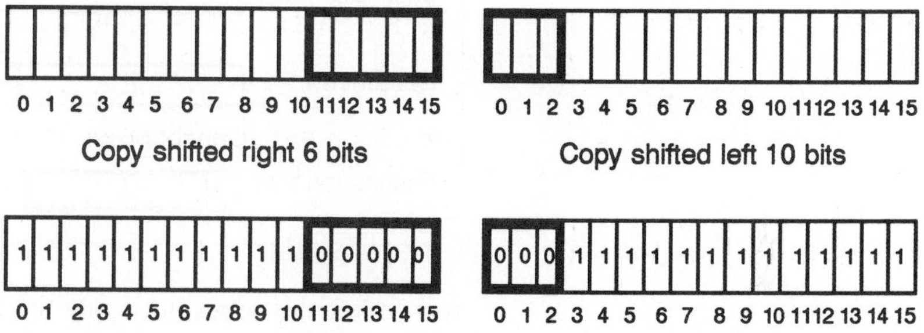

FIGURE 4.2.9

If the source covers more than one word, to create the right-shifted source the right word is shifted right and a copy of the left word is shifted left. The two words are combined by using **or.** *This result is masked before the final operation takes place.*

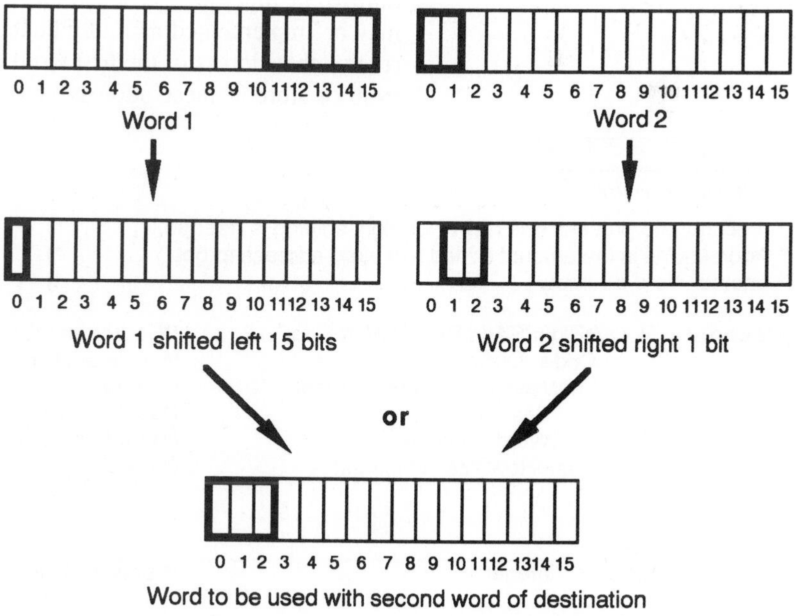

FIGURE 4.2.10

A list of all possible shifts shows that some cannot occur; therefore, Bitbit does not have to account for them.

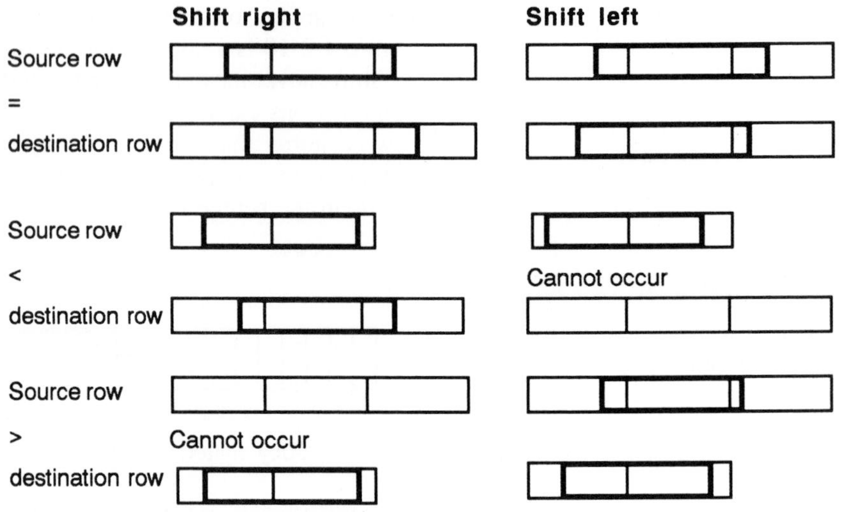

row, a left shift does not apply the left shift on the last word. In all cases, the loop size is determined by the number of words in the destination row. The differences between the tasks performed for a left shift and a right shift suggest that the procedure Rowblt be implemented as two separate procedures, **RowbltRight** and **RowbltLeft.**

The final version of RowbltRight (figure 4.2.11) uses the ShiftLeft and ShiftRight functions. Often found in new versions of Pascal, these functions may be implemented as multiplications or **div**s by powers of 2. Both Rowblts receive the address of the first word of the source and destination row. To copy from or store at these addresses, you use the ^ notation reserved for pointers.

FIGURE 4.2.11

RowbltRight procedure

```
(* procedure to process one row when right shifting is needed.       *)
(* AddressUnit is the amount added to a word address to get          *)
(* another word address.                                             *)

procedure RowbltRight(SAdd,DAdd : WordAdd;     (*Source and Destination row addresses  *)
                      Code : OpCode;           (* code applied                         *)
                      LeftMask,RightMask : integer;  (* Masks                          *)
                      ShiftBits : integer;     (* alignment shift                      *)
                      RowWords : integer;      (* words in a row                       *)
                      SameRowSize : boolean);  (* rows same length                     *)

var
  WordNo : integer;                            (* loop counter                         *)
  temp,temp1,temp2 : integer;                  (* used to hold the source during processing *)

begin (*RowbltRight *)
```

```
for WordNo := 1 to RowWords do
  begin
    if WordNo = 1 then                                   (* mask the left side              *)
       begin
          temp1 := SAdd^;                                (* get data stored at SAdd         *)
          temp1  := ShiftRight(temp1,ShiftBits);         (* align source and                *)
          (* destination *)
          if Code = cLr then                             (* must take complement of temp1   *)
             temp1 := not temp1;
          if Code in [cOr,cXor] then
             temp := temp1 and LeftMask
          else if Code in [cAnd,cLr] then
             temp := temp1 or LeftMask
          else
             temp := temp1;                              (* masking done later in cStore    *)
       end
    else
       begin
          (* take care of overflow into second word *)
          temp1 := SAdd^;                                (* get data stored at SAdd         *)
          temp := ShiftLeft(temp1,WordLength - ShiftBits);
          if SameRowSize or (WordNo <> RowWords) then(*get bits for next word           *)
             begin
               SAdd := SAdd + AddressUnit;               (* update source address to next word *)
               temp2 := SAdd^;
               temp2  := ShiftRight(temp2,ShiftBits);    (* align rows                      *)
             end;
          temp := temp1 or temp2;
          if Code = cLr then                             (*must take complement             *)
             temp := not temp;
       end;
    if WordNo = RowWords then                            (* mask the right side             *)
       if Code in [cOr,cXor] then
          temp := temp and RightMask
       else if Code in [cAnd,cLr] then
          temp := temp or RightMask
       else
          temp := temp;                                  (* masking done later in cStore    *)
       (* temp is aligned and masked, operate on temp and the DAdd *)
       case Code of
          cXor       : DAdd^ := DAdd^ xor temp;
          cOr        : DAdd^ := DAdd^  or temp;
          cAnd,cLr   : DAdd^ := DAdd^ and temp;
          cStore     :  begin
                            temp := DAdd^ xor temp;
                            if WordNo = 1 then
                               temp := temp and  LeftMask;
                            if  WordNo = RowWords then
                               temp := temp and  RightMask;
                            DAdd^ := DAdd^ xor temp
                         end
          otherwise;
       end; (* end case *)
       DAdd := DAdd + AddressUnit                        (* get next destination word       *)
    end                                                  (* end of for loop                 *)
end; (* RowbitRight *)
```

FIGURE 4.2.12

Some of the Pascal functions available for accessing memory locations

```
IBM Turbo Pascal

Add^ ⇔ MemW(Add[2],Add[1])

Macintosh LightSpeed Pascal
Addresses are long integer
var
Add : longint;
  Location : ^ integer;

Location := @Add;
Add^ ⇔ Location^
```

FIGURE 4.2.13

Bitblt clips the source rectangle by comparing it with the rect of the source bitmap. After the source rectangle is reduced to fit in this rectangle, the image of the reduced rectangle is compared with the rectangle of the destination bitmap. If this rectangle extends beyond the boundaries of the destination bitmap when it is placed at the destination point, the source rectangle is reduced again.

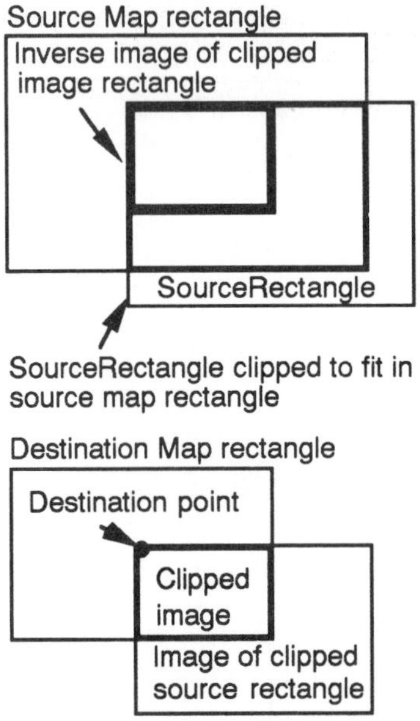

This operation is very system dependent, and implementations for some common versions of Pascal are given in figure 4.2.12. Finally, the arithmetic **and, or, xor,** and **not** found on many new versions of Pascal are used to perform the operations of the Rowblts.

All of the rows of a bitmap have exactly the same starting position with respect to word boundaries, so Bitblt may compute the shift distance as well as its direction. The masks are also fixed for all rows, so Bitblt may choose these masks once and pass them to Rowblt. The number of words in the source and destination rows are also computed by Bitblt. Three other operations are performed by Bitblt: clipping the source rectangle to ensure that the image will fit in the destination bitmap, choosing the order in which the rows will be processed, and computing the beginning address for each row of the source and the destination.

Clipping is as important in bitmap graphics as it is in the simple graphics package developed in chapter 3. If the source rectangle does not fit in the destination bitmap when it is transposed to the destination point, a clipping procedure reduces the size of the source rectangle so that the image will fit in the destination map (figure 4.2.13).

When the source and destination bitmap are the same map, it is possible for the source rectangle and destination rectangle to overlap (figure 4.2.14). In figure 4.2.14, if the first row were processed first, a later row in the source would then be altered before it was used. To avoid this problem, if the y-coordinate of the destination point is larger than the y-coordinate of the source rectangle corner, rows are processed from the bottom up.

FIGURE 4.2.14

If the source and destination maps overlap, care must be taken to perform the row-by-row operations in such a way that a row is not altered before it is applied.

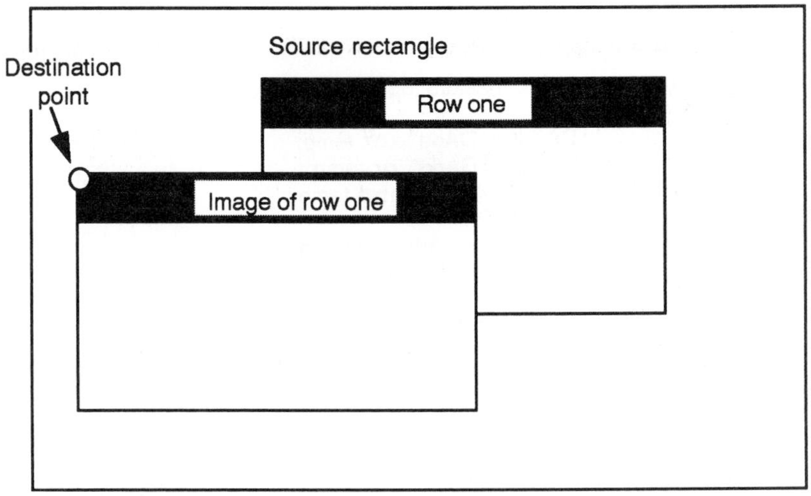

The beginning address of each row of a bitmap is difficult to compute. The process is made more complicated because the order in which rows are processed is determined at runtime. In the case of a bitmap that represents data stored in program memory, the width of the map is either added to or subtracted from the previous bitmap address (figure 4.2.15). Paging must also be taken into account in some systems. In the case of the screen buffer, the y-coordinate of the row is updated and then the address is located in a table. Multiple-page screen buffers must have both parts of the address stored in the lookup array.

The procedure Bitblt is given in figure 4.2.16.

Bitblt-like functions are available with some widely available graphics packages. Figure 4.2.17 gives examples of such functions included in two common packages.

FIGURE 4.2.15

Procedures used to calculate addresses for Bitblt

```
procedure SetAddress(var NewAdd : WordAdd;        (* the new address                 *)
                     Map : BitMap;
                     P : Point);                  (* beginning of first line processed *)
var
  Dist : integer;                                 (* distance from edge of map to P  *)
begin
    (* Find first row in map which is used*)
    if Map.Base[2] = Screen then
      NewAdd[1] := ScreenAdd[P.Y]
    else
      NewAdd[1] := Map.Base[1] + (P.Y - Map.Rect.Origin.Y) * Map.Width;
    (* Find offset in x direction *)
    Dist := (P.X - Map.Rect.Origin.X) div PixelsPerWord;
    NewAdd[1] := NewAdd[1] + Dist;
    NewAdd[2] := Map.Base[2]
end;(* SetAddress*)

procedure IncrAddress(var Addr: WordAdd;          (* address to increment            *)
                      Map : Bitmap;               (* map containing row              *)
                      WordOffset : integer;       (* words from edge                 *)
                      var Y : integer;            (* screen y-coordinate             *)

begin
  if Map.base[2] = screen then
    begin
      Y := Y + 1;
      Addr[1] := ScreenAddress[Y] + WordOffSet
    end
  else
    Addr[1] := Addr[1] + Map.Width
end;(* IncrAddress *)
```

FIGURE 4.2.16

The Bitblt procedure

```
(* We assume that there is a constant Screen, which equals the          *)
(* address of the screen; also, that there is an array, ScreenAdd,      *)
(* subscripted on the y-coordinates of the screen, which contains       *)
(* the beginning address of each row of the screen. The arrays          *)
(* LeftOrMask, RightOrMask, LeftAndMask, and RightAndMask               *)
(* are arrays of integers subscripted on the number of bits             *)
(* masked, which contain the masks for each operation                   *)


procedure Bitblt(SourceMap,DestinationMap : Bitmap;
                 DestinationPoint : Point;
                 SourceRectangle : Rectangle;
                 Code : OpCode);

var
  SAddress,DAddress : WordAdd;        (* hold beginning row addresses                     *)
  BitWidth : integer;                 (* number of bits per row of SourceRectangle        *)
  NumberOfRows : integer;             (* number of rows in SourceRectangle                *)
  row : integer;                      (* counter used to keep track of the rows for Rowblt *)
  SDist,DDist : integer;              (* number of bits from edge of bitmap to area used  *)
  SBits,DBits : integer;              (* bits from word boundary to first bit in area used *)
  SWordsOff,DWordsOff : integer;      (* offset from edge of bitmaps in words             *)
  ShiftBits : integer;                (* distance copy of source word shifted             *)
  ShiftDirection : (Left,Right);      (* direction of the shift                           *)
  SRowWords,DRowWords : integer;      (* words operated on per row                        *)
  SameRowSize : boolean;              (* are both rows the same number of words long?     *)
  Up : boolean;                       (* true if start at bottom, false if start at top   *)
  DCorner : point;                    (* lower-left corner of destination rectangle       *)
  SY1,DY1 : integer;                  (* y-coordinate of row, used for screen bitmaps     *)

begin (* Bitblt *)

  (* clip the source rectangle *)
  Clip(SourceRectangle,SourceMap,DestinationMap,DestinationPoint);

  (* find the width of the source rectangle in bits and its height in rows *)

  with SourceRectangle do
    begin
      BitWidth := Corner.X - Origin.X + 1;
      NumberOfRows := Corner.Y - Origin.Y + 1
    end;

  (* if the rectangle is non-trivial continue *)
  if (BitWidth > 0) and (NumberOfRows > 0) then
    begin
      (* calculate the number of bits in x-direction from bitmap edge   *)
      (* to SourceRectangle origin and to the DestinationPoint          *)
      SDist := SourceRectangle.Origin.X - SourceMap.Origin.X;
      DDist := DestinationPoint.X - DestinationMap.Origin.X;

      (* compute the number of bits from a word boundary to the origin*)
      (* of the SourceRectangle and the DestinationPoint               *)

      SBits := SDist mod PixelsPerWord;
      DBits := DDist mod PixelsPerWord;
```

```
(* find out how far to shift and in which direction *)

ShiftBits := DBits - SBits;
If ShiftBits < 0 then
   begin
      ShiftDirection := Left;
      ShiftBits := - ShiftBits;           (*shifts are always positive numbers              *)
   end
else
   ShiftDirection := Right;

(* how many words in a row of the source and destination? *)

SRowWords := (SBits + BitWidth + PixelsPerWord - 1) div  PixelsPerWord;
DRowWords := (DBits + BitWidth + PixelsPerWord - 1) div  PixelsPerWord;

(* are the rows the same size ?*)
SameRowSize := SRowWords = DRowWords;
(* get the masks *)

GetMasks(DBits,(DBits + BitWidth - 1) mod  PixelsPerWord,  LeftMask,RightMask,Code);

(* get the beginning address of the first row of source and              *)
(* destination. First find offset of address from address at             *)
(* beginning of row                                                      *)

SWordsOff := SDist div  PixelsPerWord;
DWordsOff := DDist div  PixelsPerWord;

(* which way do we go?*)
Up  := Direction(SourceMap,DestinationMap,SourceRectangle,  DestinationPoint);

If Up then (* start at the bottom *)
   begin
      (* must calculate lower-left corner of rectangle in destination *)
      DCorner.X  := DestinationPoint.X;
      DCorner.Y := DestinationPoint.Y + NumberOfRows - 1;
      SetAddress(SAddress,SourceMap,SourceRectangle.Corner);
      SetAddress(DAddress,DestinationMap,DCorner);
      (* save the y-coordinates in case the screen is used *)
      SY1  := SourceRectangle.Corner.Y;
      DY1 := DCorner.Y
   end
else (* start at the top *)
   begin
      SetAddress(SAddress,SourceMap,SourceRectangle.Origin);
      SetAddress(DAddress,DestinationMap,DestinationPoint);
      (* save the y-coordinates in case the screen is used *)
      SY1  := SourceRectangle.Origin.Y;
      DY1  := DestinationPoint.Y
   end;
```

(continued)

FIGURE 4.2.16 continued

```
(* do the actual operation *)

for row := 1 to NumberOfRows do
  begin
    if ShiftDirection = Right then
      RowbltRight(SAddress,DAddress,Code,
               LeftMask,RightMask,ShiftBits,DRowWords,SameRowSize)
    else
      RowbltLeft(SAddress,DAddress,Code,
               LeftMask,RightMask,ShiftBits,DRowWords,SameRowSize);
    (* get the next row addresses *)
    if Upthen
      begin
        DecAddress(SAddress,SourceMap,SWordsOff,SY1);
        DecAddress(DAddress,DestinationMap,DWordsOff,DY1)
      end
    else
      begin
        IncrAddress(SAddress,SourceMap,SWordsOff,SY1);
        IncrAddress(DAddress,DestinationMap,DWordsOff,DY1)
      end
  end
end;(* Bitblt *)
```

FIGURE 4.2.17

Several graphics systems have block transfer procedures available. While these procedures are very similar to Bitblt, care must be taken to use them properly.

Macintosh Toolbox

CopyBits (srcBits,dstBits: BitMap;srcRect,
dstRect: Rect; mode : integer;
maskRgn : RgnHandle);

(notes: a source and destination rectangle are given. The source rectangle is scaled to fit the destination. The maskRgn may be set to nil for our work. BitMap must have an even width)

Turbo Pascal

GetPic (Buffer,x1,y1,x2,y2)

PutPic (Buffer, x1,y1,mode)

(In GetPic buffer is a memory location large enough to hold the screen rectangle described by x1,y1 and x2,y2. It is not possible to specify a mode. PutPic uses x1,y1 to specify a destination point on the screen. The mode is available in Turbo versions starting with 4.0)

EXERCISES

4.2.1

Write the clipping algorithm for Bitblt.

4.2.2

Write the DecAddress procedure, used in Bitblt to compute the address of the first word of the next row of the source and destination when proceeding from the bottom up.

4.2.3

Write the procedure RowbltLeft for your system.

4.2.4

Implement Bitblt on your system.

4.2.5

What changes would you have to make to this implementation if Bitblt were to use a source point and destination rectangle rather than a source rectangle and destination point?

4.2.6

Bitblt normally has a texture added to it. Textures are patterns that are usually stored in wordlength-by-wordlength arrays. The arrays are set up so that there are wordlength words that may be **and**ed with the copy of the source word before masks are applied. Entries in the array are cycled through by using **mod** to determine the subscript of the current texture word being used. Extend Bitblt to use textures.

4.2.7

When the background color for objects is black, the texture discussed in 4.2.3 will be visible on the screen only if the source is filled with white first. This is useful if a closed area is to be textured. If, however, the texture is to show up on the entire screen, the operator **or** must be used to apply the texture.

a. Implement Bitblt with this overall texture on a black screen.
b. How would you alter the application of texture for the white background screen if you wanted to fill closed figures selectively?

4.2.8

Show that the store cperation can be achieved by the following sequence of operations on figure 4.2.18:

FIGURE 4.2.18

1	1	0	0	1	1	0	0	1	1	0	0	1	1	0	0	**Source**
1	0	1	0	1	0	1	0	1	0	1	0	1	0	1	0	**Destination before store**
0	0	0	0	1	1	1	1	1	1	1	1	0	0	0	0	**Mask**
																Intermediate value
																Destination after store

1. First, xor the source and destination storing the result in a temporary location.
2. Next, and the intermediate value with the mask. Store this in the temporary location.
3. Finally, xor the original value in the destination with the intermediate result and store in the destination.

4.2.9

Why can't the width of a bitmap always be computed from its rectangle?

4.2.10

Under what circumstances would the rectangle of a bitmap have an origin different from (0,0)?

4.2.11

What is the purpose of the masks?

4.2.12

Calculate the address of the point (5,3) in the bitmap Map given by:

```
with Map do
  begin
    Base[1] := 450; (* this pseudo address is given in decimal for simplicity*)
    Base[2] := memory;
    width := 25;
    with rect do
      begin
        origin.x := 1;
        origin.y := 1;
        corner.x := 15;
        corner.y := 20
      end
  end;
```

4.3 Using Bitblt to Draw Objects

Bitblt is often used to draw predefined images at a location on the screen. **Icons** are a broad class of such images. These are usually small graphic images used to locate positions on the screen or to draw predefined symbols in menus. Icons may be stored in a file and re-created at the time they are needed.

Icons used to point to locations on the screen are called **cursors.** Cursors are usually paired with a device that allows the user to move them. There are many devices available for moving the cursor. These range from specified keys on the keyboard to special graphics tools such as a **mouse,** a **graphics pad,** or **thumb wheels.** This section will mainly explain how to show an icon on the screen. You will integrate the cursor with an interactive device in section 5.2.

Cursors come in many shapes, but the most common are the arrow and the cross. The reason for the popularity of these two shapes is that they have a clearly defined **hotspot.** That is, the location to which the cursor is pointing is obvious in each case. In the case of the arrow, the point of the arrow is the location to which the cursor is pointing. In the case of the cross, the hotspot is the location where the lines cross.

Other common icon shapes are watches, hourglasses, paintbrushes, spray cans, and the I-bar used by many text editors. In almost all instances, these objects are stored in a file. When they are needed, they are read into a location in memory. This location is then bitmapped to the screen using the **xor** OpCode, which allows the object to be moved around the screen without destroying the underlying picture. Removal of the icon from the screen is accomplished by bitmapping it with **xor** OpCode a second time in exactly the same place on the screen. In figure 4.3.1.a, a dummy icon is mapped onto a dummy display by using the **xor** OpCode. This process is repeated on the altered image in figure 4.3.1.b.

FIGURE 4.3.1.a

Bitblt and icon onto an image in **xor** *mode*

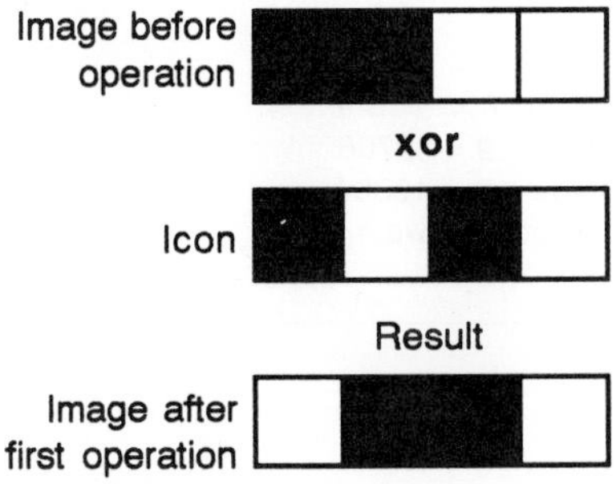

FIGURE 4.3.1.b

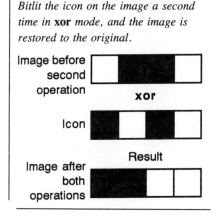

Bitlit the icon on the image a second time in **xor** *mode, and the image is restored to the original.*

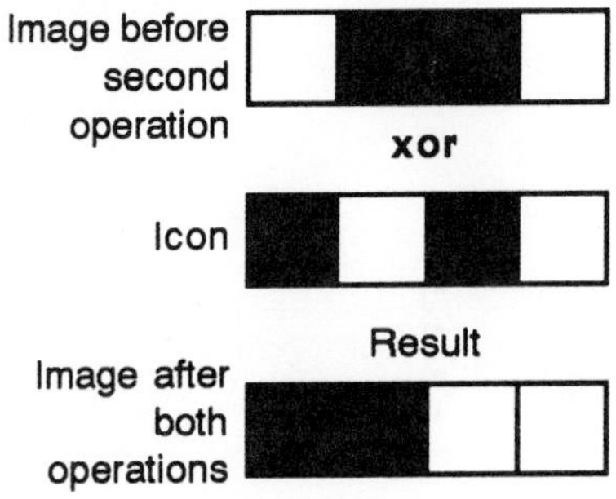

If you are going to use Bitblt to draw a cursor on the screen, you must first store the image in memory. Because you do not have the image stored in a file, you will use a program to create the image. In figure 4.3.2, the arrow icon is created for two different types of systems; first, for the Apple II system, which uses 7 pixels per 8-bit word; and, second, for Turbo Pascal on the IBM, which uses 16 pixels per word. In the Apple graphics system, the low-order bits appear to the left; in the Turbo Pascal graphics system, the high-order bits appear to the left. Bits represent $2^0, 2^1, \ldots, 2^n$, where n is the bit number. With this in mind, you can easily compute the integer value that will represent each row of the cursor.

The orientation of Turbo Pascal makes it easier to consider each row as a range type *PositiveInt* $= 0..2^{15} - 1$ instead of the type integer. In the Turbo Pascal system, icons may be stored in an **array**[1..15] **of** PositiveInt. Similarly, if byte is the range type 0..255, cursors used in the Apple II system may be stored in a **packed array**[1..7] **of** byte because this type of array uses consecutive 8-bit locations. Either of these structures will be referred to as type **IconStorage.** To initialize an icon, set each entry in the array to the value computed, and then create a bitmap that points to the array (figure 4.3.3).

To display the arrow on the screen with its hotspot at location (x,y), you need only make the following call:

FIGURE 4.3.2

Converting an icon into an array of integers

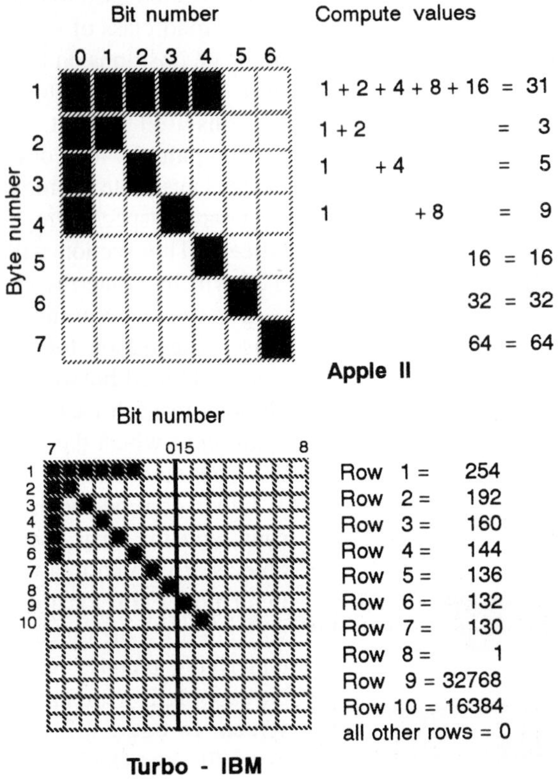

FIGURE 4.3.3

Procedure to create an arrow cursor for the Apple II

```
(* procedure used to create the arrow in figure 4.3.2 in memory *)
procedure ArrowInit;
begin
  (*store the values obtained in figure 4.3.2 in an array *)
  Aro[1] :=  31;
  Aro[2] :=   3;
  Aro[3] :=   5;
  Aro[4] :=   9;
  Aro[5] :=  16;
  Aro[6] :=  32;
  Aro[7] :=  64;
  (* initialize a bitmap which has storage Aro              *)
  (* and a coordinate system that is easy to remember*)
  with Arrow do
    begin
      Base[1] := Address(Aro);        (* connect Arrow with Aro                        *)
      Base[2] := Memory;              (* this bitmap location is not the screen        *)
      Width := 1;                     (* since this is one byte across the width is 1  *)
      SetRectangle(0,0,6,6,Rect);     (* set the corners of the rectangle              *)
    end
end;
```

FIGURE 4.3.4

An Apple II version of a cross often used for drawing operations

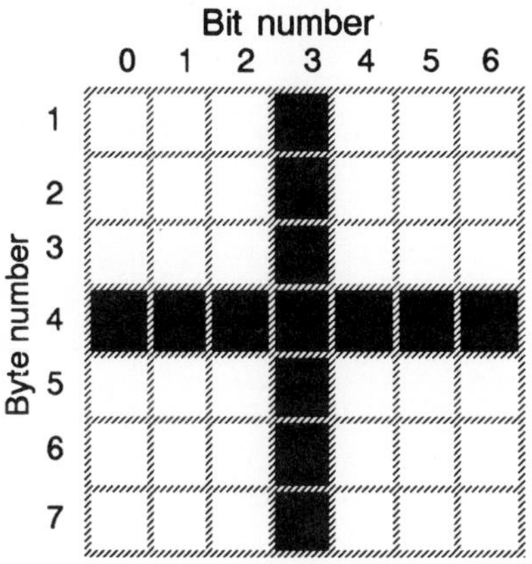


```
Bitblt(arrow,Display,Dpoint,Arrow.Rect,cXor);
```

where *Dpoint.x* = *x* and *Dpoint.y* = *y*.

Icons may be used to indicate the current condition of a program. In such cases, one bitmap is used to hold the icon currently being displayed. A file may be used to store the different icons that are displayed, and when a particular icon is needed, it is retrieved from the file and stored in the bitmap's array. It is clear that a random access file must be used to allow the appropriate icon to be retrieved.

In many common versions of Pascal, if a file of records is created sequentially, the first record is given the number 0 and succeeding records are numbered consecutively, so that the fifth record is numbered as record 4. To retrieve a given record, the command **Seek** is used to locate it. For example, to retrieve the fifth record in the file F, simply execute the following sequence of steps:

```
Seek(F,4);
Get(F);
```

After the Get, the file buffer F^ will contain the fifth record in file F.

An application may have many icons, and more than one application may use the same icon. To use multiple icons, you create them separately from the application and store them in files packaged with the application. Suppose that you are writing an application that will use the cross (figure 4.3.4), arrow, and watch icons (figure 4.3.5).

First you would write procedures to initialize arrays that could be used to draw these icons. The write code will create the file pictured in figure 4.3.6. This is a file of IconStorage with the cross in record 0, the arrow in record 1, and the watch in record 2.

Applications that use icons typically have many icons so that the record number of each icon is maintained as a constant. In this case, *CrossId* = 0; *ArrowId* = 1; and *WatchId* = 2. This allows the programmer to write

```
Seek(Icons,ArrowId);
Get(Icons);
```

to retrieve the picture of the arrow. The procedure shown in Figure 4.3.7 is used to change an icon:

FIGURE 4.3.5

An Apple II version of the watch icon used to indicate that a lengthy operation is in progress

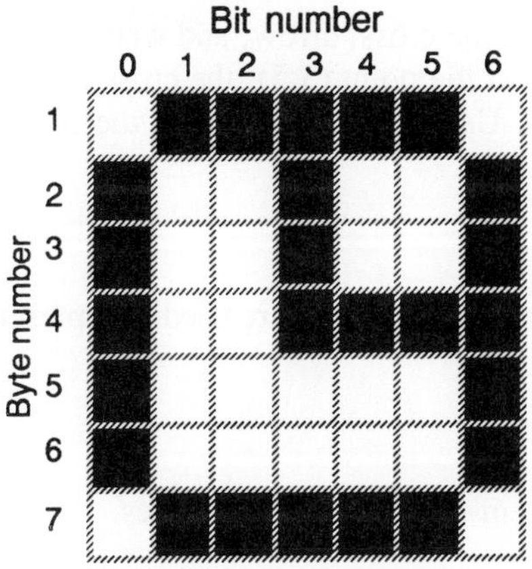

FIGURE 4.3.6

A file that stores icons

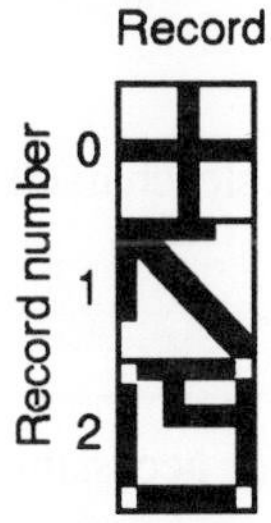

FIGURE 4.3.7

Procedure to change an icon

```
(* this procedure is used to get the icon whose record number is          *)
(* IconNumber, then replace the current Icon with this new icon           *)
(* the file Icons is of type IconFile = file of IconStorage;              *)
(* we will assume that the IconPic is the storage used by our icons       *)
(* that is, if Icon is the BitMap of the Icon, Icon.Base[1] := address(IconPic)  *)
```

(continued)

FIGURE 4.3.7 continued

```
procedure ChangeIcon(var Icons : IconFile; var IconPic : IconStorage; IconNumber : integer);
begin
  reset(Icons);                          (* open the file                  *)
  Seek(Icons,IconNumber);                (* select the appropriate record  *)
  Get(Icons);                            (* get the record                 *)
  IconPic := Icons^;                     (* transfer to the icon storage   *)
  close(Icons)                           (* close the file                 *)
end; (* ChangeIcon *)
```

EXERCISES

4.3.1

Write a program on your system to draw the icon given in figure 4.3.4 at the center of the screen.

4.3.2

Write a program to create the file containing the cross, arrow, and watch icons. Write a second program to draw the arrow at the point (3,5), the cross at point (50,150), and the watch at point (150,25). Use the file of icons in the second program.

4.3.3

If you have arrow keys on your system, what code values are used to represent these keys?

4.3.4

Find out how to create icons on your system using numerical values.

4.3.5

Do you have to store something other than the numerical values for the icon in your data structure?

4.3.6

Does your system have a special function to read single characters from the keyboard?

4.3.7

What functions does your programming language use for accessing file records directly?

4.3.8

If your system has a mouse, how can you move an icon in response to mouse movement?

4.3.9

Does your mouse have software which will allow it to mimic the keyboard input?

4.3.10

Do you have a library mouse reading procedures with predefined icons?

FIGURE 4.3.8

Create the arrow icon and Bitblt it to a point near the center of the screen

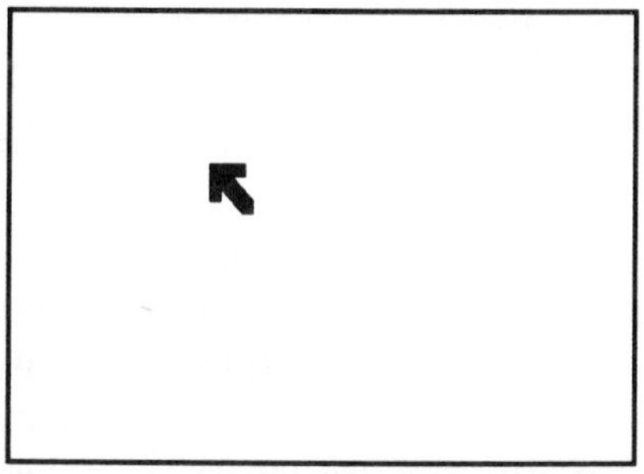

4.3.11

a. Create the arrow icon and Bitblt it to a point near the center of the screen using the cStore code (figure 4.3.8).
b. Bitblt the arrow to a point right of the first arrow using the cOr code.
c. Repeat this process using cXor, cAnd, and cLr.
d. Did all of the arrows appear? If not, why?
e. Bitblt the arrow over the first arrow using the cXor mode. What happened?

4.4 Using Bitblt to Write Text to the Graphics Screen

Every character is represented in computer memory by a binary code. Two of the most common binary codes are ASCII and EBCDIC. ASCII is found mainly on mini- and microcomputers; EBCDIC is commonly used on IBM mainframes. No matter which code a particular system uses, the code representation must be converted to an image to make it visible on a CRT screen. Any set of images that represents the set of characters may be referred to as a **font.** This term has been borrowed very loosely from typography. Each letter typically is drawn on the screen as an icon (figure 4.4.1), like those in the last section.

FIGURE 4.4.1

Letters are usually stored as icons that are Bitblt to the screen

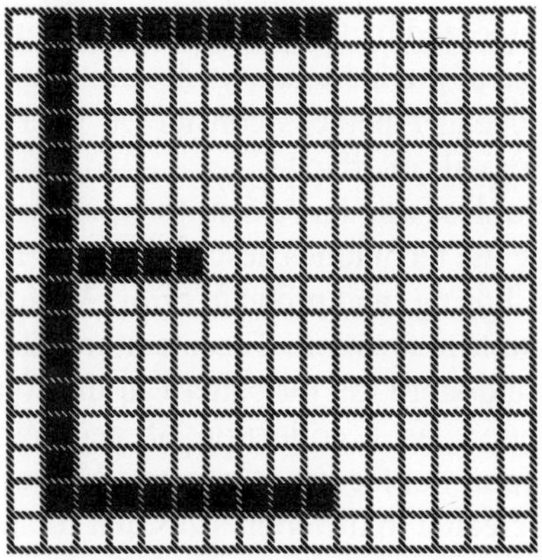

This section discusses two ways of creating a font with fixed-width letters. It also investigates specialized typefaces such as bold and italic. Assume throughout this discussion that the Pascal function ord gives the binary code for a letter. This may cause problems for numeric characters because on some systems, ord, when it is applied to numeric characters, gives the numerical value corresponding to that digit.

One way to create a font is to store the entire font in one bitmap. This representation stores all of the icons in an **array[0..255] of iconstorage.** The bitmap, Font, has a rectangle with origin at (0,0) and corner at $(256*\mathit{PixelsPerWord} - 1, \mathit{PixelsPerWord} - 1)$. Each letter's icon is contained in the rectangle with origin $(\mathrm{Ord}(\mathit{ch}) * \mathit{PixelsPerWord}, 0)$ and corner $((\mathrm{Ord}(\mathit{ch})+1)*\mathit{PixelsPerWord} - 1, \mathit{PixelsPerWord} - 1)$ (figure 4.4.2). If this rectangle is set as the source rectangle, then to show the character at a given screen point, Pt, you need only perform the operation

```
Bitblt(Font,Display,Pt,SRect,cStore);
```

An alternative storage scheme avoids the recalculation of the source rectangle for each letter. This system uses the same storage array as the first, but alters the

FIGURE 4.4.2

An alphabet may be stored in one large bitmap. Individual letters are then selected by choosing an appropriate source rectangle.

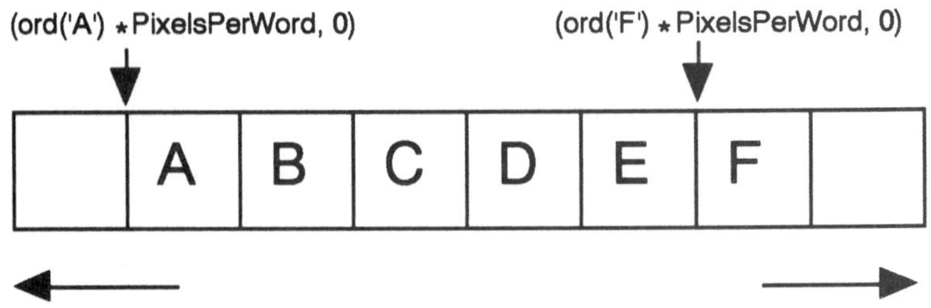

FIGURE 4.4.3

An alphabet may also be stored as an array of bitmaps. The subscript of the bitmap is used to select the desired letter.

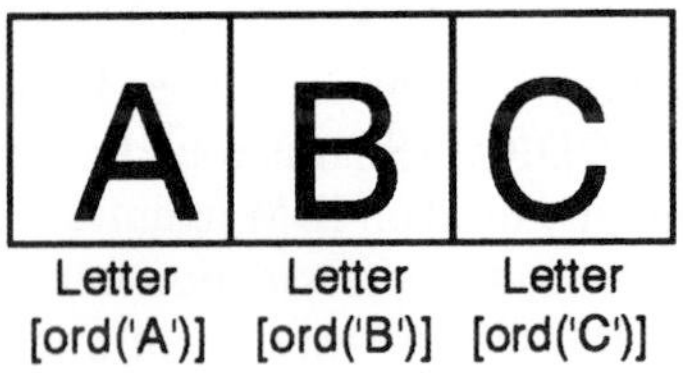

base address of one bitmap and uses the bitmap's rectangle as the source rectangle. If the array is Letters, then the character *ch* is stored in *Letters*[Ord(*ch*)] (figure 4.4.3). The bitmap Font has a fixed rectangle with origin (0,0) and corner (*PixelsPerWord* − 1, *PixelsPerWord* − 1), which is used as the source rectangle. To show the letter *ch* at the screen point *Pt*, the base address of Font is set to Address(*Letters*[Ord(*ch*)], and then the operation Bitblt(Font,Display,Pt,Font.Rect,cStore) is performed. Either method of drawing a letter will be referred to as

DrawLetter(Letter,DestPoint,Font,Code)

The procedure **WriteString(CharString, DestPoint, Font, Code)** takes a character string, CharString, and displays it on the screen below and to the right of the screen point DestPoint. The font and code are also specified. This procedure simply scans the string one letter at a time, displaying each letter at the destination point with DrawLetter. After each letter is displayed, the x-coordinate of the destination point is incremented by the number of pixels per word (or more if spacing is desired). The size of the increment is determined by the type of spacing between letters. The special typefaces considered later in this section need more spacing or the letters will overlap.

None of these procedures is much good unless one has a font to work with. Fonts may be created letter by letter by using the techniques described in the last section, but this process is time consuming, boring, and prone to error. Various font editors have been developed to facilitate font creation. These editors allow the user to draw each letter on the screen and store the bit pattern in the font. Some systems use algorithms to draw letters as a collection of geometric objects. The bit pattern is still stored in the font, but the list of geometric objects is also stored. This allows the font to be re-created in different sizes and rotated to different angles.

Once you have established a base font, you can easily create special effects like boldface and italic type. These effects are simulations of special typefaces created by typesetting machines. Boldface type is simulated by doubling each of the lines in a letter (figure 4.4.4). The procedure **DrawBoldLetter** has the same parameters as DrawLetter. It simply Bitblts the letter to the destination point, then increments both the *x*- and *y*-coordinates of the destination point by 1, and Bitblts the letter again to the new destination point.

To get the italic effect, the procedure **DrawItalicLetter** actually calls on Bitblt once for each row of the letter's icon. It starts at the bottom, displaying the last row at a destination point that has the same x-value as the destination point for the letter. A block of rows is displayed left aligned to this point. The x-value is then incremented and the next block is displayed (figure 4.4.5). If too few rows of the letter are included in the block, the letter will appear to be tipped. Too many rows in a block will cause the letter to look jagged.

Rotations of fonts in their bitmap form are limited to 90°, 180°, and 270° by the rectangular nature of a bitmap. Mirror images of text may also be used (figure 4.4.6). Both techniques are difficult to achieve and will be discussed in section 4.6.

In many applications, the same string or collection of strings is repeatedly shown on the screen. Menus are good examples of such collections of strings. To accelerate the display of these sets of strings on the screen, a single bitmap that holds the entire image is created. Only one Bitblt is needed to display the entire image, rather than at least one Bitblt per letter. This technique is particularly useful if one of the special typefaces is used or if lines are to be drawn around the image (figure 4.4.7). All parts of the image are shown with one bitmap.

FIGURE 4.4.4

Bold letters can be achieved by doubling each line in the letters

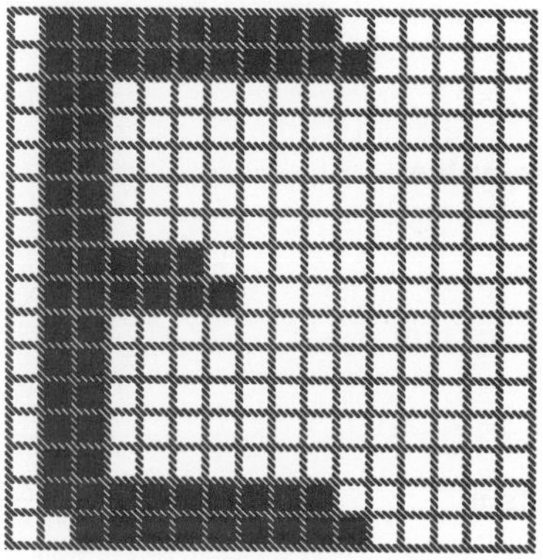

FIGURE 4.4.5

The italtic effect can be achieved by shifting groups of rows varying distances to the right.

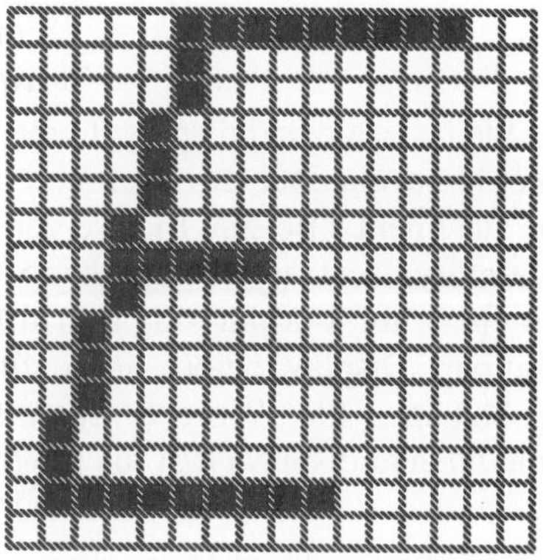

FIGURE 4.4.6

More difficult effects, such as mirror images and rotations, will be covered in section 4.6.

FIGURE 4.4.7

An example of an alert box

EXERCISES

4.4.1.

Write the procedure DrawLetter on your system by using the second representation of a font.

4.4.2

If your graphics system has a text-drawing function, create your own font by writing each of the visible characters to the screen and Bitblting it to an appropriate spot in your font.

4.4.3

Write the procedure DrawBoldLetter on your system.

4.4.4

Write the procedure DrawItalicLetter on your system.

4.4.5

Write the procedure WriteString on your system.

4.4.6

Write a procedure that will draw strings of bold characters on the screen.

4.4.7

Write a procedure that will draw strings of italic characters on the screen.

FIGURE 4.4.8

An example of a warning box

Be sure to save your file

4.4.8

Create a bitmap warning box suggesting that a file be saved and display it when the user exits a program. This warning box should have a double line around it to make it easily visible and should include the statement "Be sure to save your file" (figure 4.4.8). Compute the amount of memory necessary to hold the text and box. Use your built-in graphics system to create the warning box near the bottom of the screen; then Bitblt it into your bitmap. Display the box at the top of the screen with Bitblt. Save the warning box in a file. Write a separate program that retrieves the warning box from the file and displays it at the top of the screen.

4.4.9

What procedure does your system use for placing text on the graphics screen?

4.4.10

How do you position text with this procedure?

4.4.11

Which fonts do you have available?

4.4.12

Can you draw the letters in bold or italic?

4.4.13

Why do you think rotations of letters are usually limited to multiples of 90°?

4.4.14

Try creating a 30° rotation of the letter E.

4.5 Creating and Using Menus

In a graphics program the selection of operations available to the user is restricted. As in most programs, the list of these operations is presented to the user in a menu. The method of menu display and selection used in graphics employs the ability of bitmaps to alter rectangular areas of the screen quickly.

4.5a Creating Menus

One advantage that bitmap graphics gives to an applications programmer is an easy way to implement user-friendly menus. Anyone familiar with programs written for the Apple Macintosh or Microsoft Windows has seen the pull-down menus that are a standard feature of such programs. These menus are implemented and serviced with Bitblt.

To create a menu the programmer should follow these steps:

1. Decide on the choices that the menu will offer. Try to keep the choices related so that a given menu will consist of related actions.
2. Try to group choices in meaningful ways. For example, most frequent choices should be grouped in the location of easiest access, and similar choices should be associated. Try to make the menus easy to use.
3. Create short, meaningful menu entries for each choice.
4. Once the choices are selected and the menu entries are chosen, compute the size of the array needed to store the menu. To compute the width of the bitmap needed, find the longest entry in the menu and count the number of letters in this entry, including the blanks. Multiply this number by the width of each letter in bits to get the number of bits needed to store the letters. It is usually advisable to leave some extra bits at the beginning and end of a line to provide space at the edge of the menu. You can then use the width of the bitmap in bits to compute the width in words in the usual way. To find the number of rows in the bitmap, take the height of a letter and add one or more to that height for **leading** (space between lines) and then multiply by the number of lines. Again add two or more rows for space above and below the menu entries. See an example in Figure 4.5.1.

FIGURE 4.5.1

An example of a pull-down menu whose longest entry contains 14 letters

Notice in this example that the longest entry is **move to center,** which has 14 letters including spaces. The number of bits needed for 16-bit letters is 224 plus 2 spaces for leading, a total of 226. Thus, the width of the menu should be 15 words. There are 8 choices, including spaces, each of height 16, so if 2 rows are used for leading you have a total of 130 rows. For this menu you would need to have a menu type **array**[1..15,1..130] **of** integer. As a menu of this size takes approximately 4K of memory, it is impractical to have many menus of this size in memory at one time. One way to save space is to have a file of menus. To

FIGURE 4.5.2

A menu of icons representing tools used for drawing

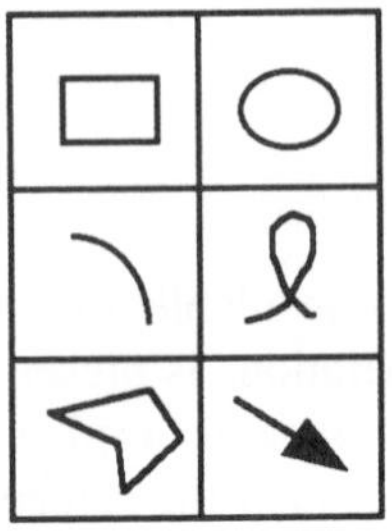

do this, compute the largest array needed for the menus and create a file of arrays of this size in which to store all large menus. Menus are retrieved as needed from the file and bitmapped directly from the file buffer. Only one array is then needed, namely, the file buffer variable. Recreating menus from a file is slow, so Microsoft Windows and Macintosh programs use a part of their program called the **resource** to store menus, icons, and other bitmap objects.

An alternative is to create menus as a collection of icons. You have already seen the arrow icon. Icons have the advantages of small size and easy user recognition. A sample of such a menu is given in figure 4.5.2. MacDraw-like menus indicate choices in pictures rather than in words. The disadvantage of icon menus is that beginning users are required to memorize a new set of symbols.

To create the menu in figure 4.5.1, first pick the most convenient coordinate system for this menu. This could be the one with origin at (1,1) and corner at (226,130) or, in the case of menus that are always displayed at the same spot on the screen, the rectangle in which the menu appears on the screen.

The origin for the text of each choice will always be along the left edge of the menu, so when creating the text, you always compute its x-location by adding the size of the edge to the x-coordinate of the menu's origin. In computing the y-coordinate of a given choice, note that the height of each row, *RowHeight,* is the height of a letter in the font plus the number of bits for leading. The main program defines **Menu** to be a bitmap with base address of a file buffer for a file of arrays and origin at (1,1) and corner computed as above. The procedure in figure 4.5.3 may be used to create a set of menus on the screen in the screen rectangle with the same boundaries as those of the menu rectangle. Each of these menus has the same number of entries and the same width. It is an easy exercise to modify the procedure so that the number of entries in a given menu may be specified at runtime. Although you could also modify the width of each menu, many of the tasks that follow would be much more complicated if this were done.

Once a file of menus has been created, you may use Bitblt to show any one of the menus. First use the Seek-Get sequence to load the file buffer. Then, if Menu is the bitmap defined above, Bitblt it to the screen. You will investigate this process in more detail in the discussion on pull-down menus in the last part of this section.

4.5.b Making Choices from Menus

This is the first application of graphics in which the user is able to alter the screen directly. These alterations are indicated by the use of graphics input devices. While there are many devices available, only the keyboard will be used here. When the user is making menu choices, only keystroke entries that represent movements between menu choices will be accepted. This will be accomplished by accepting input only from selected keys on the keyboard. Commonly used keys are the up an down arrows. If such arrows are not available, characters such as *i* and *j* can be used to indicate up an down. One other key, in this case the escape key, will be used to indicate that the currently

FIGURE 4.5.3

This procedure may be used to create a file of menus.

```
procedure createmenu;
const
    NumberMenus    = ?;          (* number of menus in the file                                  *)
    NumberChoices  = ?;          (* number of choices per menu                                   *)
    InitialYLocation = ?;        (* offset from top of the menu rectangle to first choice        *)
var
  MenuEntry  : string;
  i,j        : integer;
  down       : integer;          (* beginning location of a menu item                            *)
  DP         : Point;            (* origin of the menu on screen                                 *)
  XEdge      : integer;          (* x value of the left side of the menu                         *)
begin
  GraphOn;
  Rewrite(F);                    (* create a new file                                            *)
  DP.x := 1; DP.y := 1; XEdge := 1;
  for j := 1 to NumberMenus do
    begin
      down := InitialYLocation ;
      FillPort;                  (* clear the screen for a new menu                              *)
      for i := 1 to NumberChoices do
        begin
          readln(keyboard,MenuEntry);   (* enter the menu choice                                 *)
          WriteString(MenuEntry,standard,XEdge,down,cStore); (* blank entries produce spaces in menu bar *)
          down := down + RowHeight;
        end;
      Bitblt(Display,Menu,T,DP,Menu.Rect,cStore);
      Put(F);
      XEdge := XEdge + MenuWidth      (* update the left side of the menu                        *)
    end;
  Close(F)
end; (* CreateMenu *)
```

FIGURE 4.5.4

A solid block of color is Bitblt over selections in cXor mode to indicate the currently selected choice.

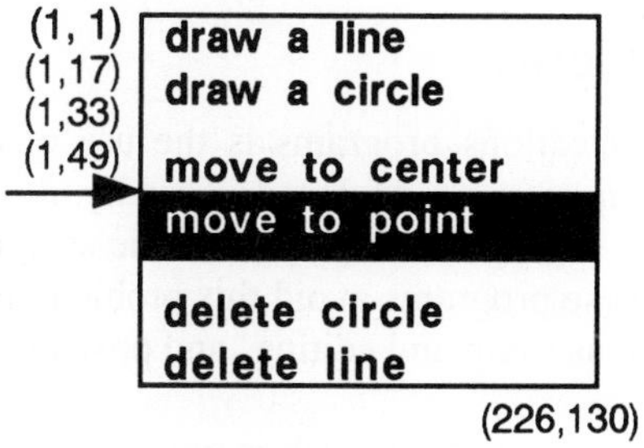

highlighted choice will be selected (figure 4.5.4). All other keys will be ignored.

The reversed, white-on-black highlight cursor is created by Bitblting a bitmap filled with ones to a location using the cXor OpCode. Let's say you would like the cursor to extend above and below the choice. The *RowHeight* already includes leading so the cursor may have *RowHeight* + leading. The highlight should also extend over the entire width of the menu. Creating a bitmap, *HighLite,* for such a cursor is not difficult. Initialize the array with the number that has a binary representation of all ones. This information should make the implementation of **MenuLocator,** shown in figure 4.5.5, clear.

The parameter *Choice* is not initialized in the procedure. This allows the user to select the most common choice for the current menu as the initial value. To focus the user's attention quickly, however, it might be best to put the initial choice in the middle of the list. This procedure does not erase the menu, so it might be called from a procedure that shows the menu, makes the choice, and then erases the menu.

FIGURE 4.5.5

Menulocator allows the user to select an operation from a pull-down menu.

```
procedure MenuLocator(var Choice : integer; MaxChoices : integer;
                          var DP : Point);
var
  BaseY : integer;
  Direction : Char;
  UpArrow, DownArrow, Done: Char;
begin
  (* initializations done in ASCII code                *)
  (* they may have to be done in the constant section  *)
  (* of the programs written for some Pascal compilers *)
  Done := chr(27);
  UpArrow := chr(11);
  DownArrow := chr(10);
  BaseY := DP.y;
  Repeat
    Bitblt(HighLite,Display,DP,HighLite.Rect,cXor);
      Read(KeyBoard,Direction);
    If Direction In [UpArrow,DownArrow] then
      case Direction of
        UpArrow     : If Choice > 1 then
                        Choice := Choice - 1
                      else
                        Choice := MaxChoices;       (* cycle to bottom of menu   *)
        DownArrow   : If Choice < MaxChoices then
                        Choice := Choice + 1
                      else
                        Choice := 1;                (* cycle back to top         *)
      end; (* case *)
    Bitblt(Highlite,Display,DP,Highlite.Rect,cXor);
    DP.y := BaseY + ((Choice - 1) * RowHeight);     (* BaseY is the origin.y     *)
  until (Direction = Done)
end; (* MenuLocator *)
```

One way to improve access to menu choices is to make the selection circular. That is, if the down arrow key is pressed when the cursor is at the bottom of the menu, the next choice highlighted is at the top of the menu. Similarly, if the cursor is at the bottom of the menu and the up arrow key is pressed, the bottom choice will then be highlighted.

4.5.c Pull-down and Pop-up Menus

One of the trends in modern graphics applications programs is the use of a main-line program from which any option may be executed. Usually it is impossible to have all the menu choices for a program displayed on the screen at one time and still have room to work. These programs avoid this problem by grouping operations together in classes such as filing and editing, and providing a menu for each group.

One way to access these menus is to display a title for each menu in a menu bar. To choose an item, the user first chooses the menu containing that item from the menu bar. Menus selected from a menu bar seem to be "pulled down" from the menu bar in much the same way a window shade is unrolled, hence the name pull-down menus. By necessity, this choice is made with a general interactive device. Figure 4.5.6 contains a screen from Microsoft Windows used on IBM-compatible PCs. The arrow pointer is selecting "Double Space" from the Paragraph menu. In this type of menu, selection is made from the top, so "Normal" is located at the top.

Instructions entered directly from an interactive device may also be used to show the menu. In the programming language SmallTalk, pressing various combinations of the mouse's multiple buttons causes different menus to appear at the current cursor location. These menus are called **pop-up menus** for obvious reasons.

Both pull-down and pop-up menus are created, displayed, and selected from in the same way. This section will only discuss the pull-down menus because they are easier to use and are less complicated to display.

After the user has chosen a menu title, the menu for that choice is retrieved from a file of menus. This menu may not simply be bitmapped to the screen because this would destroy the existing screen. To avoid this problem and save memory, the image in the rectangle that the menu will use is exchanged with the menu.

An effective way to accomplish this without the need for extra memory is to store the screen in the file buffer holding the menu (figure 4.5.7). This may be done with the following sequence of steps:

FIGURE 4.5.7

Application of Bitblt three times using the cXor operation to exchange two bitmaps without using extra memory

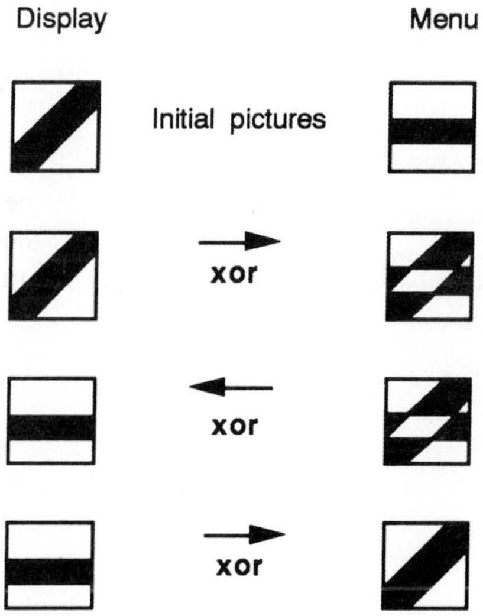

FIGURE 4.5.6

Pull-down menus can be used to choose type specifications, as in this example from a word processor in Microsoft Windows.

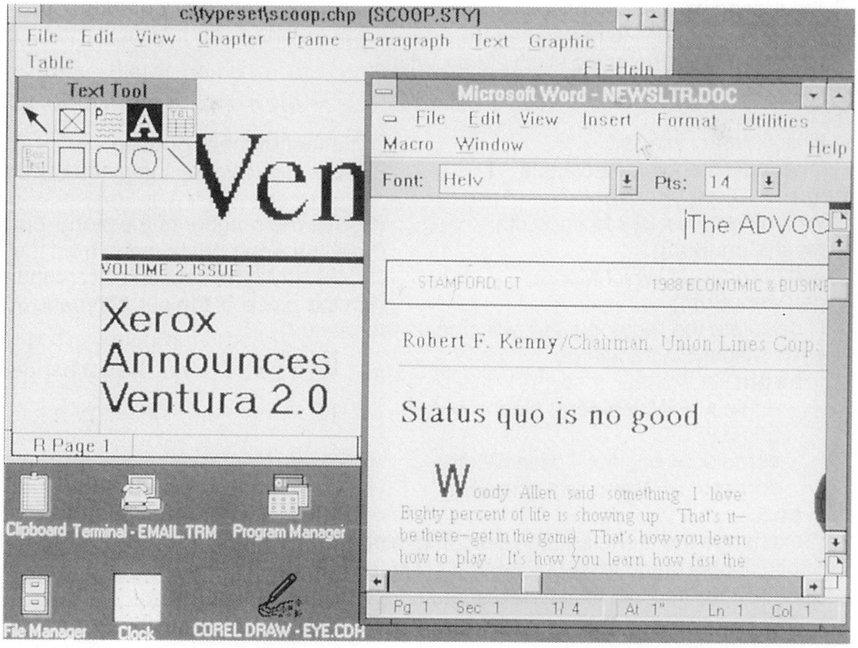

FIGURE 4.5.8

A typical layout for a menu bar

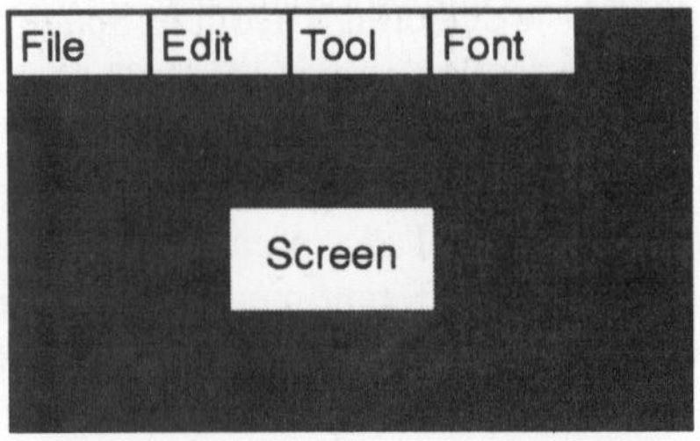

Bitblt(Display,Menu,Menu.rect.origin, DisplayRectangle,cXor);
Bitblt(Menu,Display, DisplayRectangle.origin,Menu.rect,cXor);
Bitblt(Display,Menu,Menu.rect.origin, DisplayRectangle,cXor);

This sequence has the advantage of not requiring the temporary storage needed in most swap routines. *DisplayRectangle* is the rectangle on the screen in which the menu is to appear. This rectangle is calculated by first finding its origin. The *y*-coordinate is often given as the width of the menu bar plus leading, so the menu title remains on the screen. If menus are assumed to be the same width, the menus may be numbered from left to right starting at zero. The *x*-coordinate of the origin is simply the menu number times the menu width. The number of the menu selected is then the *x*-coordinate of the selection **div** the width of each menu.

If you set up a menu bar with four entries equally spaced across the top of the screen, as in figure 4.5.8, the procedure in figure 4.5.9 may be used to display the appropriate menu. Notice that the image removed from the screen is temporarily stored in the menu file buffer. A procedure similar to that in figure 4.5.9 could be used to restore the screen and close the menu file.

FIGURE 4.5.9

The procedure DisplayPullDown exchanges the contents of a pull-down menu with the current screen contents.

```
(* in the constant section of your program                                  *)
const
  NumberofMenus = 4;
(* procedure DisplayPullDown will display the pull-down menu                *)
(* whose heading contains the point (x,y).  The x- and y-values             *)
(* are returned from the interactive read device in chapter 5               *)
(* Menu is a globally defined bitmap that holds all pull-down menus         *)
(* the procedure also stores the screen in the menu file until after choice is made *)
(* then a second call to the procedure restores the screen                  *)
(* all menus have the same width - MenuWidth                                *)
procedure DisplayPullDown(x,y : integer);
var
  WhichMenu : integer;                (* number of menu chosen                         *)
  DisplayRectangle : Rectangle;       (* rectangle in which the menu will be displayed *)
begin  (* DisplayPullDown *)
  WhichMenu := x div MenuWidth;       (* gives the number of the menu  cursor was in   *)
  reset(MenuBuff);                    (* get the appropriate menu from the file of menus *)
  seek(MenuBuff,WhichMenu);           (* or retrieve the section of screen stored temporarily *)
  get(MenuBuff);                      (* in the place of the current menu choice       *)
  (* calculate the rectangle that will contain the menu *)
  with DisplayRectangle do
    begin
      origin.x := WhichMenu * MenuWidth;
      origin.y := 0;
      corner.x := origin.x + MenuWidth;
      corner.y  :=  Menu.rect.corner.y;
    end;
  (* exchange the menu and the section of screen *)
  Bitblt(Display,Menu,Menu.rect.origin,  DisplayRectangle,cXor);
  Bitblt(Menu,Display,DisplayRectangle.origin,Menu.rect,cXor);
  Bitblt(Display,Menu,Menu.rect.origin,  DisplayRectangle,cXor);
end;  (* DisplayPullDown *)
```

FIGURE 4.5.10

Create these menus and store them in a file.

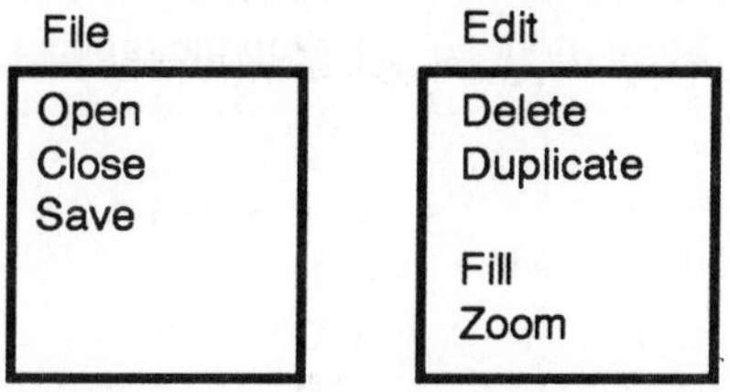

EXERCISES

4.5.1

Use the program given in figure 4.5.3 to create a file containing the two menus shown in figure 4.5.10.

4.5.2

Modify the program given in figure 4.5.3 to allow for menus offering a different number of choices.

4.5.3

How can menus of different widths be implemented? What changes in the procedures in this section would be needed if variable-width menus were implemented?

4.5.4

If the procedure given in Figure 4.5.9 displays a menu on the screen, write a procedure to restore the screen.

4.5.5

Write a program to display the arrow icon at location (50,50) on the screen and the clock icon at (150,150) on the screen. Apply the three-Bitblt exchange technique on the two icons (figure 4.5.11).

4.5.6

Do any of the programs you use have pull-down or pop-up menus? If so how are the operations divided among the various menus? How are the operations of a given menu grouped? Can you exit the menu without making a selection? If so, how?

4.5.7

Give the dimensions of an array used on your system to hold the menu in figure 4.5.1

4.5.8

Is there a fast way on your system to set all of the bits in a block of memory to 1?

4.5.9

Describe the bitmap used to hold the highlight in MenuLocator.

4.5.10

Display your arrow and clock icons on the screen as shown in figure 4.5.11. Use the method given in the book to exchange them if xor is available on your system. If you cannnot use xor, how can you exchange the two icons? If both icons are held in storage you could use the cStore mode to speed up the process.

FIGURE 4.5.11

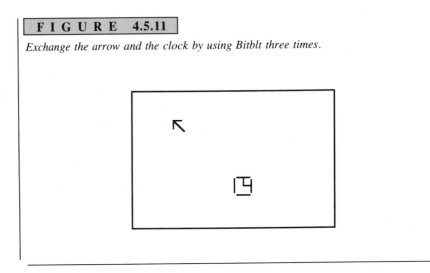

Exchange the arrow and the clock by using Bitblt three times.

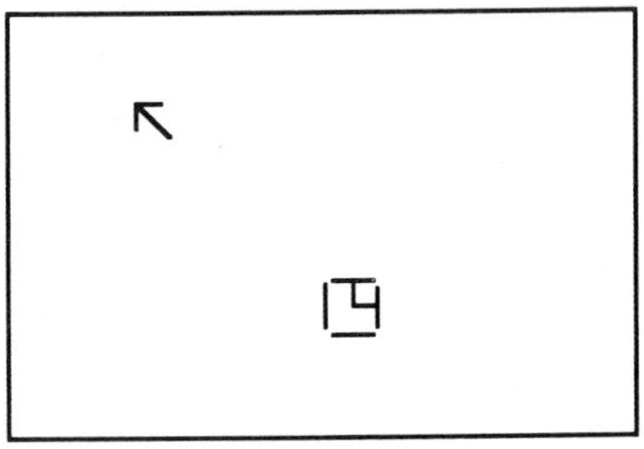

4.6 Rotations of Bitmaps

It is difficult to rotate bitmap images directly. The obvious approach is to create a copy of the storage matrix for the bitmap and then perform a rotation by interchanging appropriate rows and columns of the matrix. This type of maneuver would only give rotations of 90°, 180°, and 270°, however, and as you will shortly see, it can also be a very time-consuming operation. None of the bitmap algorithms covered here will give more flexibility with regard to the angles of rotation, but they will improve the speed of the operation by employing techniques used to create Bitblt.

Because of the limited number of angles of rotation and the inefficiency of even the best known algorithms, it is better not to rotate the images as bitmaps. Instead, try to express them in terms of their geometric parts and use the rotation formulas in section 3.5 to rotate the parts. It is not always feasible to do this conversion. In game programs, for example, images must be rotated quickly. The best way to accomplish this is to store each instance of a rotation as an array of bitmaps. When a rotation is needed, it may be quickly retrieved from this array and displayed on the screen. The rotations of the images may be created by using either a font editor or the computational techniques shown in section 4.3. Images such as CAT scans, which are generated with computation-intensive techniques, are often more difficult to create than to rotate. For this type of image and for small bitmaps that may be rotated quickly, you can use the three rotation algorithms discussed in this section. The first two algorithms will be used to rotate an image in a square matrix, one word on a side. This is the type of matrix that will be manipulated by the third algorithm.

FIGURE 4.6.1

The letter E *and the three rotations of* E *by multiples of 90°*

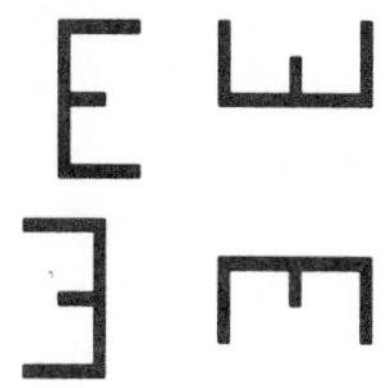

FIGURE 4.6.2

The Apple II representation of the letter E.

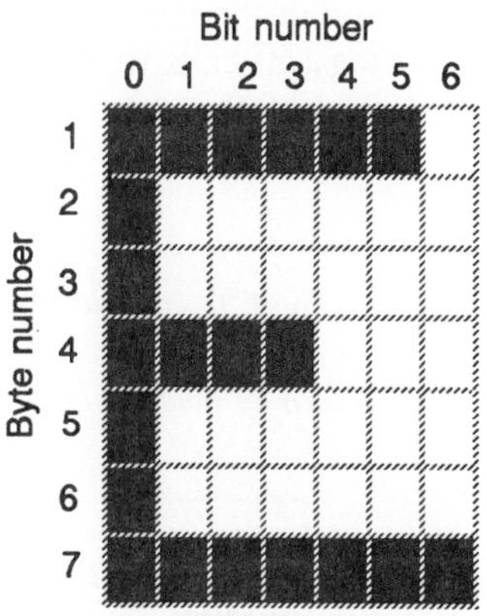

FIGURE 4.6.3

The first step in rotating the letter E *270°, after rows have been shifted to the right (with wrapping)*

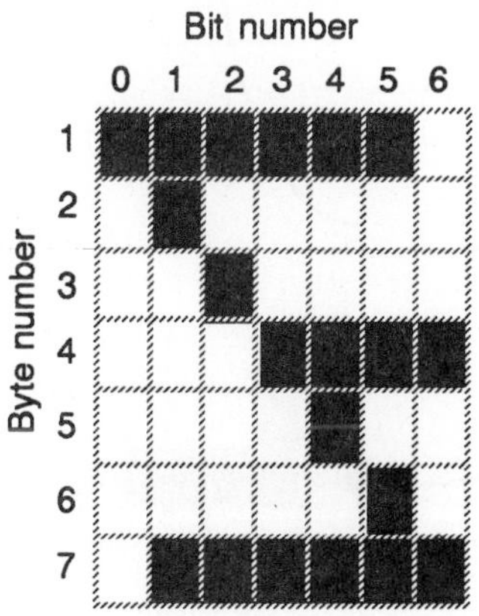

Suppose, for simplicity, that the letter *E* is stored in such a matrix. You would like to rotate it by one of three multiples of 90° (figure 4.6.1). It might seem that a 90° rotation of this matrix could be achieved by exchanging the value at the (i,j) position with the value at the (*j*, *wordsize* − i + 1). If the matrix Letter were expressed as a **packed array**[1..wordsize,1..wordsize] **of** boolean, you could then transfer the value into a temporary matrix as follows:

```
for row :=1 to wordsize do
   for column := 1 to wordsize do
      Temp[column,wordsize − row + 1] := Letter[i,j];
```

This seems innocuous and is, in fact, when wordsize is 8. In this case, 64 operations will rotate the array. If, however, wordsize is 16, the number of assignments is 256. In general, then, the number of operations coincides with the size of the matrix **squared.**

This square matrix has the same number of bits across a row as in a column, which suggests that a row should be substituted for a column by using larger units such as words. The icons, in particular, have exactly the same number of rows as there are bits in a word and are one-word wide. Here you run directly into the tyranny of the row-major form representation of matrices, that is, the screen buffer and Bitblt. While rows of an image are normally stored as consecutive bits in memory, columns are not, so there is no way to move a row to a column directly. The last method that you will examine does move larger blocks around by assignment, but you must still find a way to rotate icon-size units of memory.

There are two methods for rotating bitmaps with Bitblt that were given by Pike, Guibas, and Ingalls (1984). The first method, **shearing,** slices the bitmap into rows or columns and then, by shifting these slices, rotates the image. To rotate the *E* (figure 4.6.2) 270° or 90° counterclockwise, you start at the top of the original image and shift each row to the right, wrapping extra bits to the next row. The first row stays in place. The second moves 1 bit to the right; the last bit wraps to the first spot of the same row. The third row shifts 2 bits to the right, and so on (figure 4.6.3).

Next, starting at the right, columns are moved successively farther down, and leftover bits are wrapped around to the top (figure 4.6.4). Finally, starting from the bottom, rows are shifted successively to the left (figure 4.6.5). The left and right shifts can be considered a concatenation of bit strings because each row is a unit in memory. The columns, as always, are problematic. Bitblt is designed to resolve the difficulty and may be used here. This method would require $3*m + 6$ calls to Bitblt, where m is the size of a word.

The simplest way to implement the column shifts is to use a larger matrix with twice as many rows and columns as the original had. Each row or column is Bitblted in the direction indicated previously. No rotation of trailing bits is needed (see exercise 4.6.1 and figures 4.6.13–15). This method requires $4*m + 5$ calls to Bitblt.

The second method given by Pike, Guibas, and Ingalls is a modification of an algorithm by Floyd (1972). Even though the algorithm is called a **parallel recursive subdivision,** it iteratively applies a mask to the matrix and, by judicious placement of the destination point, rotates many submatrices as a block. A recursive description of this algorithm is fairly simple. The matrix to be rotated is assumed to be m×m, where $m = 2^n$. It is divided into four square matrices, each with side length 2^{n-1}. These matrices are rotated by the algorithm; then the rotated results are rotated as blocks (figures 4.6.6–8).

The actual iterative implementation uses a loop that is incremented between 0 and n−1. For each iteration value, k, a square of ones 2^k on a side, is placed at the origin of an m×m mask, M. The square is repeated at odd multiples of 2^k in the first row of *M*. This block of 2^k rows is repeated at rows that are odd multiples of 2^k. If, for example, the mask given in figure 4.6.9 were for a matrix with $n = 2$ ($m = 4$), then $k = 0$ and each black square is 1 pixel. On the other hand, if in the same diagram $n = 4$ ($m = 16$), then k = 2 and each black square has 4 pixels along a side.

M is applied as a texture and the source rectangle is positioned so that the solid area hits one of the four submatrices of the next larger submatrix. Then the destination point is selected in a temporary copy of the original image, and the masked squares are placed in their rotated position. For each k, four such Bitblts are necessary. With the creation of the mask at each step and the copying of the temporary matrix back to the original matrix, each step of the iteration takes 7 calls to Bitblt. Thus, this algorithm has a total of 7$\mathbf{log}_2$(m) calls to Bitblt.

FIGURE 4.6.4

In the second step of the 270° rotation of E, *the icon in figure 4.6.3 is shifted down (with wrapping). The right column is shifted by 1, and the shift is increased by 1 for successive columns to the left.*

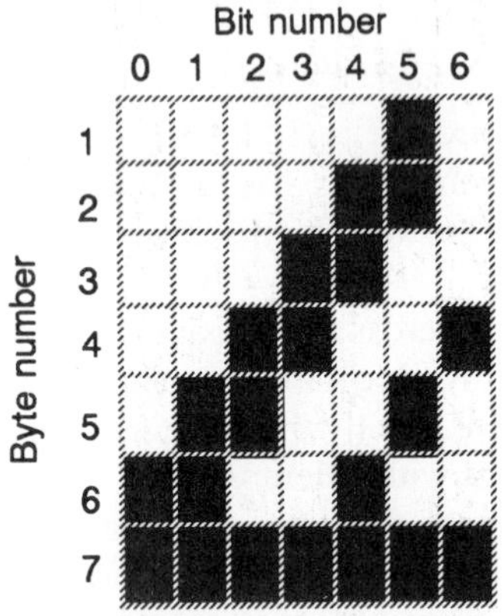

FIGURE 4.6.5

The rows of the icon in figure 4.6.4 are shifted to the left to get the final rotated E. *The bottom row is shifted 1 bit to the left, row 6 is shifted 2 bits to the left, and so on.*

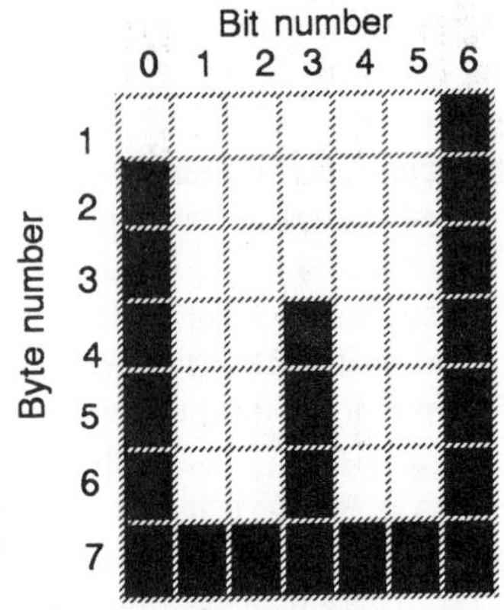

FIGURE 4.6.6

In the parallel recursive replacement algorithm, the icon holding E *is subdivided into four equal squares. These squares are rotated to replace the next square in a counterclockwise direction. Then the squares are rotated in turn by subdivision.*

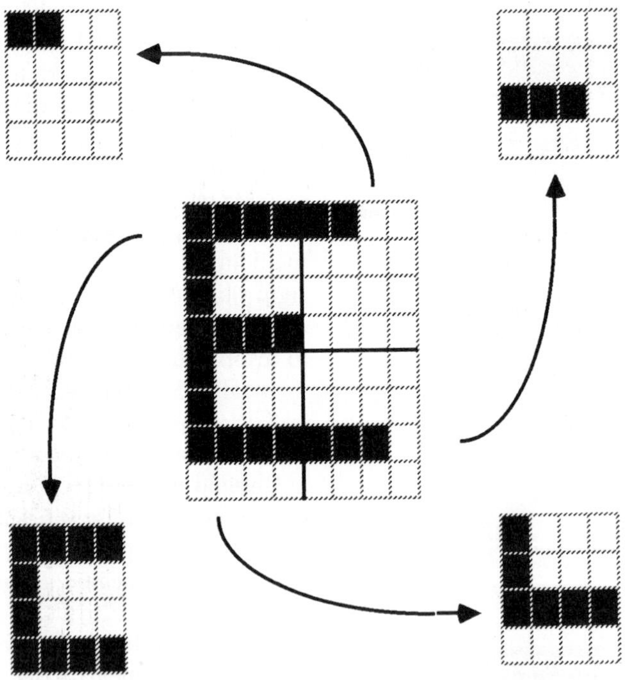

FIGURE 4.6.7

The complete set of rotations used by the parallel recursive algorithm

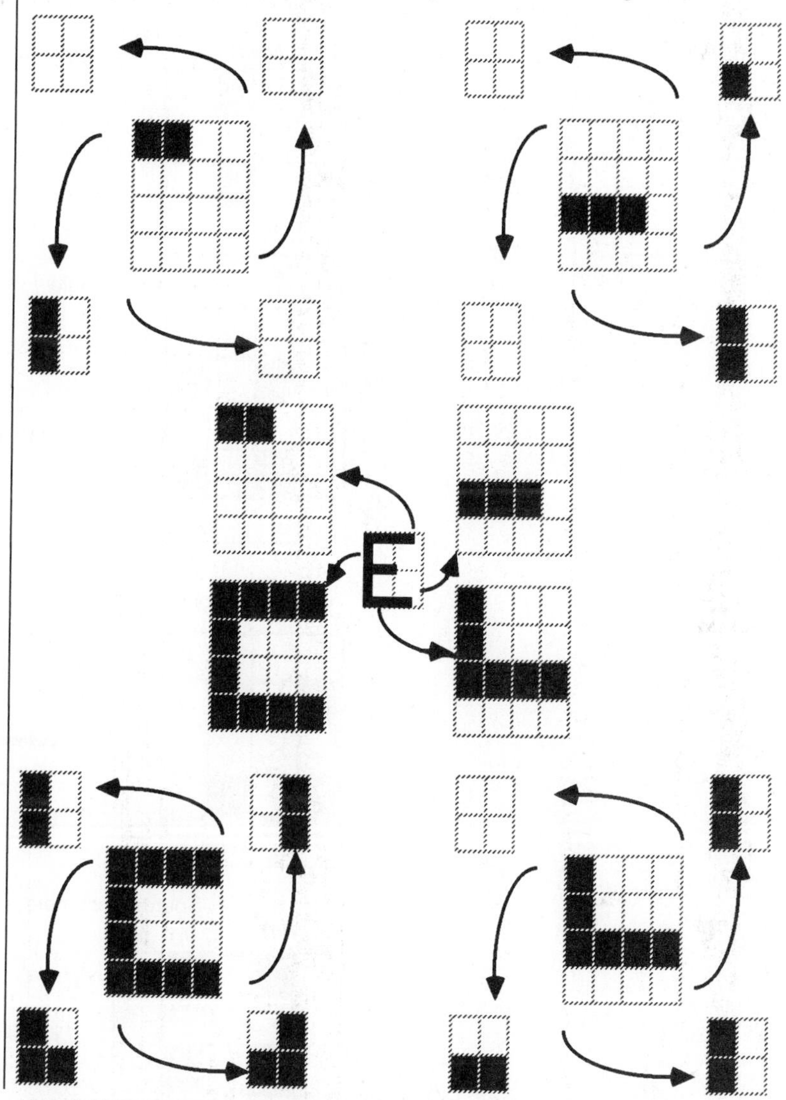

FIGURE 4.6.8

The 2 × 2 blocks from figure 4.6.7 showing their final position in the rotated E

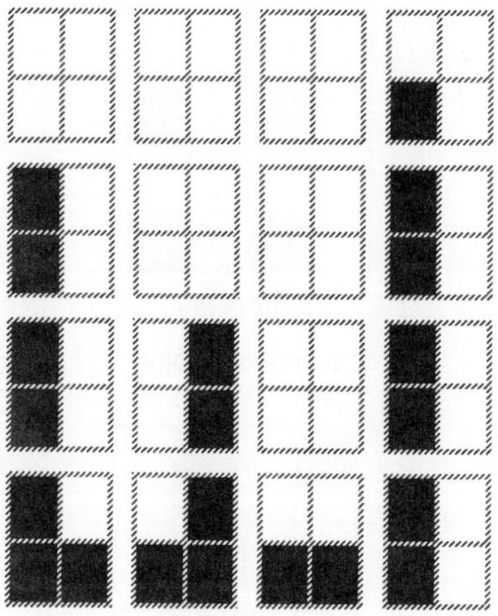

Kornfeld (1987) has proposed a way to avoid the problems involved in interchanging rows and columns with word-oriented operations. In his algorithm, bitmaps are looked at as if they were n×n matrices, where n is a multiple of the word size m. The image is broken into word-square matrices, which are transferred to a memory location of this size called a **prism.** Actual bit-level rotations are performed in the prism, and the resulting blocks are replaced in their final location in the original map. Figure 4.6.10 shows the rotation of the corner blocks in a 270° rotation. After the corner blocks are rotated, the next set of four blocks (figure 4.6.11) is rotated. This process is repeated until the outer shell is rotated. Smaller concentric shells are rotated until the whole matrix has been rotated.

FIGURE 4.6.9

The parallel recursive algorithm implemented without recursion by Bitblt using a texture mask

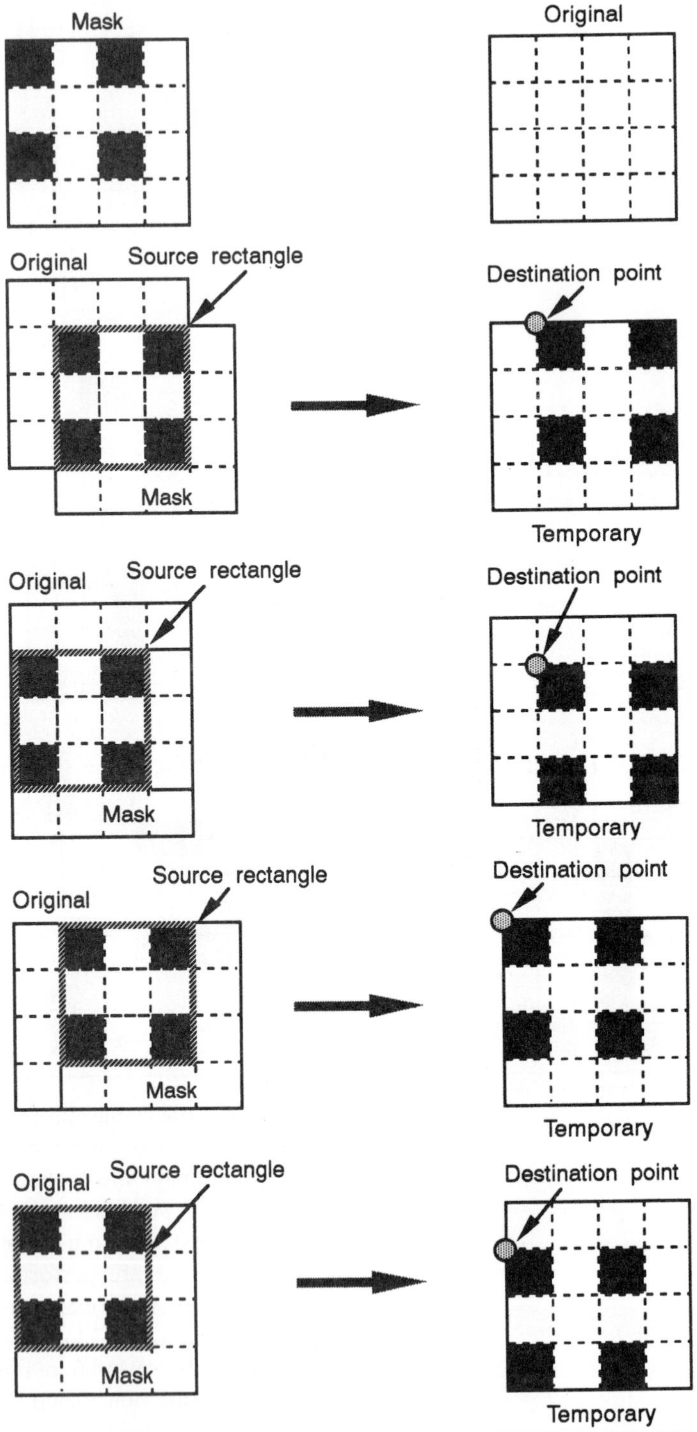

FIGURE 4.6.10

The Image Prism is a specially designed memory chip that allows access to consecutive bits in either rows or columns. This results in fast algorithms for rotations and other transformations.

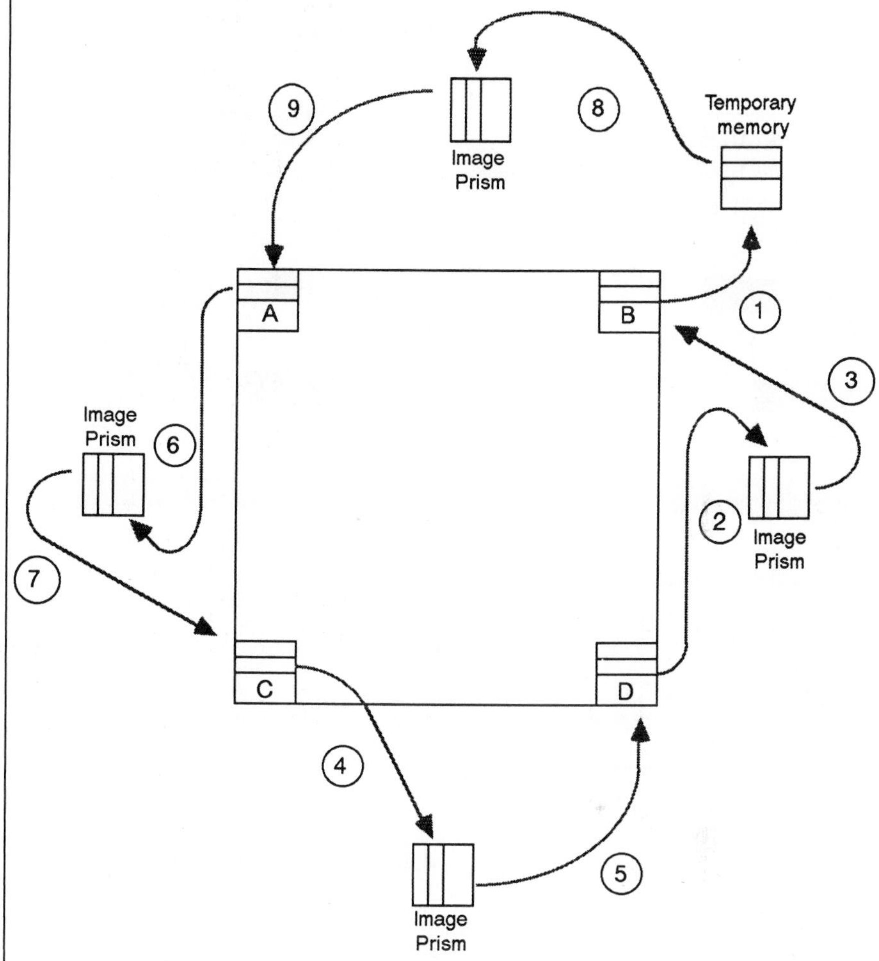

FIGURE 4.6.11

The four blocks rotated through the prism after the corner blocks have been rotated

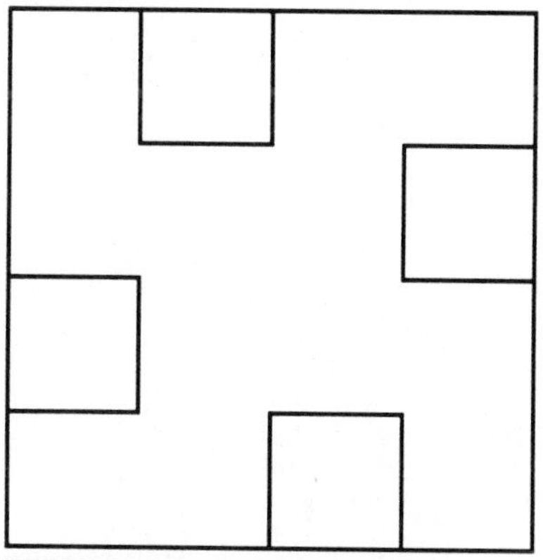

FIGURE 4.6.12

Reflecting across a vertical axis is difficult because the interchanged bits are not always placed in the same position in a word.

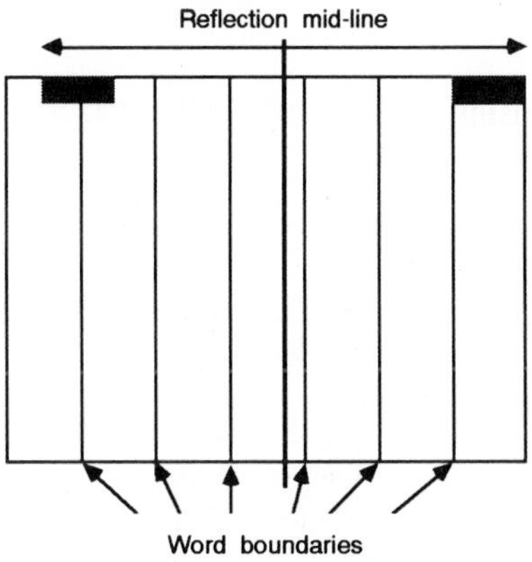

The rotation in the prism may be done with one of the Bitblt operations used previously, resulting in improved speed and memory use on larger bitmaps. In systems where rotations are often used, the prism is implemented with a biselectable memory chip. This chip allows either rows or columns to be altered as a unit.

Bitmap reflection is another difficult problem to which the prism can be applied. When a bitmap reflects across a vertical axis (figure 4.6.12), word alignment problems again make simple word interchanges difficult. By using an appropriate pattern of blocks and reflections within the prism, it is possible to speed up the process of reflection (Kornfeld, 1987).

EXERCISES

4.6.1

Implement the 270° rotation algorithm with the shear algorithm and the larger matrix (figures 4.6.13–15).

FIGURE 4.6.13

Rotate this E *using the shear algorithm and matrices larger than those needed to hold* E.

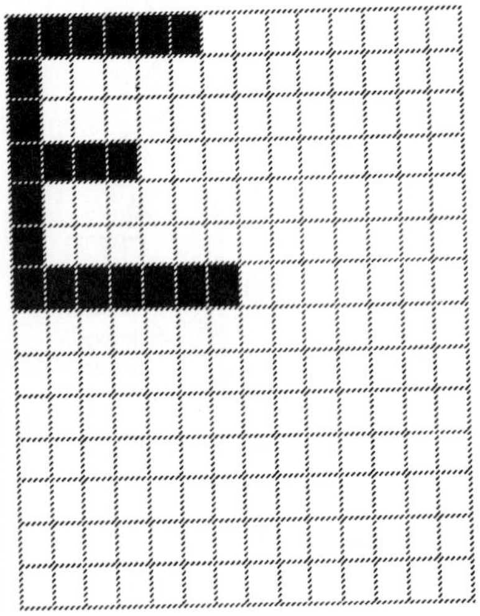

FIGURE 4.6.14

Because of the larger matrix, the right shifts need not include wrapping.

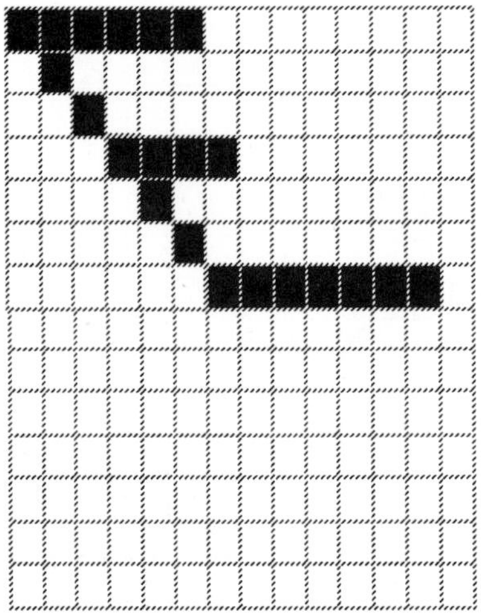

FIGURE 4.6.15

The shifts down also do not require wrapping because of the larger matrix.

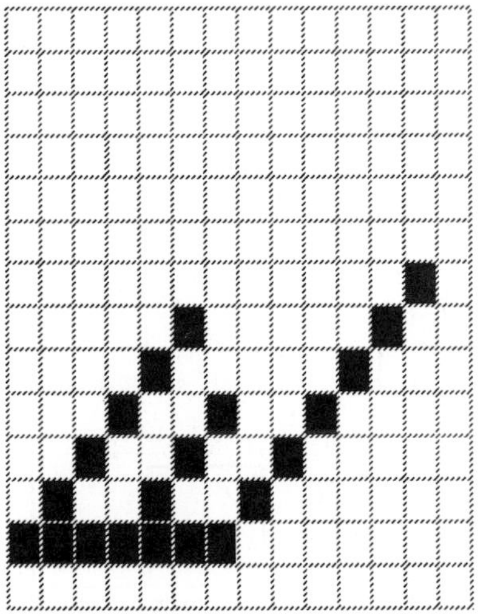

4.6.2

Implement the parallel recursive subdivision algorithm for a 270° rotation of a prism.

4.6.3

Implement the prism rotation of 270° by using the procedure from exercise 4.6.1 or 4.6.2 to rotate the prism.

4.6.4

What pattern of block replacement is used to implement the prism rotation for 90° and 180°? Is there an easier way to do rotations of 180°?

4.6.5

What set of shears would be used for a 90° rotation if you performed it with the shear method and the larger matrix?

4.6.6

How is a reflection across a horizontal line implemented?

4.6.7

What pattern of block replacement does the prism method use in a reflection across a vertical line? How is the prism altered in this operation?

4.6.8

Trace the Shearing method on a 90° rotation for the letter s given below.

4.6.9

Trace the parallel recursive subdivision algorithm on a 90° rotation for the letter s given in figure 4.6.16.

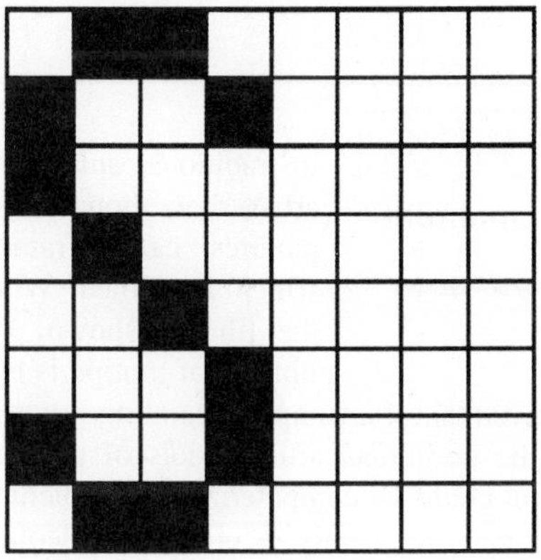

BIBLIOGRAPHY

Defanti, Tom, Rick Frankel, and Larry Leske. "A Call for the Publishing of Blt-Stones." *IEEE CG&A* 7(10):39–49 (October 1987).
A guide to addressing on graphics cards with C language interfaces.

Floyd, R. W. *Complexity of Computer Computations*. New York: Plenum, 1972.

Guibas, L., and J. Stolfi. "A Language for Bitmap Manipulation." *ACM Trans. Graphics*. (July 1982): 191–214.

Kornfeld, Cary D. "The Image Prism: A Device for Rotating and Mirroring Bitmap Images." *IEEE CG&A* 7(5):21–30 (May 1987).

Pike, R., L. Guibas, and D. Ingalls. *Bitmap Graphics*. ACM SIGGRAPH '84, July 1984. Course notes.

CHAPTER

5

Interactive Graphics

DIRECTIONS

—*Computer Animation*

In traditional animation, artists draw thousands of pictures, called frames, which are filmed. When the film is shown, the illusion of motion is created. It is easily perceived that if a computer painting program were substituted for the traditional artist's tools of pen and colored inks, animation could be computerized. The pictures created on a computer may be directly recorded on videotape for television viewing. In France, the use of computers in 2-D animation has increased dramatically the number of hours of animation broadcasted annually.

The success of computer-created cartoons in France is overshadowed by some spectacular failures by American film companies in their attempts to incorporate considerable amounts of realistic, computerized 3-D animation in films. The movies *Tron* and *The Last Starfighter* failed in part because people perceived the computer-generated images to be nothing but "very high-tech Japanese cartoons." (Sørensen 1988, p. 55)

Nevertheless, there have been some successful attempts at incorporating realistic computer animation in films such as *2010* and *The Abyss*. In both cases, more than six months of work was needed to produce a few minutes of realistic animation (Sørensen 1988, Vasilopoulos 1989). After numerous attempts to create an animation of Jupiter's surface for *2010,* the final image was finally achieved by manipulating NASA photographs of Jupiter (Sørensen 1988). The "water tentacle" in *The Abyss,* shown in figure 1.2.6, was a six-month collaborative effort among computer artists and the film's director.

The current quality of computer-generated 3-D images is only good enough to allow their use in science-fiction movies, where the audience is willing to accept an image that is not realistic. As 3-D computer images improve, they likely will be used to re-create historical sets. Location shooting of historical movies has become more difficult with the incursion of TV antennas and other vestiges of the twentieth century. Improvements in computer animation and its decreasing cost will make animated backgrounds an attractive alternative (Sørensen 1988).

Computer animation has had considerable success in some industrial applications. Walkthru (Bechtel Software Inc.) is an animation program originally developed to provide construction and maintenance planning. Engineers using this software to simulate the installation of a steam generator in a nuclear power plant discovered that there was insufficient clearance for the generator. If this installation had not been simulated, an accident might have occurred. Failure Analysis Associates reconstructs plane crashes with Walkthru, information from meteorologists' reports, and flight and cockpit voice recorders. These reconstructions, as well those of auto accidents, are now being used as courtroom evidence (Robertson 1988).

FIGURE D.5.1

A fantasy image from TRON, one of the first movies to use computer animation

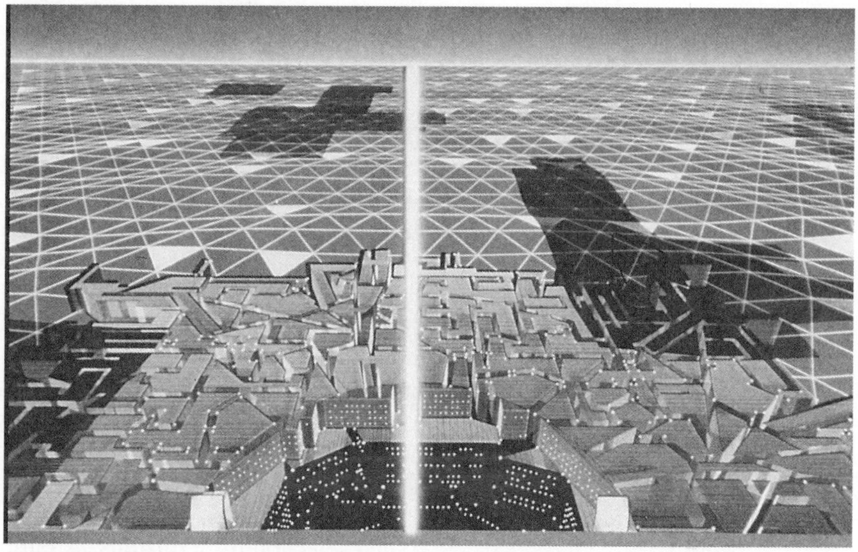

In this chapter, the menus and menu selectors created in chapter 4 will be placed in a main program. These programs allow users to access any menu or tool available in the program in all but a few selected instances. Such programs are called **event-driven.**

Event-driven programs depend heavily on user input. A classification of user input types is given in section 5.1. Section 5.2 will give a simple interactive coordinate reader, and section 5.3 will introduce a basic drawing tool that will be applied to the creation of simple animations. The chapter ends with a description of a **main-event graphics program.**

5.1 A Logical Classification of Input Devices

The pull-down menus developed in the last chapter were the first instance of direct user control of the screen image presented in this book. Readers familiar with one of the paint programs available on microcomputers know that some type of input device is used to make selections from pull-down menus or to draw screen images. The purpose of this section is to discuss the roles of interactive graphic operations independent of the actual hardware implementation of these operations.

Each of these roles may be thought of as an implementation-independent device, more commonly called a **logical device.** The logical devices that will be presented here are

- Locator–Selects a coordinate position
- Choice–Selects from choices presented on the screen
- Stroke–Specifies a sequence of points on the screen
- Pick–Points at information on the screen
- Valuator–Enters scalar values
- String–Enters strings of characters

The **locator** device is perhaps the most important logical input device because it gives the user a way to get the coordinates of a point on the screen so that pictures may be drawn without calculating the coordinates of points. This frees the artist-users from learning the technical details that might deter them from creating computer art. Locators are often implemented with light pens, mice, joysticks, and the keyboard.

Every locator device has four components. First, there has to be some way to indicate a location on the screen. Many of the physical devices display an icon on the screen at the current selection point. Second, there must be a way to move the pointer around the screen. Third, there must be a way to select a given point, and fourth, a way to return the point's coordinates to the program.

Light pens are moved by the user; when a button on the pen is pushed, the current position of the pen is calculated by reading the light from the screen. For this reason, a small icon is placed on the screen to ensure that light will be emitted. The class of devices including joysticks and mice keeps track of the position of an icon that is displayed on the screen, and a button is used to choose a given point (figure 5.1.1). The keyboard may replace a mouse for many operations. The keyboard implementation is discussed in detail in the next section.

Choice devices include selection from menus (like those presented in chapter 4) and selection from **buttons.** A button is typically selected as a choice device when the possible options in a situation are "yes" or "no." Buttons may be implemented as small areas of the screen that have either strings or icons to indicate their purposes. Selection is made by use of either a light pen or a locator device such as a mouse. Warning boxes, like the one in figure 5.1.2, typically use buttons to provide user choices. Buttons are also used when a menu is presented as a set of icons left on the screen throughout the run of a program.

FIGURE 5.1.1

A workstation with mouse and keyboard used as input devices

FIGURE 5.1.2

Buttons are used when a yes/no decision is requested.

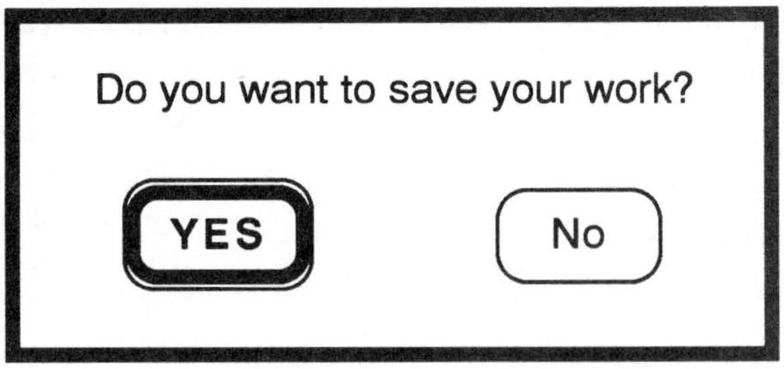
Do you want to save your work?
YES
No

These menus often present a selection of graphics tools, such as those discussed in section 6.1, or textures that may be applied to a graphic object (figure 5.1.3).

In addition, buttons may be implemented as actual buttons on a ''button box'' or functional keyboard, either as a stand-alone unit or as part of the system keyboard. Touch panels may also be used to implement choice devices.

The **stroke** device is used for drawing graphic objects directly. A locator retrieves the coordinates of a beginning location and a terminal location. The coordinates of intervening points are returned when a special button on the device is pressed (figure 5.1.4). Section 5.3 will consider a stroke device implemented from the keyboard.

The **pick** is used to select graphic objects on the screen. To select a specific object on the screen, the program must have a list of the objects on the screen and the areas of the screen that they occupy. This type of listing is created in a object-oriented graphics system, which will be discussed in detail in section 6.3. When a locator device selects a point, the list is searched for an object whose area contains the point. This object is picked and highlighted in some way to indicate the choice (figure 5.1.5). If the area surrounded by an object is used to verify selection, the choice will not always be the intended object (figure 5.1.6).

FIGURE 5.1.3

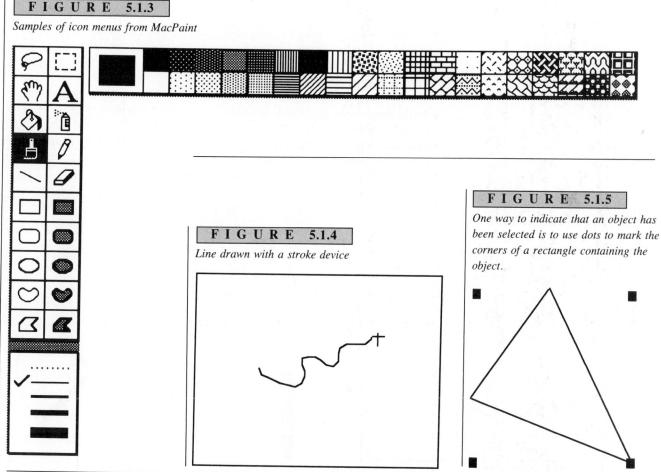

Samples of icon menus from MacPaint

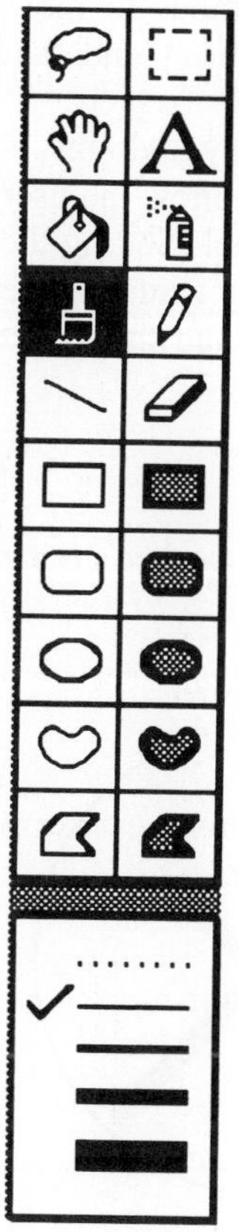

FIGURE 5.1.4

Line drawn with a stroke device

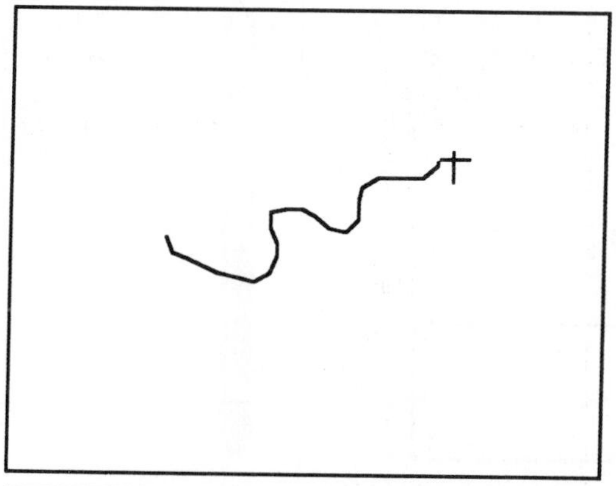

FIGURE 5.1.5

One way to indicate that an object has been selected is to use dots to mark the corners of a rectangle containing the object.

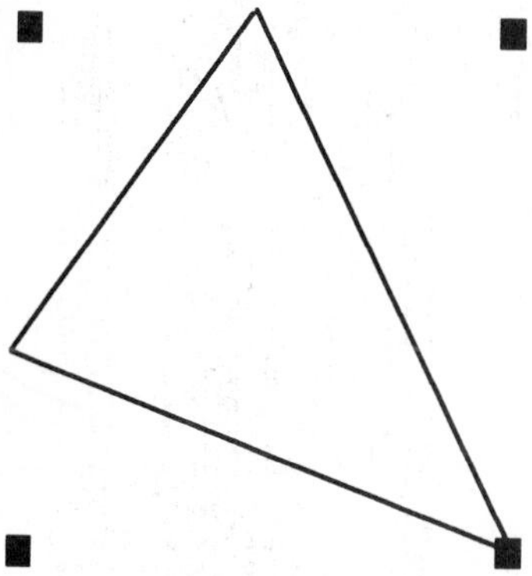

FIGURE 5.1.6

Selecting a point in a rectangle that contains an object will not necessarily select that object.

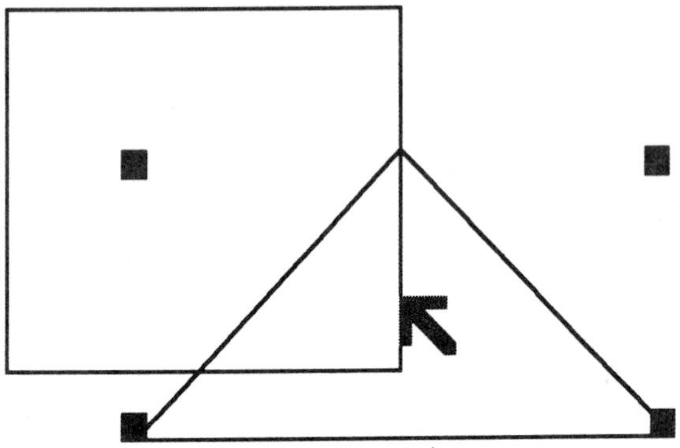

FIGURE 5.1.7

Some systems allow the user to select a region by drawing around it.

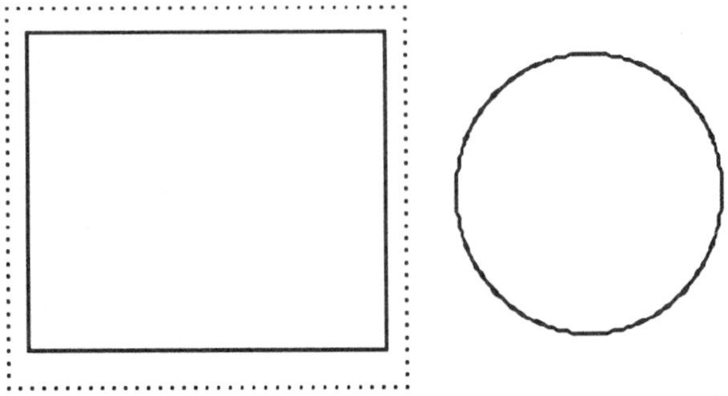

An alternative pick method is simply to select the region in which the desired object is located. The simplest way to do this is to use a rectangle (figure 5.1.7); however, irregular object placement limits the use of this method. In more sophisticated systems, a curve is drawn around the desired object and that curved region is selected (figure 5.1.8).

Valuators allow the user to enter real numbers. The easiest way to do this is directly through the keyboard. Sometimes it is more effective to allow the user to select a value indicated on an analog-type display such as a dial. Setting the time on a clock by moving its hands or regulating a temperature by adjusting the mercury in a thermometer (figure 5.1.9), while less accurate than the direct input of values, may be easier for the inexperienced user.

FIGURE 5.1.8

Selection using a rectangular region does not give enough control when objects are close to each another. Some systems provide a free-form region selector to avoid this problem.

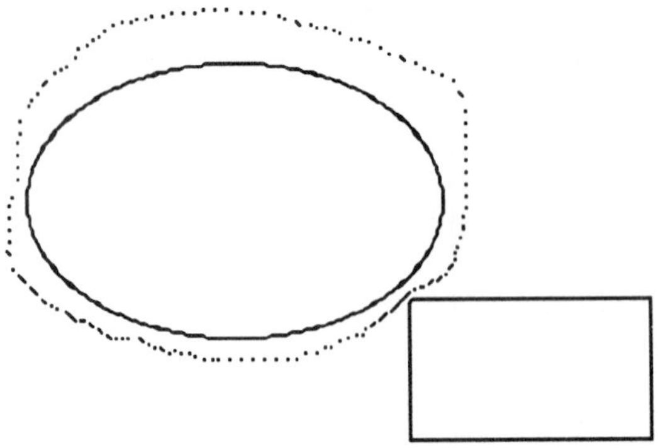

FIGURE 5.1.9

Sample graphic input. Graphic input can give the user a better sense of the required data's purpose.

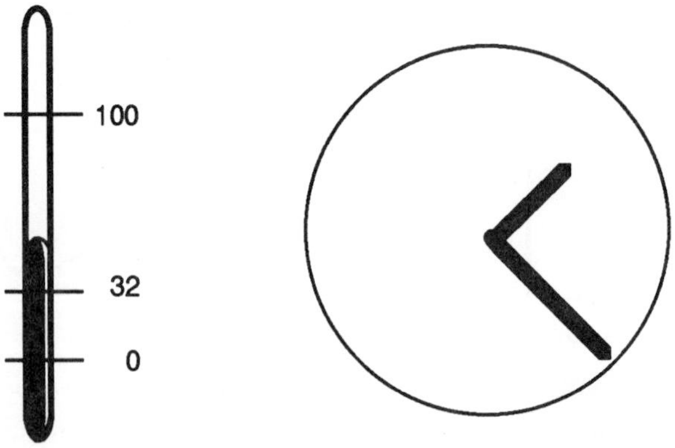

The rotary potentiometer, a dial input device, uses varying voltages to generate real numbers. The device also provides an effective way to change the parameters of a system. The slide potentiometer uses linear motion to generate real numbers. Both types of potentiometers provide physical implementations of valuator dials.

The **string** is most often implemented directly through the keyboard. As a string is typed, it is displayed on the screen. Special care is taken to display the text in XOR mode until there is an indication that the string is complete. This is done so that if the user entering the string decides to alter it by typing a backspace (left arrow), the previous letter may be deleted from the string. Such a deletion requires a second writing of the last letter of the string in XOR mode.

EXERCISES

5.1.1

What is the difference between a logical device and a physical device?

5.1.2

Which of the logical devices can be implemented with a mouse? How is a mouse used to implement these logical devices?

5.1.3

Which of the logical devices can be implemented with the keyboard? How is the keyboard used to implement these logical devices?

5.1.4

Of those logical devices that can be implemented with both a mouse and the keyboard, which are better suited to the mouse and which are better suited to the keyboard? Justify your answers.

5.2 Implementing a Locator Device

Locator devices may be implemented in many different ways using many different physical devices. The keyboard is virtually universal, so it will be used here to demonstrate the implementation of logical devices. The details of implementation will differ from device to device, but the main considerations are common to all. As you may recall, the four components of a locator device are a pointer to indicate the current position, a way for the user to move the pointer, a way for the user to select the current position, and a way to return the coordinates of the chosen point.

For the sake of this discussion, the pointer will be called a cursor to avoid confusion with the Pascal-type pointer. Cursors consist of an icon and a hotspot. The icon is, as its name suggests, a bitmap containing an image that clearly points to a particular spot, the hotspot. Images commonly used for cursors were mentioned in chapter 4. Some cursor icons, such as the I-beam used by some word processors, do not have an obvious hotspot. This makes it difficult for the user to know if the selected spot is actually the desired location.

```
Cursors may be stored in the structure
  Cursor = record
    HotSpot : Point;
    Icon    : Bitmap
  end.
```

FIGURE 5.2.1

The hotspot for the cross cursor implemented on the Apple II is at (7,7).

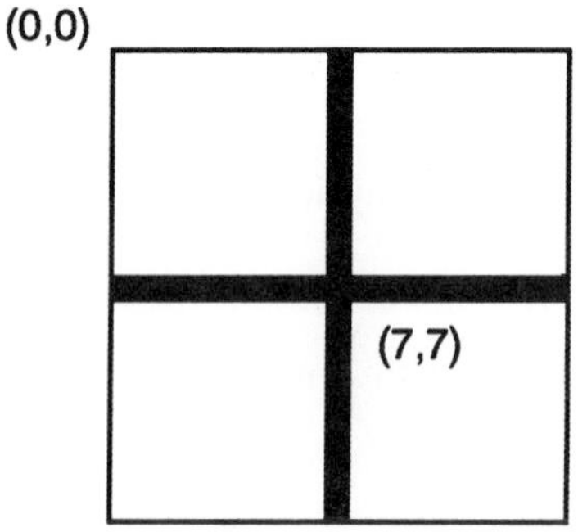

To simplify the computation of the actual point selected by an icon, assume that all cursor icons have x- and y-coordinate ranges from 0 to wordlength − 1. The cross in figure 5.2.1 has its hotspot at (7,7) in the bitmap coordinates of the icon. When the cursor is displayed, its origin coincides with the screen point where the icon appears. This point is not always the hotspot of the icon, so it is not always the point with the desired coordinates. Given the destination point (x,y) for a cursor, to access the coordinates pointed to by the cursor, you must add the offsets given by the HotSpot coordinates. The coordinates sought in this case are (x + HotSpot.x, y + HotSpot.y).

In order to move the cursor around the screen, position the cursor at a starting location (x,y) on the screen and compute an updated location in response to keyboard input. You will use predetermined keyboard keys to read the direction and to move the cursor. These keys are chosen in such a way that their locations on the keyboard relative to one another correspond to the direction of movement they indicate. Use the key **k** to indicate a move to the right; **j,** a move to the left; **i,** a move up; and **m,** a move down. To indicate that the current location is the one for which coordinates are desired, the oeprator will use the <**esc**> key. Notice that pressing the **j** key may result in either the character *j* or the character *J*. To eliminate confusion, accept either lower- or uppercase letters.

Another problem that must be addressed is the size of the movements created by the keys. When fine movements are necessary, one unit is the appropriate distance. This causes very slow movements of the cursor, so when the cursor is being moved over large distances, a larger increment is needed. Therefore, allow the operator to press the > key to increase the size of movements and the < key to decrease the size of movements. This input should be independent of the case of the key, so either < or **,** will produce smaller increments and either > or **.** will produce larger increments.

To clarify the code for this program, use the following variables of type **set of char**:

```
UP := ['i','I']; DOWN := ['m','M']; RIGHT := ['k','K'];
BIG := ['>', '.']; SMALL := ['<', ',']; LEFT := ['j','J'];
MOVES := UP + DOWN + RIGHT + LEFT;
SIZE := BIG + SMALL; LEGAL := MOVES + SIZE + [chr(27)];
```

Using these sets to indicate movements permits you to change the characters used to indicate a move without altering the locator program.

On those systems with a calculator keypad you can use the number **4** for left, **8** for up, **6** for right, and **2** for down. You can also use the keypad to add diagonal directions such as up-right, which occurs if both x and y are increased by the amount of the jump. The keypad character **9** could be used to indicate that movement, **3** for down-right, **1** for down-left, and **7** for up-left.

The coordinates returned by the locator are bitmap screen coordinates. These coordinates do not necessarily coincide with the screen coordinates of this graphics system because both the origin and direction of increasing y may be different in each system. World coordinates most likely will be different. Since the coordinates returned by the locator may be used for either bitmap display or interactive drawing with your developing graphics package, the coordinates returned will be bitmap coordinates. The procedure that uses the locator will convert to an appropriate coordinate system.

These character sets, as well as the cursor bitmap variable, may be declared globally. The appropriate cursor may be read from your file of icons as needed. Choice of cursor will affect the interpretation of the values returned from the ReadLocator function because these numbers indicate the origin of the rectangle containing the cursor. The user will assume that coordinates of the cursor's hotspot will be returned. The definition procedure ReadLocator is found in figure 5.2.2.

In a program, a call to ReadLocator will provide initial values for xmove and ymove, which place the cursor in a convenient location. Notice that xmove and ymove are variable parameters, so you must initialize two integer variables, say x and y, and then call ReadLocator(x,y,Cursor).

FIGURE 5.2.2

The first version of the interactive location-reading procedure ReadLocator

```
(* The procedure ReadLocator is used to move the cursor around the screen.                    *)
(* Sets of characters—Up, Down, Left, Right—contain the keyboard characters                 *)
(* used to move the cursor in those directions. The arrow sends back positions              *)
(* that may be used directly for drawing. With other cursors xmove and ymove                *)
(* must be adjusted for the distance of the hotspot from the origin of the bitmap.          *)
(* The user indicates a point has been selected by pressing the <esc> key, which is chr(27). *)

procedure ChangeJumpSize(Direction : Char; var AmtJump : integer);
begin
  if Direction in Big then          (* change to bigger if indicated                              *)
    AmtJump := AmtJump * 2
  else
    begin                           (* otherwise, cut jump in half, as long as the jump is bigger than 1  *)
      if AmtJump >1 then
        AmtJump := AmtJump div 2
      else
        AmtJump := 1
    end
end; (* ChangeJumpSize *)

procedure AlterCursor(Image : BitMap; var LocPt : Point; AmtJump : integer;
                      Direction : char; var xmove, ymove : integer);
  begin
    (*erase the current cursor*)
    Bitblt(Image,Display,LocPt,Image.Rect,cXor);
    if Direction in Moves then           (* if a location changes, process it  *)
```

(continued)

FIGURE 5.2.2 continued

```
        begin
           (* in all cases check to see if the cursor will                        *)
           (* stay on the screen before changing the value                        *)
           if Direction in Up then
              begin
                 if ymove >= AmtJump then
                    ymove := ymove - AmtJump
              end;
           if Direction in Down then
              begin
                 if ymove <= (Ymax - AmtJump) then
                    ymove := ymove + AmtJump
              end;
           if Direction in Left then
              begin
                 if xmove >= AmtJump then
                    xmove := xmove - AmtJump
              end;
           if Direction in Right then
              begin
                 if xmove <= Xmax - AmtJump then
                    xmove := xmove + AmtJump
              end;
           LocPt.X := xmove;        (* update point used to display the cursor *)
           LocPt.Y := ymove;
           (* display cursor at the new position *)
           Bitblt(Image,Display,LocPt,Image.Rect,cXor)
     end
  end; (* AlterCursor*)


  procedure ReadLocator(var xmove, ymove : integer; Current : Cursor);
  var
     Direction : char;
     AmtJump : integer;
     LocPt : Point;
  begin
     AmtJump := 1;                                        (* initialize the amount of cursor movement  *)
     LocPt.X := xmove;                                    (* get the initial location for the cursor   *)
     LocPt.Y := ymove;
     Bitblt(Current.Icon,Display,LocPt,Current.Icon.Rect,cXor);   (* display the cursor              *)
     repeat
        repeat
           read(keyboard,Direction);      (*read the keyboard until a direction or size changes or quit   *)
        until (Direction in Legal);
        if Direction in Size then         (* if the input indicates a change the size of the jump         *)
           ChangeJumpSize  (Direction,AmtJump);
        else
           AlterCursor(Current.Icon, LocPt , AmtJump,Direction, xmove, ymove );
     until (Direction = chr(27));
     xmove := xmove + Current.HotSpot.X;
     ymove := ymove + Current.HotSpot.Y
  end; (* ReadLocator *)
```

EXERCISES

5.2.1

What location would you use as the hot spot for each of the following icons?

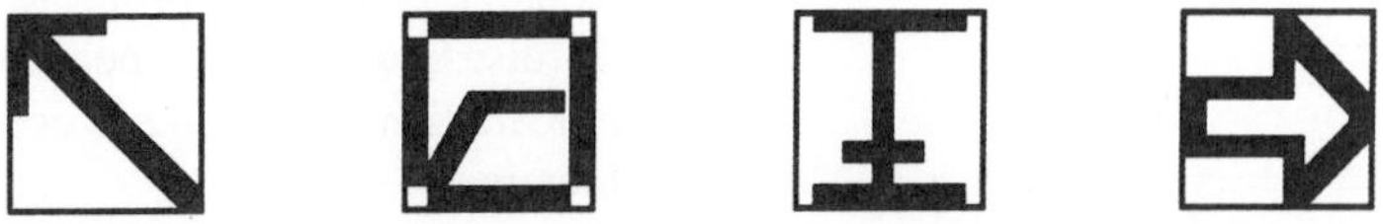

5.2.2

How would you define the sets Up, Down, Right and Left if you are using arrow keys in place of the letters i,k,j and m? (Beware of the fact that some systems use two character sequences to specify arrow keys).

5.2.3

Does your graphics library include special procedures for handling mouse input (or other non-keyboard input)? If so, how do you use these procedures?

5.2.4

Implement ReadLocator on your system.

FIGURE 5.3.1

The two cursor icons used in the sketch program (figure 5.3.2)

5.3 Constructing and Using a Sketching Program

This section combines the techniques developed in chapter 4 and in the first part of this chapter to create a simple procedure that allows the user to draw interactively. In section 5.5 you will then apply the techniques used in this procedure.

The procedure Sketch will allow the user to move a cursor around the screen and to draw. You will use two special cursors for this procedure. Both will have the same pen shape, but one will be filled to indicate that the pen is down and the other just be an outline to indicate that the pen is up (figure 5.3.1).

When the pen is down, a line is drawn from the current position of the cursor to the point the cursor is at when the <**esc**> key is pressed. If the pen is up, the cursor will be moved but no line will be drawn. This procedure is very similar to ReadLocator and will use both the ChangeJumpSize and the AlterCursor procedures from section 5.2.

As this procedure mixes both line drawing and bitmapping, it makes sense to integrate the two systems at this time. The last section presented two major problems encountered when combining these systems. First, the y screen coordinates may be defined in opposite directions in the two systems. Second, you have not as yet written a procedure to go from screen coordinates to the world coordinates used by the drawing procedures.

In this interactive drawing program, no special world coordinate system is needed, so you will not use the screen-to-world coordinate converter. Since the procedure OpenWindow sets the world coordinate system to be equal to the screen coordinate system, no calls to SetWindow or SetViewport will be needed in this section.

Your coordinate reader will return integer coordinates, but after these values have been adjusted for differences between the bitmap system and graphics package, they may be sent directly to the drawing functions. Even though the x and y parameters in these procedures are of type **real,** these parameters are value parameters so appropriate conversions are made automatically.

To raise and lower the pen, use the keyboard key **P** as a button and the **Q** key to indicate that a drawing is complete. These keys are added to the set of legal characters.

Figure 5.3.2 is a first attempt at an interactive drawing program.

FIGURE 5.3.2

This procedure is a sketch program that allows the user to draw lines interactively.

```
(* The procedure Sketch will allow a user to sketch a picture by moving  a cursor around the screen and      *)
(* selecting locations.  If the pen is down, a line will be drawn from the current point to the selected point. If *)
(* the pen is not down, then the current point will be altered to the point selected.  The bitmap Cursor will have *)
(* asits address the address of the file buffer for the Cursor file.  The characters "P" and "p" will have been *)
(* added to the set of Legal inputs to allow the pen to be raised and lowered.  The characters "Q" and "q"   *)
(* are added to allow the drawer to quit.                                                                      *)

procedure Sketch(Current : Cursor ; xmove, ymove : integer);
var
   CursorFile    : CursFile;       (* holds cursors used in the program                                        *)
   PenDown       : boolean;        (* indicates whether pen is up or down                                      *)
   Direction     : char;           (* holds user input, the direction of the cursor movement or control char   *)
   AmtJump       : integer;        (* size of the cursor jump                                                  *)
   LocPt         : Point;          (* current location of the cursor                                           *)
   DrawWindow    : Window;         (* structure holding the information about the drawing                      *)
   xloc,yloc     : real;           (* used to hold temporary x and y locations                                 *)
   PenButton     : set of char;    (* holds "P" and "p," used to indicate change of pen status                 *)
   QuitButton    : set of char;    (* holds "Q" and "q," used to indicate quit                                 *)
begin
   Initialize(CursorFile,DrawWindow,AmtJump, LocPt, PenDown,PenButton, QuitButton); (* initialize variables  *)
   repeat
      Bitblt(Current.Icon,Display,LocPt,Current.Rect,cXor);      (* display the cursor                         *)
      repeat
         repeat
            read(Direction);                                      (* read until Legal input character          *)
         until (Direction in Legal);
         if Direction in PenButton then                           (* pen changes setting                       *)
            ChangePen(CursorFile,Current,LocPt,PenDown);
         else if Direction in Size then                           (* if change in the size of the jump         *)
            ChangeJumpSize  (Direction,AmtJump);
         else
            AlterCursor(Current.Icon, LocPt, AmtJump, Direction, xmove, ymove );
      until (Direction= chr(27)) or (Direction in QuitButton);
      if ((Direction = chr(27)) then                              (* time to draw                              *)
         begin
            xloc := xmove +  Current.HotSpot.x;                   (* correct for location of pointer tip       *)
            yloc := ymax - (ymove + Current.HotSpot.y )           (* and alter y-coordinates if necessary      *)
            if PenDown then
                LineAbs(xloc,yloc,DrawWindow)
            else
                MoveAbs(xloc,yloc,DrawWindow)
         end
   until (Direction in QuitButton)
end; (* ReadLocator *)
```

The Sketch procedure allows the user to create line drawings interactively, but once the drawings are sketched, the procedure stops and nothing is printed or saved. Note that the user must now remember two specialized keys, the **P** and the **Q.** You could add more specialized keys to allow saving and printing, but this would just magnify the problem. One solution would be to add the keys and list them at a neutral location on the screen.

Even this solution has its drawbacks. For example, if you were to add the print feature, the **P** key would be the likely choice to indicate it, but the **P** key is already in use for the pen. You may also note a second problem: there is no logical separation of the loop into a section that finds a location on the screen and a section that reacts to the location. If location on the screen were the sole factor determining the action to be executed, this would solve the problem.

Still another drawback is that as the number of special commands increases, there is no longer room on the screen for commands. This often leads to a hierarchy of menus. Such menu organizations may require long sequences of keystrokes to locate a given command. You will consider an alternative method that solves these problems in section 5.6.

EXERCISES

5.3.1

How do you convert screen coordinates in your bitmap system to screen coordinates in your object-oriented system?

5.3.2

The procedure to convert screen coordinates into world coordinates is quite similar to WorldToScreen. Create new constants similar to the WV constants in your type frame, and write ScreenToWorld using these constants.

5.3.3

Write Initialize and ChangePen for the Sketch procedure given in figure 5.3.2.

5.3.4

Can you suggest other icons to replace the pen up and pen down icons given in figure 5.3.1?

5.3.5

If you have access to a paint or draw program, how do their sketch tools work?

5.3.6

The sketch program uses the ''p'' key, ''q'' key and the escape key to accomplish various tasks. What problems are caused by using keyboard keys in this way? Are there ways to avoid these problems? Why are the arrow keys better suited to interactive input?

5.3.7

If your sketch program could be used to place text on the screen, how could you distinguish between the use of the ''p'' and ''q'' keys for interactive graphic input and text input?

5.4 Using Bitblt to Save Pictures on the Screen

At this point you have only used Bitblt to map predefined images from memory to the screen. It is also possible to map images from the screen into memory. This is particularly useful if you want to save an image from the screen in a file. The entire screen can be saved, but this is not normally done because of the amount of memory needed to do it.

Figures to be saved are often a nearly standard size. To save the drawing in figure 5.4.1, you must calculate the size of an array that will store the picture. Notice that the x-distance is 56 − 24 + 1 = 33. In order to save a row of 33 bits, you must assign the bitmap a width of (33 + PixelsPerWord − 1) **div** PixelsPerWord. Therefore, each row of the array used to store this picture must be 5 bytes long. The number of rows in the array is equal to the y-distance. In this case, 67 − 30 + 1 = 38. The easiest way to define the array is **pic = array[1..Width,1..38] of Word.** Recall that in some systems it may be necessary to pack the array. If F is a **file of pic,** then it is possible to define the **bitmap saver** as follows:

Once this bitmap is initialized and the file F is rewritten, it is necessary to initialize a variable Srec of type **rectangle** with the origin and corner coordinates of the picture. In this case, the origin would be (24,30) and the corner (56,67). To move the picture to the file buffer and then to the file, execute the following steps:

```
Bitblt(Display,saver,saver.Rect.Origin,Srec,cStore);
Put(F);
```

The OpCode cStore is used in this Bitblt because the contents of the file buffer were unknown prior to moving the picture into it. You may store as many

FIGURE 5.4.1

Image saved by the bitmap saver defined in figure 5.4.2

FIGURE 5.4.2

Initializing the bitmap saver used to save images in a file

```
with saver do
  begin
    Base := Address(F^);              (* F^ is the file buffer for F *)
    Width := (33 + PixelsPerWord - 1) div  PixelsPerWord;
    with Rect do
      begin
        Origin.X : =   1;
        Origin.Y : =   1;
        Corner.X := 33;
        Corner.Y := 38
      end
  end;
```

pictures as desired in this file as long as they fit into the array used for the file buffer. After storing the pictures, close the file.

Fixed file-buffer size is the one factor that limits the use of this technique. The actual shape of the rectangle on the screen does not have to coincide with the way the buffer array is defined; bitmaps superimpose their own access methods on memory. Only the actual size of the buffer is important. If the maximum size of the screen area to be stored is known, as it would be if only specified regions of the screen were used for drawing, then this method of storing pictures is quite effective. If a wide range of picture sizes is to be stored, however, either a very large buffer must be provided or more than one file must be made available.

The problem with a large buffer is that most images will not fill it, so much of the file space is wasted. Moreover, the use of multiple files makes the program more complicated and requires that the system be capable of opening files from a program. If these problems are resolved, the procedure may be written so that the user can specify a rectangle to be saved with ReadLocator. The user is restricted to choosing a rectangle that is smaller than the largest buffer. If multiple buffers are employed, then the smallest buffer that can contain the image is chosen.

This method of storing pictures results in unnecessarily large files, and in many cases, most of the file consists mainly of bytes of background or fill color. There are many algorithms for compressing bitmap data before saving the data. One way to pack a bitmap is to create a file of pairs of bytes (figure 5.4.3). The first entry in the pair is the number of repetitions of the second byte found in the original bitmap. This will reduce the size of most bitmap files because large parts of most bitmap pictures consist of repetitions of the same byte.

FIGURE 5.4.3

One way to pack a bitmap is to create a file of pairs of bytes. The first entry in the pair is the number of repetitions of the second byte found in the original bitmap. This will reduce the size of most bitmap files because large parts of most bitmap pictures consist of repetitions of the same byte. In this case, the byte 0 0 0 0 was repeated 6 times. The packed version of this sequence consists of a byte with 6 (0110 base 2), followed by the actual byte from the picture.

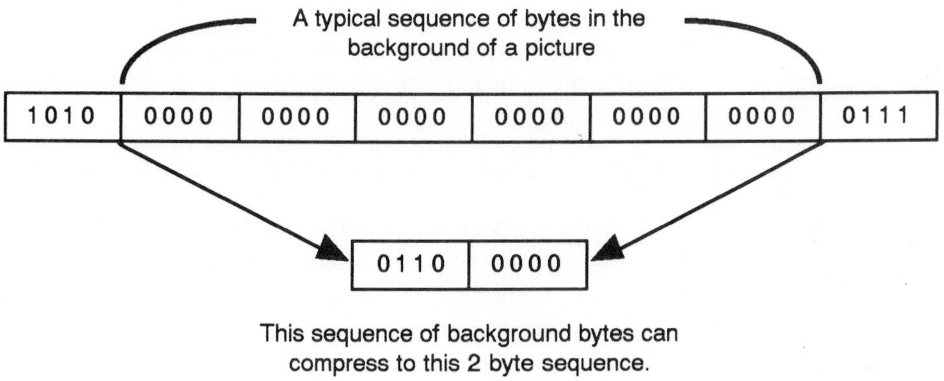
A typical sequence of bytes in the background of a picture
1010
0000
0000
0000
0000
0000
0000
0111
0110
0000
This sequence of background bytes can compress to this 2 byte sequence.

After a file of pictures has been created, any of the pictures in the file on the screen may be drawn. If the picture to be drawn were the fifth one put into the file, it would be found in file record 4 (file records are counted from 0). To get this picture into the buffer, you can use the Seek-Get sequence: Seek(F,4); Get(F). The 4 in the Seek command is the number of the record containing the desired picture. If this picture is to be displayed at point Dpoint and saver is initialized as above, you need only call on Bitblt to draw the picture: Bitblt(saver,Display,Dpoint,saver.Rect,OpCode). In this call to Bitblt, the OpCode depends on what the programmer wants to accomplish.

If more than one image will be stored in one file, you may find it useful to include a preview function that displays the images as they are stored in the file. The user may then select an image or advance to the next image. In most applications where the user picks an image to display, it is more efficient to store each image in a separate file.

EXERCISES

5.4.1

Write a save routine that saves a given rectangle on the screen into a file specified by the user.

5.4.2

Write a save procedure that will save an arbitrary rectangle from the screen to a file. Allow the user to specify the rectangle and the file name. Restrict the rectangle choice so that it does not exceed the size of the largest buffer available.

5.4.3

Write a procedure that allows a user to retrieve an image from a single-image file and display it at a place on the screen chosen at runtime with ReadLocator.

5.4.4

Calculate the storage array necessary to store the picture below on your system. Describe the bitmap Saver you would use to save the picture in figure 5.4.4 on your system.

FIGURE 5.4.4

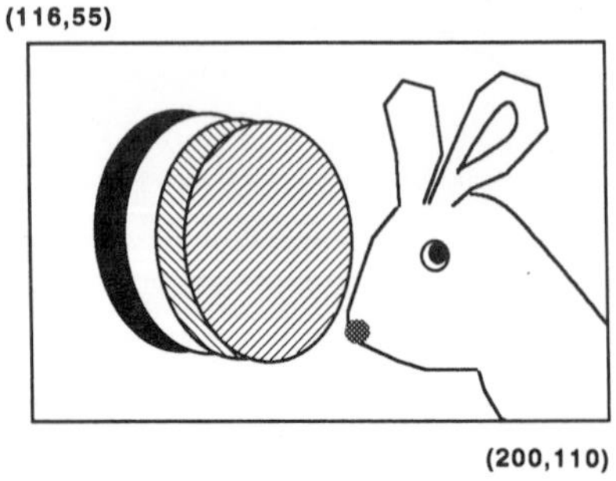

5.4.5

Will regular textures be compressed by the compression algorithm given in the text? Remember consecutive bytes represent consecutive bytes in a row of the picture.

5.4.6

Will this compression algorithm ever lead to a larger file? When?

5.4.7

If you have access to a paint type program, estimate how much memory one picture uses. Draw some sample pictures, and find out how large the files actually are compared to your estimate. Create a picture without large areas of constant color or texture. Is this file bigger than your other examples?

5.5 Simple Animation Using Bitblt

Computer-generated animation has been used for some time in video games and for instructional purposes in simulators. Computer-generated animation is also being used for special-effects sequences in movies, but it is costly. In the film *The Abyss,* a group of rescuers are sent to save a submarine disabled 2000 feet below the surface. One obstacle to the rescuers is a tube of water called a "pseudopod." This tentacle of water takes on the facial features of people it encounters. It took six months for Industrial Light & Magic to create this sequence on computers (Vasilopoulos 1989).

FIGURE 5.5.1

The five worm poses

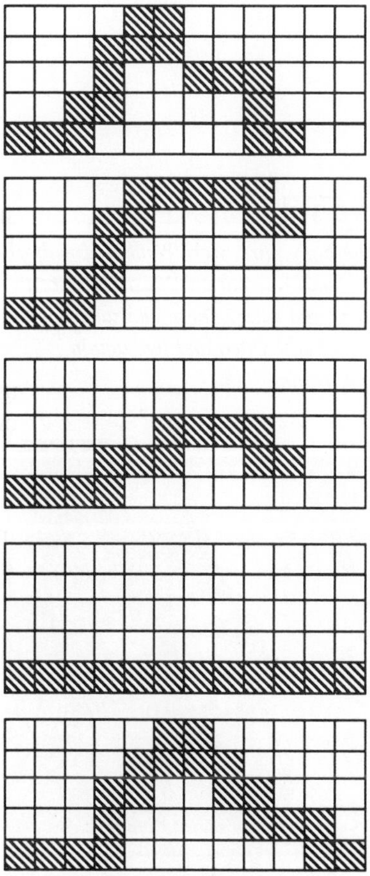

Computer animation, like traditional animation, is created by projecting a sequence of frames, each of which is slightly different from its predecessor. The sequence of pictures appears to the viewer as continuous action. Individual frames for realistic animation, such as that used in *The Abyss,* may take hours to generate so they must be recorded on film or videotape.

Images used in video games are created with extremely efficient assembly language programs so they can be seen on the CRT screen in real time. In this section you will generate an animated cartoon with Pascal. The animation will be at the level of a simple video game.

This animation sequence will show an inchworm crossing the screen. In the sequence five different frames (figure 5.5.1) are shown in a given position on the screen. This position is moved (where the frames are displayed) a distance to the right and the frames are displayed again. The length of time a frame is displayed at each position on the screen and the distance the position is shifted determine how fast the worm moves.

Using the Sketch program, you create each of the worm's poses and then save them on one file with the save technique given in section 5.4. Because all the frames are the same size, they may be created in the same rectangle. In figure 5.5.1, the worms are 12 bits wide by 5 bits high. Another possible size for the frames is 24 by 10. Larger worms take longer to display, so there is a limit on the size of the worm dictated by the speed of Bitblt. Once a size is determined, a file buffer may be defined.

When the worm is animated, the poses are stored in an array **Bworm = array[1..5] of BitMap,** so all the worm's poses may be stored in the same file. The bitmaps are identical except that each points to a different storage area that is the size of the file buffer. Before the animation begins, the poses are copied into these storage areas so that the program wastes no time reading them during the actual run.

Next, an initial point on the screen is chosen to display the worm. This point is used as the Dpoint for the first presentation of each of the five worm poses. To show each pose, use the following sequence of moves. First, Bitblt a worm at the location using the cXor OpCode. Next, pause by using a **for** loop such as **for** i := 1 **to** 100 **do;** (this **for** loop allows the viewer to see each pose before it is erased). Finally, Bitblt the same worm at the same place by using cXor again to erase the worm. After all fives poses have been shown at a given point, increase the x-value by an amount such as 3. Larger amounts make the worm move faster. Even larger amounts make it jump!

The worm has a one-part body. To create more complex creatures, you can use different poses for various body parts. A complete frame consists of combinations of these poses, possibly superimposed on a still video picture.

Figure 5.5.2 shows mouths, eyes, and noses created with a painting program, Truevision's VISTA TIPS (Young 1989). These body parts were combined with textures also created in VISTA TIPS. The resulting bunny bodies were ported to an animation program, AT&T GSL's TOPAS. TOPAS's transparency attribute was used to give the dust bunnies a dusty look. TOPAS also ports the images to videotape a frame at a time (figure 5.5.3). The resulting video is used by Pier I Imports as a maintenance training film.

FIGURE 5.5.2

Animator Monte Young created the cartoon characters Scuzz and Fuzz for a Pier 1 Imports training film produced by J. Darrell Kirkley, Inc. Computer artist Scott Beckley of J. Darrell Kirkley, Inc. then mapped various body parts of each character into polygonal representations. These representations were transformed into a variety of eyes, noses and mouths by standard polygon transformations.

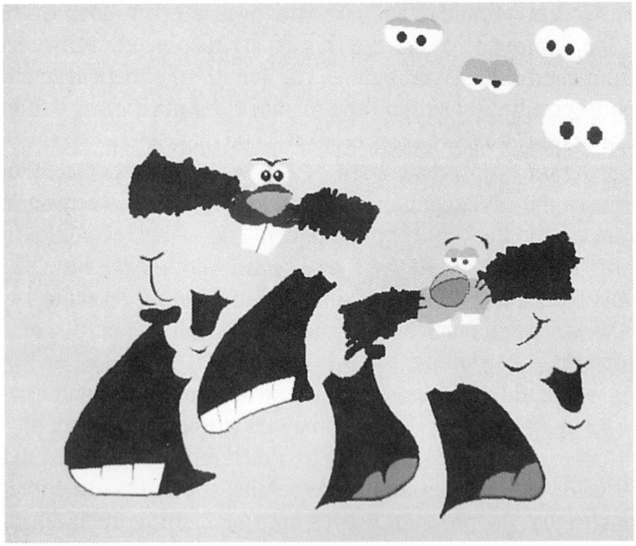

FIGURE 5.5.3

In the final animation, the body parts were combined with a plygon body filled with a semi-transparent "dust" texture to create the characters Scuzz and Fuzz. These characters were then combined with a mix of still video and live action backgrounds to create the training film.

It takes more than high-quality equipment, good software, and good drawing skills to produce animation—skill in animation techniques is also needed. Figure 5.5.4 describes techniques that make their films more realistic (Lasseter 1987). The application of the complete set of techniques is beyond the scope of this book, but the following is an example that uses two of them: squash and stretch, and slow in and out.

In this sequence a rubber ball bounces straight up and down. First the **squash and stretch principle** is applied to show that the ball is elastic and to enhance the sense of motion. The ball is stretched just before and after hitting the ground and squashed on hitting the ground to show its elasticity (figure 5.5.5).

The simple bouncing ball obeys the law of gravity, so any animation must appear to obey this law. When the ball is dropped from a height h_0, its height at time t can be computed by $h(t) = h_0 - at^2$, where a is the rate of acceleration due to gravity.

The ball, unlike the worm, does not move at a constant speed. One way to show variation in speed is to vary the time periods between poses. This is called **slow in and out.** Slow in and out is used in more complex animation when the filmmaker wants to show expressive poses.

FIGURE 5.5.4

Principles of traditional animation (Lasseter 1987)

1. **Squash and Stretch** — Define the rigidity and mass of objects by distorting their shapes during action.
2. **Timing** — The actual meaning of a pose is often determined by the speed of the movement leading up to the pose.
3. **Anticipation** — Preparation for an action.
4. **Staging** — Presentation of an idea so that it is unmistakably clear.
5. **Follow Through and Overlapping Action** — The termination of one action and the establishing of its relationship to the next action.
6. **Straight Ahead Action and Pose-To-Pose Action** — Two different approaches to creating action. In straight ahead action the artist knows the desired effects and draws a sequence of frames to achieve it. In Pose-to-pose key frames for each sequence are drawn first, then the connecting frames are drawn.
7. **Slow In and Out** — The spacing of the inbetween frames to achieve subtlety of timing and movement.
8. **Arcs** — The visual path of an action for natural movement.
9. **Exaggeration** — Accentuation of the essence of an idea via design and the action.
10. **Secondary action** — The action of an object resulting from another action.
11. **Appeal** — Creating a design or an action that the audience enjoys watching.

FIGURE 5.5.5

Squash and stretch is used to improve the animation of a bouncing ball.

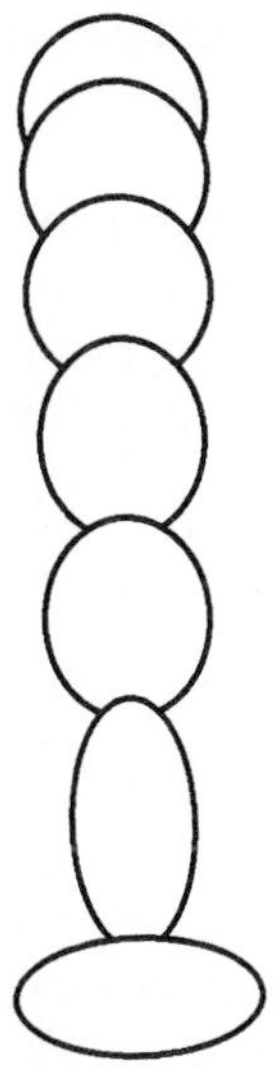

FIGURE 5.5.6

Timing chart for the bouncing-ball problem

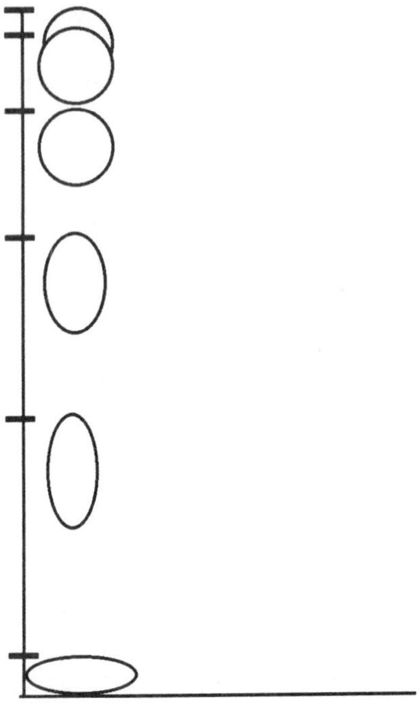

The timing of **the in-betweens,** the time during which poses change, is plotted on a timing chart (figure 5.5.6). Assuming that the ball rebounds without loss of energy, the initial velocity of the ball is then the opposite of the velocity at time of impact: $v_0 = \sqrt{h_0/a}$. The height of the ball after the bounce is h(t) $= v_0t - at^2$. This model uses the same time chart to describe both the up-and-down motions of the ball. In the real world, a small amount of energy is lost during each bounce. To incorporate this loss into the animation, a small amount can be subtracted from v_0 every time the ball hits the ground. This new initial velocity will result in the ball bouncing to a point below the initial height. Eventually the ball will come to rest.

The timing effect shown in figure 5.5.6 is accomplished by using a constant time interval while varying the distance of the jumps between images. Figure 5.5.6 assumes that the initial height of the ball is 125 and its initial position is $y_0 = 50$. The ground, in this case, is at 175. Because the ball drops from 50 to 175, the acceleration must be expressed as a negative number. If the time, t, is incremented by 1 for each unit, and the acceleration, a, is given as -5, the position of the ball at the end of each time interval is as shown in figure 5.5.7. Notice that the ground is actually located at 175 plus the height of the squashed ball.

Some of the difficulties encountered with this type of animation relate to the choice of the appropriate acceleration. If a is too large, there will be large gaps in the picture (as there are in figure 5.5.6). If a is too small, the motion of the ball will be too slow because of the number of calls to Bitblt. As a is decreased, the length of each pause should also be decreased to maintain the speed of the ball. The number of frames must also be increased as more positions are plotted on the timing chart. Finally, notice in figure 5.5.6 that the ball looks like a circle in the first three poses. This is easily achieved by repeating the initial pose for the first three poses.

Because this sequence uses balls of different shapes, a must be adjusted to position the final frame exactly at ground level. If, however, all balls are round and a is small, this precalculation is not necessary; you can calculate frame positions as the ball is displayed. When the calculated destination point is less than the height of the ball above the ground, the ball bounces and the series is shown in reverse order.

You can make the ball move across the screen by adding a constant value to the x-coordinate of the destination point. Air resistance has little effect compared to gravity; therefore, the constant horizontal direction will not give an unrealistic picture. This is a simple example using the realistic **arcs** mentioned in the list of animation techniques.

FIGURE 5.5.7

Positions of the ball calculated for evenly spaced intervals with initial height 50 and initial acceleration -5

t	$h(t) = 50 - (-5)\,t^2$
0	50
1	55
2	70
3	95
4	130
5	175

EXERCISES

5.5.1

Use Bitblt to create an animation of a worm crawling across the screen. First create five different positions used in the motion. The positions are given in figure 5.5.1.

5.5.2

Create five poses for the bouncing ball. Use these poses together with a timing chart to animate the bouncing ball.

5.5.3

Calculate a timing chart for a ball that loses a constant amount of velocity on each bounce.

5.5.4

Create the poses for a bird flying.

5.5.5

Create the poses for a stick person walking.

5.6 Constructing Icons with the Sketch and Save Procedures

This section describes two more applications that use the Sketch and the Save procedures. You will use the Sketch procedure to create icons and fonts as bitmaps. You will also investigate a way to save fonts as sets of line-drawing instructions.

First you will create icons that may be used in a program similar to the architectural draw program presented in section 3.5. In this version of the program the objects such as planters are created with Sketch and then saved. This program requires that all the objects be drawn in rectangles of the same size. All needed rotations of a given object are created and then stored in a single file. In the applications program these rotations will be shown on the screen as an icon-type menu (figure 5.6.1).

The actual creation of an object's rotations is almost identical to the creation of the worm positions in section 5.5. It is in the application of these objects to the landscape architect's draw program that you will encounter a new technique. In this program, you will read the rotations of all the objects and place them along the edge of the screen as in figure 5.6.1. Doing this permits use of screen memory to store these images.

The main program for this application will be a loop that allows the user to choose a particular object from the menu with ReadLocator. A cursor-type bitmap is changed to the specific rotation of the object chosen. It is then possible to position this object by using a variation of ReadLocator. ReadLocator may not be used in this situation because it erases the last image of the object. A more elaborate version of this idea is presented in the MacDraw demonstration program (figure 5.6.2).

The application could be modified in an obvious way to create new letters for a font. The program would allow the user to select a letter from the keyboard, display the letter, and modify the letter in a separate rectangle (figure 5.6.3). This rectangle would then be Bitblted to its final location in the array storing the font. One problem encountered with both of these examples is that the shapes created are very small, making it difficult to adjust final details at this level.

FIGURE 5.6.1

When a small set of shapes is used in a drawing, it is possible to show each as an icon. The program can make a copy from the screen of any icon requested by the user.

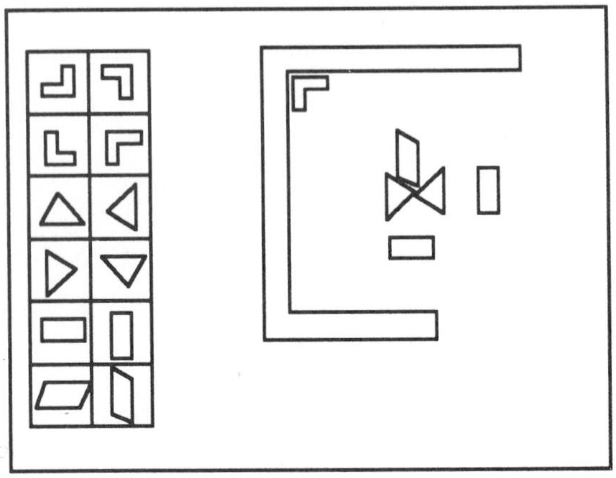

FIGURE 5.6.2

The MacDraw guided tour gives an example of an application with a restricted set of images.

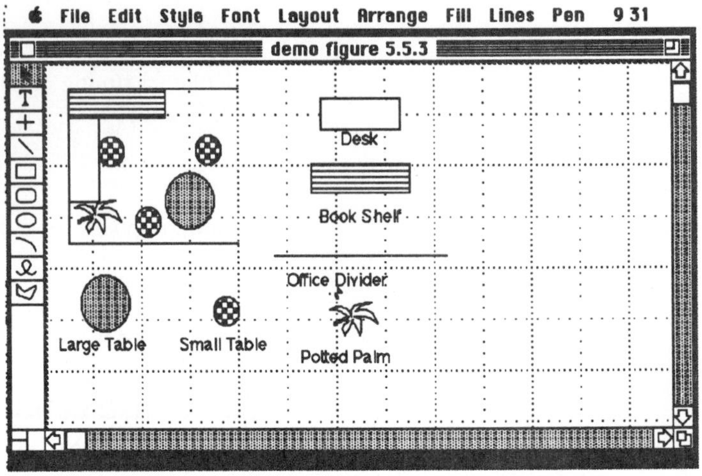

FIGURE 5.6.3

A sample screen for a font editor

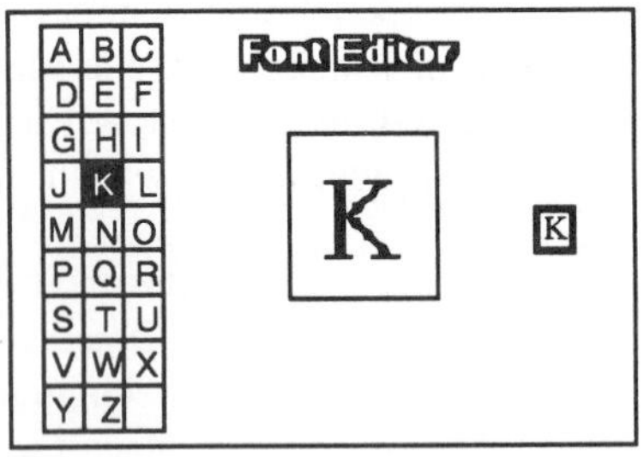

Chapter 6 discusses ways to enlarge the image to allow pixel-by-pixel alterations.

The actions taken by the draw program are all realized by calls to procedures in the simple graphics package. If these actions are recorded as relative operations, letters or icons can be reconstructed at any point on the screen. The images may also be rotated through any angle by using techniques introduced in section 3.5. The problem of rotated text introduced in sections 4.4 and 4.6 may now be solved by creating a rotated font from the list of instructions.

Saving the instructions is not difficult. Individual instructions may be put into a record of the form

```
DrawOperation = record
   Op : (Move,Line); (*make sure that these scalars do not conflict*)
                     (*with system operations*)
   Pt  : Point;      (*the end point for the operation*)
end.
```

The operations for a single image may be stored either in an array or in a linked list. An array would contain the number of operations given as the first entry and would be interpreted by a procedure similar to DrawPoly given in figure 3.5.5. A font would be an array of these images subscripted on the binary code of the characters.

Fonts created as a sequence of line segments can be easily scaled by multiplying the coordinates of each point by scaling constants. If the x-coordinates are scaled by a different amount than the y-coordinate is scaled, letters may be stretched, and italic letters may be obtained by applying a shear transformation. Bold letters can be created by using a thicker line setting when drawing.

Letters created with line segments, like *o,* do not scale well because the number of line segments does not increase as the letter is scaled (figure 5.6.4). In chapter 7 you will consider techniques for creating letters from curves. These curves are scalable and are often used to describe fonts.

FIGURE 5.6.4

To scale letters represented by line segments, you can multiply each coordinate of the vertices by a scaling factor. One problem with this technique is that letters such as o, *which look fine at small magnification, appear mechanical at larger magnification.*

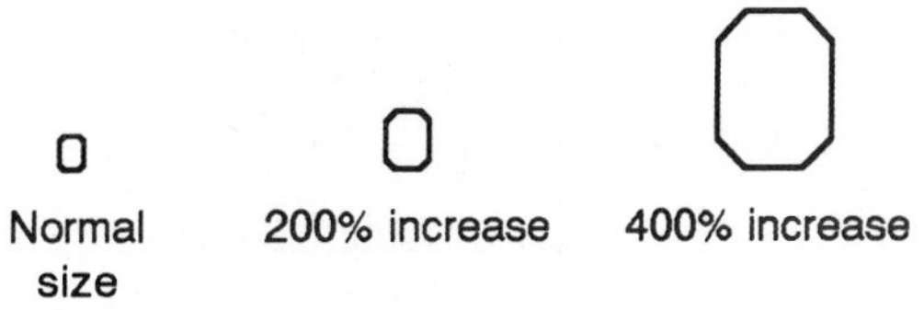

EXERCISES

5.6.1

Write the variation of ReadLocator needed to position objects from an icon menu.

5.6.2

Write a program that allows the user to create an icon with the draw program and records the steps in an array of DrawOperation records. Use this array to create the 90°, 180°, and 270° rotations of the icon. Store these rotations in a file of bitmaps.

5.6.3

Repeat exercise 5.6.2, this time storing the results in a file of DrawOperation. Write a program to exhibit these images on the screen in an icon menu. How many records must be stored for each icon?

5.6.4

Write a program that creates a font as an array of arrays of DrawOperation.

5.6.5

Write a procedure that will display a character stored as an array of DrawOperation rotated through any angle. Use this procedure to write a procedure that displays strings rotated through any angle.

5.6.6

Create a mini-font for the letters *a, e, o, r,* and *t* using the program in exercise 5.6.4; then display four different rotations of the word *rotate.*

5.6.7

In which order do you draw the objects to get the picture below?

5.6.8

Can you delete the circle without erasing part of the rectangle or part of the triangle?

5.6.9

Can you move the rectangle as a unit?

5.6.10

Is there a way to bring the rectangle infront of the other objects in figure 5.6.5?

FIGURE 5.6.5

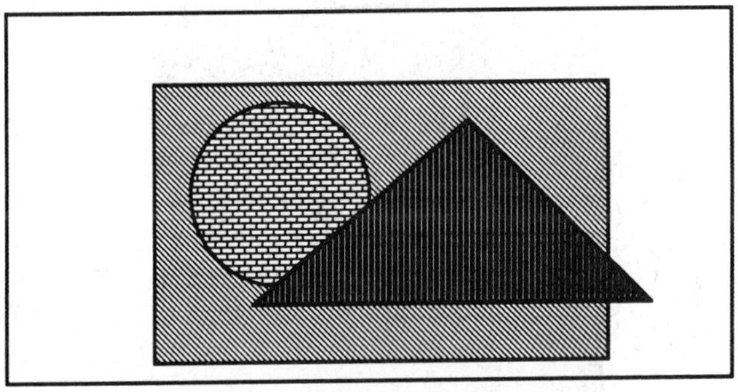

5.7 Creating a Main-Event Loop Program

This section presents an alternative to the menu and selection problems cited at the end of section 5.3: using a combination of the pull-down menus introduced in the last chapter and the icon button menus displayed along the edge of the screen. The location of the cursor at the time of choice will indicate the type of action desired. The only keystroke commands you will return are the direction indicators, the size of the jump indicator, and the select button (<**esc**>).

The main program (figure 5.7.1) consists of a loop which is only exited when Quit is set true by the procedure called when Quit is selected from the file menu. Notice that the three possible results selecting a location on the screen are derived directly from three distinct sections on the screen (figure 5.7.2).

The PullDownZone may be characterized by any point with a y-coordinate of less than 9 (the height of text plus 1). In this case, the variable PullDownZone is a set of integer defined to be [0..WordSize + 1]. Similarly, IconMenuZone = [0..WordSize] could be used to describe the set of all x-values for points in

FIGURE 5.7.1

An example of a main-event loop-drawing program

```
program MainEventLoop;
(* nonlocal references, types, constants, variables here          *)
begin
  Initialize; (* with an appropriate list of variables, display menus   *)
  repeat
    ReadLocator(x,y,Cursor);
    if y in PullDownZone then
      HandlePullDownMenu(x,y)
    else if x in IconMenuZone then
      HandleIconMenu(x,y)
    else
      HandleDrawing(x,y,PenDown,DrawFrame)
  until Quit
end.
```

FIGURE 5.7.2

One way to divide the screen into menu zones and a drawing zone

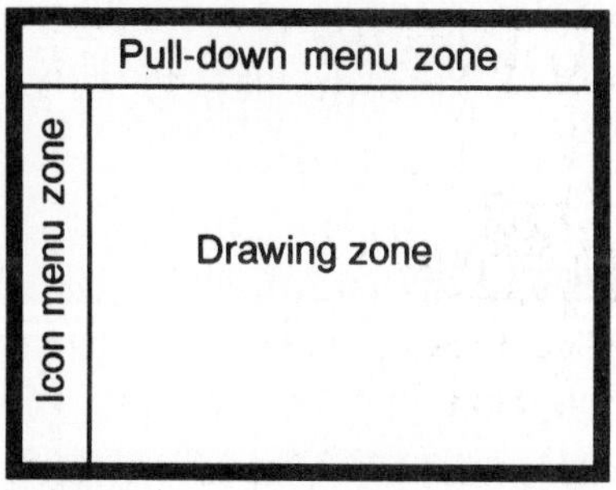

the icon menu–part of the screen. Even though these two regions overlap, the program is written in such a way as to reserve the intersection of the two regions for the pull-down menus.

This simplistic view of a main-event loop has some problems. The most obvious is that the user might be drawing something that extends into one of the menu areas. There are several ways to solve this problem. You can allow drawings to go into the menus, stop the cursor at the edge of the drawing region, or indicate to the user that the cursor no longer points to a location in the drawing region. The last solution is most consistent with the idea of restricted regions.

If different cursors are going to appear in different parts of the screen in ReadLocator, it is clear that AlterCursor musty be rewritten (figure 5.7.3). To speed the change of cursors, assume that only two cursors are used and that both are defined in global bitmaps. The example calls one the ToolCursor and the other Pointer.

The procedure HandleDrawing will call procedures like Sketch, which control the tools that will be introduced in chapter 6. Two possible tools are the circle tool and the rectangle tool. HandleIconMenu will, of course, not only change the tool icon but also the tool in use, consequently changing which procedures are called from HandleDrawing. At this point let's consider only HandlePullDownMenu; it is quite similar to the other Handle procedures, and most of the procedures it calls on are already available. HandlePullDownMenu performs four distinct tasks: displaying the correct menu, ascertaining the menu choice, processing that choice, and restoring the screen.

Some global constants must be available if the procedure is to be successful. The number of different pull-down menus will be stored in the constant NumberOfMenus. Each menu will have a constant indicating its record number in the file of records. If the first menu in the menu bar is the file menu, you would have the constant FileMenuId= 0. The constant array MaxChoice will hold the number of choices available in each menu. For example, if the file

FIGURE 5.7.3

The procedure AlterCursor changes the cursor whether it is in a menu zone or in the drawing zone.

```
(* The function InMenu determines whether or not the cursor is in one of the menu zones   *)
(* The sets IconMenuZone and PullDownZone are defined in the text.                         *)

function InMenu(x,y : integer): boolean;
begin
   InMenu := (x in IconMenuZone) or (y in PullDownZone)
end;

procedure AlterCursor(var Image : BitMap; var LocPt : Point;
                      Direction : char; var xmove, ymove : integer);
begin
   (*erase the current cursor*)
   Bitblt(Image,Display,T,LocPt,Image.Rect,cXor);
   If Direction in Moves then     (* if a location changes process it*)
      begin
         (* in all cases check to see if the cursor will           *)
         (* stay on the screen before changing the value           *)
         (* also check to see if move is out of or into menu area  *)
         If Direction in UP then
            begin
               If ymove >= AmtJump then
                  ymove := ymove - AmtJump;
               If InMenu(xmove,ymove) and (Image <> Pointer) then
                  Image := Pointer
            end;
         If Direction in Down then
            begin
               If ymove <= (Ymax - AmtJump) then
                  ymove := ymove + AmtJump;
               If (not (InMenu(xmove,ymove)) and (Image <> ToolCursor) then
                  Image := ToolCursor
            end;
         If Direction in Left then
            begin
               If xmove >= AmtJump then
                  xmove := xmove - AmtJump;
               If InMenu(xmove,ymove)and (Image <> Pointer) then
                  Image := Pointer
            end;
         If Direction in Right then
            begin
               If xmove <= Xmax - AmtJump then
                  xmove := xmove + AmtJump;
               If (not InMenu(xmove,ymove)) and (Image <> ToolCursor) then
                  Image := ToolCursor
            end;
         LocPt.X := xmove;      (* update point used to display the cursor *)
         LocPt.Y := ymove;
         (* display cursor at the new position *)
         Bitblt(Image,Display,T,LocPt,Image.Rect,cXor)
      end
end; (* AlterCursor*)
```

menu has the choice *save* and the choice *quit,* MaxChoice[FileMenuId] := 2. You will also require that all menus be the same width, MenuWidth. This will be the width of the widest menu.

With these constants defined, the procedure HandlePullDownMenu is fairly direct (figure 5.7.4).

The procedure ProcessFileChoice (figure 5.7.5) is representative of the type of procedure used to process the menu choice.

FIGURE 5.7.4

The procedure HandlePullDownMenu receives the coordinates of a point in the menu bar from ReadLocator. The x-coordinate is used to determine the menu to be displayed. This menu is displayed, and MenuLocator solicits a choice from that menu. Finally, the screen is restored by ErasePullDown, and the menu choice is processed by either ProcessFileChoice or ProcessEditChoice.

```
(* This procedure displays the pull-down menu indicated by      *)
(* the point (x,y) selected by ReadLocator                      *)
(* Then it allows the user to select a value from the menu,     *)
(* completes the process selected, and restores the screen.     *)

procedure HandlePullDownMenu(x,y : integer);
var
   DP           : point;      (* location of the highlight in the menu                *)
   Choice       : integer;    (* which operation is chosen?                           *)
   MenuChoice   : integer;    (* which menu?                                          *)
begin
   MenuChoice := x div MenuWidth;   (* which menu has been chosen                                     *)
   DisplayPullDown(x,y);            (* puts menu on screen and saves screen figure 4.5.8              *)
   DP.x := MenuChoice * MenuWidth;  (* where will the highlight appear                                *)
   DP.y := MenuOffSet;              (* how far down does the menu appear - WordSize + 1 is a good choice *)
   Choice := 1;                                             (* which menu choice will be highlighted *)
   MenuLocator(Choice,MaxChoice[MenuChoice],DP);            (* make the choice used in figure 4.5.5  *)
   ErasePullDown(x,y);                                      (* restore screen                        *)
   case MenuChoice of
      (* this program has only two pull-down menus *)
      FileMenuId : ProcessFileChoice(Choice);
      EditMenuId : ProcessEditChoice(Choice)
   end
end; (*HandlePullDownMenu*)
```

FIGURE 5.7.5

ProcessFileChoice receives a file menu selection from HandlePullDownMenu. This choice is used to determine an appropriate action.

```
procedure ProcessFileChoice(Choice : integer);
const
   SaveChoice = 1;
   QuitChoice  = 2;
begin
   case Choice of
      SaveChoice   :  SavePic;       (* procedure similar to the one described in section 4.3   *)
      QuitChoice   :  Quit := True;  (* you may want to give the user a chance to save here     *)
      otherwise;                     (* used for no-action choice                                *)
   end
end;
```

EXERCISES

5.7.1

If you have access to a draw or paint program

a. Does it have the main event organization?
b. Does this program use pull-down menus?
c. Does this program use icon menus?
d. Are different cursors used to indicate the user is in one of the menu zones?
e. What type of cursors are used to indicate to the user that different tools are in use?

5.7.2

Write the procedure HandleIconMenu if there are four choices corresponding to line, rectangle, triangle and circle and the choices are arranged as shown below. You may assume that the pull-down zone and each icon are two bits (rows) higher than a letter on your system.

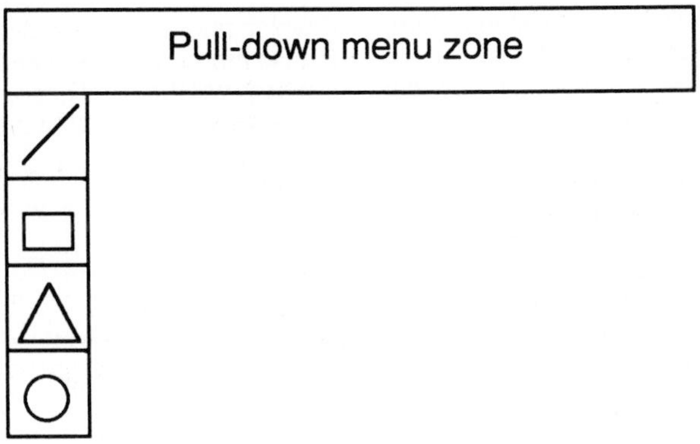

BIBLIOGRAPHY

Buxton, William, Ralph Hill, and Peter Rowley. ''Issues and Techniques in Touch-Sensitive Tablet Input.'' *Computer Graphics* (SIGGRAPH '85): 215–24 (July 1985).

Cardelli, Luca, and Rob Pike. ''Squeak: A Language for Communicating With Mice.'' *Computer Graphics* (SIGGRAPH '85): 199–204 (July 1985).

Emmett, Arielle. ''Cartooning in France.'' *Computer Graphics World* 12 (7): 97–102 (July 1989).

Green, Mark. ''The University of Alberta User Interface Management System.'' *Computer Graphics* (SIGGRAPH '85): 205–13 (July 1985).

Lasseter, John. ''Principles of Traditional Animation applied to 3D Computer Animation.'' *Computer Graphics* 21 (4): 35–44 (July 1987).

Lieberman, Henry. ''There's More to Menu Systems Than Meets the Screen.'' *Computer Graphics* (SIGGRAPH '85): 181–89 (July 1985).

Magnenat-Thalmann, N., and D. Thalmann. ''Special Cinematographic Effects with Virtual Movie Cameras.'' *CG&A* 6 (4): 43–50 (April 1986).

Myers, Brad A. ''Creating Interaction Techniques by Demonstration.'' *IEEE CG&A* 7 (9): 51–60 (September 1987).

Myers, Brad A., and William Buxton. ''Creating Highly-Interactive and Graphical User Interfaces by Demonstration.'' *Computer Graphics* (SIGGRAPH '86): 249–58 (August 1986).

Olsen, Dan R., Jr., Elizabeth P. Dempsey, and Roy Rogge. ''Input/Output Linkage in a User Interface Management System.'' *Computer Graphics* (SIGGRAPH '85): 191–97 (July 1985).

Robertson, Barbara. ''Animation Goes to Work.'' *Computer Graphics World* 11 (7): 38–48 (July 1988).

Sibert, John L., William Hurley, and Teresa W. Bleser. ''An Object-Oriented User Interface Management System.'' *Computer Graphics* (SIGGRAPH '86): 259–68 (August 1986).

Smith, Randall B. ''Experiences With the Alternate Reality Kit: An Example of the Tension Between Literalism and Magic.'' *IEEE CG&A* 7 (9) 42–50 (September 1987).

Sørensen, P. ''Graphics in Film.'' *Computer Graphics World* 11 (4): 53–56 (November 1988).

Young, Monte, ''Cartoon Animation with TOPAS,'' MicroCAD News, Vol 4 (10), October, 1989, pp. 30–32.

Vasilopoulos, Audrey. ''Exploring the Unknown.'' *Computer Graphics World* 12 (10) 76–82 (October 1989).

CHAPTER

6

Integrated Graphics Applications

DIRECTIONS

Window Managers

Chapter 3 introduced windows to give the user a bridge between world coordinates and screen coordinates. Throughout the intervening sections your work was restricted to one window on the screen. Most new graphics systems allow the user to work in more than one window at a given time (figure D.6.1). The software controlling the use of these windows is called a **window manager.** Window managers control the use of multiple programs in a workstation or a multiple-activity environment on a microcomputer. Applications programs usually inherit window managers from the computer system. Only the parts of window manager implementation that use graphics techniques will be discussed in this section.

Generally, window managers are responsible for the size, shape, border, and presentation of a window on the screen. They may also provide such control mechanisms as **scroll bars** and **zoom boxes** (figure D.6.2). Window managers may also provide for special windows, such as dialog boxes and menus.

In all cases where multiple windows appear on the screen, one of the windows must be designated as the window that reacts to user input. This window is called the **listener** or **focus.** At one time this was called the active window, but in a modern system, windows other than the listener may be active with such activities as printing. The window containing the cursor or the window in which the locator button was most recently pushed is generally designated as the listener.
Because Bitblt is normally used to display a window, windows are usually rectangular, but some systems, such as Sun's NeWS and the Macintosh, allow for nonrectangular windows. Each window typically has a border to set it off from other windows, and the listener is often designated by a special border. The border also may have a title line, making it easier for the user to discern the window containing a given picture.

Users are often allowed to change the location or size of the window as well as the section of the picture displayed in the window. The controls for these functions are displayed as part of the border. Windows are moved when the user selects a specified area in the border and drags the window with the locator device. The size of a window can be changed by selecting an icon in a corner of the window. That icon is dragged across the screen until the window is the desired size. Another icon, the ''zoom'' icon, responds to a click by altering the size of the window, which can range from its normal size to the size of the screen. Changing the section of the picture that appears on the screen without changing its size is called **panning.** Scroll bars are normally provided to allow the user to pan text and pictures.

Windows may be placed on the screen in a non-overlapping manner, as you would place tiles on a floor. This procedure is called **tiling** (figure D.6.3.). When a system employs tiling, the windows can be restricted to shapes such as rectangles, triangles, and hexagons, and may be placed side by side to save space. Systems that employ tiling generally restrict the placement of windows to allow for easier alteration of the screen when window sizes are changed or new windows are added. The Cedar system, for example, puts all windows in two columns. Windows may be moved between columns, and the column sizes may be changed. All windows in a column have the same width. Tiling has the advantage that the user can see the contents of all windows simultaneously and may easily

FIGURE D.6.1

Windows displayed by X windows with the PEX extension. The PEX extension allows the user direct access to all PHIGS primitives and a selection of the PHIGS+ primitives.

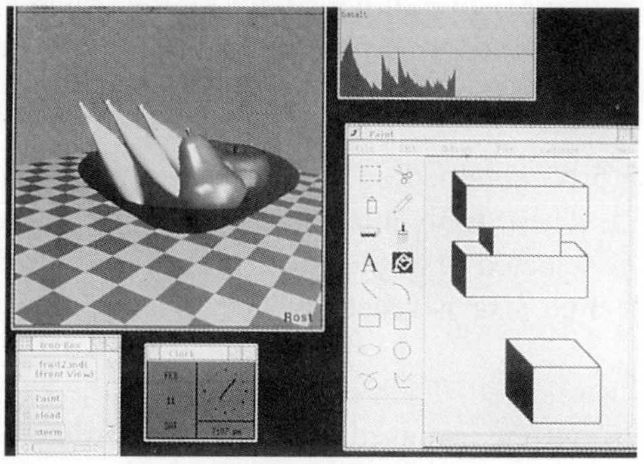

FIGURE D.6.2

Scroll bars and a zoom box from the Macintosh system

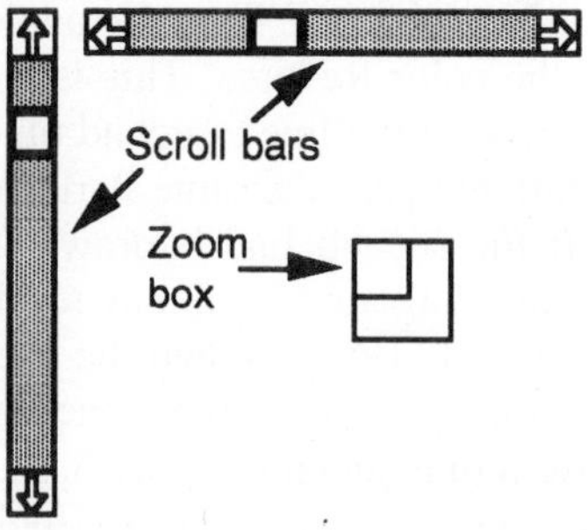

FIGURE D.6.3

An example of a non-overlapping, tiled window system

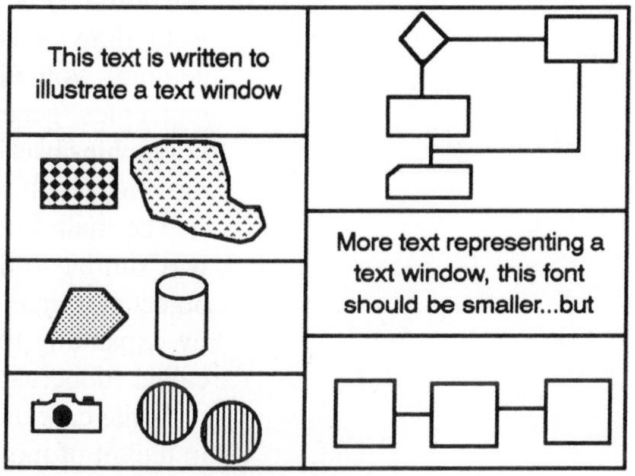

FIGURE D.6.4

Example from the window manager Microsoft Windows.

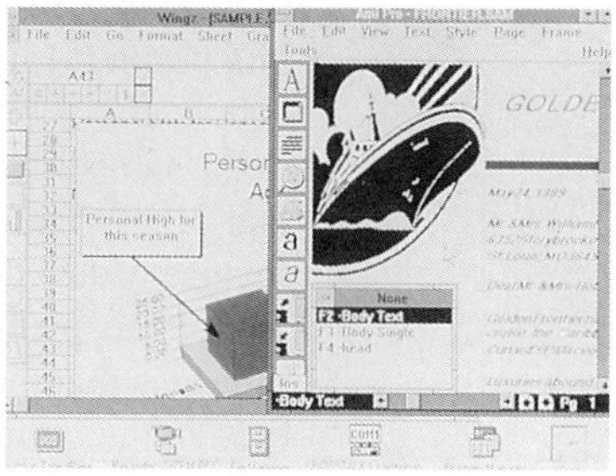

move from window to window. It is also easier to implement non-overlapping windows because no complicated clipping is needed.

Overlapping windows may be used when screen space is at a premium or when it is desirable to give the user more freedom (see figure D.6.4). These windows give the appearance of papers lying on a desk; thus the name **desk top** is often used to describe these systems. The freedom to place windows at any position on the screen, including over other windows, has one disadvantage: windows can disappear from view. Clipping may also be a problem, because overlapping windows may create very irregular polygonal regions.

Whether tiling or overlapping windows are used, it is still possible to run out of room on the screen. Windows that are not in use may be replaced by icons representing them. Most window managers have fixed icons to represent windows or applications that are not currently open. The X/uwm manager creates an icon by reducing the window to icon size. This reduction is called **iconifying;** the technique for creating these icons is covered in section 6.7.

Often the window manager or application restricts the user's freedom—for example, when a yes or no answer is required before the program can take an action such as saving a file. To implement this restricted states, it displays a special window, called a **dialog box**. Dialog boxes generally appear over existing windows or in specified regions of the screen and can be used for many types of interactions. User activity is restricted to the specific set of responses listed in the dialog box. For example, when a user wants to save the current work, the name of the file is usually needed before saving can take place. A dialog box with space to type the name of the file is provided, and unless the save is canceled, the only activity allowed is typing the name of the file.

While window managers provide flexibility for the experienced user, they make it more difficult for the novice user to learn to use the system. Myers (1988) gives a detailed discussion of various techniques used by window managers as well as examples from major systems in use today.

6.1 Drawing Tools

This section expands your set of drawing tools. Recall that the Sketch procedure (section 5.3) is essentially a line-drawing tool. In this section you will modify it to draw a continuous line with a technique called **rubberbanding.** In addition, you will create tools that draw other two-dimensional figures, such as rectangles, general polygons, and circles. Unlike the graphics primitives found in graphics packages, these tools provide the user with an interactive method for drawing graphics primitives.

The main-line program in section 5.6 contained an icon menu of tools that was similar to the pen in section 5.3. These tools allow the user to draw one object at a time. A starting location is selected first; then a final size is selected by expanding the object until the desired size is reached. This is the process called rubberbanding.

In the case of a line, one endpoint is selected. Then each time one of the keys in the set of moves is pressed, the current line is erased, the current coordinates are updated, and a line is drawn from the end point to the point with the current coordinates. The user gets the impression that the line is growing in response to the keystrokes.

Intermediate lines cannot be drawn in their final color, because the process of erasing the lines will also erase other objects along each of the lines. To avoid this problem, intermediate lines are drawn with the color Reverse. This is the equivalent of bitmapping the line in **xor** mode. Drawing the line a second time in the same direction restores the screen. It is important to use the same start and end points the second time the line is drawn. If the second line is drawn in reverse order, then round-off choices, in the line-drawing algorithm may result in isolated pixels remaining on the screen (Bresenham, 1987.) When the user indicates that the final end point is the current position, the line is drawn one last time in the current pen color. A version of the **line tool** is given in figure 6.1.1.

You create the **rectangle tool** exactly the same way you create the line tool. A call to a procedure DrawRectangle replaces the MoveAbs-LineAbs sequence in the LineTool procedure. In each case the call might be

DrawRectangle(BeginX,BeginY,xmove,ymove)

The points (BeginX,BeginY) and (xmove,ymove) are corners of a rectangle, but not necessarily the lower-left and upper-right corners respectively. To make sure that the proper corners are passed to DrawRectangle, you must use a procedure that compares the coordinates of the two points and returns the corners used in DrawRectangle.

A tool closely related to the rectangle tool is the **square tool.** Not all systems implement this as a separate tool. The square differs from the rectangle in that either the cursor's movement is restricted so that the x- and y-distances from the initial point are always the same, or only a square is drawn in response to indicator movements. The square's size may be either the larger or the smaller of the x- and y-distances.

The **circle tool** may have the same general structure as the square tool, but there are some significant differences. For both the rectangle and the line, the first point selected is at one extreme on the figure while the second point marks a second extreme. Some graphics systems will treat the circle as an object

FIGURE 6.1.1

This procedure is used for interactive line drawing.

```
procedure LineTool ( xmove, ymove : integer; Current : Cursor, var Picture : Window);
var
  Direction     : char;         (* records the user's keystroke                                          *)
  AmtJump       : integer;      (* amount that the cursor moves in response to each keyboard command     *)
  LocPt         : Point;        (* point used to display the cursor                                      *)
  BeginX        : integer;      (* x-coordinate of the first end point of the line                       *)
  BeginY        : integer;      (* y-coordinate of the first end point of the line                       *)
  CurrentColor  : ScreenColor;  (* used to store the current pen color so it can be restored at the end of LineTool *)
begin (*LineTool *)
  AmtJump := 1;                                            (* initialize the size of cursor movement          *)
  LocPt.x := xmove;                                        (* get the initial location for the cursor         *)
  LocPt.y := ymove;
  Bitblt(Current.Icon,Display,LocPt,Cursor.Icon.Rect,cXor);   (* display the cursor                           *)
  repeat
    repeat
      read(Direction);                                     (*read until a direction or size change, or quit   *)
    until (Direction in Legal);
    if Direction in Size then                              (* if the input is change the size of the jump     *)
      ChangeJumpSize (Direction,AmtJump);
    else
      AlterCursor(Cursor.Icon, LocPt , Direction, xmove, ymove );
  until (Direction = chr(27));
  BeginX := xmove + Current.HotSpot.x;
  BeginY := YMax - (ymove + Current.HotSpot.y);            (* correct for different orientation of coordinates *)
  CurrentColor := Picture.PenColor;
  SetPenColor(Reverse,Picture);
  Bitblt(Current.Icon,Display,LocPt,Current.Icon.Rect,cXor);  (* display the cursor                           *)
  repeat
    repeat
      read(Direction);                                     (*read until a direction or size change, or quit   *)
    until (Direction in Legal);
    MoveAbs(BeginX,BeginY,Picture);                        (* erase old line                                  *)
    LineAbs(xmove + Current.HotSpot.x,YMax-(ymove + Current.HotSpot.y),Picture);
    if Direction in Size then                              (* if the input indicates change the size of the jump*)
      ChangeJumpSize (Direction,AmtJump);
    else
      AlterCursor(Cursor.Icon, LocPt , Direction, xmove, ymove );
    MoveAbs(BeginX,BeginY,Picture);                        (* draw new line                                   *)
    LineAbs(xmove + Current.HotSpot.x,YMax-(ymove + Current.HotSpot.y),Picture);
  until (Direction = chr(27));
  (* draw the final line *)
  SetPenColor(CurrentColor,Picture);                       (* restore original pen color                      *)
  MoveAbs(BeginX,BeginY,Picture);
  LineAbs(xmove + Current.HotSpot.x,YMax-(ymove + Current.HotSpot.y),Picture);
  Current := Pointer;                                      (* restore the selector cursor                     *)
  Bitblt(Current.Icon,Display,LocPt,Current.Icon.Rect,cXor);  (* display the pointer                          *)
end; (* LineTool *)
```

inscribed in a square drawn from the corners. In these systems, the points plotted by the user are assumed to be the opposite corners of this square (figure 6.1.2). Other graphics systems assume that the user picks the center first and then indicates the radius by moving the cursor away from that point. In both cases, the fastest way to indicate the size of the circle is to draw the square that circumscribes it. The radius of the circle is one-half the side length of the square.

The main problem with drawing circles is that you do not have a good algorithm to draw them because of the primitive operations in your graphics package. Many graphics packages provide a circle-drawing primitive, and if this primitive is provided it should be used. If your package does not provide a circle-drawing primitive, the following method may be used to construct one.

Mathematicians would use the equation of a circle to compute points (x,y) on the circle: $(x - center.X)^2 + (y - center.Y)^2 = radius^2$. For all values of x between −radius and radius, the values of y may be computed as the positive and negative of $SQRT(radius^2 - (x - center.x)^2)$. Even if only a few values of x are used and lines are employed to connect these computed points, this computation leads to a very slow circle generator.

The number of points computed may be reduced to one-quarter of the points plotted by using the symmetry of a circle. You will also use the PointRel function to plot the points, because with this function the center has effective coordinates (0,0). Thus, all symmetry is symmetry with respect to the origin, which leads to much simpler computations. These considerations allow you to reduce the set of computed points to those with relative coordinates between (0,r) and $(r/\sqrt{2}, r/\sqrt{2})$, where r is the radius (figure 6.1.3).

The procedure PlotSymmetricPoints (figure 6.1.4) plots the point with coordinates (x0,y0) relative to the center and all the other points determined by symmetry. Because of the relative nature of this procedure, the initial point used

FIGURE 6.1.2

The initial cursor position for the circle tool can be either a corner of the square that circumscribes the circle or the center of the circle.

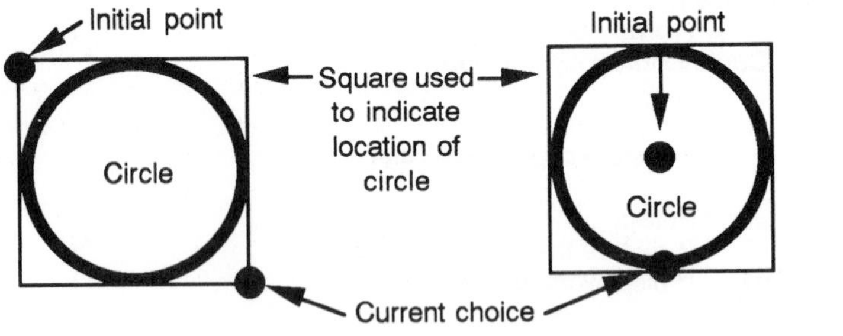

FIGURE 6.1.3

Once the point (x0,y0) is computed, symmetry can be used to plot seven other points on the circle.

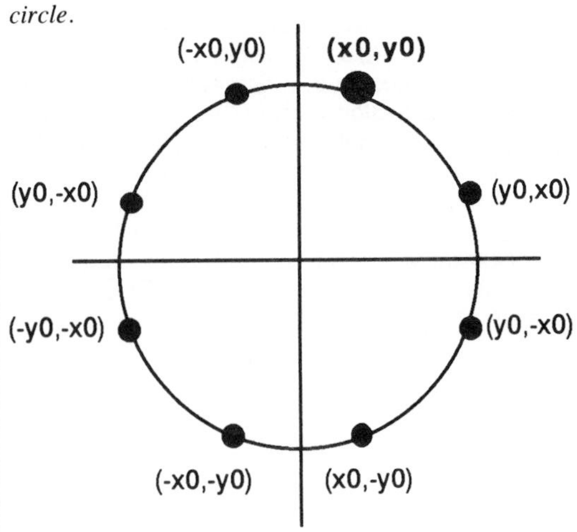

FIGURE 6.1.4

PlotSymmetricPoints uses the symmetry of a circle about the origin to plot eight points on a circle.

```
(* This procedure plots eight symmetric points on a circle          *)
(* given one of the points has coordinates (x,y). It uses the       *)
(* procedure PlotRel for which the Window place is a value          *)
(* parameter so that the center value is not altered by the         *)
(* PointRel procedure.                                              *)

procedure PlotRel(x,y : integer; Place : Window);
begin
  PointRel(x,y,Place)
end;

procedure PlotSymmetricPoints(x,y : integer; Place : Window);
begin
  PlotRel( x,  y,  Place);
  PlotRel( y,  x,  Place);
  PlotRel(-y,  x,  Place);
  PlotRel(-x,  y,  Place);
  PlotRel(-x, -y,  Place);
  PlotRel(-y, -x,  Place);
  PlotRel( y, -x,  Place);
  PlotRel( x, -y,  Place)
end;
```

FIGURE 6.1.5

In the first quadrant of the circle, any one of three points may be the closest successor to the point (x_i, y_i).

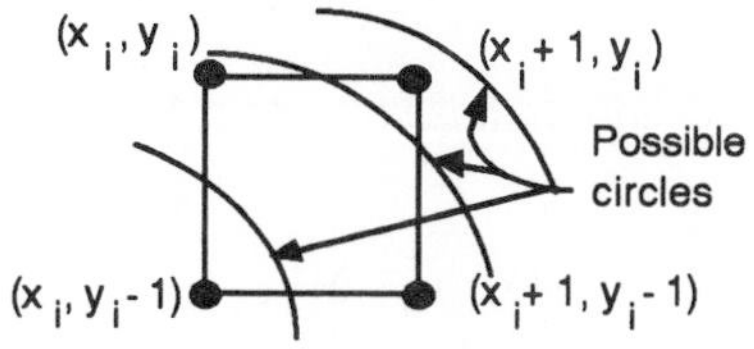

FIGURE 6.1.6

The number of points that can be plotted is reduced to two because the slope of the circle is between 0 and −1 for this part of the circle.

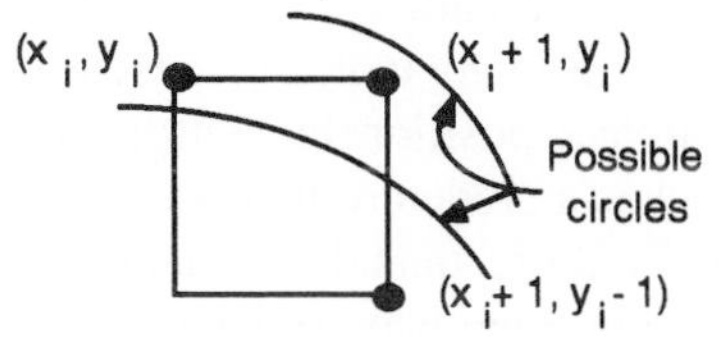

to plot each point is the center of the circle. To preserve this initial point, PlotSymmetricPoints does not call on PointRel directly; instead, a special function, PlotRel, which has the frame as a value parameter, calls on PointRel.

Even with this reduction in the number of points to be plotted, the use of squares and square roots will require substantial computation time. Fortunately, there is a faster algorithm based on theoretical work by J. Bresenham. This algorithm, like the Bresenham algorithm for lines, uses an indicator to choose the screen point closest to the actual point on the circle.

The algorithm is based on the fact that all points plotted have integer coordinates, and thus are not necessarily on the circle. If you start with the point (0,r) on a circle of radius r, it will be plotted as $(0,y_0)$, where $y_0 = \text{round}(r)$. The point $(0,y_0)$ is the screen point closest to a point on the circle with a positive y-coordinate and 0 for its x-coordinate. If a point (x_1,y_1) is chosen to be plotted, the next point may be any one of three points in figure 6.1.5. Recall that you are only plotting first quadrant points between (0,r) and $(r/\sqrt{2}, r/\sqrt{2})$, and that the slope of the circle is between 0 and −1. Therefore, the x-value must be increased by 1, and you need only decide whether y will remain the same or be decremented (figure 6.1.6).

A difference variable, d, is used to determine which of these points is the best approximation of the actual point on the circle. As in the case of the line algorithm, the distance is computed from each of the points $(x_i + 1, y_i)$ and $(x_i + 1, y_i - 1)$ to the point $(x_i + 1, y)$, where y is the actual point on the circle. The value of y may be computed directly by using the equation of a circle

$$y^2 = r^2 - (x_i + 1)^2$$

FIGURE 6.1.7

The distances d1 and d2 are used to decide which point is closest to the circle.

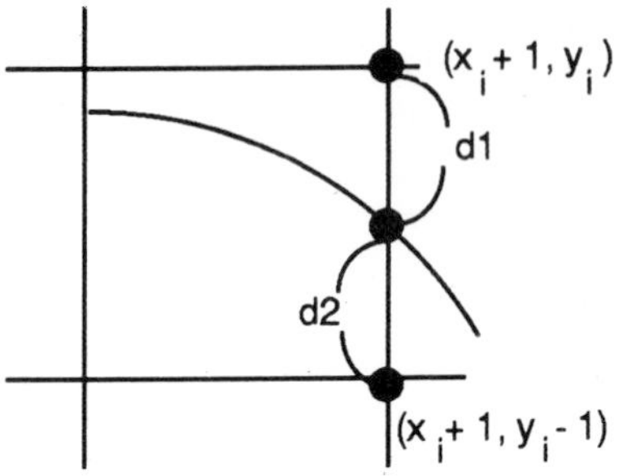

A measure of distance from $(x_i + 1, y_i)$ to $(x_i + 1, y)$ can be arrived at by computing

$$d_1 = y_i^2 - y^2 = y_i^2 - r^2 + (x_i + 1)^2$$

Similarly, a measure of the distance from $(x_i + 1, y_i - 1)$ to $(x_i + 1, y)$ (figure 6.1.7) is given by

$$d_2 = y^2 - (y_i - 1)^2 = r^2 - (x_1 + 1)^2 - (y_i - 1)^2$$

The indicator you will use is the difference between d_1 and d_2:

$$\begin{aligned} S_i &= d_1 - d_2 \\ &= 2(x_i + 1)^2 + y_i^2 + (y_i - 1)^2 - 2r^2 \end{aligned}$$

When the value of S_i is negative, then the point $(x_i + 1, y_i)$ is closer to the circle; otherwise, the point $(x_i + 1, y_i - 1)$ is closer. This computation appears to require more operations than simply calculating the coordinates of the points on the circle and using the round function. The arithmetic may be simplified if the current value of S_i is used to compute S_{i+1}. The first value S_1 may be computed directly from the equation for S_i with $x_1 = 0$ and $y_1 = r$:

$$S_1 = 3 - 2r$$

The value of S_{i+1}, which is computed by substituting x_{i+1} and y_{i+1} for x_i and y_i respectively

$$S_{i+1} = 2(x_{i+1} + 1)^2 + y_{i+1}^2 + (y_{i+1} - 1)^2 - 2r^2$$

may be simplified to

$$S_{i+1} = 2(x_i + 2)^2 + y_{i+1}^2 + (y_{i+1} - 1)^2 - 2r^2$$

when it is noted that $x_{i+1} = x_i + 1$.

If S_i is subtracted from S_{i+1} and the resulting equation is solved for S_{i+1}, you get the equation

$$S_{i+1} = S_i + 4x_i + 6 + 2(y_{i+1}^2 - y_i^2) - 2(y_{i+1} - y_i)$$

The value of y_{i+1} is determined by S_i. If $S_i < 0$, then $y_{i+1} = y_i$ and you can compute S_{i+1} as

$$S_{i+1} = S_i + 4x_i + 6$$

Otherwise, if $S_i \geq 0$, then $y_{i+1} = y_i - 1$ and you can compute S_{i+1} as

$$S_{i+1} = S_i + 4(x_i + y_i) + 10$$

In either case, the computation no longer requires floating-point arithmetic or squares. Figure 6.1.8 gives the complete algorithm for DrawCircle.

Even with the efficiency of this algorithm, a rubberband-type circle tool may be slow to respond. This is why the square is used to indicate the circle's location. It is also possible to indicate the circle's position by plotting only selected points on the circle after the radius reaches a predetermined value. This can be achieved by incrementing the x-value by more than 1, the amount of incrementation determined by the size of the circle. One way to determine this amount is to require the number of x-values computed always to be less than a fixed upper limit.

FIGURE 6.1.8

This procedure draws a circle around the current location stored in place.

```
(* This procedure draws a circle around the current location              *)
(* stored in place.  Place is a value parameter so the                   *)
(* current location is not altered by this procedure.  This allows       *)
(* for multiple calls to DrawCircle without the need to move to the center. *)

procedure DrawCircle(radius : integer;  place : Window);
var
  x, y, d : integer;
begin
  x := 0;
  y := radius;
  d := 3 - 2 * radius;
  while x < y do
    begin
      PlotSymmetricPoints(x,y,place);
      if d < 0 then
        d := d + 4 * x + 6                 (* y value is unaltered    *)
      else
        begin
          d := d + 4 *(x-y) + 10;          (* y = y-1                 *)
          y := y - 1
        end;
      x := x + 1
    end;
  if  x = y then
    PlotSymmetricPoints(x,y,place)
end;
```

A **triangle tool** could be constructed by adding a third loop to the line tool that draws both of the remaining lines of the triangle until a final choice is made (figure 6.1.9).

In the case of the **polygonal tool,** the number of sides is unknown; therefore, it is impossible to draw the entire figure while the cursor is moving, as was done with the triangle. If the Sketch procedure is modified to rubberband the current line segment, it will make a usable polygonal tool. A closed polygon may or may not be required in a given application. If the polygon must be closed, you need only keep track of the initial point, and at the end of the procedure, draw one last line from the current point to the initial point if they are not the same point.

FIGURE 6.1.9

Cursor movement during the creation of a triangle with the triangle tool

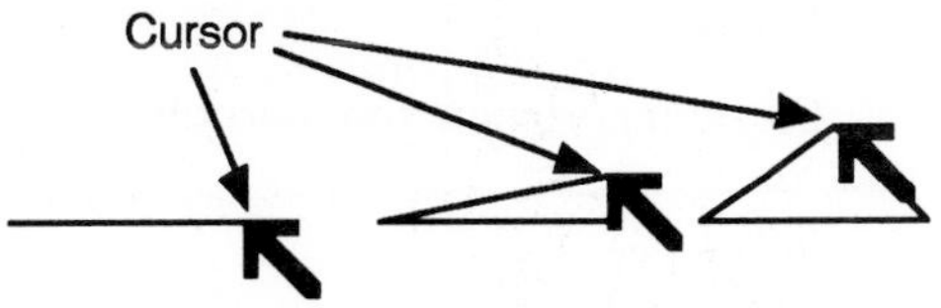

Figure 6.1.10 summarizes the tools available in some of the standard graphics packages.

FIGURE 6.1.10

Primitives available in some standard graphics packages

Function	GKS	Turbo Pascal	Macintosh Toolbox
Polygon	Polyline	DrawPoly	FramePoly FrameRect
Circle ellipse		Circle ellipse	FrameOval
Arcs		Arc	FrameArc

EXERCISES

6.1.1

Write the procedure DrawRectangle and the procedure RectangleTool.

6.1.2

Write the SquareTool procedure.

6.1.3

Write the CircleTool procedure that draws the circle from the corner of the square.

6.1.4

Write the CircleTool procedure that draws from the center of the circle.

6.1.5

Experiment with the circle tool to see which type of feedback in the circle tool gives the best combination of position information and performance.

6.1.6

Create the triangle tool described in the text.

6.1.7

Create the polygonal tool described in the text.

FIGURE 6.1.11

The I-beam cursor used for the text tool

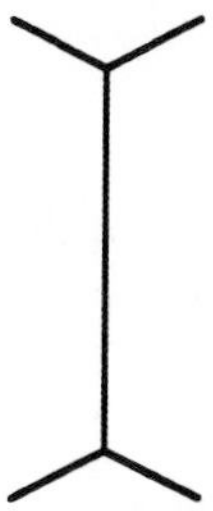

6.1.8

Create a text tool that will allow interactive placement of text in a drawing. Note that the cursor for text is usually in the form of an I-beam (figure 6.1.11).

6.1.9

Trace the circle drawing algorithm for a circle of radius 5.

6.1.10

Trace the following simplified Bresenham's line algorithm twice for a line between (0,0) and (4,1). First with x1 = 0, y1 = 0 and x2 = 4, y2 = 1, then with x1 = 4,y1 = 1 and x2 =0 and y2 = 0. If you were drawing your line in **xor** mode which pixels would remain on the screen if you drew your lines in opposite directions? How does our version of Bresenham's algorithm (figure 3.1.7) avoid this problem?

FIGURE 6.1.12

(*Bresenham's line drawing algorithm for 0 <= m <= 1*)

```
procedure NewBresenham(x1,y1,x2,y2 : integer);
var
  dx,dy,x,y,r,xChange,yChange,PositiveAddon, NegativeAddon : integer;
begin (*DrawLine*)
  if y1 <= y2 then
    yChange := 1
  else
    yChange := -1;
  if x1 <= x2 then
    xChange := 1
  else
    xChange := -1;
  dx := abs(x2 - x1);
  dy := abs(y2 - y1);
  r := 2 * dy - dx;                  (*the initial value of the indicator          *)
  PositiveAddon := 2 * (dy - dx);    (*constant added if previous indicator >=0    *)
  NegativeAddon := 2 * dy;           (*constant added if previous indicator < 0    *)
  y := y1;
  x := x1;
  while x <= x2 do
    begin
      SetPixel(x,y);
      x := x + xChange;
      if r < 0 then                  (*choose current y value and compute r        *)
        r := r + NegativeAddon
      else                           (*increment y value and compute r             *)
        begin
          y := y + yChange;
          r := r + PostiveAddon
        end;
      SetPixel(x,y)
    end (*while x <= x2*)
end;(*DrawLine*)
```

6.1.11

Draw the lines from (0,0) to (4,1) and from (4,1) to (0,0) in **xor** mode on your system. Were there pixels left on the screen?

6.1.12

Where does the version of Bresenham's algorithm given in this section draw different pixels when the order of the points is changed?

6.1.13

What will the rectangle tool show if the user begins with a series of horizontal or vertical cursor movements? How can you indicate that a rectangle is being drawn?

6.2 Segments and Object-oriented Graphics

With the tools you have just created the user may draw many of the shapes used in graphics programs. But what if the user wants to delete or move one or more of the objects? This problem has not yet been addressed because once an object has been drawn, if it overlaps other objects, those objects will be altered if the overlapping object is moved or deleted. In figure 6.2.1, the original picture shows rectangle B overlapping rectangle A. When rectangle B is deleted (by drawing it in either reverse color or background color), a part of rectangle A is also deleted. If you had a record of all the objects in a picture, then you could redraw the picture after deleting rectangle B.

As you may recall, the structure used to record the groups of objects in a picture is called a segment. The objects forming a segment are called **primitives.** Segments were originally used in vector graphics systems. In those systems, the only way to erase an object on a screen was to erase the whole screen. Each time the screen was erased, it had to be completely redrawn. In raster graphics systems, it is possible to redraw just those objects in the vicinity of the object being deleted.

FIGURE 6.2.1

A part of rectangle A is deleted when rectangle B is deleted. To restore a picture after deletions, you must maintain a list of the objects in the picture.

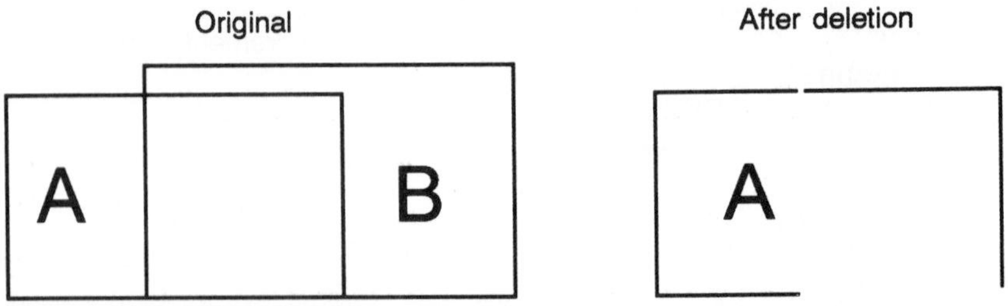

If you can redraw the picture from the list of its segments, that gives you another way to save the picture. To re-create the pictures, you need only create a file of the segments, re-create the list of segments from this file, and redraw the picture. An added benefit is that when a picture is transported to a graphics device with better resolution, it can be reconstructed at the higher resolution.

The dynamic nature of a graphic image suggests that a linked list is the most natural structure for storing a segment (figure 6.2.2). Each object is a node in this list, which holds all the information necessary to reconstruct the object. The procedure that redraws the picture traverses the list and has a draw routine that reconstructs the picture from the information in each node of the list. Segments may also store bitmaps in addition to graphics primitives such as polygons and circles. What information is needed in order to redraw the picture?

If the objects are filled with a solid color, the first objects in the list that are drawn will be partially covered. This gives the impression that the first objects in the list are being drawn underneath the existing objects. To show the most recently drawn objects on top of previously drawn objects, you either add objects at the end of the list or use a doubly linked list to store the segment list. You will see that if a singly linked list is used, placing recent additions at the end of the list makes interactive selection of the top object difficult. Therefore, you should use singly linked lists only when no filling is required. In this case, put the most recent objects at the head of the list.

To draw a rectangle that has the hotspot at one of its corners, you only need to know the hotspot and the relative coordinates of the corner opposite the hotspot. This is possible because all rectangles constructed with the rectangle tool have only vertical and horizontal sides. At this time you should consider rotations of a rectangle that result in sides that are neither vertical nor horizontal as general polygons. In a later section you will look at a rotation tool.

All that is needed in order to draw a circle is the center point and the radius. Drawing a polygon requires that the coordinates of all its vertices be relative to the preceding vertex. The first vertex is given in coordinates relative to the hotspot, the hotspot, the number of vertices, and the angle of rotation. This disparity of representation suggests that each segment be held in a variant record. A partial record structure is given in figure 6.2.3.

FIGURE 6.2.2

A segment contains a list of objects.

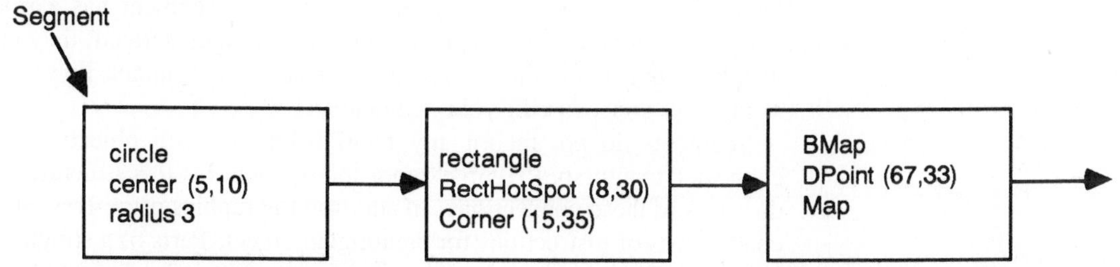

FIGURE 6.2.3

Record structure used to store objects in a segment

```
(* A sample of the record structure of a graphic segment *)
ObjectType = (lineObject,rectObject, circleObject, polygonObject,bitMapObject);
SegmentPtr = ^Segment;
Segment = record
  NextObject      : SegmentPtr;              (* pointer to the next object in a segment        *)
  SelectRegion    : rectangle;               (* region used to select an object with a pointer *)
  case Object     : ObjectType of
    lineObject    : (Beginning : point;      (* beginning of the line                          *)
                       LineEnd  : point );   (* end of the line                                *)
    rectObject    : (RectHotSpot : point;    (* hotspot for rectangle                          *)
                       OppositeCorner : point); (* opposite corner of rectangle                *)
    circleObject  : (Center : point;         (* center of circle                               *)
                       Radius : integer);    (* radius of the circle                           *)
    polygonObject : (PolyHotSpot : point;    (* hotspot for polygon                            *)
                       RotationAngle : real; (* angle of rotation                              *)
                       Poly : Polygon);      (* contains number of vertices and coordinates    *)
                                             (* of the vertices                                *)
    bitMapObject  : (DPoint : point;         (* destination point for the bitmap               *)
                       Map : BitMap);        (* actual bitmap                                  *)

end; (*segment*)
```

One field of the record that appears as a permanent part of the record but has not yet been mentioned is the **SelectRegion** or **extent.** This is a rectangle region surrounding an object. To point to the object, the user need only select a point in the region. The creation and use of SelectRegion will be covered in section 6.3.

When a picture consists of more than one segment, the segment may be maintained in a list. Each segment in the list may be the list of objects that construct a single complex item in the picture. A person, for example, may consist of a head, two arms, two legs, and a torso (figure 6.2.4). In most cases a segment is located in a restricted part of the screen. If this is the case, interactive selection can be speeded up if each segment has a select region. Segments can be opened, defined, and closed. Once defined, they can be made visible or invisible or they can be transformed. They cannot, however, be edited in the way you will edit your segments.

Segments do not record any relationship between objects, such as arms connected to a torso. PHIGS extends the segment list to a structure, a graph that does record these connections. In addition to graphics primitives, structures can contain lists of instructions for creating an object. Parts of a structure are called **elements.** Elements may be interactively inserted and deleted from a structure.

FIGURE 6.2.4

A segment can be used to hold related objects such as parts of a body. A list of segments can be used to keep track of all the segments. Nodes in this list may contain a select region to narrow searches for selected items.

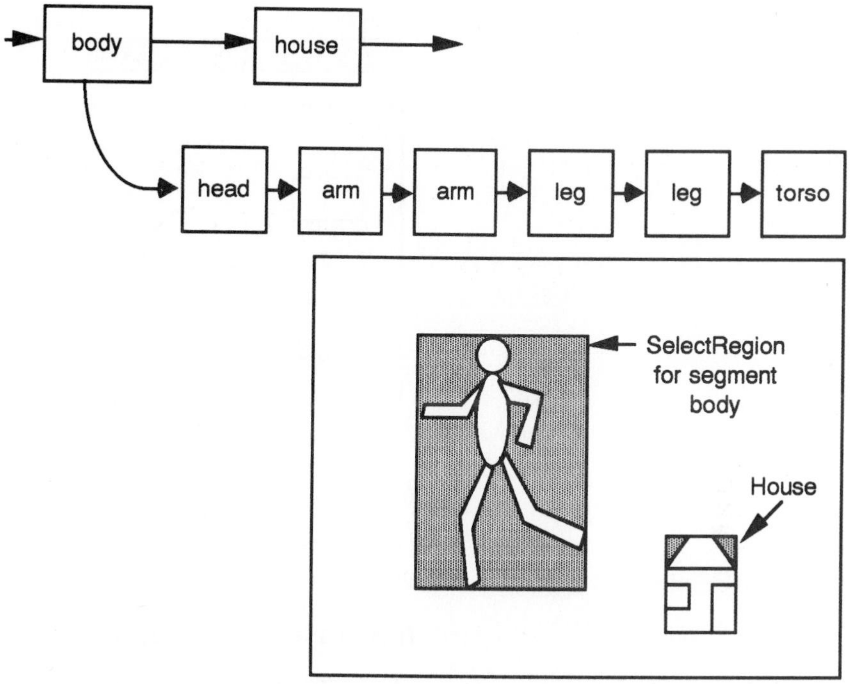

EXERCISES

6.2.1

If you had created a text tool in section 6.1, what would an entry in a segment representing text contain?

6.2.2

Write a procedure to draw an object stored in a segment.

6.2.3

Write a procedure to save a list of segments in a file of segments.

6.2.4

Write a procedure to create a list of segments read from a file of segments.

6.2.5

Give the record structure for a file used to store a segmented graphic image.

6.2.6

Compare the amount of data stored in a bitmap file of the following image with the amount of data stored in a file if this image where stored as a segmented image.

FIGURE 6.2.5

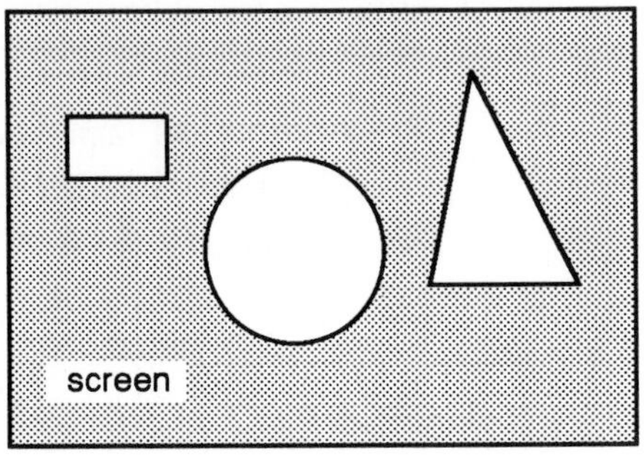

6.2.7

Does size of either file in exercise 6.2.6 change if more objects are added to the picture?

6.3 Inserting Objects into Segmented Pictures

This section concentrates on techniques to alter the tool procedures discussed in section 6.1 so that they enter the objects they create in your list of segments.

For simplicity, all the objects in your picture will be in one segment. To maintain access to this list, you will have one pointer, **SegmentList,** of type **SegmentPtr.** This pointer must be passed as a variable parameter to all your tool procedures and to any other procedure that alters your picture. When a tool procedure adds a new element to the picture, that element is added to the SegmentList.

You will add new objects to the front of the list for two reasons. First, it is faster to add an object at that point. Second, when you alter the picture, you must search the list for the object to be altered. Because alterations to recently placed objects are the most common, placing these at the front of the list allows for faster alteration.

Even though insertions are made at the beginning of the list, the order in which the list is maintained plays an important role when objects in the list are accessed. It is easier to maintain a list as an ordered list if the list begins with a dummy node. This node is sometimes called a head node. The ordering of the segment will be considered later in this chapter.

The diverse nature of the objects suggests that separate procedures are needed to insert each type of object. At this time you will consider the alterations needed in the line tool; you will work with the others in the exercises.

The procedure to insert a line into the list of objects would be called from the end of the line tool (see figure 6.3.1 for a revised version of figure 6.1.1).

FIGURE 6.3.1

If lines created in the drawing program are to be recorded in a segment, a call to procedure InsertLine is added to the procedure LineTool (figure 6.1.1).

```
SetPenColor(CurrentColor,Picture);                    (* restore original pen color     *)
MoveAbs(BeginX,BeginY,Picture);
LineAbs(xmove,YMax-ymove);
InsertLine(BeginX,BeginY,xmove,ymove,ObjectList);     (* added to LineTool              *)
Current:= Pointer;                                    (* restore the selector cursor    *)
Bitblt(Current.Icon,Display,LocPt,Current.Icon.Rect,cXor);  (* display the pointer      *)
```

Two features of the insert routine (figure 6.3.2) should be noted. First, each of the records for type **Segment** takes different amounts of memory. To minimize the amount of memory used, the procedure New is called with the record type specified by the second parameter. A few worlds of warning about this method of generating nodes: Not all Pascal compilers support this standard, and the second parameter of New must be a constant. So the call is new(temp,line).

The second interesting feature of this procedure is the computation of the SelectRegion. In the case of the line, you choose a rectangle that has the line as a diagonal (figure 6.3.3).

FIGURE 6.3.2

Procedure to insert a line into a segment

```
procedure InsertLine(BeginX,BeginY,EndX,EndY : integer;   (* coordinates of ends of line     *)
                     ObjectList : SegmentPtr);
var
  temp : SegmentPtr;                                      (* new node for this line segment  *)
begin
  new(temp,line);                                         (* get a new node of the proper type *)
  with temp^ do                                           (* initialize the new node         *)
    begin
      object := line;
      Beginning.x := BeginX;
      Beginning.y := BeginY;
      LineEnd.x := EndX;
      LineEnd.y := YMax - EndY;
      with SelectRegion do
        begin
          Origin.x : = min(BeginX,EndX);
          Origin.y : = min(BeginY,EndY);
          Corner.x := max(BeginX,EndX);
          Corner.y := max(BeginY,EndY)
        end
    end;
  Insert(Temp,ObjectList)                                 (* insert the new node in the list *)
end;
```

FIGURE 6.3.3

Rectangular select regions for line segments

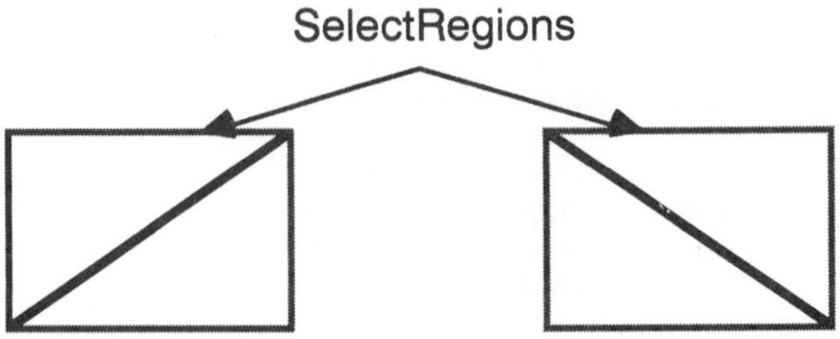

FIGURE 6.3.4

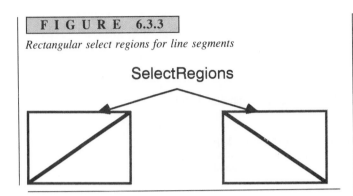

A square can be used for the select region of a circle.

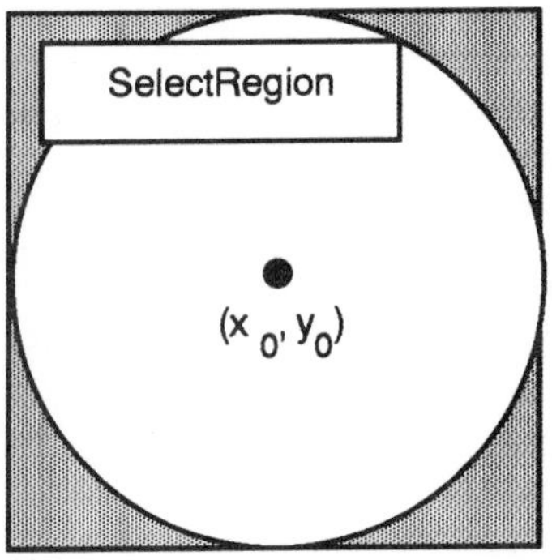

In the case of a rectangle, the SelectRegion is the rectangle. Circles may have as their SelectRegion the rectangle with origin (center.X − radius, center.Y − radius) and corner (center.X + radius, center.Y + radius) (figure 6.3.4). For a polygon, the select rectangle has as its origin the point whose x-coordinate is the smallest x-value from the set of x-values of the vertices, and whose y-coordinate is the smallest y-value from the set of y-values of the vertices. The corner for polygons will have the largest value from each of the sets (figure 6.3.5).

In more complex situations when objects completely overlap, the order of the list of objects may be used to indicate which object is in the background and which is in the foreground. For more complicated hierarchies, the order in which objects appear in the list indicates their levels.

In figure 6.3.6, the triangle is above the circle, which, in turn, is above the rectangle. If the user selects any point in the triangle, the triangle would be

FIGURE 6.3.5

The select region for a polygon is determined by the smallest and largest values of x and y at vertices.

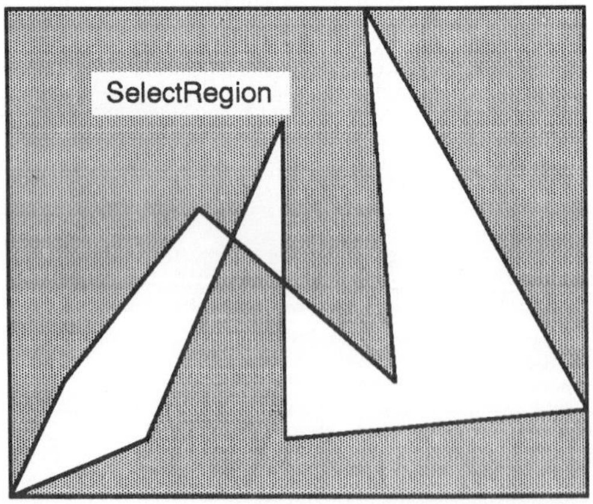

FIGURE 6.3.6

Overlapping of objects may make one or more objects inaccessible.

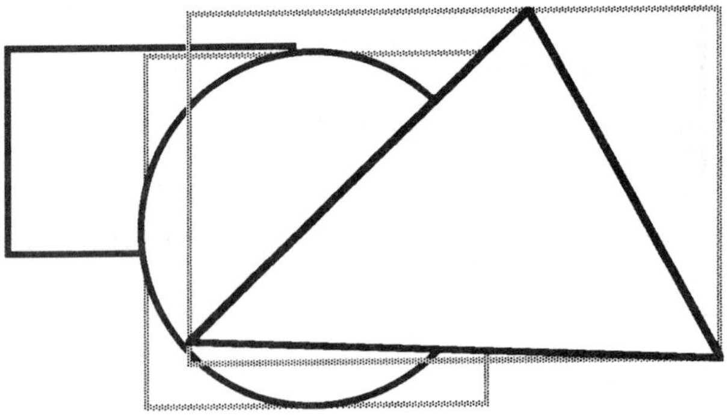

selected because its area is the first encountered on the list. Similarly, the choice of any point in the circle other than those in the triangular region will select the circle. Only points in the rectangle other than those in the circle or triangle can be selected to choose the rectangle. In other words, the overlapping of objects may make one or more of the underlying objects inaccessible. The next section will take up the problem of selecting existing objects and altering the order of the objects in the list to allow access to the underlying objects.

EXERCISES

6.3.1

Implement an insert procedure for a doubly linked list.

6.3.2

Given the (simplified) segment list for an image:

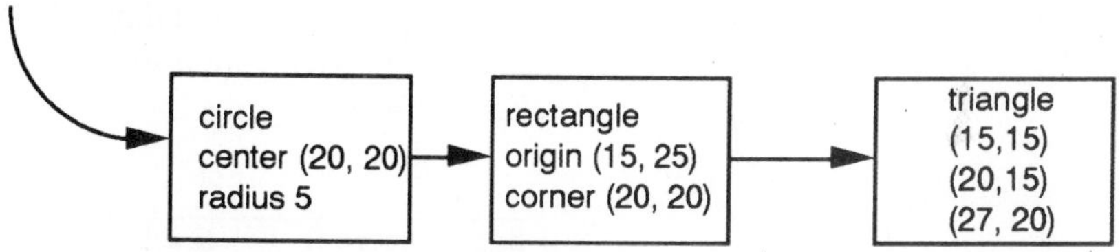

with all of the objects are filled with patterns. If the objects are drawn in the order that they appear in the list, which picture would be drawn from this list?

FIGURE 6.3.7

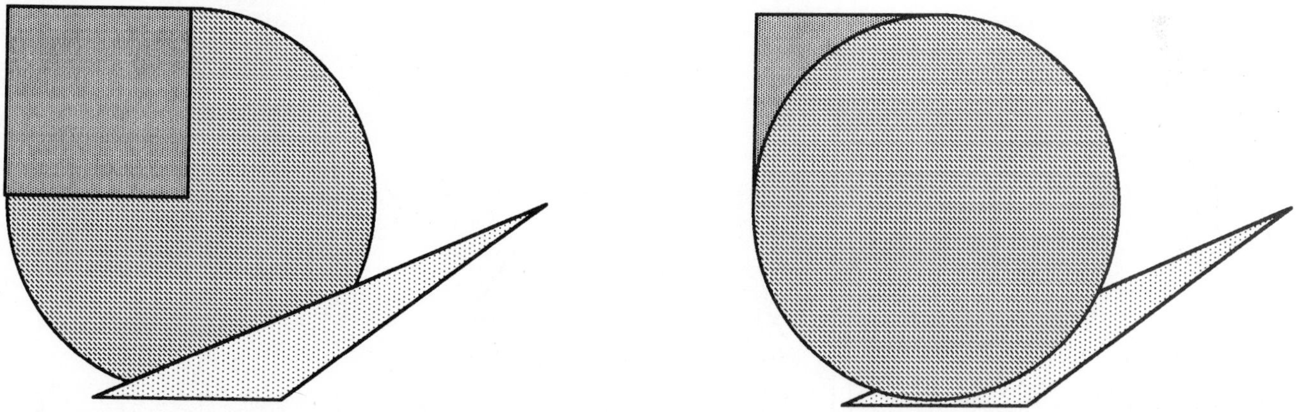

6.3.3

Alter the tool procedures you created in section 6.1 to insert the objects created by the tool into a segment.

6.4 Selecting Objects in a Segmented Picture

In this section you will consider the process of selecting an object in a segmented picture in order to move or remove it.

The arrow will be the cursor for the **select tool.** The user will use ReadLocator to obtain the location of the desired object. The location of the cursor at the time of selection is returned to the select tool, and the list of objects is searched in order to locate an object with the given selected point in its select region (figures 6.4.1 and 6.4.2). To indicate which object has been selected, each of the corners of its select region is drawn in reverse mode. Notice that the procedure does not return a pointer to the object selected, but to the object that precedes it in the object list. This is done because if the singly linked object list is altered (as it would be in a delete), a pointer to the predecessor of the chosen object is needed.

It is clear from the discussion in the last section that it may be impossible to select an object in this manner if much of its select region is covered by the select regions of objects appearing earlier in the list (figures 6.4.3 and 6.4.4).

In order to make things more or less accessible, the edit menu may contain the **move to front** and **move to back** options. If an object has been selected, the move to front option will move the object to the head of the segment. Similarly, the move to back option moves the selected object to the back of the segment (figure 6.4.5).

FIGURE 6.4.1

The corners of the select region of the triangle are marked by dots to indicate that the region has been selected.

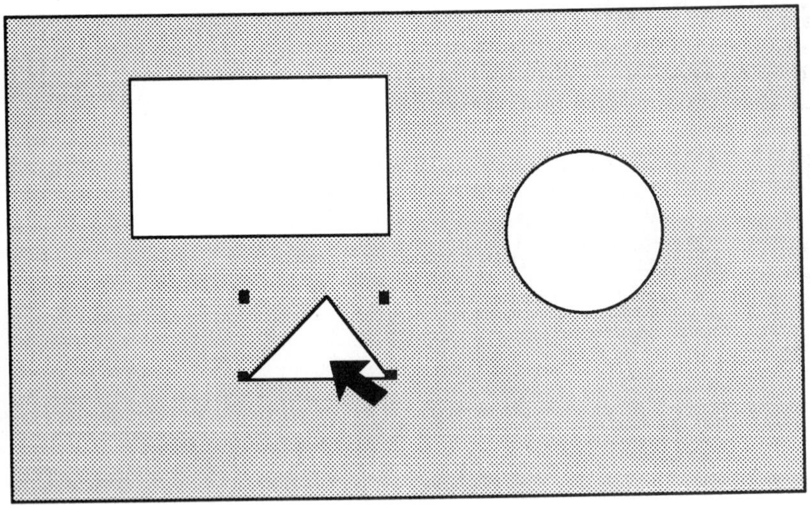

FIGURE 6.4.2

SelectObject finds the topmost object in a segment whose select region contains the point (x,y).

```
(* This procedure is used to select a object from a object list.  The values x and y are the          *)
(* coordinates of a point inside the desired object. The object list is searched for the first object *)
(* with the point (x,y) in its select region.  The procedure returns the segment preceding the         *)
(* selected object in the segment list.  The parameter Selected is set to true if the point (x,y) is   *)
(* in the select region of an object.  If no object in the segment list has the point in its select    *)
(* region, Selected is set to false and the pointer to the selected object is set to nil.              *)
(* The object list is assumed to start with a dummy node to make the look-ahead process simpler.       *)
(* Function InRegion tests whether the point (x,y) is in the select region of the  current segment.    *)

function InRegion(x,y : integer; R : rectangle):boolean;
begin (*InRegion *)
  with R do
    InRegion :=  ((Origin.X <= x) and (x <= Corner.X))  and
                 ((Origin.Y <= y) and (y <= Corner.Y))
end; (* InRegion*)

procedure SelectObject(x,y : integer; ObjectList : SegmentPtr;
                       var ObjectSelected : SegmentPtr;
                       var Selected : boolean);
var
  Temp : SegmentPtr;                      (* used to chain the segment list                  *)
begin  (*SelectObject*)
  Temp := SegmentList;
  Selected := false;                      (* if no object is found, Selected stays false     *)
  while (Temp^.NextObject <> nil) and (not Selected) do
    begin
      Selected := InRegion (x,y,Temp^.next^.SelectRegion);
      if not Selected then
        Temp := Temp^.NextObject
    end;
  if Selected then
    ObjectSelected := Temp
  else
    ObjectSelected := nil
end; (* SelectObject *)
```

FIGURE 6.4.3

The select region of the triangle is covered by the two rectangles that appear earlier in the object list.

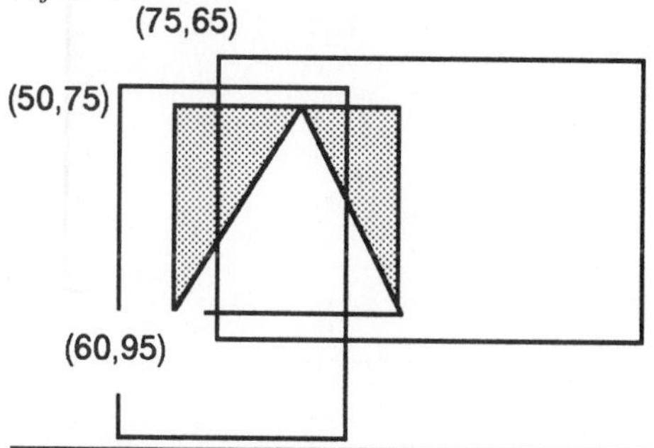

FIGURE 6.4.4

The object list for the picture in figure 6.4.3

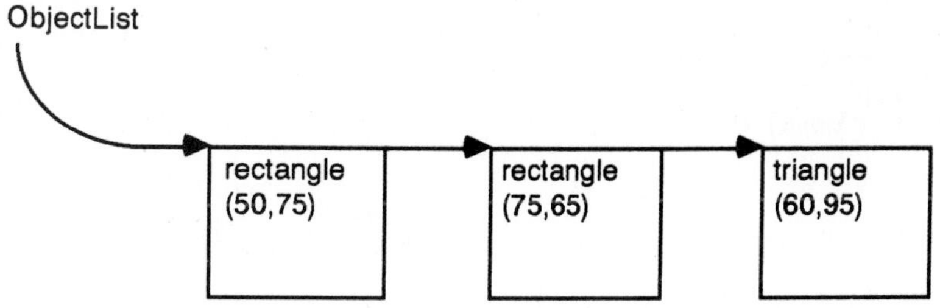

FIGURE 6.4.5

These procedures move objects to the front or back of a segment.

```
(* These procedures move a selected object to the front or rear of the object list.  This list is assumed       *)
(* to have a dummy record as its first record.  The pointer received is assumed to be that of the record        *)
(* preceding the selected record in the object list as in figure 6.4.2.  The pointer SelectedObject is sent to the *)
(* front of the list to be consistent with the principle that SelectedObject is the record  prior to the selected *)
(* object in the object list.                                                                                    *)

procedure MoveToFront (var ObjectList : SegmentPtr;      (* the list of segments                         *)
                       var SelectedObject: SegmentPtr);
var
  Temp : SegmentPtr;                                     (* used to hold onto the segment to be moved     *)
begin  (*MoveToFront *)
  Temp := SelectedObject^.NextObject;                    (* Temp holds the record of the object selected  *)
  (* deleted object from current position in list *)
  SelectedObject^.NextObject := Temp^.NextObject;
  (* insert object at head of the list *)
  Temp^.NextObject := ObjectList^.NextObject;
  SementList^.NextObject:= Temp;
  (* make adjustment in the pointer to the selected object *)
  SelectedObject := ObjectList
end; (*MoveToFront*)

(* Function used to find the last node in the segment list *)

function FindLast(List : SegmentPtr):SegmentPtr;
var
  Temp : SegmentPtr;
begin (* FindLast *)
  Temp := List;
  while Temp^.NextObject <> nil do
    Temp := Temp^.NextObject;
  FindLast := Temp
end; (* FindLast *)

procedure MoveToBack ( var SelectedObject : SegmentPtr);
var
  Temp : SegmentPtr;                                     (* used to hold onto the segment to be moved     *)
begin  (*MoveToBack*)
  Temp := SelectedObject^.NextObject;                    (* get the selected object                       *)
  (* remove selected object from current position in list *)
  SelectedObject^.NextObject := Temp^.NextObject;
  (* alter SelectedObject to indicate new position of selected object *)
  SelectedObject := FindLast(SelectedObject);            (* end must be after this                        *)
  (* insert selected object at end of list *)
  SelectedObject^.NextObject := Temp;
  Temp^.NextObject := nil
end; (*MoveToBack*)
```

It is clear that in order for the move operations to work, an object must be selected, so there should be an indication that some object has been selected. A boolean variable may be set to true whenever an object has been selected, and access to the move to front and move to back should be allowed only if the boolean is set to true.

In several of the more sophisticated systems, menu selections that depend on an action prior to their being chosen—such as the selection of an object before a deletion—are shown to be inactive if the required action has not been taken. In Macintosh programs, the currently inactive choices are shown in light gray.

There must also be a way to deselect an object. After a move to front or back operation, the selected object remains selected. A simple way to deselect an object would be to move the cursor to an empty area of the screen and select at this point, as is done in figure 6.4.2. If an object is deleted (section 6.5), it will automatically be deselected.

EXERCISES

FIGURE 6.4.6

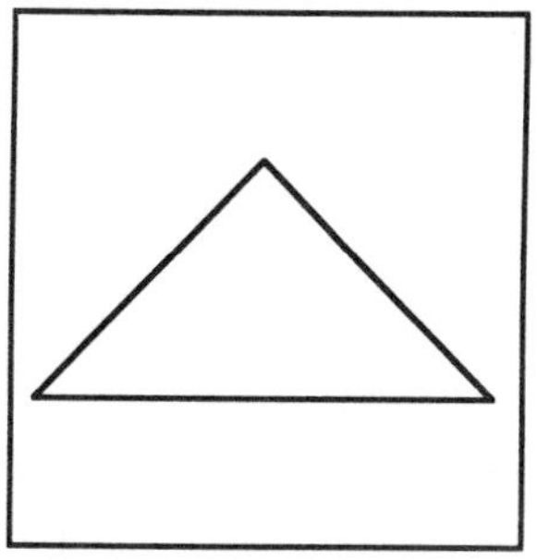

6.4.1

If the list for figure 6.4.6 has the rectangle listed earlier than the triangle, it is imposible to select the triangle in our system. If you have the options move to the front and move to the back, what would you do if you wanted to be able to select the triangle?

6.5 Deleting, Moving, and Rotating Selected Objects in a Segmented Picture

Once an object has been selected, deleting, moving, or rotating will be handled by procedures called by selecting delete, move, rotate right, or rotate left, respectively, from the edit menu. Recall that one could deselect an object by moving the select cursor to a neutral area of the drawing screen and then pressing <**esc**>**.** Moving the cursor to the pull-down menu area of the screen will not deselect the current object, so selecting an operation from the edit menu will not cause the current selection to be lost.

In order to delete an object from a segmented picture, you only need to Bitblt the SelectRegion of the object chosen over itself in **xor** mode, delete the object from the list, and then redraw the picture with the DrawObjectList procedure, created in exercise 6.2.2. In this procedure (figure 6.5.1), assume that the SelectedObject is a pointer to the record preceding the selected objects record (see figure 6.4.2). Figure 6.5.2 shows the reconstruction of the object list needed to delete an object. Notice that the procedure DrawObjectList redraws all the objects that remain in the picture, even though only those intersecting the deleted rectangle require redrawing. To increase the efficiency of the redraw process, check to see if the select region of an object intersects the deleted rectangle.

Moving an object is more difficult because the user must be given a method to indicate the new position of the object. This device must provide some user feedback as to the effect of the change on the picture, yet the picture often

FIGURE 6.5.1

This procedure deletes an object from a segment. It also erases everything in the select region of that object and redraws the remaining objects in the list.

```
(* This procedure deletes the object following SelectedObject from a        *)
(* segmented picture.  It uses the simple process of Bitblting the selected *)
(* region of the screen with itself in xor  mode to erase both the object and *)
(* the selection marks.  The selected switch is also turned off.            *)

procedure DeleteObject(ObjectList : SegmentPtr;
                          var SelectedObject : SegmentPtr;
                          var Selected : boolean);
var
  TempRec : rectangle;                    (* the region to be deleted         *)
begin  (* DeleteObject *)
  TempRec := SelectedObject^.NextObject^.SelectRegion;
  (* delete object by setting the NextObject pointer of SelectedObject to the  *)
  (* object following the object that will be deleted               *)
  SelectedObject^.NextObject := SelectedObject^.NextObject^.NextObject;
  (* erase the region around the selected object *)
  Bitblt(Display,Display,TempRec.Origin,TempRec,cXor);
  (* redraw the picture *)
  DrawObjectList(ObjectList);
  Selected := false
end;(* DeleteObject *)
```

FIGURE 6.5.2

The adjustment of pointers in the DeleteObject procedure

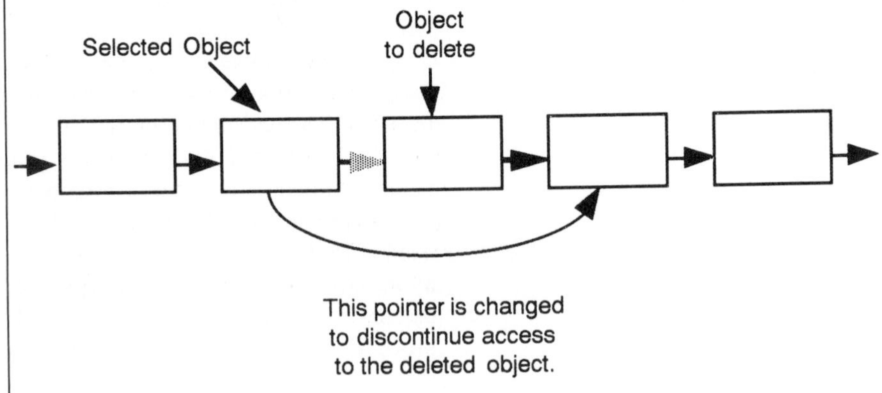

cannot be redrawn after each move. In the case of small disjointed objects, an object may be moved by Bitblting it into the cursor and by moving the cursor (object) into its final position with ReadLocator.

In a more general case, a fixed cursor may be moved in response to the user's keyboard commands until a final location is chosen. The object is erased as in the case of delete, the coordinates of the object's new hotspot are recorded in its node, and the picture is redrawn by using the procedure from exercise 6.2.2.

Next you will look at the Bitblt method for moving objects. The general method is similar and will not be covered here. Because all your objects have a rectangular SelectRegion, this rectangle makes the ideal rectangle for the initial source rectangle. All these objects are on the screen and will return to the screen, so it would seem logical that both the source bitmap and the destination bitmap could be Display. This, however, is not possible. Even if the initial picture does not overlap another object, the first redrawing of the object will overlap the initial picture, resulting in a confused picture.

To circumvent these problems, assume all objects to be smaller than a given size (in bytes). This will allow you to create a packed array with the number of bytes allowed by your storage. The rectangle for the bitmap may be just the SelectRegion. Because the points used to indicate that an object has been selected are the corners of this rectangle, these points will also move with the object during the selection process.

The object will be stored in the bitmap, Object, which will be passed to ReadLocator as the cursor. After the final position is selected, Object will be drawn on the screen in store mode. In order for the original object to be erased, it is bitmapped to the screen before ReadLocator is called. This ensures that the calls to Bitblt within ReadLocator will be done in the proper order (figure 6.5.3).

Object data is altered in AdjustObject. This procedure simply adds XMove and YMove to the corners of the SelectRegion and the hotspot. These values could be added to various variables depending on the structure of objects.

Non-overlapping objects are required by this procedure because it gets its original version of the object from the object to be moved. If the initialization of Object in the procedure can be done from a neutral area of the screen or from a file of objects, overlapping images may be moved with this procedure.

The alternative is to move some fixed cursor, such as a small rectangle, that has its upper-left corner at the hotspot of the object to be moved. The one problem encountered here is that the object must be deselected before it is erased and reselected after the picture is redrawn. If this is not done, the selection marks will remain around the original position of the object.

Finally, you must consider the rotation of objects in your list. To simplify your menu choices, restrict the rotations to **rotate left** and **rotate right**. Rotate left can be thought of as a 90° rotation in a counterclockwise direction, and rotate right as a 90° rotation in the clockwise direction. In both cases the rotation will be around the hotspot. Only allow rotations of polynomials because text rotation is difficult.

For polygons and triangles, the rotation formula given in figure 3.5.5 may be applied to their vertices to get the new coordinates. Notice that because of the restricted rotations, the sine will be either 1 or -1 and the cosine will be 0, so the formula may be simplified. In the case of a rectangle, you need only apply

FIGURE 6.5.3

This procedure uses Bitblt to move small non-overlapping objects.

```
(* This version of move works on small non-overlapping objects. It uses the ability of ReadLocator to move      *)
(* a bitmapped object around the screen without destroying the picture. The maximum size of an object that     *)
(* can be moved is given in bytes as byteSize, a constant for the main program. The procedure AdjustObject     *)
(* will use the displacements XMove and YMove to change the information in the segment to reflect the object's *)
(*  new position. Remember that the pointer SelectedObject actually points to the object preceding the          *)
(* selected object in the ObjectList.                                                                            *)

procedure BitMove(ObjectList : SegmentPtr; var SelectedObject : SegmentPtr);
var
  Object : BitMap;                               (* will hold the image of the object to be moved          *)
  Storage : packed array[1..byteSize] of Byte;   (* storage for this bitmap                                *)
  XMove,YMove : integer;                         (* relative change in the position of any point of the object *)
begin (*BitMove*)
  SelectedObject := SelectedObject^.NextObject;  (* move to the actual object selected                     *)
  with SelectedObject^ do
    begin
      with Object do                             (* initialize the cursor as the object to be moved        *)
        begin
          Base:= address(Storage);
          Width := (SelectRegion.Corner.X - SelectRegion.Origin.X + PixelsPerWord - 1) div PixelsPerWord;
          Rect := SelectRegion
        end;
      (* move the object into the bitmap *)
      Bitblt(Display,Object,SelectRegion.Origin,SelectRegion,cStore);
      (* erase the object from its current position *)
      Bitblt(Object,Display,SelectRegion.Origin,SelectRegion,cXor);
      (* get the new location for the object *)
      with SelectRegion do
        begin
          ReadLocator(Origin.X,Origin.Y,Object);
          (* place the object in its final position *)
          Bitblt(Object,Display,Origin,Object.Rect,cStore)
        end;
      (* compute the change in position of the region's origin*)
      XMove := SelectRegion.Origin.X - Object.Rect.Origin.X;
      YMove := SelectRegion.Origin.Y - Object.Rect.Origin.Y;
      (* change the other information in the object *)
      AdjustObject(SelectedObject,XMove,YMove);
    end;
  (* redraw picture to ensure erasures are covered *)
  DrawObjectList(ObjectList)
end; (*BitMove*)
```

the rotation formula to the opposite corner to get the new coordinates. The SelectRegion should be recalculated to the state it was in when it was created. Once the new coordinates have been established, the old picture may be erased as before and redrawn as in the move or delete operation.

EXERCISES

6.5.1

Write the rotate right and rotate left procedures.

6.5.2

Develop a test to determine if two rectangles overlap. Use this test to write a procedure that draws an object only if its SelectRegion intersects a given rectangle. This procedure can replace DrawObjectList in the procedure DeleteObject (figure 6.5.1).

6.6 Object-oriented Graphics Using Object-oriented Programming

Your segments store objects from a list of graphics primitives. Many of the operations on these primitive objects are similar to one another. For example, graphic objects are moved by erasing them, changing their locations, and then redrawing them. The only difference between moving a point, a polygon, or a circle is in the functions that erase and draw these objects. Object-oriented languages provide mechanisms to take advantage of the similarities among objects and support the differences among them.

The foundations of object-oriented programming can be traced to the language Smalltalk, developed in the 1970s. An entire Smalltalk program consists of **objects** that communicate with one another by passing **messages.** Messages have a role similar to that of parameters in other languages; however, there is a difference in emphasis on the role of objects and messages. In other languages, procedures receive data through parameters and pass back data to the main program or other procedures. Objects hold data and have access to certain procedures, called **methods.** In Smalltalk, even constants are objects. Messages are passed between objects, and these messages tell the objects to use methods.

Objects can respond only to certain messages. An object representing a number will accept messages asking it to do arithmetic, but will not necessarily accept a message requesting string handling. Similar objects share methods and accept the same set of messages. These objects are grouped into **classes.** Classes, in turn, are grouped into more general classes. Each class contains a list of methods shared by all objects in that class. At the highest level, there is a superclass composed of all objects and classes. This superclass contains only those methods shared by all objects. Objects may **inherit** methods from any class of which they are a direct descendant.

Object-oriented versions of Pascal and C have recently become available for both IBM-compatible PCs and the Macintosh. Object-oriented Pascal uses a simpler hierarchy than Smalltalk does. Classes are replaced by types designated as objects. The type **object** is used to define the data fields and methods of a given type's variables (figure 6.6.1). Each of your primitive graphic objects may be considered members of the class GraphicObject.

FIGURE 6.6.1

The object structure used in Turbo Pascal and Think Pascal. The method type ***virtual*** *or* ***override*** *is used to indicate that the methods Show and Hide are polymorphic.*

```
type
  GraphicObject = object
     Location :   point;
     procedure Init (x,y : integer);
     procedure Show  :   virtual;       (*override in Think Pascal*)
     procedure Hide  :   virtual;
     procedure MoveTo(NewX,NewY:integer);
  end; (* GraphicObject*)
```

While polygons, circles, and points may share the MoveTo operation, they do use different Show and Hide methods. These methods draw the figures. Circles have to access circle-drawing methods as well as MoveTo. The type **Circle** inherits MoveTo from the type **GraphicObject** (figure 6.6.2).

Each object type may have some data fields and some methods specific to that type. If a type is a direct descendant of this type, these data fields and methods may be inherited. The method definitions may also be overidden by local declarations. In the example, Init will be different for every definition of graphic object. The Show and Hide methods also differ from type to type but are used by the method MoveTo (figure 6.6.3).

FIGURE 6.6.2

Circles, points, and polygons share the property location and the operation MoveTo. The operations Show and Erase are also common to the three types of objects, but each uses a different implementation of these operations.

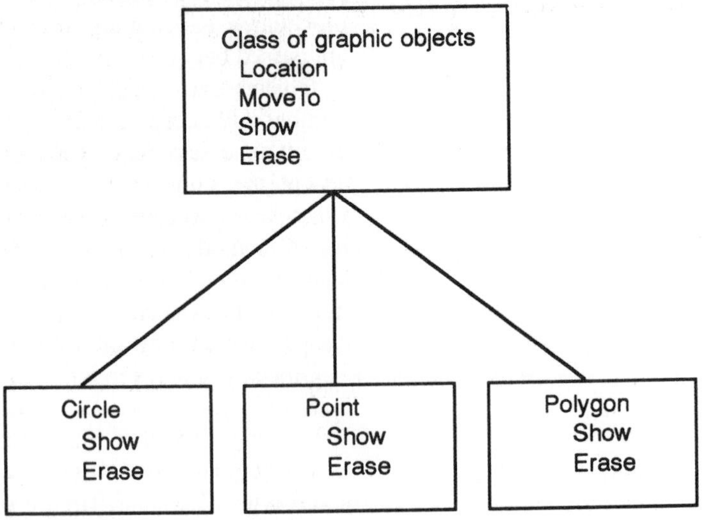

FIGURE 6.6.3

The MoveTo procedure defined for all graphic objects uses the polymorphic actions Hide and Show. Procedures with these names are defined for each type of graphic object.

```
(* This is a generic procedure used to move any graphic object.*)

procedure GraphicObject.MoveTo (NewX,NewY: integer);
begin
  Hide;
  Location.X := NewX;
  Location.Y := NewY;
  Show
end;
```

While you could declare Show as a method to show the point where the object is located, this is not an appropriate definition of Show for a circle. The method names Show and Hide are shared by various graphic objects, but the implementations differ from object to object. Non-local actions like Show and Hide that lend their names to different methods are called **polymorphic.**

Specific types of graphic objects, such as circles, are defined as objects of type **GraphicObject** (figure 6.6.4). Each circle inherits the field Location from **GraphicObject.** In addition, the type **Circle** has a field of its own, namely radius. Methods defined for **Circle** access these fields directly. There is not need to make specific reference to **Circle** when you are accessing radius with these methods. The methods for showing and hiding circles must also be defined. The

FIGURE 6.6.4

The polymorphic action Show, implemented for the graphic object Circle with a generic circle-drawing procedure. The Location parameter of DrawCircle is inherited from GraphicObject, and the radius parameter is one of the fields of Circle.

```
type
Circle = object(GraphicObject);    (* Circle is defined as an object that inherits from GraphicObject*)
  radius : integer;
  procedure Init (InitX,InitY, InitRadius : integer);
  procedure Show : virtual;
  procedure Hide  : virtual
end;

procedure Init(InitX,InitY,InitRadius: integer);
begin
  GraphicObject.Init(InitX,InitY);
  radius := InitRadius
end;
procedure Circle.Show;
begin
  DrawCircle(Location, radius)
end;
```

method Init has the same name as a method defined for **GraphicObject** but is private to **Circle.**

Actual circles are defined as variables (figure 6.6.5). In the program segment given in figure 6.6.5, the circle MyCircle has its fields initialized; then it is displayed and finally moved. The fact that MyCircle is of type **Circle** determines that the method Show used by MyCircle is Circle.Show.

If you add the fields NextObject and SelectRegion to the type **GraphicObject** (figure 6.6.6), you have a structure similar to the record Segment (figure 6.2.3). There is no need for a variant record structure because each graphics primitive is described as an object of type **GraphicObject**.

Object-oriented programming encourages programmers to group structures so that similar structures may share methods. Insight gained by charting these similarities and differences should improve the quality of the final program. While object-oriented programming is not a magic cure-all, it is yet another tool for creating well-organized programs.

FIGURE 6.6.5

This segment of a program shows how a variable of type ***Circle*** *is manipulated in an object-oriented program.*

```
var
  MyCircle : Circle;

begin (*main program*)

   MyCircle.Init(25,34,5);
   MyCircle.Show;
   MyCircle.MoveTo(65,78);

end. (* main program*)
```

FIGURE 6.6.6

The type ***GraphicObject*** *is a Pascal object.*

```
type
  ObjectPtr      = ^GraphicObject;
  GraphicObject = object
    Location       : point;
    NextObject     : ObjectPtr;
    SelectRegion   : rectangle;
    procedure Init (x,y : integer);
    procedure Show   :         virtual;          (* override in Think Pascal*)
    procedure Hide   :         virtual;
    procedure MoveTo(NewX,NewY:integer);
end; (* GraphicObject*)
```

EXERCISES

6.6.1

Find out if your compiler supports object-oriented programming. If it does, create the types **GraphicObject, Circle, Point,** and **polygon**. Implement the methods Init, Hide, Show, and MoveTo on your system.

6.6.2

Change your implementation of the segment structure to make use of an object-oriented system.

6.6.3

Rewrite the functions for selecting, moving, and deleting graphic objects given in sections 6.4 and 6.5 in an object-oriented manner.

6.7 Zooming

Many graphics applications require a change to the degree of magnification used on a given image during the run of the program. This change in magnification is called **zooming.** For some applications the user may need to see an enlargement of part of the screen as in figure 6.7.1; this is called **zooming in.** For other applications the user may need to see the current image in the context of a larger image. The current screen image is then reduced to show it in relation to the rest of the image (see figure 6.7.2). This form of zooming is called **zooming out.**

FIGURE 6.7.1

An example of zooming in

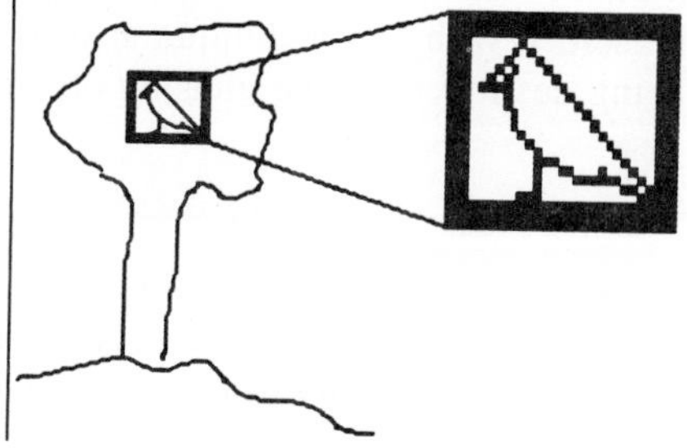

FIGURE 6.7.2

An example of zooming out to show the whole picture containing the original image

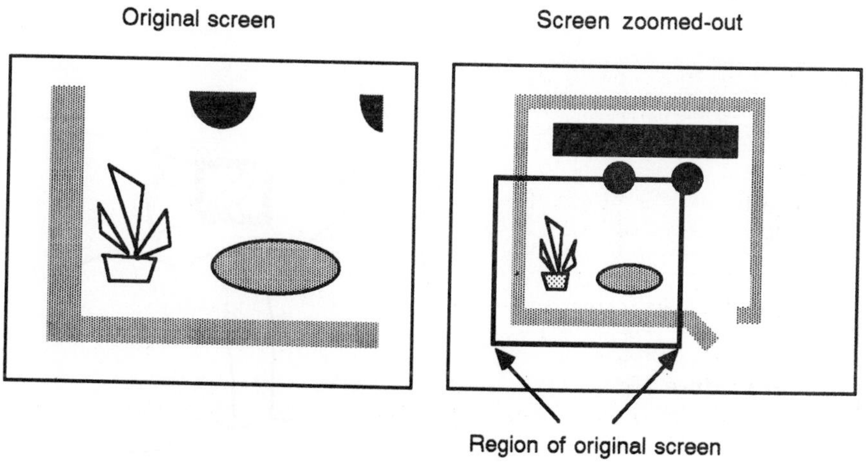

In figure 6.7.1, Bitblt was employed to create the zoomed image. This technique reconstructs bits as rectangular blocks of bits. If the picture is stretched to n-times its original horizontal length, then each block has a horizontal length of n bits. Similarly, if the picture is stretched to m-times its original vertical height, then each block has a vertical height of m bits. The result of this stretching is a pronounced sawtooth appearance typical of this type of zoom. Zooming in with Bitblt is valuable when it is important to see the actual placement of bits in the picture, but fine-tuning of pictures may often require a bit-by-bit alteration of the picture. This can be achieved easily only when each bit is enlarged, as it is when Bitblt is used for zooming. Most graphics hardware implements this form of zooming by allowing the CRT controller to repeat bits or scan lines.

In figure 6.7.3, the picture in figure 6.7.1 was enlarged by redrawing it in a window with world coordinates coinciding with the coordinates of the corner of the zoom rectangle. This type of zooming can be achieved only if the program has access to a list of all objects in the picture and their locations. Its use, therefore, is normally restricted to segmented graphics programs. The zoom-out in figure 6.7.2 is achieved by changing the corners of a new window to encompass a larger area and redrawing the picture in the new window coordinates.

Bitblt may also be used to zoom out, but only to reduce the size of the area being zoomed, because there is no record of objects outside the screen area. Procedures that use Bitblt to zoom out sample bits at fixed intervals and reconstruct the picture using the sample bits. This form of zooming is mainly useful in reducing objects that have been edited with the bit-by-bit technique described earlier. Reducing sections of the screen with this technique at other settings can result in parts of the image being destroyed by the aliasing effect (figure 6.7.4).

FIGURE 6.7.3

One way to zoom is to set the window coordinates of a larger viewport to the values at the corners of a small rectangle on the screen, and then redraw the picture in the window.

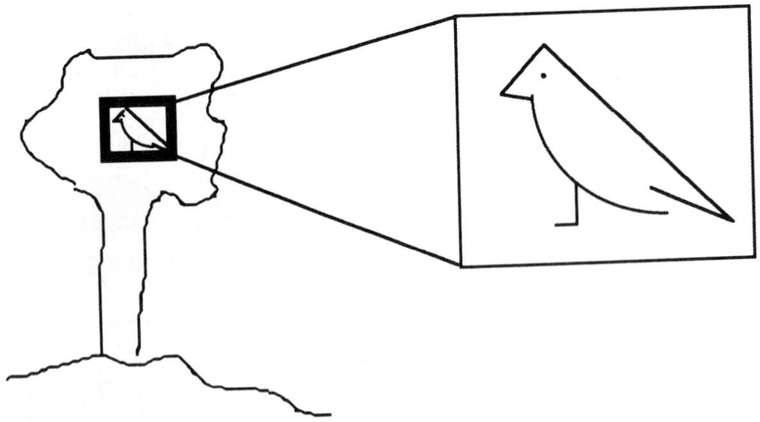

FIGURE 6.7.4

Parts of figures are lost or aliased when zooming out.

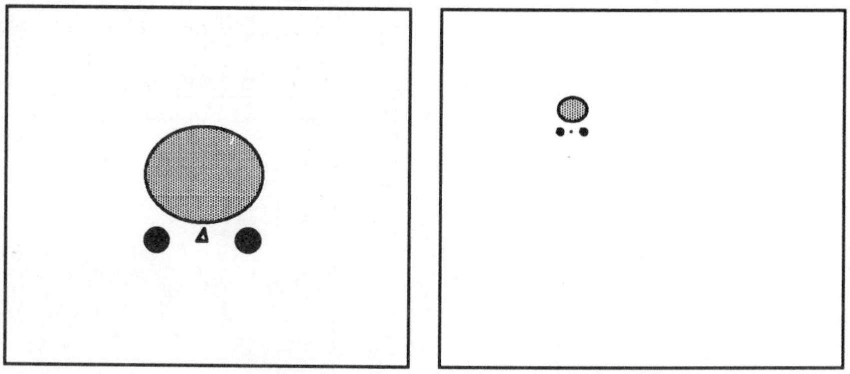

FIGURE 6.7.5

A possible screen layout for a font editor

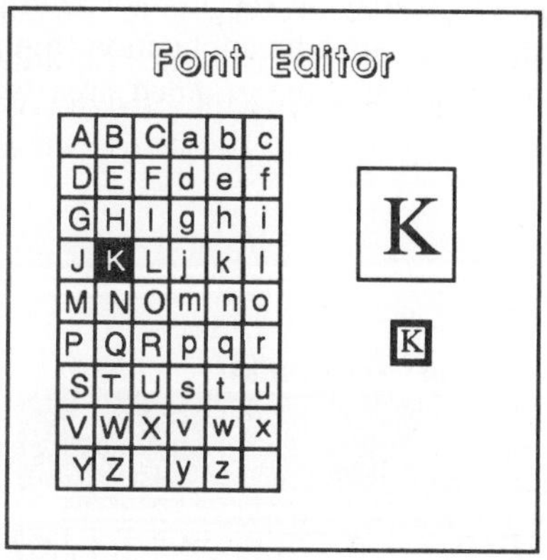

The **zoom tool** is somewhat independent of the technique used for the actual zooming. Basically, a rectangular region of the screen must be specified, and a percentage of increase or decrease in size must be chosen. In addition, a zoom window must be provided. Font editors use perhaps the simplest methods for making these choices. Letters appear at different predetermined magnifications in predetermined windows (figure 6.7.5). No choice is provided for the user. During zooming out, the zoom rectangle normally is the current window. The user selects the percentage of the new screen that the current screen will occupy. More complicated draw and paint programs allow the user to zoom in on a user-specified rectangle at a user-selected percentage. The results can then be placed in a predefined or user-defined window.

There are two ways to select a zoom rectangle. In segmented systems, it is often assumed that the currently selected item will be zoomed. Figure 6.7.6 is an example of zooming in SuperPaint. A rectangle of predetermined size is constructed so that the selected object is at its center. This rectangle is then zoomed the specified amount. An alternative method for constructing the zoom region is to draw a rubberband rectangle around the region to be zoomed and then to zoom this rectangle. The difficulty with this method is that if a large increase in size is coupled with a large rectangle, the resulting image may not fit in the window provided. This problem can be handled in different ways. Some programs simply ignore such requests; others issue a warning and do nothing; still others try to zoom part of the image selected. The user is often confused if no warning is given, especially if nothing happens. A warning should be a part of any resolution of this problem. In systems where menu options can be deactivated, attempts to zoom oversized areas may result in the zoom choice being deactivated.

When constructing the zoom-out tool, which allows the user to show the current screen as a percentage of a larger area, the developer normally determines the section of the new image in which the original will appear. If, after zooming, the entire image is not on the screen, at least the zoomed part of

FIGURE 6.7.6

An example of zooming in SuperPaint

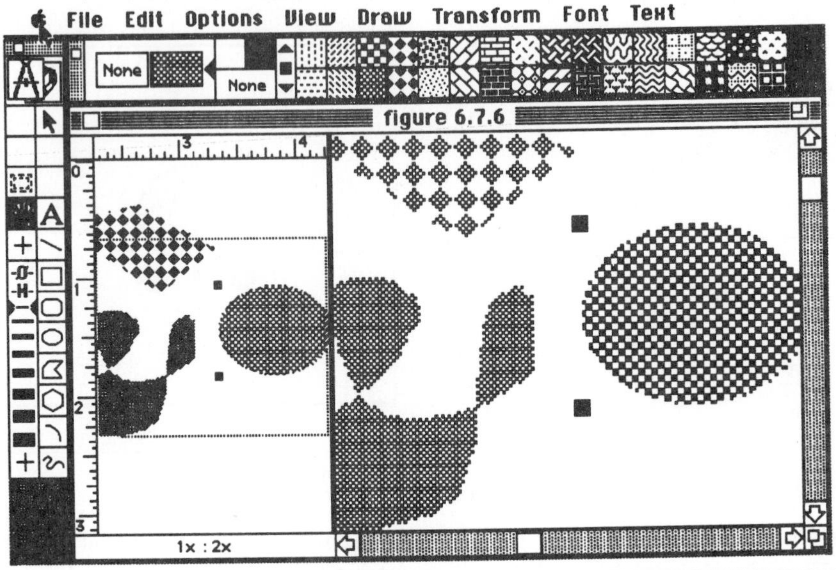

the image must still be positioned on the screen. It may appear in the center of the screen or in one of the corners, depending on the specific application (figure 6.7.7). When the entire image appears on the screen, the zoomed area will appear in its normal position in the image.

FIGURE 6.7.7

An example of zooming out in SuperPaint

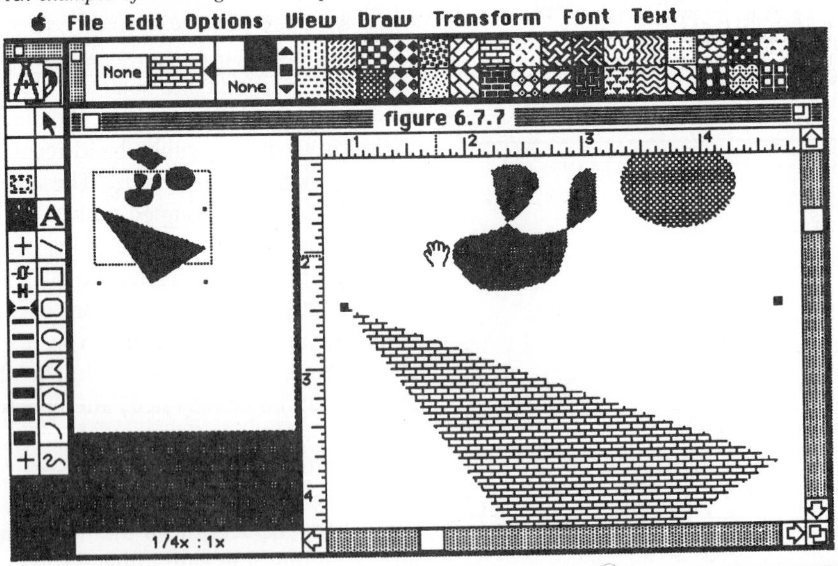

FIGURE 6.7.8

Original image to be zoomed

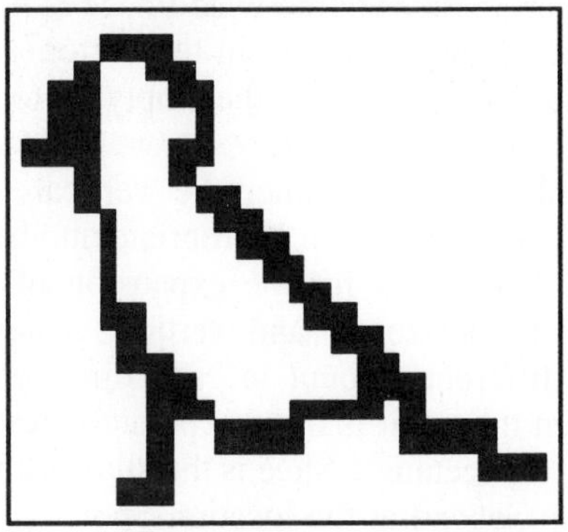

The percentage of zoom is often fixed in a program. In such a program, successive zooms always alter the size of the image by the predetermined percentage. Usually a limit on the number of zooms is provided. In some cases, such as the original MacPaint, this limit is one zoom in, but newer paint and draw programs now provide for many zooms in either direction. If the zoom is accomplished by redrawing the picture, the coordinate system of the zoom window is preset by the application. When Bitblt is used to zoom in, the size of the block that replaces each bit is predetermined. In the case of zoom-out, the sampling interval is built into the program.

Using Bitblt to zoom in so that each bit is represented by a block m bits wide and n bits high is a two-part process. First the picture (figure 6.7.8) is enlarged horizontally; then this new picture is enlarged vertically to the final size. To enlarge the picture horizontally, it is sectioned into a sequence of vertical rectangles 1 bit wide and the same height as the zoom area (figure 6.7.9). Each of these rectangles is then reproduced $(m - 1)$ times to stretch the picture in the horizontal direction (see figure 6.7.10).

To enlarge the picture vertically, each row is reproduced $(n - 1)$ times to produce the final image (see figure 6.7.11).

FIGURE 6.7.9

The slices that are repeated in the horizontal spread of this zoom

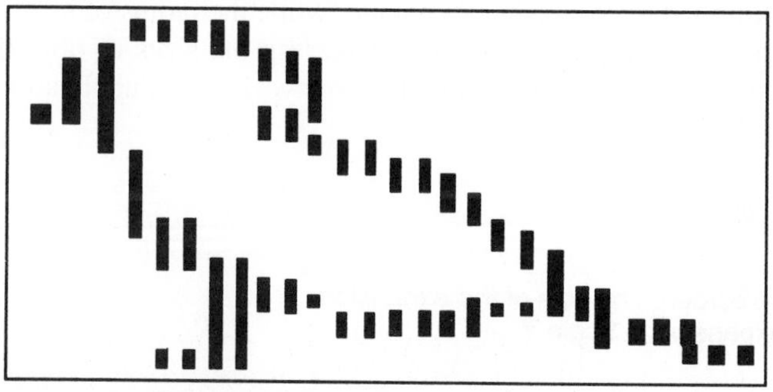

FIGURE 6.7.10

The image from figure 6.7.9 after the slices have been repeated to fill in the horizontally stretched image

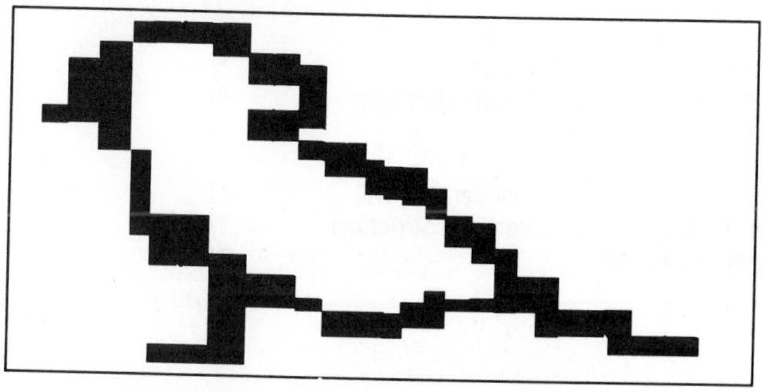

FIGURE 6.7.11

The image from figure 6.7.8 after zooming is complete

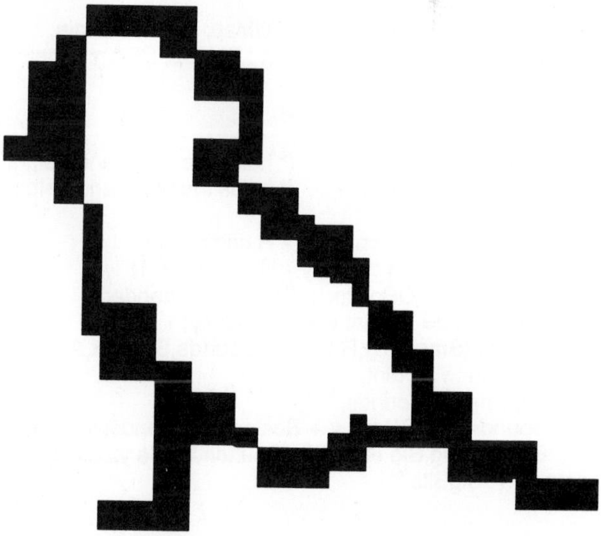

In the following code, Small represents the beginning bitmap and Big represents the final bitmap. The bitmap Big is assumed to be properly initialized in the main program. An intermediate bitmap for storing the wide image is not needed because the vertical slicing and spreading is done from the bottom of Big. Thus, the bottom row of the wide image is spread into the empty bottom row of Big.

The procedure Spread cuts bitmaps into slices in either the vertical or horizontal direction. It also reproduces each of the slices an appropriate number of times. Notice that BigBits (figure 6.7.12) allows for the expansion of a subrectangle of a bitmap. It also has both horizontal and vertical scales, allowing a picture to be expanded by a different amount in each direction. Spread is a local procedure of BigBits, even though it is listed separately here.

In the procedure Spread (figure 6.7.13), the rectangle Slice is the slice of the bitmap First to be transferred to the bitmap Second at the location Spot.

The process of scaling an object is similar to zooming, in that the size of an object or area of the screen is altered by a percentage usually specified by the user. The difference is that the scaled object or area still appears in its original window; nothing else in that window is altered by the scaling process. If the process of scaling is done with Bitblt, an area is specified and the Bitblt zoom algorithms are applied. When an object in a segmented system is zoomed, it is erased and redrawn after its description has been altered by the percentage specified. A polygon given in relative coordinates will simply have each of those coordinates multiplied by the scale percentage, while the radius of a circle will multiplied by the scale percentage. When increasing the sizes of objects, take care to make sure that they will still fit in the window. In some applications

FIGURE 6.7.12

This procedure zooms a rectangle by stretching it horizontally and then vertically.

```
(* This procedure uses Bitblt to zoom a given rectangle on the screen. The size of the expansion    *)
(* is given in Scale.  The x-expansion is Scale.X and the y-expansion is Scale.Y.                   *)

procedure BigBits(Small : BitMap; R : Rectangle;
                  var Big : BitMap; DPoint, Scale : Point);
type
  Direction = (Down,Across);
var
  Extender  : Point;     (* holds the width and height of R in bits              *)
  Bounds    : Point;     (* holds the width and height of Wide and Big in bits   *)
begin
  Extender.x := R.corner.x - R.origin.x +1;          (* get the width of R in bits                *)
  Extender.y := R.corner.y - R.origin.y + 1;         (* get the height of R in bits               *)
  Bounds.x := DPoint.x + Scale.x * Extender.x;       (* get the corner of the scaled image        *)
  Bounds.y := DPoint.y + Extender.y;                 (* no vertical scaling yet                   *)
  Spread(Small,Big,R,DPoint,Bounds,Scale.x,Across);
  R.origin := DPoint;                                (* set up a rectangle in Wide that will      *)
  R.corner := Bounds;                                (* be extended in the vertical direction     *)
  Bounds.y := DPoint.y + Scale.y * (Extender.y + 1); (* scale vertically                          *)
  Spread(Big,Big,R,DPoint,Bounds,Scale.y,Down)
end; (* BigBits *)
```

FIGURE 6.7.13

The procedure Spread is used by BigBits to spread the zoom rectangle horizontally or vertically.

```
(* Procedure that slices and spreads a picture during the bitmap zoom procedure.        *)
procedure Spread(First,Second : BitMap; R : Rectangle;
                    DP,DCorn :Point;Space : Integer; D : Direction);
var
  I     : integer;
  Slice : Rectangle;
  Spot  : Point;
  T     : Texture;
begin
  If D = Across then                                  (* start at right and work left        *)
    begin
      Spot.x := DCorn.x;
      Spot.y := DP.y;
      Slice := R;
      Slice.origin.x := Slice.Corner.x                (* Slice is one bit wide at bottom    *)
      for I := 1 to Extender.x + 1 do
        begin
          for J := 1 to Space do
            begin
              Bitblt(First,Second,T,Spot,Slice,Cstore);
              Spot.x := Spot.x-1
            end;
          Slice.Origin.x := Slice.Origin.x - 1;
          Slice.Corner.x := Slice.Origin.x
        end
    end
  else
    begin                                             (* start at the bottom and work up   *)
      Spot.x := DP.x;
      Spot.y := DCorn.y;
      Slice := r;
      Slice.origin.y := R.corner.y;
      for I := 1 to Extender.y + 1 do
        begin
          for J := 1 to Space do
            begin
              Bitblt(First,Second,T,Spot,Slice,Cstore);
              Spot.y := Spot.y - 1;
            end;
          Slice.Origin.y := Slice.Origin.y - 1;
          Slice.Corner.y := Slice.Origin.y
        end
    end
end; (* Spread *)
```

it is acceptable to have only part of an object visible. In other applications, however, a partial view should not be allowed. As in the case of zooming a rectangle to a size that does not fit in the zoom window, a warning should be issued if a scaling is not feasible.

EXERCISES

6.7.1

Create an algorithm and write a procedure that allows the user to select a zoom rectangle and create a fixed-size zoom to a predetermined window in a segmented system. Use either of the zooming algorithms.

6.7.2

Create an algorithm and write a procedure that scales circles, polygons, and lines to a specified percentage.

PROJECTS

6.7.1

Create a font editor that allows the user to create a new font for use by your graphics system. This editor should do the following:

1. Show the font being altered
2. Allow the user to specify the letter to be altered
3. Enlarge a specified letter in a fixed window
4. Have a cursor that only moves from enlarged pixel to enlarged pixel in this window
5. Allow the user to alter any pixel in the enlarged window
6. Show the altered version of the letter in normal size on the screen
7. Allow the user to revert to the original version of a given letter or to the original version of the entire font
8. Allow the user save the new font or cancel the entire session

Notice that the zoom used in this project is much simpler than the general zoom described in the chapter. Each bit of the original letter may be replaced by a block of the same color that is 1 byte on a side. If a similar block is used as a cursor, it should blink. A timing loop may be used to get the cursor to blink. This type of cursor provides an easy device for altering bit blocks in the enlarged drawing; simply Bitblt the cursor one extra time in **xor** mode if the user indicates a change. The array structure of both the enlarged version of the letter and its smaller companion can be used to speed up the update process. See figure 6.7.5 for a sample screen layout that could be used in this project.

6.7.2

Create an animation workshop program. This program improves the sketch program used to create animations in section 5.5. It should display a number of consecutive frames on the screen (figure 6.7.14) and allow any one of these frames to be selected and zoomed. In addition, just like the font editor in project 6.7.1, it should allow the zoomed frame to be edited on a bit-by-bit basis. After

FIGURE 6.7.14

The screen layout for project 6.7.2

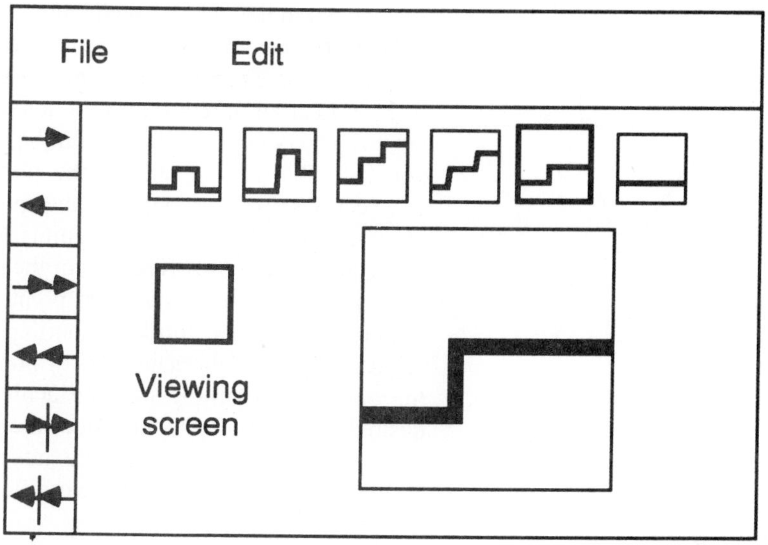

editing, the frame would replace the original frame. The program should also allow the sequence to be viewed in the screen section of the screen in either forward or backward sequence, at normal or slow speed, or one frame at a time.

6.8 Filling Regions

This section begins with a presentation of the **scan method** for filling a polygon. In this algorithm, the intersections of the sides of the polygon and a scan line are calculated. A horizontal line is then drawn between these intersections if that line lies inside the polygon. The scan algorithm can be modified to fill circles and other regions for which the boundary points can be computed directly (figure 6.8.1). When intersections are not easily calculated, another fill algorithm must be used—the **seed-fill algorithm.** This algorithm, also discussed in the this section, works for closed regions when only one point in the region's interior is known. That point is given to the seed-fill procedure; if the color of the point is not already the fill color, the pixel is set in that color. Then the procedure is called for pixels adjacent to the given pixel. Both of these fill algorithms use screen coordinates for their calculations because they do their manipulations with scan lines or pixels. The **scan-line seed fill method,** which combines many advantages of the scan method and seed-fill method, will also be described here.

FIGURE 6.8.1

Examples of filled regions

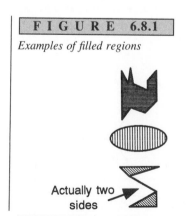

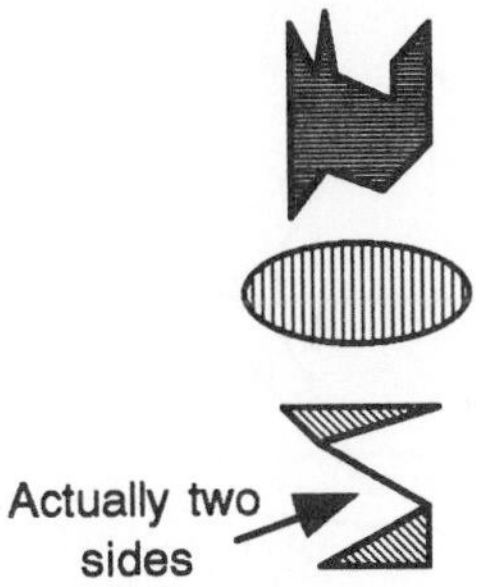

The **scan-filling algorithm** is based on the fact that any line that intersects a polygon intersects more than one side. This allows you to determine if a pixel is inside or outside of a polygon. If a pixel on a scan line is inside a polygon, adjacent pixels on that scan line are inside the polygon. This property is called **scan-line coherence.** In figure 6.8.2.a and 6.8.2.b, the line *a* seems to intersect the polygon on only one side. The line in figure 6.8.2.a hits a vertex at point P, and that vertex lies on two sides. The line joining A and B in figure 6.8.2.b must

FIGURE 6.8.2

The scan-line algorithm computes the intersection of scan lines and the sides of polygons.

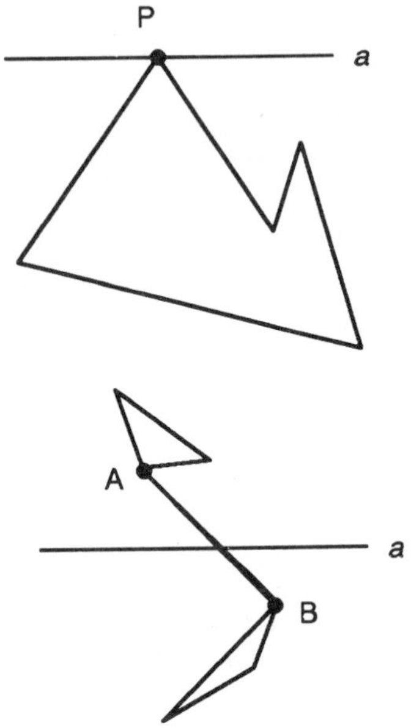

represent two sides because a polygon must begin and end on the same vertex. In order to use the scan-fill algorithm, the program must have a description of the region's boundary. Segmented programs always have such a description for each object in the picture, while nonsegmented programs have such information only at the time an object is created. Hence, nonsegmented programs normally use the scan-fill technique during the creation of an object.

If the set of intersections of a polygon and a scan line are ordered by increasing x-value, the point with the smallest x-value has the property that all points to the left lie outside the polygon. If you assume that none of the intersections is a vertex of the polygon, you can make the following observations: The first pair of points will describe a line contained within the polygon (figure 6.8.3). The part of the scan line between the second intersection point and the third intersection point will lie outside the polygon, while the segment between the third and fourth points will be inside the polygon. The line segment between alternate pairs of non-vertex intersections is contained within the polygon, so filling may be achieved by drawing these segments in the desired fill color. Horizontal sides are not included because they coincide with a segment of a scan line and are automatically filled.

Vertices are end points for two different sides of a polygon; when a vertex is crossed, it normally counts as two intersections. This convention causes problems when the vertex occurs between two lines that have decreasing or increasing y-values, as in vertex 4 in figure 6.8.4. If this vertex were to be counted twice, the line between 4 and 5 would be drawn, and the part of the drawing lying outside the polygon would be shaded. To avoid this, vertices that join two lines having increasing or decreasing y-values are counted as only one intersection. This convention leads to the numbering of intersections in figure 6.8.4 and allows continued use of the technique of drawing segments between alternate pairs of intersections.

A polygon may be filled by creating a list of scan lines that intersect it, and for each such scan line, a list of its intersections with the polygon in order of increasing x-values (figure 6.8.5). If provision has been made for the

FIGURE 6.8.3

The scan-line fill algorithm connects alternate pairs of intersection points of a scan line and sides of the polygon.

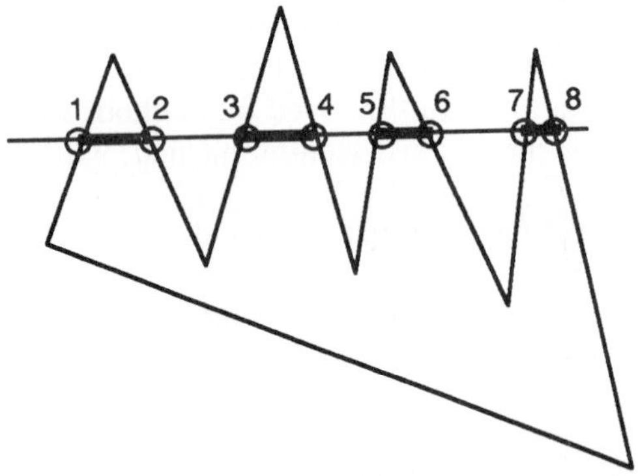

FIGURE 6.8.4

The vertex 4 must be counted only once as an intersection or the segment between 4 and and intersection 5 will be filled by the scan-line fill algorithm.

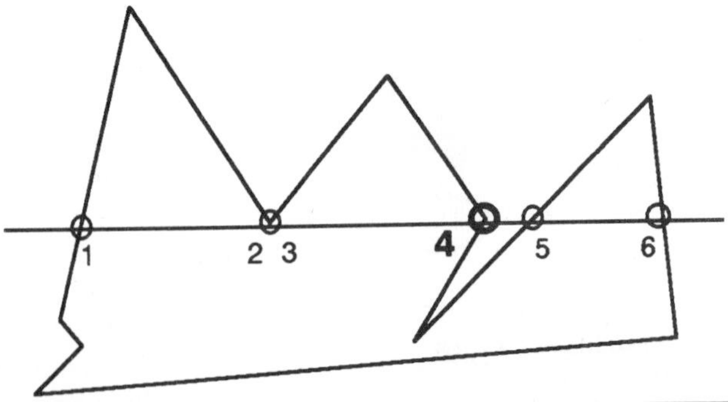

FIGURE 6.8.5

The list of each scan-line's intersections with sides of the polygon is ordered by increasing x-values.

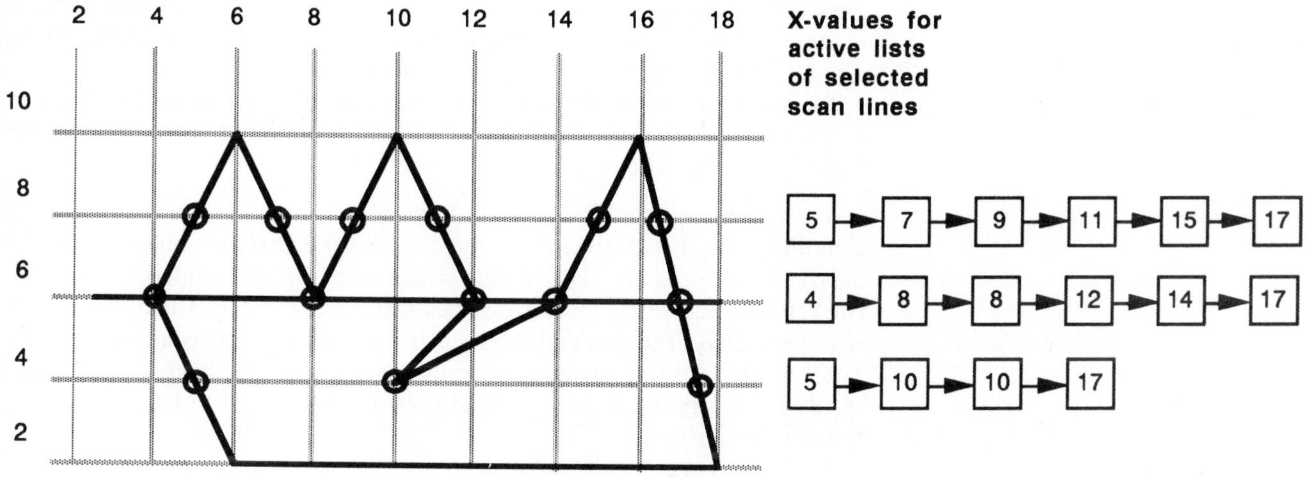

exceptional cases listed earlier, lines are drawn between alternate pairs of intersections. A scan line is determined uniquely by its y-coordinate, so you must determine the set of y-values for each side of the polygon. An orderly method for making this determination is to find the largest y-value for the vertices of each side that is not horizontal. Nonhorizontal sides are then listed in descending order of these y-values. The first side in this list has the vertex with the largest y-value in the polygon, hence the largest scan-line value.

The filling process begins with the scan line corresponding the largest y-value. A side will intersect a scan line only if its vertex with largest y-value is on or above the scan line and its other vertex is on or below the scan line. One way to represent a side is by recording the following information: the coordinates of the vertex with the largest y-value, the number of scan lines it intersects, and the change in x associated with a decrease of 1 in the value of y. The Pascal record given in figure 6.8.6 may be used for this structure. This representation is used as follows:

FIGURE 6.8.6

The record structure used to represent one side of a polygon in the scan-line fill algorithm

```
type
  orderedList = ^SideNode;
  SideNode = record
    TopY : integer;             (* largest y-value on side          *)
    XIntersection : real;       (* intersection with scan line      *)
    ScansUndone : integer;      (* scans left to do on this side    *)
    ChangeInX : real;           (* change in x for decrease of 1 in y *)
    Next : orderedList          (* next side in list                *)
  end;
```

- When the scan line reaches the y-value of the top vertex, TopY, it is entered into the current list of intersections.
- Each time the scan line changes, the ScansUndone is decremented by 1, and the XIntersection has ChangeInX subtracted from it. If the new XIntersection value is smaller than the XIntersection of the previous point, the node is removed from the list and reinserted with xOrderInsert.
- The side is removed from the list of intersections when ScansUndone = 0.
- When all sides have entered the list of intersections and been removed, the process is complete.

The procedure ScanFill shown in figure 6.8.7 is an implementation of this algorithm. The list ActiveList is the list of sides that the current scan line intersects. This list is kept in increasing order of the XIntersections. The NotYetProcessed list is the set of sides that have TopY less than the current scan-line value. The NotYetProcessed list is kept in decreasing order of the TopY values. All sides ending above the current scan line have been disposed of. Both lists employ a dummy head node to allow sides to be added with a simple insertion sort.

The procedure CreateList (figure 6.8.8) traverses the list of vertices in the polynomial (given here in screen coordinates because scan lines are in screen coordinates), creating the list of nonhorizontal sides. This procedure also draws horizontal lines in the color chosen for the fill. NewList, which is left to the reader, creates a head node with XIntersection of zero and nil next pointer. The head node has XIntersection of 0 to facilitate the sort that follows each evaluation of points in the ActiveList. The boolean function Empty checks a list to see if there are any nodes other than the head node. If NotYetProcessed is not the empty list, then ActivateSides (figure 6.8.9) checks this list to see if any of its sides should be transferred to the ActiveList. If so, it deletes that side from NotYetProcessed and inserts it in the ActiveList. Insertions into ActiveList maintain this list in increasing order of XIntersection.

FIGURE 6.8.7

The scan-line fill algorithm

```
procedure ScanFill (p : polygon);
var
  ActiveList, NotYetProcessed : orderedList;
  ScanLine : integer;
begin
  CreateSideList(P, NotYetProcessed, ScanLine);
  NewList(ActiveList);
  repeat
    if not Empty(NotYetProcessed) then
      ActivateSides(ActiveList, ScanLine, NotYetProcessed);
    DrawFillLines(ActiveList, ScanLine);
    UpdateActiveList(ActiveList);
    ScanLine := ScanLine - 1
  until Empty(ActiveList) and Empty(NotYetProcessed)
end;
```

FIGURE 6.8.8

This procedure called from ScanLine adds nonhorizontal sides of the polygon to the list to be processed and draws horizontal sides of the polygon.

```
procedure CreateSideList (P : polygon;
                          var NotYetProcessed : orderedList;
                          var ScanLine : integer);
  var
    side : integer;
    SideNumbers : integer;
    x1, y1, x2, y2 : integer;
begin
(* process line from the last vertex to prime the pump *)
  SideNumbers := P.NumberOfSides;
  y1 := P.Vertex[SideNumbers].y;
  x1 := P.Vertex[SideNumbers].x;
  NewList(NotYetProcessed);
  for Side := 1 to SideNumbers do
    begin
      if y1 <> P.Vertex[Side].y then          (* if not horizontal, add to list       *)
        AddToList(NotYetProcessed, x1, y1, P.Vertex[Side].x, P.Vertex[Side].y, NextY(P, Side, SideNumbers))
      else                                     (* if horizontal, draw it now in fill color *)
        DrawLine(x1, y1, P.Vertex[Side].x, y1);
      (* save the last vertex since it is at one end of the next side *)
      y1 := P.Vertex[side].y;
      x1 := P.Vertex[side].x
    end;
  ScanLine := NotYetProcessed^.Next^.TopY     (* first side has largest y-value      *)
end;
```

FIGURE 6.8.9

Before each scan line is processed, sides not yet active are checked to see if they intersect the new scan line. If they do, they are activated.

```
procedureActivateSides (var ActiveList : orderedList;
                        ScanLine : integer;
                        var NotYetProcessed : orderedList);
var
  Current : OrderedList;
  finished : boolean;
begin
  Current := NotYetProcessed^.Next;      (* get first actual unused side          *)
  finished := false;
  while (Current <> nil) and (not finished) do
    if Current^.TopY >= ScanLine then    (* if TopY >= scanline, activate side   *)
      begin
        NotYetProcessed^.next := Current^.next
        xOrderInsert(Current, ActiveList); (* ascending-order XIntersection      *)
        Current := NotYetProcessed^.next
      end
    else                                 (* rest of list still not activated       *)
      finished := true
end;
```

The procedure DrawFillLines (figure 6.8.10) connects alternate pairs of intersections on the ActiveList with lines in the fill color. The exceptional cases when a vertex will only count as one side are eliminated by the procedure, which creates the representation of the sides. This will be discussed later in this section. After each scan line has been filled, the sides on the active list are updated. UpDateActiveList (figure 6.8.11) checks whether a side has additional scan lines that it crosses. If ScansUndone is greater than 1, the number is decremented and the XIntersection for the next scan line is computed; otherwise the side is deleted from the active list. Sides of a polygon may intersect at points other than the vertices (figure 6.8.12). Such intersections result in points being out of order in the ActiveList. Newly computed XIntersection values are compared with the value in the node preceding them. If this new value is smaller, the point is removed from the list and placed in the list OutOfOrder. After all values have been updated, points in the OutOfOrder list are reinserted in the ActiveList with xOrderInsert.

The procedure AddToList (figure 6.8.13) creates a representation for a side from each pair of vertices of the polygon P. The vertex (x1,y1) has already been used to create the previous side of the polygon, and the point (x2,y2) represents the next vertex in the polygon. Each time a new vertex is considered, a check is made to see if it represents an intersection of two sides, both of which have

FIGURE 6.8.10

This procedure draws lines between alternate pairs of points in the active list.

```
procedure DrawFillLines (ActiveList : orderedList;
                         ScanLine : integer);
var
  First, Last : orderedList;
begin
  if ActiveList^.next <> nil then
    begin
      First := ActiveList^.next;
      Last := First^.next;
      while First <> nil do
        begin
          if Last <> nil then
            begin
              (* DrawLine could be replaced by a loop that sets consecutive     *)
              (* pixels. This is useful when patterns are used for fill.        *)
              DrawLine(round(First^.xIntersection), ScanLine,
                          round(Last^.xIntersection), Scanline);
              First := Last^.next
            end
          else
            First := nil;
          if First <> nil then
            Last := First^.next
        end
    end
end;
```

FIGURE 6.8.11

After each scan line is drawn, the list of active points is updated by this procedure.

```
procedure UpdateActiveList (var ActiveList: orderedList);
var
   NextNode: orderedList;
   Current: orderedList;
   OutOfOrder: orderedList;       (* holds all nodes that are out of order after XIntersection is recomputed *)
begin
   Current := ActiveList;
   NextNode := Current^.next;
   OutOfOrder := nil;
   while NextNode <> nil do
      begin
         (* is the node still active?*)
         if NextNode^.ScansUndone > 1 then    (* update node data *)
            begin
               (* get the next x-value for the node*)
               with NextNode^ do
                  begin
                     ScansUndone := ScansUndone - 1;
                     XIntersection := XIntersection - ChangeInX
                  end;
               (* if new value is out of order, delete it for reinsertion later; otherwise, go to next node *)
               if NextNode^.XIntersection < Current^.XIntersection then
                  begin
                     (*delete NextNode from ActiveList and put it on OutOfOrder list*)
                     Current^.next := NextNode^.Next;
                     NextNode^.next := OutOfOrder;
                     OutOfOrder := NextNode;
                     (*don't reset Current*)
                  end
               else                               (* get next node              *)
                  Current := NextNode
            end                                   (* update active node         *)
         else                                     (* node no longer active, delete it   *)
            begin
               Current^.Next := NextNode^.Next;   (* delete NextNode; it's done       *)
               dispose(NextNode)
            end;
         NextNode := Current^.Next
      end;                                        (* end update x-values for active list*)
   (* reinsert those things that were out of order *)
   while OutOfOrder <> nil do
      begin
         Current := OutOfOrder;
         OutOfOrder := OutOfOrder^.next;
         xOrderInsert(Current, ActiveList);
      end
end; (* UpdateActiveList *)
```

FIGURE 6.8.12

In this polygon the intersection of the scan line and the polygon side P_1P_3 is placed above the intersection with side P_2P_4 in the active list. Below the intersection these points reverse positions.

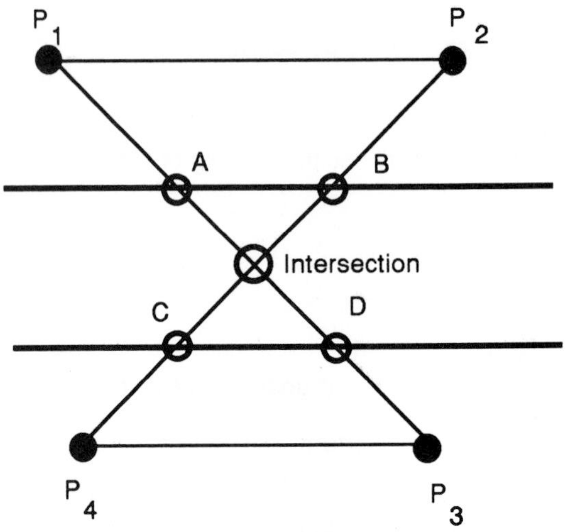

FIGURE 6.8.13

The procedure AddToList creates a node to represent each side of the polygon and adds this node to the list of sides to be processed.

```
(* This function gets the y-value of the vertex  of the next nonhorizontal side.        *)
  function NextY (  P : polygon;
                    Side : integer;
                    SideNumbers : integer) : integer;
  var
    next : integer;
  begin
    Next := Side mod SideNumbers + 1;
    while  (P.Vertex[Side].y  =  P.Vertex[next].y)  do
      Next := Next mod SideNumbers + 1;
    NextY  :=  P.Vertex[Next].y
  end;

  procedure AddToList (var  NotYetProcessed : orderedList;
                          x1, y1, x2, y2, NextYValue : integer);
  var
    mInverse : real;
    x2Adjusted : real;
    NewSide : OrderedList;
  begin
    mInverse := (x2 - x1) / (y2 - y1);
    x2Adjusted := x2;
    (* take care of the exceptional vertices *)
    if (y1 < y2) and (y2 < NextYValue) then          (*increasing *)
```

FIGURE 6.8.13 continued

```
      begin
        y2 := y2 - 1;
        x2Adjusted := x2Adjusted - mInverse
      end
    else if (y1 > y2) and (y2 > NextYValue) then  (*decreasing*)
      begin
        y2 := y2 + 1;
        x2Adjusted := x2Adjusted + mInverse
      end;
    new(NewSide);
    if y1 > y2 then
      begin
        NewSide^.TopY := y1;
        NewSide^.XIntersection := x1
      end
    else
      begin
        NewSide^.Topy := y2;
        NewSide^.XIntersection := x2Adjusted
      end;
    NewSide^.ScansUndone := abs(y2 - y1) + 1;
    NewSide^.ChangeInX := mInverse;
    (* insert in decreasing order of TopY*)
    yOrderInsert(NewSide, NotYetProcessed)
  end;
```

either increasing or decreasing y-values. To make this determination you need only find out if y1, y2, and the y-value of the next vertex NextYValue are in increasing or decreasing order—that is, y1 < y2 < NextYValue or y1 > y2 > NextYValue. If this is the case, the vertex (x2,y2) should appear in the active list only once. This can be achieved by reducing by 1 the number of scan lines for the current side. If both lines have increasing y-values, y2 is reduced by 1. If, on the other hand, both are decreasing, then y2 is increased by 1 (see figure 6.8.14). In all cases, x2Adjusted represents the x-coordinate of vertex as a real number.

Once the adjustments are made to the vertex (x2,y2), the larger of y1 and y2 is assigned to TopY and the corresponding x-value is assigned to XIntersection. Finally, the number of scan lines is determined by taking the absolute value of y1 − y2 and adding 1, and the change in x is set to be the inverse of the slope of the side.

It is possible to fill irregularly shaped regions by using the scan-fill algorithm, but the techniques involved are beyond this text. Another filling technique, the seed-fill algorithm, reads pixels on the screen to determine the boundaries of a region and the pixels that are already filled. This algorithm, given in figure 6.8.15, is so named because a "seed point" inside the figure is colored with the fill color, and then, by recursion, the seed spreads to the pixels surrounding it. The seed-fill method works only on raster systems with a function PixelColor, which returns the color of the given pixel. In two-color systems, this is often a

FIGURE 6.8.14

When y-values are increasing or decreasing for consecutive sides of polynomial, the end point of the second side is changed so the vertex is counted as only one intersection.

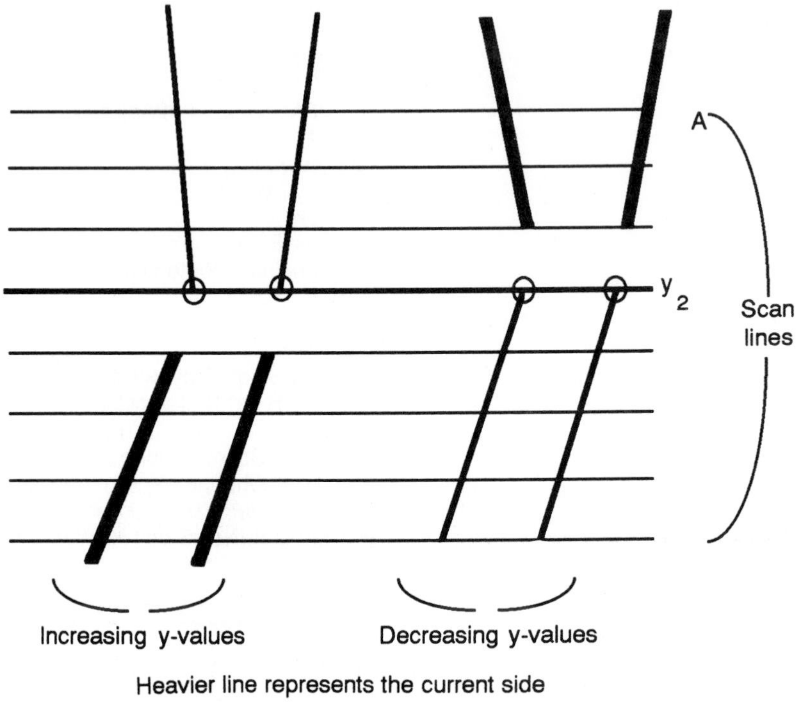

FIGURE 6.8.15

The seed-fill algorithm

```
(* This procedure tests the pixel at the coordinates it receives.            *)
(* If the color is not the fill color or the boundary color, it is changed   *)
(* and the four neighboring pixels are visited. The function PixelColor      *)
(* returns the current color of the given pixel.                             *)

procedure SeedFill(x,y : integer; FillColor, BoundaryColor : ScreenColor);
var
  CurrentColor : ScreenColor;
begin
  CurrentColor := PixelColor(x,y);
  if (CurrentColor <> FillColor) and (CurrentColor <> BoundaryColor) then
    begin
      SetPixel(x,y,FillColor);
      SeedFill(x, y + 1, FillColor,BoundaryColor);
      SeedFill(x, y - 1, FillColor,BoundaryColor);
      SeedFill(x + 1, y, FillColor,BoundaryColor);
      SeedFill(x - 1, y, FillColor,BoundaryColor);
    end
end;
```

boolean function that returns true if the pixel is on and false if it is off. In these systems, the boundary and fill colors are the same, so only one color needs to be passed to the procedure.

The method for determining the neighbors of a given pixel differs depending on the nature of the region to be filled. The algorithm given in figure 6.8.15 uses four-connected regions, regions in which every interior pixel may be reached from any other interior pixel by a path that uses only horizontal and vertical steps. In the region shown in figure 6.8.16, there is no such path from pixel A to pixel B. If such a region is to be filled, the algorithm must be augmented to visit all eight adjacent neighbors of a pixel. Boundaries having isolated interior pixels cannot be filled by one application of the seed fill.

The advantage of the seed-fill algorithm over the scan-fill algorithm is that a mathematical description of the region being filled is not needed. This allows the seed-fill algorithm to fill regions such as the simply connected intersection of two curved regions (figure 6.8.17) or regions constructed in nonsegmented systems. If the boundary of a region is not completely connected, the seed-fill technique will **break out** of the region to fill the entire plane, except for those regions enclosed by other boundaries. This can ruin many hours of work when no undo command is available.

The scan-line algorithm has the advantage that there is no danger of stack overflow because it does not use recursion. The **scan-line seed fill method,** a combination of the scan-fill and seed-fill algorithms, reduces the chance of stack overflow. A seed point (s in figure 6.8.18) is passed to the scan-line seed fill algorithm. Instead of checking neighboring pixels recursively, the scan-line

FIGURE 6.8.16

If the seed point is in region B of this polygon, the region A will not be filled by a seed-fill algorithm using four-way adjacency.

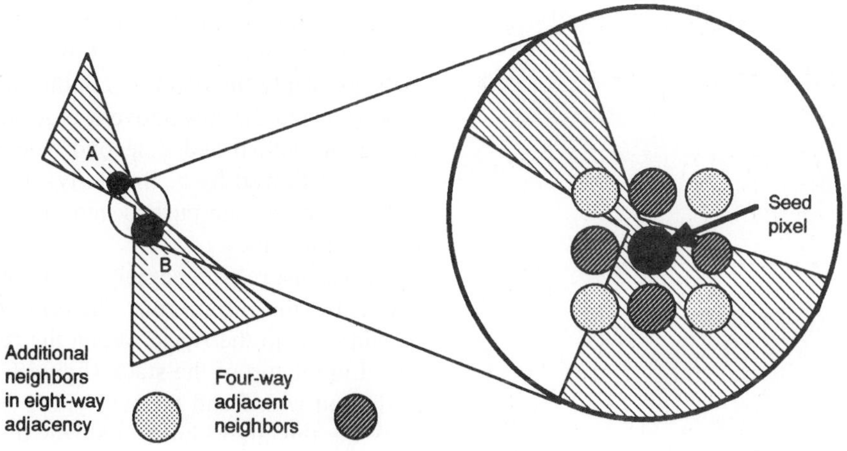

FIGURE 6.8.17

The seed-fill algorithm may be used to fill a simply connected intersection of two irregular regions.

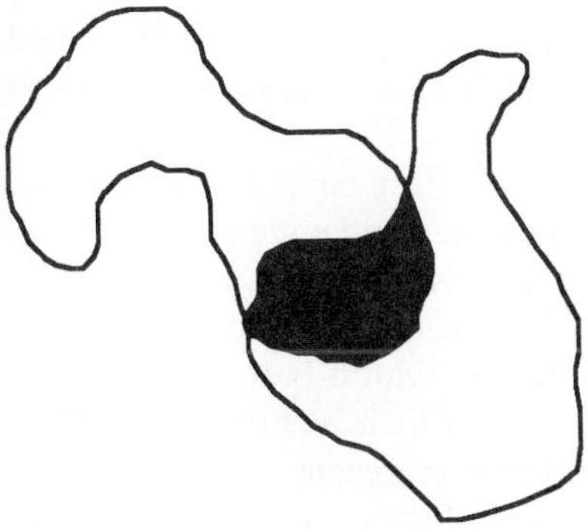

FIGURE 6.8.18

The scan-line seed-fill algorithm may be applied to the following diagram with seed pixel s. Other label pixels are left end points of runs discussed in the text and in figure 6.8.19.

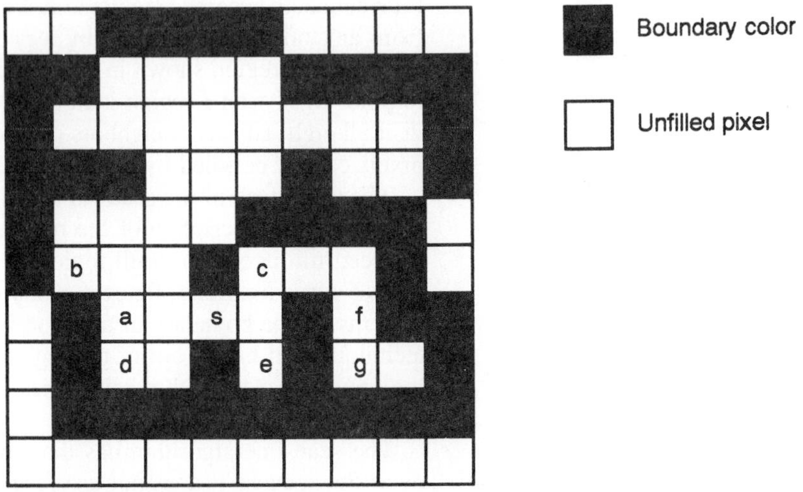

seed algorithm searches for the longest sequence of pixels in a scan line that can be filled. This sequence is called a **run of pixels.** The leftmost pixel in the run containing the seed is found and pushed into a stack of left end points (figure 6.8.19) to begin the process.

While the stack is not empty, the stack is popped to get the left end point of the current run. The current run is checked for runs adjacent to it. The left end points of these runs are pushed into the stack. Next, the row below the run is checked for adjacent runs, and left end points of these runs are also pushed into the stack. Finally, the current run is filled by using a line-drawing primitive. A Pascal version of this algorithm is given in figure 6.8.19.

The seed point, s, in figure 6.8.20 has a run with left end a that is pushed into the stack. Only the point a is in the stack at the beginning of the **while** loop. It is popped and the row above it is searched left to right for runs. Two runs, one beginning with b and a second beginning with c, are found. The point b is pushed, followed by c. Similarly, the runs beginning with d and e are found, and these points are pushed into the stack (figure 6.8.20 contains a copy of the stack at this time).

Notice that the run beginning with g is not in the stack because this run is not adjacent to the current run. The runs beginning with d and e are processed with no additions to the stack. When the run with c at its left end is processed, f is added to the top of the stack (figure 6.8.21). This sequence leads to the filling of the run with f and the run with g before the run with b is filled.

While this algorithm minimizes the use of a stack, it is still susceptible to break out if the boundary around the region is not complete.

It is also possible to fill regions with a **pattern.** Patterns can be described in much the same way as icons—that is, as a square array, usually one word on

FIGURE 6.8.19

The scan-line seed-fill algorithm

```
type
  Direction = (left,right,upOne,downOne);
  ColorSet = set of ScreenColor;

(* The procedure FindEnd finds the EndPoint of a sequence of points with color          *)
(* in a given set  if the sequence begins at BeginPoint and moves in Way left or right.  *)

procedure FindEnd (BeginPoint : Point; Way : Direction; BlockColor : ColorSet; var EndPoint : Point);

var
  XIncrement  :  integer;  (* the increment is determined by whether the Direction is left or right     *)
begin
  if Way = left then
    XIncrement := -1;
  else
    XIncrement := 1;
  EndPoint := BeginPoint;
  while (PixelColor(EndPoint.x + XIncrement,EndPoint.y) in BlockColor)
          and (EndPoint.x < XMax)
          and (EndPoint.x > 0) do
    EndPoint.x := EndPoint.x + XIncrement
end;

(*The procedure StackSeedPoints finds left end points for runs of unfilled bits in the rows above or   *)
(* below the run starting at Start and ending at RightEnd.  The left end points found are pushed into  *)
(* the stack PointStack.                                                                                 *)

procedure StackSeedPoints(Start,FarRightEnd  : Point;
                          FillOff,FillOn : ColorSet;
                          UpOrDown : Direction;
                          var PointStack : StackOfPoints);

var
  LeftEndPoint     :  Point;     (* left end point of a run of pixels in a given color set        *)
  RightEndPoint  :  Point;      (* right end point of a run of pixels in a given color set       *)
  CurrentColorSet  :  ColorSet;
begin
    (* do the row above the run                          *)
    LeftEndPoint.x  :=  Start.x;
    if UpOrDown = downOne then
      LeftEndPoint.y  :=  Start.y+1
    else
      LeftEndPoint.y  :=  Start.y-1;
    (* if there is a run above this point, find its left end     *)
    if  PixelColor(LeftEndPoint.x,LeftEndPoint.y)  in FillOn then
      begin
        FindEnd(LeftEndPoint,Left,FillOn,LeftEndPoint);           (* find the left end point          *)
        Push(LeftEndPoint,PointStack);                            (* push left end point              *)
        FindEnd(LeftEndPoint,Right,FillOn,LeftEndPoint);          (* find right end of run            *)
        LeftEndPoint.x := LeftEndPoint.x + 1
      end;
    RightEndPoint  :=  LeftEndPoint;
    CurrentColorSet := FillOff;                                   (*color of LeftEndPoint is in FillOff   *)
```

(continued)

FIGURE 6.8.19 continued

```
    while RightEndPoint.x <= FarRightEnd.x do
      begin
        FindEnd(LeftEndPoint,Left,FillOff,RightEndPoint);          (* find end of current run                 *)
            If CurrentColorSet = FillOn then
          begin
            Push(LeftEndPoint,PointStack);
            CurrentColorSet := FillOff
          end
        else
          CurrentColorSet := FillOn
        If  RightEnd.x < FarRightEnd then
          LeftEndPoint.x := RightEndPoint.x + 1;
      end;
end;     (*StackSeedPoints *)

procedure ScanLineSeedFill( seed : Point; FillColor,BoundaryColor : ScreenColor);
var
  CurrentPoint    :    Point;              (* left end point of the current fill run                    *)
  RightEnd        :    Point;              (* right end of current run                                  *)
  PointStack      :    StackOfPoints;      (* stack that contains points                                *)
  FillOff,FillOn  :    ColorSet;           (* colors that indicate whether fill is needed or not        *)
begin
  NewStack(PointStack);
  FillOff := [FillColor,BoundaryColor];    (* Pixels in these colors will not be filled                 *)
  FillOn := Complement(FillOff);           (* Pixels of this color will be filled. Complement will often be *)
                                           (* computed as [Black..White] - FillOff, but this is system   *)
                                           (* dependent                                                 *)
  (* find the left end point of the run with the seed point in it                                       *)
  FindEnd(seed,Left,FillOn,CurrentPoint);
  Push(CurrentPoint,  PointStack);
  while  not Empty(Pointstack) do
    begin
      Pop(CurrentPoint,Pointstack);
      FindEnd(CurrentPoint,right,FillOn,RightEnd);
      (* check line above for runs                  *)
      If CurrentPoint.y < YMax then
        StackSeedPoints(CurrentPoint,RightEnd,FillOff,FillOn,upOne,PointStack);
      (* check line below for runs                  *)
      If CurrentPoint.y > 0 then
        StackSeedPoints(CurrentPoint,RightEnd,FillOff,FillOn,downOne,PointStack);
      (* fill Current run                           *)
      DrawLine(CurrentPoint.x,CurrentPoint.y,  RightEnd.x,RightEnd.y);
    end
 end;
```

FIGURE 6.8.20

After the first row is filled, the stack contains points b, c, and d. The top of the stack is d.

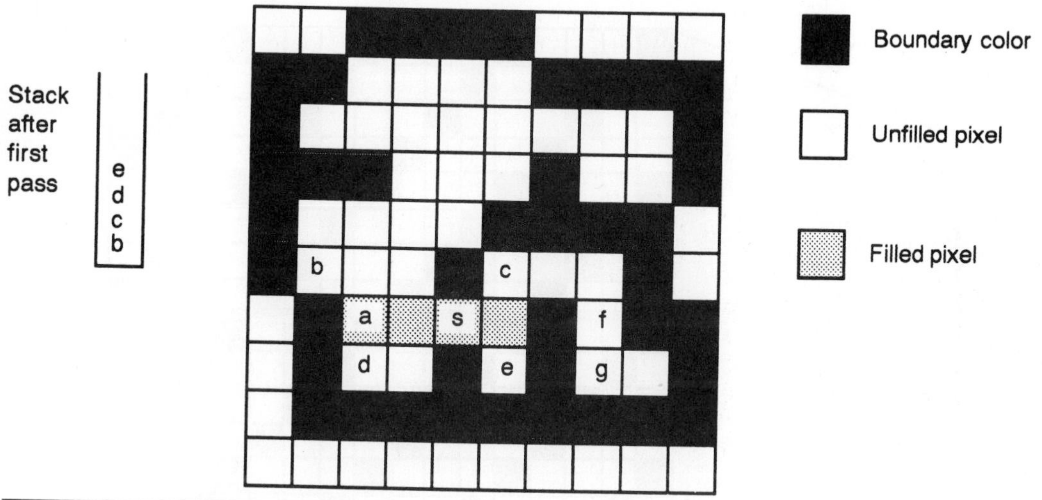

FIGURE 6.8.21

After the run containing c is processed, the stack contains b and f.

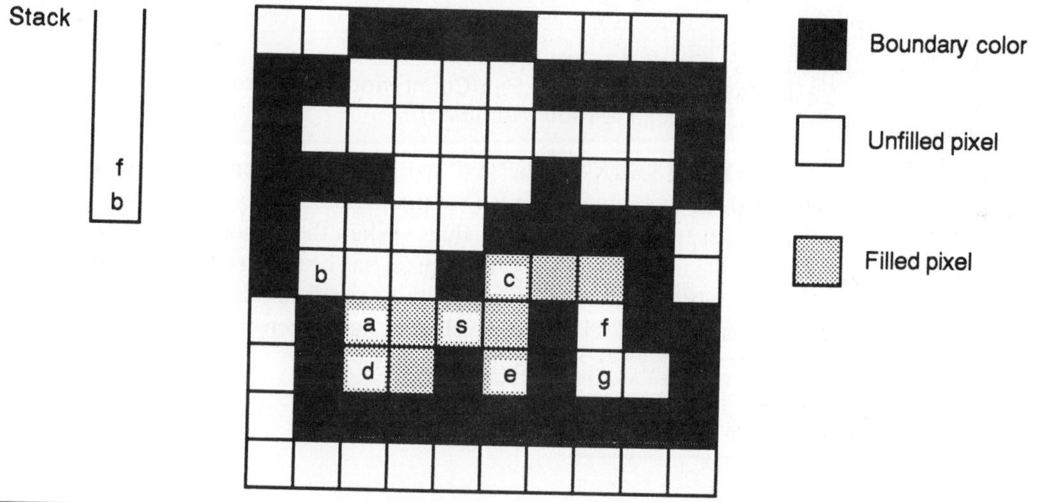

a side, in which bits are set as "on" or "off" (figure 6.8.22). Unlike icons, the pattern is repeated so the sides of a pattern must mesh smoothly. In figure 6.8.22, the diagonal lines extend continuously from square to square. This type of repetition is the same as that required for matching wallpaper.

The scan-line algorithm is well suited to filling with a pattern, Pat. The call to DrawLine in procedures CreateSide (figure 6.8.8) and DrawFillLines (figure 6.8.10) can be replaced by the following loop:

FIGURE 6.8.22

A pattern used to fill a region

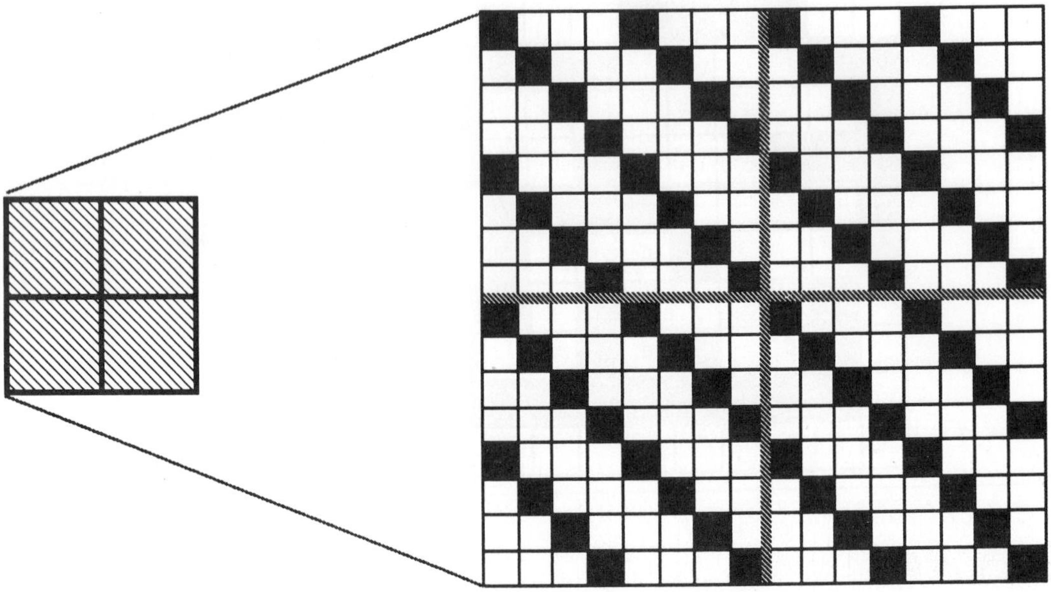

```
for count := FirstX toLastX do
    SetPixel(Count,ScanLine,Pat((Count mod WordSize),
            (ScanLine mod WordSize)));
```

where FirstX and LastX are the first and last x-values in the DrawLine.

The seed-fill technique can also set pixel color by computing the subscripts for the pattern from the x- and y-values. When the region is filled with white, it is impossible to tell whether a white pixel has been filled if the pattern for that pixel is also white. To solve this problem, the seed-fill algorithm can be adapted to keep a background record of pixels that have been visited.

EXERCISES

6.8.1

Adapt the scan-fill algorithm to fill with a pattern.

6.8.2

Develop some patterns that can be used to fill regions.

6.8.3

Adapt the seed-fill algorithm to fill with a pattern.

6.8.4

An algorithm that can be used to fill a polygonal region on a raster screen is the **edge-fill algorithm.** In this algorithm, a vertical is constructed with an x-value 1 larger than any in the polygon, and for each side of the polygon, all points between the line and side are filled in **xor** mode (figure 6.8.23). Write a program to implement this algorithm. The filling can be done by drawing successive lines in much the same way as they were drawn for the scan-line algorithm. Notice that many points have their values set more than once, but some computation is saved by not finding intersections.

FIGURE 6.8.23

The sequence of fills used by the edge-fill algorithm

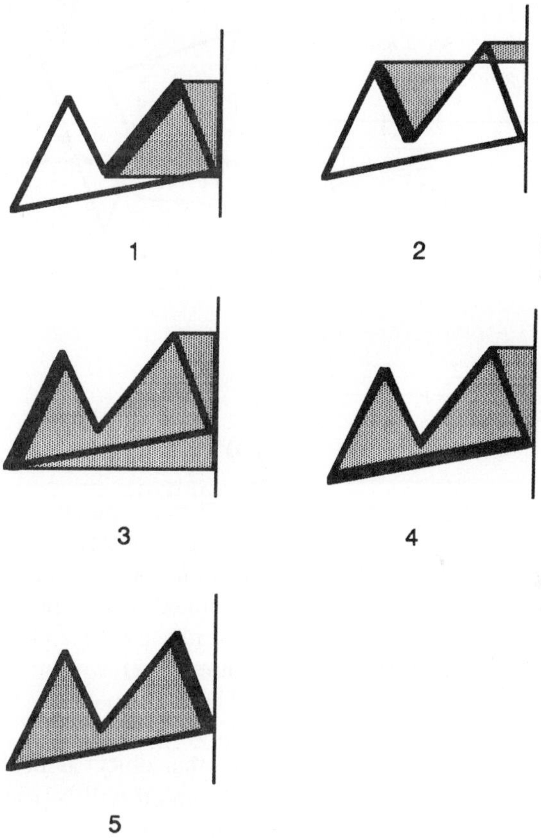

6.8.5

What simplifications can be made to the scan line seed fill algorithm if you can restrict its use to convex regions?

6.8.6

Implement the scan line seed fill for convex regions.

6.8.7

Make a list of the scan line intersection for each of the following diagrams.

a.

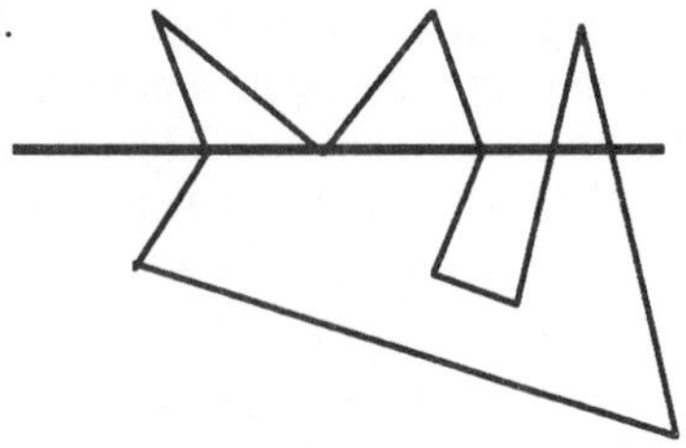

b.

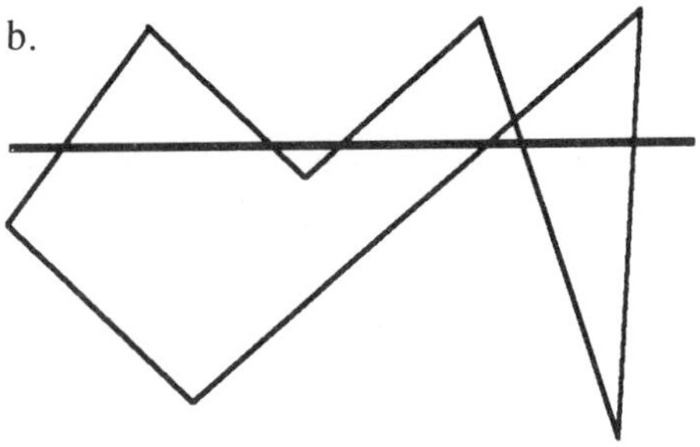

c.

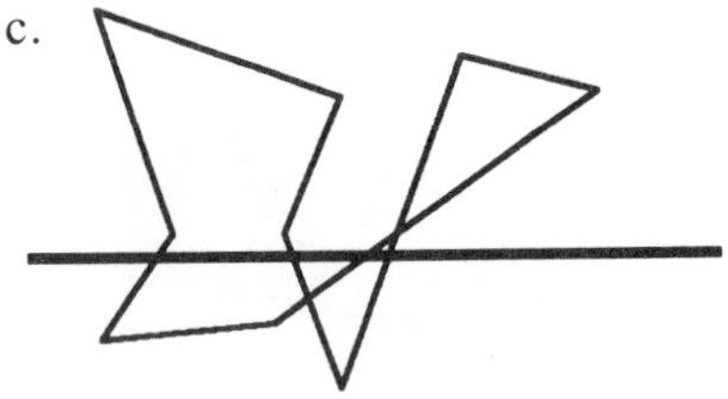

FIGURE 6.9.1

A common screen layout for a main-event graphics program

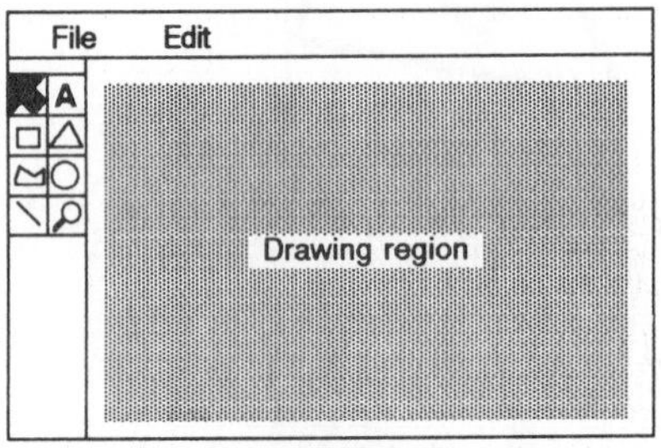

6.9 Summary of the Main-Event Line Graphics Program

Section 5.6 introduced the idea of a main-event graphics program, in which all operations were available at the top level of the system. Now that you are acquainted with segments and some tools and choices from the edit menu, you are ready to take a closer look at the screen (figure 6.9.1) and the edit menu (figure 6.9.2).

The tools menu has a two icons you have not encountered before. The first is the *A* in the first row. It is used to indicate that the user wants the text tool. The other object is in the lower-right box. This is meant to be a magnifying glass, and it will be used in the next chapter to indicate that the user wants to zoom.

The edit menu (figure 6.9.2), which is bitmapped to the screen, is only the portion of the screen below the line under the word *Edit*.

This section reviews the main-event program from section 5.6 and looks at the procedure **ProcessEditChoice** from the HandlePullDownMenu. The procedures **HandleIconMenu** and **HandleDrawing,** alluded to in section 5.6, will also be outlined here.

With the addition of segments and tool choices the main-event program (figure 6.9.3) must now handle more information. Recall that Selected is a boolean that indicates whether or not an object has been selected.

FIGURE 6.9.2

An example of an edit menu used in a draw program

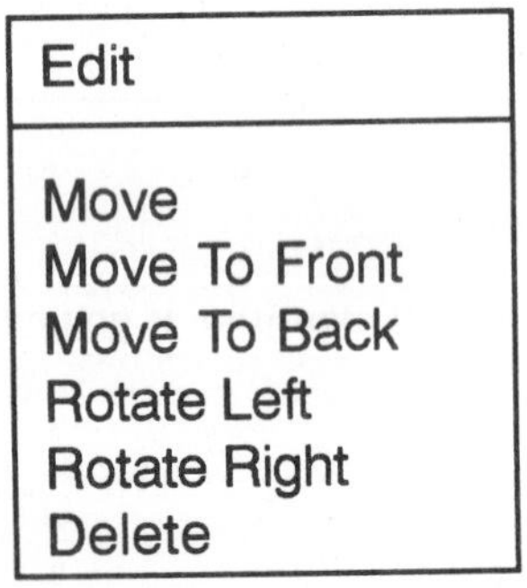

FIGURE 6.9.3

An example of a main-event program

```
program MainEvent;
(* nonlocal references, types, constants, variables here                    *)
begin
   Initialize;         (* with an appropriate list of variables, display menus   *)
   repeat
      ReadLocator(x,y,Cursor);
      if y in PullDownZone then
         HandlePullDownMenu(x, y, SegmentList, SelectedSegment,Selected )
      else if x in IconMenuZone then
         HandleIconMenu(x,y,Tool)
      else
         HandleDrawing(x,y,Tool)
   until Quit
end.
```

When no object has been selected, the edit menu may be made unusable by restricting calls to ProcessEditChoice from HandlePullDownMenu only if Selected is true. The procedure ProcessEditChoice would be very similar to ProcessFileChoice (figure 5.6.5).

HandleIconMenu is a more complicated procedure because not only does it facilitate the user's choice of tool, but it must also change the tool cursor. As in the case of pull-down menus, the location at which selection is made dictates the choice. Here, however, the choice depends on whether or not the cursor is in a predetermined rectangle. Not all of the region reserved for icon-menu use will actually correspond to a tool. Therefore, as in the case of the edit menu, a selection that is in the icon-menu region but is not an actual icon choice should result in no action.

The actual rectangles may be stored in a global array subscripted on the set of ObjectType form your definition of segment (figure 6.2.3) if this set is extended to include the text tool, select tool, and zoom tool. A sequential search similar to that in your segment list can be used to locate the rectangle in which the selection was made. The tool will be set to the subscript of the selected rectangle. Once the tool has been selected, its cursor may be Bitblted into the ToolCursor bitmap defined in section 5.6. A sketch of HandleIconMenu is given in figure 6.9.4.

This chapter concludes with a brief mention of HandleDrawing. HandleDrawing receives the cursor position at selection time and has the current tool as a parameter. It is only necessary to use a **case** statement to select the appropriate tool procedure from among those defined in sections 6.1, 6.4, and, in the case of zooming, 6.7.

The following projects should be implemented as main-event programs. The file menu should include open, close, quit, and print commands; the edit and icon menus vary from project to project.

FIGURE 6.9.4

This procedure activates a tool selected from an icon menu. It also shows that the tool has been selected by highlighting the tool's icon in the menu and changing the cursor icon to indicate which tool is active.

```
(* This procedure tests to see which of the tools is requested by the selection of point (x,y).  The procedure      *)
(* WhichTool searches the array of rectangles, ToolChoice, and returns the subscript of the rectangle that          *)
(* contains (x,y). If (x,y) is not in one of the given rectangles, a bell is sounded.  The boolean variable         *)
(* parameter Found is set to true or false depending on whether or not the choice is in a rectangle.  The main      *)
(* procedure uses the rectangle of the tool to bitmap the correct cursor into the ToolCursor, and the procedure     *)
(* ReverseIt is used to reverse the rectangle of the currently selected tool.  It is similar to the highlight       *)
(* technique used in pull-down menus.                                                                               *)

procedure HandleIconMenu(x,y : integer;
                         var Tool : ObjectType        (*figure 4.5.5*));
var
   NewTool : ObjectType;                  (* contains the choice of tool corresponding to point (x,y)  *)
   Found : boolean;                       (* indicates whether or not the selection is legal           *)
begin  (* HandleIconMenu *)
   WhichTool(x,y,NewTool,Found);
   if Found and (NewTool <> Tool) then
      begin
         ReverseIt(ToolChoice[Tool]);     (* reverse the rectangle of the old tool                      *)
         (* move the new cursor into the ToolCursor *)
         Bitblt(Display,ToolCursor,ToolCursor.Rect.Origin,ToolChoice[NewTool],CStore);
         ReverseIt(ToolChoice[NewTool]);  (* highlight new tool                                          *)
         Tool := NewTool                  (* set the tool choice                                         *)
      end
end; (* HandleIconMenu *)
```

PROJECTS

6.9.1

A paint program usually allows the user to do freehand drawing, something that is difficult to record in a segment. In addition to the drawing tool, these programs usually include the line, polygon, circle, and text tools. Closed figures may be filled. Rectangular sections of the screen may be selected and moved by the user. Sections of the screen may also be zoomed. Write a paint program.

6.9.2

A draw program is usually a segmented graphics program that does not include the freehand draw tool. In addition to the standard tools, these programs have a select tool that is used to specify an object to be moved, deleted, or duplicated. To facilitate these operations, it is also necessary to have the move to front and move to rear operations. Many of the operations on selected items are chosen from the edit menu; however, some, such as delete, may be done in response to keystrokes. Write a draw program. Curve-drawing techniques introduced in chapter 7 will allow the inclusion of the freehand draw tool in this project.

6.9.3

A flowchart-building program may be implemented as a segmented graphics system. A fixed set of icons correspond to the boxes used in a flowchart. Additions of a line-drawing tool and a text tool are needed to create a complete system. The user should have the freedom to move, duplicate, and delete parts of the flowchart. The BitMove procedure (figure 6.5.3) can do much of the work in this program. Write a flowchart program.

6.9.4

A program used to design architectural floor plans may employ a set of symbols to represent doors, window, and other common architectural features. The user specifies scale, so these symbols would not be stored as bitmaps. Tools such as the line, rectangle, and circle tools are necessary, as is a method for entering the scale. A useful addition to such a program would be a display including line lengths, side lengths of a rectangle, and the radius of a circle in world coordinates as they are drawn. Write a floor-plan design program.

BIBLIOGRAPHY

Buxton, William, Ralph Hill, and Peter Rowley. "Issues and Techniques in Touch-Sensitive Tablet Input." *Computer Graphics* (SIGGRAPH '85); 215–24 (July 1985).

Cardelli, Luca, and Rob Pike. "Squeak: A Language for Communicating With Mice." *Computer Graphics* (SIGGRAPH '85): 199–204 (July 1985).

Green, Mark. "The University of Alberta User Interface Management System." *Computer Graphics* (SIGGRAPH '85): 205–13 (July 1985).

Gregg, W. "The Apple Macintosh Computer." *Byte* 9 (2): 30–54 (February 1984).

Lieberman, Henry. "There's More to Menu Systems Than Meets the Screen," *Computer Graphics* (SIGGRAPH '85): 181–89 (July 1985).

Myers, B. A. "The User Interface for Sapphire." *IEEE CG&A* 4 (12): 13–23 (December 1984).

Myers, Brad A. "A Taxonomy of Window Manger User Interfaces." *IEEE CG&A* 8 (5): 65–83 (September 1988).
Discussion of the parts of a window manager and a comparison of the major window managers. Extensive bibliography covers technical articles on different window managers.

Myers, Brad A. "Creating Interaction Techniques by Demonstration." *IEEE CG&A* 7 (9): 51–60 (September 1987).

Myers, Brad A., and William Buxton. "Creating Highly-Interactive and Graphical User Interfaces by Demonstration." *Computer Graphics* (SIGGRAPH '86): 249–58 (August 1986).

Olsen, Dan R., Jr., Elizabeth P. Dempsey, and Roy Rogge. "Input/Output Linkage in a User Interface Management System." *Computer Graphics* (SIGGRAPH '85): 191–97 (July 1985).

Rubinstein, David, Jeffrey Shallit, and Mario Szegedy. "A Subset Coloring Algorithm and Its Applications to Computer Graphics." *Commun ACM* 31 (10): 1228–32 (October 1988).
Theorems for reaching various parts of regions.

Scheifler, R. W., and J. Gettys. "The X Window System." *ACM Trans. on Graphics* 5 (2): 79–109 (April 1986).

Schmucker, Kurt J. *Macintosh Library: Object-Oriented Programming for the Macintosh*. Hasbrouck Heights, N.J.: Hayden, 1986.

Sibert, John L., William Hurley, and Teresa W. Bleser. "An Object-Oriented User Interface Management System." *Computer Graphics* (SIGGRAPH '86): 259–68 (August 1986).

Smith, D. C., et al. "Designing the Star User Interface." *Byte* 7 (4): 242–82 (April 1982).

Smith Randall B. "Experiences with the Alternate Reality Kit: An Example of the Tension between Literalism and Magic." *IEEE CG&A* 7 (9): 42–50 (September 1987).

Teitelman, W. "A Tour Through CEDAR." *IEEE Software* 1 (2): 44–73 (April 1984).

Tesler, L. "The Smalltalk Environment." *Byte* 6 (8): 90–147 (August 1981).

Tesler, Larry. *Object Pascal Report*. Cupertino, Calif.: Apple Computer, 1985.

Bresenham, Jack E., "Ambiguities in Incremental Line Rastering." *IEEE CG&A*, Vol 7 (5) May 1987, pp 31–43.

CHAPTER

7

Spline Curves

DIRECTIONS

Flexible Fonts

The application of computer graphics to graphic design has created a need for flexible type fonts. Graphic designers spend much of their time working with typography as a visual design element. Type must be easily enlarged, rotated, and flipped while remaining readable.

As you have seen, enlarged bitmapped type is jagged. Rotation of this type is essentially limited to multiples of 90°; other transformations, such as stretching, will exaggerate the jaggies. If type could be specified as a set of lines, circles, and other regular geometric objects, you could apply scaling and rotating procedures to letters with no loss of quality.

For a given graphics device, each letter of a given size could be specified as a polygon with enough vertices so that the letter appears to have smoothly curved edges. If a letter specified by a polygon is enlarged or drawn on a device of higher resolution, curved sections of the letter would be seen as polygons.

An alternative to describing a letter as a polygon is to create a formula that describes the points of a letter. For a given size of letter on a device of a given resolution, the vertices of a polygon can be calculated from the formula. The number of vertices may be specified when the letter is drawn so that the letter will appear to have smooth curves. Such a system has the advantages that each letter has one specification that is device independent, and that letters are drawn using a polygon-drawing procedure found in most graphics systems.

The page description language PostScript uses a technique invented by P. E. Bézier to create formulas for letters. The Bézier curves employed to create letters are quadratic or cubic polynomials whose coefficients are determined from a set of points called control points (figure D.7.1). Each letter is fully described by its control points, so fonts are stored as a set of control points.

Letters used in high-resolution printing with laser printers or typesetting machines are described by outline curves. For such uses, a letter is created as a polygon with enough vertices to appear smooth at the resolution of the device used. After the outline has been drawn, a fill algorithm, such as the scan-line algorithm, fills the letter. The letter is then bitmapped to a storage location. It may then be bitmapped to the device each time it is used.

FIGURE D.7.1

Letters are described by specifying control points for Bézier curves. This figure is an example of Altys Corporation's Fontographer®

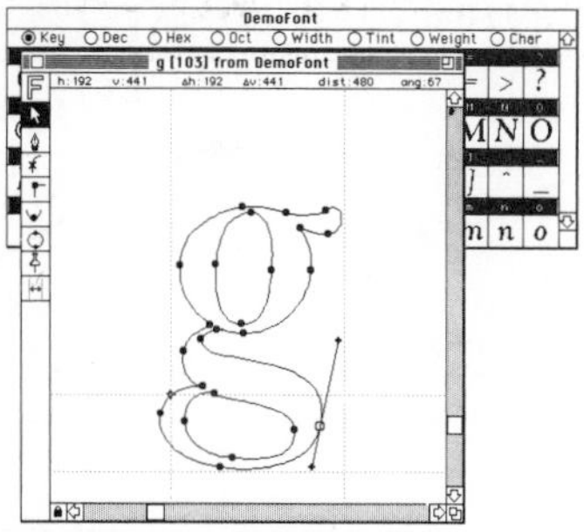

7.1 Overview Cubic Splines

Many applications of computer graphics require smooth curves other than circles or ellipses. Fonts used by many laser printers have their letters described in terms of such curves. CAD/CAM systems use curves for drawing machinery; and animators use curves to describe the trajectory of objects. In all cases, the curves must be displayed quickly and must be modifiable by interactive means.

Curves used in computer graphics are often described by **parametric equations.** The x- and y-coordinates are computed as a function of a third variable, called a **parameter.** In section 3.3 you used a parametric representation of a line between two points in the Liang-Barsky clipping algorithm. The coordinates of points on the line between points (x_1,y_1) and (x_2,y_2) can be computed by the equations $x(u) := x_1 + (x_2 - x_1)u$ and $y(u) := y_1 + (y_2 - y_1)u$, where u is in (0,1). Parametric techniques used to create two-dimensional curves have the advantage of being easily generalized to techniques for creating curved surfaces.

Curves may be created by smoothly connecting a series of specified points, $P_0, P_1, P_2 \ldots P_n$, called **control points.** The most obvious way to create such a curve is to require that it pass through each of the points. This is called **interpolation** (figure 7.1.1). In computer graphics it is not always important to have a curve pass through a set of points, but it is important to have a smooth curve. It is possible to create an easily modified smooth curve that only passes close to the set of points. These curves are called **approximations** (figure 7.1.2).

With interpolation, if a single polynomial is used to fit a curve to a large number of points, the degree of the polynomial is large. This creates two problems. First, the curve "wiggles" so that the resulting curve does not truly reflect the distribution of points. This problem is pronounced when the points are widely spread (figure 7.1.3).

To avoid the "wiggles," it is best to use polynomials of low degree. But these polynomials will not give even a good approximation of a large point set, much less an interpolation of such a set. The compromise is to create a set of polynomials in which each matches three or four of the points. If this process is to result in single curve, the end points of consecutive polynomial segments must meet. This does not, however, ensure a smooth curve (figure 7.1.4).

FIGURE 7.1.1

A curve created by interpolation

FIGURE 7.1.2

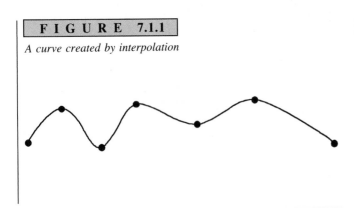

A curve created to approximate the set of points

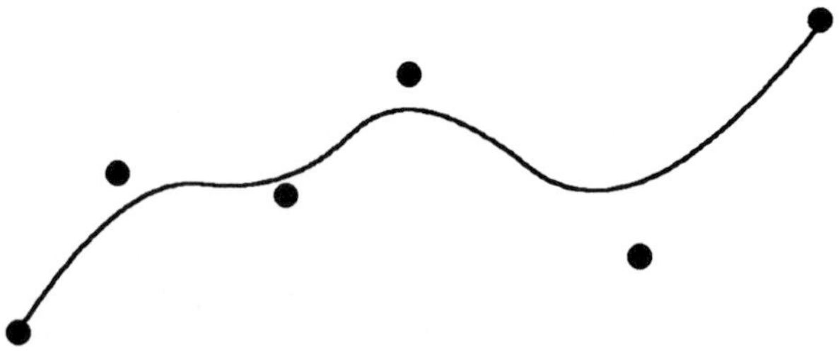

FIGURE 7.1.3

"Wiggle" caused by interpolation from a single polynomial passing through a large number of points

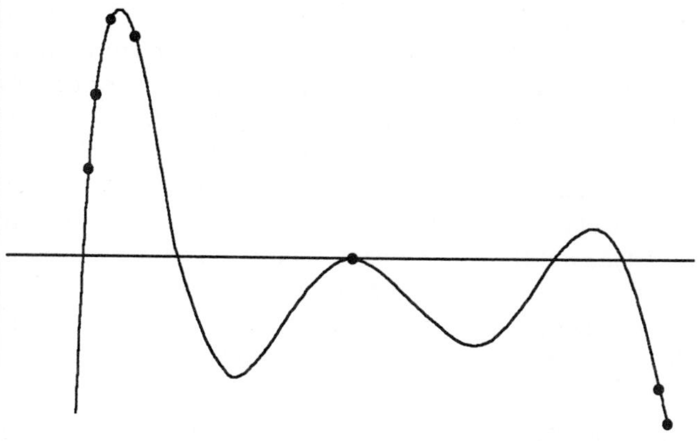

FIGURE 7.1.4

When you are fitting more than one polygon to a set of points, the curves must not only match at end points; they must also have the same slopes or the resulting curve will have corners.

Several methods are used to ensure that the intersections are smooth. One of the simplest is to require that the derivatives of the parametric functions of two consecutive curves agree at the point of intersection. When the curve is used for animation, the parameter often represents time. In these cases, the second derivatives of consecutive polynomials must also be equal at the point of intersection to ensure smooth motion.

The most popular curves generated by this technique are the **spline curves.** Splines are flexible rods used by drafters to draw a smooth curve through a series of points. A spline curve, C(u), composed of cubic polynomials that interpolate the points $P_0, P_1, \ldots, P_n$ on an interval [0,n] could be constructed by using the following technique. Divide the interval [0,n] into n intervals $[u_{i-1},u_i]$, for i = 1 to n. The numbers u_1 are called **knots.** On each of these intervals define a polynomial q_i such that $C(u) := q_i(u)$ for u in $[u_{i-1},u_i]$. The value of C(u) for each u is a point.

To simplify this discussion, you will look at only one coordinate of each point generated by C. All properties that hold for one coordinate will hold for the second. For example, using p_i to represent a single coordinate of P_i, you can describe the properties you desire for a spline:

$$q_i(u_{i-1}) = p_{i-1} \text{ and } q_i(u_i) = p_i \qquad \text{for } i := 1 \text{ to } n$$
$$q_i'(u_i) = q_{i+1}'(u_i) \qquad \text{for } i := 1 \text{ to } n-1$$
$$q_i''(u_i) = q_{i+1}''(u_i) \qquad \text{for } i := 1 \text{ to } n-1$$

The fact that this curve interpolates the points is given in the first two equations; the remaining two equations guarantee smoothness. In addition to these requirements at the knots, requirements are imposed on q_1 and q_n at 0 and n. Either their derivatives at the end points must be constant, or the second derivatives must be zero.

Each polynomial q_i is given by $q_i(u) = a_iu^3 + b_iu^2 + c_iu + d_i$. The conditions indicated above lead to the following equations:

$$a_i u_{i-1}^3 + b_i u_{i-1}^2 + c_i u_{i-1} + d_i = p_{i-1}$$
$$a_i u_i^3 + b_i u_i^2 + c_i u_i + d_i = p_i$$
$$3a_i u_i^2 + 2b_i u_i + c_i = 3a_{i+1} u_i^2 + 2b_{i+1} u_i + c_{i+1}$$
$$6a_i u_i + 2b_i = 6a_{i+1} u_i + 2b_{i+1}$$

If you add the extra conditions on the polynomials q_1 and q_n, you get 4n linear equations in 4n unknowns. These equations may be simplified to make them easily solved. This technique creates a problem for interactive applications because if one of the points P_i changes, the entire curve is altered. If the curve C is close to the desired result except at one point, moving this point will cause the whole curve to change. These changes may lead to the need for changes at other points, which could lead to a long series of minor changes. To avoid these global changes, you can take a different approach: The B-spline introduced in section 7.2 can be modified locally at the expense of other controls.

This chapter will present three commonly used curve-generating techniques. Many similar methods in use are beyond the scope of this book.

7.2 Uniform B-Splines

The problem of non-local changes leads to a different approach to creating spline curves: you try to find a set of polynomials b_i that are non-zero only on an interval near u_1, such that the spline curve can be written as

$$C(u) = \sum_{j=0}^{n} b_j(u) p_j$$

The functions b_i are called **basic splines** and are said to form a **basis** for the curve. Splines can be made local by requiring that $b_i(u_i)$ be non-zero on a minimal interval around u_i. You also want each b_i to be continuous with continuous first and second derivatives. Because of continuity requirements, b_i may not be identically zero outside of the interval $[u_{i-1}, u_{i+1}]$. It is possible to construct b_i by using four distinct polynomials on the four consecutive intervals beginning with $[u_{i-2}, u_{i-1}]$ and ending with $[u_{i+1}, u_{i+2}]$. In addition to these requirements, let's say you would like to require that b_i be identically zero outside of these four intervals. This requirement is one too many for the number of equations, so a compromise must be reached.

The **uniform cubic B-spline** is the cubic spline with equally spaced knots that is non-zero on the smallest interval. It satisfies these requirements by passing through the control points P_i. Uniform B-splines are approximations rather than interpolations. Note first that each b_i satisfies exactly the same set of conditions. This means that all b_i have a curve with the same shape. This general curve can be defined by the polynomial b(u) for u in the interval $[-2,2]$. The polynomials that describe b are

$$\begin{aligned}
b(u) &= 0 && \text{if } u \le -2 \\
b(u) &= (2 + u)^3/6 && \text{if } -2 \le u \le -1 \\
b(u) &= (2 + u)^3/6 - 2(1 + u)^3/3 && \text{if } -1 \le u \le 0 \\
b(u) &= (1 - u)^3/6 - 2(2 - u)^3/3 && \text{if } 0 \le u \le 1 \\
b(u) &= (2 - u)^3/6 && \text{if } 1 \le u \le 2 \\
b(u) &= 0 && \text{i } u \ge 2
\end{aligned}$$

The graph of b (figure 7.2.1) shows that the polynomials composing b create a smooth curve. The splines b_i are then defined by $b_i(u) = b(u - i)$ for all u in [0,n]. Notice that each b_i is non-zero only on the interval $(i - 2, i + 2)$.

The curve C(u) can be expressed in terms of the four non-zero b_i for the interval around u (figure 7.2.2). If u is in $[u_i, u_{i+1}]$, then C(u) can be expressed as

$$C(u) = b_{i-1}(u)p_{i-1} + b_i(u)p_i + b_{i+1}(u)p_{i+1} + b_{i+2}(u)p_{i+2}$$

You can substitute given that $b_i(t) = b(t - i)$. The curve $C_i(t)$ can be given for the interval [i,i+1] as

$$\begin{aligned} C_i(t) = {} & ((1 - t)^3/6)p_{i-1} \\ & + (-2(1 - t)^3/3 + (2 - t)^3/6)p_i \\ & + ((1 + t)^3/6 - 2t^3/3)p_{i+1} \\ & + (t^3/6)p_{i+2} \end{aligned}$$

where t is between 0 and 1.

B-splines can be drawn by drawing $C_i(t)$ for each i between 1 and n − 2. You can then evaluate $C_i(t)$ for a sequence of evenly spaced t values between 0 and 1. The coefficients pass through the same values for each i, so they can be calculated before the curve is sketched. These coefficients are also referred to as the **blending functions.** The procedure in figure 7.2.3 computes and draws an approximation of a B-spline curve for a given polynomial.

The curve generated by this procedure will normally not come close to the first or last control point (figure 7.2.4) because drawing starts in the second interval and ends in the second interval from the end. One way to alter this is to repeat the first and last points in the polygon. If any control point is listed three consecutive times in the polygon of control points, then the B-spline curve will pass through the repeated point. You can alter the procedure that draws the B-spline curve so that it augments the control-point polygon with three copies

FIGURE 7.2.1

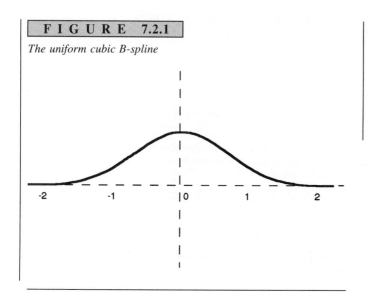

The uniform cubic B-spline

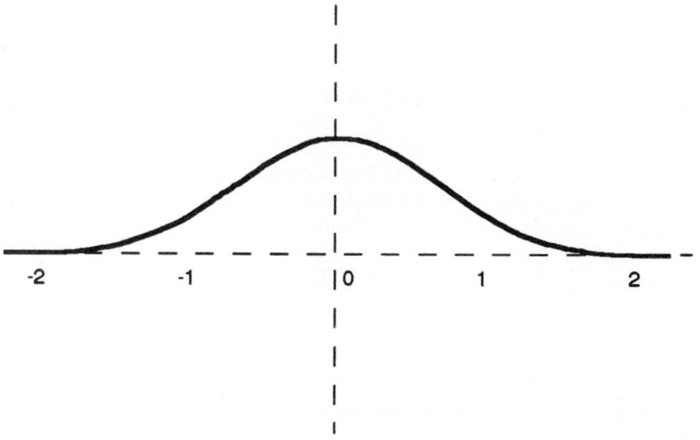

FIGURE 7.2.2

Only the functions b_{i-1}, b_i, b_{i+1}, and b_{i+2} are non-zero at u.

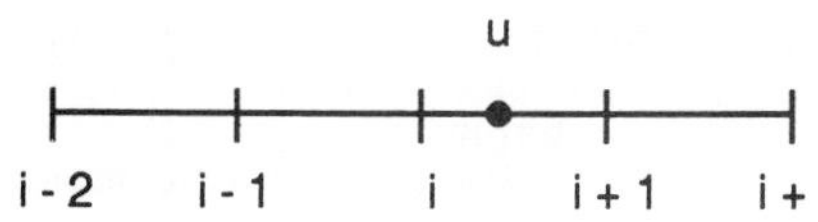

FIGURE 7.2.3

A procedure for drawing B-splines

```
const
  density = 20;               (* number of values of u computed for each interval   *)
  PolySize = 20;              (* maximum number of control points for the spline    *)
  OneThird := 1 / 3;          (* real constants used to compute blending functions  *)
  FourThirds := 4 / 3;
type
  point = record
      x, y: integer
    end;
  polygon = record
      NumVert   : integer;
      Verts     : array[0..PolySize] of point
    end;
  spline = array[0..density] of point;
  Curve = array[1..PolySize] of spline;
  BlendType = array[1..4, 0..density] of real;

procedure InitializeBlendingFunctions (var Blend: BlendType);
  var
    parameter         : integer;
    PointCount        : integer;
    increment         : real;
    u, uSquared, uCubed, OneMinusUCubed: real;
begin
  increment := 1 / density;
  u := 0;
  for parameter := 0 to density do
    begin
      uSquared := u * u;
      uCubed := uSquared * u;
      OneMinusuCubed := (1.0 - u) * Sqr(1.0 - u);
      Blend[1, parameter] := OneMinusuCubed / 6;
      Blend[2, parameter] := (uCubed - 2 * uSquared + FourThirds) / 2;
      Blend[3, parameter] := (-uCubed + uSquared + u + OneThird) / 2;
      Blend[4, parameter] := uCubed / 6;
      u := u + increment;
    end;
end;
procedure DrawSpline (p: polygon; var SCurve: Curve; Blend: BlendType; var Port : window);
  var
    PointCount: integer;
    Parameter: integer;
begin
  for PointCount := 1 to P.NumVert - 2 do
    for parameter := 0 to density do
      begin
        SCurve[PointCount, parameter].x := round(blend[1, parameter] * p.verts[PointCount - 1].x
                                             + blend[2, parameter] * p.verts[PointCount].x
                                             + blend[3, parameter] * p.verts[PointCount + 1].x
                                             + blend[4, parameter] * p.verts[PointCount + 2].x);
        SCurve[PointCount, parameter].y := round(blend[1, parameter] * p.verts[PointCount - 1].y
                                             + blend[2, parameter] * p.verts[PointCount].y
                                             + blend[3, parameter] * p.verts[PointCount + 1].y
                                             + blend[4, parameter] * p.verts[PointCount + 2].y);

      end;
  MoveAbs(SCurve[1, 0].x, SCurve[1, 0].y,Port);
  for PointCount := 1 to P.NumVert - 2 do
    for parameter := 0 to density do
      LineAbs(SCurve[PointCount, parameter].x, SCurve[PointCount, parameter].y,Port);
end;
```

FIGURE 7.2.4

B-spline curves do not usually pass near the first and last control points.

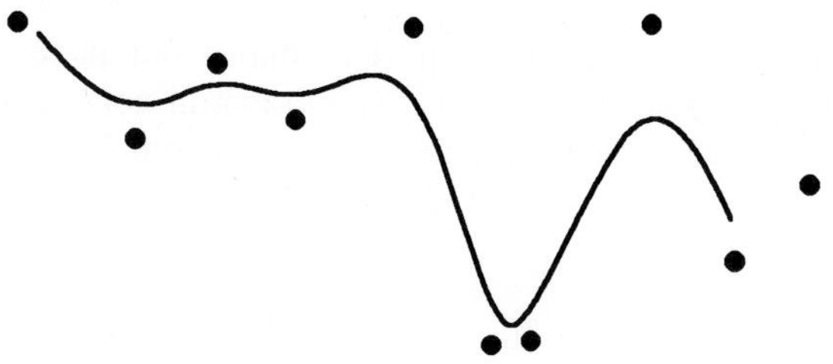

FIGURE 7.2.5

To get this B-spline curve to pass through the first and last control points, the points are repeated three times in the polygon.

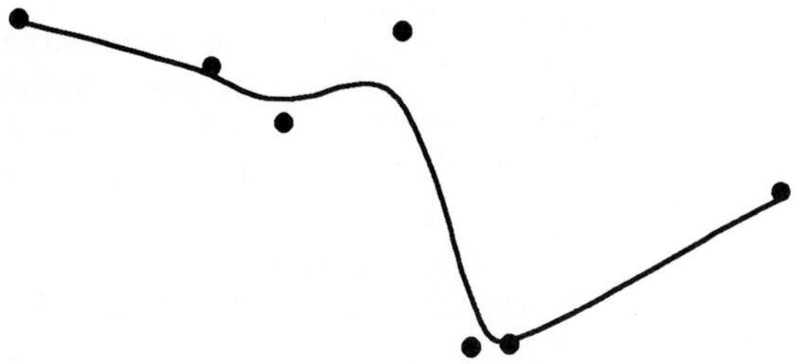

of the first and last control points. The B-spline curve drawn by this procedure will pass through the first and last control points (figure 7.2.5).

B-splines can be altered interactively if the user is provided with a way to move a control point. If ReadLocator is used to get the coordinates of a control point, a simple linear search of the polygon of control points will reveal which control point is to be moved. Because the influence of each control point is restricted to the four intervals adjacent to its knot, only those four segments of the curve will be altered by moving a control point. These segments can be drawn in **xor** mode in response to every movement of the control point. This gives you a way to rubberband B-splines.

MacDraw uses **uniform quadratic B-splines** in its smooth function. Uniform quadratic B-splines stretch over the four knots $-3/2$, $-1/2$, $1/2$, and $3/2$ in the interval $[-1.5,1.5]$. The polynomials describing the basic blending function are

$$
\begin{array}{ll}
b(u) = 0 & u \le -3/2 \\
b(u) = (u + 3/2)^2/2 & -3/2 \le u \le -1/2 \\
b(u) = -u^2 + 3/4 & -1/2 \le u \le 1/2 \\
b(u) = (u - 3/2)^2/2 & 1/2 \le u \le 3/2 \\
b(u) = 0 & 3/2 \le u
\end{array}
$$

Substituting $b_i(t) = b(t - i)$ yields

$$
\begin{aligned}
C(t) &+ p_{i-1}(u^2 - 2u + u)/2 \\
&+ p_i(-2u^2 + 2u + u)/2 \\
&+ p_{i+1}\, u^2/2.
\end{aligned}
$$

EXERCISES

7.2.1

Implement a procedure to initialize the blending functions for quadratic B-splines.

7.2.2

Implement the B-spline drawing procedure on your system.

7.2.3

Use a rubberband polygon-drawing program to specify control points for a B-spline. Notice that once the polygon is drawn, if it is redrawn in **xor** mode, only the control points remain on the screen. Pass the polygon to your B-spline drawing procedure.

7.2.4

Rewrite your B-spline drawing procedure to repeat the first and last control points three times.

7.2.5

Create a procedure that will interactively alter your B-spline curve.

7.2.6

Show that the splines $b_i(u)$ defined in this section are in fact only non-zero when u is in $(i-2,i+2)$.

7.2.7

Plot the uniform quadratic B-spline with control points {(1,1), (5,7), (7,3), (10,1)} if the points are each counted as one control point and their order is as given.

7.2.8

Repeat exercise 7.2.7. with the endpoints repeated twice.

7.2.9

Repeat exercise 7.2.7. with the endpoints repeated three times.

7.2.10

Repeat exercise 7.2.7. with the control points each counted once, but with the order {(1,1), (7,3), (5,7), (10,1)}.

7.2.11

Repeat exercise 7.2.7. with all of the control points except (7,3) counted once. Sketch the graph once with (7,3) repeated twice and once with (7,3) repeated three times.

PROJECTS

7.2.1

Extend the draw or paint project from section 6.9 to include a smooth curve tool. This tool should allow the user to plot a series of control points and then create the B-spline curve for these points. In addition, once the curve is plotted the user should be allowed to move the control points interactively and the spline curve should be redrawn in response to these changes. If your program is a draw type program and the user selects the curve, the control points should be displayed and the user should then be able to reshape the curve by moving the control points.

7.3 Bézier Curves

One of the most commonly used types of splines are the Bézier curves, named after P. E. Bézier, who used them at Renault. They are popular partly because the first and last control points are on the curve. Repositioning of any control point causes a reshaping of the entire curve, so modifications are not localized. Also, the degree of the polynomial increases as the number of control points increases. To avoid the problems inherent with polynomials of higher order and to localize modifications caused by moving control points, Bézier curves of second, third, and fourth order are often pieced together to create a single curve. These pieced Bézier curves are used in popular Macintosh programs such as SuperPaint and Freehand.

Each point, $\mathbf{p}(t)$, on a Bézier curve with $n+1$ control points is computed with the formula

$$\mathbf{p}(t) = \sum_{k:=0}^{n} B_{k,n}(t)\mathbf{p_k}$$

where the blending functions are given by

$$B_{k,n}(t) = \text{CombinationsOf}(n,k)\ t^k(1 - t)^{n-k}$$

where t ranges from 0 to 1, and CombinationsOf(n,k) is the number of combinations of n things taken k at a time. The standard formula for the combination coefficients, CombinationsOf(n,k) = $n!/(k!\ (n - k)!)$, contains many multiplications and divisions, making it subject to overflow and round-off errors. For most applications these values are computed and stored in an array to save time during a run.

As in B-splines, the blending functions determine the contribution to a given curve value of a given control point. If you consider the most commonly used Bézier curve that has four control points, the parametric equation is

$$\mathbf{p}(t) = (1 - t)^3\mathbf{p_0} + 3t(1 - t)^2\mathbf{p_1} + 3t^2(1 - t)\mathbf{p_2} + t^3\mathbf{p_3}$$

Figure 7.3.1 shows the graphs of each of the blending functions for this polynomial. The multiplier $B_{0,3}$ is largest when $t = 0$ and is zero when $t = 1$, while the multiplier $B_{3,3}$ acts in exactly the opposite way. The two middle

FIGURE 7.3.1

The blending functions for a third-order Bézier curve

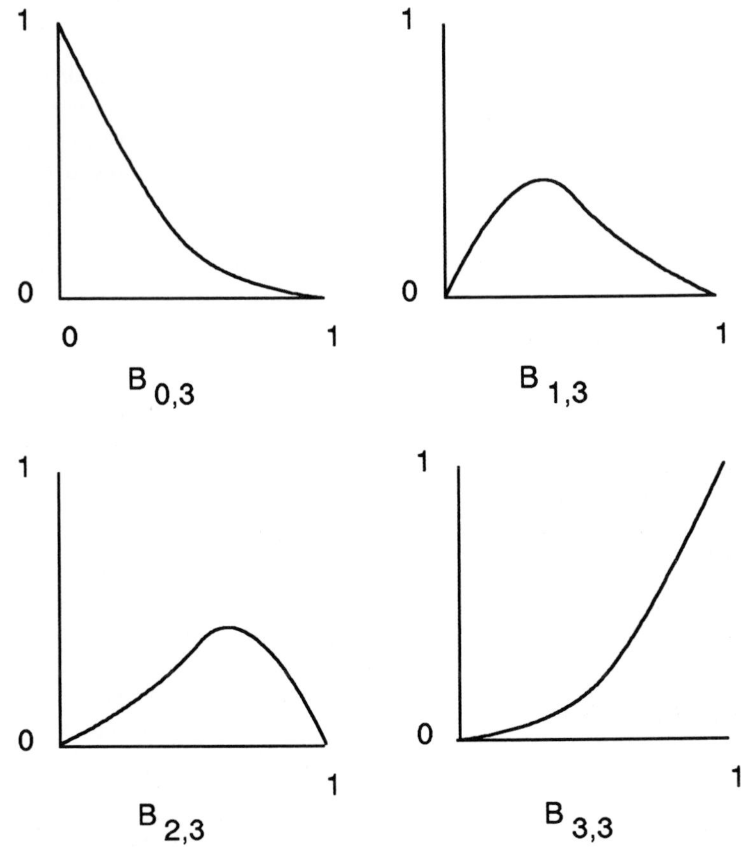

functions, $B_{1,3}$ and $B_{2,3}$, have their maximum values at t = ⅓ and t = ⅔ respectively, so that the points $\mathbf{p}_1$ and $\mathbf{p}_2$ respectively reach their maximum impact at these same values of t.

The polynomial **p** is computed for only a finite number of values of t in the interval [0,1]. The points computed in this manner are connected by line segments. Clearly the number of values of t computed must be large compared to the number of control points or the curve will still appear to be a polygon. The Bézier curve with control points (20,20), (35,40), (45,25), and (55,35) is shown in figure 7.3.2. Values for **p** are given at t = ⅓ and t = ⅔. You also know that **p**(0) = (20,20) and **p**(1) = (55,35). Since most of the control points lie to the right of the diagram, **p**(⅓) = (34,37) has an x-value larger than 32 and roughly ⅓ of the x-distance from 20 to 55. If the values of t are evenly distributed, it is clear that all the segments connecting values of **p** need not be of the same length. This suggests that control points should be distributed relatively evenly or that a large number of t-values should be computed to avoid jagged curves. A procedure for computing the blending functions for the Bézier curve with four control points is given in figure 7.3.3.

FIGURE 7.3.2

An example of a Bézier curve with control points (20,20), (35,40), (45,25), and (55,35)

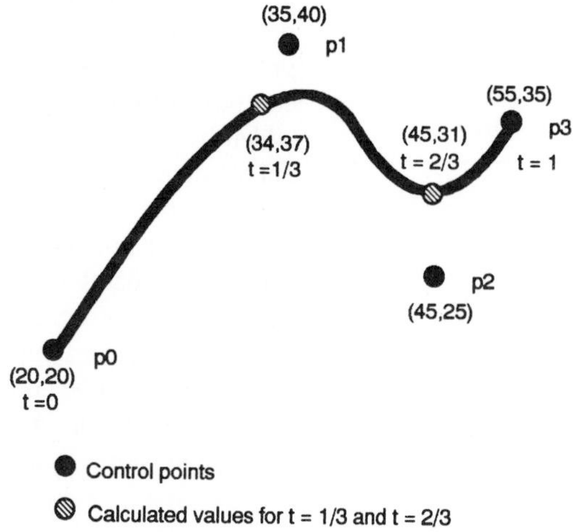

FIGURE 7.3.3

Initialization of the blending functions for a Bézier curve with four control points

```
(* This procedure initializes the blending functions for a Bézier curve with four control   *)
(* points. Density is a constant which is the number of points at which t is evaluated.      *)

type
  BlendingFunction = array[0..3,0..density] of real;

procedure SetBezierBlendingFunctions(var Blend : BlendingFunction);
var
  parameter              : integer;     (* counts the intervals                    *)
  t, tSquared, tCubed    : real;        (*parameter and its powers                 *)
  OneMinust,
  OneMinustSquared,
  OneMinustCubed         : real;        (* one minus the parameter raised to power  *)
  tIncrement             : real;        (* the amount t is incremented at each step *)
begin
  tIncrement := 1/density;
  t := 0;
  for parameter := 0 to density do
    begin
      tSquared := sqr(t);
      tCubed := t*tSquared;
      OneMinust := 1.0 - t;
      OneMinustSquared := OneMinust * OneMinust;
      OneMinustCubed := OneMinust * OneMinustSquared;
      Blend[0,parameter] := OneMinustCubed;
      Blend[1,parameter] := 3 * t * OneMinustSquared;
      Blend[2,parameter] := 3 * tSquared * OneMinust;
      Blend[3,parameter] := tCubed;
      t := t + tIncrement
    end
end;
```

Curves can be broken into segments to avoid polynomials of degree larger than 3 while still retaining a large number of control points. Each segment is then generated as a Bézier curve with four control points. When a user of a paint program wants to convert a curve drawn freehand to a Bézier curve, the program places sample points at intervals on the curve. These points are used as end points for each piece of the piecewise curves. Auxiliary control points are added by the program between each of the sample points (figure 7.3.4). Cubic curves have two auxiliary points added between each pair of sample points, so that each pair of sample points is joined by one piece of the piecewise curve.

Each piece of the piecewise curve begins and ends on a sample point of the original freehand curve, so these curves are continuous. The slopes of the curves need not be continuous, however (figure 7.3.5). If the auxiliary point before and after a sample point is co-linear with the sample point, then the slope of the curve will be continuous. SuperPaint allows the user to decide if the slope will be continuous at a sample point. Figure 7.3.6 shows an example with continuous slope at the join of two pieces.

FIGURE 7.3.4

A Bézier curve from SuperPaint with control points showing

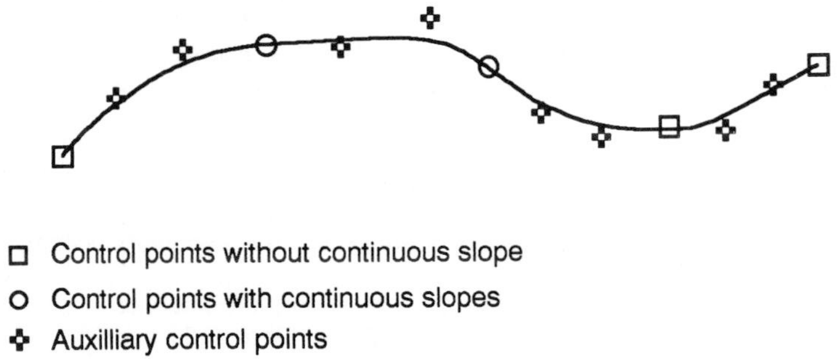

FIGURE 7.3.5

In this example from SuperPaint, the control points P1, P2, and P3 are not co-linear; therefore the curve does not have continuous slope.

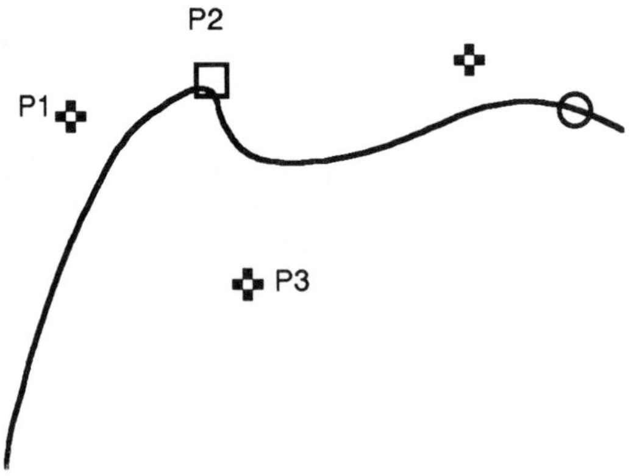

FIGURE 7.3.6

In SuperPaint, the user may choose to have pieces of a Bézier curve joined with continuous slope. To do this, the auxilliary control points surrounding the sample point are placed on the same line.

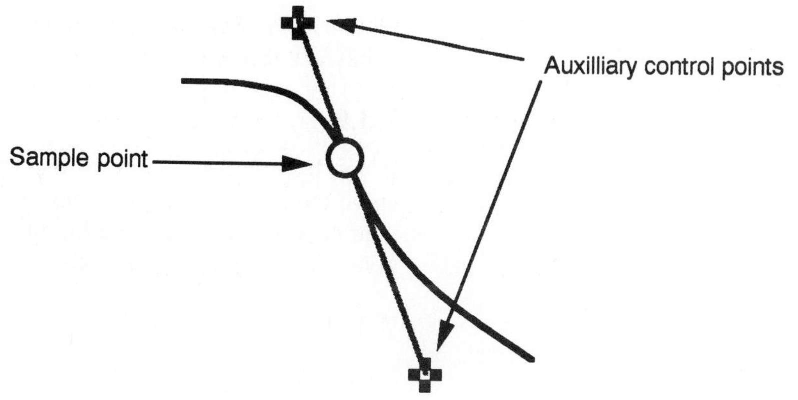

EXERCISES

7.3.1

Write a procedure to create blending functions for the quadratic Bézier curve.

7.3.2

Write a procedure to draw cubic Bézier curves.

7.3.3

Write a procedure that augments a polygon of points with two auxiliary points for each pair of points.

7.3.4

Repeat exercise 7.3.3 with the additional requirement that each point in the polygon is on the same line as the two auxiliary points adjacent to it.

7.3.5

Write a procedure to draw a cubic, piecewise, Bézier curve.

7.3.6

Write a procedure to alter piecewise Bézier curves without maintaining continuous slopes at the join of pieces.

7.3.7

Write a procedure to alter piecewise Bézier curves maintaining continuous slopes at the join of pieces.

7.3.8

Plot the cubic Bézier curve with control points {(1,1), (5,7), (7,3), (10,1)} if the points are each counted as one control point and their order is as given.

7.3.9

If you have access to any of the draw or paint programs that provide Bézier curve tools, draw a curve using the tool, then try to reshape the curve. Does your program always give a smooth curve at control points? Does your program give you the option of smooth corners or "hinged" corners?

7.3.10

Plot the Bézier curve with control points {(1,1), (7,5), (7,5), (10,2)}.

7.3.11

Plot the Bézier curve with control points {(1,1), (1,1), (7,5), (10,2)}.

PROJECTS

7.3.1

Extend the draw project from section 6.9 to include a free hand draw tool that records the curve as a polygon. Allow the user to select the curve and smooth it by converting it to a Bézier curve. To convert this curve, you can select every third, fourth or nth point to be a control point. Use the selected points as the endpoints for a four-point Bézier curve. The method used to select the two internal control points for each interval will determine whether or not the joint of consecutive sections of the curve will be smooth or not.

7.3.2

Create a font editor that can create and edit letters described by Bézier curves.

7.4 Catmull-Rom Curves and Splines under Tension

The discussion on B-splines approached the problem of fitting a curve to a set of control points by requiring continuous first- and second-order derivatives while requiring the curve to pass through the control points. If the curve must pass through the control points, the requirement for second-order continuity can be dropped.

Curves without continuous second derivatives will still appear to be smooth. In the case of cubic splines, requiring the curve to pass through the control points with first-order continuity results in 13 equations in 16 unknowns. One way to complete the specification of the curve is to specify the slopes of the curve at the three middle knots. The **Catmull-Rom curve** is the special case when the three slopes are ½ at the left knot, 0 at the middle knot, and −½ at the right knot.

The slopes at the middle knots can be given more generally as m at the left knot, 0 at the middle knot, and −m at the right knot. The value m is often called the **tension,** because as the value of m decreases to 0, the curve appears to be stretched more tightly through the control points (figure 7.4.1, 7.4.2 and 7.4.3). These curves are often called **splines under tension** even though mathematically they are not really splines.

Values of m greater than 1 or less than 0 lead to curves that loop around the control point (figure 7.4.4); therefore m is usually restricted to the interval [0,1]. The most commonly used spline under tension is the Catmull-Rom curve, that is, m = ½.

FIGURE 7.4.1

A spline under tension with m=0.1

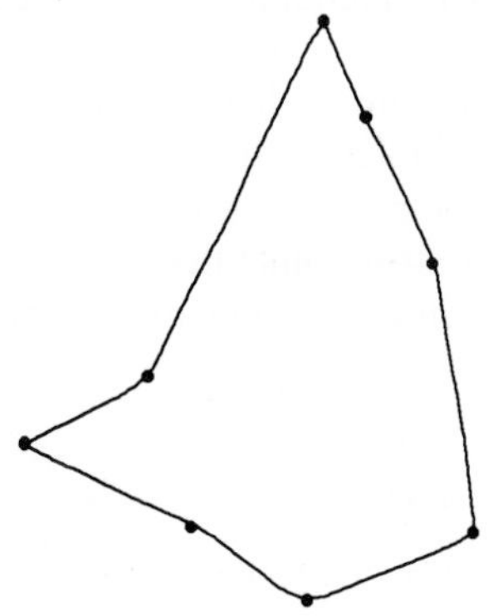

FIGURE 7.4.2

A spline under tension with m=0.3

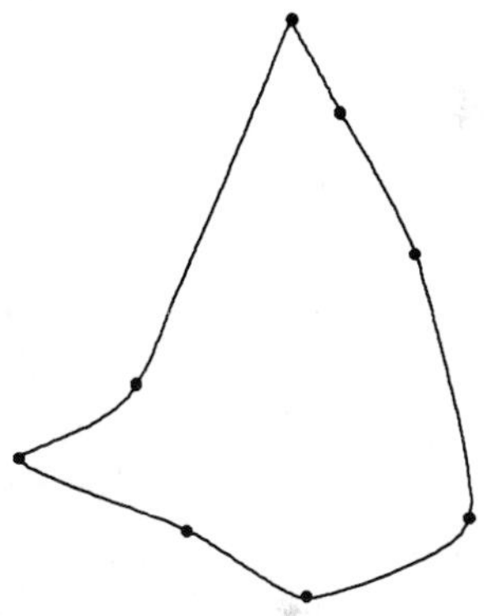

FIGURE 7.4.3

A spline under tension with m=0.5

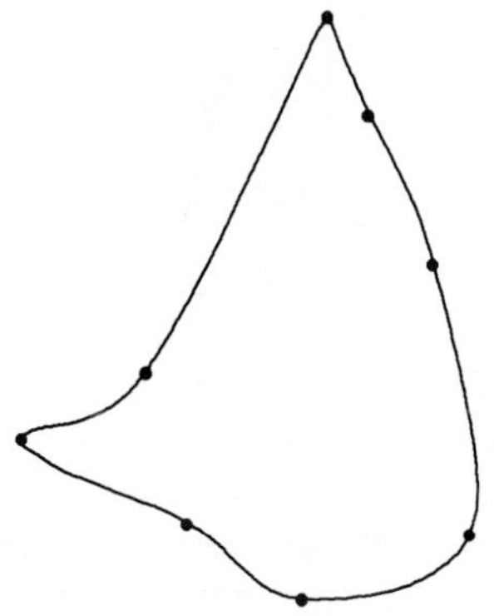

FIGURE 7.4.4

A spline under tension with m=2.0.

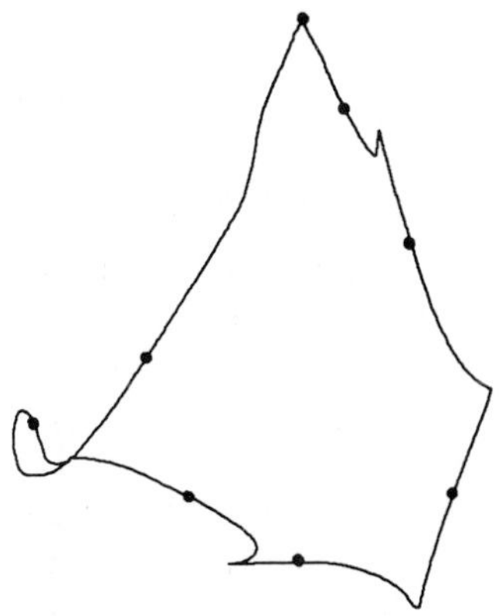

The equation for the interpolating curve of these curves is the same as that for B-splines, namely

$$C(u) = \sum_{i=0}^{n} b_i(u)*\mathbf{p}_i$$

As in the case of B-splines, a general basis function for Catmull-Rom curves can be defined on the interval [−2,2]. The curve of this basis function is seen in figure 7.4.5. Each blending function, b_i, can be described as the transformation $b_i(u) = b(u-i)$ of the general basis function. With this transformation the formula for C on the interval [i,i+1] is given by

$$\begin{aligned} C(u) = &(-mu^3 + 2mu^2 - u)p_{i-1} \\ &+((2 - m)u^3 + (m - 3)u^2 + 1)p_i \\ &+((m - 2)u^3 + (3 - 2m)u^2 + mu)p_{i+1} \\ &+(mu^3 - mu^2)p_{i+2} \end{aligned}$$

FIGURE 7.4.5

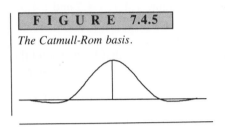

The Catmull-Rom basis.

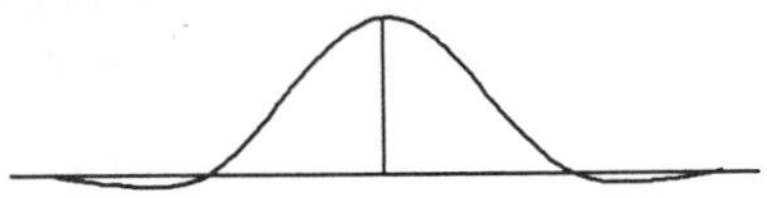

The procedures that draw and modify B-splines will also draw and modify splines under tension if the Catmull-Rom blending functions are substituted for the B-spline blending functions.

The first and last control points of Catmull-Rom curves must be specified twice or the curve will not pass through them. If these points are repeated three times, the curve will overshoot the point and form a cross at the end. The overshot cross will occur at middle control points that are repeated twice. If a middle control point is specified three times, a loop will form around the control point (figure 7.4.6).

FIGURE 7.4.6

Catmull-Rom curve with multiple, specified control points

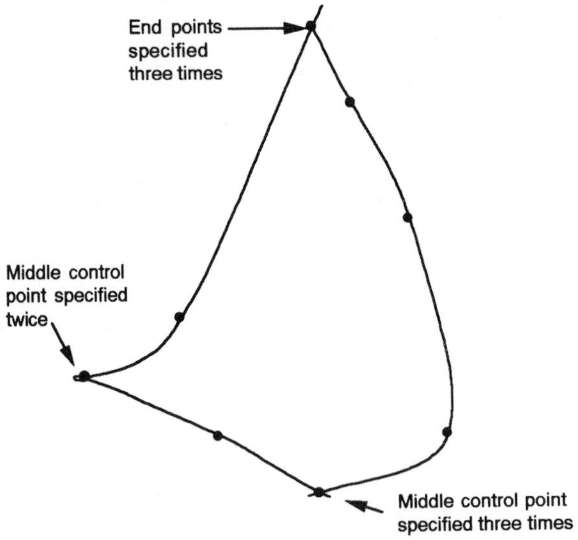

EXERCISES

7.4.1

Write a procedure to create the Catmull-Rom blending functions.

7.4.2

Use the procedure created to draw B-splines to draw the splines under tension for m = −1, 0, 0.1, 0.3, 0.5, 0.8, 1.0, 2.0, and 3.0.

7.4.3

Create a Catmull-Rom curve with first and last control points specified three times, one middle control point specified twice, and another middle control points specified three times.

BIBLIOGRAPHY

Barry, Phillip J., and Ronald N. Goldman. "A Recursive Evaluation Algorithm for a Class of Catmull-Rom Splines." *Computer Graphics* 22 (4) (SIGGRAPH '88): 199–204 (August 1988).
Recursive procedures for computing blending functions using Pascal's triangle.

Barsky, Brian A., and Tony D. DeRose. "Geometric Continuity of Parametric Curves: Three Equivalent Characterizations." *CG&A* 9 (6): 60–68 (November 1989).

———. "Geometric Continuity of Parametric Curves: Constructions of Geometrically Continuous Splines." *CG&A* 10 (1): 60–68 (January 1990).

Cox, M. G. "The Numerical Evaluation of B-Splines." *J. Institute for Mathematics & Applications* 10: 134–49 (1972).

de Boor, C. "On Calculating with B-Splines." *J. Approximation Theory* 6: 50–62 (1972).

Farouki, Rida T., and John K. Hinds. "A Hierarchy of Geometric Forms." *IEEE CG&A* 5 (5): 51–78 (May 1985).
Great survey of the different types of splines: accurate descriptions, good bibliography.

Gerald C. F., and P. O. Wheatley. *Applied Numerical Analysis*. Reading, Mass.: Addison Wesley, 1984.

Goldman, Ronald N. "Urn Models and Beta-Splines." *IEEE CG&A* 6 (2): 57–64 (February 1986).

Goodman, T. N. T., and K. Unsworth. ''Manipulating Shape and Producing Geometric Continuity in β-spline Curves.'' *IEEE CG&A* 6 (2): 50–56 (February 1986).
Features of β-splines that make them suitable for computer-aided design.

Pavlidis, Theo. ''Scan Conversion of Regions Bounded by Parabolic Splines.'' *IEEE CG&A* 5 (6): 47–53 (June 1985).

Piegl, L. ''Interactive Data Interpolation by Rational Bézier Curves.'' *IEEE CG&A* 7 (4): 45–58 (April 1987).
Interactive techniques with interpolation methods allow user intervention.

Rogers, D. F., and J. A. Adams. *Mathematical Elements of Computer Graphics*. New York: McGraw-Hill, 1976.

CHAPTER

8

Matrix Representations and Three-Dimensional Graphics

DIRECTIONS

"Space: The Final Frontier"

This introduction begins every episode of "Star Trek" as the starship Enterprise embarks on another mission. When the television series was introduced in the mid 1960s, satellite photography and computer graphics were in their infancy. To create the opening sequence of the ship, a large model was pulled by cables past the camera.

"Star Trek" and movies such as *Star Wars* and *2010* appeal to the imaginations of viewers who have grown up with moon landings and television images of places "where no man has gone before." These movies must maintain credibility with their audience and so they must provide images of at least the same quality as the actual ones.

A typical "fly-by" sequence shows a spaceship traversing above a planet's surface. In the filming of such sequences, model ships are still commonly superimposed on images of planets produced by computers. There are many different types of planetary surfaces. Some planets have cratered surfaces like that of the moon. Some have a mixture of cratered and desert-canyon surfaces similar to that of Mars. The outer, gas-giant planets of the solar system are surrounded by bands of turbulent clouds, while some of their moons are covered by an almost mirrorlike ice. The techniques used to create these surface textures are presented in chapter 11.

Computer graphics has progressed to the point where a fly-by sequence can now be generated entirely by computer. Newtonian physics dictates the motions of two or more bodies relative to each other and is the starting point for creating a realistic scene. Once an orbital system has been modeled, it must be rotated and translated to appear in an advantageous position on the screen. In addition, physical models are traditionally created in a righthand coordinate system, while graphics systems have a left-hand orientation. Therefore, all points computed from physical models must be transformed into left-hand orientation, then rotated and translated to be appropriately aligned with the camera. Finally, the image must be projected into screen coordinates.

8.1 Three-Dimensional Graphics

The move from two-dimensional to three-dimensional graphics creates two categories of problems. The first concerns the extension of the two-dimensional tools you have developed to three-dimensional tools. The second class of problems deals with the representation of three-dimensional objects in two dimensions.

In this chapter you will work only with the extension to three dimensions. While coordinate systems may be extended by adding one coordinate, the orientation of positive axes is more complicated in three dimensions. If you assume the xy-plane is the graphics screen, you must decide whether the positive z-axis will point out of or into the screen.

Polygons in two dimensions consist of vertices and edges. When you move to three dimensions, polygons also have faces. The representations of polygonal surfaces and curved surfaces are presented in section 8.2.

Three-dimensional transformations are also more complicated than transformations in two dimensions. In addition to rotations about a point, you must now consider rotations about a line. It is often necessary to describe a transformation as a sequence of simpler transformations. Matrix algebra becomes an indispensable tool for creating these composite transformations. The matrix forms of three dimensional transformations such as translation and rotation are given in this chapter. These solutions are applied to the problem of establishing the viewer's position in a graphics system.

The remaining chapters address the projection of three-dimensional images on a two-dimensional surface, the hiding of surfaces and lines that are not visible from the viewer's position, and the creation of realistic images. The solutions to these problems rely heavily on vector operations. The vector products also provide an alternative approach to finding the matrix representations of some commonly used three-dimensional transformations. An example of this approach is given in section 8.7.

8.2 Representing Graphic Objects in Three-Dimensions

Representing three-dimensional objects is considerably more difficult than adding an extra coordinate to the Cartesian system used in two-dimensional systems. Even if you elect to retain the normal screen position of the x- and y-axes, the positive part of the z-axis can point either into or out of the screen. It is also possible to have the z-axis in the plane of the screen and one of the other axes perpendicular to the screen. It is equally possible to have none of the axes in the plane of the screen. In this section you determine the orientation of the z-axis relative to the x- and y-axes. You also look at various methods used to represent objects in such a system. The more difficult problem of positioning the axes relative to the screen and viewer is covered later in the chapter.

The position of the positive z-axis points relative to the xy-plane determines whether the coordinates of a specific point will be (x,y,z) or or (x,y,−z). If the z-axis points out of the screen when the x- and y-axes are in their normal positions on the screen, the coordinate system is called a **right-hand system.** If you align your right hand so that your fingers curve from the x-axis to the y-axis, then your thumb points along the positive z-axis (figure 8.2.1). If,

FIGURE 8.2.1

The right-hand reference system

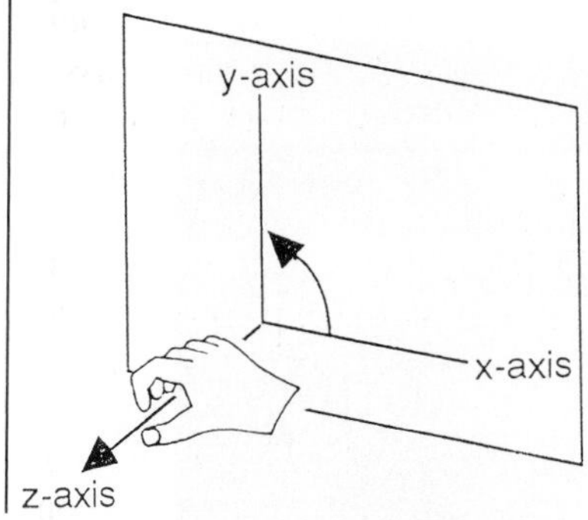

FIGURE 8.2.2

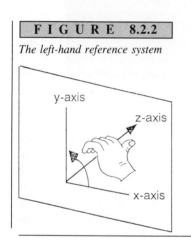

The left-hand reference system

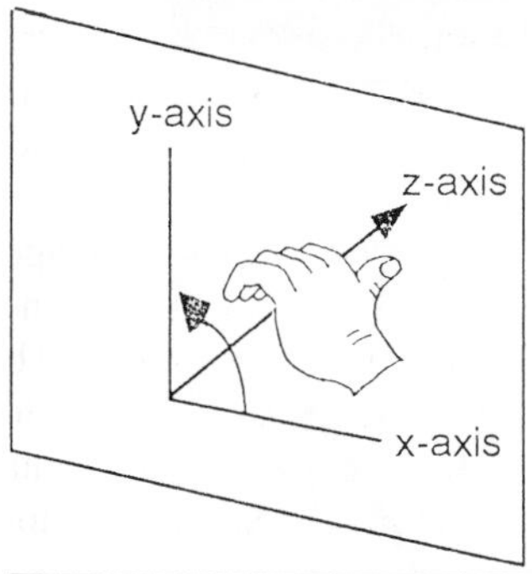

however, your thumb points along the negative z-axis, then the system is a **left-hand system.** In this system, if the fingers of your left hand are positioned so that they curl from the x-axis to the y-axis, then your left thumb points in the positive z-direction (figure 8.2.2).

Whether to use the right- or left-hand system often depends on the positions of the important objects in the application you are working with. For some applications, the solution is easier to derive with one orientation than with the other. In such cases, right- and left-handed systems may be used in the same problem (Blinn 1988).

Many problems are easier to solve within a coordinate system other than the Cartesian system. Both the cylindrical and spherical coordinate systems can provide simple descriptions of objects that would be difficult to derive in the Cartesian system. Nevertheless, most graphics packages use the Cartesian system, which, as a result, limits the usefulness of non-Cartesian systems in computer graphics because objects represented in these systems must be converted to the Cartesian system before they can be displayed.

Once objects are represented in world coordinates, they must be converted into screen coordinates. Methods used to convert world coordinates to normalized screen coordinates in two-dimensional systems are also used in three-dimensional systems. Homogeneous coordinates are often used in three dimensions as they were in two dimensions to simplify certain matrix representations. The homogeneous coordinates of a point (x,y,z) are usually given as (x,y,z,1).

Images of solid objects can be created in many ways, with varying levels of complexity, depending on the type of information required by an application. When the surface appearance of an object is the only requirement, **geometric** or **shape modeling** is used to create the descriptions of the solid objects used in creating their images. This section presents two commonly used methods for performing geometric modeling of three-dimensional surfaces; polygonal meshes and spline surfaces. Objects with regular geometric surfaces, such as buildings and furniture, can be decomposed into a set of polygonal surfaces. This representation is called a **polygon mesh.**

A polygon mesh can also approximate curved surfaces (figure 8.2.3). When this technique is applied, picture quality can be improved by using a finer mesh in the curved areas, but the result will not be realistic. To achieve realistic curved surfaces, the spline techniques discussed in chapter 7 can be extended to three dimensions. The parametric equations utilized in this extension have two parameters rather than one and are normally cubic polynomials. Because of these characteristics, they are often called **bicubic patches.**

Engineers construct mechanical devices by combining pieces such as blocks, pyramids, and cylinders as well as spline surfaces. This type of constructive representation is called **solid modeling.** It is more complicated than geometric modeling and will be covered in chapter 11.

You have displayed polygons in two dimensions by connecting successive vertices with line segments. If you attempt the same type of construction with three-dimensional objects, one set of lines may represent many different polygonal surfaces. In figure 8.2.4 *(left),* the polygon mesh and vertices **A**, **B**, **C**, and **D**, can be interpreted in different ways. One interpretation (figure 8.2.4 [*center*]) is the solid with four triangular surfaces, while another (figure 8.2.4

FIGURE 8.2.3

An example of a surface rendered with a polygon mesh

FIGURE 8.2.4

*The polygon mesh with vertices **A, B, C** and **D*** (left) *can be interpreted in different ways. One way is as a solid with four triangular sides* (center); *another* (right) *is as the same solid with the side **ACD** missing.*

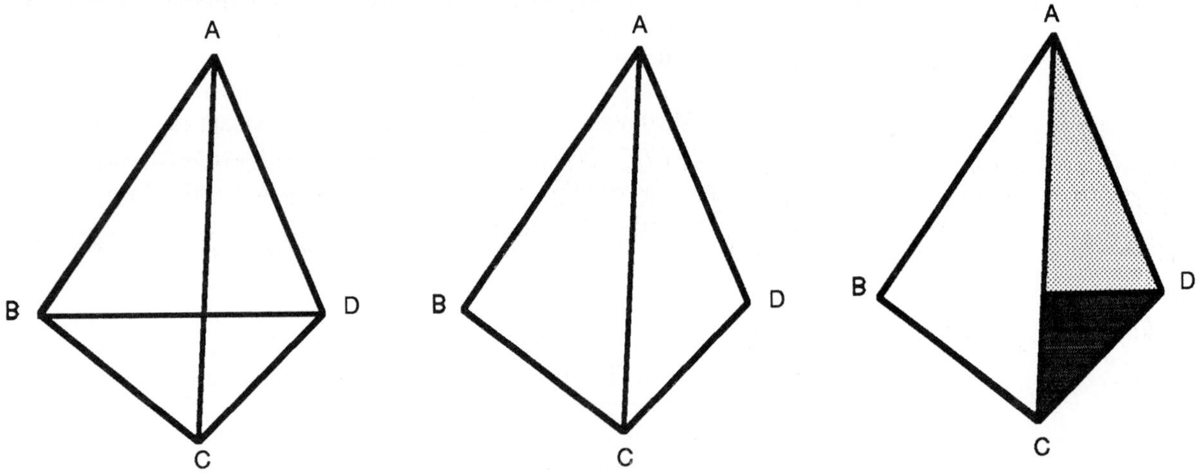

[*right*]) is the same solid without the side **ACD.** To avoid this ambiguity, any representation of such a solid must include a way to determine its polygonal surfaces.

A polygon mesh consists of vertices, edges, and polygons. Figure 8.2.5 is an example of a polygon mesh with vertices {$\mathbf{V}_1$, $\mathbf{V}_2$, $\mathbf{V}_3$, $\mathbf{V}_4$, $\mathbf{V}_5$, $\mathbf{V}_6$, $\mathbf{V}_7$}, edges {$\mathbf{E}_1$, $\mathbf{E}_2$, $\mathbf{E}_3$, $\mathbf{E}_4$, $\mathbf{E}_5$, $\mathbf{E}_6$, $\mathbf{E}_7$, $\mathbf{E}_8$, $\mathbf{E}_9$}, and polygons { $\mathbf{P}_1$, $\mathbf{P}_2$, $\mathbf{P}_3$}. The vertices are defined by their coordinates. The polygons can be defined by listing their vertices in clockwise or counterclockwise order. All polygons should have their

FIGURE 8.2.5

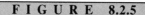

A cube with vertices, edges, and polygons labeled

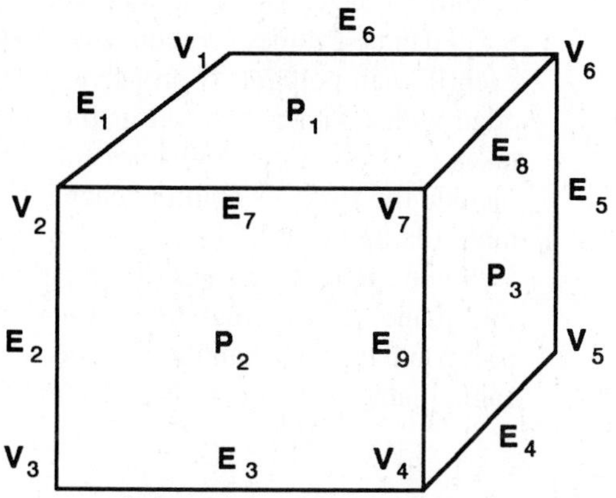

vertices listed in the same order. The polygon P_1 in figure 8.2.5 could be described by ((x_1, y_1, z_1), (x_2, y_2, z_2), (x_7, y_7, z_7), (x_6, y_6, z_6)), where the vertex V_i is assumed to have coordinates (x_i, y_i, z_i).

For a single polygon this type of representation is relatively efficient. Yet even in the comparatively small polygon mesh given in figure 8.2.5, the vertex $\mathbf{V}_7$ has its coordinates listed for each polygon. Other vertices, such as V_2, also appear in more than one vertex list. To save room, a **vertex table** listing the coordinates of a vertex is created, and references to a given vertex are made through its subscript in the table (figure 8.2.6). Representing polygons as the list of vertex subscripts improves storage efficiency but does not provide explicit methods for determining shared edges and vertices.

To expedite the retrieval of relationships between parts of the polygon mesh, a list of edges and their end points is kept in an **edge table,** and the polygons are described in terms of the subscripts of the edges in the table. The edge table for figure 8.2.5 is given in figure 8.2.7, and the polygon table is given in figure 8.2.8.

FIGURE 8.2.6

The vertex table for figure 8.2.5

Vertex Table

$\mathbf{V}_1$: x_1, y_1, z_1
$\mathbf{V}_2$: x_2, y_2, z_2
$\mathbf{V}_3$: x_3, y_3, z_3
$\mathbf{V}_4$: x_4, y_4, z_4
$\mathbf{V}_5$: x_5, y_5, z_5
$\mathbf{V}_6$: x_6, y_6, z_6
$\mathbf{V}_7$: x_7, y_7, z_7

FIGURE 8.2.7

The edge table for figure 8.2.5

Edge Table

$\mathbf{E}_1 : \mathbf{V}_1 \quad \mathbf{V}_2$
$\mathbf{E}_2 : \mathbf{V}_2 \quad \mathbf{V}_3$
$\mathbf{E}_3 : \mathbf{V}_3 \quad \mathbf{V}_4$
$\mathbf{E}_4 : \mathbf{V}_4 \quad \mathbf{V}_5$
$\mathbf{E}_5 : \mathbf{V}_5 \quad \mathbf{V}_6$
$\mathbf{E}_6 : \mathbf{V}_6 \quad \mathbf{V}_1$
$\mathbf{E}_7 : \mathbf{V}_7 \quad \mathbf{V}_2$
$\mathbf{E}_8 : \mathbf{V}_6 \quad \mathbf{V}_7$
$\mathbf{E}_9 : \mathbf{V}_7 \quad \mathbf{V}_4$

FIGURE 8.2.8

The polygon table for figure 8.2.5

Polygon Table

$\mathbf{P}_1$: $\mathbf{E}_1\ \mathbf{E}_6\ \mathbf{E}_8\ \mathbf{E}_7$
$\mathbf{P}_2$: $\mathbf{E}_2\ \mathbf{E}_7\ \mathbf{E}_9\ \mathbf{E}_3$
$\mathbf{P}_3$: $\mathbf{E}_4\ \mathbf{E}_9\ \mathbf{E}_8\ \mathbf{E}_5$

FIGURE 8.2.9

The vertex A is not on any edge; therefore, A cannot be listed as part of this polygon.

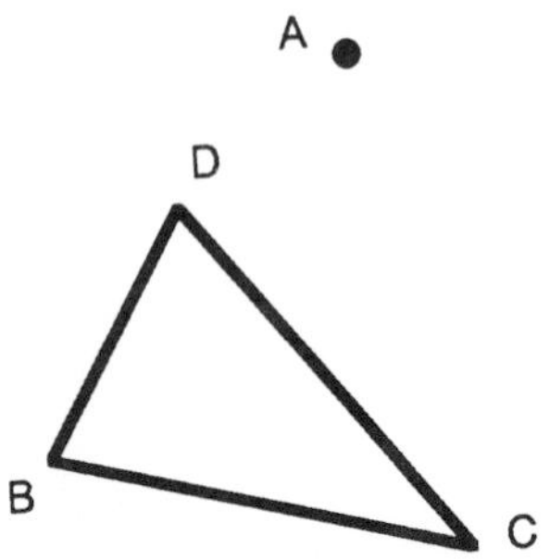

FIGURE 8.2.10

This is not a polygon mesh because A is an isolated point.

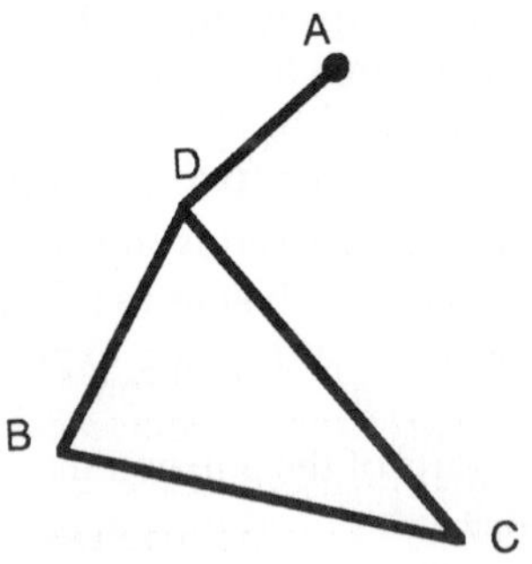

Not all lists of vertices, edges, and surfaces describe real objects. Tables that describe real objects are called **consistent.** Figure 8.2.9 is an example of a vertex not on any edge. If an edge is drawn from **D** to **A** (figure 8.2.10), the resulting image is still not a polygon mesh. Isolated points such as A in figure 8.2.9 can be avoided by requiring all points to be on at least two edges. Finally, even if each polygon is properly formed, all polygons must share at least one edge with another polygon or the surface is not connected (figure 8.2.11). It takes less time to check tables for consistency if the edge table is extended to include the surfaces abutting each edge. Figure 8.2.12 gives the extended edge table for figure 8.2.5.

Some implementations of the polygon mesh require that each polygon lie in one plane. Recall that three non-collinear points determine a plane. If the polygon has more than three vertices, you must check that all vertices are in the same plane. The equation of a plane has the form

$$Ax + By + Cz + D = 0$$

The coordinates (x,y,z) of any point in a plane will satisfy the equation of the plane.

Any three non-collinear points determine a plane. By choosing any three non-collinear vertices of a polygon (x_1,y_1,z_1), (x_2,y_2,z_2), and (x_3,y_3,z_3), you can substitute each into the equation of the plane and normalize to get the three equations

$$(A/D)\ x_1 + (B/D)\ y_i + (C/D)\ z_i = -1$$
$$i = 1,2,3$$

in the three unknowns $A' = A/D$, $B' = B/D$, and $C' = C/D$; or

$$A'\ x_1 + B'\ y_1 + C'\ z_1 = -1$$
$$A'\ x_2 + B'\ y_2 + C'\ z_2 = -1$$
$$A'\ x_3 + B'\ y_3 + C'\ z_3 = -1$$

These equations can be solved using Cramer's rule, provided the determinant of the coefficients

FIGURE 8.2.11

This figure does not represent a polygon mesh because the two polygons do not share a common edge.

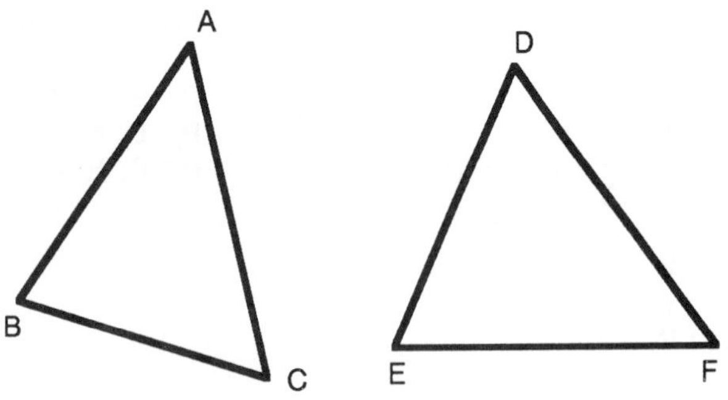

FIGURE 8.2.12

The extended edge table for the polygon mesh in figure 8.2.5

Edge Table

E_1 :	V_1	V_2	P_1	
E_2 :	V_2	V_3	P_2	
E_3 :	V_3	V_4	P_2	
E_4 :	V_4	V_5	P_3	
E_5 :	V_5	V_6	P_3	
E_6 :	V_6	V_1	P_1	
E_7 :	V_7	V_2	P_1	P_2
E_8 :	V_6	V_7	P_1	P_3
E_9 :	V_4	V_7	P_2	P_3

$$\begin{vmatrix} x_1 & y_1 & z_1 \\ x_2 & y_2 & z_2 \\ x_3 & y_3 & z_3 \end{vmatrix}$$

is not zero. This will always be true if the vertices are chosen so that they are not collinear, and every non-degenerate polygon has at least three non-collinear vertices. (Why?)

If the determinant of the coefficients is d, then the solutions are given as

$$A' = \begin{vmatrix} -1 & y_1 & z_1 \\ -1 & y_2 & z_2 \\ -1 & y_3 & z_3 \end{vmatrix} / d$$

$$B' = \begin{vmatrix} x_1 & -1 & z_1 \\ x_2 & -1 & z_2 \\ x_3 & -1 & z_3 \end{vmatrix} / d$$

$$C' = \begin{vmatrix} x_1 & y_1 & -1 \\ x_2 & y_2 & -1 \\ x_3 & y_3 & -1 \end{vmatrix} / d$$

FIGURE 8.2.13

The vector [A,B,C] normal to a plane can be computed from the equations of the plane.

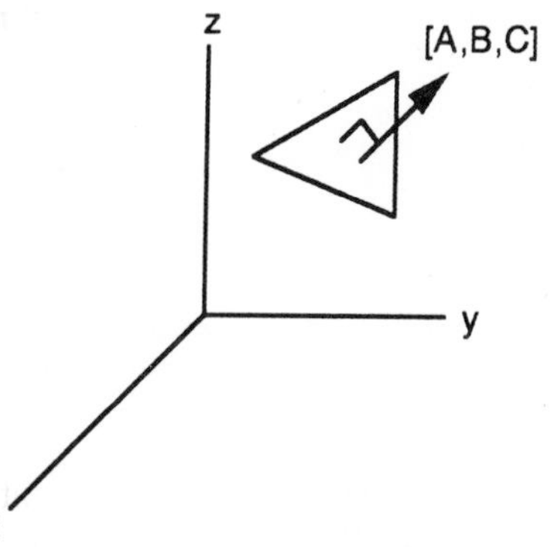

To avoid repeated division by d, apply simple algebra to get an alternative set of solutions: A = A′*d, B = B′*d, C = C′*d, and D = d. These reduce to

$$\begin{aligned} A &= y_1(z_2 - z_3) + y_2(z_3 - z_1) + y_3(z_1 - z_2) \\ B &= z_1(x_2 - x_3) + z_2(x_3 - x_1) + z_3(x_1 - x_2) \\ C &= x_1(y_2 - y_3) + x_2(y_3 - y_1) + x_3(y_1 - y_2) \\ D &= -x_1(y_2z_3 - y_3z_2) - x_2(y_3z_1 - y_1z_3) - x_3(y_1z_2 - y_2z_1) \end{aligned}$$

The vector (A, B, C) is normal to the plane (figure 8.2.13). Hence, for fixed A, B, and C, different D values give planes that are parallel.

When a polygon mesh does not produce a smooth enough representation of an object, it is replaced by one of the bicubic models. These models are the three-dimensional counterparts of the spline curves introduced in chapter 7. A major difference between spline curves and spline surfaces is that parametric equations of a surface have two variables. Linear interpolation is a simple example of a parametric representation of a surface. If, for example, you want to develop linear interpolation of the surface bounded by the four points $\mathbf{P}_{00}, \mathbf{P}_{10}, \mathbf{P}_{01}, \mathbf{P}_{11}$, (figure 8.2.14), then the parametric equation for this surface is

$$\mathbf{P}(u,v) = \mathbf{P}_{00}*(1-u)*(1-v) + \mathbf{P}_{10}*u*(1-v) + \mathbf{P}_{01}*v*(1-u) + \mathbf{P}_{11}*u*v$$

where u and v range from 0 to 1.

FIGURE 8.2.14

The boundary values for the parameters in the parametric representation of a polygon

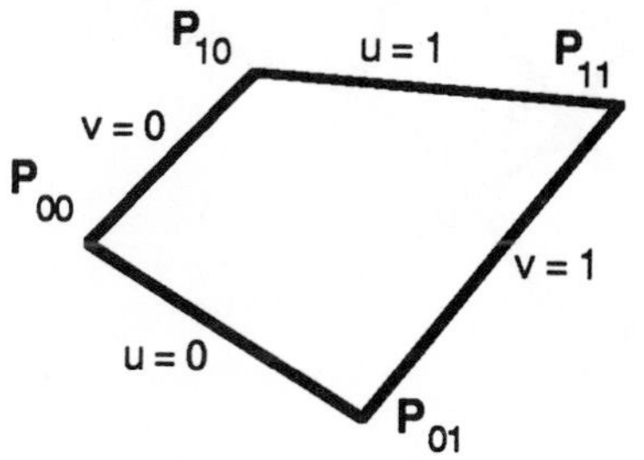

The region bounded by the four points is called a **patch.**

A smoother, more adjustable surface can be achieved by extending the Bézier curves to three dimensions. Recall that two-dimensional Bézier curves are defined by

$$\mathbf{p}(t) = \sum_{k=0}^{n} B_{k,n}(t)\mathbf{p}_k$$

where the blending functions $B_{k,n}$ are given as

$$B_{k,n}(t) = \binom{n}{k}^{k} (1 - t)^{n-k}$$

The parametric form of **Bézier surfaces** is given by

$$\mathbf{P}(u,v) = \sum_{j=0}^{m} \sum_{k=0}^{n} B_{j,m}(u) B_{k,n}(v) \mathbf{p}_{j,k}$$

where the (m + 1)-by-(n + 1) control points $\mathbf{p}_{j,k}$ are distributed over the patch. It is possible to construct Bézier surfaces for arbitrarily large m and n. Normally m and n are restricted to 3 so the blending functions will be cubic polynomials. Figure 8.2.15 shows a patch with a polygon mesh formed by the control points, while figure 8.2.16 illustrates the Bézier surface for this set of control points.

If greater numbers of control points are needed for a desired effect, the surface can be divided into more than one patch. To maintain continuity along the common edge of two successive patches, certain properties must be maintained. In figure 8.2.17, the triples of control points $(\mathbf{P}_1,\mathbf{Q}_1,\mathbf{R}_1)$, $(\mathbf{P}_2,\mathbf{Q}_2,\mathbf{R}_2)$, $(\mathbf{P}_3,\mathbf{Q}_3,\mathbf{R}_3)$, and $(\mathbf{P}_4,\mathbf{Q}_4,\mathbf{R}_4)$ must be collinear. In addition, the ratios

$$\frac{\text{length } (\mathbf{P}_i\mathbf{Q}_i)}{\text{length } (\mathbf{Q}_i\mathbf{R}_i)}$$

must be the same constant for i = 1, 2, 3, 4.

FIGURE 8.2.15

A patch with the polygon mesh formed by the control points

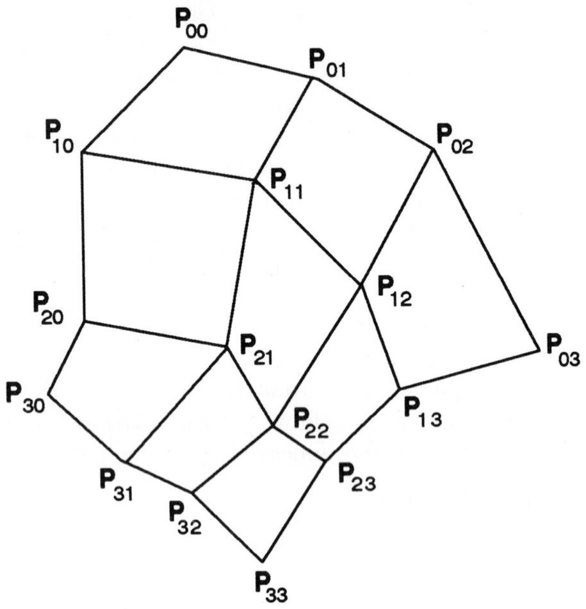

FIGURE 8.2.16

The Bézier surface constructed from the set of control points in figure 8.2.15

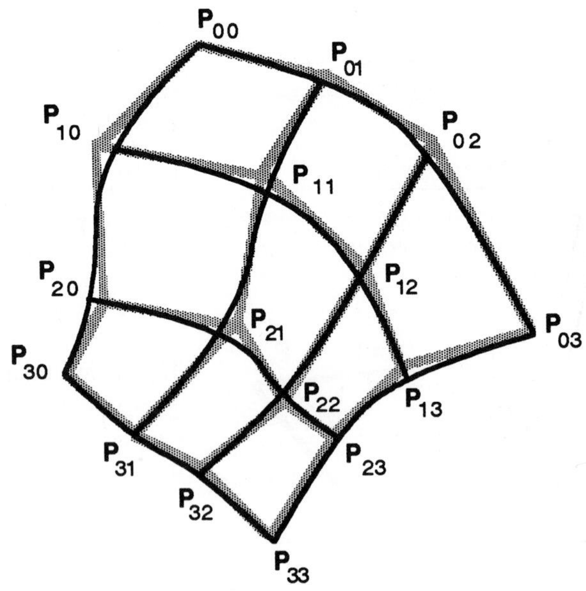

B-splines can be generalized to three dimensions in much the same way that Béizer curves are generalized. The parametric equation for B-spline surfaces is

$$P(u,v) = \sum_{j=0}^{m} \sum_{k=0}^{n} \mathbf{p}_{j,k} N_{j,s}(u) N_{k,t}(v)$$

where the blending functions $N_{j,s}$ and $N_{k,t}$ are of degree $s - 1$ and $t - 1$ respectively. The control points $\mathbf{p}_{j,k}$ define the patch, but are generally not on the patch.

For any type of spline construction, the set of patches depends heavily on the shape of the object being modeled. The density of control points in an area is proportional to the curvature of the object. Planar areas can be treated with 1 patch and 16 control points; areas of high curvature require more control points and, hence, a large number of patches (figure 8.2.18). Most systems allow the user to specify the smoothness of the surface but reserve the actual subdivision into patches for the program. Subdivision is usually done recursively.

Computing the values for a parametric bicubic surface requires numerous multiplications. The number of multiplications can be reduced by applying Horner's rule for factoring:

$$f(u) = au^3 + bu^2 + cu + d = [(au + b)u + c]u + d$$

But all the multiplications are real multiplications. The values can be computed more efficiently by using differences in function values between consecutive points.

FIGURE 8.2.17

Two successive patches with common edge Q1,Q2,Q3,Q4

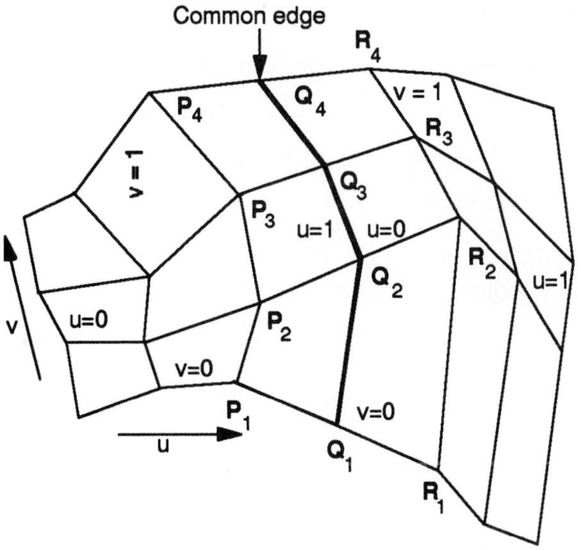

FIGURE 8.2.18

Areas with high curvature, such as the bottom section of this surface, require more patches for a realistic rendering.

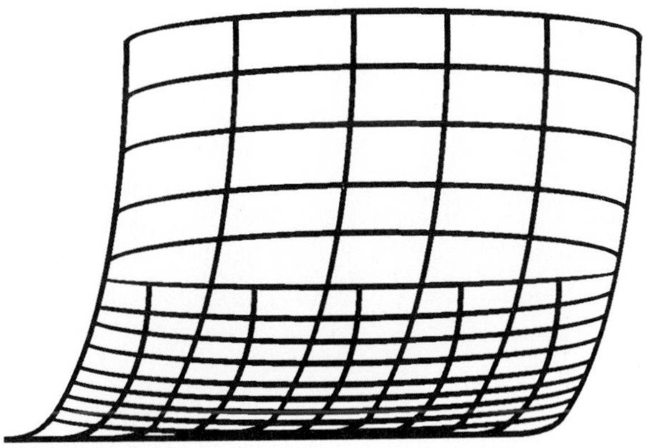

When the value of the parameter u is increased by a small amount, $\delta > 0$, the amount of change in the function value Δf is computed by

$$\Delta f(u) = f(u + \delta) - f(u)$$

This difference is called the **forward difference.** The value of $f(u + \delta)$ can be computed directly from $\Delta f(u)$:

$$f(u + \delta) = f(u) + \Delta f(u)$$

If the values of f are computed iteratively, then f_i is associated with f(u), and f_{i+1} with $f(u + \delta)$. With these substitutions the equation becomes

$$f_{i+1} = f_i + \Delta f_i$$

The forward difference for the cubic polynomial can be computed directly as follows:

$$\Delta f(u) = f(u + \delta) - f(u) = 3au^2\delta + u(3a\delta^2 + 2b\delta) + a\delta^2 + b\delta^2 + c\delta$$

Unfortunately, this formula is still quadratic. To reduce the degree of Δf, you find its forward difference, $\Delta^2 f$:

$$\Delta^2 f(u) = \Delta f(u + \delta) - \Delta f(u)$$

In an iterated process:

$$\Delta^2 f_i = \Delta f_{i+1} - \Delta f_i$$

Evaluating $\Delta^2 f(u)$, you get

$$\Delta^2 f(u) = 6a\delta^2 u + 6a\delta^3 + 2b\delta^2$$

You now have reduced the problem to a linear equation, but if you find the forward difference for $\Delta^2 f$ you get the constant equation

$$\Delta^3 f = 6a\delta^3$$

The iterative evaluation of the parametric equation begins with u = 0, so the initial values for f_0, Δf_0, $\Delta^2 f_0$ are

$$\begin{aligned} f_0 &= f(0) = d \\ \Delta f_0 &= \Delta f(0) = a\delta^3 + b\delta^2 + c\delta \\ \Delta^2 f_0 &= \Delta^2 f(0) = 6a\delta^3 + 2b\delta^2 \end{aligned}$$

At the ith iteration, f_i, Δf_i, and $\Delta^2 f_i$ are known. Their $(i + 1)^{th}$ counterparts are computed with the following sequence of equations:

$$\begin{aligned} f_{i+1} &= f_i + \Delta f_i \\ \Delta f_{i+1} &= \Delta f_i + \Delta^2 f_i \\ \Delta^2 f_{i+1} &= \Delta^2 f_i + \Delta^3 f_0 \end{aligned}$$

Figure 8.2.19 is an example of forward differences applied to the parametric function $f(u) = 2u^3 + u^2 - 2u + 1$ for u in [0,1] and $\delta = 0.1$.

For spline surfaces, there are separate parametric equations for each of the coordinate directions—that is, x(u), y(u), and z(u).

FIGURE 8.2.19

Forward differences applied to the function $f(u) = 2u^3 + u^2 - 2u + 1$.

i	u	f(u)	Δ fi	Δ^2 fi	Δ^3 fi
0	0.00	1.0000	-0.1880	0.0320	0.0120
1	0.10	0.8120	-0.1560	0.0440	0.0120
2	0.20	0.6560	-0.1120	0.0560	0.0120
3	0.30	0.5440	-0.0560	0.0680	0.0120
4	0.40	0.4880	0.0120	0.0800	0.0120
5	0.50	0.5000	0.0920	0.0920	0.0120
6	0.60	0.5920	0.1840	0.1040	0.0120
7	0.70	0.7760	0.2880	0.1160	0.0120
8	0.80	1.0640	0.4040	0.1280	0.0120
9	0.90	1.4680	0.5320	0.1400	0.0120
10	1.00	2.0000	0.6720	0.1520	0.0120

EXERCISES

8.2.1

Create vertex, edge, and polygon tables similar to those in figures 8.2.6, 8.2.7, and 8.2.8 for the unit cube shown in figure 8.2.20.

FIGURE 8.2.20

Unit cube used in exercises 8.2.1 and 8.2.2

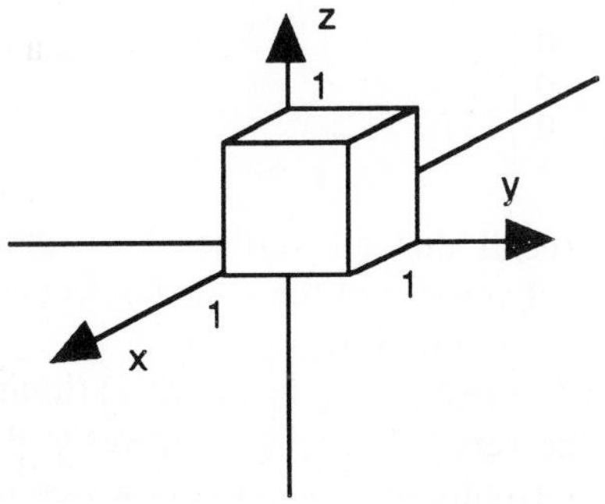

8.2.2

Create the extended edge table (figure 8.2.12) for the cube shown in figure 8.2.20.

8.2.3

Write an efficient program to compute the coefficients for the equation of a plane from the coordinates of three non-collinear points.

8.2.4

Write a procedure that checks the consistency of data tables for a polygon mesh.

8.2.5

Using forward differences on the parametric equations, write a procedure that uses forward differences on parametric equations to compute the set of points on a spline surface.

8.2.6

Use forward differences to compute the value of $f(u) = u^3 + 2u^2 - u + 1$, when u is incremented by 0.1.

8.3 Matrix Representation of Translation and Scaling

Each two dimensional matrix representation introduced in section 3.6 has its three-dimensional counterpart. Translation and scaling are realized in three dimensions by simply adding one row and column to their matrix representations to account for the transformation of the third coordinate.

Homogeneous coordinates must again be used to represent points for translations, and as in two dimensions, the amount of translation in each direction is entered in the last row of the matrix. If the amounts of translation in each direction are given as T_x, T_y, and T_z, then the representation matrix is

$$\begin{bmatrix} 1 & 0 & 0 & 0 \\ 0 & 1 & 0 & 0 \\ 0 & 0 & 1 & 0 \\ T_x & T_y & T_z & 1 \end{bmatrix}$$

It is often necessary to translate a point to the origin (figure 8.3.1). If the homogeneous coordinates of the point are (a,b,c, 1), then the translation matrix is given by

$$\begin{bmatrix} 1 & 0 & 0 & 0 \\ 0 & 1 & 0 & 0 \\ 0 & 0 & 1 & 0 \\ -a & -b & -c & 1 \end{bmatrix}$$

To invert a translation, points must be moved an equal distance in the opposite direction. What is the matrix representation of this translation?

Scaling is done by multiplying the homogeneous coordinates of a point by a matrix with the scaling factors on the main diagonal. The following is an example of such multiplication:

$$[x'\ y'\ z'\ 1] = [x\ y\ z\ 1] \begin{bmatrix} S_x & 0 & 0 & 0 \\ 0 & S_y & 0 & 0 \\ 0 & 0 & S_z & 0 \\ 0 & 0 & 0 & 1 \end{bmatrix}$$

Here S_x, S_y, S_z are the scaling factors. Recall that all vertices have their coordinates multiplied by scaling factors, so all vertices of the scaled object are moved unless one of the vertices is the origin (figure 8.3.2).

To scale a polygonal object and fix one of its vertices, say $(x_0,y_0,z_0,1)$ (figure 8.3.3), you first translate the object so that the vertex $(x_0,y_0,z_0,1)$ moves to the origin (figure 8.3.4). The scaling takes place (figure 8.3.5) and is followed by the inverse of the original translation (figure 8.3.6).

FIGURE 8.3.1

Translation of the point (a,b,c,1) to the origin

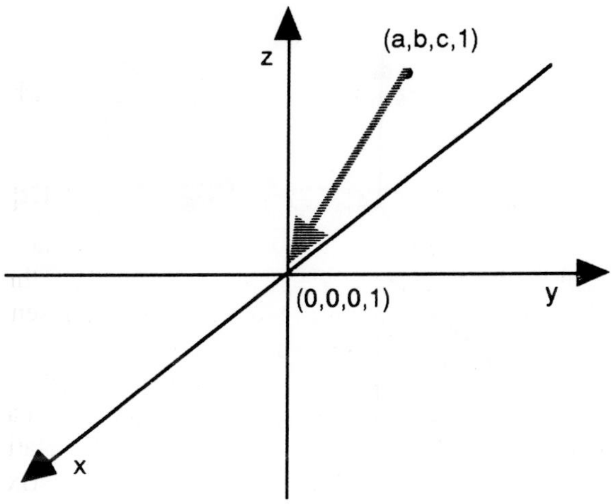

FIGURE 8.3.2

All vertices of a polygon are moved by scaling unless one of the vertices is the origin.

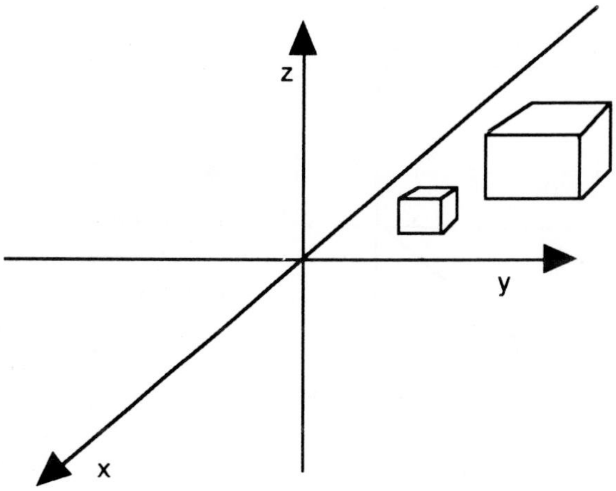

FIGURE 8.3.3

It is possible to scale a polygon and fix a vertex, but it must be done through a sequence of transformations.

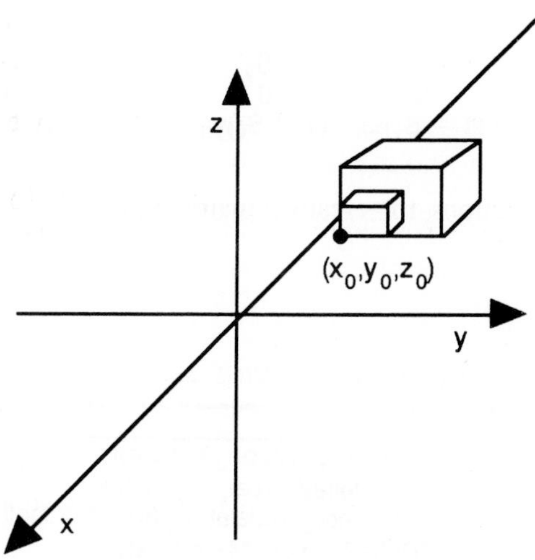

FIGURE 8.3.4

The first transformation in scaling with a fixed point is the translation of the fixed point to the origin.

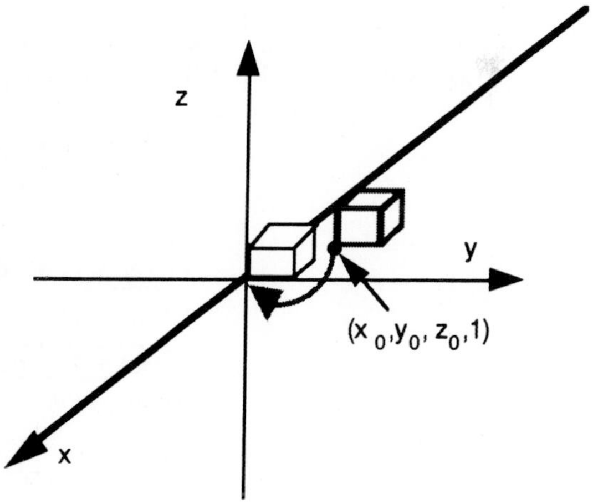

FIGURE 8.3.5

Next, the polygon is scaled by the desired factors.

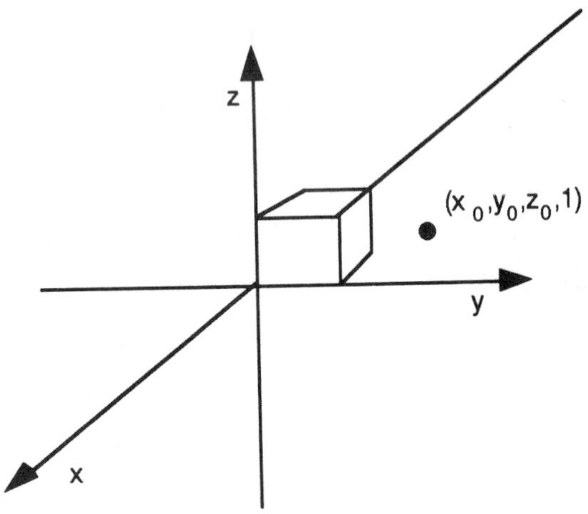

FIGURE 8.3.6

Finally, the polygon is translated so that the origin is back to the fixed point.

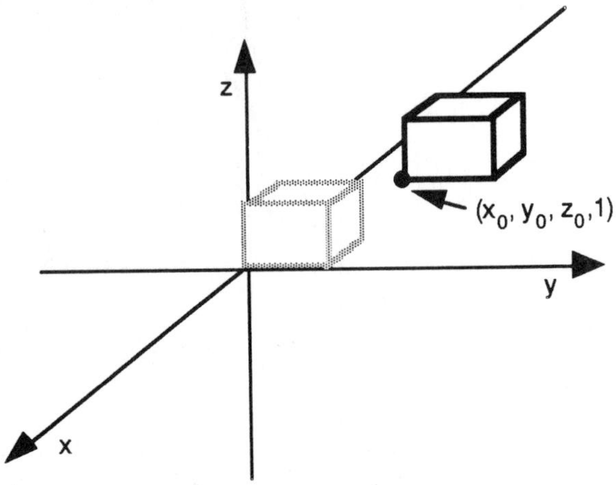

You may recall that this sequence of operations can be realized by consecutive multiplications of matrices representing each operation. Associativity of matrix multiplication allows you to compute the product of matrices before performing the transformation. Thus, the matrix representing the whole process can be computed as

$$\begin{bmatrix} 1 & 0 & 0 & 0 \\ 0 & 1 & 0 & 0 \\ 0 & 0 & 1 & 0 \\ -x_0 & -y_0 & -z_0 & 1 \end{bmatrix} \begin{bmatrix} S_x & 0 & 0 & 0 \\ 0 & S_y & 0 & 0 \\ 0 & 0 & S_z & 0 \\ 0 & 0 & 0 & 1 \end{bmatrix} \begin{bmatrix} 1 & 0 & 0 & 0 \\ 0 & 1 & 0 & 0 \\ 0 & 0 & 1 & 0 \\ x_0 & y_0 & z_0 & 1 \end{bmatrix} = \begin{bmatrix} S_x & 0 & 0 & 0 \\ 0 & S_y & 0 & 0 \\ 0 & 0 & S_z & 0 \\ (1 - S_x)x_0 & (1 - S_y)y_0 & (1 - S_z)z_0 & 1 \end{bmatrix}$$

Both PHIGS and GKS-3D have functions for creating matrices representing translations and scaling (figure 8.3.7).

FIGURE 8.3.7

Functions used to create translation and scaling matrices in PHIGS and GKS-3D.

Matrix Created	PHIGS	GKS-3D
translation	translate(DeltaX, DeltaY, DeltaZ : real)	Create_Translation_3(DeltaX, DeltaY,DeltaZ : real; M : matrix); Accumulate_Translation_3(DeltaX,DeltaY,DeltaZ : real; M : matrix);
scaling	scale (ScaleX,ScaleY, ScaleZ : real)	Create_Scale_3(ScaleX,ScaleY, ScaleZ : real; M : matrix); Accumulate_Scale_3 (ScaleX, ScaleY, ScaleZ : real; M : matrix);

EXERCISES

8.3.1

Give the matrix representing the inverse of the translation

$$\begin{bmatrix} 1 & 0 & 0 & 0 \\ 0 & 1 & 0 & 0 \\ 0 & 0 & 1 & 0 \\ T_x & T_y & T_z & 1 \end{bmatrix}$$

8.3.2

Give the matrix representing the inverse of the scaling

$$\begin{bmatrix} S_x & 0 & 0 & 0 \\ 0 & S_y & 0 & 0 \\ 0 & 0 & S_z & 0 \\ 0 & 0 & 0 & 1 \end{bmatrix}$$

8.3.3

List, in order, each operation needed to compute the inverse of a scaling operation that has fixed point $(x_0, y_0, z_0, 1)$. Give the matrix product for this inverse scaling.

8.3.4

Write a procedure to multiply two 3×3 matrices.

8.3.5

Write a procedure to implement translation that does not use matrix multiplication.

8.3.6

Write a procedure that scales a polygon by a given set of scaling factors, fixing a specified vertex of the polygon.

8.3.7

Give the transformation matrix that will translate the point $(1, -2, 3, 1)$ to $(0,0,0,1)$.

8.3.8

Give a transformation matrix that transforms a line into a line with twice the length of the original. Try your transformation on the line from (1,1,1,1) to (2,1,1,1). What line does this transformation create?

8.3.9

Give a transformation matrix that creates a line with twice the length of the line between (1,1,1,1) and (2,1,1,1) that starts at (1,1,1,1) and passes through (2,1,1,1).

FIGURE 8.4.1

The vector joining the point P_1 to the point P_2

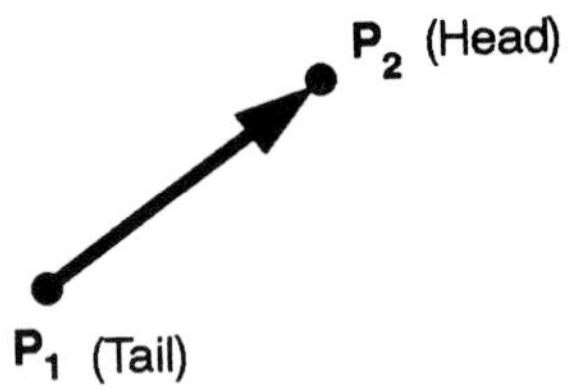

8.4 Review of Vector Operations

Just as a plane is best described by the equation given in section 8.2, lines in three dimensions are most efficiently described by vectors. A vector can be defined as the directed line segment joining two points (figure 8.4.1). The point toward which the segment is directed is called the **head,** while the other end point is called the **tail.**

This definition can be somewhat misleading because the directed line segment is actually a representative of a vector. All line segments of equal length directed in the same way, relative to a given coordinate system, are considered representatives of the same vector. A vector can be described numerically as the coordinates of the head of its representative that has its tail at the origin. A vector joining two arbitrary points, $\mathbf{P_1}$ and $\mathbf{P_2}$ (figure 8.4.2), is described numerically by the coordinates (x,y,z), where the line joining the origin to (x,y,z) is a representative of the vector joining $\mathbf{P_1}$ and $\mathbf{P_2}$.

Addition of two vectors can be defined in much the same way as addition of two matrices is defined. If $\mathbf{V}_1 = (x_1,y_1,z_1)$ and $\mathbf{V}_2 = (x_2,y_2,z_2)$ are vectors, then the sum is

$$\mathbf{V}_1 + \mathbf{V}_2 = (x_1 + x_2, y_1 + y_2, z_1 + z_2)$$

The sum has a geometric interpretation. The head of the representative of $\mathbf{V}_2$ with tail at the head of $\mathbf{V}_1$ is the head of the sum vector (figure 8.4.3).

While vector addition is important in many applications, you will find vector subtraction even more useful. Vector subtraction is defined by

$$\mathbf{V}_1 - \mathbf{V}_2 = (x_1 - x_2, y_1 - y_2, z_1 - z_2)$$

FIGURE 8.4.2

The vector joining P_1 and P_2 can be written as the triple (x,y,z)

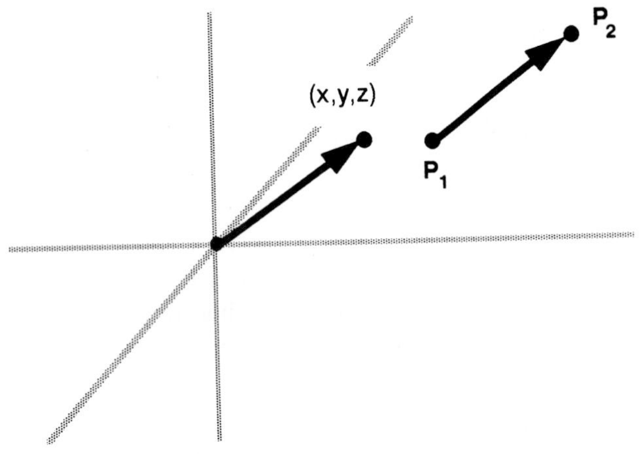

FIGURE 8.4.3

*The sum of vectors **b** + **c** can be constructed by connecting the tail of **b** with the head of the representative of **c** with the tail at the head of **b**.*

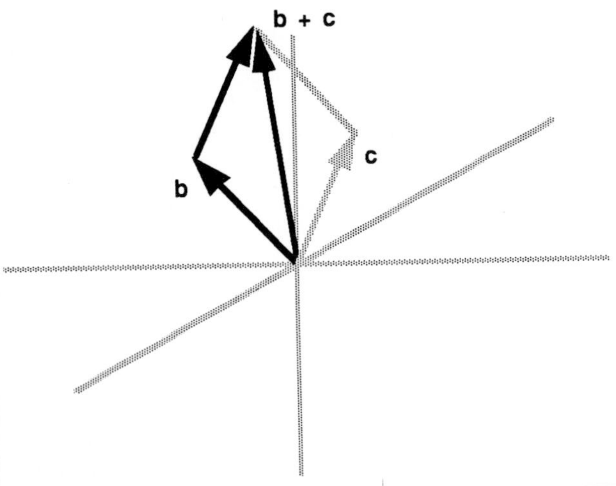

FIGURE 8.4.4

*The difference **c** − **b** can be seen as the sum **c** + −**b**.*

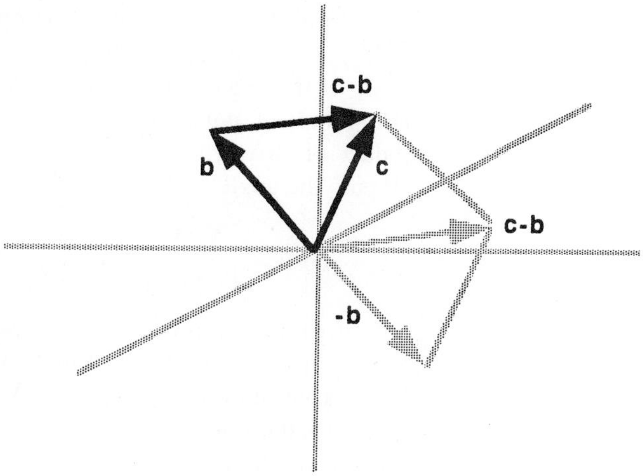

If $-\mathbf{V} = (-x,-y,-z)$ when $\mathbf{V} = (x,y,z)$, then $\mathbf{V}_1 - \mathbf{V}_2 = \mathbf{V}_1 + (-\mathbf{V}_2)$ and the geometric interpretation of a vector computed by subtraction is just the vector joining the head of $\mathbf{V}_2$ to the head of $\mathbf{V}_1$ (figure 8.4.4). Thus, the vector representing the line joining two points (x_1,y_1,z_1) and (x_2,y_2,z_2) (figure 8.4.5) is computed by

$$(x_1 - x_2,\ y_1 - y_2,\ z_1 - z_2)$$

FIGURE 8.4.5

To compute the numerical representation of the vector joining the point with coordinates (x_2,y_2,z_2) and (x_1,y_1,z_1), you need only subtract the vector (x_2,y_2,z_2) from the vector (x_1,y_1,z_1) to get $(x_1 - x_2,\ y_1 - y_2,\ z_1 - z_2)$.

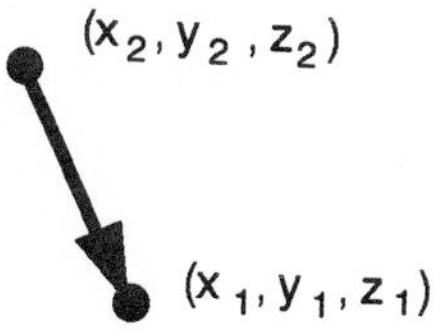

There are three different types of multiplication associated with vectors: multiplication by a real number, the scalar or dot product, and the cross or vector product. A vector $\mathbf{V} = (x,y,z)$ is multiplied by a real number r when all its coordinates are multiplied by r:

$$r\mathbf{V} = (rx,ry,rz)$$

The **length of a vector,** $\mathbf{V} = (x,y,z)$, is computed by

$$|\mathbf{V}| = \sqrt{x^2 + y^2 + z^2}$$

When the direction of a vector is more important than its length, it is convenient to use the **unit vector** in that direction. The unit vector **u** in the direction of vector **V** is computed from **V** by multiplying by real number $1/|\mathbf{V}|$—that is,

$$\mathbf{u} = (1/|\mathbf{V}|)\mathbf{V}$$

The **scalar** or **dot product** of two vectors, $\mathbf{V}_i = (x_1,y_1,z_1)$ and $\mathbf{V}_2 = (x_2,y_2,z_2)$, is the real number

$$\mathbf{V}_1 \cdot \mathbf{V}_2 = x_1x_2 + y_1y_2 + z_1z_2$$

The length of a vector, **V,** can also be computed by using the scalar product

$$|\mathbf{V}| = \sqrt{\mathbf{V}\cdot\mathbf{V}}$$

The scalar product can also be defined in terms of the angle θ between the vectors $\mathbf{V}_1$ and $\mathbf{V}_2$;

$$\mathbf{V}_1 \cdot \mathbf{V}_2 = |\mathbf{V}_1|\,|\mathbf{V}_2| \cos\theta$$

In this form, the dot product is the product of the length of one of the vectors, say $\mathbf{V}_2$, and the length of the projection of the other vector, $\mathbf{V}_1$, onto it (figure 8.4.6). If the angle between the two vectors is 90°, the vectors are said to be **orthogonal,** or **perpendicular,** to each other. Since cos90° = 0, the scalar product of two orthogonal vectors is 0. This formula also can be used to compute the angle between two vectors because

$$\cos\theta = \frac{\mathbf{V}_1 \cdot \mathbf{V}_2}{|\mathbf{V}_1|\,|\mathbf{V}_2|}$$

While the scalar product can be used to tell if two vectors are perpendicular to each other, the **vector product, or cross product,** of two vectors, $\mathbf{V}_1$ and $\mathbf{V}_2$, produces a third vector, $\mathbf{V}_1 \times \mathbf{V}_2$, which is perpendicular to each of these vectors (figure 8.4.7).

To determine the direction of the perpendicular vector, apply the right-hand rule—that is, position the fingers of your right hand so they point from the first vector in the product toward the second vector. The direction your thumb points is the direction of the vector product. To compute the vector product of vectors $\mathbf{V}_1 = (x_1,y_1,z_1)$ and $\mathbf{V}_2 = (x_2,y_2,z_2)$, use the following formula:

$$\mathbf{V}_1 \times \mathbf{V}_2 = (y_1z_2 - z_1y_2,\ z_1x_2 - x_1z_2,\ x_1y_2 - y_1x_2)$$

This form of the vector product is difficult to remember, so the following determinant form is often used as a memory aid:

$$\mathbf{V}_1 \times \mathbf{V}_2 = \left[\begin{vmatrix} 1 & 0 & 0 \\ x_1 & y_1 & z_1 \\ x_2 & y_2 & z_2 \end{vmatrix}, \begin{vmatrix} 0 & 1 & 0 \\ x_1 & y_1 & z_1 \\ x_2 & y_2 & z_2 \end{vmatrix}, \begin{vmatrix} 0 & 0 & 1 \\ x_1 & y_1 & z_1 \\ x_2 & y_2 & z_2 \end{vmatrix} \right]$$

FIGURE 8.4.6

The projection of V_1 onto V_2 has length $|V_1|$ cosθ.

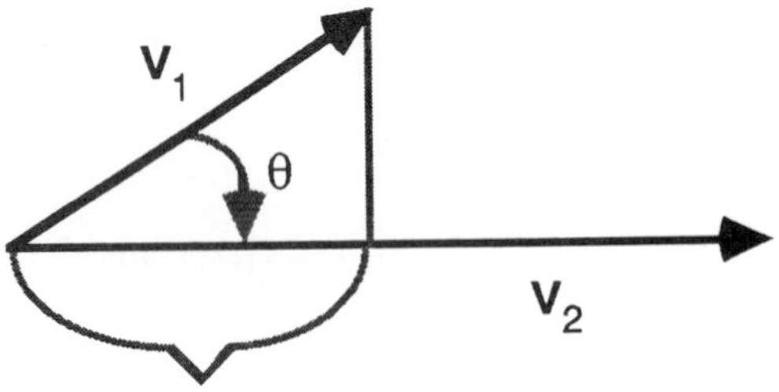

FIGURE 8.4.7

*The vector product of two vectors **v** × **u** is a vector perpendicular to the plane of **v** and **u, v, u** and **v** × **u** forming a right-hand system.*

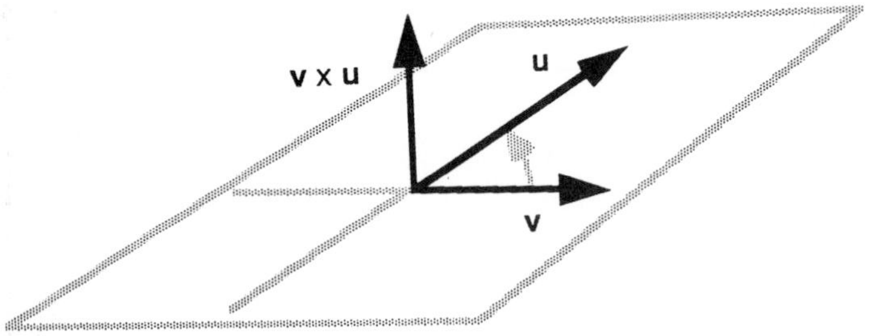

If vectors $\mathbf{V}_1$ and $\mathbf{V}_2$ have the angle θ from $\mathbf{V}_1$ to $\mathbf{V}_2$ then the vector product can be computed with

$$\mathbf{V}_1 \times \mathbf{V}_2 = \mathbf{U}\,|\mathbf{V}_1|\,|\mathbf{V}_2|\,\sin\theta$$

where **U** is the unit vector perpendicular to the plane containing $\mathbf{V}_1$ and $\mathbf{V}_2$, and for which $\mathbf{V}_1$, V_2, and **U,** in that order, form a right-handed system.

EXERCISES

8.4.1

Given the two unit vectors (1,0,0) and (0,1,0), use the scalar product to show that these vectors are perpendicular to each other.

8.4.2

Given the two unit vectors (1,0,0) and (0,1,0), use the vector product (1,0,0) × (0,1,0) to find a vector perpendicular to them. Compute the vector product of these two vectors in reverse order. What is the difference? Are either of the products unit vectors?

8.4.3

Use one of the vector products from exercise 8.4.2 to compute the equation of the xy-plane.

8.4.4

In the two-dimensional matrix representation of a rotation it is necessary to compute the sine and cosine of the angle between a line and its rotated form. The cosine of the angle between two vectors can be computed directly from its scalar product, while the sine can be computed from the vector product. Create a formula for the cosine that uses the scalar product, and a formula for the sine from the vector product.

8.4.5

Write a procedure to subtract one vector from another.

8.4.6

Write procedures for computing the dot product and the vector product of two vectors.

8.4.7

Write a procedure to create a unit vector in the direction of a given vector.

8.5 Rotations

In three-dimensional spaces, objects may be rotated about a line called an axis. Rotations about the x-, y-, or z-axes are relatively simple, corresponding closely to a rotation about the origin in a plane. Rotations about an arbitrary axis are implemented as a sequence of simpler transformations.

When an object is rotated about the z-axis, the z-coordinate of every point is maintained while the x- and y-coordinates are changed (figure 8.5.1). The new coordinates are computed as they were for rotations about the origin in two dimensions.

$$\begin{aligned} x' &= x\cos\theta - y\sin\theta \\ y' &= x\sin\theta + y\cos\theta \\ z' &= z \end{aligned}$$

where θ is the angle of rotation. This set of equations can be represented by the matrix equation in homogeneous coordinates

$$[x'\ y'\ z'\ 1] = [x\ y\ z\ 1]\begin{bmatrix} \cos\theta & \sin\theta & 0 & 0 \\ -\sin\theta & \cos\theta & 0 & 0 \\ 0 & 0 & 1 & 0 \\ 0 & 0 & 0 & 1 \end{bmatrix}$$

A rotation about the x-axis will fix all x-coordinates while y and z are recalculated (figure 8.5.2). To maintain the proper relationship between the three axes, the three coordinates are transformed by the cyclic permutation; x replaces z, y replaces x, and z replaces y. This permutation results in the following rotation equations:

$$\begin{aligned} x' &= x \\ y' &= y\cos\theta - z\sin\theta \\ z' &= y\sin\theta + z\cos\theta \end{aligned}$$

FIGURE 8.5.1

A point rotated about the z-axis has its z-coordinate fixed.

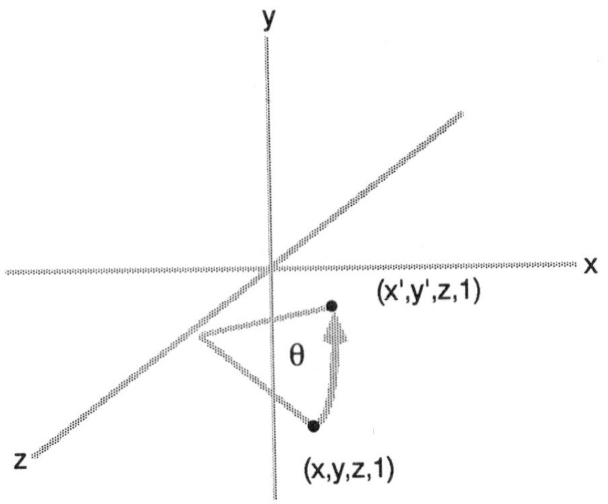

FIGURE 8.5.2

A point rotated about the x-axis has its x-coordinate fixed.

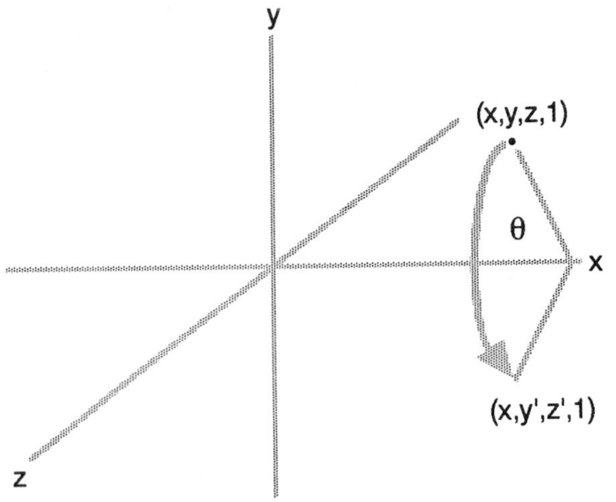

The matrix equation that represents this set of equations is

$$[x'\ y'\ z'\ 1] = [x\ y\ z\ 1]\begin{bmatrix}1 & 0 & 0 & 0\\ 0 & \cos\theta & \sin\theta & 0\\ 0 & -\sin\theta & \cos\theta & 0\\ 0 & 0 & 0 & 1\end{bmatrix}$$

The equations for a rotation about the y-axis (figure 8.5.3) are obtained by applying the permutation z replaces x, x replaces y, and y replaces z to the equations for a rotation about the z-axis:

$$\begin{aligned} x' &= z\sin\theta + x\cos\theta \\ y' &= y \\ z' &= z\cos\theta - x\sin\theta \end{aligned}$$

The matrix equation for the rotation about the y-axis is

$$[x'\ y'\ z'\ 1] = [x\ y\ z\ 1]\begin{bmatrix}\cos\theta & 0 & -\sin\theta & 0\\ 0 & 1 & 0 & 0\\ \sin\theta & 0 & \cos\theta & 0\\ 0 & 0 & 0 & 1\end{bmatrix}$$

Each of the rotations about one of the coordinate axes has the property that its inverse function is represented by the transpose of the matrix representing it.

Rotation about an arbitrary axis would be difficult if it were not broken down into a series of transformations. First, the axis of rotation is transformed to the z-axis. Next, the rotation is performed as a rotation about the z-axis. Last, the inverse of the transformation on the axis of rotation restores objects to their final rotated positions. To summarize, the transformation of the axis of rotation involves three steps:

FIGURE 8.5.3

A point rotated about the y-axis has its y-coordinate fixed.

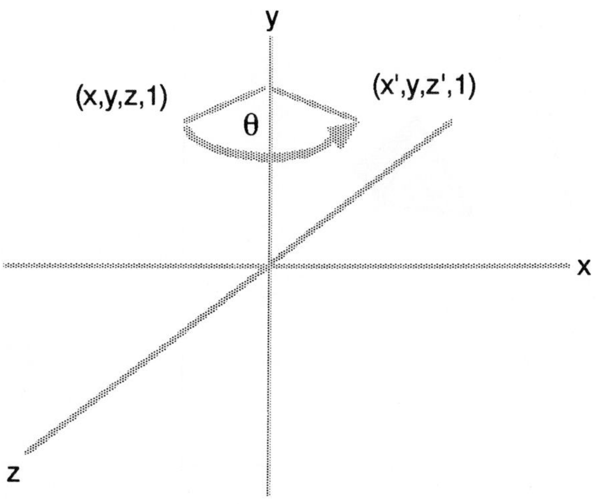

1. Translation of the axis of rotation so that it passes through the origin.
2. Rotation about the x-axis so that the axis of rotation is in the xz-plane.
3. Rotation about the y-axis so that the axis of rotation coincides with the z-axis.

The axis of rotation may be specified as the line passing through two points, say (x_1, y_1, z_1) and (x_2, y_2, z_2) (figure 8.5.4). The transformation represented by the matrix

$$T = \begin{bmatrix} 1 & 0 & 0 & 0 \\ 0 & 1 & 0 & 0 \\ 0 & 0 & 1 & 0 \\ -x_1 & -y_1 & -z_1 & 1 \end{bmatrix}$$

translates the axis so that the point (x_1, y_1, z_1) is transformed to the origin (figure 8.5.5).

The original points also define the vector

$$\mathbf{V} = (x_2 - x_1, y_2 - y_1, z_2 - z_1) = (x,y,z)$$

along the axis of rotation.

Following the translation, the axis of rotation passes through the origin and the point (x,y,z). Here you use the scalar and vector products to compute the sines and cosines in the rotation matrices, so it is useful to replace **V** with its unit vector **u** in the same direction.

$$\mathbf{u} = \frac{\mathbf{V}}{|\mathbf{V}|} = (a,b,c)$$

FIGURE 8.5.4

The axis of rotation may be specified as the line passing through two points.

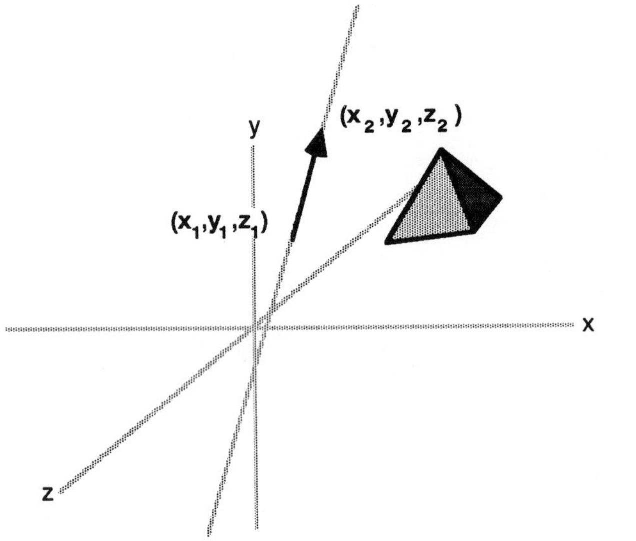

FIGURE 8.5.5

The first step in a rotation about an arbitrary axis is to translate the axis of rotation so it passes through the origin.

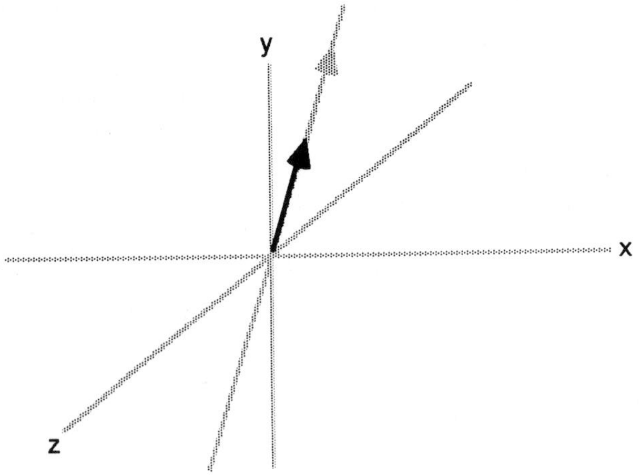

You want to rotate the vector u around the x-axis into the xz-plane (figure 8.5.6). To create this rotation matrix, you could compute the angle of rotation and then compute the appropriate sines and cosines. But you can use vector operations to compute the sine and cosine values directly. First, consider $\mathbf{u}' = (0,b,c)$, the projection of **u** into the yz-plane (figure 8.5.7). The rotation that takes **u** into the xz-plane also takes **u**′ to the z-axis. Hence, if you could calculate the sine and cosine of the angles between **u**′ and the z-axis, you could easily create the desired rotation matrix.

Let $\mathbf{u}_x = (1,0,0)$, $\mathbf{u}_y = (0,1,0)$, and $\mathbf{u}_z = (0,0,1)$ be the unit vectors along the coordinate axes. Then the formula for the scalar product gives you the following formula for the cosine of the angle, θ, between **u**′ and $\mathbf{u}_z$:

$$\cos\theta = \frac{\mathbf{u}' \cdot \mathbf{u}_z}{|\mathbf{u}'||\mathbf{u}_z|} = \frac{c}{d}$$

where $d = \sqrt{b^2 + c^2}$ is the length of **u**′.

The vector product gives you a formula for sinθ. The vector product of **u**′ and $\mathbf{u}_z$ is

$$\begin{aligned} \mathbf{u}' \times \mathbf{u}_z &= \mathbf{u}_x \, |\mathbf{u}'| \, |\mathbf{u}_z| \sin\theta \\ &= \mathbf{u}_x \, d \sin\theta \end{aligned}$$

The vector $\mathbf{u}_z$ is a unit vector, so its length is 1. The vector **u**′ has length d; thus, using the determinate form of the vector product, you get

$$\mathbf{u}' \times \mathbf{u}_z = (b,0,0) = b\,\mathbf{u}_x$$

FIGURE 8.5.6

The second step in the general rotation is to rotate the axis of rotation about the x-axis until it is in the xz-plane.

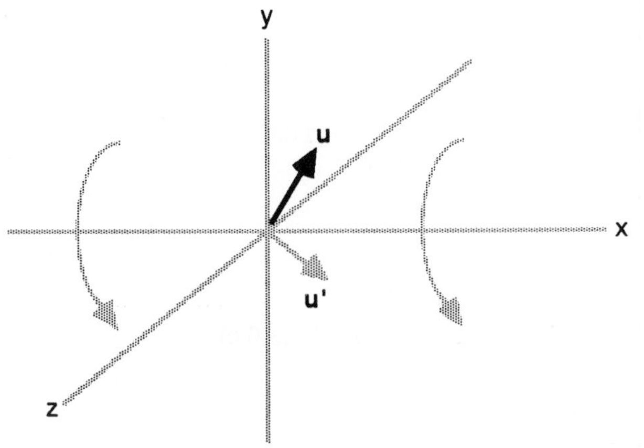

FIGURE 8.5.7

The entries in the rotation matrix may be computed directly from the coordinates' unit vectors.

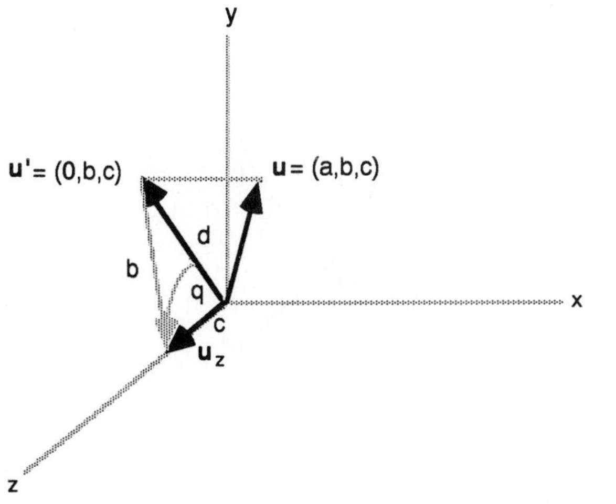

The vector d sinθ $\mathbf{u}_x$ equals the vector b $\mathbf{u}_x$, so

$$\sin\theta = b/d$$

You can substitute these values for sine and cosine directly into the matrix formulation for a rotation about the x-axis to get

$$R_x = \begin{bmatrix} 1 & 0 & 0 & 0 \\ 0 & c/d & b/d & 0 \\ 0 & -b/d & c/d & 0 \\ 0 & 0 & 0 & 1 \end{bmatrix}$$

Let $\mathbf{u}''$ be the rotation of $\mathbf{u}$ onto the xz-plane (figure 8.5.8). The projection of $\mathbf{u}''$ onto the z-axis is also the rotation of $\mathbf{u}'$ onto the z-axis. Because rotation does not change the length of a vector, the rotated form of $\mathbf{u}'$ is (0,0,d). The x-component of $\mathbf{u}$ is not altered by the rotation, so $\mathbf{u}'' = (a,0,d)$.

To rotate $\mathbf{u}''$ around the y-axis until it coincides with the z-axis (figure 8.5.9), you repeat the operations used earlier to find the sine and cosine of the angle ϕ between $\mathbf{u}''$ and the z-axis. Because the vector $\mathbf{u}''$ is already in the xz-plane, it is unnecessary to use a projection of it in the computations.

First, use the scalar product to compute cosϕ:

$$\cos\phi = \frac{\mathbf{u}'' \cdot \mathbf{u}_z}{|\mathbf{u}''||\mathbf{u}_z|} = d$$

where the value d is computed directly because both $\mathbf{u}''$ and $\mathbf{u}_z$ are unit vectors.

The sine is computed by combining the two formulas for the vector product

$$\mathbf{u}'' \times \mathbf{u}_z = \mathbf{u}_y\, |\mathbf{u}''|\, |\mathbf{u}_z| \sin\phi$$

FIGURE 8.5.8

*the vector **u**″ is the rotation of vector **u** into the xz-plane.*

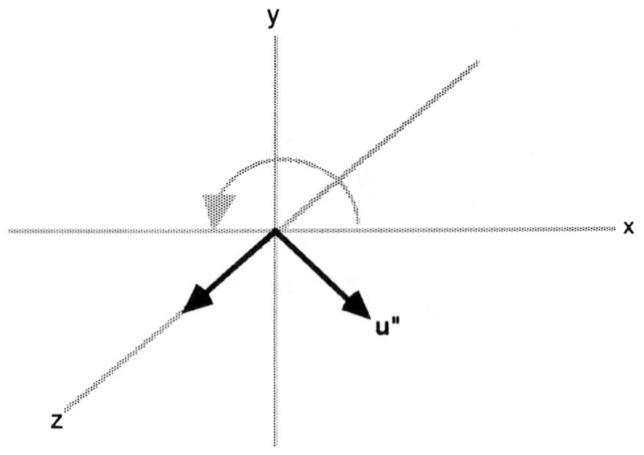

FIGURE 8.5.9

*The vector **u**″ is rotated about the y-axis unit it coincides*

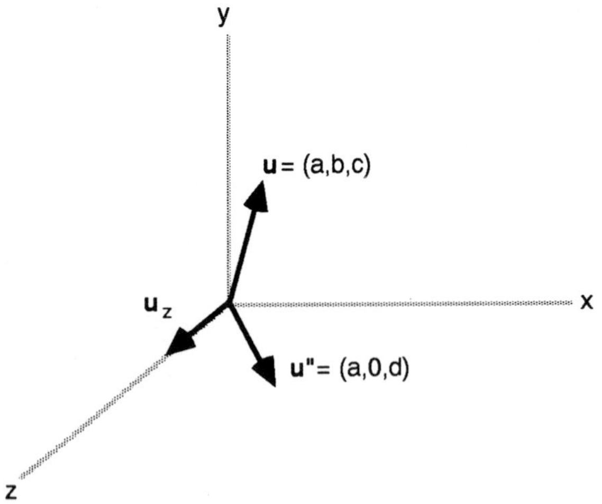

and

$$\mathbf{u}'' \times \mathbf{u}_z = (-a)\,\mathbf{u}_y$$

As both $\mathbf{u}''$ and $\mathbf{u}_z$ have length 1,

$$\sin\phi = -a$$

These values for the sine and cosine are substituted into the general matrix representation for a rotation about the y-axis to get

$$R_y = \begin{bmatrix} d & 0 & a & 0 \\ 0 & 1 & 0 & 0 \\ -a & 0 & d & 0 \\ 0 & 0 & 0 & 1 \end{bmatrix}$$

Finally, if the angle of the original rotation is ϕ, you rotate through this angle about the z-axis. This transformation is represented by

$$R_\phi = \begin{bmatrix} \cos\phi & \sin\phi & 0 & 0 \\ -\sin\phi & \cos\phi & 0 & 0 \\ 0 & 0 & 1 & 0 \\ 0 & 0 & 0 & 1 \end{bmatrix}$$

To get the matrix representation of rotation $R(\phi)$ about the arbitrary axis, you compute the matrix product

$$R(\phi) = T\,R_x\,R_y\,R_\phi\,R_y^{-1}\,R_x^{-1}\,T^{-1}$$

PHIGS and GKS-3D provide functions for creating matrices to represent rotations about coordinate axes and the matrix products used to represent general rotations (figure 8.5.10).

FIGURE 8.5.10

PHIGS and GKS-3D provide a means to create matrices representing rotations about the coordinate axes, and a method for composing these matrices with other transformation matrices to create the matrices representing general rotations.

Matrix Created	PHIGS	GKS-3D
rotations about a coordinate axis	RotateX(Angle : real); RotateY(Angle : real); RotateZ(Angle : real);	Create_Rotation_3X(theata,phi : real; m : matrix); Create_Rotation_3Y(theata,phi : real; m : matrix); Create_Rotation_3Y(theata,phi : real; m : matrix);
compostion	SetLocalTransformation (Maxtrix : matrix_4by4; mode : (Replace, PreConcatenate, PostConatenate))	Accumulate_Rotation_3X(theata,phi : real; m : matrix); Accumulate_Rotation_3Y(theata,phi : real; m : matrix); Accumulate_Rotation_3Z(theata,phi : real;m : matrix);

EXERCISES

8.5.1

Compute the matrices R_y^{-1}, R_x^{-1}, and T^{-1}.

8.5.2

Compute the matrix representing R(ϕ).

8.5.3

Write a procedure to rotate an object through a given angle about a specified axis.

8.6 Reflections and Shears

Two simple transformations that have many applications are reflections and shears. Conversion from a right-hand coordinate system to a left-hand coordinate system is a reflection through the xy-plane. A point with coordinates (x,y,z,1) in a right-hand system has coordinates (x,y,−z,1) in the corresponding left-hand system. To convert from the right-hand system to the left-hand system, one need only apply the reflection represented by

$$\begin{bmatrix} 1 & 0 & 0 & 0 \\ 0 & 1 & 0 & 0 \\ 0 & 0 & -1 & 0 \\ 0 & 0 & 0 & 1 \end{bmatrix}$$

Similar matrices represent reflections through the other coordinate planes. Reflections through an arbitrary plane are realized by applying a sequence of rotations and reflections.

Shears in three dimensions are similar to those in two dimensions because one of the coordinates is fixed while the other coordinates have multiples of the fixed coordinate added to them. The following matrix represents a y-axis shear.

$$\begin{bmatrix} 1 & 0 & 0 & 0 \\ a & 1 & b & 0 \\ 0 & 0 & 1 & 0 \\ 0 & 0 & 0 & 1 \end{bmatrix}$$

In this transformation, the y-coordinate of a point is held constant while constants are added to the x- and z-coordinates.

EXERCISES

8.6.1

Write a procedure that returns the matrix representing a specified reflection through the x-, y-, or z-plane.

8.6.2

Write a procedure that returns the matrix representing a specified x-, y-, or z-shear.

8.6.3

Find the sequence of transformations needed to reflect through an arbitrary plane. Write the matrix representation of this transformation.

8.6.4

Find the sequence of transformations needed for a shear in an arbitrary plane. Write the matrix representation of this transformation.

8.7 Transformation of Coordinate Systems

Recall that for right-hand coordinate systems, one standard orientation uses the graphics screen as the xy-plane. This orientation results in the positive z-axis pointing out of the screen (figure 8.7.1). If the left-hand system has the xy-plane coinciding with the screen, then the positive z-axis points into the screen (figure 8.7.2). In either of these orientations, the viewer is looking directly down the z-axis.

While this orientation simplifies the display of an object, it does not always present the desired view. This can be a particularly vexing problem with animation. An example of this type of situation is camera (viewer) placement in space movies (Blinn 1988). A typical sequence in such movies shows a spaceship at point **f** orbiting a planet at point **a.** Both the planet and ship are moving along different curved paths at different rates of speed. To create

FIGURE 8.7.1

The right-hand orientation of a coordinate system results in the positive z-axis pointing out of the screen.

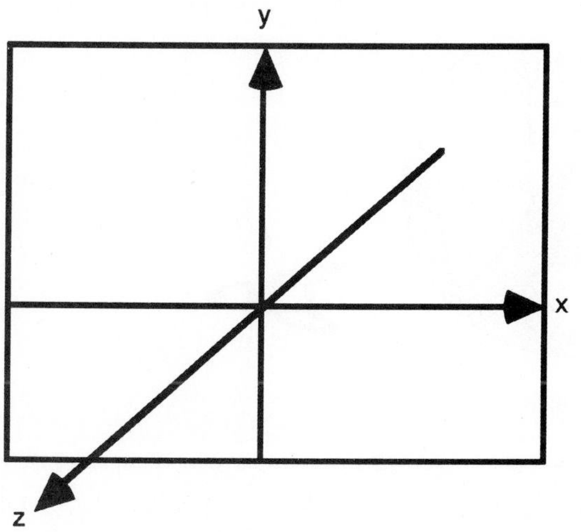

FIGURE 8.7.2

The left-hand orientation of a coordinate system results in the positive z-axis pointing into the screen.

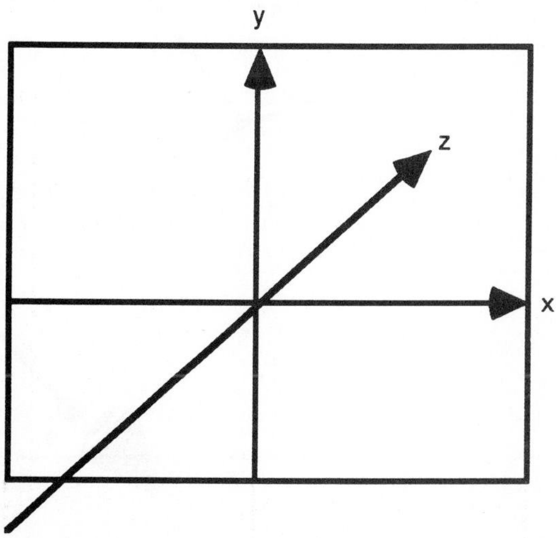

realistic motion, the paths of both ship and planet are computed in world coordinates by means of Kepler's methods for computing orbital motion (figure 8.7.3). The camera is normally placed at point **e,** so both the object being tracked by the camera and the camera are on the z-axis. To facilitate such camera placement, all positions are converted to a new coordinate system called **view coordinates.**

Other considerations in this problem include the separation of the ship and planet on the screen, the distance from the camera to the object being tracked, and the need to track one or the other object. This brief discussion considers only the change of coordinates.

Suppose the camera is to track the planet. You then need to create a new coordinate system with the camera and the planet on the z-axis. In addition, you want to choose the coordinate system so that the ship will appear right side up. The up direction is defined by the vector **U.** To maintain these conditions as well as position the camera and image plane in the desired place, you translate the coordinate system so that **a** is at the origin. Then the vector $\mathbf{T} = (\mathbf{a} - \mathbf{e})$, is rotated to lie along the z-axis (figures 8.7.4 and 8.7.5).

When this transformation is applied to **U**, the resulting vector should also point as close to up as possible; that is, the image of **U** should have x-component 0 (figure 8.7.6). If you assume initially that both **T** and **U** are unit vectors and that **M** is the matrix representing the rotation, you have the following matrix equations:

$$\mathbf{TM} = (0,0,1)$$

FIGURE 8.7.3

In order to create an image from a desired viewpoint, you must convert points given in the world coordinate system that are used to compute the motion of the spaceship and planets to coordinates determined by the new z-axis and the up vector ***u***.

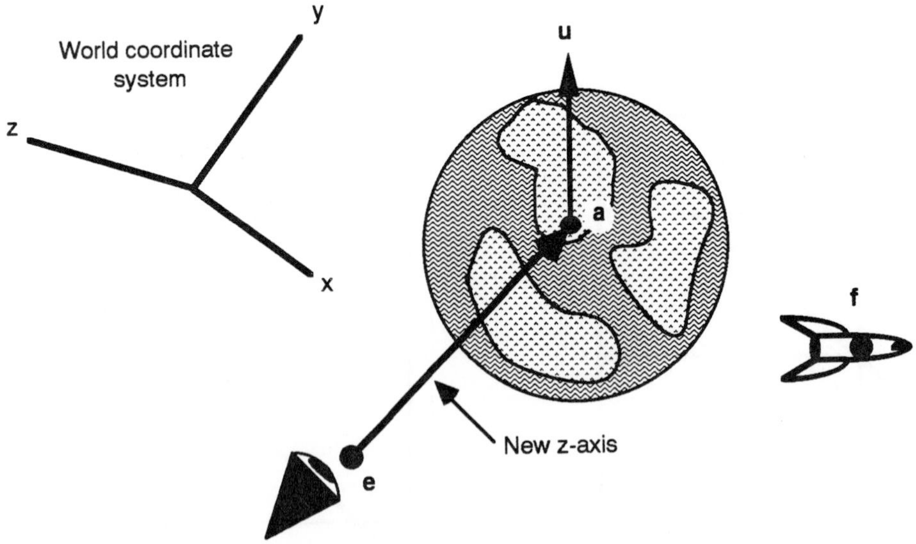

FIGURE 8.7.4

Figure 8.7.3 with the spaceship and planet removed

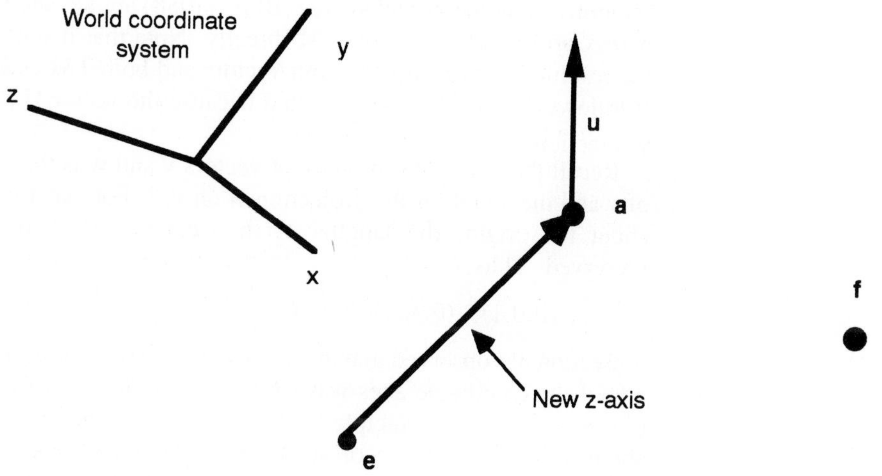

FIGURE 8.7.5

*The first step in the transformation is to translate the point **a** to the origin.*

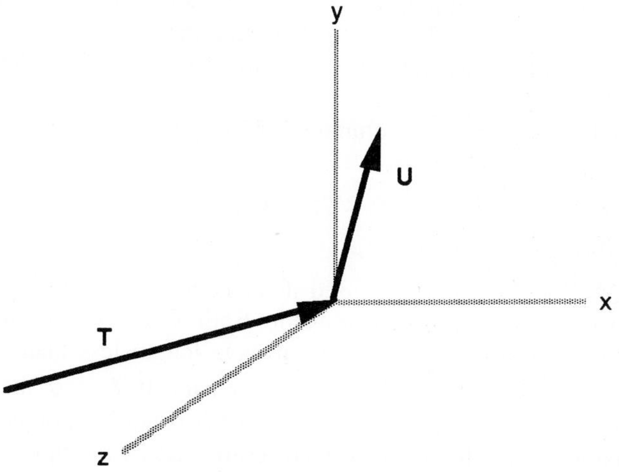

FIGURE 8.7.6

*The vector **T** is rotated by a transformation with matrix **M** so it coincides with the z-axis.*

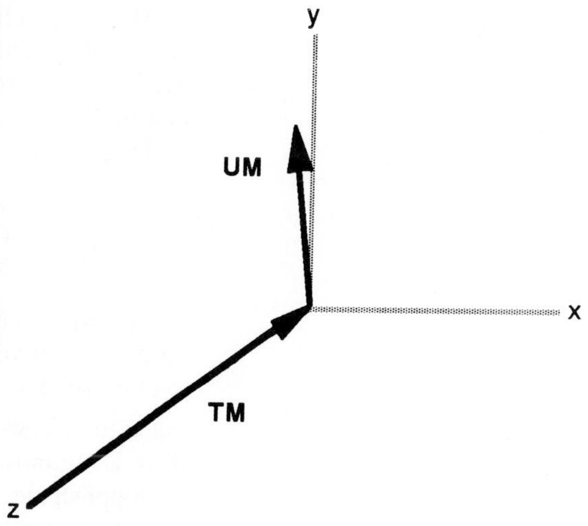

and

$$\mathbf{UM} = (0,V_y,V_z)$$

The matrix **M** may be calculated by breaking the rotation process into a series of rotations about the x- and y-axes. Blinn (1988) applies the following vector and matrix arithmetic to compute **M** directly. Note that if unit vectors are rotated, the resulting vectors are also unit vectors and both **TM** and **UM** have length 1. It follows that $V_y^2 = 1 - V_z^2$, and because the vector **U** points in the positive y-direction, $V_y = \sqrt{1 - V_z^2}$.

Recall that the scalar product of vectors **v** and **w** is the product of the length of **v** and the length of the projection **w** on **v.** If both vectors are rotated equally about the origin, the lengths of the vectors and their projections will be preserved. Thus,

$$(0,0,1) \cdot (0,V_y,V_z) = \mathbf{T} \cdot \mathbf{U}$$

Section 8.5 observed that the inverse of a matrix representing a rotation about any of the coordinate axes was, in fact, the transpose of that matrix. It is easy to demonstrate this principle because a matrix is the product of three rotations about axes. The inverse of such a product is the product of the inverses in reverse order ($(\mathbf{ABC})^{-1} = \mathbf{C}^{-1}\mathbf{B}^{-1}\ \mathbf{A}^{-1}$)). The transpose of a product of matrices is the product of the transposes in reverse order ($\mathbf{C}^t\mathbf{B}^t\mathbf{A}^t = (\mathbf{ABC})^t$). Solving the original transformation equations using $\mathbf{M}^{-1} = \mathbf{M}^t$ you get

$$\mathbf{T} = (0,0,1)\mathbf{M}^t = \mathbf{M}_3$$
$$\mathbf{U} = (0,V_y,V_z)\ \mathbf{M}^t = V_y\mathbf{M}_2 + V_z\mathbf{M}_3$$

where $\mathbf{M}_i$ is the ith row of $\mathbf{M}^t$ and therefore also the ith column of **M**. The first equation shows that the third row of $\mathbf{M}^t$ is simply **T**.

The equation $\mathbf{M}^t\mathbf{M} = \mathbf{I}$, the identity matrix, shows that the scalar product of the second row of $\mathbf{M}^t$(second column of **M**) and the first column of **M** is zero. Thus, the first and second columns of **M** are perpendicular. In fact, each column of **M** is perpendicular to the other columns of **M.** This, along with the fact that you want a right-handed system, is sufficient to show that the first column of **M**, $\mathbf{M}_1$ is the cross-product of the second ($\mathbf{M}_2$) and third ($\mathbf{M}_3$) columns of **M**, that is, $\mathbf{M}_i = \mathbf{M}_2 \times \mathbf{M}_3$.

These equations can be solved for the columns of **M** to give

$$\mathbf{M}_3 = \mathbf{T}$$
$$\mathbf{M}_2 = (1/V_y)\ \mathbf{U} - (V_z/V_y)\ \mathbf{T} = [\mathbf{U} - (\mathbf{U} \cdot \mathbf{T})\mathbf{T}]/V_y$$
$$\mathbf{M}_1 = \mathbf{M}_2 \times \mathbf{M}_3 = [\mathbf{U} \times \mathbf{T}]/V_y$$

The equations for $\mathbf{M}_2$ and $\mathbf{M}_1$ cannot be used if V_y is either imaginary or zero. Neither of these cases occurs in this problem. Both **T** and **U** are unit vectors so that $|\mathbf{T}\cdot\mathbf{U}| \leq 1$; hence, $V_z = \mathbf{T}\cdot\mathbf{U}$ must have length less than or equal to 1. Thus, the value of $V_y = \sqrt{1 - V_z^2}$ is not imaginary. If $V_y = 0$, then $\mathbf{T} = \mathbf{U}$. In most real problems, **U** can be adjusted so that it is not **T.** You can accomplish the conversion from right- to left-handed coordinates by multiplying the z-coordinate of each vector by -1 before transforming it into view coordinates.

While placement of a movie camera may not be a common application of transformations, the solution to this problem is the first step in creating realistic projections of three-dimensional objects onto graphics screens. In addition, it shows the importance of knowing the geometric interpolation of vector operations when you are solving such problems.

EXERCISE

8.7.1

Given a viewer position (e_1, e_2, e_3), planet position (a_1, a_2, a_3), and up vector (u_1, u_2, u_3), use Blinn's method to compute the transformation matrix from world to view coordinates.

BIBLIOGRAPHY

Blinn, Jim. ''Where Am I? What Am I Looking At?'' *IEEE CC&A* 8 (4): 76–81 (July 1988).

Rogers, David F., and J. Alan Adams. *Mathematical Elements for Computer Graphics*. New York: McGraw-Hill, 1976.

Strang, Gilbert. *Linear Algebra and its Applications*. 2d ed. New York: Academic Press, 1980.

Yaeger, Larry, Craig Upson, and Robert Meyers. ''Combining Physical and Visual Simulation-Creation of the Planet Jupiter for the Film ''2010.'' '' *Computer Graphics* 20 (4): 85–93 (August 1986).

CHAPTER

9

Projecting Solids Onto a Plane

DIRECTIONS

—Computer Art

The words *computer* and *art* are often taken to be a contradiction in terms conjuring up visions of a war between right and left brain. While technology and art seem to be opposites, artists have always used technology. Even the flint tools used to make bone carvings 26,000 years ago [Marshack 88] represented the best technology of their time. Since computer art presents us with a marriage between technology and art, why does computer art have so many critics?

There seem to be three main objections to computer art: it is mechanical; it is easily reproduced in quantity; and it may be employed in many different settings. Photography faced similar objections at the beginning of the twentieth century. The photographic community responded that the camera is simply a tool that captures the image the photographer sees. It is the photographer who has final control over the photographic image as well as the number of images made from a given negative. Computer artists may reasonably respond to critics as photographers did.

Image reusability sets computer art and photography apart from traditional art forms. One of the reasons paintings are valuable is that you cannot cut them up and use the pieces in a new work without destroying the originals. Critics have always conceded that using multiple negatives to create composite photographic images, or reusing parts of negatives in several images, are legitimate techniques. Critics of computer art claim that any computer art work may be cut into pieces and reassembled with other computer art to create new images, thus devaluing both the old and the new works.

Photographers in the late nineteenth century attempted to simulate work created in other media ([Cox 89] and [LeWinter 90]). Not until photographers demonstrated the uniqueness of their medium did critics begin to see photography as an art form. Like nineteenth century photographers, many computer artists today are attempting to simulate other media as they search for something that makes their medium and tools unique.

The computer's ability to produce images, such as fractals, with little human intervention except for the choice of colors is, in fact, unique. For many years artists have used this computer property to create a sequence of distortions of a given image. Interactive art is another area in which computer artists may find new directions for expression. Here the artist generates images on the computer and specifies a list of images that may be seen next. Viewers of this art, equipped with special viewing systems and interactive devices, enter a world of virtual reality where their response to the currect image dictates the next image they see. Thus, the images and the viewer's responses to them combine to form a unique art experience.

As the number of computer artists and the diversity of their work continue to grow, art critics are seeking ways to evaluate this new medium. These critics will eventually have to decide just how much human intervention is required before an image is considered to be art. In the final analysis, the success of computer art will depend on the ability of the artist to create exciting images uniquely suited to the medium.

9.1 Historical Perspective

Attempts to represent three-dimensional objects on two-dimensional surfaces date back about 35,000 years, and much of the knowledge of optics necessary to create ''realistic'' drawings comes from the ancient Greeks. Yet the depiction of scenes on two-dimensional surfaces reflects the philosophy of a culture as much as its science. When comparing the view of Florence in a fresco created about 1350 (figure 9.1.1) to a painting of the city from about 1480 (figure 9.1.2), Edgerton (1975) points out the philosophical differences between the two eras:

FIGURE 9.1.1

A view of Florence, Italy, in a fresco dating from about 1350. (Alinari/Art Resource).

FIGURE 9.1.2

A view of Florence, Italy, in a painting dating from about 1480. (Alinari/Art Resource).

Unlike the Renaissance painter depicting his scene in perspective, the medieval artist viewed his world quite subjectively. He saw each element in his composition separately and independently, and thus paid little attention to anything in the way of systematic spatial relationship between objects. He was absorbed within the visual world he was representing rather than, as with the perspective painter, standing without it, observing from a single, removed viewpoint.(21)

The two views of Florence are strikingly different because of the types of **projections** used to create them. In the medieval painting, each face of a building is projected onto the painting's plane without much regard for the other faces of that building or for the faces or positions of other buildings in the scene. This may appear to be a primitive view of the world, but mathematicians used a similar projection to illustrate a cylinder as late as the seventeenth century (figure 9.1.3). To these mathematicians, the cylinder was, in fact, two circles connected by parallel lines, and so it was pictured as such. In more recent times, Cézanne, Picasso, and other artists depicted more than one side of an object in their paintings, and even today technical drawings commonly show more than one face of an object.

FIGURE 9.1.3

Seventeenth-century mathematicians pictured a cylinder as two circles connected by parallel lines. Adapted from Edgerton 1975, 25.

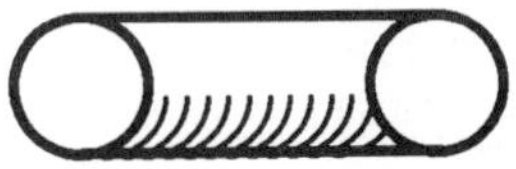

During the century spanning those two paintings of Florence, Greek and Arabic mathematics and science were reintroduced to Italy. Greek interest in optics can be traced back as far as Plato and Aristotle; however, it was Euclid's *Optica,* written in the fourth century B.C., that recorded the first uniform mathematical model of optics. Euclid's basic rule was that the diminishing apparent size of distant objects was determined by the visual angle. He used this rule to insist that parallel lines do not converge (Edgerton 1975).

Even though Euclid and Ptolemy, who lived in the second century A.D. believed that vision depended on rays emanating from the eye in a cone, their theory of linear perspective was essentially correct. While there are some written references (Edgerton 1975) that indicate linear perspective was used to create stage backdrops, no actual examples of these backdrops exit. Roman painters experimented with perspective on murals such as those at Pompeii, but did not use the linear perspective of Euclid and Ptolemy. This led to cases of visual ambiguity where it was not possible for the viewer to deduce relative distances of objects.

FIGURE 9.1.4

Euclid and Ptolemay believed that vision depended on a cone of rays emanating from the eye. Adapted from Edgerton 1975, 67.

Both Euclid and Ptolemy, who lived in the second century A.D., believed that vision depended on rays that emanated and fanned out in a cone shape from the eye (figure 9.1.4). The Greeks and Romans may have applied the ideas of Euclid and Ptolemy to art, but no examples of such art survive today.

Even before the fall of Rome, with all of the questions about geometry seemingly answered, interest in Euclidean geometry was on the decline in the Roman Empire. Then, after Roman civilization collapsed, the study of Greek mathematics and science moved to the Arab world. The Arabs not only preserved but also expanded much of the Classical Greek work in mathematics and science.

The most influential book on Arab optics was Alhazen's *Kitab al-Manazir,* or *Perspectiva.* This eleventh-century work theorized that objects are seen because of the light that they reflect, not, as Euclid thought, because of rays emanating from the eye. Alhazen also explained how the eye's lens focused light.

The work of Alhazen might not have reached Italy by the early 1400s had it not been for the small book *Perspectiva communis* (ca. 1265), by the English Franciscan John Pecham. This book incorporated some of the work of Pecham's fellow Englishmen Robert Grosseteste and Roger Bacon, but gave credit mainly to Alhazen, whom Pecham called *auctor perspectivae*.

Book such as *Perspectiva communis* spurred experiments with perspective drawing. Filippo Brunelleschi is credited with being the first person known to incorporate the principles of perspective in pictures since classical antiquity. In 1425, Brunelleschi set up a mirror in front of the Baptistery in Florence. There he carefully painted the image in the mirror on a panel of the same size. When the painting was complete, Brunelleschi drilled a hole in the panel at the position where his eye appeared in the mirror. He then held a mirror behind the hole in the picture, noting that all lines in the drawing converged to that hole. This experiment demonstrated the concept of the **vanishing point** (figure 9.1.5).

Within ten years of Brunelleschi's experiment, Leon Battista Alberti, one of his friends, recorded his experiment in the book *Della pittura* (*De pictura* in its Latin version). This book presented techniques such as how to draw a checkerboard-like floor pattern in perspective. Once the vanishing point is established, a horizontal baseline is divided into even intervals, and then a ray is drawn from the vanishing point to each mark on the baseline. A second point is plotted on a horizontal line passing through the vanishing point. Finally, a line is drawn from the second point to each intersection of a ray with the base line. In figure 9.1.6, dashed lines lead from the second point. Intersections of these lines with a ray perpendicular to the base line establish the spacing for the horizontal lines in the checkerboard pattern.

FIGURE 9.1.5

Brunelleschi's experiment demonstrated the concept of vanishing point. Adapted from Edgerton 1975, 137.

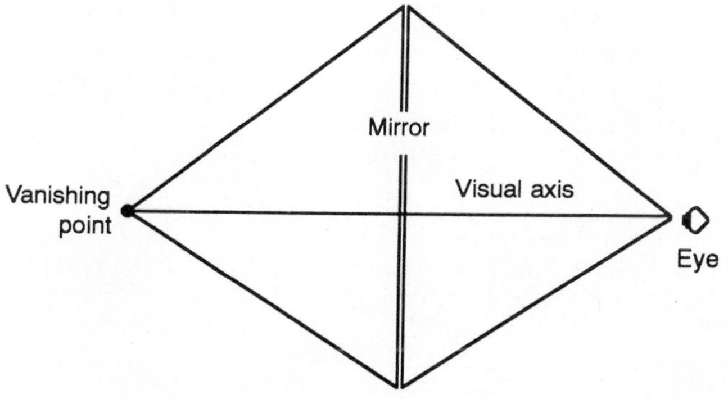

FIGURE 9.1.6

One of Brunelleschi's friends, Leon Battista Albert, demonstrated this technique for drawing a tile floor in perspective.

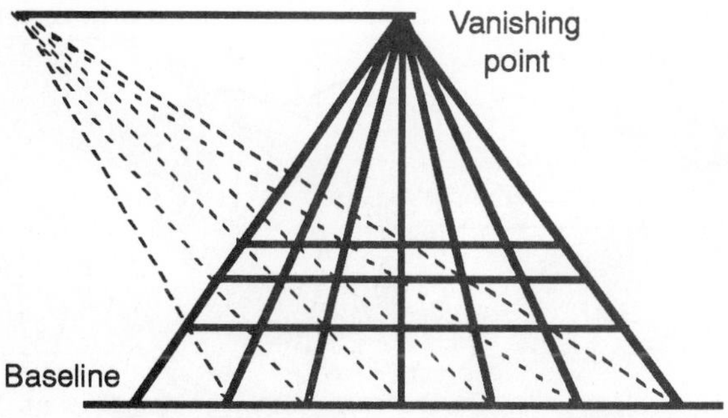

The influence of the Alberti book on artists was widespread. By 1506 German artist Albrecht Dürer had traveled to Italy, where he learned "the secret art of perspective," and throughout the 1520s and 1530s Dürer illustrated the techniques of perspective in a series of woodcuts. The Dürer woodcut in figure 9.1.7 (ca. 1538) is of particular interest to anyone creating three-dimensional computer images. The painter depicted in the woodcut faces a grid of threads stretched in a frame. The frame stands between the painter and his model, and the painter's viewpoint is fixed by a sighting post. The painter duplicates what he sees in each square of the grid in a corresponding square of the grid drawn on a piece of paper. For the computer graphics programmer trying to produce a perspective drawing, the frame with the grid (figure 9.1.8) is the computer screen, and the viewpoint is fixed as the distance from the screen to the viewer (figure 9.1.9).

One might conclude that the perspective paintings of the Renaissance period replaced the subjective representations of the medieval painters, yet, both methods of projection have proved useful in computer graphics. Technical artists project each side of an object directly onto the screen, while perspective projections are often used to create natural-looking scenes.

9.2 Projections

Artists and technicians faced with the problem of reproducing three-dimensional objects on a plane surface frequently use variations of two basic projections: the **parallel projection** and the **perspective projection.** Objects are re-created on a surface, called the **projective plane,** by projecting every point on the object along a line to the projective plane. The lines used in a parallel projection are parallel to one another (figure 9.2.1), and the lines used in the perspective projection meet at a point called the **center of projection** (figure 9.2.2).

FIGURE 9.1.7

During the 1520s and 1530s Albrecht Dürer created a series of woodcut prints to illustrate the techniques of perspective. (Art Resource).

FIGURE 9.1.8

The Renaissance painters employed a grid of threads to reproduce objects in perspective.

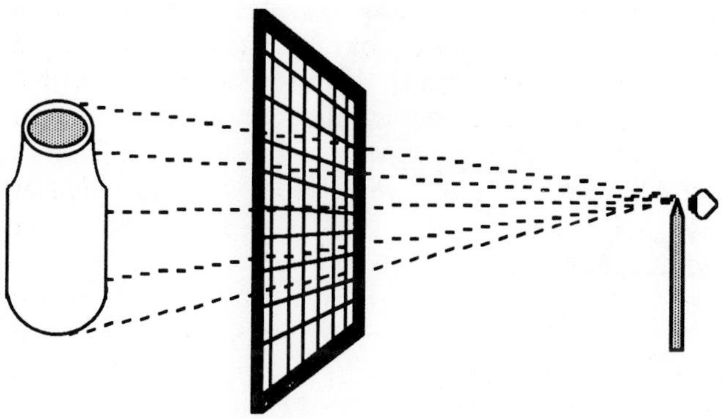

FIGURE 9.1.9

For the computer graphics programmer, the pixels of a CRT screen replace Dürer's grid of threads.

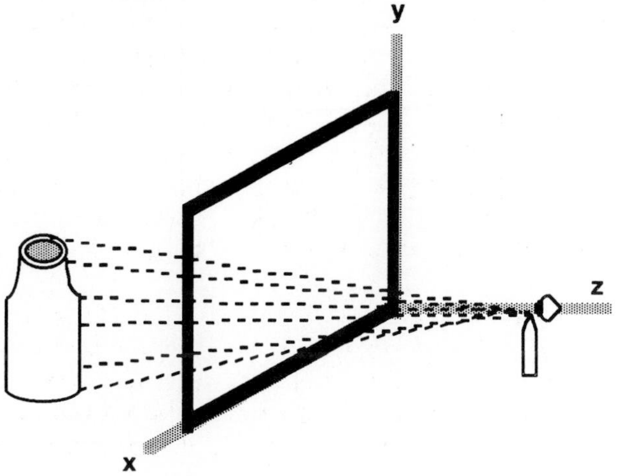

FIGURE 9.2.1

The projection lines are parallel to one another in a parallel projection.

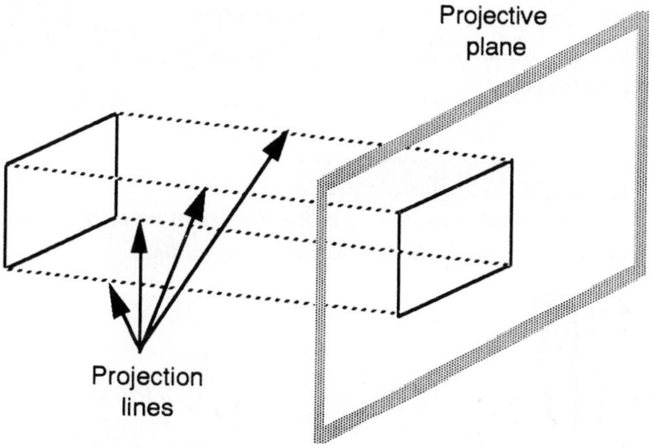

FIGURE 9.2.2

The lines of a perspective projection pass through a point called the center of projection.

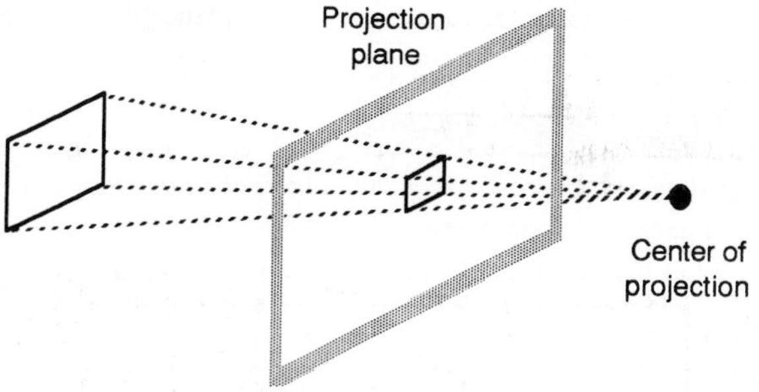

Parallel projections are the easiest type of projection to implement. The distance from an object to the projective plane does not affect the drawing because the projection lines are parallel. The angle at which the projection lines intersect the projective plane does, however, alter the appearance of an image, so parallel projections are classified by this angle. As you may recall, when the lines of projection are perpendicular to the projective plane (figure 9.2.3), the projection is called orthogonal.

FIGURE 9.2.3

A parallel projection in which the lines of projection are perpendicular to the projective plane

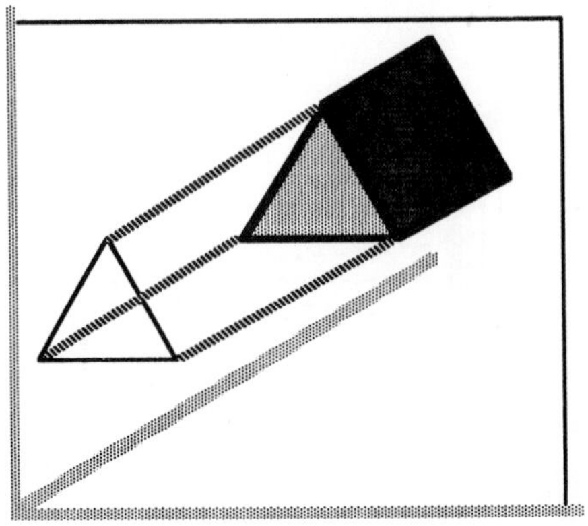

Drafters use orthogonal projections, called **elevations,** to show the front, sides, and back of an object, as well as to show top views called **plans.** Distances and angles can be measured directly from these projections because the projective plane is parallel to faces of the objects.

Orthogonal projections may also show more than one face of an object (figure 9.2.4). These projections are called **axonometric.** Lines that are not parallel to the projective plane are shortened in these projections (figure 9.2.5). Axonometric projections that equally foreshorten lines along each of the principal axes are called **isometric.**

FIGURE 9.2.4

An orthogonal projection that shows more than one face of an object is called axonometric.

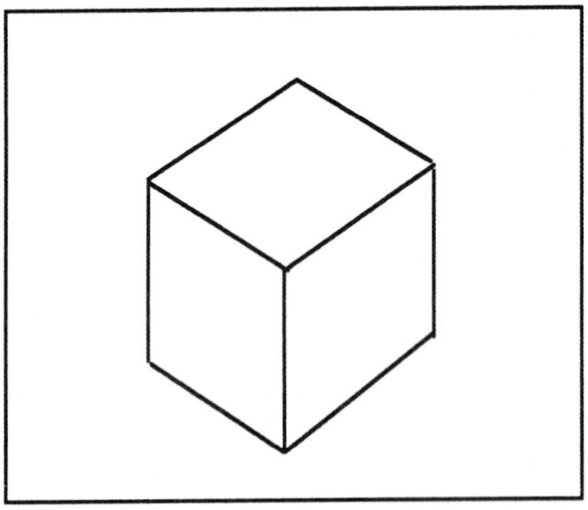

FIGURE 9.2.5

An orthogonal projection of a line that is not parallel to the projective plane is shorter than the original line.

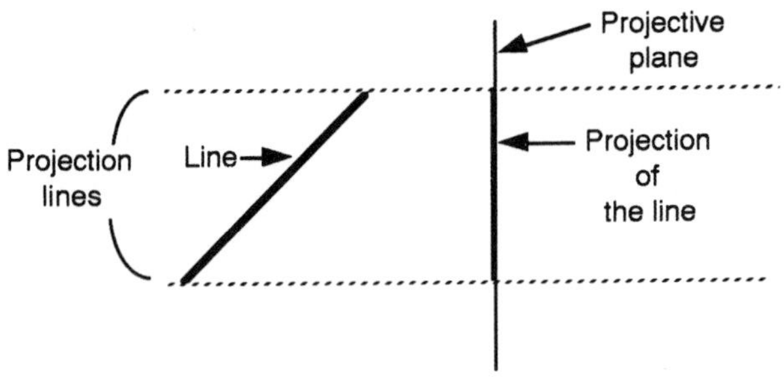

Orthogonal projections can be implemented by rotating an object so that the lines of projection are perpendicular to the xy-plane, and then projecting every point (x,y,z) of the rotated image to (x,y,0).

When the points of an object are projected along parallel lines that are not perpendicular to the projective plane, the projection is called **oblique.** If a point (x,y,z) is projected to the point (x′,y′,0) along the direction of vector (x_p,y_p,z_p) (figure 9.2.6), then the vector, (x_p,y_p,z_p), is called the **projection vector.** Properties of an oblique projection are established by the choice of the projection vector. The projection vector may be defined in terms of two angles. The first of these angles, φ, is the angle that the projection vector makes with the z-axis. The second angle, θ, is determined by projecting a line parallel to the z-axis into the xy-plane. The angle θ is the angle this projection makes with the horizontal.

The equations for x′ and y′ can be expressed in terms of the angles φ and θ (figure 9.2.7)—

$$x' = x + dx = x + L\cos\theta$$
$$y' = y + dy = y + L\sin\theta$$

where L is the length of the projection of the line from (x,y,z) to (x,y,0) onto the xy-plane—

$$L = z \tan\phi$$

After substituting for L, you get the following equations for the projection:

$$x' = x + z \tan\phi \cos\theta$$
$$y' = y + z \tan\phi \sin\theta$$

FIGURE 9.2.6

The direction of the lines of projection is represented by the projection vector (x_p, y_p, z_p).

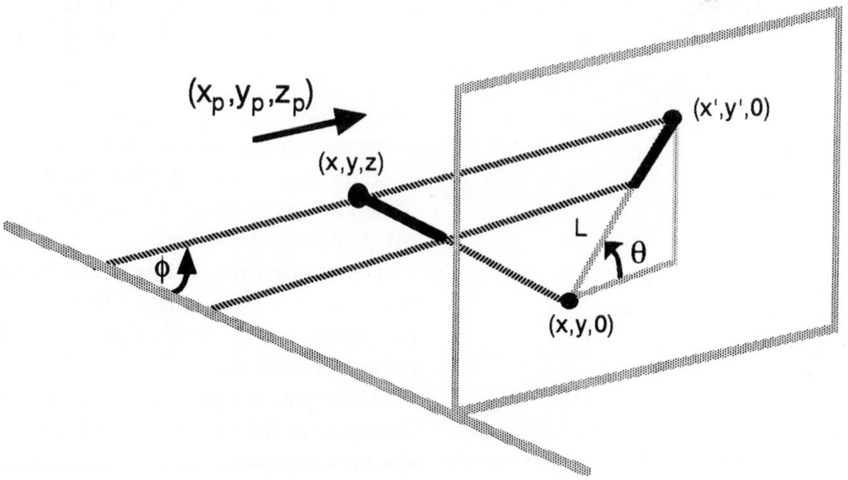

FIGURE 9.2.7

The values x' and y' of the projections of x and y can be computed with the trigonometric relationships dx = Lcosθ and dy = Lsinθ. L can be computed directly from L = ztanϕ.

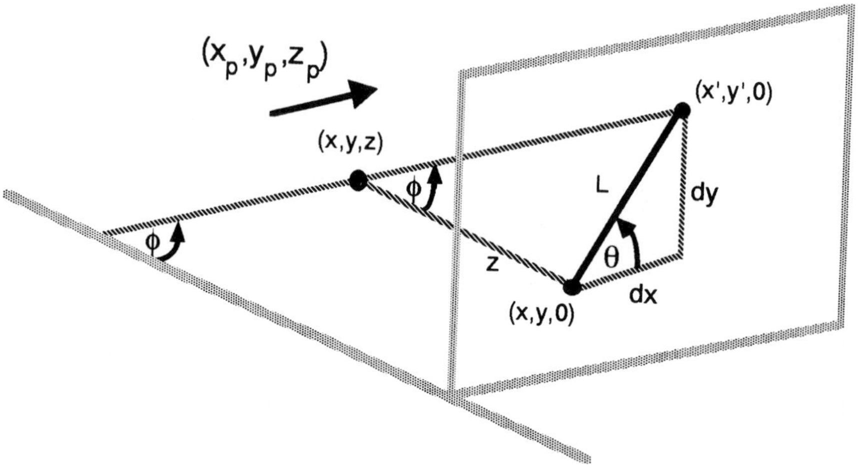

For a given projection the angles are constant, so the factors

$$\text{xfactor} = \tan\phi \cos\theta \text{ and}$$
$$\text{yfactor} = \tan\phi \sin\theta$$

can be calculated before the transformation is applied. The matrix representing this transformation is

$$\begin{bmatrix} 1 & 0 & 0 & 0 \\ 0 & 1 & 0 & 0 \\ \text{xfactor} & \text{yfactor} & 0 & 0 \\ 0 & 0 & 0 & 1 \end{bmatrix}$$

One standard oblique projection, the **cavalier projection,** preserves the lengths of lines perpendicular to the projective plane. To accomplish this, tanϕ must be 1, so the cavalier projection uses ϕ = 45° (figure 9.2.8). The second angle θ is often chosen as either 45° or 30°. Figure 9.2.9 shows a cube with 45° and 30° cavalier projections for θ.

The **cabinet projection** sends lines perpendicular to the projective plane into lines one-half their length. This is accomplished by requiring tanϕ = ½, or ϕ of approximately 26.6°. Figure 9.2.10 shows a cube with 45° and 30° cabinet projections for θ

While parallel projections are useful in technical drawing because they allow control over the orientation and size of an object's various components, they do not preserve perspective. Perspective projections are more difficult to implement because they require control of the observer's position relative to the screen.

FIGURE 9.2.8

If the lines of projection make a 45° angle with the projective plane, lines perpendicular to the projective plane have their lengths preserved.

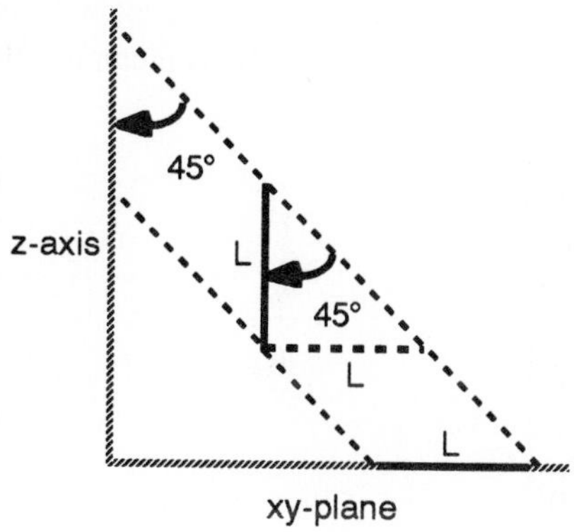

FIGURE 9.2.9

Two popular values for θ in the cavalier projection are 45° and 30°.

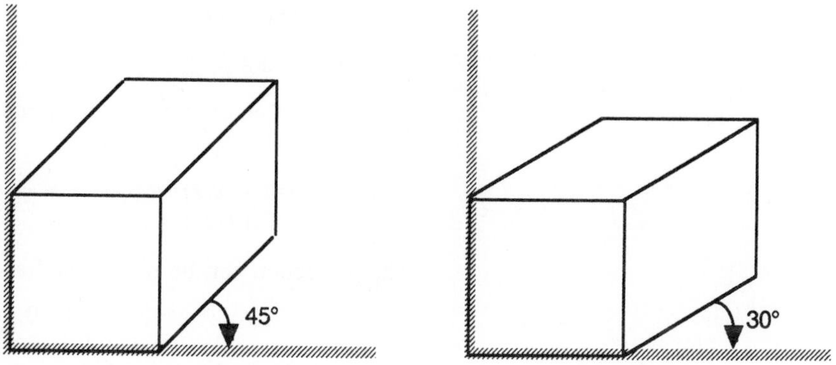

FIGURE 9.2.10

Two popular values for θ in the cabinet projection are 45° and 30°.

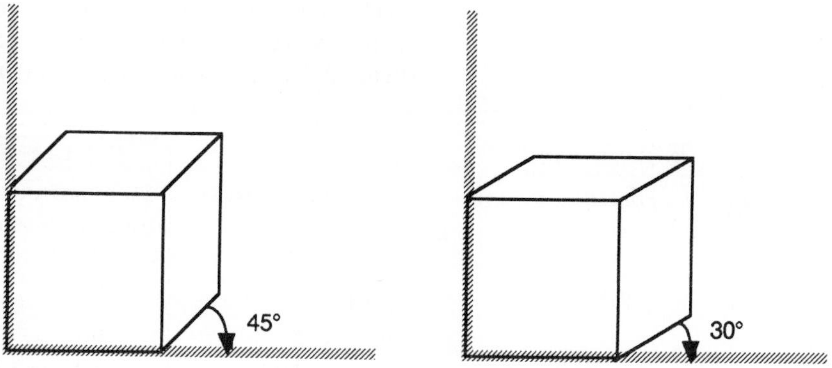

Section 8.7 noted that before an image is projected, it is transformed from world coordinates to view coordinates. View coordinates are a left-handed system with the observer positioned at the origin and the projective plane given as z = d (figure 9.2.11).

Therefore, the perspective projection of the point (x_0,y_0,z_0) is the point of intersection of the line joining (x_0,y_0,z_0) and (0,0,0) and the plane z = d. The line joining (x,y,z) and (0,0,0) can be represented by the following parametric equations:

$$x_t(t) = xt$$
$$y_t(t) = yt$$
$$z_t(t) = zt \qquad 0 \le t \le 1$$

Projection lines intersect the plane z = d for t such that $z_t(t) = d$. Solving this equation for t, you get

$$t = d/z$$

If the projection of (x,y,z) is the point (x′,y′,d) (figure 9.2.12), you can use the value of t to compute x′ and y′:

$$x' = d\,(x/z)$$
$$y' = d\,(y/z)$$

The projection can be represented as

$$[x,y,z,z/d] = [x,y,z,1]\begin{bmatrix} 1 & 0 & 0 & 0 \\ 0 & 1 & 0 & 0 \\ 0 & 0 & 1 & \frac{1}{d} \\ 0 & 0 & 0 & 0 \end{bmatrix}$$

where w = z/d.

When using this representation, the coordinates of the projection are computed from the homogeneous coordinates by the following:

$$[x',y',z',1] = [d(x/z),d(y/z),d,1]$$

The equations for x′ and y′ show that as a point moves farther from the origin (that is, z gets larger), its projection moves closer to the point (0,0,d). Thus, if an object moves farther from the origin, its projection will appear smaller (figure 9.2.13). It is also clear from the equations for x′ and y′ that if the plane

FIGURE 9.2.11

In the perspective projection, the origin of the view coordinates is the observer and the projective plane is given as z = d.

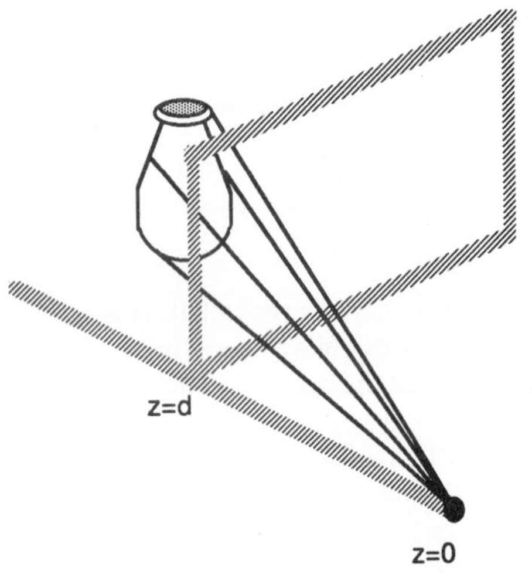

FIGURE 9.2.12

The x- and y-coordinates of the projection of a point can be computed from the equations x′ = d(x/z) and y′ = d(y/z).

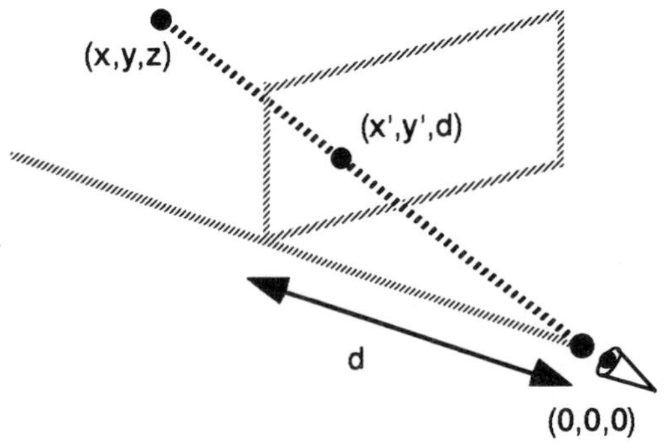

FIGURE 9.2.13

In a perspective projection, the farther an object from the center of projection, the smaller it appears.

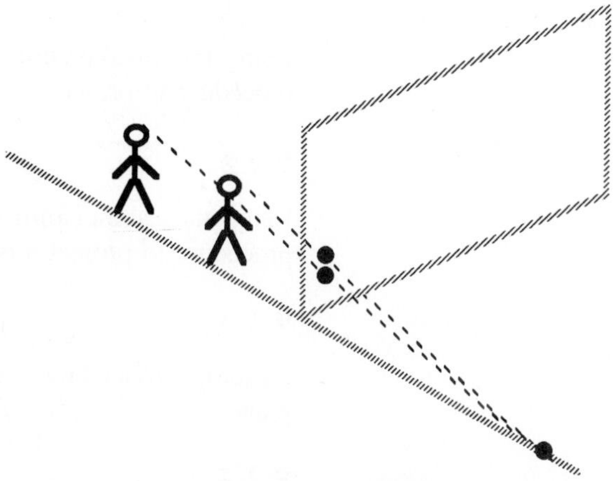

z = d is moved farther from the origin, the projection of a fixed point will move farther from the point (0,0,d) and an object at a fixed distance will appear larger.

Any set of parallel lines that are not parallel to the projective plane are projected to a set of intersecting lines. This intersection is the vanishing point demonstrated by Brunelleschi. Each set of parallel lines has a vanishing point, but those lines parallel to one of the coordinate axes converge to a **principal vanishing point.** The number of principal vanishing points depends on how many axes are parallel or contained in the projective plane. In standard view coordinates, parallel lines that are also parallel to the x- or y-axis will be projected to parallel lines. Those lines parallel to the z-axis will appear to intersect at the vanishing point (0,0,d). This type of projection has one principal vanishing point. Other orientations of the projective plane can result in two or three vanishing points (figure 9.2.14).

FIGURE 9.2.14

A projection with two vanishing points

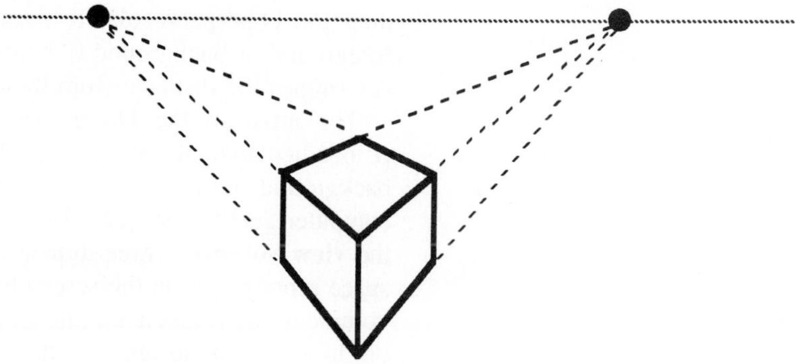

EXERCISES

9.2.1

Using the cavalier projection with fixed angle θ specified in radians, write a procedure to project a point into the xy-plane.

9.2.2

Using the cabinet projection with fixed angle θ specified in radians, write a procedure to project a point into the xy-plane.

9.2.3

Develop a procedure that computes the parallel projection of any point onto the plane $z = 0$ in a left-handed system through any angles ϕ and θ.

9.2.4

Write a procedure to implement a perspective projection with the projective plane $z = d$ for a fixed d.

9.2.5

Apply the transformations listed below on the unit cube with corners at (0,0,0), (1,0,0), (0,1,0), (1,1,0), (0,0,1), (1,0,1), (0,1,1) and (1,1,1). Draw the projections of each point for each of these:

a. The orthogonal parallel projection.
b. The cavalier projection $\theta = 45°$.
c. The cabinet projection with $\theta = 45°$.
d. The perspective projection with $d = 2$.

9.3 Clipping in Three-Dimensions

Setting a movie camera at the appropriate position to capture the movements of a spaceship in a science fiction epic is a relatively simple procedure. The view direction is perpendicular to the projective plane, there are no objects in the foreground or background to be hidden, and the desired image size of the ship determines the distance from the center of projection to the projective plane.

The artist in the Dürer print (figure 9.1.7) also had a view direction perpendicular to the projective plane as well as the problem of hiding some background items. Three-dimensional clipping hides background items on a computer graphics system. The volume of space visible after clipping is called the **view volume**. Three-dimensional clipping is used to limit the volume of space represented on the screen to a region called the **view volume.** The view volume for a perspective projection is the frustum of a pyramid. Once a window on the screen is designated, the edges of the pyramid are formed by the lines connecting the corners of this window to the center of projection (figure 9.3.1).

FIGURE 9.3.1

The view volume is the volume of space to be represented on the screen.

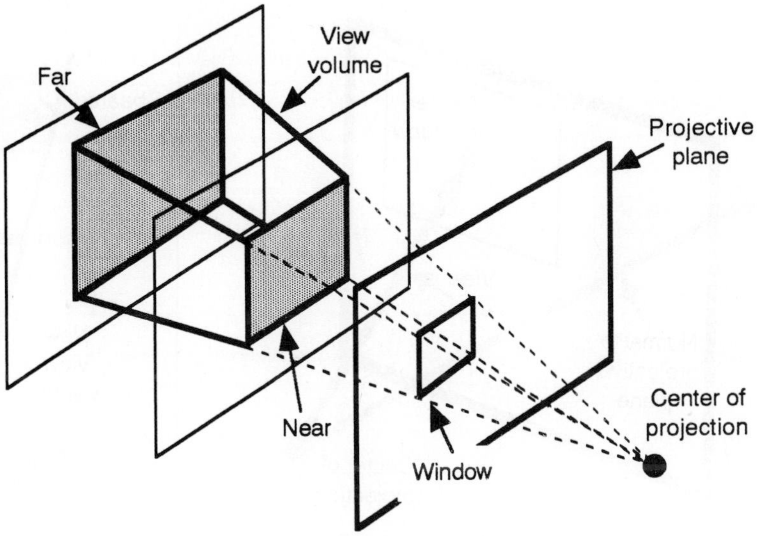

Two planes parallel to the projective plane form the top and bottom of the frustum. The plane closest to the projective plane is called the **near plane.** The other plane is called the **far plane.**

In some applications, the view vector is not perpendicular to the projective plane (figure 9.3.2). In such cases, a z-shear is used to transform the view vector so that it points to the center of the window (figure 9.3.3).
Recall that the matrix form of a z-shear is

$$\begin{bmatrix} 0 & 1 & 0 & 0 \\ s_x & s_y & 1 & 0 \\ 0 & 0 & 0 & 1 \end{bmatrix}$$

where s_x and s_y are the shear factors. The view vector points to the center of the window (XCenter,YCenter,d) (figure 9.3.4). It is sheared to become the vector (0,0,d), which is perpendicular to the projective plane. If the shear function is applied to (XCenter,YCenter,d), the shear factors s_x and s_y satisfy the equations

$$0 = \text{XCenter} + s_x d$$
$$0 = \text{YCenter} + s_y d$$

or

$$s_x = -\text{XCenter}/d$$
$$s_y = -\text{YCenter}/d$$

Once this z-shear is applied, the view vector is perpendicular to the projective plane (figure 9.3.5).

FIGURE 9.3.2

The view vector may not be perpendicular to the projection plane.

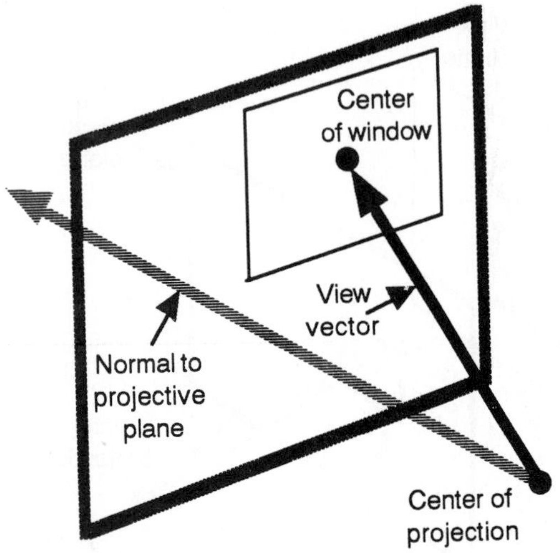

FIGURE 9.3.3

A shear can be applied to make the view vector perpendicular to the projective plane.

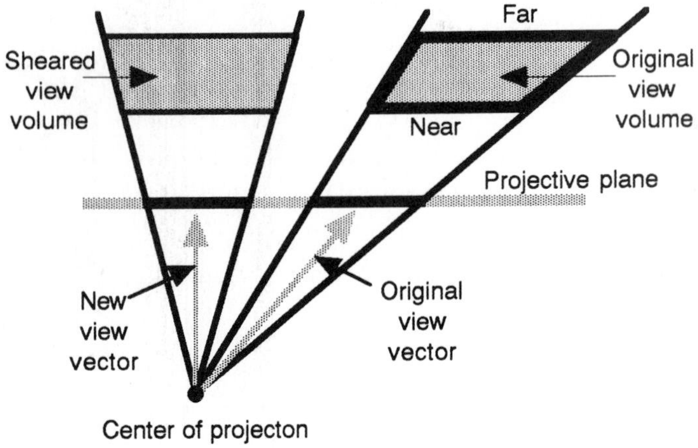

FIGURE 9.3.4

The shear transforms the center of the window to (0,0,d).

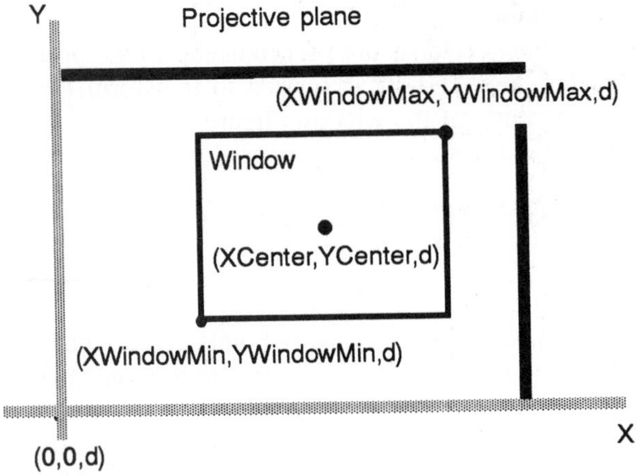

FIGURE 9.3.5

The view volume seen in cross-section

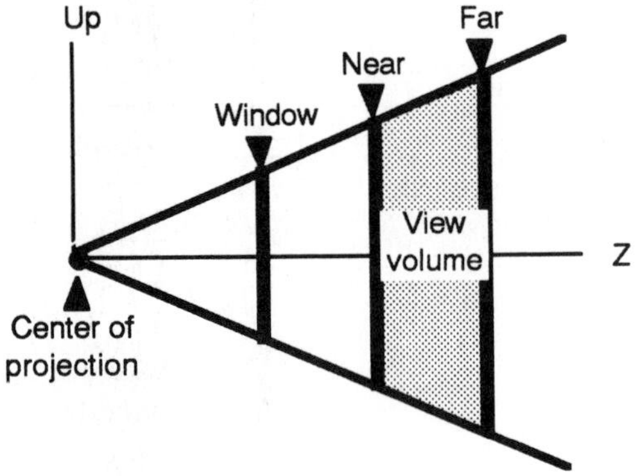

The clipping algorithms for two-dimensional systems depend on the viewport being defined by a rectangle whose boundaries are described by constant values of x and y. The regular parallelepiped view volume has front and rear defined by planes of constant z-value, but the sides cannot be so simply described. If a point (x,y,z) is projected to the point (x′,y′,d) in the projective plane, the point (x′,y′,d) is shown on the screen only if it is within the designated viewport—that is, the x′ and y′ values are in the viewport. It is tempting at this point to assume that if the z-value of a point is between the near and far bounds, the point will be visible. With this in mind, the transformation of (x,y,z) into (x′,y′,z) is often used to convert the clipping region to the regular parallelepiped bounded by the viewport boundaries of x and y and the near and far values for z (figure 9.3.6).

While this transformation is acceptable for wire-frame drawings, it will not maintain depth information if hidden surface removal is attempted. If z is used to decide on depth, the problem presented in figure 9.3.7 occurs. The **C** is

FIGURE 9.3.6

If x′ is the projection of x and if y′ is the projection of y, the point (x,y,z) may be transformed to the point (x′,y′,z) for clipping. This transformation will not work properly if depth information must be preserved.

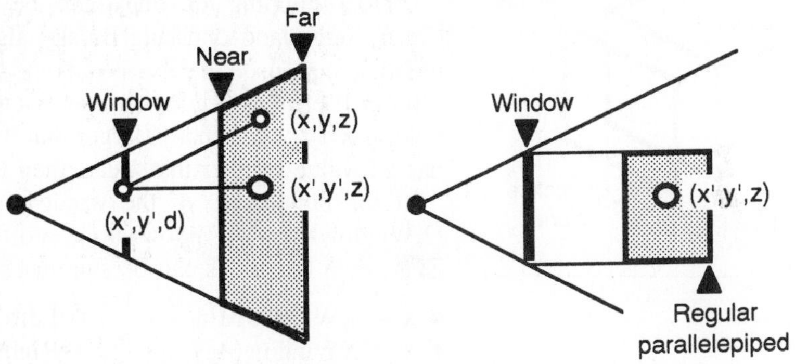

FIGURE 9.3.7

The point C lies behind the line AB, but if its z-coordinate is not transformed, C′, its representative in the view volume, will be in front of the transformation A′B′ of the line AB.

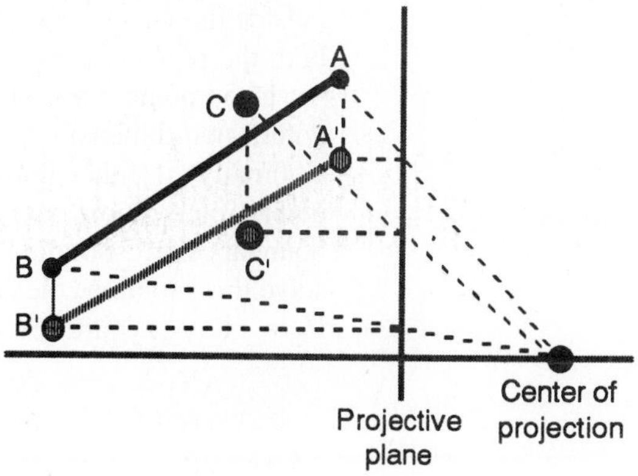

behind the line **AB,** while the transformation **C′** of **C** with z-coordinate fixed lies in front of the transformation **A′B′** of **AB.** If depth information is to be maintained, z must also be transformed. In this case, the complete transformation, modified from (Pokorny and Gerald 1989), is given as

$$x' = d\,(x/z)$$
$$y' = d\,(y/z)$$
$$z' = (z - d/z)$$

Clipping can be done with the window coordinates of the view volume or by converting points to viewport coordinates and clipping against the viewport coordinates of the view volume (figure 9.3.8). Here you will clip with the window coordinates of the view volume because if a line lies outside the view volume, there is no point in converting it. Also, unless a scan-line hidden-surface algorithm (section 10.4) is used, the z-coordinate will be discarded after clipping, so there is no need to convert it into viewport coordinates.

FIGURE 9.3.8

Points in the view volume may be clipped in window coordinates or viewport coordinates.

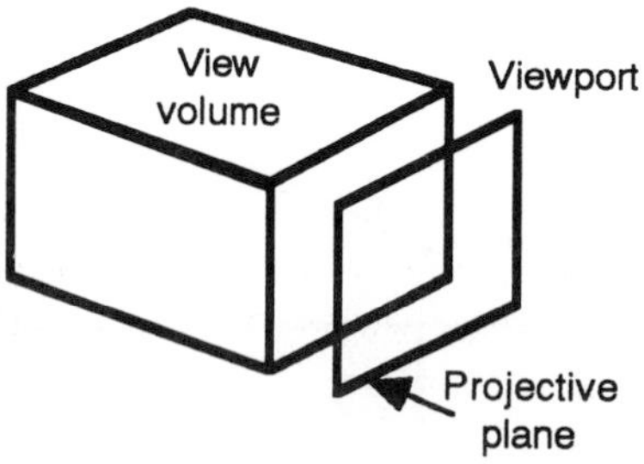

Actual clipping of lines can be done by an extension of either the Cohen-Sutherland or Liang-Barsky algorithm. In the Cohen-Sutherland case, the four codes used to describe a point's position relative to the viewport—Top, Bottom, Left, and Right—are augmented with the codes Front and Back. If a point has a z-value that is larger than Far, then the code Back is set. If a point has a z-value smaller than near, then the code Front is set.

If the boundaries of the window are (XWindowMin,YWindowMin) and (XWindowMax,YWindowMax), and the near and far z-values are ZNear and ZFar, then the codes can be summarized as follows:

- $x <$ XWindowMin — Left
- $x >$ XWindowMax — Right
- $y <$ YWindowMin — Bottom
- $y >$ YWindowMax — Top
- $z <$ ZNear — Front
- $z >$ ZFar — Back

Each end point of a line can be classified by a code set describing its relationship to the view volume. The intersection of the code sets for the two end points is computed, and if the two points share a code, the line will be outside the viewport and clipping will stop. If the two code sets are empty, then both the points are in the viewport and may be projected onto the screen. The projected points are converted to screen coordinates, and the line can be drawn with a two-dimensional line-drawing algorithm.

Finally, if either point has a non-empty code set and the two sets have an empty intersection, you need to find the intersection of the line and a window boundary corresponding to one of the members of the non-empty code set. To solve this problem, the equations of the line between points $P_1 = (x_1,y_1,z_1)$ and $P_2 = (x_2,y_2,z_2)$ are given parametrically by

$$x(t) = x_1 + (x_2 - x_1)t$$
$$y(t) = y_1 + (y_2 - y_1)t$$
$$z(t) = z_1 + (z_2 - z_1)t$$

where t ranges from 0 to 1.

If, for example, $z_1 < \text{ZNear}$, then Front will be in the code set for P_1. A new end point P_1' must be computed to replace P_1. Replace z_1 by ZNear and compute t for this intersection as follows:

$$\text{ZNear} = z_1 + (z_2 - z_1)t$$

Therefore,

$$t = (\text{ZNear} - z_1)/(z_2 - z_1)$$

The x- and y-values for this new point are computed by substituting this t-value into the parametric equations. As in the two-dimensional case, the code sets are recalculated for this new end point. The intersection of the code set for the new end point and the other end point is found, and the process is repeated.

EXERCISES

9.3.1

Develop a clipping algorithm that checks the front and rear values for the end points of a line, and after clipping front and rear, uses the two-dimensional LineAbs to draw the line. What are the advantages of this algorithm if the two-dimensional clipping is done by hardware?

9.3.2

Modify the Cohen-Sutherland algorithm to clip lines to the three-dimensional view volume.

9.3.3

Modify the Liang-Barsky algorithm for use in three-dimensional clipping.

9.3.4

Create a procedure for converting the world coordinates of a point in the view volume to the viewport coordinates of its projection.

9.4 Implementing a Three-Dimensional Graphics Package

Simple graphics packages in two-dimensions have relatively simple and standard forms. This is not the case for three-dimensional packages, in part because of the difficulty in projecting three-dimensional objects onto the two-dimensional screen. This is also because the requirements of various applications can be met only with varied types of projections and representations of data.

This section presents the basic operations for displaying perspective projections. This implementation is not intended to be the exclusive paradigm for three-dimensional graphics systems, but will illustrate how some of the theoretical considerations presented in the last 4 sections may be converted to reasonably efficient code.

Figure 9.4.1 outlines the sequence of events presented in the last three sections. This is the actual sequence of events if the viewing operations are implemented with hardware. If the three-dimensional package is being implemented as software added onto an existing two-dimensional package, the resulting sequence will not be as clear-cut.

The first step is to list those conversion factors that should be computed beforehand in order to speed up the drawing process. This information is stored in a record referred to as the type ThreeWindow. A sample of a record that could be used in conjunction with an existing two-dimensional Window system is given in figure 9.4.2. The two-dimensional Window system already holds the x- and y-coordinates of the current position. The z-coordinate of the current position is to be stored as CurrentZ.

Homogeneous coordinates were introduced to allow translations and perspective projections to be expressed as matrix operations. The only translation needed for this conversion from world coordinates to screen coordinates is the translation of the view vector to the origin in the first step. If this translation is implemented as a vector subtraction and the perspective operation is applied to the x- and y-coordinates only at the very end of the operation, all other operations can be achieved as multiplications with 3×3 matrices rather than 4×4 matrices.

FIGURE 9.4.1

This is the sequence of events used in displaying perspective projections.

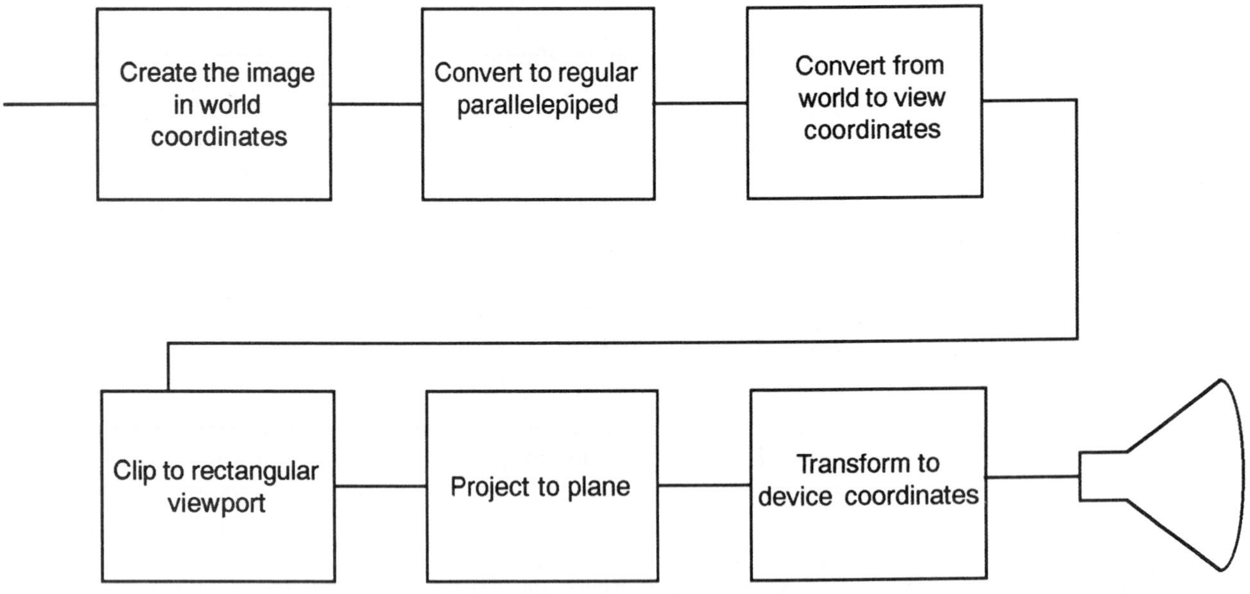

FIGURE 9.4.2

Use this record structure for your three-dimensional graphics package

```
ThreeWindow = record
    Port                 : Window;   (* 2-dimensional window information; include x,y coordinate    *)
    CurrentZ             : real;     (* z-coordinate of current point                               *)
    Near, Far            : real;     (* near and far plane for clipping                             *)
    RotateShearMatrix    : matrix;   (* rotation matrix                                             *)
    TranslateFactor      : vector;   (* used to translate viewpoint to origin before rotating       *)
    Distance             : real;     (* distance from origin to projection plane                    *)
    XShear, YShear       : real;     (* shear factors                                               *)
end;
```

Additional simplification can be achieved by combining the rotation and shearing matrices. Figure 9.4.3 gives a procedure for creating this matrix. The first part of this procedure creates the rotation matrix by means of the techniques discussed in section 8.7. It is important to create the rotation matrix first because matrix multiplication is not commutative and the rotation is done before shearing. The alterations to the rotation matrix due to shearing are calculated directly, by multiplying the rotation matrix by the shearing matrix.

FIGURE 9.4.3

This procedure creates a matrix combining the shear and rotation operations in the perspective projection.

```
procedure CreateRotationShearMatrix (var RotationShear   : matrix;
                                         ViewVector      : vector;
                                         UpVector        : vector;
                                         WindowCenter    : vector);
var
    NormalizedView     : vector;
    TempVector         : vector;
    ScalarY, ScalarZ   : real;
    i                  : integer;
    XShear, YShear     : real;
begin
    XShear := WindowCenter[1] / WindowCenter[3];
    YShear := WindowCenter[2] / WindowCenter[3];

    (*compute the ViewVector and normalize both the view and up vectors*)
    Normalize(ViewVector, NormalizedView);
    Normalize(UpVector, UpVector);

    (* third column is the view vector with minus sign to convert from right to left coordinates *)
    for i := 1 to vectorsize do
        RotationShear[i, 3] := NormalizedView[i];

    (* compute the columns of the rotation matrix *)
    ScalarZ := DotProduct(NormalizedView, UpVector);
    ScalarY := Sqrt(1 - ScalarZ * ScalarZ);
    if ScalarY > 0 then
```

(continued)

FIGURE 9.4.3 continued

```
      begin
         (*compute the second column of the rotation matrix *)
         for i := 1 to vectorsize do
            TempVector[i] := NormalizedView[i] * ScalarZ;
         SubtractVector(UpVector, TempVector, TempVector);
         for i := 1 to vectorsize do
            RotationShear[i, 2] := TempVector[i] / ScalarY;

         (*compute the first column of the rotation matrix*)
         CrossProduct(UpVector, NormalizedView, TempVector);
         for i := 1 to vectorsize do
            RotationShear[i, 1] := TempVector[i] / ScalarY;

         (* include shear factor *)
         for i := 1 to vectorsize do
            RotationShear[i, 1] := RotationShear[i, 1] - RotationShear[i, 3] * XShear;
         for i := 1 to vectorsize do
            RotationShear[i, 2] := RotationShear[i, 2] - RotationShear[i, 3] * YShear;
      end
   else
      writeln('The UpVector and ViewVector cannot be parallel');
end;
```

The procedure for converting from world coordinates to view coordinates suitable for clipping—the x- and y-coordinates in screen-window coordinates and the z-coordinate in view coordinates—are given in figure 9.4.4. At this point it is easy to construct a three-dimensional line-drawing algorithm,

FIGURE 9.4.4

This procedure calculates the perspective projection of a point.

```
(* Converts a point in world coordinates into its projection *)
procedure ConvertToView (WorldPoint      : vector;        (* world coordinates of a point     *)
                        var ViewPoint   : vector;        (* projected coordinates            *)
                        W               : ThreeWindow);  (* distance from projective plane   *)
                                                         (* to center                        *)
   var
      TranslateFactor: vector;
begin
   with W do
      begin
         (*translate*)
         SubtractVector(WorldPoint, TranslateFactor, ViewPoint);
         (*rotate and shear *)
         MultiplyVector(ViewPoint, RotateShearMatrix, ViewPoint);
         (*project x-coordinate*)
         ViewPoint[1] := (Distance * ViewPoint[1]) / ViewPoint[3];
         (*project y-coordinate*)
         ViewPoint[2] := (Distance * ViewPoint[2]) / ViewPoint[3];
         end
   end;
```

FIGURE 9.4.5

The procedure draws the perspective projection of a three-dimensional line.

```
procedure LineAbs3(x,y,z : real;        (* view coordinates of end point after rotation shearing   *)
                                         (* x and y are projected while z remains in view coordinates *)
               var TheWindow   :ThreeWindow);
begin
   ClipFrontBack(x,y,z,TheWindow);
   LineAbs(x,y,TheWindow.Port);          (* recall that LineAbs updates the current x and y positions *)
   TheWindow.CurrentZ := z               (* current z position is needed for the next front-back clip *)
end;
```

LineAbs3 (figure 9.4.5). The procedure receives the x, y, and z values computed by ConvertToView and ThreeWindow. The values of x and y are adjusted by clipping back and front if needed. Those values along with the windows port, are passed to LineAbs to complete the process. Notice that LineAbs completes the clipping and conversion to screen coordinates.

EXERCISES

9.4.1

Create a ThreeWindow record structure that will facilitate construction of a three-dimensional graphics system based on your two-dimensional system.

9.4.2

What procedures are needed so the user can establish and alter your ThreeWindow? Write these procedures.

9.4.3

Create a three-dimensional perspective graphics package based on your two-dimensional system.

9.4.4

Write the procedures necessary to create the projection matrices for parallel projections.

9.4.5

How would your window structure be altered if more than one type of projection were available to the user? How would the procedures developed in exercise 9.4.2 be altered to accomplish this task?

9.4.6

Extend the system developed in 9.4.3 to allow for different types of projections.

BIBLIOGRAPHY

Cox, Donna J. "The Tao of Postmodernism: Computer Art, Scientific Visualization and Other Paradoxes." *Leonardo* (Supplemental Issue, 1989): 7–12.

Desargues, Pierre. *Perspective*. New York: Harry N. Abrams, 1976.

Edgerton, Samuel Y., Jr. *The Renaissance Rediscovery of Linear Perspective*. New York: Basic Books, 1975. Excellent introduction to the history and theory of perspective.

Holt, Michael. *Mathematics and Art*. New York: Studio Vista, Van Nostrand Reinhold, 1971.

Ivins, William M., Jr. *Art & Geometry. A Study of Space Intuitions*. New York: Dover, 1964.

LeWinter, Renee, and Cynthia Barron. "Artistic Challenge Establishing Aesthetic Standards in Computer Art." *Computer Graphics World* 13 (2): 49–54 (February 1990).

Marshack, Alexander, "An Ice Age Ancestor?" *National Geographic* 174 (4): 478–81 (October 1988).

Pokorny, Cornel K., and Curtis F. Gerald. *Computer Graphics: The Principles Behind the Art and Science*. Irvine, Calif.: Franklin, Beedle & Associates, 1989.

White, John. *The Birth and Rebirth of Pictorial Space*. Boston: The Boston Book and Art Shop, 1967.

Wright, Richard. "The Image in Art and Computer Art." *Leonardo,* (Supplemental Issue, 1989), 49–53.

CHAPTER

10

Hidden-Line and Hidden-Surface Removal

DIRECTIONS

—Technical Illustration

Advertisements for CAD systems often include beautifully shaded, multicolored technical drawings of machinery alongside wire-frame drawings of the same machinery. These flashy images sell the machinery as well as the CAD systems, but the output from CAD systems are often two-dimensional plans. Plans are the orthographic projections of front, top, and side views with detailed measurements of the components.

Once a device has been designed and built, users need drawings to learn how to use and repair it. For their purposes orthographic projections are often too detailed because the parts have been standardized and replacements are ordered by number rather than size. Technical drawings simplify plans by giving only the information needed for instruction and maintenance. Part numbers replace exact measurements, and one axonometric view replaces the three views of the plan. Objects are often shown in exploded form (figure D.10.1), the parts separated from the main body. Parts are joined by lines to show their positions in the object.

Widely used three-dimensional CAD files can provide all of the information needed to produce wire-frame technical drawings, but programs to transfer data from CAD systems to the drawing systems used by technical artists are still under development. Currently, digitizers are used to capture information from plans, and libraries of images of standard parts such as screws and gaskets help simplify the transformation from plans to technical drawings. Once the data has been transferred, programs used by technical artists display a wire-frame image of the object.

The wire-frame image may be rotated and zoomed so that the illustrator may choose the best position from which to view the drawing. Even after the best viewing position has been found, however, the wire-frame drawing reveals many boundaries not normally seen by the viewer. These boundaries, called **hidden lines,** make drawings difficult to interpret. In most instances it is desirable to erase hidden lines; this can be done with the algorithms presented in this chapter. Some of the hidden lines in technical drawings may help the user understand the relationship between various parts, so these technical drawing systems provide semi-automatic hidden-line removal.

The final step in creating technical drawings is to print hard copies. Until recently, most output has been through plotters, but the advent of device-independent output has extended the assortment of devices available, one of which is the laser printer. Laser printers can provide inexpensive prints of sufficient quality for the technical artist.

FIGURE D.10.1

Technical drawings often show objects in an exploded form with parts separated from the main body

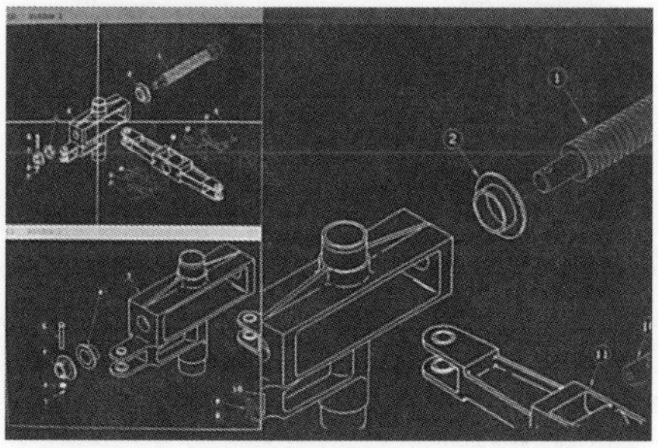

10.1 Overview of Hidden Line and Surface Removal

All drawing algorithms defined in chapter 9 have a major drawback: they draw all the lines in a given picture. This is not normally a problem with two-dimensional drawings, but in 3-dimensional pictures too much information can be presented when all lines are drawn. The object in figure 10.1.1, for example, is difficult to interpret because we are not accustomed to seeing all edges of such an object.

In the real world we see only those edges not obscured by the object's sides (figure 10.1.2). Even this is not always sufficient to give a clear impression of an object unless some shading or texturing is added to provide more optical clues (figure 10.1.3).

Two broad classes of algorithms are used to eliminate invisible objects from an image. **Hidden surface removal** algorithms determine which surface is closest to each pixel, and then set the pixel to the color value of that surface. **Hidden line removal** algorithms find parts of each line that are closest to the screen and draw only those segments.

This chapter considers techniques for removing invisible edges from a drawing and for assuring that the correct color of an edge is visible. Chapter 11 will deal with the problems of rendering a surface with appropriate texture and shading.

10.2 Back-face Removal

Each face of a polygonal solid has an inside and an outside. Faces can be represented by normal vectors that point outside. A face with a normal vector representation pointing away from the viewer is likely to be hidden. In this section you will develop an algorithm for deleting those faces from a drawing.

The faces of a polygonal solid, viewed from outside the solid, may be described by listing the vertices on the boundary in clockwise order. In figure 10.2.1 the vertices of the top face of the cube can be listed in clockwise order as v_1, v_2, v_3, v_4. Notice that the same labeling would result in a counterclockwise ordering when the face is viewed from inside the cube. To see this,

FIGURE 10.1.1

If all edges of a polygon mesh are shown, it is difficult to interpret the image.

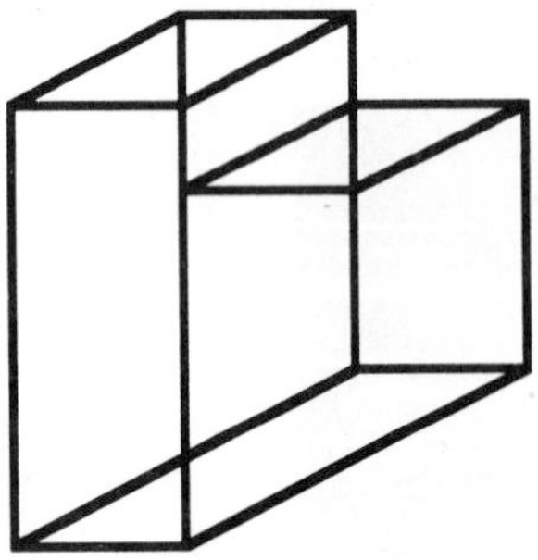

FIGURE 10.1.2

In the real world we normally see only those edges that are not obscured by the object's sides.

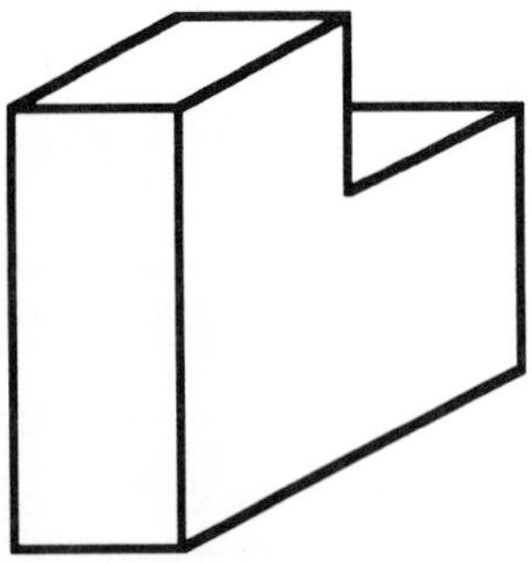

FIGURE 10.1.3

Shading and texturing provide more optical clues to an object's true nature.

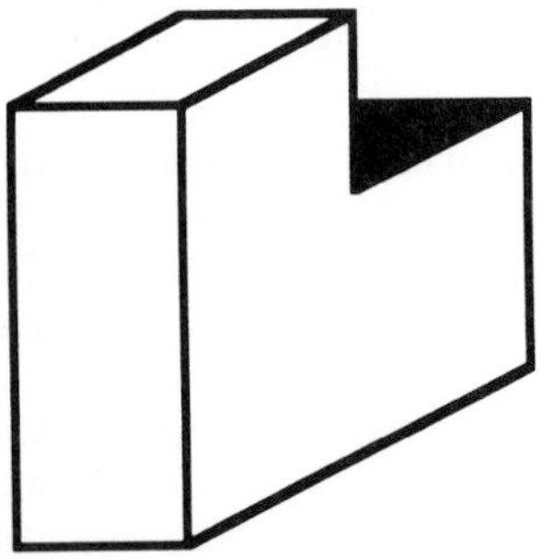

label the corners of a piece of paper in clockwise order with the numbers 1 through 4. Hold the paper up to a light with numbered side away from you. The sequence 1 through 4 will now be in counterclockwise order.

This ordering of vertices suggests the use of the cross product in the left-hand coordinate system to get a vector pointing outside the cube. The cross product of two vectors in the plane of this surface will indicate if the vectors establish the clockwise direction. Let $\mathbf{E}_1 = v_2 - v_1$ and $\mathbf{E}_2 = v_3 - v_2$ (figure 10.2.2). The cross product $\mathbf{N} = \mathbf{E}_1 \times \mathbf{E}_2$ is a vector pointing out of the cube.

If the angle, θ, between the vector **N** and the vector **V** from the center of projection to a vertex of the face is between 90° and 180°, then the outside of the face is pointing away from the viewer (figure 10.2.3). If, however, θ is between 0° and 90°, the outside of the face is pointing toward the viewer (figure 10.2.4). The vector **V** can be set to any of the vertices of the face because the center of perspective is the origin (figure 10.2.5).

FIGURE 10.2.1

A face of a cube is described by listing the vertices in clockwise order (with the face viewed from the outside of the cube).

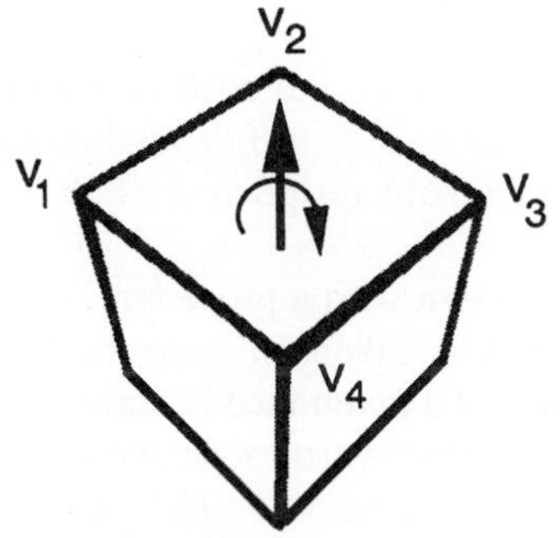

FIGURE 10.2.2

The cross-product of two consecutive edge vectors gives a normal vector pointing out of the cube.

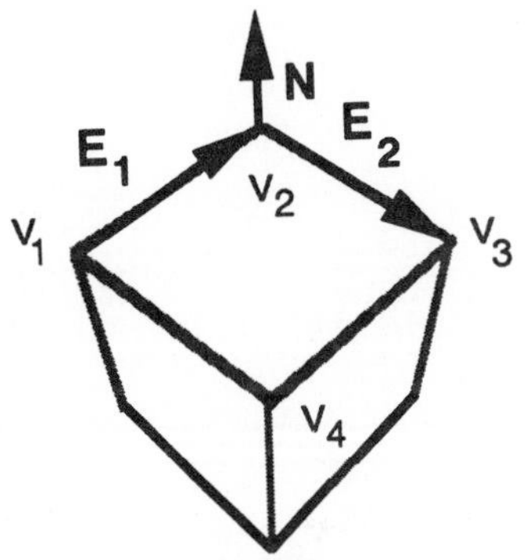

FIGURE 10.2.3

A face is not visible if the normal vector to the face and the view vector form an angle between 0° and 90°.

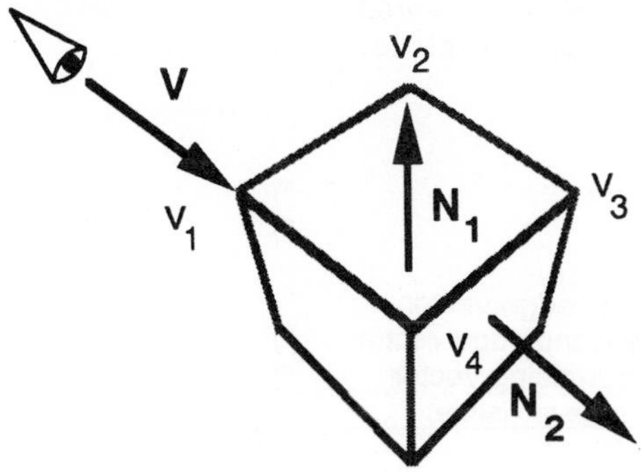

FIGURE 10.2.4

If the normal vector to a face and the new vector form an angle between 90° and 180°, then that face is visible.

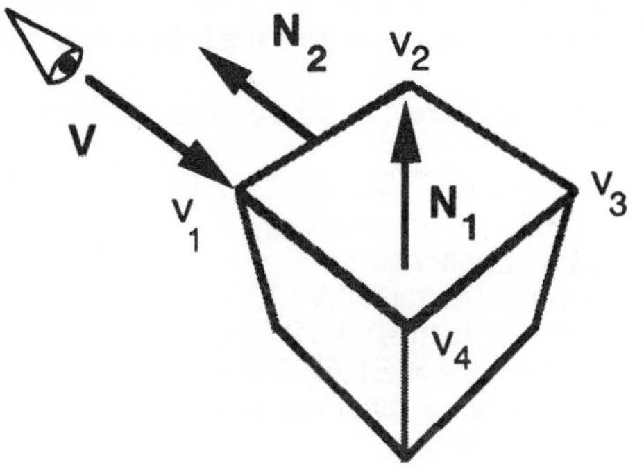

F I G U R E 10.2.5

The view vector can be set to any vertex of a face because the center of projection is the origin.

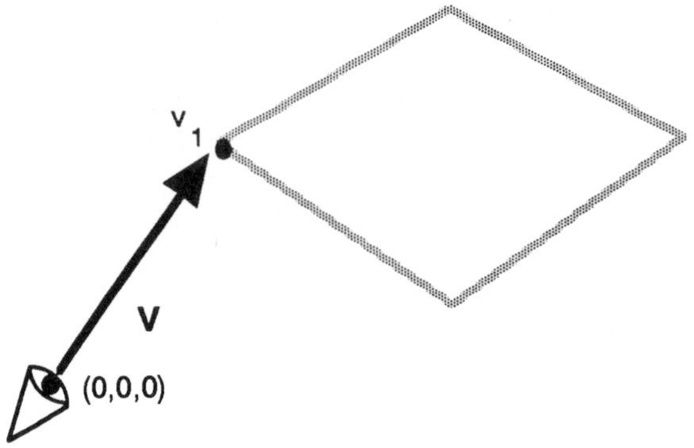

To find out if a face is visible, you only need to know the quadrant of θ. The sign of the dot product presented in section 8.4,

$$\mathbf{N} \cdot \mathbf{V} = |\mathbf{N}|\ |\mathbf{V}|\ \cos\theta$$

reveals the location of θ. If $90° < \theta < 180$, the cosθ is negative; and if $0° < \theta < 90°$, the cosθ is positive. The sign of the cosθ depends entirely on the sign of $\mathbf{N} \cdot \mathbf{V}$ because lengths of vectors are always positive. If $\mathbf{N} \cdot \mathbf{V} > 0$, the side is invisible; otherwise it is visible.

Faces of polygonal solid can be drawn with a procedure, DrawPolygon, that is similar to the procedure DrawPoly given in section 3.5. The function BackFace in figure 10.2.6 determines if a given face is drawn. The three vectors passed to BackFace are three consecutive vertices of the face that have been translated by subtracting the center of perspective. This function can be made more efficient if normal vectors for each face are stored in the face's extended

F I G U R E 10.2.6

This function may be used to determine if a face with consecutive vertices V1, V2, and V3 is visible.

```
(* The vectors are vertices of a face that have translated but have not rotated or sheared.   *)
(* This function returns true if the face is not visible, and false if the face is visible.   *)

function BackFace (V1,V2,V3: vector): boolean;
   var
      OutVector   : vector;                     (* vector facing out               *)
      E1,E2       : vector;                     (* edge vectors                    *)
   begin (* BackFace*)
      SubtractVector(V2,V1,E1);                 (* compute the first edge vector   *)
      SubtractVector(V3,V2,E2);                 (* compute the second edge vector  *)
      CrossProduct(E1,E2,OutVector);            (* compute the out-facing vector   *)
      BackFace := (DotProduct(V1,OutVector)>0)  (* find out if the face is visible *)
   end; (* BackFace*)
```

table. In this case, the function BackFace need only compute the dot product of one vertex with the normal vector to determine if the face is visible.

Back-face removal is the simplest method for removing hidden surfaces. It works well for single convex polygonal solids because faces are either visible or hidden. For more complex structures, like that in figure 10.2.1, the algorithm is not entirely effective (figure 10.2.7). In addition, if any faces of a figure are open, the inside back-facing surfaces become visible (figure 10.2.8). This situation causes difficulty if back-face removal is used as a first step in hidden-surface removal because visible inside faces are removed. Open figures should have each face labeled twice, so both the inside and outside faces are judged for visibility.

FIGURE 10.2.7

Back-face removal applied to the object in figure 10.1.1 does not result in an acceptable rendering of the object.

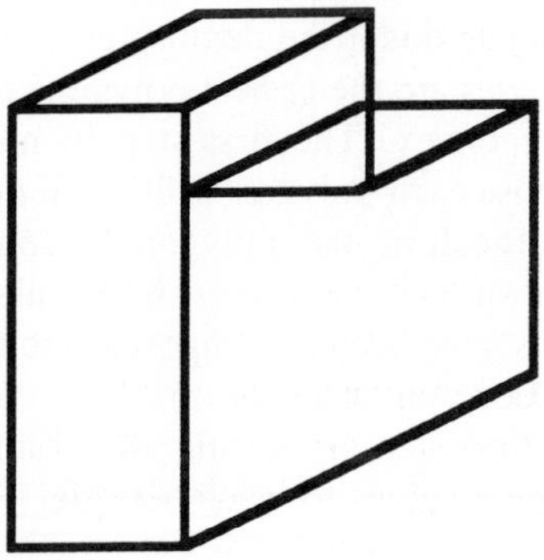

FIGURE 10.2.8

Open figures should have their faces labeled twice so both the inside and outside may be judged for visibility.

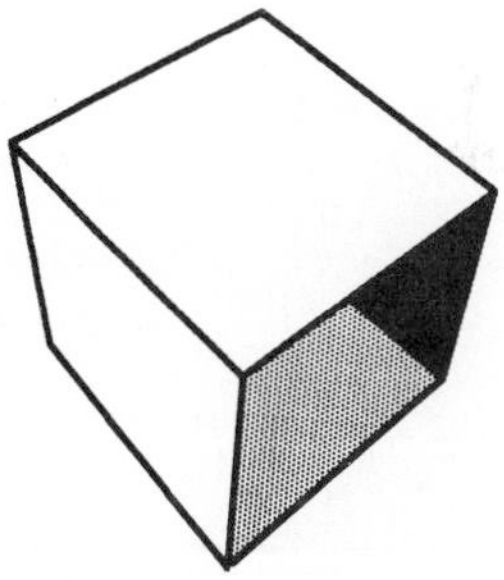

EXERCISES

10.2.1

Create a representation of a cube that could be used by the back-face-removal algorithm.

10.2.2

Create a representation for the solid in figure 10.1.1 that could be used by the back-face-removal algorithm.

10.2.3

Write a procedure that uses back-face removal to draw polygonal solids. Test your procedure on the edge tables you created in exercises 10.2.1 and 10.2.2.

10.3 Depth-sorting Method

The back-face removal method simplifies the images of solid objects by not drawing the boundary lines for hidden faces. If the faces remaining after back-face removal will be filled with a texture or color, you can replace or supplement the call to DrawPolygon with a call to FillPolygon. In figure 10.3.1, the surface S_1 is to be filled with white and surface S_2 is to be filled with gray. When S_1 is drawn before S_2, the resulting image is not in the desired form. If, however, S_2 is drawn before S_1, the solid appears in the desired form.

The **depth-sorting,** or **painter's, algorithm** makes use of this idea by first drawing the filled surfaces farthest from the center of projection. For all the computations in the following sections, assume that the depth-preserving transformation

$$x' = d\,(x/z)$$
$$y' = d\,(y/z)$$
$$z' = (z - d)/z$$

has been used to compute z-values. Keep in mind that you are using the left-hand system; the farther a point from the center of projection, the larger its z-coordinate under the depth-preserving transformation.

Triangles are the easiest polygons to sort because they have only three sides and are convex. The first step in many depth-sorting implementations is to decompose each polygon with more than three sides into triangles. This can be quite difficult if the polygon is convex. For a detailed discussion of this decomposition see Pokorny and Gerald (1989). Assume for this example that all polygons have been decomposed into triangles and that all of your comparisons will be done on triangles.

The first step in sorting the triangles is to compute the maximum and minimum z-values for each triangle. These values occur at vertices, so they are

FIGURE 10.3.1

The order in which filled faces are drawn affects the final appearance of the image.

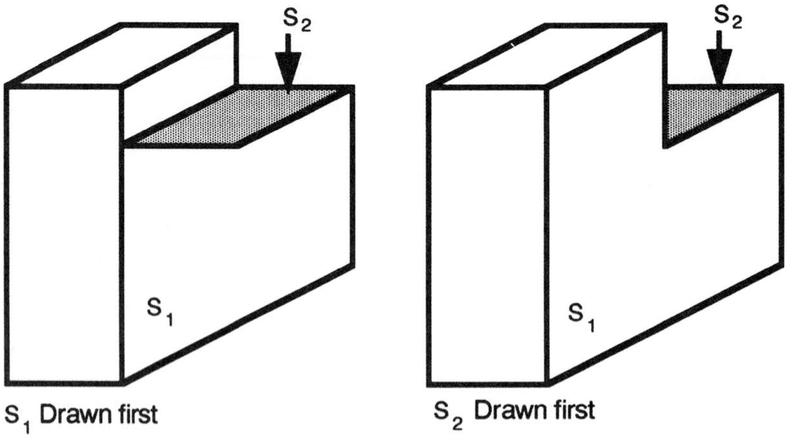

easily obtained. The surfaces are then sorted in order of decreasing maximum z-value. The surface with the largest such value is the first to be considered. This surface is behind all other surfaces if its minimum z-value is larger than their maximum z-values (figure 10.3.2). Because this test is relatively quick, it is performed first. If the chosen surface passes the test, it is drawn and removed from the list of surfaces to be drawn.

If the chosen surface has a minimum z-value smaller than the maximum z-value for one of the surfaces yet to be drawn, other tests are applied so see if the surface can be drawn. If the surface overlaps another in the z-direction, it may not overlap in the x- or y-direction. A **minimax,** or **boxing, test** can be applied to see if this is the case. Maximum and minimum x- and y-values are computed for each surface. If the minimum y-value for one surface is larger than the maximum y-value for the other surface (figure 10.3.3), then the

FIGURE 10.3.2

The triangle S is clearly behind the triangle S', so it is drawn before S'.

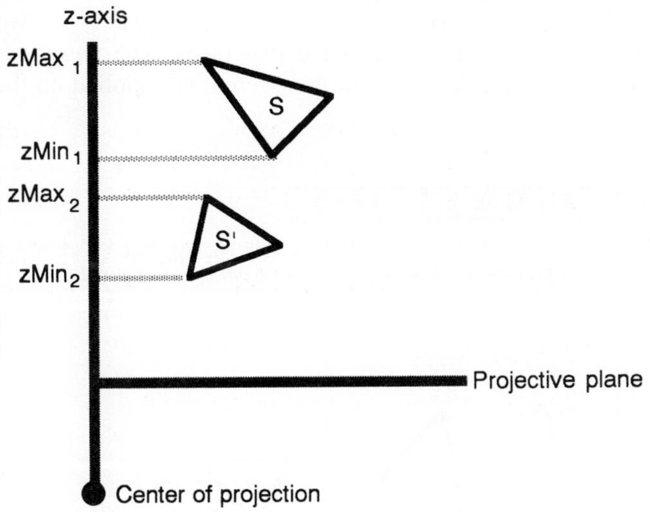

FIGURE 10.3.3

The triangles S and S' do not overlap in the y-direction. The farther of the two may be drawn first because their projections do not overlap.

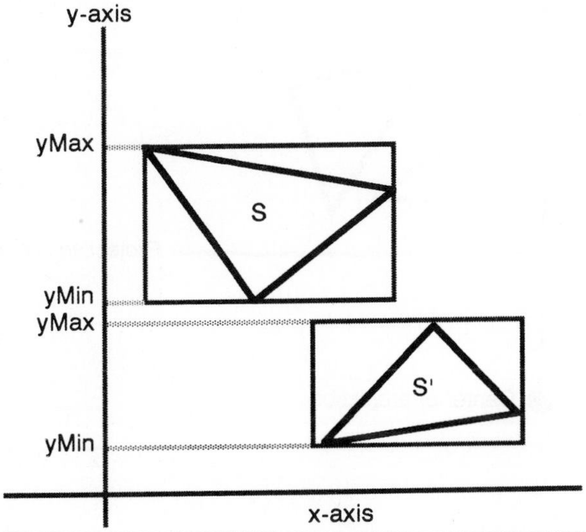

surfaces do not overlap. The same test can be applied in the x-direction. It is possible for this test to fail and have the images of the two surfaces not overlap. Because the test for this condition is difficult, it is postponed until simpler tests have failed.

This algorithm makes it possible to create an unambiguous drawing even if the projections of two surfaces overlap in all directions, as they do in figure 10.3.1. If all vertices of one of the surfaces lie on the same side of the plane containing the other surface, then all of one surface is in front of the other (figures 10.3.4 and 10.3.5). If a pair of surfaces are related in this way, draw the farther surface and eliminate is from the list.

Finally, if all other tests fail, it is still possible that the projections of two surfaces do not overlap, even though they do not satisfy the minimax criterion (figure 10.3.6). The edges of the projections of the surfaces are checked to see where they intersect. This is time consuming because every edge in one projection must be compared with every edge in the other projection. As long as no intersection lies between the vertices of an edge, the projections will not intersect.

When the planes of two surfaces intersect and the projections overlap (figures 10.3.7 and 10.3.8), the tests given here fail. One method considers the intersection of two planes to be a face boundary. A plane surface that is divided into two pieces by such a boundary is considered two faces. The two faces replace the original face, and the rules given in this section are applied on the new set of faces.

FIGURE 10.3.4

All points on S′ are on the same side of the plane containing S; therefore, each point on S′ is in front of every point on S.

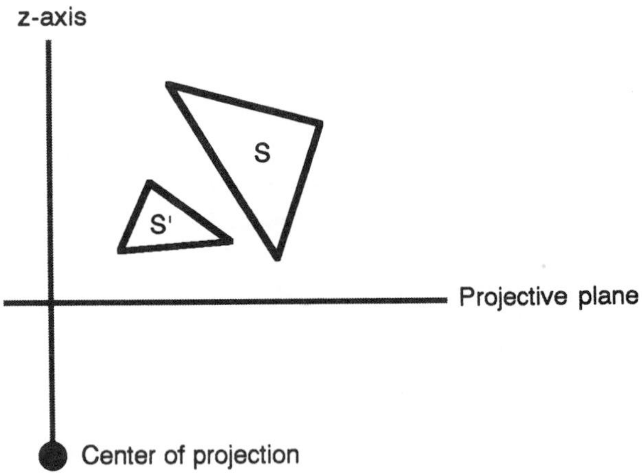

FIGURE 10.3.5

All points on S′ are on the same side of the plane containing S; therefore, each point on S is in front of every point on S′.

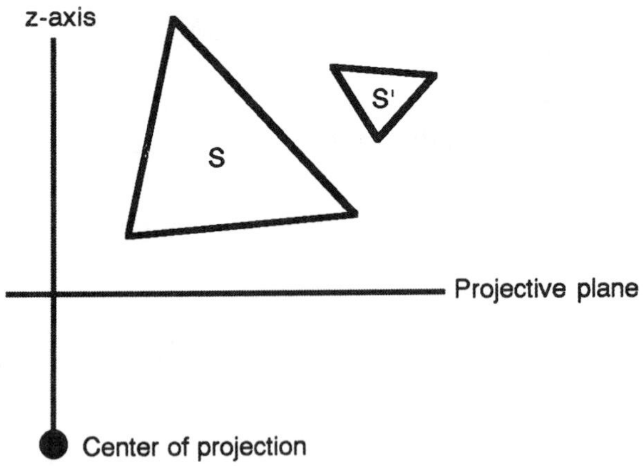

FIGURE 10.3.6

The sides of the projections of these triangles do not intersect, so neither will cover the other.

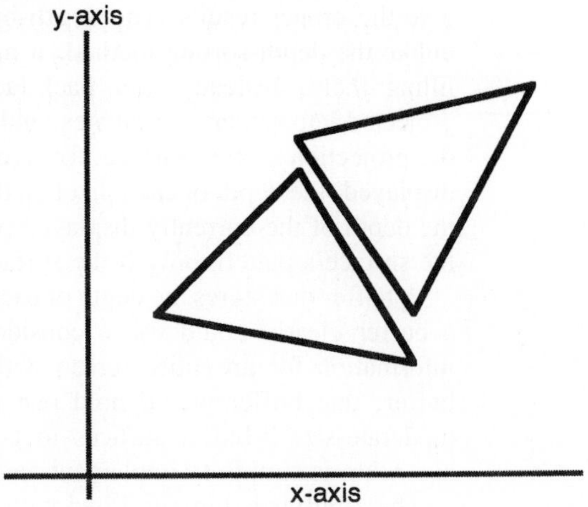

FIGURE 10.3.7

The surface S_1 passes through the surface S_2, so the painter's algorithm will not work here. In this drawing, S_1 is drawn first.

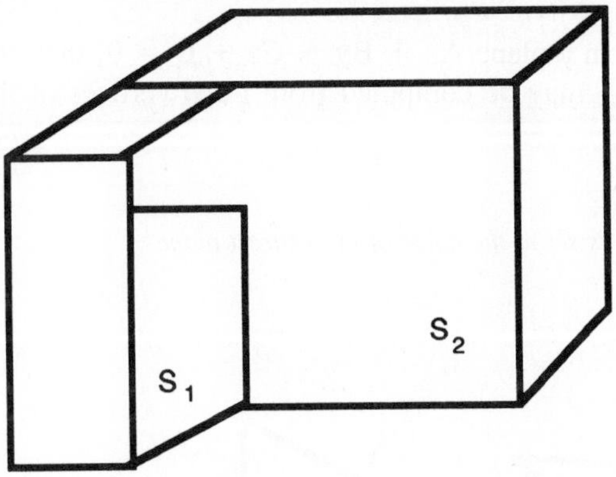

FIGURE 10.3.8

The surface S_1 passes through the surface S_2, so the painter's algorithm will not work here. In this drawing, S_2 is drawn first.

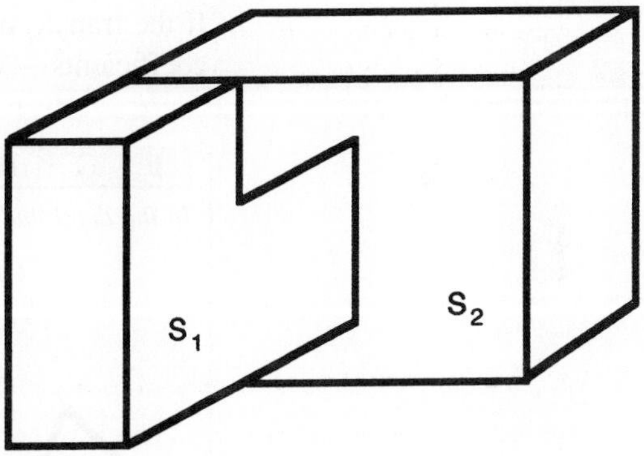

EXERCISES

10.3.1

Write a procedure to sort the projections of triangles by decreasing z-values.

10.3.2

Write a procedure to implement the minimax test for projections of triangles.

10.4 Depth-Buffer Methods

The depth-sorting method discussed in section 10.3 is complicated by the number of methods used to sort polygonal surfaces, and in some cases will not give the proper results. The **depth-buffer method** also fills the surfaces, but unlike the depth-sorting method, it makes no attempt to order surfaces before filling them. Instead, after back-face removal, each remaining surface is projected into screen coordinates, and a modified scan-line filing algorithm fills the projection of this surface. To avoid filling pixels behind the pixel already displayed, the depth of each pixel on the projection's scan line is compared with the depth of the currently displayed pixel (figure 10.4.1) A pixel is filled with the surface's pattern only if the surface point is in front of the screen pixel.

A buffer that stores the depth of each screen point is called the **z-buffer**. Such a buffer clearly could use a considerable amount of memory. If the depth information for an entire screen with 1000 × 1000 pixels were stored in a buffer, that buffer would hold one million real numbers. In cases where a moderate-size z-buffer suffices to hold the screen information, the z-buffer algorithm is simple to implement and works for all types of surfaces.

The z-buffer is initially filled with a value larger than the rear value for the view volume, and the screen is filled with a background color. Then the vertices of each polygonal surface are transformed by the depth-preserving transformation

$$x' = d\,(x/z)$$
$$y' = d\,(y/z)$$
$$z' = (z - d)/z$$

If the transformed polygon lies in a plane $Ax + By + Cz + D = 0$, then the coefficients—A, B, C, and D—may be computed from three vertices of the

FIGURE 10.4.1

In the depth-buffer method, a pixel is set to the color of the nearest plane.

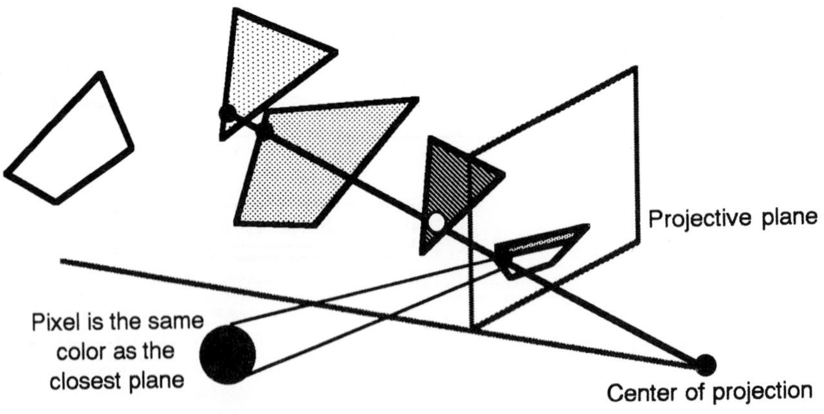

transformed polygon by means of the equations given in section 8.2. The depth-preserving transformation ensures that these coefficients properly reflect the depth of the plane.

Next, the transformed polygon is projected into the view plane by the simple process of discarding the z-coordinate. Clipping of line segments is done as needed, and the world coordinates are converted to screen coordinates. The conversion to screen coordinates takes place before scan conversion because scan conversion is a pixel-oriented operation. It is only necessary to compute the equation of the plane once for each polygonal surface. The projection of a point (x′,y′,z′) in the plane of the transformed polygon is the point (x,y). Thus, given the world coordinates (x′,y′) of such a point, its depth, z, can be computed directly from the equation of the plane:

$$z(x',y') = \frac{-Ax' - By' - D}{C}$$

This computation can be simplified to eliminate the computation of x′ and y′. The simplification is accomplished by computing the change in z for consecutive x-values. Consecutive points on a given scan line differ by 1 in their screen-coordinate x-values. Recall that x-distances in world coordinates are converted to x-distances in screen coordinates by multiplying by XConvertMult. To convert x-distances from screen to world coordinates, simply multiply by

ToWorldX = 1/XConvertMult

If an x-value is incremented by 1 in screen coordinates, its world x-coordinate is incremented by ToWorldX (figure 10.4.2). You use this and the equation of

FIGURE 10.4.2

A screen-coordinate change of 1 in x results in a change of ToWorldX in world coordinates of the corresponding point.

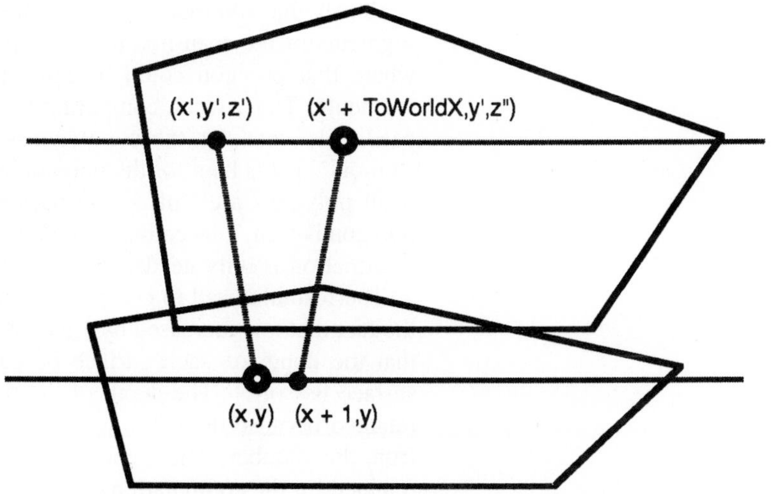

the plane to compute the difference between z-values for consecutive points on a scan line:

$$z(x' + \text{ToWorldX}, y') - z(x', y') = \frac{-A(x' + \text{ToWorldX}) - By' - D + Ax' + By' + D}{C} = \frac{-A * \text{ToWorldX}}{C}$$

Therefore, if the depth for one point (x,y) on the scan line is known, the depth of the next point is computed by

$$\text{depth}(x + 1, y) = \text{depth}(x, y) - \frac{A * \text{ToWorldX}}{C}$$

When moving from one scan line to the next, y-values are decreased by 1 in screen coordinates. A conversion of this change in y back to world coordinates corresponds to a change of ToWorldY in world coordinates, where ToWorldY is the reciprocal of YConvertMult. Computation similar to that above gives the change in depth for a point on one scan line to the point directly below it:

$$z(x', y' - \text{ToWorldY}) = z(x', y') + \frac{B * \text{ToWorldY}}{C}$$

When filling a polygon by means of the scan-line algorithm, each intersection of that polygon with the scan line is inserted into a list in order of increasing x-coordinates. If all the intersection lists for each of the polygons are combined into one larger list, it is possible to eliminate the z-buffer entirely. Each intersection on this larger list may come from any of the polygons representing projections of surfaces. To keep track of which polygons intersect at a given point, each intersection node must also have a list of polygons that intersect the scan line at that point.

Recall that alternate pairs of intersections for a given polygon represent segments of the scan line that lie within that polygon, so that the only places where that polygon could be represented on the screen are in the alternate segments. Thus, when computing which polygon is closest to the screen, you need only consider those polygons active in the current line segment. An "on-off" list is kept for the polygon projections of the surfaces (figure 10.4.3); if all polygons are "off," the background color is filled in. When only one polygon is "on," its color automatically is the fill color for that segment. Depth information is only needed when more than one polygon is "on."

The formula used to compute the depth of a given point takes advantage of the fact that x is increased by 1 as the scan line is traversed. This would require that the depth of each surface be calculated for each point even when that surface is "off." The depth of the first intersection of each polygon must be retained because the depth at the beginning of the next scan line is computed from this number. The x-coordinate of this first intersection point must also be retained for the computation of the first intersection with the next scan line. The depth function is easily modified to be a function of the depth of the first

FIGURE 10.4.3

A list of intersections of the sides of polygons can be maintained. For each intersection on this list, a second list indicates which polygon is projected to this point and which is not.

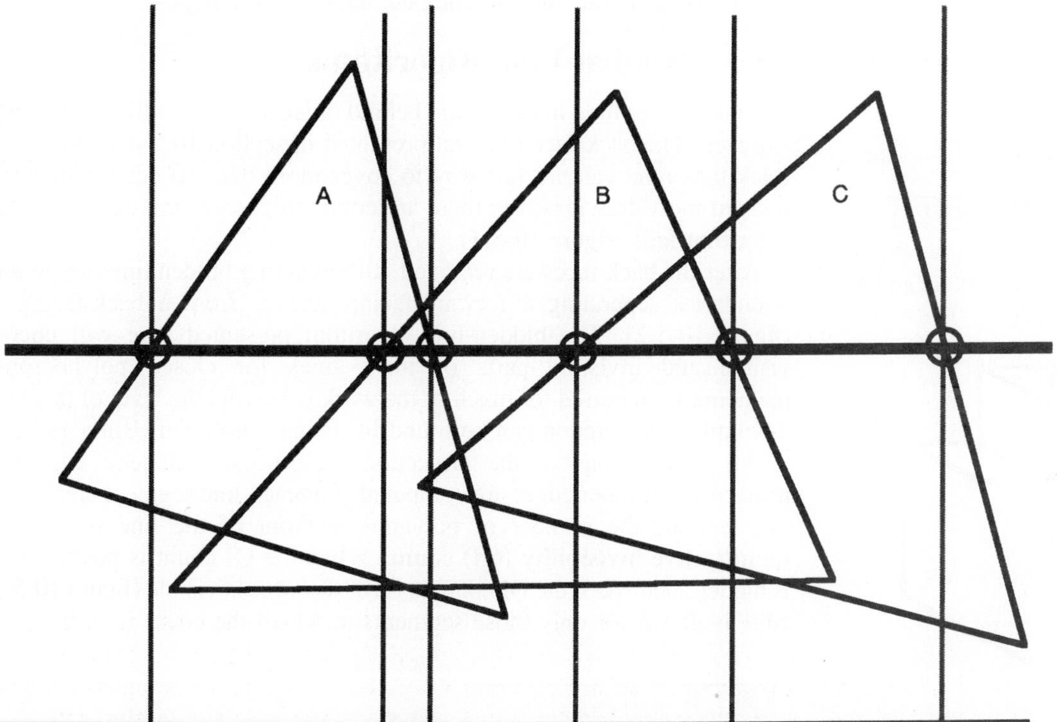

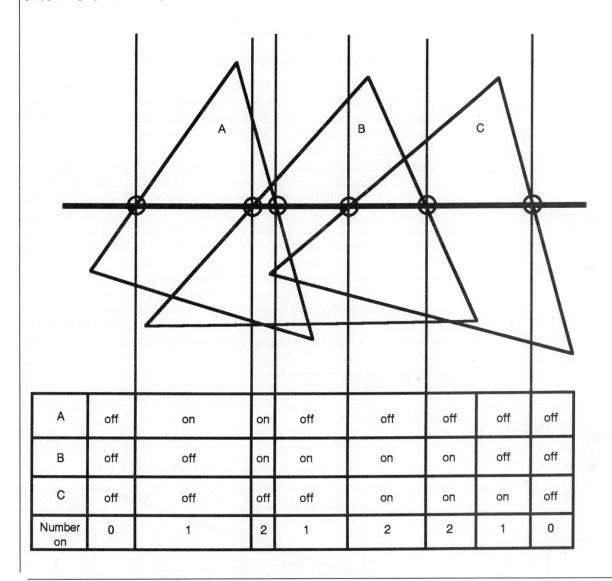

A	off	on	on	off	off	off	off	off
B	off	off	on	on	on	on	off	off
C	off	off	off	off	on	on	on	off
Number on	0	1	2	1	2	2	1	0

intersection and the current x-coordinate (exercise 10.4.1). It is possible to begin the depth computation for a polygon whenever it is ''on'' and drop this computation when it is ''off.'' This allows the depth calculations to be restricted to only those polygons marked ''on.'' If the surfaces are nonintersecting, then for every segment of the scan line the front surface at the left end of the segment will be in front, at least until the next intersection point. Here, depth computations using the formula in exercise 10.4.1 need only be performed for polygons marked ''on'' at the intersection point.

EXERCISE

10.4.1

Adapt the depth equation to compute depth (x + k,y).

10.5 Hidden-Line Algorithms

It is possible to hide lines that are behind objects without filling the overlapping surfaces. The back-face removal presented in section 10.2 does not use filling. Back-face removal is a fast way to cover more than 50 percent of the hidden lines in most drawings, but there are commonly occurring cases for which the algorithm fails (figure 10.5.1).

After the back faces are removed, all remaining hidden lines are in the set of boundaries separating a forward-facing surface from a back-facing surface (figure 10.5.2). The hidden-line algorithm presented here will uncover the visible and invisible parts of these lines for closed polyhedrons. The mathematics required for much of the work is beyond the level of this book, but a complete description can be found in (Blinn 1988) and (Blinn 1978).

All intersections of the projection of a possible hidden edge with the projections of other edges are computed. For each line segment created by these intersections the number of polygons in front of the line is stored in the **quantitative invisibility (QI) count.** When the QI count is positive, the edge is hidden, and when the QI count is zero, the edge is visible (figure 10.5.3). The edge is drawn for only those segments in which the count is zero.

FIGURE 10.5.1

You have seen that back-face removal applied to this figure does not give an acceptable final image.

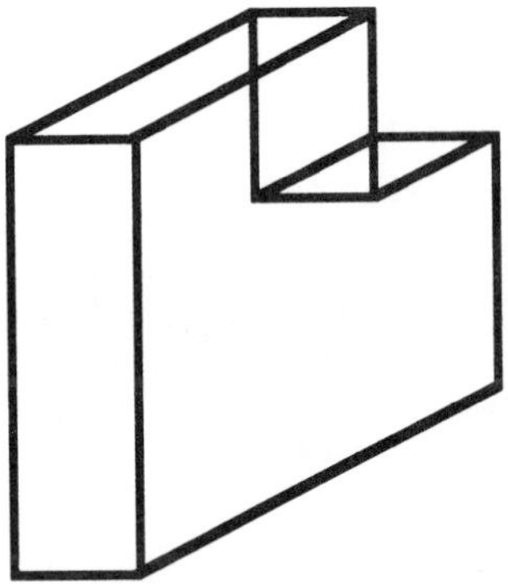

FIGURE 10.5.2

After back-face removal all the lines that must be eliminated to give an acceptable image are contained in the set of lines that separate a front face from a back face.

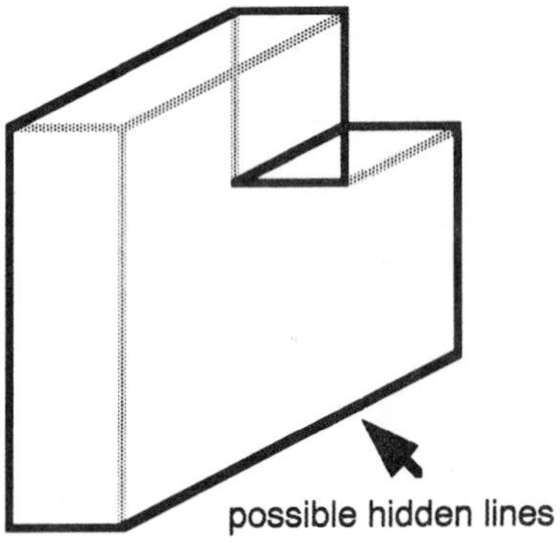

FIGURE 10.5.3

The QI count tells how many polygons are in front of a given edge. The edge is drawn only when the QI count is zero.

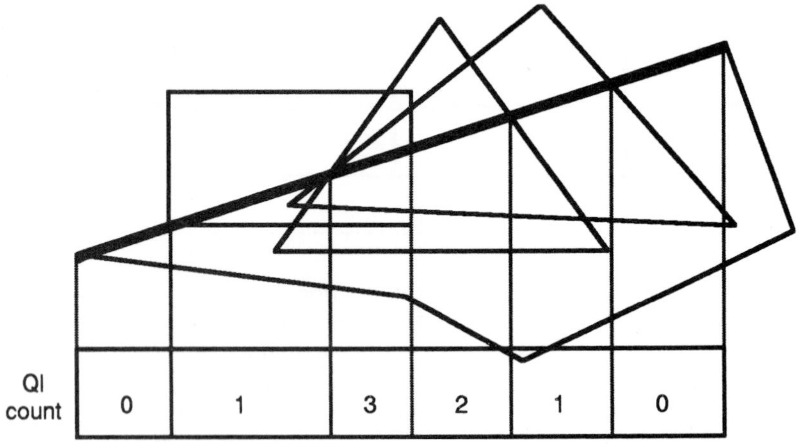

The QI count is initialized for each vertex by a face-vertex comparison. A vertex will be hidden by a face if it is farther than the face from the center of projection, and if it is inside the projection of the polygon face to the screen. The comparative depths of the vertex of one surface and that of another can be computed from the plane equations as they were in section 10.4. One way to find out if a point in a plane is surrounded by the polygon in that plane is to draw a ray from the point in the negative x-direction and count the number of times that line intersects the polygon. If the number of intersections is odd, the polygon surrounds the point; otherwise it does not (figure 10.5.4).

This algorithm for discovering whether a polygon surrounds a point works well unless the ray intersects a vertex (figure 10.5.5). If vertices were to be counted as two intersections, the ray in figure 10.5.5.a would intersect the polygon in three places. The test would therefore indicate that the polygon

FIGURE 10.5.4

One way to determine if a point in the same plane as a polygon is inside or outside of the polygon is to draw a ray from the point and count the number of intersections of that ray with the edges of the polygon. If the number of intersections is odd, the polygon surrounds the point; otherwise it does not.

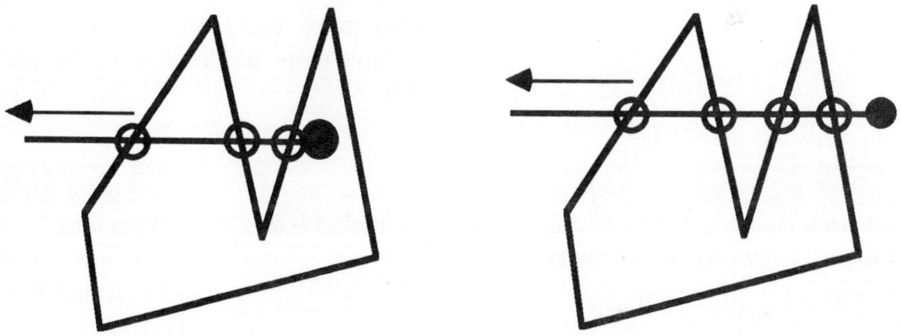

FIGURE 10.5.5

If a ray passes through a vertex, the count will not always work properly.

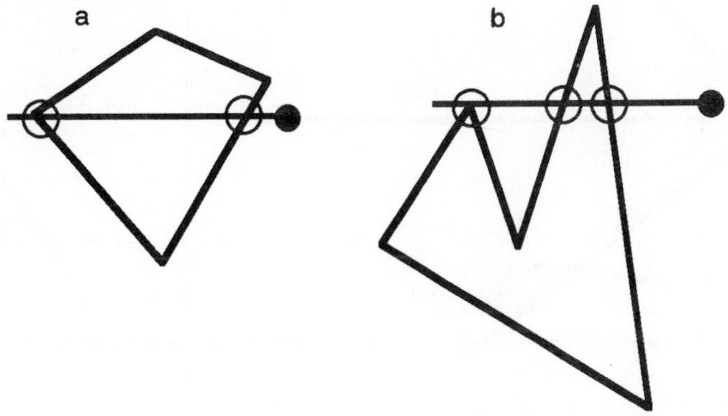

surrounds the point. But if the vertices were to count as 1 in the QI count, the count of intersections for the ray in figure 10.5.5.b would be 3. Again, the count shows that the point is surrounded by the polygon.

A solution to the vertex problem is to count vertices as an increment of ½ (Blinn 1988). When the ray passes through a vertex formed by two edges, the QI is incremented by ½ if the ray enters the polygon through an edge and decremented by ½ if the ray exits through an edge. In figure 10.5.6, the ray is entering the polygon through both edges; therefore, the QI is incremented by ½ twice. In figure 10.5.7, however, the ray enters through edge E_1 and exits through edge E_2. Thus, the QI is incremented by ½ and decremented by ½ at this vertex. In figure 10.5.5.a, the fraction ½ is added twice, giving a total count of 2. In figure 10.5.5.b, the fraction is added once and subtracted once; hence, the count in this case is also 2.

Once the QI count has been initialized for a vertex of an edge, it can be computed for each point on the edge. You want to know where an edge passes behind or emerges from behind another polygon. First, all intersections of the projection of that edge with the projections of the edges of other faces are computed. This can be determined by vector calculations without computing the actual point of intersection (Blinn 1978). For each intersection the clockwise ordering of the vertices will determine if the edge is moving behind the surface or moving from behind the surface. In figure 10.5.8, the subscripts show the vertex order, and the QI count is being computed for edge $\mathbf{P}_1\mathbf{P}_2$.

Many more hidden-line techniques are presented in (Pokorny and Gerald 1989).

FIGURE 10.5.6

When a ray through a vertex enters the polygon through both edges, the QI count is incremented twice by 1/2.

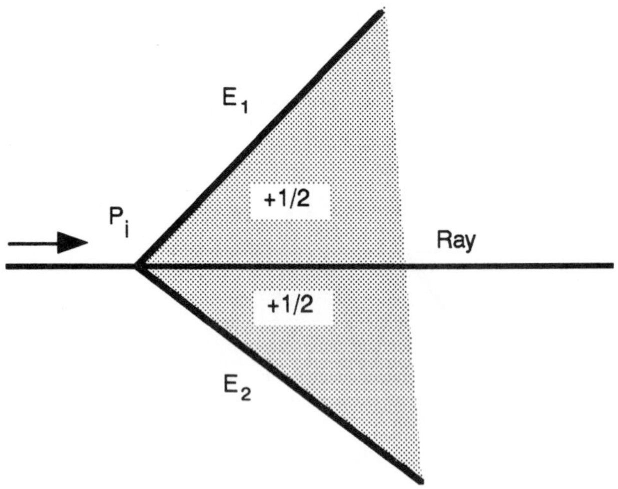

FIGURE 10.5.7

When a ray through a vertex enters the polygon through one edge and exits through another, the QI count is incremented by 1/2 and decremented by 1/2.

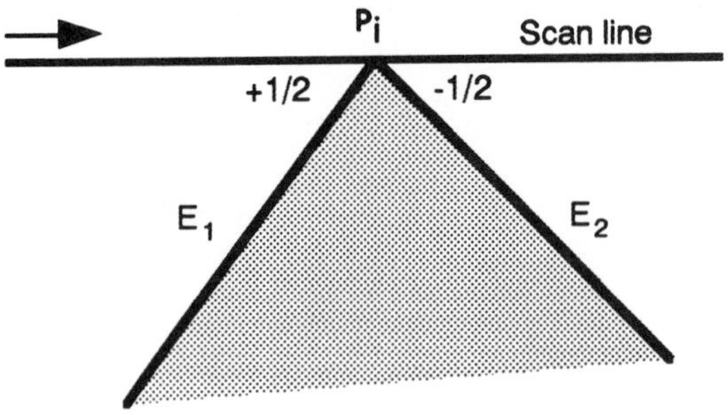

FIGURE 10.5.8

The QI is updated for each intersection of an edge with the projection of a polygon. If the edge goes behind a polygon, the QI is incremented. If the edge emerges from behind a polygon, the QI is decremented.

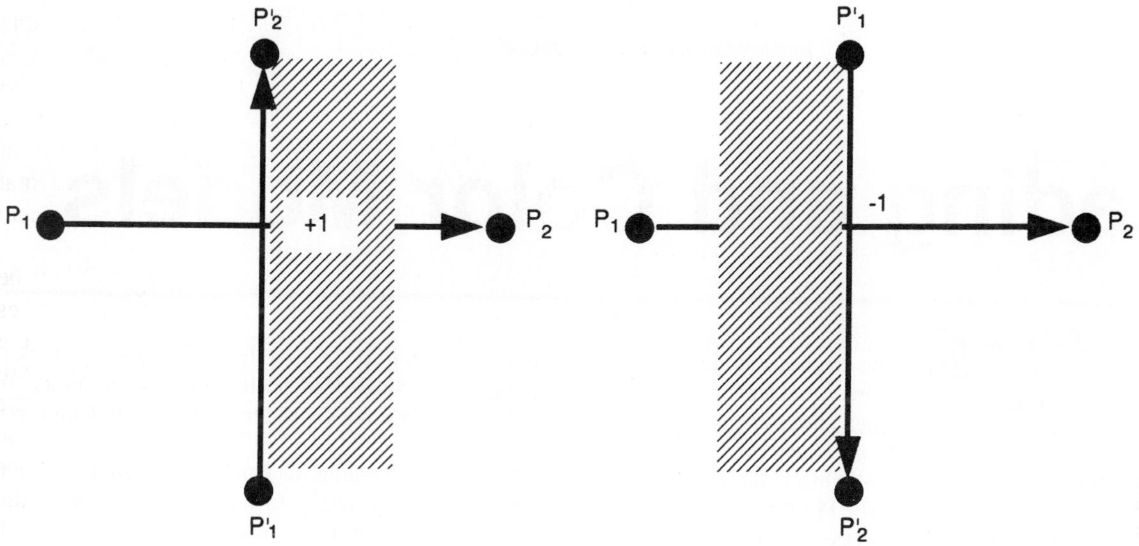

BIBLIOGRAPHY

Blinn, James F., "Fractional Invisiblity." *IEEE CG&A* 8 (6): 77–84 (November 1988).
Overview of the complete hidden-line process.

______. "Clipping Using Homogeneous Coordinates" *Computer Graphics* (Proc SIGGRAPH) 12 (3): 245, August 1978.

Pokorny, Cornel K., and Curtis F. Gerald. *Computer Graphics: The Principles Behind the Art and Science*. Irvine, Calif.: Franklin, Beedle & Associates, 1989.

CHAPTER

11

Shading and Color Models

DIRECTIONS

Computer Graphics in Medicine

The diagnosis of tumors, heart problems, and other diseases depends on the physician's ability to see inside the patient. Until 1895 the only way to look inside the human body was to operate on the patient. In that year, Wihelm Konrad Röntgen used X rays to photograph his wife's hand. Physicians finally had a noninvasive method of seeing inside patient. X rays give good images of dense structures such as bones, but indistinct images of soft tissues, which do not absorb the rays.

A major improvement in the quality of X-ray images of both bone and soft tissues came with the invention of the **CT (Computed Tomography) scan**. CT scanners produce X-ray images from more than one angle. These multiple scans are digitized, and a computer uses this information to create a three-dimensional model of the scanned region. Slices of the model may then be examined. CT scans allow physicians to locate problems with great precision.

The computers that made CT scanning possible led to the development of other scanning technologies. One widely hailed method is **MRI (Magnetic Resonance Imaging)**. Strong magnets cause the hydrogen atoms in the body to align in a given direction. A radio pulse knocks them temporarily out of alignment, but when the pulse is removed they return to their aligned position. Because they all return simultaneously, they generate radio waves of their own. The strength of these signals reveals the distribution of hydrogen atoms in the body, and this distribution indicates the amount of water in various locations in the body. The advantage of MRI is that it depicts soft tissue in high contrast. Many other imaging technologies are being explored. All depend on the computer's ability to discover patterns in data quickly and to enhance digital images.

The possibilities of imaging techniques are endless, and already the computer's capacity to represent slices of three-dimensional data is used for more than locating medical problems. For example, solid models of body parts such as the skull, the femur, and the knee have been used to create custom-made prostheses (Rhodes, Kuo, and Rothman 1987). The upper leg and its ball-like hip joint are routinely replaced with a proximal femoral prosthesis held in place by a bone cement. Standard premanufactured prostheses are much cheaper than custom-fitted models. For young or active patients, however, these prostheses are not always satisfactory, and they must be custom fitted.

One answer to the expense of custom-fitted prostheses is the CAD/CAM approach taken by Rhodes, Kuo, and Rothman (1987). Cross-sectional slices of the patient's leg are obtained by CT scans and converted to contour outlines of the bone's outer and inner surfaces (figure D.11.1). The contour cross-sections are transmitted as bitmaps to another facility where they are scan converted to vector representations. The vectors can then be used to create a machine tool to create the prosthesis.

Some systems show some soft tissue as a transparent layer, while selected organs or bones are rendered opaque (Drebin, Carpenter, and Hanrahan 1988). Surface-shading techniques and volume-rendering data structures needed for these applications are covered in this chapter.

FIGURE D.11.1

Cross-sectional slices of a patient's leg obtained by CT scans

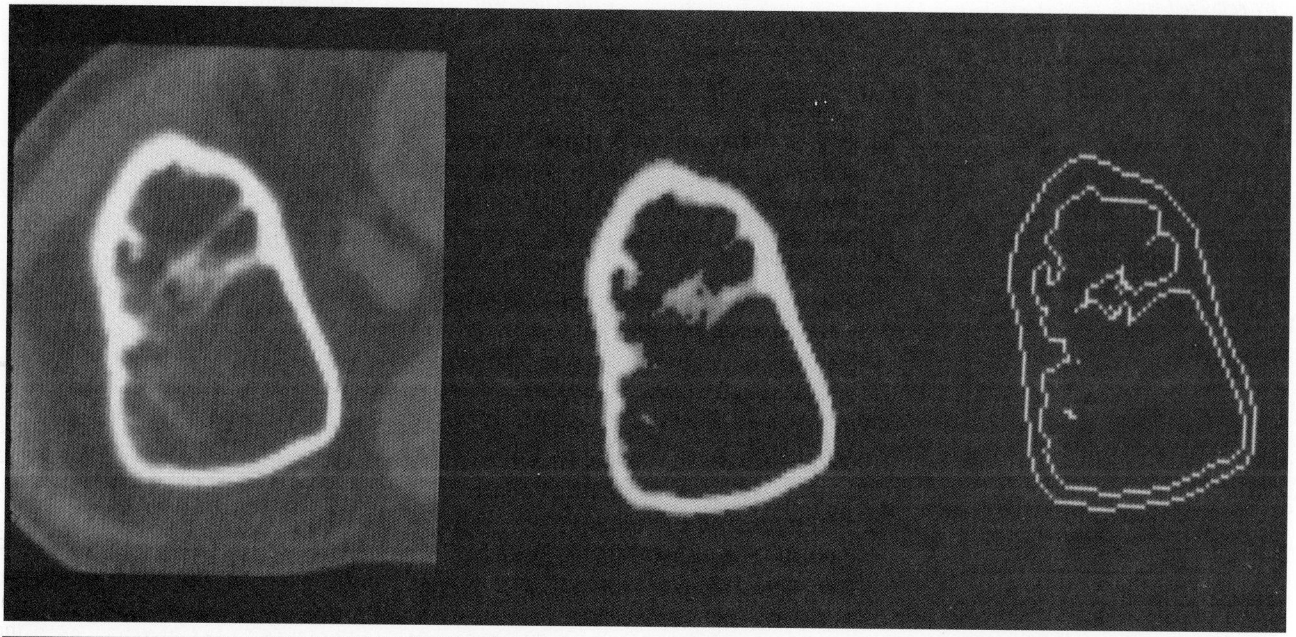

11.1 Reflected Light

The basic methods for producing three-dimensional images discussed in chapters 8 through 10 do not produce *realistic* images. To simulate a real scene, it is necessary to re-create the effects of light on surfaces which is accomplished through a process called **rendering**. Most of what we see is the reflection of light off surfaces, and we determine the shapes, textures, and colors of objects from this reflected light. The complex interactions of light coming from different directions at varying intensities are impossible to duplicate, but elaborate methods have been developed to create extremely good approximations. This section will introduce methods for computing the intensity of reflected light.

Objects may be illuminated by light coming directly from a light source such as the sun or by light reflected from other surfaces. The surface A in figure 11.1.1 is lighted directly, while side B receives only reflected light. **Emitted** light comes directly from a light source. Light generated by multiple reflections is often called **ambient**, or **background, light**.

Emitted light may appear to come from a single point or from a non-point surface. Light emanating from small surfaces is called **point source light**. Light rays from a point source have a fixed direction when they are viewed from a given point in space (figure 11.1.2). When light emanates from a surface of significant area, the source is called a **distributed light source**. Light beams

FIGURE 11.1.1

Surface A is illuminated by direct light; surface B is illuminated by reflected light.

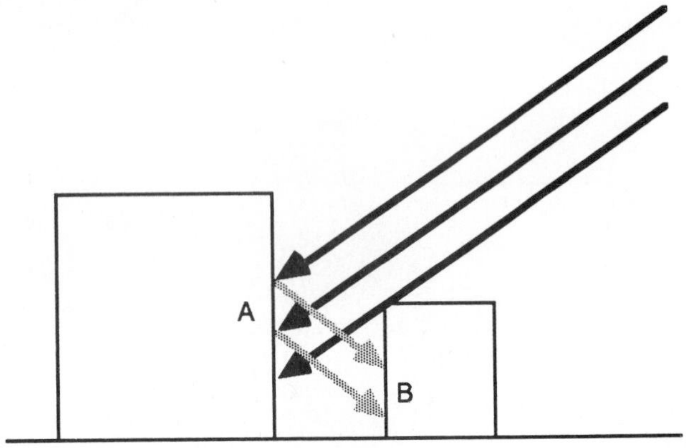

FIGURE 11.1.2

Light from a point source comes from a uniquely defined direction when it is viewed from any point in space.

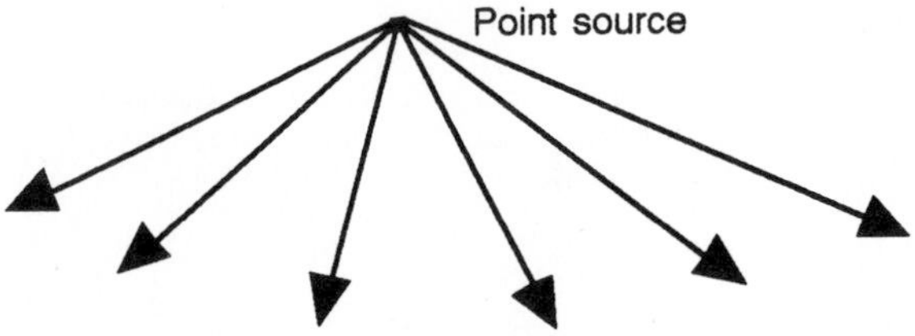

from different parts of a distributed source strike a given point on a surface at many different angles and with many different intensities (figure 11.1.3). The resulting "soft light" has shadows without sharp edges (figure 11.1.4). Even though the sun is not a small surface, because of its great distance from the Earth, it acts as a point. The farther away a surface is from a light source, the more that source resembles a point source.

FIGURE 11.1.3

Light from a distributed source strikes a given point from many different directions, the intensity varying in each direction.

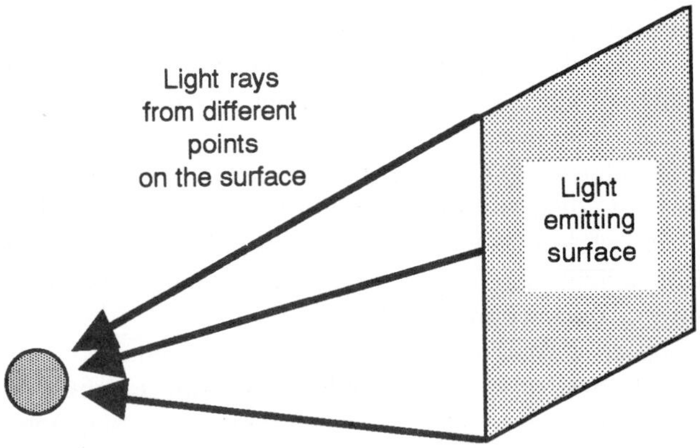

FIGURE 11.1.4

Shadows created by distributed light sources are "soft" because rays come from many directions.

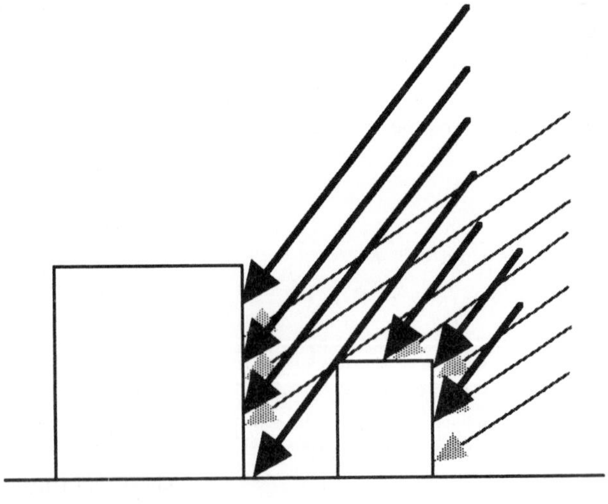

FIGURE 11.1.5

The angle of incidence for a light ray with a surface is the angle that ray makes with the normal to that surface.

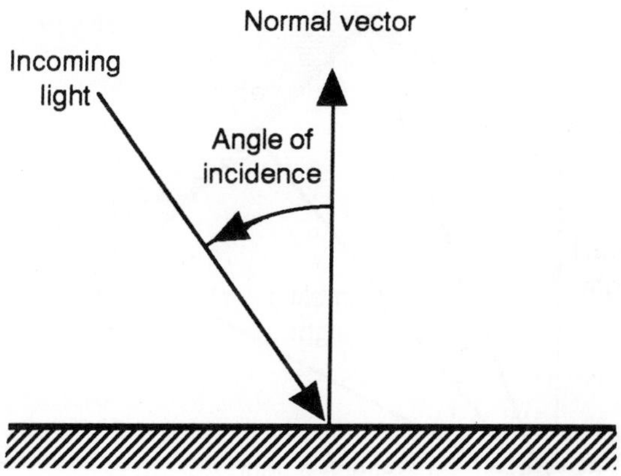

FIGURE 11.1.6

Light rays from a distant source strike all points on a planar surface at the same angle of incidence and with the same intensity.

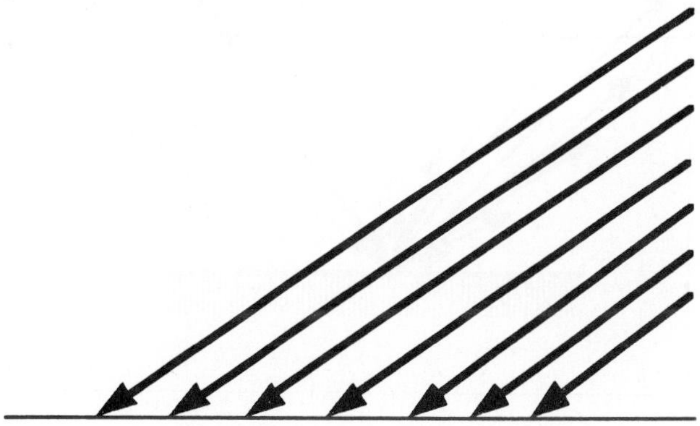

Light that has traveled a great distance has parallel rays; thus, they strike every point on a planar surface at the same angle. This angle is called the **angle of incidence** (figure 11.1.5). Because all points on a planar surface are at almost the same distance from a remote light source, the surface will be evenly lit. Models constructed for distant light sources have the advantage that light strikes all points on a given surface at the same angle of incidence and with the same intensity (figure 11.1.6).

The qualities of reflected light vary with the texture and color of the surface as well as with the nature of the light striking the surface. **Diffuse reflection** occurs when light penetrates a surface and the surface, having absorbed the light, reemits it in all directions. Surface detail such as texture and color are revealed by diffuse reflection (figure 11.1.7).

Specular reflection is the direct reflection of light by a surface. Shiny surfaces reflect almost all incident light and therefore have bright specular **highlights**, or **hot spots**. Rougher surfaces reflect less light directly, so they have few or no highlights (figure 11.1.8).

The light reflected from a typical surface is a combination of direct and ambient light (figure 11.1.9). The total light reflected is the sum of the ambient and direct light reflected by both diffuse reflection and specular reflection. This can be expressed by the equation.

$$I = R_a + R_d + R_s$$

where R_a is the ambient light reflected, R_d is the direct light diffusely reflected, and R_s is the specular reflection. Specular reflection clearly overpowers the other two sources of reflected light at hotspots. On less shiny surfaces, however, there is a region around the hotspot in which reflection gradually dominates the other two sources.

FIGURE 11.1.7

Incoming light that is absorbed by a surface and re-radiated in all directions is called diffuse reflection.

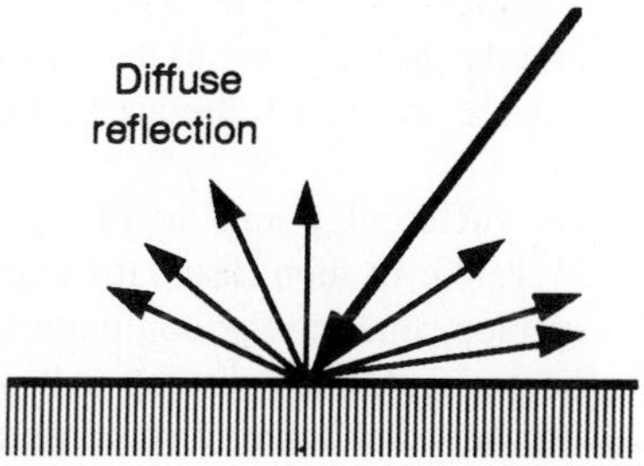

FIGURE 11.1.8

Light reflected directly by a surface is called specular reflection.

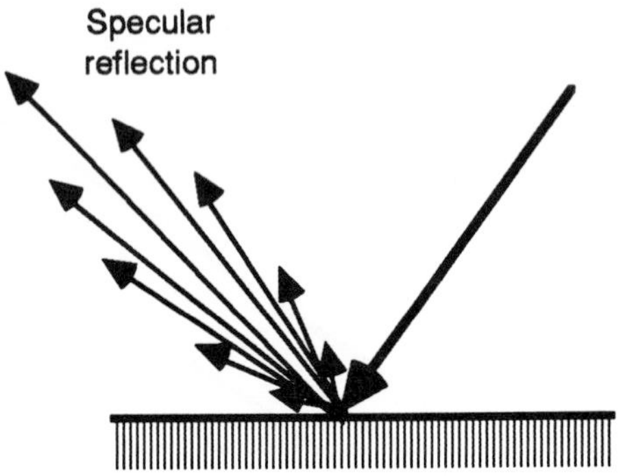

FIGURE 11.1.9

Light striking a surface can be direct or ambient.

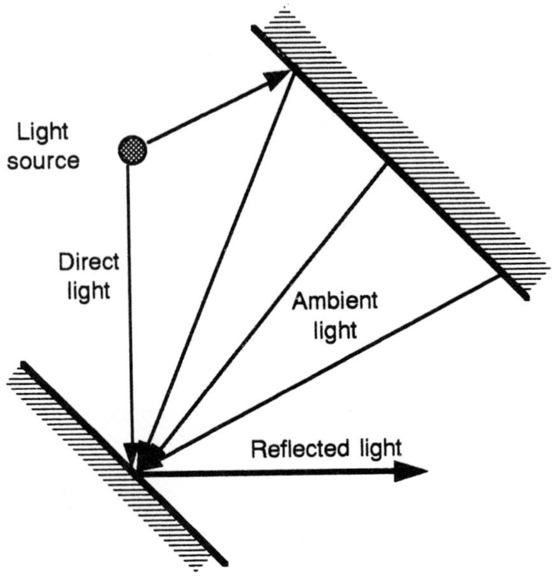

Ambient light strikes a surface simultaneously and with the same intensity from many different directions; therefore, it is reflected uniformly in all directions. If the intensity of ambient light is represented by I_a, then ambient light reflected can be computed by

$$R_a = k_d I_a$$

where k_d is the **coefficient of reflectivity**, or **reflectivity**, of the surface. White surfaces have reflectivity of nearly 1, while black surfaces have reflectivity of nearly 0.

Direct light from a point source strikes a point on a surface from a single direction and is reflected in all directions. As the angle of incidence increases, the surface intercepts fewer and fewer light rays, so it reflects less light (figure 11.1.10). This relationship is described by **Lambert's consine law**, which states that the intensity of diffuse reflection is directly proportional to the cosine of the angle of incidence. As the angle of incidence increases, the amount of light reflected decreases.

When light sources are nearby, light strikes different points at different angles because the rays are not parallel (figure 11.1.11). In such cases, the angle of incidence varies for different points on the surface, making the computation of reflected light very difficult. To simplify the computation, assume that all light sources are far enough from surfaces to be considered distant point sources. This allows you to consider the same angle of incidence for all points on the surface.

FIGURE 11.1.10

The number of parallel light rays striking a surface decreases as the angle of incidence increases. Lambert's law of cosines says that the amount of light reflected from a surface is proportional to the cosine of the angle of incidence.

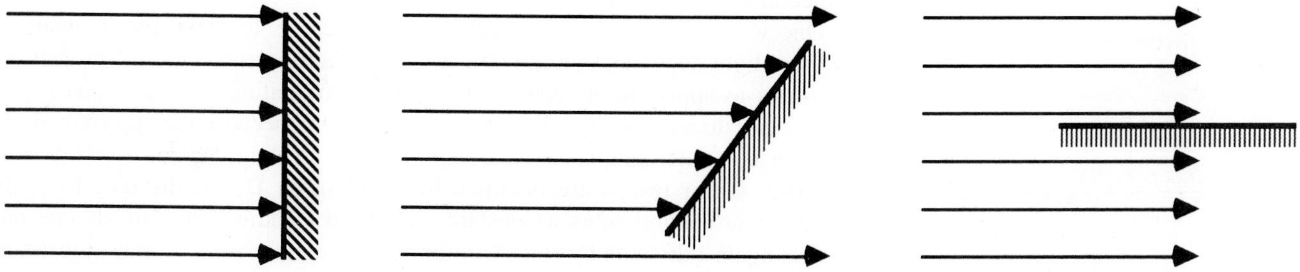

For distant point sources, the cosine of the angle of incidence for all points on a planar surface can be calculated from the dot product of a unit vector that is perpendicular to the surface, **N**, and a unit vector pointing in the direction of the light source, **L** (figure 11.1.12):

$$\cos\theta = \mathbf{N} \cdot \mathbf{L}$$

If the light source has power E_p, the amount of light reaching a surface depends on the distance from the surface to the light source. The intensity of point light striking a surface, I_p, decreases with the square of the distance, D, between the source and the surface.

$$I_p = \frac{E_p}{D^2}$$

FIGURE 11.1.11

Light from a source near a surface strikes that surface at many different angles.

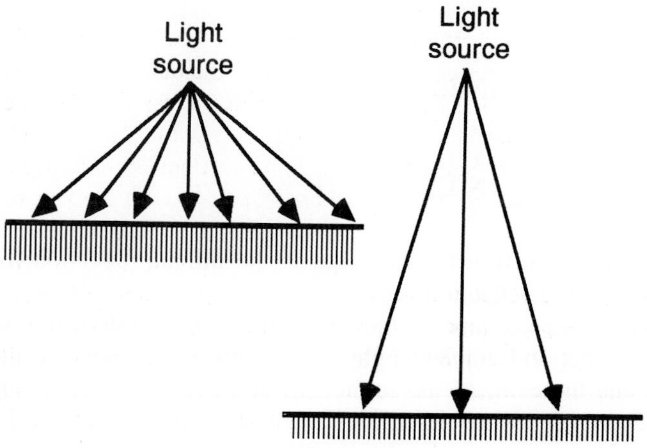

FIGURE 11.1.12

*The cosine of the angle of incidence for point source light can be computed by taking the scalar product of a unit vector, **N**, normal to the surface, and a unit vector, **L**, pointing in the direction of the light source.*

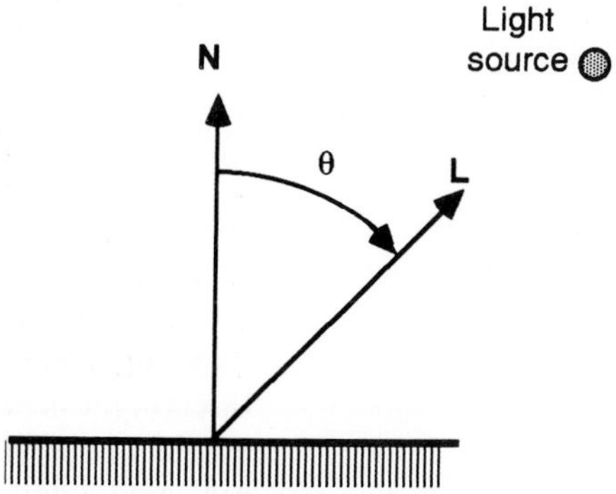

In a scene illuminated by a distant light source, these distances differ by so little that the intensity of light on the scene may be considered constant. This can be confusing if the projections of two parallel surfaces with the same reflectivity overlap. Both will reflect the same amount of light, and their projections will be indistinguishable.

One way to distinguish between such surfaces is to make the intensity of incident light dependent on the object's distance from the center of projection. Attempts to apply the inverse square rule to computing the light intensity in these cases do not give a realistic rendering. This is because the approximations used in computer graphics make light appear to diminish too quickly with distance. Better results are obtained by dividing by D, the distance from the center of projection, plus a constant, D_0, used to adjust the fall-off-rate and protect against division by zero. Combining Lambert's law with this adjustment for distance, you can find that the intensity of diffuse reflection is

$$R_d = \frac{k_d E_p}{D + D_0} (\mathbf{N} \cdot \mathbf{L})$$

The total diffuse reflection is the sum of the diffusely reflected direct and ambient light:

$$R_{td} = k_d I_a + \frac{k_d E_p}{D + D_0} (\mathbf{N} \cdot \mathbf{L})$$

Both of these forms of reflection are highly dependent on the reflectivity, k_d, of the surface.

When color is included in the model, it is created by mixing the red, green, and blue (RGB) of the color monitor. Here the reflectivity of a surface is decomposed into three components: k_{dr}, k_{dg}, and k_{db}, one for each of the primary colors. A pure bright red surface will have $k_{dr} = 1$ and other reflectivities at 0 while a purple surface will have all three constants greater than zero.

There are three equations for diffuse reflection when color is included:

$$R_{tdr} = k_{dr} I_{ar} + \frac{k_{dr} E_{pr}}{D + D_0} (\mathbf{N} \cdot \mathbf{L})$$

$$R_{tdg} = k_{dg} I_{ag} + \frac{k_{dg} E_{pg}}{D + D_0} (\mathbf{N} \cdot \mathbf{L})$$

$$R_{tdb} = k_{db} I_{ab} + \frac{k_{db} E_{pb}}{D + D_0} (\mathbf{N} \cdot \mathbf{L})$$

where R_{tdr} is the diffuse reflection for red, R_{tdg} is the diffuse reflection for green, and R_{tdb} is the diffuse reflection for blue.

Notice that in each of these equations, the incident light is also divided into its components. The direct and ambient light may be different colors. If the direct light is white and the color of the surfaces is predominantly green, the ambient light will be green. The three intensities are used to set the output of the red, green, and blue electron guns in the RGB color monitor.

While the color of a surface is determined mostly for its diffuse reflection, the shine and shape of surface are determined largely by its specular highlights. Smooth surfaces have specular highlights; rough surfaces do not. Flat surfaces often have larger specular highlights than curved surfaces. The following discussion presents one method, the **Phong model**, for simulating specular reflection (Phong 1975).

The **angle of reflection** is the angle that reflected light from a surface makes with the normal to that surface. In simplified, idealistic models of reflection, the angle of reflection is equal to the angle of incidence (figure 11.1.13). If this were true for all surfaces, a point source would be reflected as a point of light and all surfaces would be mirrors. As you have seen, some light is reflected through random angles off most surfaces. Even highlights are seldom points of light reflected solely along a vector at the angle of reflection. There is, instead, a cone of specular reflection. The amount of specular reflection decreases as the angle of view deviates from the angle of reflection (figure 11.1.14)

FIGURE 11.1.13

In simplified, idealistic models of reflection, the angle of incidence is equal to the angle of reflection.

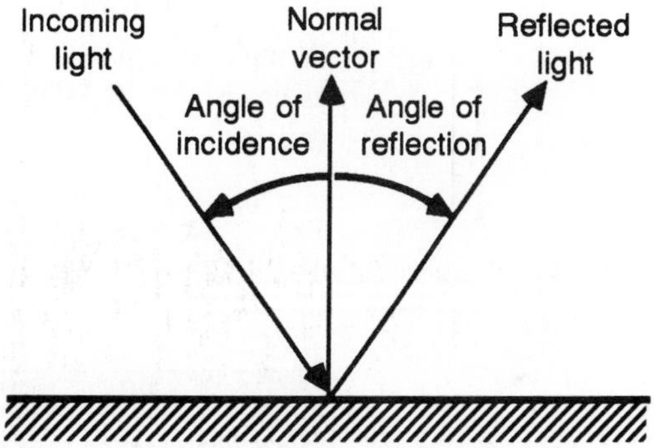

FIGURE 11.1.14

Specular reflection from a dull surface can be seen over a wider range of angles than reflection from a shiny surface.

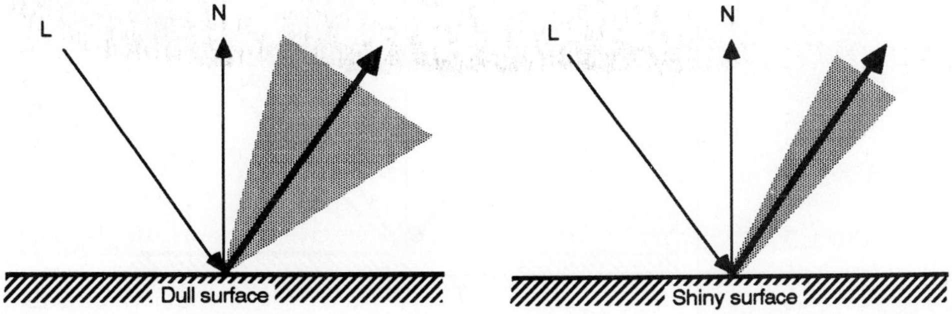

In the Phong model, the intensity of the light along a vector at an angle ϕ from the angle of reflection (figure 11.1.15) is proportional to $\cos^n\phi$, where n is determined by the shininess of the surface. Clearly, when the angle ϕ is 0, the $\cos^n\phi = 1$; hence, the specular reflection is greatest at the angle of reflection. If $n = 1$, the intensity decreases gradually as ϕ approaches $\pm\pi/2$. Thus, surfaces with $n = 1$ are dull surfaces, such as cardboard or fabric-covered surfaces. Metallic surfaces such as silver have large n values, of 150 or more. For these surfaces the intensity of specular reflection drops off rapidly as the line of sight moves away from the angle of reflection. Shiny objects have smaller, more intense highlights.

Another consideration is that the reflectivity of the surface changes with the angle of incidence. Surfaces such as water or glass have a high reflectivity when the angle of incidence is large, and small reflectivity when the angle of incidence is small (figure 11.1.16). This variation, which is also dependent on the wavelength, λ, of the incoming light is expressed by $W(\theta,\lambda)$, the **specular reflection coefficient**, or **specular reflectance**.

All these factors combine to give the following equation for R_s, the specular reflection:

$$R_s = \frac{E_p}{D + D_0} W(\theta,\lambda) \cos^n\phi$$

For most surfaces, variations in specular reflection are small so the function W may be replaced by a constant, k_s. The $\cos\phi$ can also be computed directly as $\cos\phi = \mathbf{V}\cdot\mathbf{R}$ if **V** and **R** are normalized. Combining these simplifications, you get

$$R_s = \frac{E_p}{D + D_0} k_s (\mathbf{V}\cdot\mathbf{R})^n$$

FIGURE 11.1.15

Specular reflection is visible when the view vector is at an angle that is close to the angle of reflection.

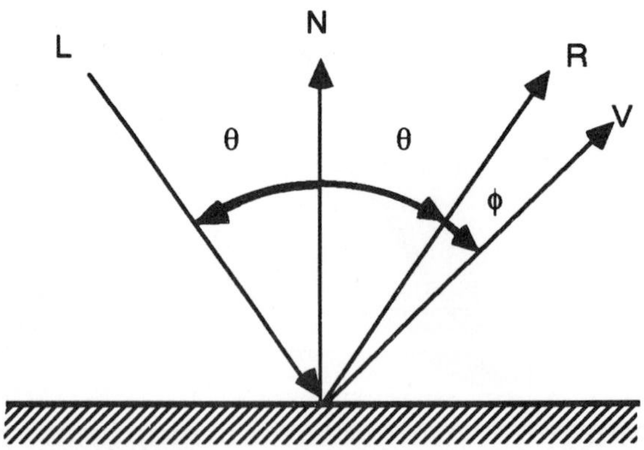

FIGURE 11.1.16

The amount of light reflected from a surface such as water is dependent on the view vector.

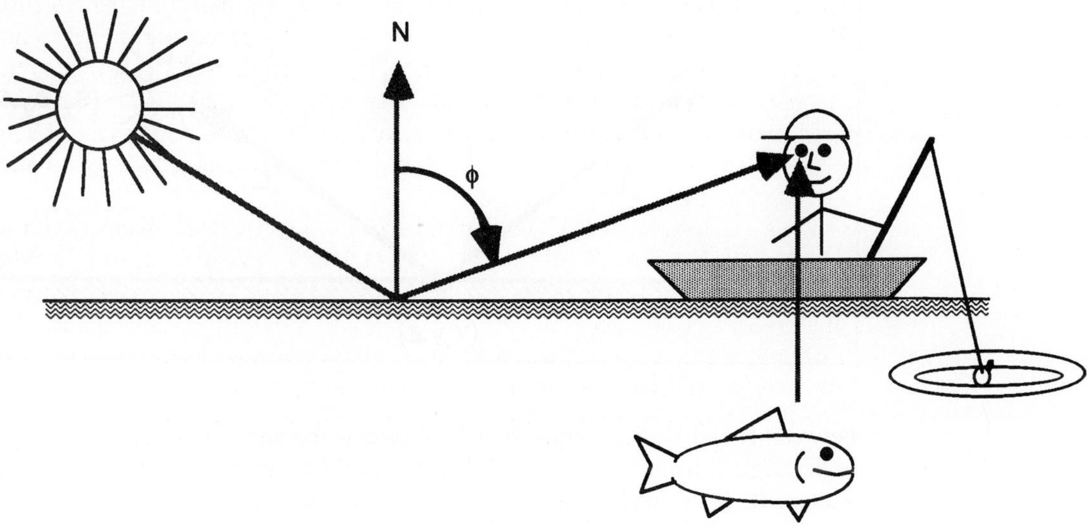

The equation for reflected light may now be given as

$$I = k_d I_a + \frac{E_p}{D + D_o}(k_d(\mathbf{N}\cdot\mathbf{L}) + k_s(\mathbf{V}\cdot\mathbf{R})^n)$$

Reflected light displayed by color monitors may be computed for each of the primary colors. The equation for red is

$$I_r = k_{dr} I_{ar} + \frac{E_{pr}}{D + D_0}(k_{dr}(\mathbf{N}\cdot\mathbf{L}) + k_s(\mathbf{V}\cdot\mathbf{R})^n)$$

Similar equations may be developed for green and blue.

If both the light source and the viewer are sufficiently far from the reflecting surface, it is possible to assume that both **N·L** and **V·R** are constant for all points on the surface. When this is not the case, the dot products are computed for a beginning point. Incremental methods similar to the scan-line algorithm are used to approximate them for other points.

The vectors **L** and **V** can be computed for a given point, (x,y,z), on a surface by simple vector arithmetic. If the viewer's eye is at the point (v_x, v_y, v_z), then the vector $\mathbf{V} = (v_x - x, v_y - y, v_z - z)$. Similarly, if the light source is at (s_x, s_y, s_z), then the vector $\mathbf{L} = (s_x - x, s_y - y, s_z - z)$ (figure 11.1.17). The normal vector **N** is easily computed for plane surfaces. If the surface is a polygon mesh, then each of the polygonal regions is a plane for which a normal vector may be computed. Normal vectors for more complex surfaces are not easy to compute, however.

For reflections from a plane surface, if ϕ is small, the $\cos\phi$ may be approximated (Hearn and Baker 1986) without computing **R**. Because the angle if incidence equals the angle of reflection, the vector **N** bisects the angle

FIGURE 11.1.17

*The vectors **V** and **L** can be computed easily if the coordinates of the view point, light source, and point on the surface are known.*

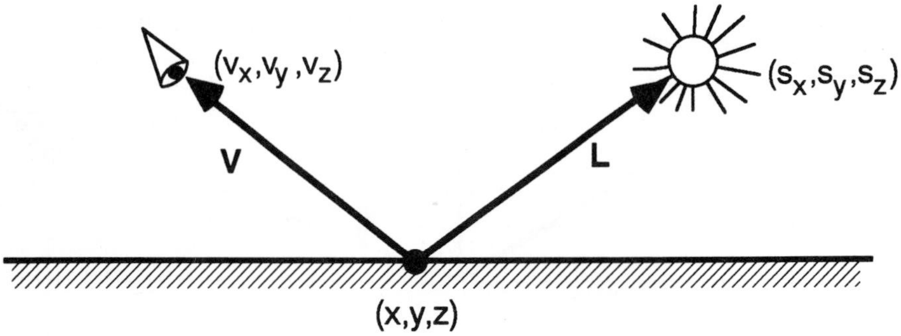

between **R** and **L**. The vector **B**, which bisects the angle between **R** and **L**, is at the angle β from **N** (figure 11.1.18). If, for the moment, you assume that the vectors **R**, **L**, **V**, and **N** are coplanar, you can see that

$$\phi = 2\mu - 2\theta = 2(\mu - \theta) = 2\beta$$

For small values of φ, the value of cosφ is close to the value of cosβ, so that **N**·**B** = cosβ may be used as an approximation of **V**·**R** = cosφ. The vector **B** is easy to compute for the vectors **V** and **L**.

$$\mathbf{B} = \frac{\mathbf{V} + \mathbf{L}}{|\mathbf{V} + \mathbf{L}|}$$

FIGURE 11.1.18

*If the angle of incidence, θ, is not near 90° and the angle φ is near zero, then **N•B** is approximately **R•V** = cosθ.*

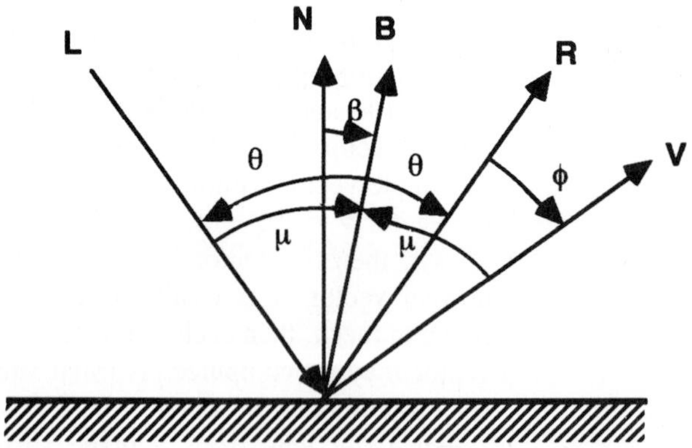

As long as the angle ϕ is small, the vector **V** need not be in the plane of **L** and **R** for this to be a usable approximation.

When it is necessary to compute the vector **R**, geometry can be applied to devise a formula for **R**. Recall that both **L** and **N** are unit vectors. Construct the vector **R′** so that it is parallel and in the same direction as − **L** from **N** to **R** (figure 11.1.19). **R′** is parallel to **L**, so the angle that **R′** makes with **N** is ϕ. The triangle formed by **N**, **R**, and **R′** is isosceles, with the length of **R** equal to the length of **R′**. The length, d, of these vectors is calculated from the law of cosines: $d^2 = d^2 + 1 - 2d\cos\phi$. Solving for d, you get $d = 1/(2\cos\phi)$, so $\mathbf{R}' = d(-\mathbf{L}) = -\mathbf{L}/(2\cos\phi)$. From the construction you can see that $\mathbf{R} = \mathbf{N} + \mathbf{R}'$. This, together with the fact that $\cos\phi = \mathbf{N}\cdot\mathbf{L}$, results in the equation

$$\mathbf{R} = \mathbf{N} + -\mathbf{L}/(2\mathbf{N}\cdot\mathbf{L})$$

FIGURE 11.1.19

*The reflection vector **R** may be computed directly from the vector **L** to the light source and the normal vector **N**.*

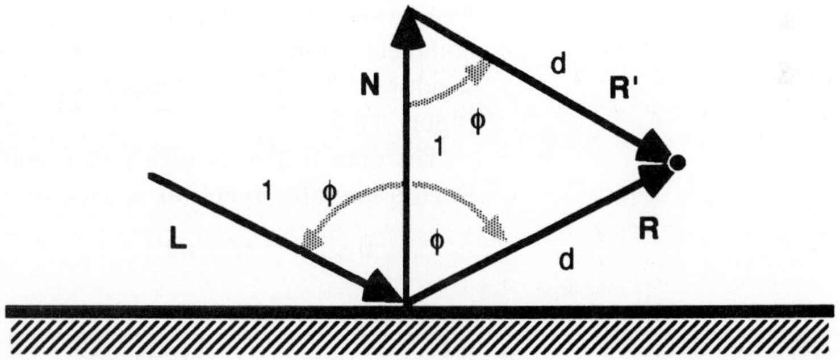

EXERCISES

11.1.1

Using Lambert's law with no correction for distance, write a procedure to compute the diffuse reflection of a single white light source from a surface.

11.1.2

Using Lambert's law with modifications for distance, write a procedure to compute the diffuse reflection of a single white light source from a surface. Assume that the power of the light source, the distance of the surface from the light source, the reflectivity, and the angle of incidence are passed to the procedure, and that D_0 is a constant.

11.2 Refraction, Transparency, and Scattering

Most of what we see is reflected light, but this light seldom passes directly to our eyes without interference from other substances. This interference is called *scattering*. Windows separate us from the world outside, and smoke or dust interfere with our view inside. **Ray tracing** is used to model the effects of transparent and mirrorlike objects. When scattering is important, the medium causing the scattering is translucent. Combinations of transparent and translucent media are usually modeled by using **radiosity**. Ray tracing and radiosity are the subjects of section 11.4. A simple model of transparency and refraction is presented here.

Transparent media are substances that allow light to pass through without a large amount of scattering. At the boundary between two transparent media, light is bent. This bending is called **refraction**. The amount and direction of the bending depends on the two substances involved. The speed of light is a constant in a vacuum, but it has different values when it passes through substances. If the speed of light is slower in one substance than in a second substance, the first substance is **optically denser** than the second. Light entering an optically denser substance is bent toward the normal vector to the surface (figure 11.2.1). Light entering a substance that is less optically dense is bent away from the normal to the interface (figure 11.2.2). When light passes completely through a transparent object with parallel plane edges such as a window, every ray is transformed into a ray that is parallel to the original ray (figure 11.2.3).

The optical density of a given material is given as the **index of refraction**. **Snell's law of refraction** is used to compute **angle of refraction** θ':

$$n \sin\theta = n' \sin\theta'$$

FIGURE 11.2.1

Light is bent toward the normal to the interface when it passes from a medium of lower optical density to a medium of higher optical density.

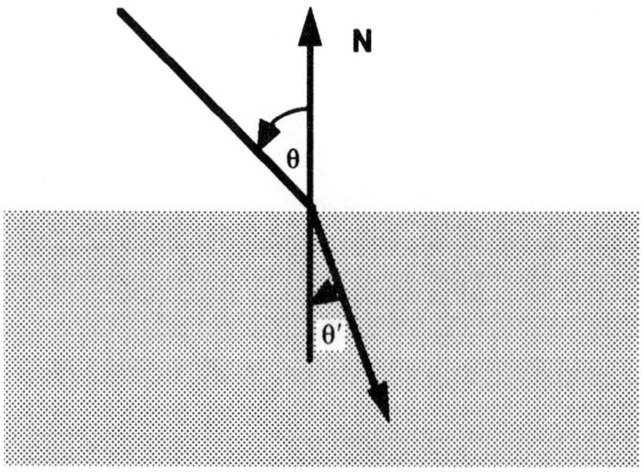

FIGURE 11.2.2

Light is bent away from the normal to the interface when it passes from a medium of higher optical density to a medium of lower optical density.

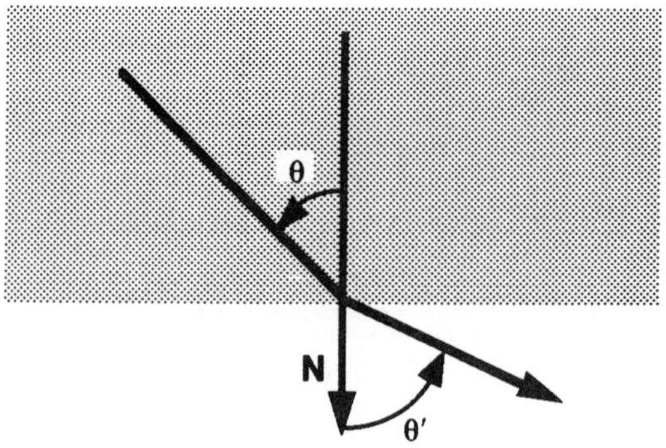

Here n and n′ are the indices of refraction, and θ is the angle of incidence. Snell's law is usually not used to calculate the path of light passing through a transparent object such as a window because of the computation of the sine. It is quicker to simulate refraction using the fact that a ray leaving the glass is parallel to the original ray, and simply translate the ray by a small amount. When the transparent material is very thin, the amount of translation is small enough that it may be ignored.

The light intensity, I, coming from a transparent surface must incorporate both the light reflected from that surface and the light transmitted by the surface (figure 11.2.4). Very transparent substances reflect little light while opaque substances absorb or reflect all their light. The transparency of an object can be expressed as a **refraction coefficient**, r, in the equation

$$I = rI_f + (1 - r)I_b$$

where I_f is the intensity of light striking the front surface of the object and I_b is the light striking the surface directly behind the front surface. Highly transparent objects have $r \approx 0$ while opaque objects have $r = 1$.

When hidden-surface algorithms, such as the z-buffer algorithm, are used to create surfaces, rI_f is the value associated with the transparent surface. The value I_b is obtained from the surface directly behind the transparent object.

This is a very simple model that fails to take into account curved transparent surfaces, absorption of light, and specular highlights. More complicated models are used for such surfaces (Kay 1979; Kay and Greenberg 1979). Problems of translucency are treated in Cohen et al. (1988).

Light passing through a medium may be altered by small particles distributed through the substance. These particles absorb, scatter, and reflect light. The effects of this scattering have been modeled in Rushmeier and Torrance (1987) and Nishita, Miyawaki, and Nakamae (1987).

FIGURE 11.2.3

When light passes completely through a transparent medium, the ray entering the medium is parallel to the ray after it leaves the medium.

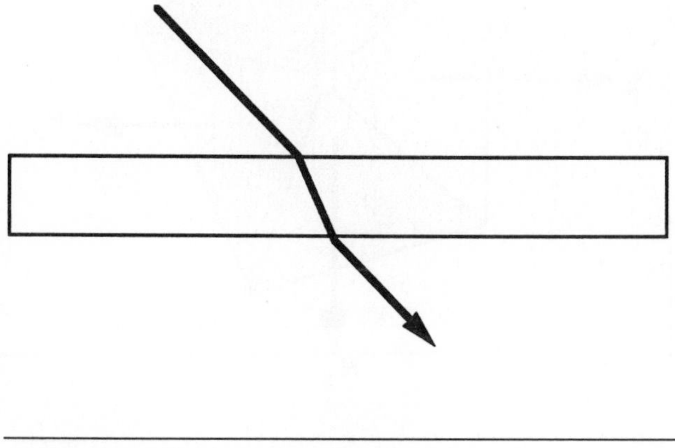

FIGURE 11.2.4

The light coming from a transparent surface must incorporate both the light reflected from the surface and the light transmitted by the surface.

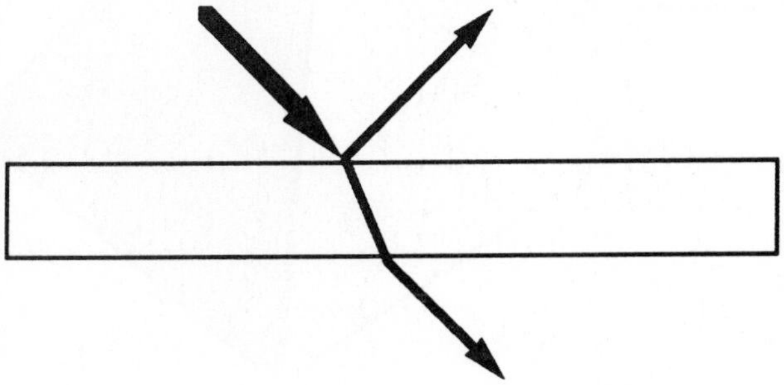

11.3 Shading Surfaces

Methods for computing the light intensity at a point on a given surface lead to several ways of rendering a surface. You will start by shading simple objects with plane faces; then you will consider ways to use surface shading techniques on a polygon mesh to give the impression of a smoothly curved surface.

A single polygon mesh illuminated by a distant point source and viewed from a distance can be rendered by using a **constant shading** model (figure 11.3.1). A plane surface has one easily computed normal vector, **N**. The distant point source ensures that the angle of incidence is constant over each surface so that **N·L** will be constant for each face. The product **V·R** will be constant because the viewer is at a distance. Even if the light source is not a point source or the viewer is closer, good results are achieved when the dot products are computed for average **V** and **L**, or **V** and **L** are computed at the center of each face.

The constant shading model used on a polygon mesh is always acceptable if the mesh approximates a smooth, curved surface. It is possible to use interpolation to create the impression that a polygon mesh is a smooth surface. Two forms of interpolation are often used for this purpose: **Gouraud**, or **intensity**, **interpolation**; and **Phong**, or **normal-vector**, **interpolation**.

The Gouraud shading model uses a modified scan-fill algorithm to assign an interpolated intensity value for each point. First, intensities are assigned to each vertex of the mesh. To incorporate all the adjacent faces in these computations, the normal vector used for each vertex is the average of the normal vectors to the adjacent faces. The normal vector used for vertex V in figure 11.3.2 is

FIGURE 11.3.1

The constant shading model assumes that a scene is lighted with a distant point source light and is viewed from a distance.

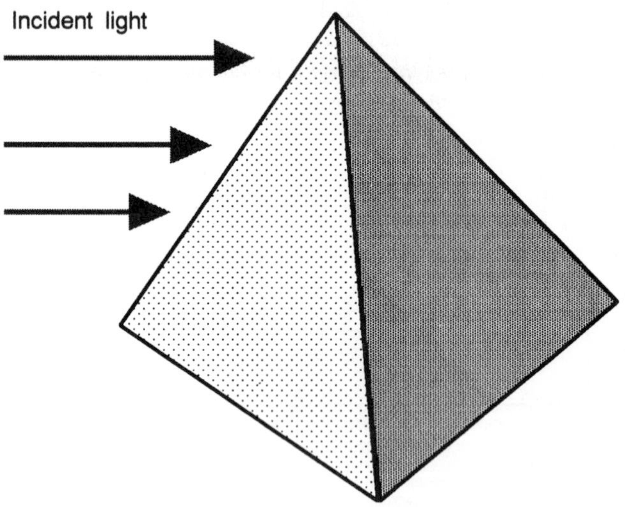

FIGURE 11.3.2

You can compute the normal vector at a vertex by adding the normal vectors to the faces adjacent to the vertex and then normalizing that sum.

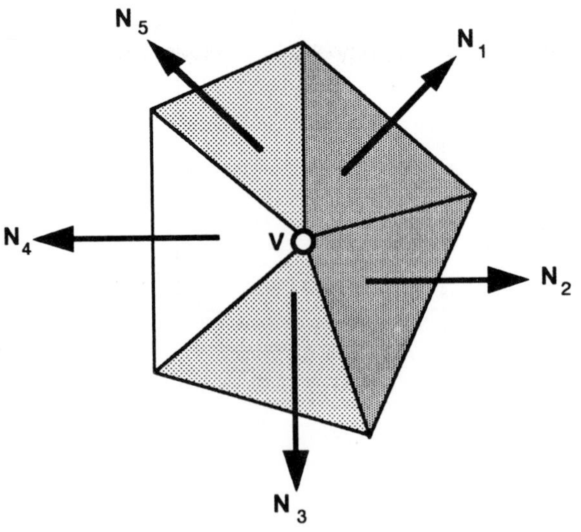

FIGURE 11.3.3

You can compute the intensity of reflected light at a point on a surface by interpolating the intensity values at the two end points for the scan line.

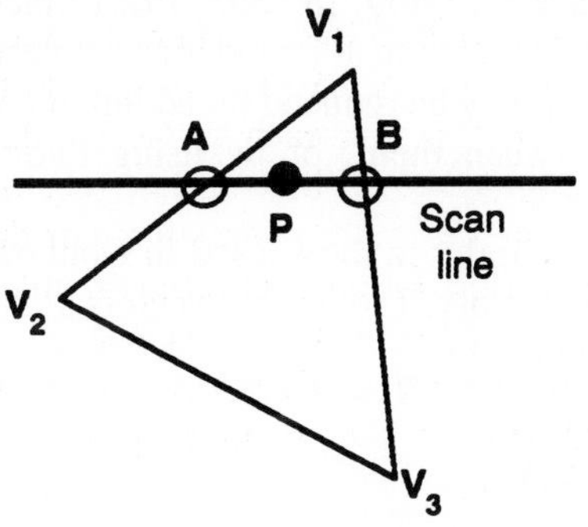

computed by adding the vectors $\mathbf{N}_1$ to $\mathbf{N}_5$ and then normalizing the sum. Once normals have been computed for each vertex, the intensity at each vertex is computed by using these normals in an intensity model.

To compute the intensity at a point **P** (figure 11.3.3), compute the intensities I_A and I_B for the end points **A** and **B** of the scan line containing **P**. The intensity at point **A** can be computed by interpolation from the values I_1 and I_2 at vertices by using the formula

$$I_{\mathbf{A}} = (1 - t)I_1 + tI_2$$
$$t = \mathbf{V}_1\mathbf{A}/\mathbf{V}_1\mathbf{V}_2$$

Similarly,

$$I_{\mathbf{B}} = (1 - s)I_1 + sI_3$$
$$s = \mathbf{V}_1\mathbf{B}/\mathbf{V}_1\mathbf{V}_3$$

After the intensities at the end points of the scan line are computed, intensity values for points on the line are computed incrementally. The amount of the increment is also computed by using interpolation on two consecutive points on the scan line. If **Q** is the point preceding, **P**, $u_{\mathbf{P}} = \mathbf{AP}/\mathbf{AB}$ and $u_{\mathbf{Q}} = \mathbf{AQ}/\mathbf{AB}$. Then the intensity at each point may be computed as

$$I_{\mathbf{P}} = (1 - u_{\mathbf{P}})I_{\mathbf{A}} + u_{\mathbf{P}}I_{\mathbf{B}}$$
$$I_{\mathbf{Q}} = (1 - u_{\mathbf{Q}})I_{\mathbf{A}} + u_{\mathbf{Q}}I_{\mathbf{B}}$$

The difference between these values is the constant

$$\Delta I = (u_{\mathbf{P}} - u_{\mathbf{Q}})\ (I_{\mathbf{B}} - I_{\mathbf{A}})$$

This value is computed once for each scan line. The intensity at a given point is computed by adding ΔI to the intensity at the previous point on the scan line.

When Gouraud shading is used to fill a surface such as that in figure 11.3.4, all the averaged normals may be parallel. This will lead to the same intensity for

FIGURE 11.3.4

When Gouraud shading is used to calculate light intensity, all the averaged normals may be parallel, leading to one intensity for all surfaces in the mesh.

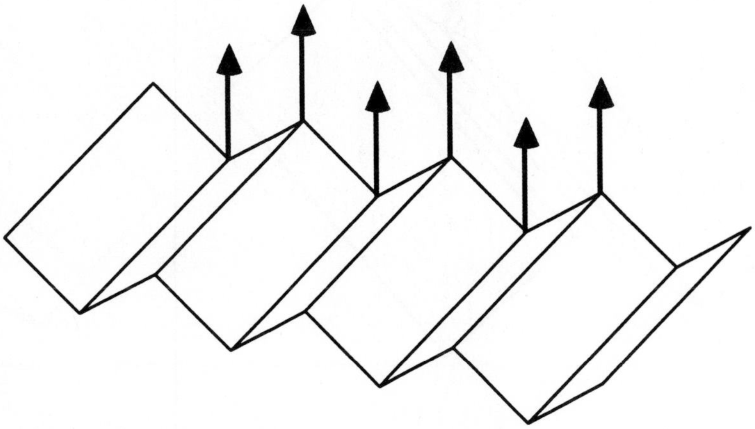

the entire area. Smoother shading can be achieved by creating additional polygons (figure 11.3.5). If the shading on one face is substantially different from that on the other—that is, there is a crease—then two normals may be associated with a given vertex. In figure 11.3.6, the vertex **V** lies on a crease. The shading of F_1 is determined from the normal vector $\mathbf{N}_1$ at **V**, and the intensity of F_2 is determined from the normal vector $\mathbf{N}_2$ at **V**.

Gouraud shading is also susceptible to **Mach banding**. In 1865, Ernst Mach discovered that the eye perceives bright or dark streaking at boundaries between two areas of different intensities. This problem may be reduced by adding more polygons with smaller intensity changes between them, or by using Phong shading.

Phong shading uses interpolation formulas similar to those used in Gouraud shading but with intensity replaced by normal vectors. The normal vectors at the beginning and end of the scan line are computed by

$$\mathbf{N_A} = (1 - t)\mathbf{N}_1 + t\mathbf{N}_2, \quad t = \mathbf{V_1A/V_1V_2}$$
$$\mathbf{N_B} = (1 - s)\mathbf{N}_1 + s\mathbf{N}_3, \quad s = \mathbf{V_1B/V_1V_3}$$

Normal vectors at consecutive points on a scan line are computed by

$$\mathbf{N_P} = (1 - u_P)\,\mathbf{N_A} + u_P\mathbf{N_B}, \quad u_P = \mathbf{AP/AB}$$
$$\mathbf{N_Q} = (1 - u_Q)\,\mathbf{N_A} + u_Q\mathbf{N_B}, \quad u_Q = \mathbf{AQ/AB}$$

The change in the normal vector between consecutive scan-line points can be computed by

$$\Delta \mathbf{N} = (u_P - u_Q)\,(\mathbf{N_B} - \mathbf{N_A})$$

FIGURE 11.3.5

To get better definition with Gouraud shading, subdivide polygons into additional polygons before computing the normals.

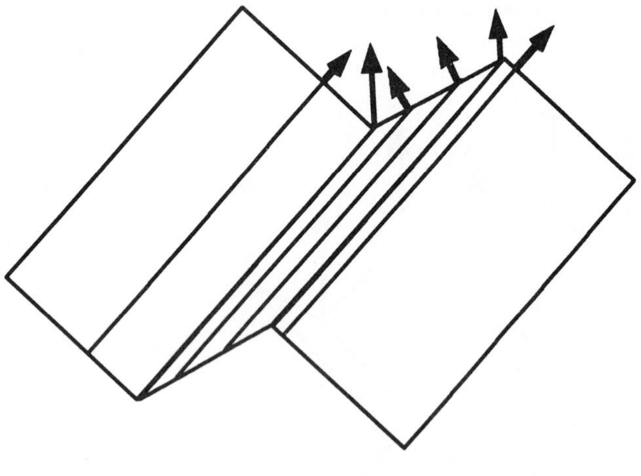

FIGURE 11.3.6

A crease is created, when there is a substantial difference between two faces. This can be achieved with Gouraud shading if two normals are associated with vertices shared by the two faces.

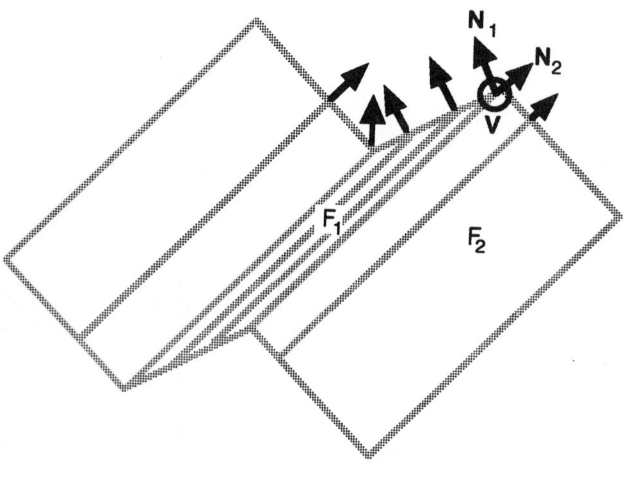

Generally, Phong shading reduces the amount of Mach banding that Gouraud shading produces; however, Phong shading sometimes increases the amount of Mach banding as shown by Duff (1979) (figure 11.3.7). Phong shading also takes loner than Gouraud shading because it has a much larger number of vector computations.

All the shading models discussed in this section assume a uniformly colored smooth surface. While the shape of an orange is closely approximated by a sphere, its surface has a distinctive texture that shading alone cannot duplicate. Textures or patterns on a surface can be regular repeating patterns like those used in filling regions, or irregular, seemingly random patterns such as those formed by stones on a beach.

Regular patterns can be generated mathematically, but natural or random patterns often come from digitized photographs. In either case, the two-dimensional pattern must be displayed on a three-dimensional surface. Texture planes can be coordinatized, and the value of a texture at a point, (u,v), can be given by T(u,v). Many three-dimensional surfaces may be described by parametric equations in two variables. A sphere can be described as the set of all points (x,y,z) satisfying the equations

$$x(u,v) = R\cos(2\pi u)\sin(\pi v)$$
$$y(u,v) = R\cos(\pi v)$$
$$z(u,v) = R\sin(2\pi u)\sin(\pi v) \quad 0 \leq u,\ v \leq 1$$

FIGURE 11.3.7

A comparison of flat shading, Gouraud shading, and Phong shading. The normal vectors used to create the flat shading were chosen incorrectly so the rectangular patches appear to be subdivided into triangles. The close-up view of the pawn's head shows flat shading with a better choice of normal vectors. Reprinted from Bishop et al. 1986, 106.

The texture can be associated with such a surface by letting the intensity at (x(u,v),y(u,v),z(u,v)) be T(u,v).

One way to make this association is to step through values of u and v, calculate (x,y,z), and assign T(u,v) to this point. With this method it is important to choose the correct increment. If the increment is too large, there will be gaps in the texture because not all pixels will be associated with a point s(u,v) = (x(u),y(u),z(u)). If the increments are too small, more than one value s(u,v) will be contained in each pixel, so that more than one texture value will be associated with a pixel. Clearly it is better to choose an increment that is small, but the method of choice used to determine the shading value in case of conflict is important. It is possible to take just the current color value. This results in pixel color T(u,v), where (u,v) is the last pair of values mapping to the pixel. Because this can result in aliasing problems, an alternative is to take the average color value for the set of points (u,v) that map to a given pixel.

An alternative to guessing the size of the increments for u and v is to find the pair (u,v) for which s(u,v) is at the center of a pixel. Each pixel may then be associated with a unique pair (u,v). This process works well if the pattern is large compared to the area covered by a pixel. If, however, the pattern is on a scale similar to that of the pixel, the resulting texture may be random. To avoid this problem, the inverse image of a pixel is used to determine a quadrilateral in texture space (figure 11.3.8). The texture values for this quadrilateral are averaged and the result used for the pixel color.

More complex methods have been used to map textures directly onto surfaces. A two-part map that first maps the texture onto a plane and then transforms the plane onto a curved surface is given by Bier and Sloan (1986).

FIGURE 11.3.8

You can obtain the value of pixel in a textured area by computing the average texture value for the inverse image of that pixel.

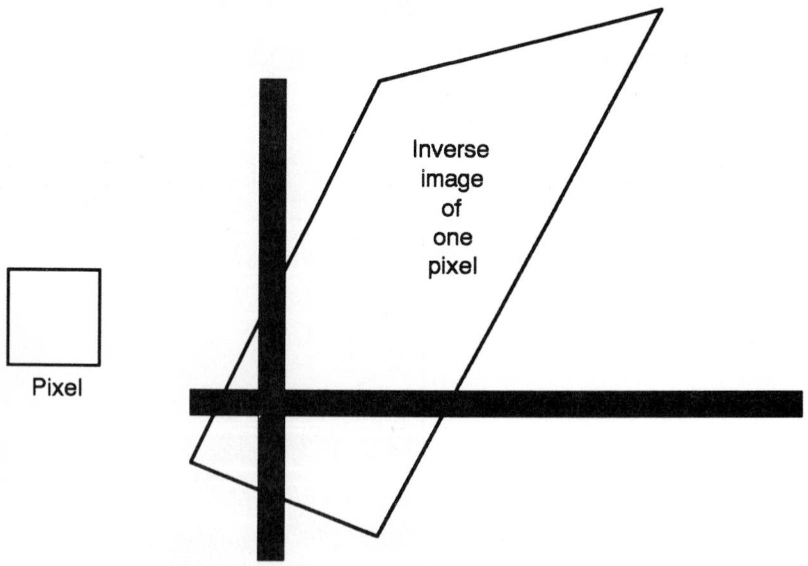

Oka et al. (1987) use linear approximations to create interactive texture maps. Texture maps give a life-like appearance to animated creatures. Matt Elson employed two different types of texture maps when creating Lotta Desire (figure 11.3.9) for his visual poem ''A Little Death.'' The first texture, leopard skin, was used to give Lotta the appearance of natural breathing. The second version of Lotta featured a realistic face created by mapping a scanned photo onto the free-hand sculpted head.

FIGURE 11.3.9

The character Lotta Desire from the animated poem ''The Little Death'' was created by Matt Elson of Symbolics. A leopard skin texture (middle) on a free-hand sculpted wireframe model (left) to give Lotta the appearance of natural breathing. The second version (right) of Lotta features a realistic face created by mapping a scanned photo onto the wireframe head.

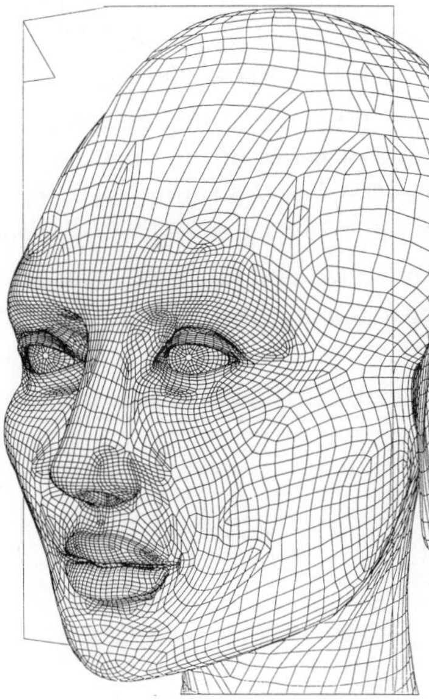

EXERCISES

11.3.1

Modify the data structure used for a polygon side in the scan-line algorithm to facilitate the Phong shading algorithm.

11.3.2

Modify the scan-line algorithm to compute intensity values for the Phong shading algorithm.

11.3.3

Modify the data structure used for a polygon side in the scan-line algorithm to facilitate the Gouraud shading algorithm.

11.3.4

Modify the scan-line algorithm to compute intensity values for the Gouraud shading algorithm.

11.4 Ray Tracing and Radiosity

The calculations of reflected and refracted intensities in sections 11.1 and 11.2 depend on incident light intensity. A single object illuminated by a distant point source can be rendered by means of shading techniques covered in section 11.3. Scenes with more than one object require more sophisticated approaches to reveal the interplay of reflected and refracted light. One theoretically simple approach is ray tracing. If it were possible to trace every ray from the light source, it would be possible to calculate the total amount of incident, reflected, and refracted light hitting any point in the scene. There are an infinite number of such paths, so this is not a feasible technique. There are, however, only a finite number of pixels on the screen. It is possible to generate a ray from the center of projection through each pixel. These rays may be traced through all their reflections and refractions until they pass out of the view volume, strike a surface of known illumination, or hit the light source (figure 11.4.1). The initial intensity is assigned at this point. As the paths are traced in reverse order, techniques for computing intensity of reflected and refracted light are applied to compute each ray's contribution to the intensity of the next ray on the path.

FIGURE 11.4.1

Rays are traced from the center of projection until they hit a surface of known illumination, a light source, or pass out of the view volume.

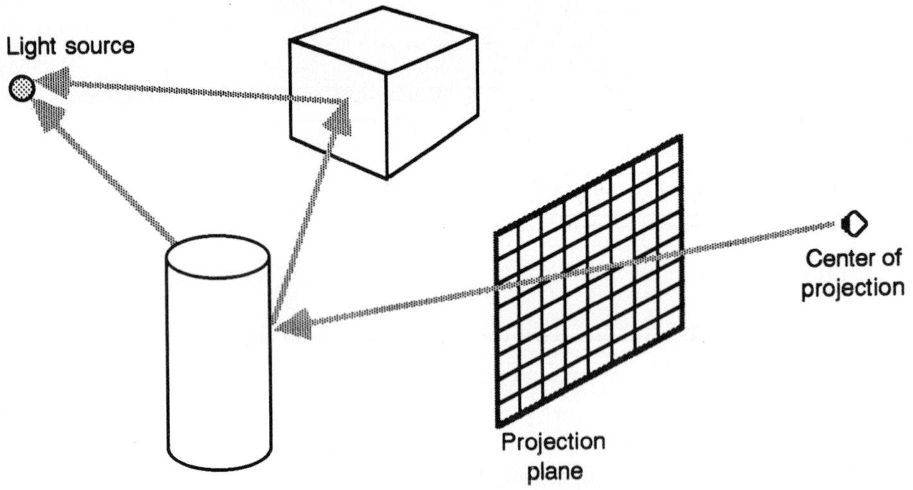

A ray traced to a diffuse surface can be traced no farther because it splits into an infinite number of possible rays. Thus, ray tracing is mainly used to depict mirrored and perfectly refracting surfaces. To establish the light intensities on diffuse surfaces, illumination and shading models, such as those introduced in sections 11.1 through 11.3, are applied to the scene before ray tracing begins.

Tracing a ray from a given pixel begins with the formulation of the parametric equations of a line joining that pixel with the center of projection. The view coordinates of pixel (x_0,y_0) are (x_0,y_0,d), and the center of projection is at the origin (figure 11.4.2). The parametric equations of a line joining these two points are

$$x(t) = x_0\, t$$
$$y(t) = y_0\, t$$
$$z(t) = d\, t$$

Intersections of this line with all scene surfaces are calculated (figure 11.4.3). To do this, a list of all surfaces must be maintained. List entries hold the equation of the surface and the illumination of the surface. This process is easily demonstrated with a sphere. The equation of a sphere of radius r with center (x_c, y_c, z_c) is $(x - x_c)^2 + (y - y_c)^2 + (z - z_c)^2 - r^2 = 0$. To compute the intersection of a ray with this or any other surface, substitute the parametric form of x, y, and z into the equation for the surface and solve for the parameter. In the case of the sphere, the value of the parameter t can be computed by using the quadratic formula on

$$t^2(x_0^2 + y_0^2 + d^2) - 2t(x_0\, x_c + y_0\, y_c + d\, z_c) + x_c^2 + y_c^2 + z_c^2 - r^2 = 0$$

F I G U R E 11.4.2

For each pixel (x,y) the parametric equation of the line from the center of projection to the pixel is created.

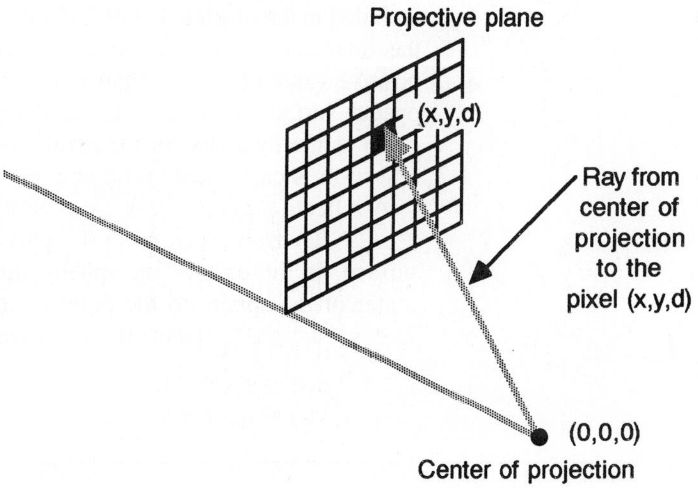

FIGURE 11.4.3

The intersection of a given ray with all surfaces in the scene is computed. The number of computations can be reduced if back faces are removed before ray tracing is begun.

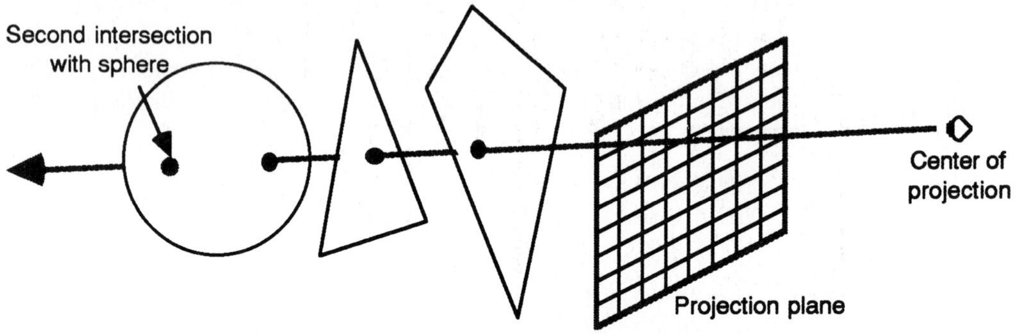

Only real values of t correspond to intersections of the ray and the sphere, and in the case of two real solutions, the smallest value of $t > 1$ corresponds to the intersection closest to the viewer.

Testing for the intersection of a ray and a polygon is more difficult. A polygon lies in the plane with equation $Ax + By + Cz + D = 0$, where (A,B,C) is the normal vector for the polygon. Finding the intersection of a ray and this plane can be done in the same way as for the intersection of the ray and the sphere. While this solution will indicate where a ray strikes the plane, it will not disclose whether the ray has passed through a polygon in this plane. The ray will pass through the polygon if the intersection point is inside the polygon. This test is beyond the scope of this book.

The number of computations can be reduced if back faces of solids are not included in the original list of surfaces. Light reaching the pixel must come from the intersection nearest the projective plane, the intersection with smallest positive value of t larger than 1. If the surface containing this point is a rough, opaque surface, then ray tracing is complete; the intensity at the intersection is given as the intensity for the pixel. If the surface is a mirror, then the angle of reflection is calculated and a new ray is generated (figure 11.4.4).

A reflection vector $(x_r\ y_r,\ z_r)$ can be computed with the equation $\mathbf{R} = \mathbf{N} + -\mathbf{L}/(2\mathbf{N}\cdot\mathbf{L})$ from section 11.1. This formula uses the vector normal to the surface. In the case of the sphere, this normal is just a vector connecting the center of the sphere to the point of intersection $(x_i,\ y_i,\ z_i)$, namely $(x_i - x_c,\ y_i - y_c,\ z_i - z_c)$. Parametric equations for this ray follow directly:

$$x(t) = x_i + t\,x_r$$
$$y(t) = y_i + t\,y_r$$
$$z(t) = z_i + t\,z_r$$

Intersections of this ray with all surfaces, including back-facing surfaces, are calculated. The intersection nearest the origin of this ray is used to assign a light

FIGURE 11.4.4

A new ray is generated from the point where the incoming ray strikes a surface.

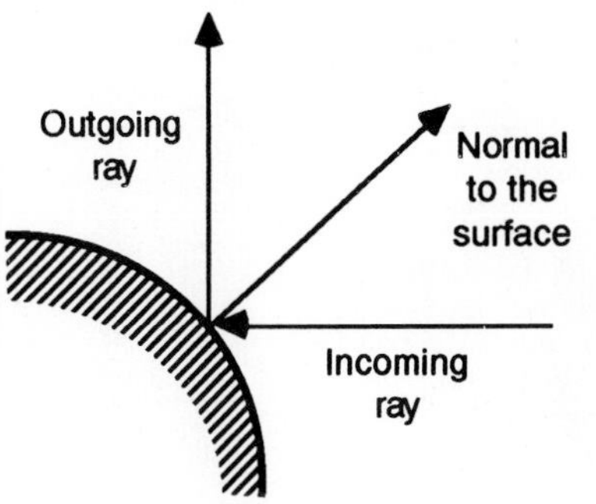

intensity value or to compute the next ray in the path. An upper limit is set for the number of reflections allowed in order to prevent infinite loops.

Rays striking transparent objects may be traced by creating a new ray that is parallel but slightly offset from the incident ray. The offset may be calculated once for a given object or set as a constant that gives a realistic representation. The new ray is then traced in the same way as the original ray.

If none of the intersections for a given ray is within the view volume, then either the line points to the light source or it is assumed to pass through the background. Those rays parallel to the light rays are assigned the highest intensity, while those passing through to the background are assigned a predetermined background intensity. This background color is often blue or black.

Ray tracing may also be used to show shadows in a scene. A ray from a rough surface in the direction of the light source can be used to check whether the light at that point is obscured by another object (figure 11.4.5). If such a ray strikes an object in the scene, then this object makes a shadow on the surface at that point. Shadows may be simulated by reducing the light intensity (figure 11.4.6).

The simplest applications of ray tracing are scenes with a small number of plane surfaces and spheres (figure 11.4.7). A sample of computations for such a scene are given by Pokorny and Gerald (1989). Scenes with more complex objects or many different surfaces are treated by creating simpler bounding surfaces for each object (Kay and Kajiya) or by representing the view volume with a data structure such as an octree, discussed in section 11.8 (Fujimoto, Tanaka, and Iwata (1986). Antialiasing can be incorporated in ray tracing by tracing cones (Amanatides 1984). While much success has been had from the use of ray-tracing algorithms on general-purpose computers, the time needed for such operations has led some researchers to explore the possibility of specialized ray-tracing hardware (Pulleyblank and Rapenga 1987). Ray tracing has also been extended to diffuse surfaces (Ward, Rubinstein, and Clear 1988).

FIGURE 11.4.5

If a ray from a rough surface strikes an object in the direction of the light source, the tail of the ray will lie in the shadow of the surface struck by the ray.

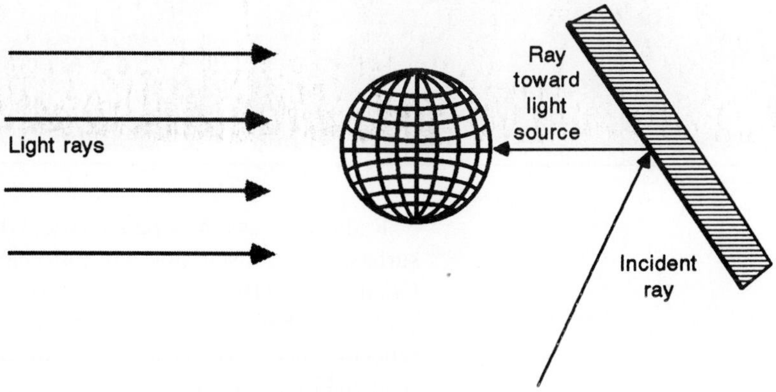

FIGURE 11.4.6

Shadows may be simulated by reducing the light intensity.

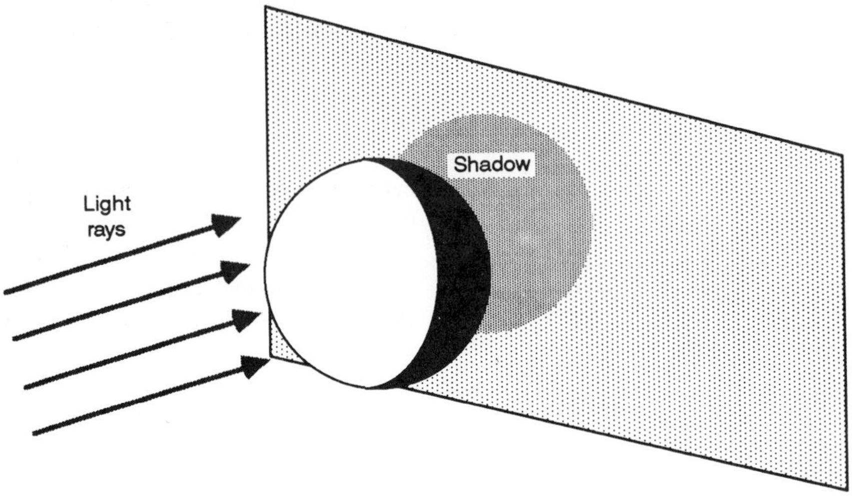

FIGURE 11.4.7

Two examples of ray tracing with cones created by John Amanatides, University of Toronto.

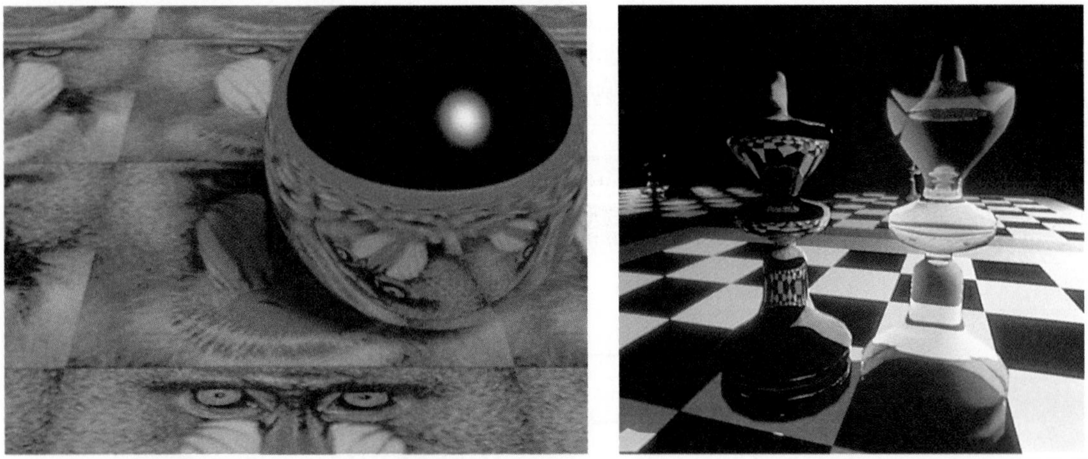

Radiosity was developed to model the interplay of diffuse reflections between surfaces. This discussion will introduce radiosity with the model introduced by Goral et al. (1984). The set of surfaces and light sources is defined as an enclosure. Each surface in the enclosure is assumed to be a perfect diffuse reflector that may be a source of light emission. Directional light can be modeled by identifying those surface areas struck directly by the light. The light directly reflected off of these surfaces is treated as a diffuse light source. If only part of a surface is directly illuminated, then the surface is divided into the illuminated part, considered a light source, and the reflector part.

For each surface in the enclosure, the radiosity is the rate at which radiant energy leaves the surface per unit area. The radiosity is composed of the light emitted by the surface plus the light reflected from the surface. A surface, j, has radiosity B_j given by

$$B_j = E_j + \rho_j H_j$$

where E_j is the rate at which light is emitted from the surface, ρ_j is the reflectivity of the surface, and H_j is the incident radiant energy for the surface.

The incident radiant energy for a surface in the enclosure is the sum of the radiant energy from all surfaces in the enclosure that strikes the given surface. The fraction of the radiosity of surface i striking surface j is called the **form factor**, F_{ji}. You can use these form factors to calculate the light incident on surface j.

$$H_j = \sum_{i=1}^{n} B_i F_{ji}$$

where the enclosure contains n surfaces. The incident light reaching surface j from surface j is included in this sum because curved surfaces may add to their own illumination. Plane surface j has form factor $F_{jj} = 0$.

Form factors depend on the distance between two surfaces and the angle between those surfaces. Light reaching a surface is inversely proportional to the square of the distance from the source to that surface, and directly proportional to the cosine of the angle of incidence (figure 11.4.8). Each surface in the sample enclosure can be thought of as many infinitesimal light sources. The form factor F_{ij} can be computed by integrating the infinitesimal light sources

FIGURE 11.4.8

Light reaching a surface is inversely proportional to the square of the distance from the source to that surface, and directly proportional to the cosine of the angle of incidence.

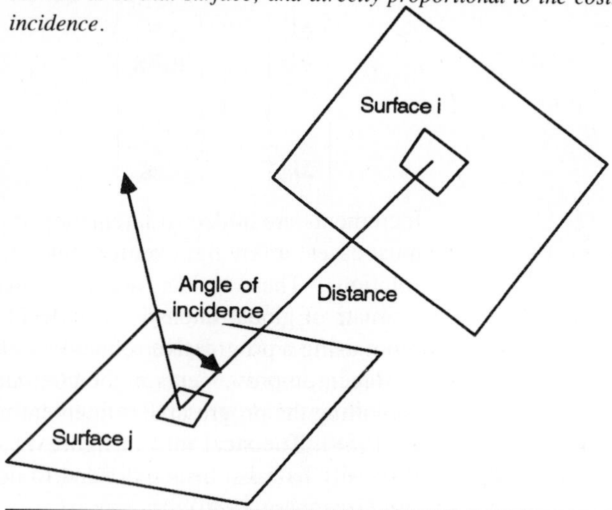

over surface i. The reciprocity relation, $A_iF_{ij} = A_jF_{ji}$, allows F_{ij} to be computed from F_{ji} and areas A_i and A_j of the two surfaces. This reduces the time spent computing form factors. This computation is still time consuming, however, and is normally carried out once at the beginning of the program.

Once the computation of incident radiation is computed by using form factors, the radiosity for surface j is given as

$$B_j = E_j + \rho_j \sum_{i=1}^{n} B_jF_{ji}$$

The radiosity problem is solved by solving the n equations for radiosity, which can be given in matrix form as

$$\begin{bmatrix} (1-\rho_1)F_{11} & -\rho_1F_{12} & \cdots & -\rho_1F_{1n} \\ -\rho_2F_{21} & (1-\rho_2)F_{22} & \cdots & -\rho_2F_{2n} \\ \cdots & \cdots & \cdots & \cdots \\ -\rho_nF_{n1} & -\rho_nF_{n2} & \cdots & (1-\rho_n)F_{nn} \end{bmatrix} \begin{bmatrix} B_1 \\ B_2 \\ \cdots \\ B_n \end{bmatrix} = \begin{bmatrix} E_1 \\ E_2 \\ \cdots \\ E_n \end{bmatrix}$$

This system of equations can be solved by standard matrix-solving techniques if few surfaces are involved. Some recent applications use as many as 50,000 surfaces. To solve large systems of equations used in such applications, the iterative Gauss-Seidel method is employed.

When color is added to the problem, the radiosity equations must be solved for red, green, and blue. The form factors do not vary with color, so only the reflectivity and emission for each surface is altered. In figure 11.4.9, you see the color from the red and blue walls bleeding on the gray walls. This occurs because the light from the red and blue walls strikes the gray wall. Also notice that as each wall is divided into more surfaces, the effect becomes more realistic.

An alternative to solving the radiosity matrix equation is **progressive refinement.** This method can be viewed either as backward ray tracing (Cohen et al. 1988) or two-way ray tracing (Zhu et al. 1988). The change of light intensity on environmental surfaces contributed by each surface is computed using the equations

$$\begin{bmatrix} \Delta I_1 \\ \Delta I_2 \\ \cdot \\ \cdot \\ \cdot \\ \Delta I_N \end{bmatrix} = I_i \begin{bmatrix} \rho_1F_{1i} \\ \rho_2F_{2i} \\ \cdot \\ \cdot \\ \cdot \\ \rho_NN_{Ni} \end{bmatrix}$$

Increments are added to intensities at each step and the process is repeated. In most cases, a few light sources and large bright surfaces contribute most to the solutions. These values are computed first, and quickly give a very good estimate of global intensity. Figure 11.4.10 shows the flat shading of a cubical room using a progressive refinement algorithm developed by Baum et al. 1989.

Recent improvements in the computation of radiosity have been obtained by exploiting the progressive refinement method and reciprocity relation (Cohen et al. 1988). The steel mill in figure 11.4.11 was created from 50,000 surfaces. Radiosity has also been extended to non-diffuse environments (Immel, Cohen, and Greenberg 1986).

FIGURE 11.4.9

The color from the red and blue walls bleeds on the gray walls in this image created using the full-matrix radiosity method. Reprinted from Baum et al. 1989, 329.

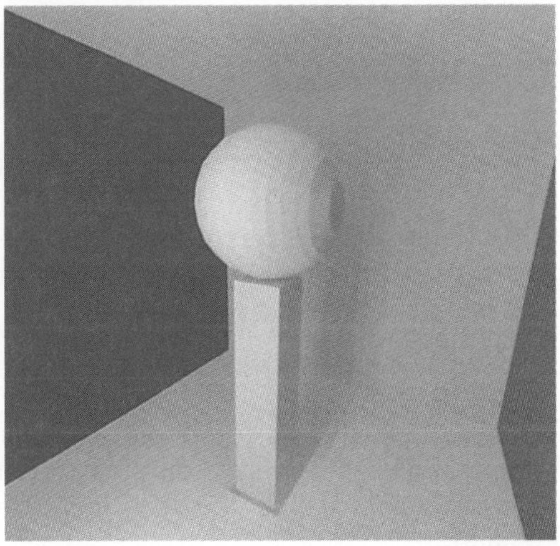

FIGURE 11.4.10

In this image the color from the red and blue walls bleeds on the gray walls by using the modified progressive refinement radiosity method. Reprinted from Baum et al. 1989, 332.

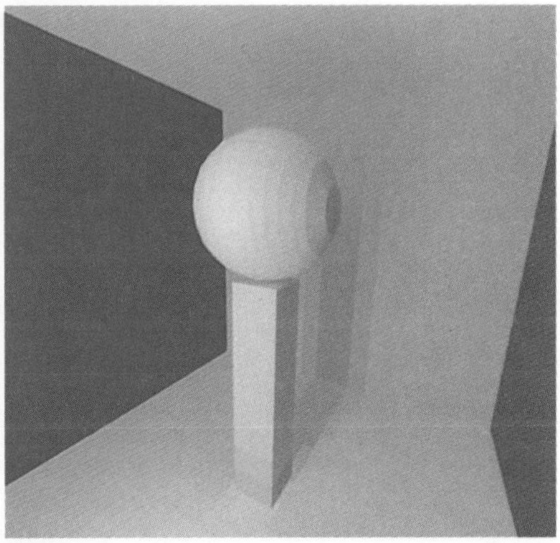

FIGURE 11.4.11

This simulated steel mill was created by using a modified version of the hemi-cube radiosity algorithm and 30,000 patches that were subdivided into 55,000 elements. A close approximation of the final product was created in 5 hours. Over 190 hours of post-production were required to create this final form. Reprinted from Cohen et al. 1988, 83.

EXERCISES

11.4.1

Compute the general solutions for the parameter at the intersections of a ray and a sphere. Simplify this solution as much as possible.

11.4.2

Write a procedure to implement the solution found in exercise 11.4.1.

11.4.3

Write a procedure to compute the parametric equations of a ray reflected from a spherical surface.

11.4.4

Write a procedure to do ray tracing for a scene with two spheres and one distant point source. You may assume that the plane y = 0 is white and that your scene has black sides and a top of a predetermined distance (that is, z = front, z = back, x = left, x = right, and y = top).

11.5 Depicting Light Intensities and Halftoning

Once the light intensities for the surfaces in a picture have been calculated, these intensities must be converted into emission levels for pixels. Often the range of intensities exceeds the range of pixel emission levels.

After you have calculated the brightness of the surfaces in a picture, you must associate these values with possible screen values. The intensity levels are usually expressed as numbers between 0 and 1. Black is associated with 0, and white is associated with 1. Only a finite number of different intensity values are available within the range of the screen. If there are n non-zero levels and you label the levels above 0 as $I_1, I_2, \ldots I_n$, what relationship must exist between consecutive levels to ensure realistic reproduction? We perceive light changes on a logarithmic scale, that is, the change of intensity between .2 and .22 is perceived to be the same as the change between .6 and .66. To maintain this logarithmic relationship, you must require that consecutive intensity levels have a constant ratio, r. This leads to the equations

$$r = \frac{I_2}{I_1} = \frac{I_3}{I_2} = \ldots = \frac{I_{n+1}}{I_n}$$

For each value of k between 1 and n you can solve for I_k to get

$$I_k = r^{k-1} I_1$$

The value I_n is associated with 1, so you also have a way to compute r for a given number of levels and a lowest gray level I_1.

$$1 = r^{n-1} I_1$$

or

$$r = (1/I_1)^{1/(n-1)}$$

The number of gray levels, n, is usually a power of 2. If, for example, there are eight levels of gray above zero, then $n - 1 = 7$. In order to simplify the computations, pick I_1 to be a seventh power less than 1. A simple choice for I_1 is $(1/2)^7$, or 1/128. For this value of I_1, $r = 2$.

Many monochrome monitors have pixels that are either "on" or "off." One method used to achieve more than one gray level on such monitors is **halftoning**. Halftoning has long been used to reproduce photos in print. A rectangular grid is imposed on the photo; then the level of gray at each intersection on the grid determines the size of the dot to be printed at that point. The larger the dot size, the darker the area. Graphics display devices can approximate the varying dot size of the halftone process by replacing each dot with a square of pixels called a **dither matrix** (figure 11.5.1).

As in the construction of patterns, care must be taken so that the dither matrices do not create patterns on their own. Dots should not align in such a way that in combination they form a pattern. Clearly symmetrical patterns should be avoided, but even non-symmetric arrays (figure 11.5.2) can align to create an unforeseen pattern.

FIGURE 11.5.1

You can simulate the halftone process by replacing dots with squares of pixels called dither matrices.

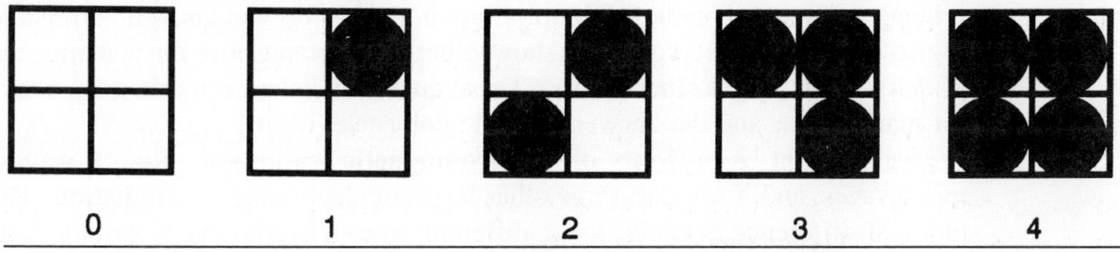

FIGURE 11.5.2

Non-symmetrical patterns can be combined to form a larger pattern.

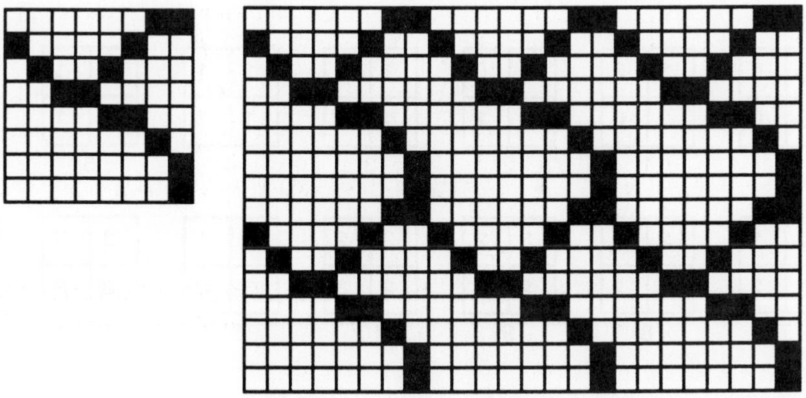

Normally, the dither matrices are 2 × 2 or 3 × 3, but larger squares may be used to create additional levels of gray. Be careful that the squares do not significantly reduce the resolution of the final image. When a 2 × 2 grid is used in a 1024 × 1024 monitor, the result is an image with a resolution of 512 in each direction.

Halftoning may also be applied when pixels have more than two levels of intensity. For example, if pixels can be set at four levels including black, then you may set a display to 12 different levels by using the 2 × 2 arrays in figure 11.5.3. Notice that the pixel values represented in each array sum to the intensity level represented by that array.

Halftoning can also be used to print images whose gray scale needs to exceed the capability of a printer. If, for example, 16 levels of gray are represented on a 640 × 400 screen, each pixel may be printed as a 4 × 4 dither matrix. The printer would need to be able to print 2560 dots per line for this halftone image. If this is not possible, the screen can be grouped into 2 × 2-pixel matrices. The average intensity value for the four pixels can be computed, and the block of four pixels can be replaced by a dither matrix representing the average intensity (figure 11.5.4). The printer would require 1280 dots per line to print this image, using dither matrices to replace the 2 × 2-pixel blocks.

11.6 Color Models

Earlier sections in this chapter, we have discussed the reflectivity of surfaces with respect to the colors red, green, and blue. These colors are the three primary colors used by the RGB color monitor. How do you know it is possible to use just these three colors to show other colors, and how do you mix the primary colors to get other colors? These questions have been asked by artists for many years, and the answers predate color television.

Visible light is a form of **electromagnetic radiation**. Radio waves, microwaves, and X rays are some other forms of electromagnetic radiation. The physical difference between these different types of radiation is simply their wavelengths. Radio waves and microwaves have very long wavelengths, while

FIGURE 11.5.3

cluding black, then a display may be set to 12 different levels using the 2 × 2 arrays.

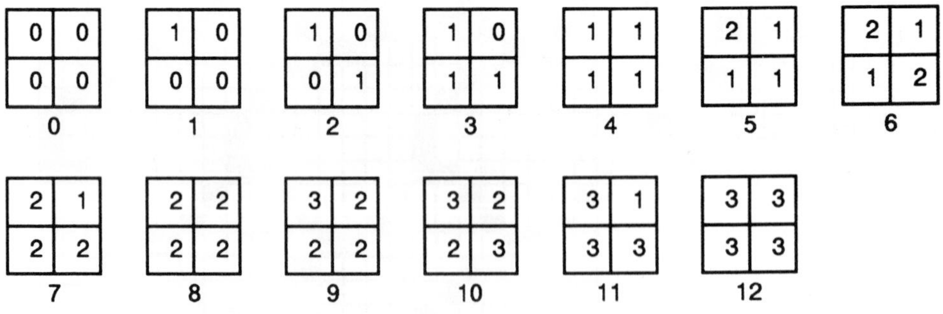

FIGURE 11.5.4

The average intensity value for the four pixels can be computed and the block of four pixels replaced by a dither matrix representing the average intensity.

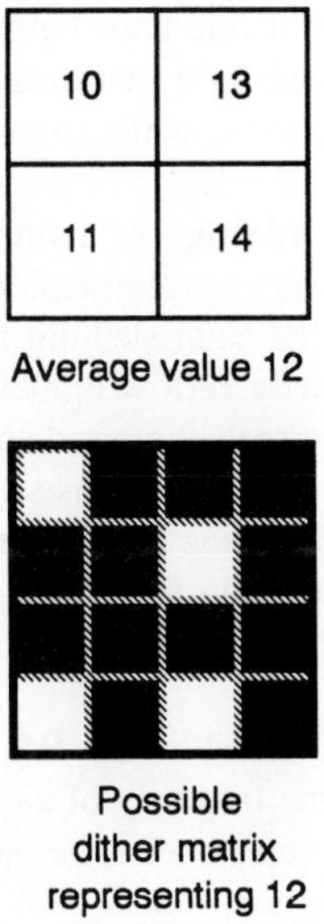

X rays have short wavelengths. Visible light occupies a very small section of this continuum. Infrared light (heat) and visible light are the only forms of electromagnetic radiation that humans can detect with their senses (figure 11.6.1).

The range of wavelengths of visible light, called the **visible spectrum**, is between 400 and 700 nanometers. A **nanometer (nm)** is 10^{-9} meters, or one billionth of a meter. **Color**, or **hue**, is strictly the human brain's interpretation of the wavelength of a light source. The theory of color vision assumes that the cones of our eyes have tissues sensitive to three different wavelengths—630 nm (red), 530 nm (green), and 450 nm (blue)—and that light of a dominant wavelength simulates each of the receptors differently. Red light stimulates the red sensitive tissues more than the green or blue, so we perceive that light as red. Yellow light (~600 nm) stimulates the red and green more than the blue. This combination is perceived as yellow. The human brain perceives the color of light by stimulation of the three types of cones, which allows us to simulate color of any wavelength as a mixture of these **primary colors**. This **tri-stimulus theory** serves as the basis for most color models.

When the amounts of red, green, and blue light present are perceived to be equal, then the mixture appears to be white light. Other colors can be simulated by mixtures of red, green, and blue. As noted, yellow light can be simulated by a mixture of red and green light. Cyan (~500 nm) can be created as a mixture of green and blue (figure 11.6.2). A color formed by the combination of red and blue is magenta. Magenta is an artificial color because it corresponds to no wavelength of light.

Cyan, magenta, and yellow can also be thought of as white light minus one of the primary colors. Yellow, for example, is white light minus blue. Stated another way, if you add blue to yellow, you get white. Because of this property, cyan, magenta, and yellow are called the **complements** of blue, red, and green respectively.

FIGURE 11.6.1

Visible light is a narrow band of wavelengths in the electromagnetic spectrum.

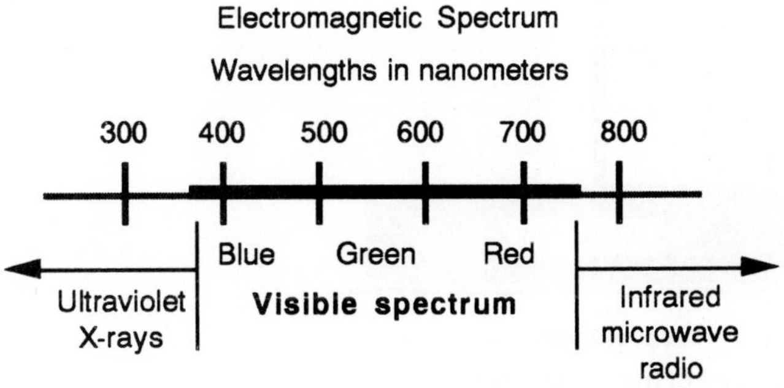

FIGURE 11.6.2

Colors such as cyan and yellow may be created by mixture of two primary colors.

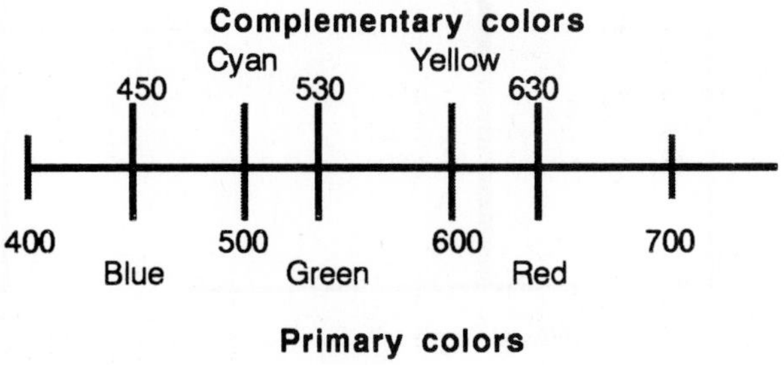

It is possible to base the tri-stimulus model on primary colors other than red, green, and blue, but the complementary colors cannot be used as primaries. Consider what happens if the color yellow is mixed with cyan. Yellow is a mixture of red and green and cyan is a mixture of green and blue. The red, green, and blue components of yellow and cyan combine to form white light. There is probably a surplus of green light, giving the combination a greenish appearance.

Pure color mixed with white light is called a **tint**. Light of one wavelength is called **saturated light**. As white light is added to saturated light, saturation decreases from 100 percent to 0 percent, at which point the light is white (figure 11.6.3).

The mixing process just described is called **additive mixing**, so named because light of a given primary color is being added. Artists mix pigments to get colors. Cyan pigment is cyan because it absorbs most red light striking it. But yellow pigment absorbs blue light, thus reflecting primarily yellow light. If cyan and yellow pigments are mixed, the resulting pigment absorbs both red and blue light and reflects only green. This is called **subtractive mixing** because the absorption property of the pigment determines its color. The complementary colors for the additive primaries that will be used in the example here are the primary subtractive colors. CRTs create color by adding light, so the discussion will mainly focus on additive color models.

The color model corresponding most closely to the RGB CRT is the **RGB color model**. This model represents a color by specifying the intensity of each of the primary colors. The intensity of each primary color can be set independently on an RGB monitor, so values represented by this model can be easily transferred to the screen.

FIGURE 11.6.3

As white light is added to saturated light, saturation decreases from 100 percent to 0 percent. At 0 percent the light is white.

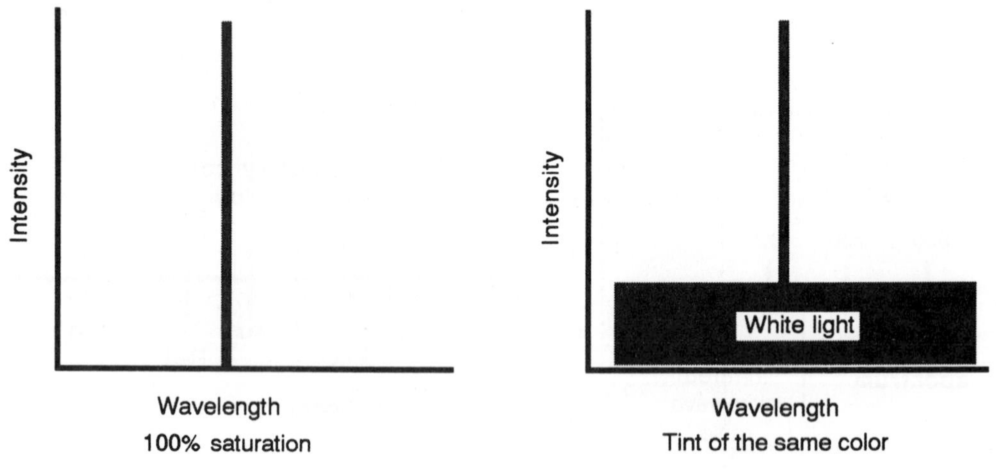

The intensity of each primary color is unbounded in the real world, but color monitors typically allow between 8 and 256 intensities for each primary color. The number of colors such a system can generate in n^3, where n is the number of intensities allowed for each primary color. A system with 8 intensity levels can generate 512 different colors, while one with 256 intensity levels can generate over 16 million different colors. Sixteen million colors well exceeds the approximately 350,000 different colors that tests have shown humans are capable of distinguishing.

A system with 256 different intensities per primary color would require 3 bytes per pixel. It is not cost effective to use this much memory if the user can distinguish 350,000 different colors at most. The majority of applications can use far fewer colors. A **color table** is one method for storing a wide range of colors without using excessive amounts of memory. If, for example, an application needs only 256 different colors, these colors can be stored in a color table (figure 11.6.4). Each pixel would then refer to a position in the table. In such a scheme, a restricted palette could be chosen from a broad range of colors, and each pixel would need only 1 byte.

Intensities of each primary color in the RGB system can be represented as a number between 0 and 1 to allow for machine-independent descriptions. Every color can be represented by the coordinates of a point in the unit cube (figure 11.6.5). The line joining the corner (0,0,0) and (1,1,1) passes through all neutral grays between black and white (figure 11.6.6).

Hard-copy devices work with pigments, so it is not surprising that a color model based on the subtractive primaries cyan, magenta, and yellow (the **CMY model**) is used for these devices. This model is designed to maintain

FIGURE 11.6.4

A color table allows a program to reference a color with one integer rather than three real numbers.

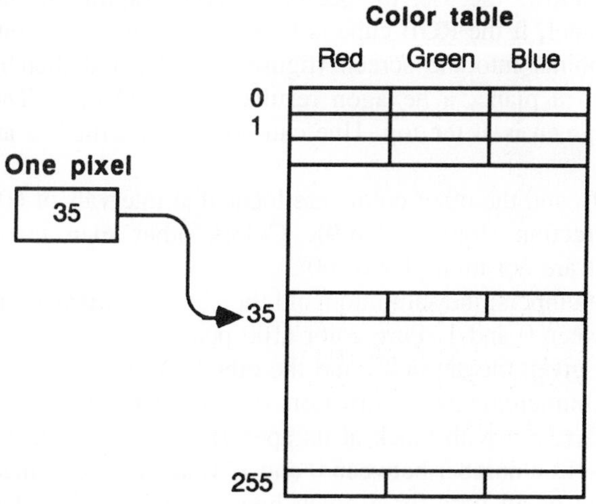

FIGURE 11.6.5

Every color can be represented by the coordinates of a point in the unit cube.

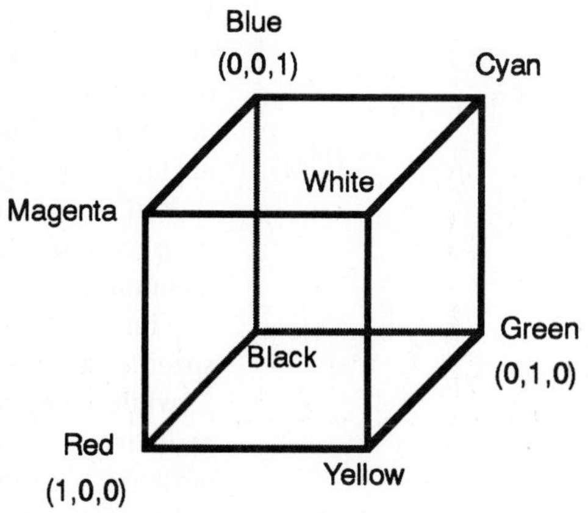

FIGURE 11.6.6

The line joining the corner (0,0,0) and (1,1,1) passes through all neutral grays between black and white.

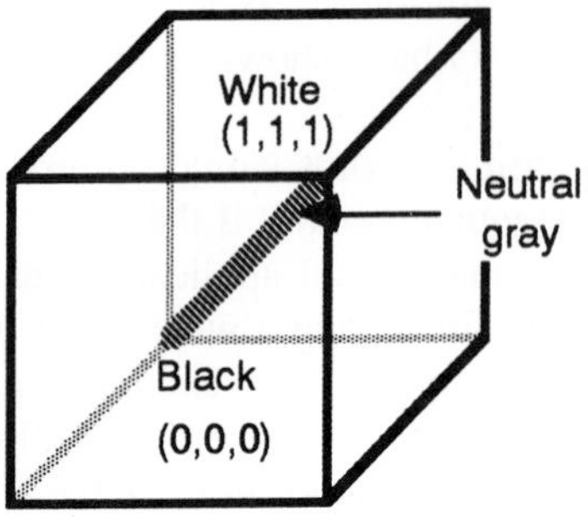

consistency between the CRT image and the hard copy. To achieve this, the intensity of each subtractive primary is computed by subtracting the intensity of its complement from 1.

$$
\begin{aligned}
C &= 1 - R \\
M &= 1 - G \\
Y &= 1 - B
\end{aligned}
$$

In theory, if cyan, magenta, and yellow are mixed, the resulting color should be black. In practice, commercial dyes are not ideal, so the mixture is not black. To compensate for this, commercial printers normally use a four-color process based on mixtures of cyan, magenta, yellow, and black. Formulas for computing the amounts of extended subtractive primaries in this system are

$$
\begin{aligned}
C &= \max(RGB) - R \\
M &= \max(RGB) - G \\
Y &= \max(RGB) - B \\
Black &= 1 - \max(RGB)
\end{aligned}
$$

Recall that neutral gray results when all three additive primaries have the same value. The conversion formula applied to neutral gray give cyan, magenta, and blue values of zero, and a black value based on the intensity of the point.

An example of a non-neutral gray occurs with the RGB value (0.6, 0.2, 0.8). The value is converted as

$$
\begin{aligned}
C &= 0.8 - 0.6 = 0.2 \\
M &= 0.8 - 0.2 = 0.6 \\
Y &= 0.8 - 0.8 = 0 \\
Black &= 1 - 0.8 = 0.2
\end{aligned}
$$

Conversion from CMY to RGB is not needed because conversions of hard copy to digital images are handled by digitizers that produce the RGB values directly.

Specifying a color by using the intensity of each of the primary colors may be the most direct approach to describing color, but it is not a method most people would find usable. Most would rather specify a color and brightness directly. The **HSV model** allows the user to specify the *H*ue, *S*aturation and *V*alue of a color. In this model, if the RGB cube is rotated so white points out of the screen and black points into the screen (figure 11.6.7), and then is orthogonally projected onto a plane, a hexagon results (figure 11.6.8). The hexagon is rotated so that green is at the top. Hue can now be specified as an angle.

Red is given the angle 0°, and the other colors are located at intervals of 60° in a counterclockwise direction (figure 11.6.9). Colors other than those mentioned have angles that are not multiples of 60°.

Tint is specified by two numbers: the saturation and the value. **Saturation** is specified by a number between 0 and 1. Pure color (100 percent saturation) is 1, while white is 0. Red is given the angle 0°, and the other colors are located at intervals of 60° in a counterclockwise direction (figure 11.6.10). If the hexagon is extended to a pyramid with black at its apex (figure 11.6.11), the **value of a color** is specified as a number between 0 and 1. Black is represented by 0 and white by 1. A set of all tints for a given hue can be found on the intersection of a vertical half-plane along its angle and the hexpyramid (figure 11.6.12).

FIGURE 11.6.7

If the RGB cube is rotated so white points out of the screen and black points into the screen, the hexagon of colors around the edge of the cube form a basis for the HSV color model.

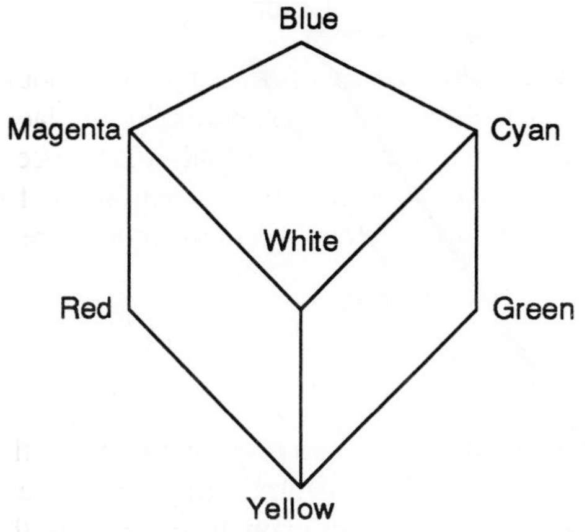

FIGURE 11.6.8

When the rotated cube is orthogonally projected onto a plane, a hexagon results.

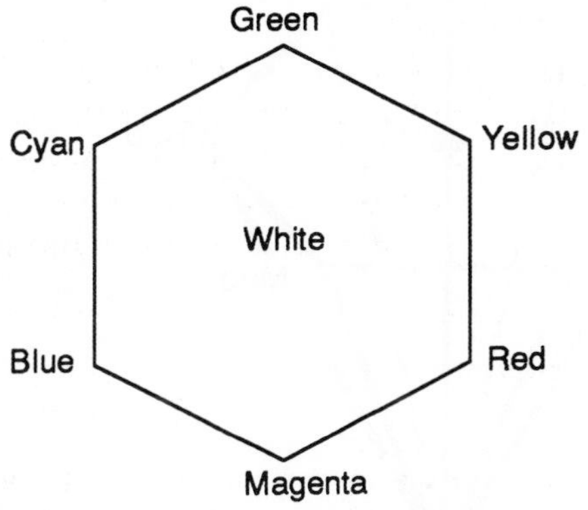

FIGURE 11.6.9

Red is given the angel 0°, and the other colors are located at intervals of 60° in a counterclockwise direction.

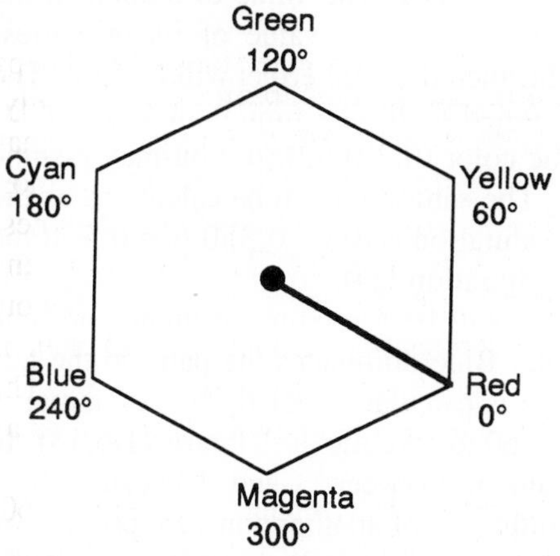

FIGURE 11.6.10

The saturation is specified by a number between 0 and 1, and represented by a position on the line joining the center of the hexagon and the location of the color on the perimeter.

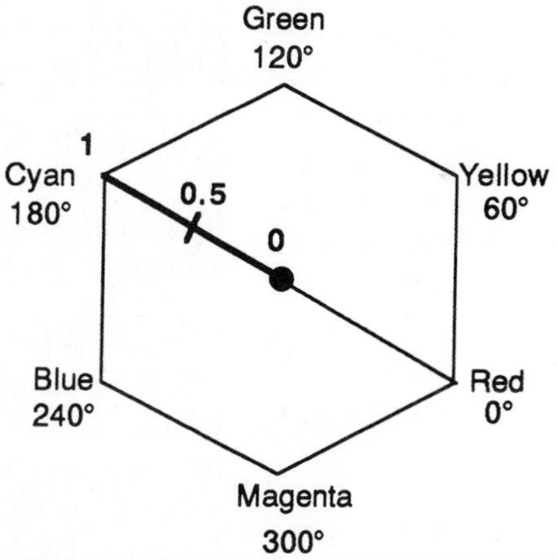

In practice, when the user picks a color, the hue is specified and the saturation and value are set to 1. This is a pure color at its brightest. The user can darken the color by decreasing the value and can decrease the saturation by reducing its value. A dark magenta would be specified as (300,1,0.3), while a bright tint of light green would be (120,0.5,1). Again, the line representing neutral gray is the line joining white and black. A neutral midgray would be specified as (n,0,0.5), where n can take any value between 0 and 360.

FIGURE 11.6.11

If the hexagon is extended to a pyramid with black at its apex, the value of a color is specified as a number between 0 and 1.

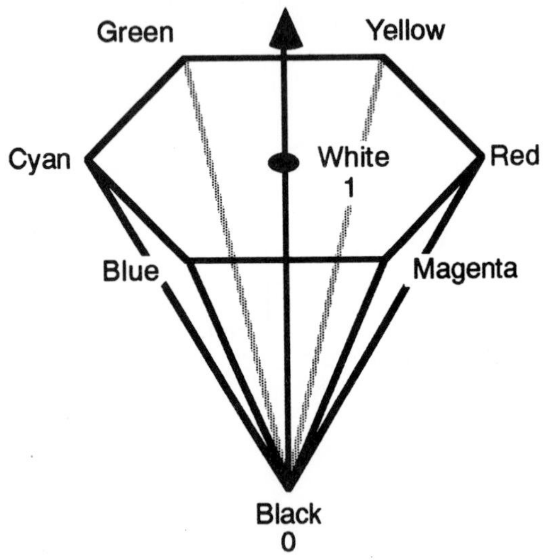

FIGURE 11.6.12

A set of all tints for a given hue can be found on the intersection of a vertical half-plane along its angle and the hexpyramid.

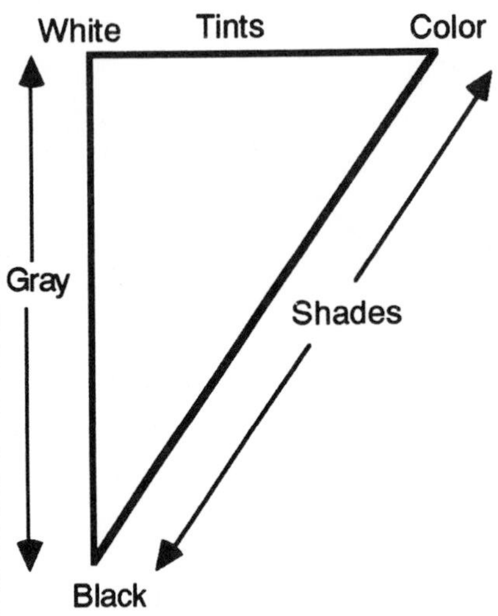

Conversion between RGB and HSV is important because many graphics packages use HSV, and color monitors use RGB. The value of a color in the RGB system may be assumed to be the maximum value of its primaries. Clearly, if none of the primaries is bright, then the total effect will be dark. The amount of white in a color can be assumed to be the minimum value of its primaries. If, for example, you have the color (0.3,0.5,0.6), you may assume 0.3 of each color mixed to form white. The saturation can be calculated as the fraction of the value above white. Here saturation is $(0.6-0.3)/0.6 = 0.5$. If the value is 0, then the color is black and saturation is 0.

The hue associated with (0.3,0.5,0.6) will be a mixture of green and blue because the red was neutralized to white. Blue dominates the pair, so the hue should be an angle near 240°. The angle is calculated exactly by computing a section number that can be multiplied by 60 to give the hue (figure 11.6.13). In the example, the section number should be between 3 and 5 because these values cover the region near blue. The influence of another non-zero primary on the color, computed as a percentage of the maximum above white, is called a distance. This distance is

$$\text{Primary Distance} = \frac{\text{Maximum} - \text{Primary Value}}{\text{Maximum} - \text{Minimum}}$$

In the example, Green Distance $= 0.1/0.3 = 0.33$. The section value, 3.33, is the distance added to 3 (the multiple associated with cyan) (figure 11.6.13). The hue is $3.33 \times 60 = 200$. The complete conversion algorithm is given in figure 11.6.14.

FIGURE 11.6.13

The hue is calculated by multiplying its section number by 60.

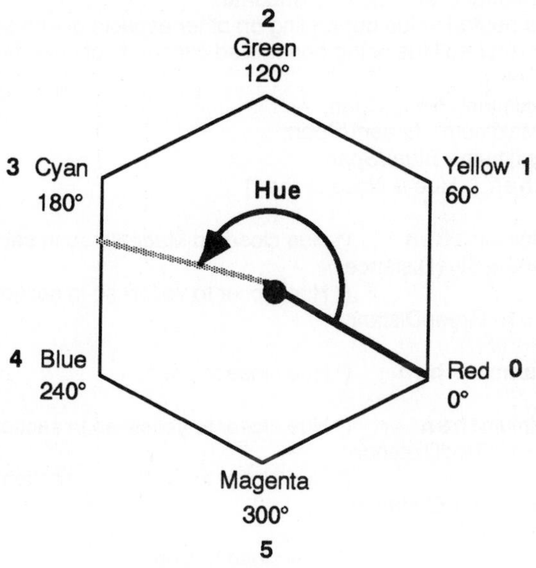

FIGURE 11.6.14

Procedure to convert from the RGB model to the HSV model

```
(* This procedure is used to convert from the RGB system to the HSV system.     *)
(* The procedure receives the intensities Red, Green, and Blue, and returns     *)
(* the values Hue, Saturation, and Value.                                       *)

procedure RGB_to_HSV (Red,Green,Blue : real; var Hue, Saturation, Value : real);
var
   Maximum        : real;     (* largest value from Red, Green, and Blue      *)
   Minimum        : real;     (* smallest value from the same colors          *)
   Span           : real;     (* difference between maximum and minimum       *)
   RedDistance,
   GreenDistance,
   BlueDistance   : real;     (* normalized distances of color from RGB       *)
   Section        : real;     (* section of hexagon where the hue is          *)
begin
   Maximum := Max(Red,Green,Blue);
   Minimum := Min(Red,Green,Blue);
   Value := Maximum;
   Span := Maximum - Minimum;

   if Value = 0 then
      Saturation := 0
   else
      Saturation := Span /Maximum;
```

(continued)

FIGURE 11.6.14 continued

```
(* calculate Hue *)
if Saturation = 0 then (* neutral gray, Hue is unimportant                                   *)
   Hue := Undefined    (* a neutral value depending on other aspects of implementation     *)
else                   (* calculate Hue using normalized distances of color from RGB       *)
   begin
      RedDistance := (Maximum - Red)/ Span;
      GreenDistance := (Maximum - Green)/Span;
      BlueDistance := (Maximum - Blue)/Span;
      if Red = Maximum then (* Hue is close to red *)
         begin
            if Green = Minimum then      (* Hue closer to Magenta so in section 5    *)
               Section := 5 + BlueDistance
            else                         (* Hue closer to yellow so in section 0     *)
               Section := 1 - GreenDistance
         end
      else if  Green = Maximum then      (* Hue close to green                       *)
         begin
            if Blue = Minimum then       (* Hue closer to yellow so in section 1     *)
               Section := 1 + RedDistance
            else                         (* Hue closer to cyan so in section 2       *)
               Section := 3 - BlueDistance
         end
      else                               (* Hue close to blue                        *)
         begin
            if Red = Minimum then        (* Hue closer to cyan so in section 3       *)
               Section := 3 + GreenDistance
            else                         (* Hue closer to magenta so in section 4    *)
               Section := 5 - RedDistance
         end;
      Hue := 60 * Section
   end
end; (* RGB_To_HVS *)
```

Reverse these operations to convert from HSV to RGB. The details of the algorithm are found in figure 11.6.15.

The **HLS model**, used by Tektronix, is similar to the HSV model. In this model color is specified by hue, lightness, and saturation. A double hexpyramid (figure 11.6.16) represents the HLS model. Hue is still computed as an angle, but blue corresponds to angle 0. White and black are at opposite ends of the axis joining the two apices. Lightness is a measure of the distance from black to white along this axis; black is 0 and white is 1. Neutral gray lies on this line. Saturation can be considered the distance that a point lies off the axis, 1 being on the perimeter of the pyramid.

Conversions between RGB and HLS are similar to those between RGB and HSV. For a complete discussion of these conversions, see Rogers (1985).

There is yet another way to describe color in terms of the additive primaries. In the RGB model, each color is the sum of a constant times each of the primaries:

$$C = rR + gG + bB$$

URE 11.6.16

hexpyramid represents the HLS model.

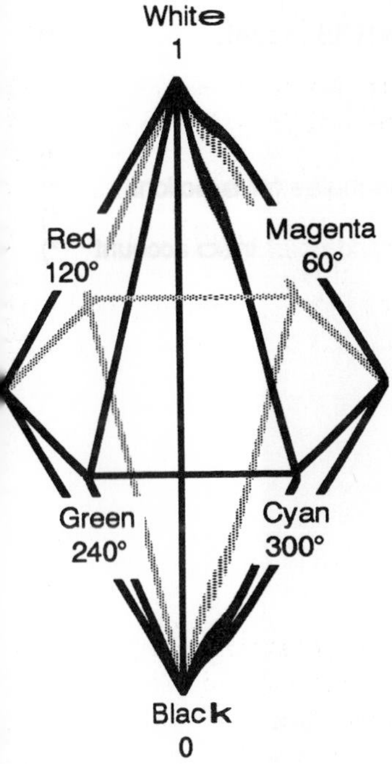

FIGURE 11.6.17

The intersection of the unit plane and the vector C can be computed directly.

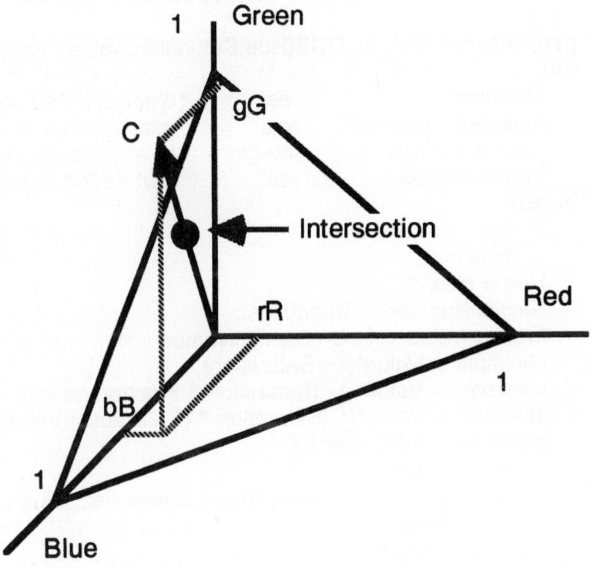

The advantage of these coefficients is that they total 1. Once two of the coefficients are known, the third can be retrieved by subtracting the sum of the other two from 1. This allows a two-dimensional representation of the model.

One problem with this model is that the weights are not always positive. Suppose you wish to create blue-green, but the combination of blue and green light used is too light. You could add red, but this only creates a lighter blue-green. If the blue-green is denoted by C, and your current mixture is gG + bB, then you add red to C to lighten it so that C + rR = gG + bB. This tells you that C = −rR + gG + bB. While the equation balances, you cannot subtract light.

The Commission Internationale de L'Eclairage (CIE) solved this problem with a model using a normalized coordinate system and a two-dimensional chromaticity diagram. The **CIE model** uses three hypothetical primaries. X, Y, and Z. These can be combined to form any color by using only positive weights. Although the primaries are defined by energy distribution curves, real colors can be defined by these primaries and the model can be used to describe theoretical properties of color.

If X, Y, and Z are the amount of each primary used to create a color, then the normalized weights, x, y, and z are calculated with the formulas

$$x = \frac{X}{X + Y + Z}$$

FIGURE 11.6.15

A procedure to convert from the HSV color model to the RGB color model

```
(* This procedure receives a  color specified in the HSV model and converts it to the RGB mo

procedure HSV_To_RGB(Hue,Saturation,Value : real; var  Red,Green,Blue : real);
var
    Minimum                : real;       (* smallest RGB value
    Inverse1,  Inverse2    : real;       (* middle value found by inverting one of the formulas fo
    SectionNumber          : integer;    (* in which section is the computation occurring
    FractionValue          : real;       (* part added to multiplier of 60 to take the second color
begin
    if Hue = 360 then
        Hue := 0;
    Hue := Hue/60;
    SectionNumber := Trunc(Hue);
    FractionValue := Hue - SectionNumber;
    Minimum := Value*(1 - Saturation);
    Inverse1 := Value*(1- (Saturation * FractionValue));
    Inverse2 := Value*(1-(Saturation * (1 - FractionValue));
    case SectionNumber of
        0 :  begin
                 Red := Value; Green := Inverse2; Blue := Minimum
             end;
        1 :  begin
                 Red := Inverse1; Green := Value; Blue := Minimum
             end;
        2 :  begin
                 Red := Minimum; Green := Value; Blue := Inverse2
             end;
        3 :  begin
                 Red := Minimum; Green := Inverse1; Blue := Value
             end;
        4 :  begin
                 Red := Inverse2; Green := Minimum; Blue := Value
             end;
        5 :  begin
                 Red := Value; Green := Minimum; Blue := Inverse1
             end
    end (* Case *)
end; (* HSV_To_RGB*)
```

The intersection of the vector C and the unit plan
coefficients

$$\bar{r} = \frac{r}{r + g + b}$$

$$\bar{g} = \frac{g}{r + g + b}$$

$$\bar{b} = \frac{b}{r + g + b}$$

$$y = \frac{Y}{X + Y + Z}$$

$$z = \frac{Z}{X + Y + Z}$$

where x + y + z = 1. The XYZ triangle is projected into the xy-plane (figure 11.6.18). This projection is the **CIE chromaticity diagram**. The coordinates x and y, called the **chromaticity coordinates**, represent only the relative amounts of the three primary colors, XYZ, needed to create a color. They do not represent the **luminance**, or intensity of the resulting light. Luminance is represented by Y, and the other values, X and Z, are scaled to incorporate this value. Colors in the CIE model is specified by (x,y,Y). Given this specification, the amount of each primary present in a color is computed by the equations

$$X = x\frac{Y}{y}$$

$$Y = Y$$

$$Z = (1 - x - y)\frac{Y}{y}$$

The CIE model is interesting mainly for its graphic representation of color relationships. Pure colors are found on the boundary curve of the CIE chromaticity diagram at the locations shown. Tints of a color are found along a line joining that color's point on the boundary with the point C (figure 11.6.19).

FIGURE 11.6.18

The projection of the XYZ triangle into the xy-plane yields the CIE chromaticity diagram.

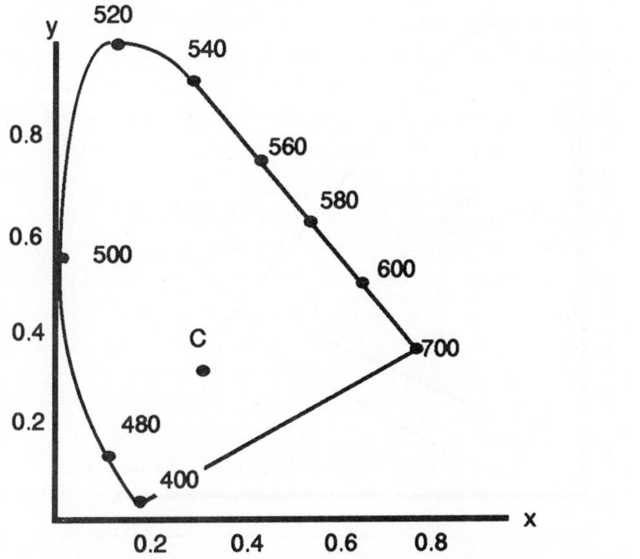

FIGURE 11.6.19

Tints of a color are found along a line joining that color's point on the boundary with the point.

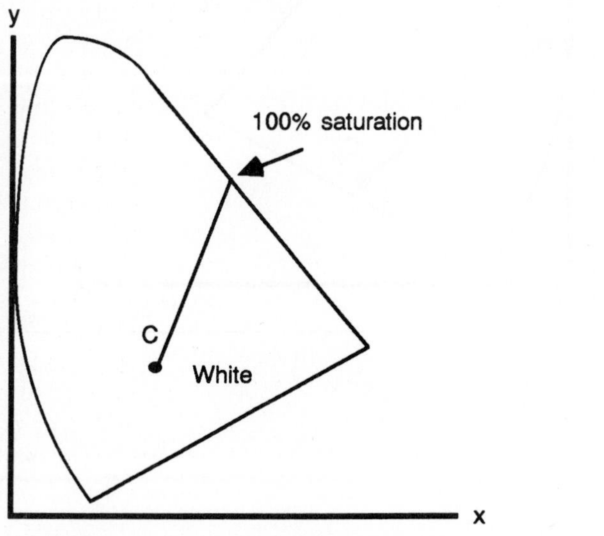

The joint C represents pure white. Complementary colors are found on opposite end points of lines passing through C (figure 11.6.20).

Color models depending on three primary colors to produce a range of colors cannot produce all colors. The **color gamut** of a set of primary colors is the set of all colors resulting from linear mixtures of those primary colors. The color gamut for three colors is the triangle created by the three points representing those colors (figure 11.6.21). Notice that no triangle that contains all the points in the chromaticity diagram can be constructed. This shows that no three colors can generate all colors.

Standards for various models can be established in terms of the CIE model. For example, the primaries for a RGB color monitor given in CIE form are

- Red (0.628,0.346)
- Green (0.268,0.588)
- Blue (0.150,0.070)

The color gamut for such a CRT is given in figure 11.6.22. Conversions between RGB and CIE models given as matrix products can be found in Rogers (1985).

FIGURE 11.6.20

The point C represents pure white. Complementary colors are found on opposite end points of lines passing through C.

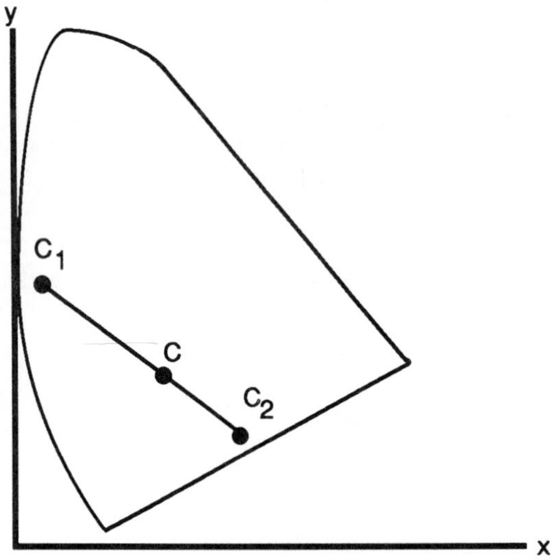

FIGURE 11.6.21

The color gamut for three colors is the triangle created by the three points representing those colors.

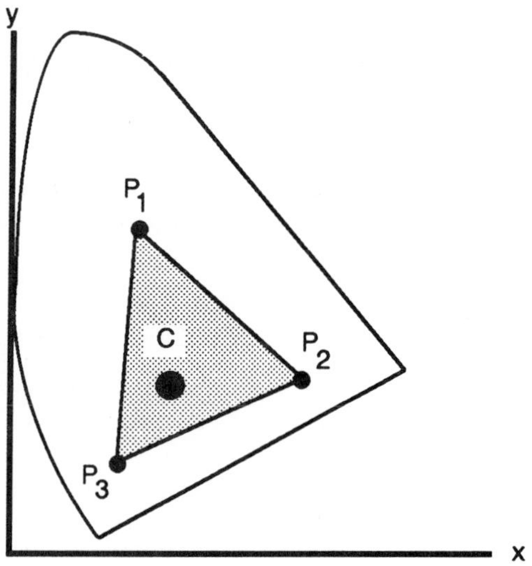

FIGURE 11.6.22

The triangle in this diagram represents the color gamut for a typical CRT.

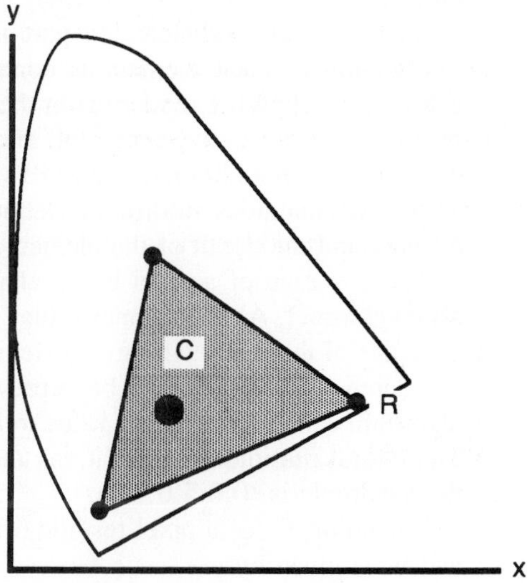

EXERCISES

11.6.1

If a color is given as (0.5,0.25,0.7) in the RGB model, find its representation in the HSV model.

11.6.2

If a color is given as (90,0.9,0.4) in the HSV model, give its RGB coordinates.

11.6.3

Show that the values of Red, Green, and Blue computed by HSV_To_RGB invert to the original hue, saturation, and value when they are passed to RGB_To_HSV.

11.7 Compositing and Antialiasing

Rendering techniques such as ray tracing and texture mapping have complicated implementations requiring large programs. Creating complex scenes may call for the use of many techniques in one picture, and programs large enough to combine several rendering operations are very difficult to debug. Over the years, many programming strategies have been developed to modularize large projects so debugging takes place in a restricted environment. It is possible to divide many images into parts, each of which is created with only one of the rendering methods. These images could be combined with z-buffer techniques, but aliasing is difficult to deal with when the z-buffer is applied. Porter and Duff (1984) and Duff (1985) introduced **compositing** to combine and antialias in one operation.

Each independently created part is an element. The shape and coverage information of each element is contained in a **matte**. Antialiasing is often achieved by applying rendering on the average intensity for a pixel, rather than on the intensity at the center of the pixel. A similar strategy is utilized in compositing. In addition to the RGB values, the data structure for each pixel of an element includes information about the area of the pixel covered by the element and the depth of the element.

The coverage of a pixel by an element is stored in a coordinate called the **alpha channel**. Alpha channel values range from 0 for no coverage to 1 for full coverage of that pixel. If a green element covers half of a pixel and you ignore the depth value, it might be represented as (0,1,0,0.5). The compositing algorithm calls for the green value to be premultiplied by the alpha value, 0.5. This avoids runtime multiplications and accelerates the calculation. In this case, the quadruple is (0,0.5,0,0.5).

The color, C, of a pixel resulting from the compositing of two elements, A and B, is given by

$$C = C_A F_A + C_B F_B$$

where the pixel has colors C_A and C_B in elements A and B respectively. F_A and F_B represent the fractions of the total pixel area covered by A and B after compositing. These fractions depend on the depth of each element and the compositing operation used, and are determined as shown in figure 11.7.1. The actual area of a pixel occupied by an element is already incorporated in the color values C_A and C_B.

Basic rules of set arithmetic are used to compute the fraction of a pixel covered by an element. If A has alpha value α_A, then the part of the pixel outside A has area $1 - \alpha_A$. The intersection of two regions A and B has area $\alpha_A \times \alpha_B$. Both rules are used to show that the intersection of the complements of two areas is $(1 - \alpha_A) \times (1 - \alpha_B)$. Every pixel can be partitioned into the regions

$$A^c \cap B^c$$
$$A \cap B^c$$
$$A^c \cap B$$
$$A \cap B$$

where A^c and B^c represent the complements of A and B. The coverage of these regions can be represented by a quadruple listing the front element for each region. The background is represented by 0, and if all of an element is visible, its fraction is 1.

Consider the case when B is *over* A. Both A and B are present in the pixel, but A shows only in that part of the pixel outside B. That is, A is visible only in region $A \cap B^c$, which occupies $\alpha_A(1 - \alpha_B)$. Each of the colors in this situation is premultiplied by its alpha factor, so the fraction $F_A = (1 - \alpha_B)$. All of B is visible, so $F_B = 1$.

FIGURE 11.7.1

F_A and F_B represent the fractions of the total pixel area covered by A and B after compositing. These fractions depend on the depth of each element and the compositing operation used, and are determined as shown. Adapted from Porter and Duff 1984, 255.

Operation	Coverage	Diagram	F_A	F_B
Clear	(0,0,0,0)		0	0
A	(0,A,0,A)	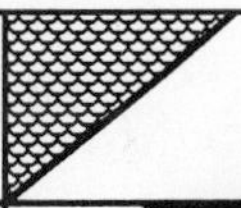	1	0
B	(0,0,B,B)		0	1
A over B	(0,A,B,A)		1	$1-\alpha_B$
B over A	(0,A,B,B)	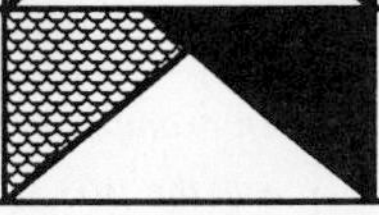	$1-\alpha_A$	1
A in B	(0,0,0,A)		α_B	0
B in A	(0,0,0,B)		0	α_A
A out B	(0,A,0,0)	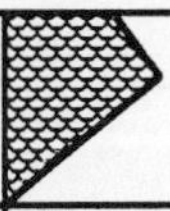	$1-\alpha_B$	0
B out A	(0,0,B,0)		0	$1-\alpha_A$
A atop B	(0,0,B,A)		α_B	$1-\alpha_A$
B atop A	(0,A,0,B)	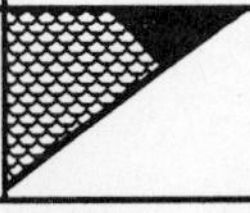	$1-\alpha_B$	α_A
A xor B	(0,A,B,0)	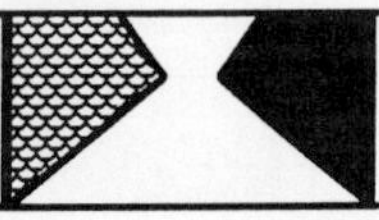	$1-\alpha_B$	$1-\alpha_A$

Mixing images is controlled by three functions and a binary operator. The functions **darken**, **dissolve**, and **opaque** are used to alter the contribution of an element and are defined by

$$\textbf{darken}(A,\phi) = (\phi r_A,\ \phi g_A,\ \phi b_A,\ \alpha_A)$$

$$\textbf{dissolve}(A,\delta) = (\delta r_A,\ \delta g_A,\ \delta b_A,\ \delta\alpha_A)$$

$$\textbf{opaque}(A,\omega) = (r_A,\ g_A,\ b_A,\ \omega\alpha_A)$$

The function **darken** changes each color of an area, A, without altering the size of the A's contribution to the color mix of a pixel, and decreases the value of ϕ. **Dissolve** increases or reduces an element's brightness as well as its area of coverage. The function **opaque** changes the coverage of an element from normal coverage when $\omega = 1$ to no coverage when $\omega = 0$.

The binary operator **plus** simply adds the effect of two elements together in each pixel. It is often used in combination with one of the functions. Two images can be merged by **dissolve**(A,α) **plus** **dissolve**(B, $1-\alpha$). An example of a composited image is the *Road to Point Reyes* (figure 11.7.2). Figure 11.7.3 shows the compositing in sections of that image.

FIGURE 11.7.2

An example of a composited image is the Road to Point Reyes. *The Road to Point Reyes landscape was the first very detailed modeling of a complex scene using patches, polygons, fractals, particle systems and a variety of procedural models. (© 1983 Pixar) Reprinted from Cook 1984, 229.*

FIGURE 11.7.3

The compositing used to create figure 11.7.2 is shown for sections of that image. Reprinted from Porter and Duff 1984, 257. (© 1983 Pixar)

11.8 Volume Visualization

Up to this point the discussion of three-dimensional computer graphics has focused on the realistic presentation of surfaces. No attempt has been made to model physical phenomena. The graphic presentation of data created by a physical model or by an actual data sampling often requires more sophisticated storage techniques, because it is often necessary to look beneath the surface of objects. This section surveys some data structures used in **volume visualization**. A picture of a face, for example, is just a skin-deep representation. The faces in figure 11.8.1. are not simply surfaces created by techniques you have

FIGURE 11.8.1

Waters modeled contractions of various facial muscles when people were exposed to different stimuli. Reprinted from Waters 1987, 24.

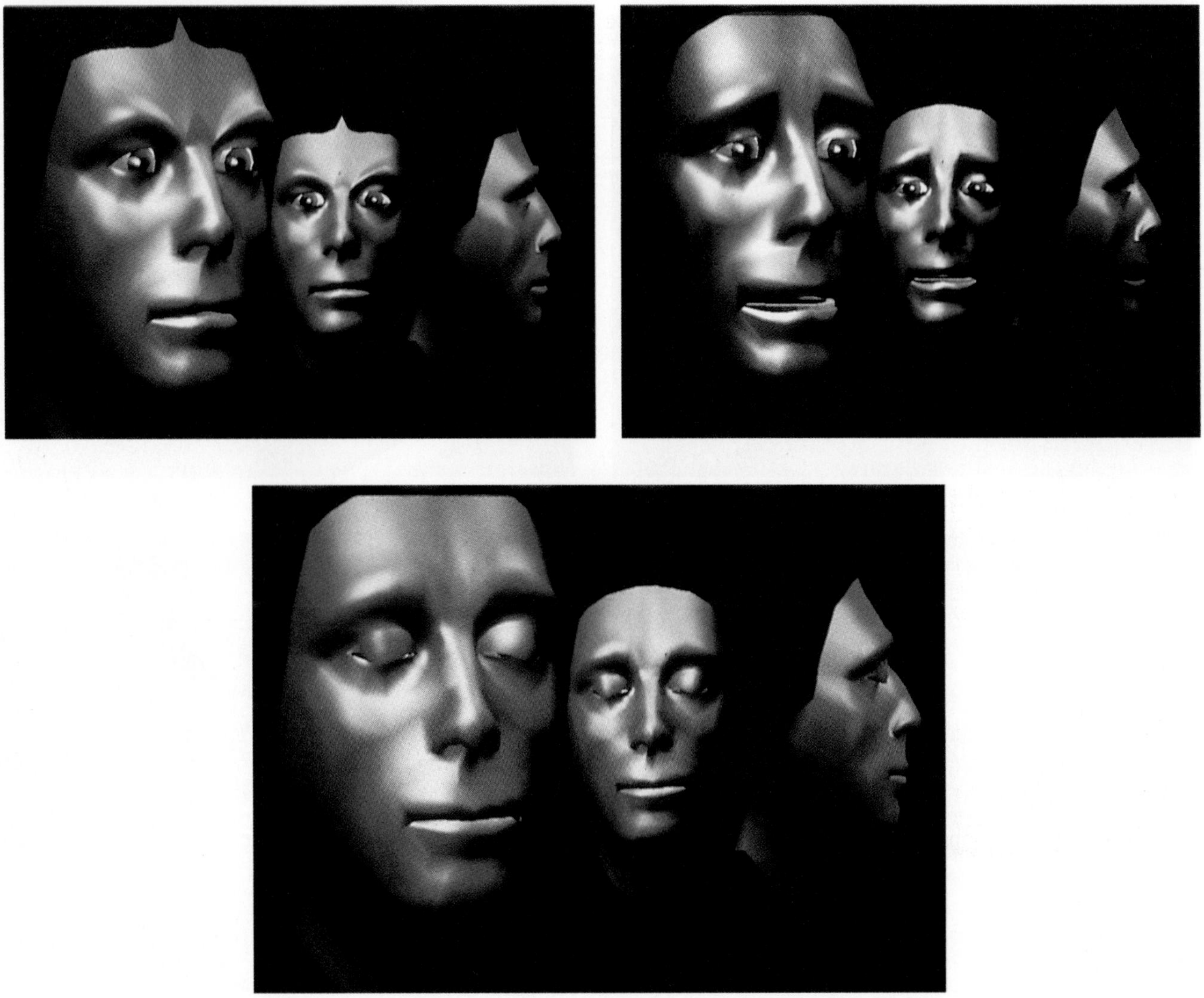

seen. Waters (1987) modeled contractions of various facial muscles when people were exposed to different stimuli: these muscle contractions translate directly into changes in the surface of a face. Figure 11.8.1 presents this surface after it has been rendered by means of techniques presented earlier in this chapter.

While it is possible to ''fake'' images like those in figure 11.8.1, the purpose here was not merely to create lifelike representations, but also to present images created by that model in order to test a mathematical model. In order to make hip replacement and skull plates that fit tightly technicians must have an accurate cross-section of the region where the device will be placed. No faking is possible in applications calling for volume visualization, such as when CAD/CAM is used in the construction of custom-designed prostheses. Hip replacements and plates fitted to the skull (Rhodes, Kuo, and Rothman 1987), require the accurate presentation of cross-sections of solid objects so they fit tightly (figure 11.8.2). Another application where surface information is insufficient is the rendering of images from a CT scan (figure 11.8.3). In this application, it is important to be able to see more than one layer at a time (Drebin, Carpenter, and Hanrahan 1988). Compositing is used in these images to create transparent and opaque layers. Mattes are used to create cross-sections (figure 11.8.4).

FIGURE 11.8.2

The plastic mandible model made by CAD/CAM from CT scan data, and a custom mandible reconstructive prosthesis fitted from this model. Reprinted from Rhodes et al. 1987, 20. © DE 1987 IEEE

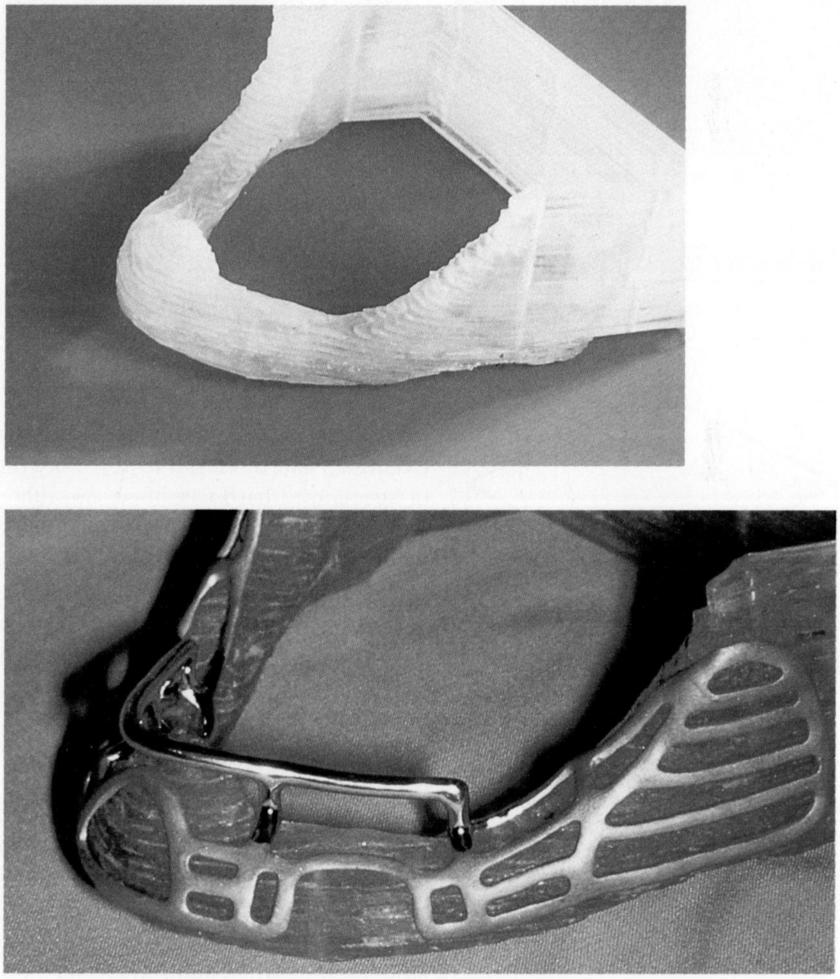

FIGURE 11.8.3

Another application in which surface information is insufficient is the rendering of images from a CT scan. In this application it is important to be able to see more than one layer at a time. Reprinted form Drebin et al. 1988, 72.

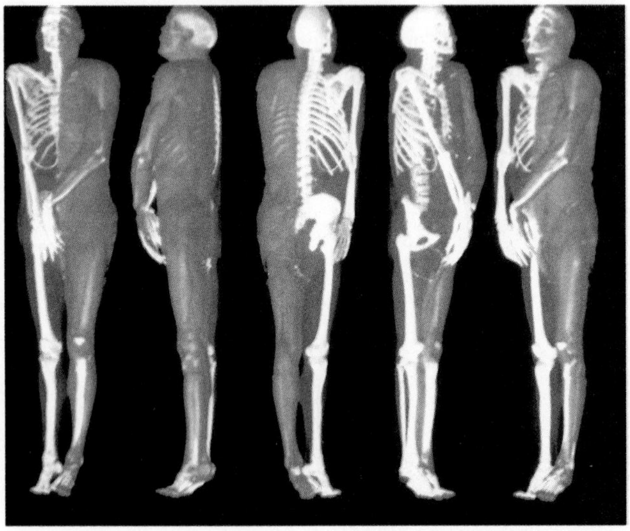

FIGURE 11.8.4

Mattes like these are used to create cross-sections. Reprinted from Drebin et al. 1988, 71.

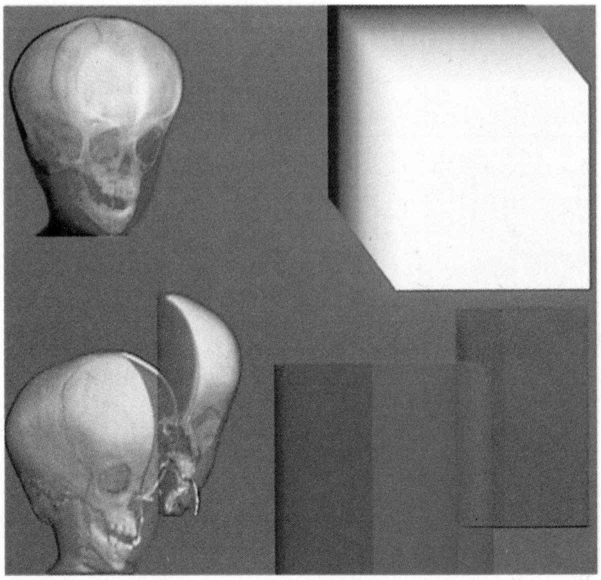

FIGURE 11.8.5

Data for this application is stored in small volume elements, or voxels.

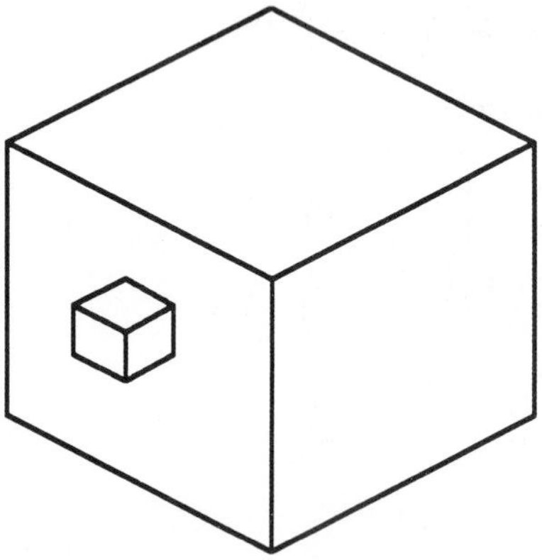

Data for this application is stored in small **volume elements**, or **voxels** (figure 11.8.5). These units represent the volumes mapped to a single pixel. A cube with 512^3 voxels, each represented by 1 byte, requires a huge amount of memory. But with memory prices decreasing, the main problem in processing voxels is the time needed to select and display those voxels concurrently on the screen. Specialized hardware has been developed to give realtime processing (Kaufman and Bakalash 1988). For computers that do not have enough memory or specialized hardware there are other techniques for handling solids.

While it is possible for adjacent voxels to have different colors, most images have blocks of adjacent voxels of the same color. The **octree** takes advantage of the homogeneous nature of images to reduce storage requirements. The following discussion will use **quadtrees**, the two-dimensional counterparts of the octree, to introduce this hierarchial data structure.

To represent the two-dimensional image in figure 11.8.6 with a quadtree, areas of the screen are subdivided until all pixels in a region are the same color. Begin by dividing the screen into four regions (figure 11.8.7). All pixels in region 1 are white, while all pixels in region 4 are black. Both regions may be completely described by one entry in a data structure. Regions 2 and 3 have pixels of both colors, so they are subdivided into four regions (figure 11.8.8). After renumbering the regions, you see that regions 2, 3, 4, 5, 6, and 8 are either entirely black or entirely white. These regions can now be added to the quadtree. Regions 7 and 9 must be divided into four regions (figure 11.8.9). Now no region has more than one color in it.

FIGURE 11.8.6

Most graphic images have large areas of adjacent pixels in a single color.

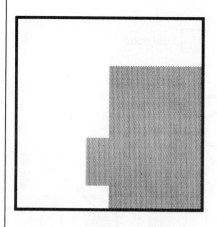

FIGURE 11.8.7

The quadtree takes advantage of the fact that adjacent pixels often have the same color. Regions 1 and 4 are composed of pixels of one color; therefore all pixels in these two squares have the same value.

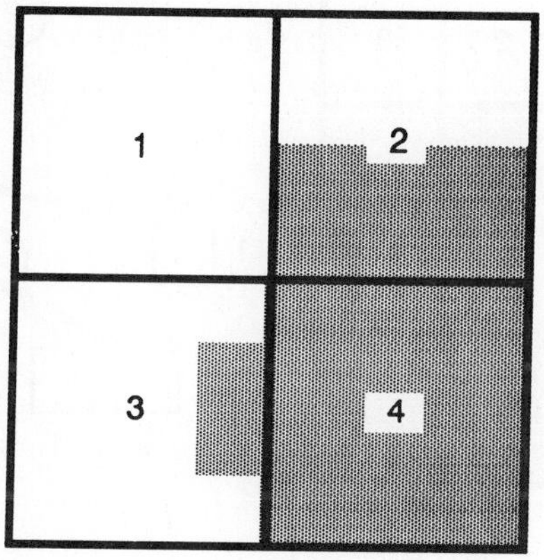

FIGURE 11.8.8

All pixels in the upper-right square are not the same color. When this square is subdivided into four equal squares, each of the resulting squares contains pixels of one color. When the technique is applied to the lower-left square, squares 7 and 9 contain pixels of both colors.

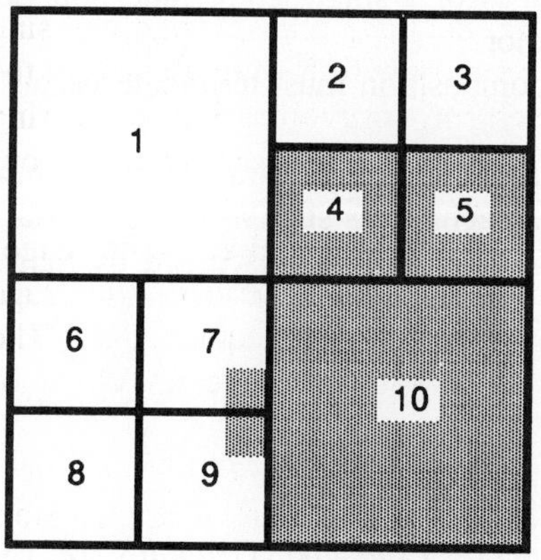

FIGURE 11.8.9

The remaining multicolor squares are again divided into four squares. Now all the squares are one color.

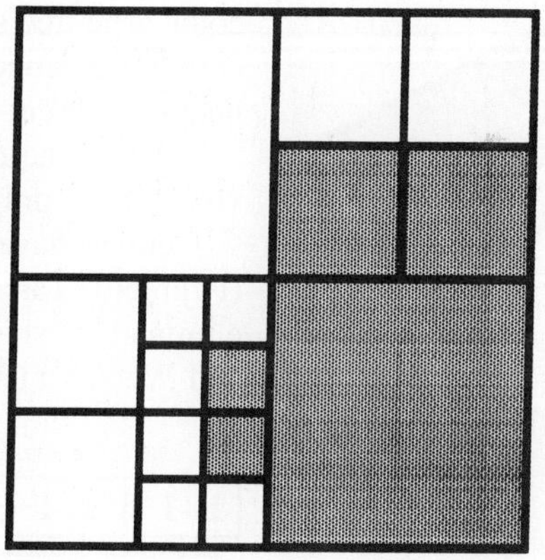

The quadtree generated by this decomposition is shown in figure 11.8.10. Only regions of homogeneous color are numbered in this diagram, and these numbers are used as labels for leaf nodes. Leaf nodes in this tree represent regions of homogeneous color; non-leaf nodes represent regions of mixed color.

FIGURE 11.8.10

After the scene is subdivided into unicolor squares, it can be represented by a quadtree. Leaf nodes represent a square of one color. A node is a child of another node if it is contained in the square representing that node.

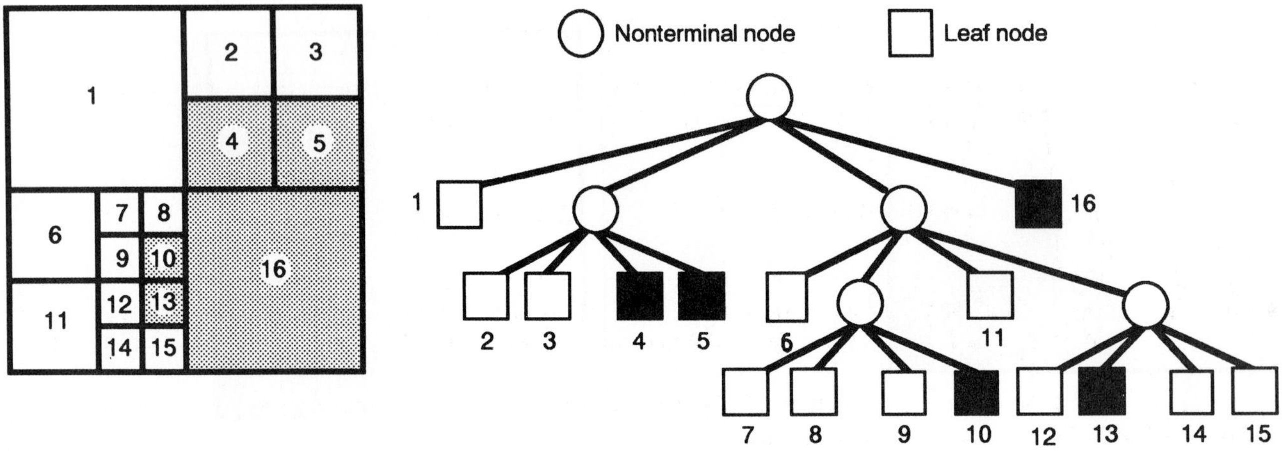

FIGURE 11.8.11

A volume subdivided for storage in an octree.

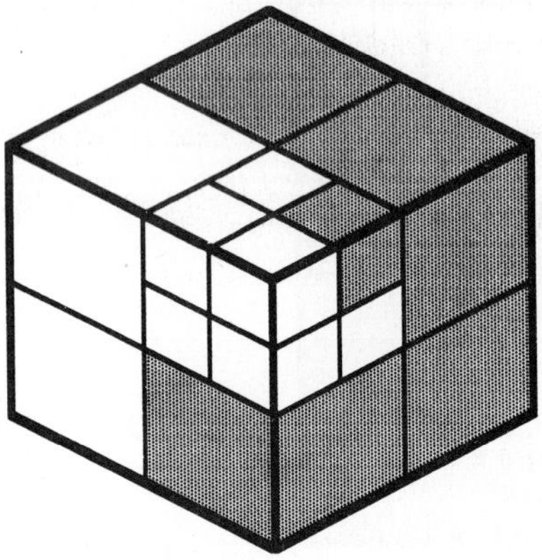

The subdivision process used to create a quadtree must terminate because pixels are the smallest regions of one color.

Figure 11.8.11 shows a volume subdivided for storage in an octree. Here squares of homogeneous colored pixels are replaced by voxel cubes of a single color. The tree structure used to store this decomposition has nodes with eight children or none. Leaf nodes represent cubes of a single color, and non-leaf nodes represent cubes of more than one color.

As with the quadtree, the recursive decomposition must terminate because voxels have only one color.

Octrees have proved most useful in speeding up ray-tracing algorithms (Fujimoto, Tanaka, and Iwata 1986). Other techniques such as hidden-surface elimination, shading, and displaying curved surfaces are discussed by Samet and Webber (1988).

BIBLIOGRAPHY

Amanatides, J. ''Ray Tracing with Cones.'' *Computer Graphics* 18 (3): 287–96 (July 1984).

Arvo, James, and David Kirk. ''Fast Ray Tracing by Ray Classification.'' *Computer Graphics* 21 (4): 55–64 (July 1987).

Barr, Alan H. ''Ray Tracing Deformed Surfaces.'' *Computer Graphics* 20 (4): 287–96 (August 1986).

Baum, Daniel R., Holly E. Rushmeier, and James M. Winget. ''Improving Radiosity Solutions Through the Use of Analytically Determined Form-Factors.'' *Computer Graphics* 23(3): 325–334 (July 1989). Excellent comparison of methods used to speed up radiosity computations.

Bier, Eric A., and Kenneth R. Sloan, Jr. ''Two-Part Texture Mappings.'' *IEEE CG&A* 6 (9): 40–53 (September 1986).

Cohen, Michael F., et al. ''A Progressive Refinement Approach to Fast Radiosity Image Generation.'' *Computer Graphics* 22 (4): 75–84 (August 1988).

Cook, Robert L. ''Shade Trees.'' *Computer Graphics* 18 (3): 223–31 (July 1984).

Cook, Robert L., Loren Carpenter, and Edwin Catmul. ''The Reyes Image Rendering Architecture.'' *Computer Graphics* 21 (4): 95–102 (July 1987).

Drebin, Robert A., Loren Carpenter, and Pat Hanrahan. ''Volume Rendering.'' *Computer Graphics* 22 (4): 65–74 (August 1988).

Duff, T ''Smooth Shaded Renderings of Polynomial Objects on Raster Displays.'' *Computer Graphics* 13: 270–5 (1979).

———. ''Composting 3D Rendering Images.'' *Computer Graphics* 19 (3): 41–44 (July 1985).

Foley, James D., and Won Chul Kim. ''Image Composition via Lookup Table Manipulation.'' *IEEE CG&A* 7 (11): 26–35 (November 1987).

Fournier, Alain, and William Reeves. ''A Solid Model of Ocean Waves.'' *Computer Graphics* 20 (4): 75–84 (August 1986).

Frenkel, Karen A. ''The Art and Science of Visualizing Data.'' *Communications of the ACM* 31 (2): 111–21 (February 1988).

Fujimoto, Akira, Takayuki Tanaka, and Kansei Iwata. ''Arts: Accelerated Ray-Tracing System.'' *IEEE CG&A* 6 (4): 16–26 (April 1986).

Glassner, Andrew. ''Adaptive Precision in Texture Mapping.'' *Computer Graphics* 20 (4): 297–306 (August 1986).

Goldfeather, Jack, Jeff P. M. Hultquist, and Henry Fuchs. ''Fast Constructive Solid Geometric Display in the Pixel-Powers Graphics Systems.'' *Computer Graphics* 20 (4): 107–16 (August 1986).

Goldfeather, Jack, et al. ''Near Real-Time CSG Rendering Using Tree Normalization and Geometric Prunning.'' *IEEE CG&A* 9 (3): 20–28 (May 1989).

Goral, Cindy M., et al. ''Modeling the Interaction of Light Between Diffuse Surfaces.'' *Computer Graphics* 18 (3): 213–22 (July 1984).

Greenberg, Donald P. ''Coons Award Lecture.'' *Communications of the ACM* 31 (2): 123–29 (February 1988).

Hearn, Donald, and M. Pauline Baker. *Computer Graphics*. Englewood Cliffs, N.J.: Prentice-Hall, 1986.

Heckbert, P. S., and P. Hanrahan. ''Beam Tracing Polygonal Objects.'' *Computer Graphics* 18 (3): 119–27 (July 1984).

Immel, David S., Michael F. Cohen, and Donald P. Greenberg. ''A Radiosity Method for Non-Diffuse Environments.'' *Computer Graphics* 20 (4): 133–42 (August 1986).

Joy, Kenneth I. ''Ray Tracing Parametric Surface Patches Utilizing Numerical Techniques and Ray Coherence.'' *Computer Graphics* 20 (4): 279–85 (August 1986).

Kajiya, James T. ''The Rendering Equation.'' *Computer Graphics* 20 (4): 143–50 (August 1986).

Kaufman, Arie, and Reuven Bakalash. ''Memory and Processing Architecture for 3D Voxel-Based Imagery.'' *IEEE CG&A* 8 (6): 10–23 (November 1988).

Kay, D. G. ''Transparency, Refraction and Ray Tracing for Computer-Synthesized Images.'' Master's thesis, Cornell University, 1979.

Kay D. G., and D. Greenberg. ''Transparency for Computer Synthesized Images.'' *Computer Graphics* 13: 158–64 (1979).

Kay, Timothy L., and James T. Kajiya. ''Ray Tracing Complex Scenes.'' *Computer Graphics* 20 (4): 269–78 (August 1986).

Lee, Y. C., and K. S. Fu. ''Machine Understanding of CSG: Extraction and Unification of Manufacturing Features.'' *IEEE CG&A* 7 (1): 20–32 (January 1987).

Max, Nelson L. ''Atmospheric Illumination and Shadows.'' *Computer Graphics* 20 (4): 117–24 (August 1986).

Nakamae, Eihachiro, et al. ''Compositing 3D Images with Antialiasing and Various Shading Effects.'' *IEEE CG&A* 9 (2): 21–29 (March 1989).

Nishita, Tomoyuki, and Eihachiro Nakamae. ''Continuous Tone Representation of Three-Dimensional Objects Illuminated by Sky Light.'' *Computer Graphics* 20 (4): 125–32 (August 1986).

Nishita, Tomoyuki, Yasuhiro Miyawaki, and Eihachiro Nakamae. ''A Shading Model for Atmospheric Scattering Considering Luminous Intensity Distribution of Light Sources.'' *Computer Graphics* 21 (3): 303–10 (July 1987).

Oka, Masaaki, et al. ''Real-Time Manipulation of Texture-Mapped Surfaces.'' *Computer Graphics* 21 (4): 181–88 (July 1987).

Phong, Bui-Tuong. ''Illumination for Computer Generated Images.'' *Communications of the ACM* 18 (6): 311–17 (June 1975).

Pokorny, Cornel K., and Curtis F. Gerald. *Computer Graphics: the Principles Behind the Art and Science*. Irvine, Calif.: Franklin, Beedle & Associates, 1989.

Porter T., and T. Duff. ''Compositing Digital Images.'' *Computer Graphics* 18 (3): 253–59 (July 1984).

Pulleyblank, Ron, and John Kapenga. ''The Feasibility of a VLSI Chip for Ray Tracing Bicubic Patches.'' *IEEE CG&A* 7 (3): 33–44 (March 1987).

Rhodes, Michael L., Yu-Ming Kuo, and Stephen L. G. Rothman. ''An Application of Computer Graphics and Networks to Anatomic Model and Prosthesis Manufacturing.'' *IEEE CG&A* 7 (2): 12–25 (February 1987).

Rogers, David F. *Procedural Elements of Computer Graphics*. New York: McGraw-Hill, 1985.

Rushmeier, Holly, and Kenneth E. Torrance. ''The Zonal Method for Calculating Light Intensities in the Presence of a Participating Medium.'' *Computer Graphics* 21 (4): 293–302 (July 1987).

Samet, Hanan, and Robert E. Webber. ''Hierarchical Data Structures and Algorithms for Computer Graphics Part I: Fundametnals.'' *IEEE CG&A* 8 (3): 48–68 (May 1988).

———. ''Hierarchical Data Structures and Algorithms for Computer Graphics Part II: Applications.'' *IEEE CG&A* 8 (4): 59–75 (July 1988).

Shao, Min-Zhi, Qun-Sheng Peng, and You-Dong Liang. ''A New Radiosity Approach by Procedural Refinements for Realistic Image Synthesis.'' *Computer Graphics* 22 (4): 93–101 (August 1988).

Shinya, Mikio, Tokiichiro Takahashi, and Seiichiro Naito. ''Principles and Applications of Pencil Tracing.'' *Computer Graphics* 21 (4): 45–54 (July 1987).

Snyder, John M., and Allan H. Barr. ''Ray Tracing Complex Models Containing Surface Tessellations.'' *Computer Graphics* 21 (4): 119–28 (July 1987).

Strang, Gilbert. *Linear Algebra and its Applications*. 2d ed. New York: Academic Press, 1980.

Upson, Craig, and Michael Keeler. ''V-Buffer: Visible Volume Rendering.'' *Computer Graphics* 22 (4): 59–64 (August 1988).

Wallace, John R., Michael F. Cohen, and Donald P. Greenberg. ''A Two-Pass Solution to the Rendering Equation: A Synthesis of Ray Tracing and Radiosity Methods.'' *Computer Graphics* 21 (4): 311–20 (July 1987).

Ward, Gregory J., Francis M. Rubinstein, and Robert D. Clear. ''A Ray Tracing Solution for Diffuse Interreflection.'' *Computer Graphics* 22 (4): 85–92 (August 1988).

Waters, Keith, ''A Muscle Model for Animating Three-Dimensional Facial Expression,'' *Computer Graphics*, 21 (4): 17–24 (July 1987).

Yaeger, Larry, Craig Upson, and Robert Meyers. ''Combining Physical and Visual Simulation—Creation of the Planet Jupiter for the Film '2010.' '' *Computer Graphics* 20 (4): 85–93 (August 1986).

Zhu, Yinning, Qunsheng Peng, Youdong Liang. ''PERIS: A Programming Environment for Realistic Image Synthesis.'' *Computers and Graphics* 12(3/4): 299–308 (1988).

Appendix

A program to produce the Sierpinski Curve in figure 3.7.1.

```
program Sierpinski1;
   uses
      MyGraph;
   const
      order = 4;
      h0 = 256;
   var
      i, h, x, y, x0, y0 : integer;
   procedure A (i,h : integer;var x,y real,var Place : Window);
   forward;
   procedure B (i,h : integer;var x,y real,var Place : Window);
   forward;
   procedure C (i,h : integer;var x,y real,var Place : Window);
   forward;
   procedure D (i,h : integer;var x,y real,var Place : Window);
   forward;
   procedure A;
   begin
      if i > 0 then
         begin
            A(i - 1,h,x,y,Place);
            x := x + h;
            y := y - h;
            LineAbs(x, y,Place);
            B(i - 1,h,x,y,Place );
            x := x + 2 * h;
            LineAbs(x, y,Place);
            D(i - 1,h,x,y,Place );
            x := x + h;
            y := y + h;
            LineAbs(x, y,Place);
            A(i - 1,h,x,y,Place )
         end
   end;
```

(program continued)

Appendix A continued

```
procedure B;
begin
   if i > 0 then
      begin
         B(i - 1,h,x,y,Place );
         x := x - h;
         y := y - h;
         LineAbs(x,  y,Place);
         C(i - 1,h,x,y,Place );
         y := y - 2 * h;
         LineAbs(x,  y,Place);
         A(i - 1,h,x,y,Place );
         x := x + h;
         y := y - h;
         LineAbs(x,  y,Place);
         B(i - 1,h,x,y,Place )
      end
end;
procedure C;
begin
   if i > 0 then
      begin
         C(i - 1,h,x,y,Place );
         x := x - h;
         y := y + h;
         LineAbs(x,  y,Place);
         D(i - 1,h,x,y,Place );
         x := x - 2 * h;
         LineAbs(x,  y,Place);
         B(i - 1,h,x,y,Place );
         x := x - h;
         y := y - h;
         LineAbs(x,  y,Place);
         C(i - 1,h,x,y,Place )
      end
end;
procedure D;
begin
   if i > 0 then
      begin
         D(i - 1,h,x,y,Place );
         x := x + h;
         y := y + h;
         LineAbs(x,  y,Place);
         A(i - 1,h,x,y,Place );
         y := y + 2 * h;
         LineAbs(x,  y,Place);
         C(i - 1,h,x,y,Place );
         x := x - h;
         y := y + h;
         LineAbs(x,  y,Place);
         D(i - 1,h,x,y,Place )
      end
end;
```

```
begin
   GraphOn;
   OpenWindow(World);
   SetViewPort(0,0,1,1,World);
   SetWindow(0,0,h0,h0,World);
   i := 0;
   h := h0 div 4;
   x0 := 2 * h;
   y0 := 3 * h;
   repeat
      i := i + 1;
      x0 := x0 - h;
      h := h DIV 2;
      y0 := y0 + h;
      x := x0;
      y := y0;
      MoveAbs(x,  y,World);
      A(i,h,x,y,World);
      x := x + h;
      y := y - h;
      LineAbs(x,  y,World);
      B(i,h,x,y,World);
      x := x - h;
      y := y - h;
      LineAbs(x,  y,World);
      C(i,h,x,y,World);
      x := x - h;
      y := y + h;
      LineAbs(x,  y,World);
      D(i,h,x,y,World);
      x := x + h;
      y := y + h;
      LineAbs(x,  y,World);
   until i = order
end.
```

Glossary

aliasing The term aliasing is used in sampling theory applied to signal processing. If too few samples of a waveform are taken, the precise nature of the waveform is lost.
antialiasing Antialiasing techniques are used to reduce the effects of sampling errors by adjusting each pixel's gray level to better match the pixels position relative to the actual line.
aperture grille Replaces the holes of a shaddow mask with long vertical slits to help align the red blue and green beams of some color CRTs.
aspect ratio The aspect ratio is the ratio of the number of rows of a display to the number of columns of a display. Also see pixel ratio
Bézier surfaces A class of spline curves often used to create letters for fonts.
bicubic patches A small segment of a surface described by cubic polynomials in both parameters.
Bit-boundary Block Transfer (Bitblt) The fundamental procedure used to compose one bitmap with another.
bitmap A data structure used to describe a set of pixels in a raster graphics system.
CIE The color model created in 1931 by the Commission Internationale de l'Éclairage based on the three standard primaries, called X, Y, and Z. All visible colors can be matched with positive weights of these three primary colors.
clipping A collection of techniques used to draw graphic objects in a restricted region.
clipping pipe The sequence of operations used to clip a given class of graphic objects.
color *additive mixing* Method of creating colors by adding varying amounts of the primary colors. This type of mixing is associated with creating colored light.
color *chromaticity coordinates* Coordinate system used in the chromaticity diagram of the CIE color model.
color *complementary* Two colors which when mixed produce white.
color *gamut* The triangle in the CIE diagram showing the colors that can be achieved if the corners of the diagram are used as primary colors.
color *hue* Distinct colors such as red, green, purple, etc.
color *primary* A color belonging to one of three groups used to generate all colors.
color *subtractive mixing* The method use to create colors by reducing the amount of a given primary color in a mixture. This type of mixing is usually associated with pigments.
color *table* A table used to associate the colors available on a given system with a set of numbers.
color *tint* The result of adding white pigment to a pure pigment.
compositing Combining images to create a new image.
compositing *alpha channel* Used in compositing to hold the amount of coverage of each pixel
coordinates *homogeneous* The coordinate system used to allow all afine transformations to be represented by matrices.
coordinates *normalized device* The device-independent coordinate system that represents all coordinates as pairs of real numbers between 0 and 1.
coordinates *screen* The coordinates used to represent pixels on a given device. Also called device coordinates.
coordinates *view* Coordinates associated with a given viewport.
coordinates *window* The coordinates of points in a given window. Sometimes called world coordinates.

coordinates ***world*** Coordinates that represent a real-world problem.
cursor A object displayed on the screen that shows the user the area of the screen an interactive input device is currently pointing to.
cursor ***hotspot*** The point on the cursor that points to the exact screen location.
density ***optical*** Property of matter that changes the direction of light as it passes through an object.
digitizers Machines used to convert images into digital representation.
direct-view storage tube (DVST) A CRT in where the picture is created on a storage surface between the electron gun and the phosphors on the screen.
display controller Refreshes the display on a raster scan CRT.
display file program A set of device dependent opcodes such as line and move instructions. It is stored in the refresh display file and executed once during every refresh cycle by the display processor.
display file translator A program that translates the output of application programs into display file programs.
display processor The collection of special software and hardware responsible for controlling output to display devices.
dither matrix A matrix of binary values used to represent pixel patterns that can create gray levels.
dithering Techniques used with halftoning methods to smooth edges of displayed objects.
edge table A table that lists the edges of a polygon in terms of the edges vertex end points.
film recorder Records graphic images on film.
font A set of shapes used to represent letters of the alphabet.
font ***leading*** The amount of space between lines of type.
fractal A class of graphic objects used to create realistic images of mountains and other natural objects. Fractal images are often associated with the mathematical study of chaos.
fractal ***attractor*** The limit point of a series points computed by iterated application of a function.
frame buffer A special block of memory from which raster-scan systems generate a display.
geometric modeling A technique for decomposing structures into simple geometric objects like cubes, cylinders and spheres.
graphic primitives Simple drawing procedures available in a graphics system.
Graphics Kernal System (GKS) A two- and three-dimensional graphics (GKS-3D)standards.
graphics tablet A flat surface on which a user can point to various locations by activating a hand cursor or stylus.
graphtals Graphic objects that are generated using L-grammars and that appear to be plants.
halftoning A method used to create gray levels using small patterns of black dots
hidden lines Lines in a three-dimensional scene obscured by surfaces closer to the viewer.
icon A small graphic shape used to represent an idea or operation.
joystick An interactive input device that allows the user to move a cursor by moving a small lever.
L-system or grammar A collection of formal grammars used to generate plant-like graphic objects.
light ***ambient*** Uniform illumination of a surface produced by multiple reflections off of nearby objects.
light ***distributed*** Light emanating from a large nearby source.
light ***point-source*** Light emanating from a small source such as a single light bulb.
light pens Pointing device that allows the user to point at a location on the screen and select that location.
liquid crystal display (LCD) A thin display device that creates images using the polarizing effect of liquid crystals.
logical input device A classification system used to describe types of input and their purpose.
luminance The brightness of light.
Mach bands Bright bands of light that appear along boundaries that have a large change in intensity. The bands are caused by a physiological phenomenon called lateral inhibition.
main-event graphics program A program that is organized to be event-driven to give the user more flexibility.
menu A list of operations available to the user at a given time.
menu bar A list of menus available to the user. This list stays on the screen, and a user can pick a menu by pointing to its name in the list.
mouse An interactive input device that can be used for most pointing, choosing and drawing activities.
octree A data structure used to represent sets of voxels of the same color.
output primitives Procedures used to create simple graphic objects such as lines and points.
panning Shifting the graphic image to allow the user to see areas not currently displayed on the screen.

pixel The smallest addressable screen location on a display device.
pixel ratio The ratio of the height of a pixel to its width. Also see aspect ratio
Plasma panel display A flat display device with low flicker and high resolution.
plotters Hard-copy devices that produce images by moving instruments such as pens, styluses, or electrostatic devices over paper or another appropriate medium.
polygon mesh A collection small polygonal surfaces used to approximate a surface.
Programmers Hierarchical Interactive Graphics System (PHIGS) A graphics standard that attempts to organize graphic objects into hierarchies of primitive components.
projection ***axonometric*** Orthographic projections that show more than one face of an object.
projection ***cabinet*** A commonly used oblique projection with a projection angle of approximately 63.4°.
projection ***cavalier*** A commonly used oblique projection with a projection angle of 45°
projection ***center of*** The point through which projection lines pass in a perspective projection.
projection ***elevations*** Orthographic projections used by architects
projection ***isometric*** An axomometric projection in which all three principal axes are foreshortened by equal amounts.
projection ***oblique*** A projection that is not perpendicular to the projection plane.
projection ***parallel*** A projection in which the lines of projection are parallel.
projection ***perspective*** A projection in which the lines of projection all pass through one point called the center of projection.
projection ***plans*** Orthographic front, side and top views used in engineering drawings.
projective plane The plane used to plot the two-dimensional representation of a three-dimensional image.
pull-down menu An interactive display window in which users choose an operation from the set of available operations.
quadtree A data structure used to represent blocks of pixels of the same color.
radiosity A technique used to create realistic lighting effects.
radiosity ***form factor*** The number used to compute the amount of light reaching a given surface that emanates from another surface.
random scan A CRT in which the electron gun is free to draw in any direction.
raster scan A CRT in which the electron gun always draws horizontal scan lines in sequence.
ray tracing A method for creating realistic reflections and shadows by tracing individual light rays from the center of projection back to light sources and sinks.
rendering Methods used to create realistic images.
rubberbanding Interactive drawing of graphic objects such as lines and circles.
scan line The horizontal line traced by the electron gun in a raster scan system.
segment A grouping of graphic objects used by the GKS system.
spline curves Smooth, easily modified curves.
structure The data structure used in PHIGS to represent the relationship between parts of a graphic object.
touch panel Device put on the front of a display device that allows the user to select locations on the screen by pointing at them.
trackball An interactive input device which incorporates a ball mounted in a base. Using a finger the user rolls the ball to move a cursor on the screen.
vanishing point The point at which groups of parallel lines appear to intersect in a perspective projection.
vector graphics The graphics system in which all objects are specified as a sequence of end points of vectors. It was originally developed for use with random scan graphics systems.
vertex table A look-up table used to store the vertices of a polygonal mesh.
view volume The three-dimensional counterpart of a viewport.
viewport An area of the screen corresponding to a given window.
virtual device coordinate space (VDC) A flexible coordinate system introduced in the Computer Graphics Metafile (CGM) standard.
virtual reality High-level, interactive graphics environments that attempt to give the user the feeling of actually being part of the environment.
voxels Volume elements that are the three-dimensional equivalent of pixels.
window A rectangular region of the screen specified in world coordinates.
window manager A program that coordinates the use of one or more windows on the screen.
workstation In the GKS system, the logical interface through which an application program controls physical

systems. Also a CPU capable of executing several million instructions per second, a large disk and display with at least 1000 × 800. Usually networked with other work-stations.

world coordinates (WC) The coordinates used in an application.

zooming Enlarging an area of the screen to show more detail, or enlarging the viewing area to show parts of a graphics image not currently on the screen.

Index

Intergraph Corporation. **1.2.22** © 1988-Aminática-Sev'88 for TVE. **1.2.21** Published with permission of Evans and Sutherland Computer Company; **1.2.19** Provided through the courtesy of the Jet Propulsion Laboratory, California Institute of Technology, Pasadena, California; **1.2.15** Photos courtesy of Silicon Graphics Computer Systems; **1.2.16** Photos courtesy of Silicon Graphics Computer Systems; **2.2.2** Courtesy of Apple Computer; **2.2.4** Photo compliments of Calcomp Canada, Inc.; **2.2.5** Pen Ploter Photos courtesy of Houston Instrument, a Summargaphics Company; **2.3.1** Photo courtesy of Logitech; **2.3.2** TurboMouse® photo courtesy of Kensington Microware Limited; **2.3.3** MicroTouch Systems, Inc., Wilmington, MA: **2.3.4** Photos courtesy of Silicon Graphics Computer Systems; **2.3.5** Photos courtesy of Silicon Graphics Computer Systems; **2.5.11** (left) Photo courtesy of Microsoft, Inc. (right) © 1989 Digital Equipment Corporation, Randy Post; (center) Courtesy of Visix Software, Inc. © 1989; **D.3.1** Images of H. Jurgens, H.O. Peitgen, D. Saupe, from "The Beauty of Fractals", H.O. Peitgen, P. Richter, Springer-Verlag, Heidelberg, 1986; **D.3-2** Robert B. Wilhelmson, Crystal Shaw, Lou Wicker, Stefen Fangmeier, NCSA Visualization Production Team; **3.1.11** Lines drawn using Codonics 4096 Graphics Terminal, Codonics, Inc., Middleburg Heights, OH; **3.7.17** © 1989 F. Kenton Musgrave and Benoit B. Mandelbrot **3.7.18** Images by H. Jurgens, H.O. Peitgen, D. Saupe, from "The Beauty of Fractals", H.O. Peitgen, P. Richter, Springer-Verlag, Heidelberg, 1986; **3.7.21** Images by H. Jurgens, H.O. Peitgen, D. Saupe, from "The Beauty of Fractals", H.O. Peitgen, P. Richter, Springer-Verlag, Heidelberg, 1986; Mandelbrot set by J. Milnor; **D.4.1** Courtesy of Borland International; **4.5.6** Photo Courtesy of Microsoft, Inc.; **D.5.1** Courtesy of Robert Abel & Assoc.; **5.1.1** Courtesy of Visix Software Inc. © 1989; **5.1.3** Claris and McPain are registered trademarks of Claris Corporation; **5.5.2** Courtesy of J. Darrell Kirkley, Inc; **5.5.3** Courtesy of J. Darrell Kirkley, Inc; **5.6.2** Courtesy of J. Darrell Kirkley, Inc; Claris and McDraw are registered trademarks of Claris Corporation; **D.6.1** © 1989 Digital Equipment Corporation, Randy Rost; **D.6.4** Photo courtesy of Microsoft, Inc.; **6.7.6** Silicon Beach Software, Inc., a Subsidiary of Aldus Corporation; **6.7.7** Silicon Beach Software, Inc., a Subsidiary of Aldus Corporation; **7.3.4** Silicon Beach Software, Inc., a Subsidiary of Aldus Corporation; **7.3.5** Silicon Beach Software, Inc., a Subsidiary of Aldus Corporation; **7.3.6** Silicon Beach Software, Inc., a Subsidiary of Aldus Corporation; **8.2.3** Courtesy of Autodesk, Inc.; **9.1.1** Credit: Alinari/Art Resource; **9.1.2** Credit: Alinari/Art Resource; **9.1.7** Credit: Alinari/Art Resource; **D.10.1** Photo courtesy of Auto-trol Technology Corporation; **D.11.1** (© 1987 1EEE) Rhodes, Kuo and Rothman, 1987; **11.3.9** Artist: Matt Elson, Sumbolics © 1990, All works created using Symbolics Unified Graphics Environment; **11.4.7** John Amanatides, University of Toronto; **11.4.9** Photos courtesy of Silicon Graphics Computer Systems; **11.4.10** Photos courtesy of Silicon Graphics Computer Systems; **11.7.2** ©1983 Pixar; **11.7.3** G1983 Pixar; **11.3.7** Courtesy of Gary Bishop, David Weimer, ATT Bell Laboratories; **11.8.1** © Keith Waters, 1987; **11.8.2** (©1987 IEEE) Rhodes, Kuo and Rothman, 1987; **11.8.3** © 1988 Pixar; **11.8.4** © 1988 Pixar;